The Radical Spanish Empire

The Radical Spanish Empire

HOW PAPERWORK POLITICS REMADE THE NEW WORLD

Jorge Cañizares-Esguerra and Adrian Masters

Harvard University Press • Cambridge, Massachusetts
London, England • 2026

Printed in the United States of America
First printing

EU GPSR Authorised Representative
LOGOS EUROPE, 9 rue Nicolas Poussin, 17000, LA ROCHELLE, France
E-mail: Contact@logoseurope.eu

Library of Congress Cataloging-in-Publication Data

Names: Cañizares-Esguerra, Jorge author | Masters, Adrian, 1988– author
Title: The radical Spanish Empire : how paperwork politics remade the New World / Jorge Cañizares-Esguerra and Adrian Masters.
Description: Cambridge, Massachusetts ; London, England : Harvard University Press, 2026. | Includes bibliographical references and index.
Identifiers: LCCN 2025026879 (print) | LCCN 2025026880 (ebook) | ISBN 9780674986640 cloth | ISBN 9780674304116 epub | ISBN 9780674304123 pdf
Subjects: LCSH: Radicalism—New Spain—History—16th century | Lawfare—New Spain—History—16th century—Sources | New Spain—History—16th century | New Spain—Social conditions—16th century | Spain—Colonies—America—Administration—History—16th century—Sources | New Spain—Archival resources
Classification: LCC F1231 .C256 2026 (print) | LCC F1231 (ebook) | DDC 956/.404—dc23/eng/20250903
LC record available at https://lccn.loc.gov/2025026879
LC ebook record available at https://lccn.loc.gov/2025026880

CONTENTS

NOTE ON ORTHOGRAPHY

This book features a great number of Spanish, Nahuatl, Otomi, Mixtec, Muisca, Quechua, and other words. Our main concern has been making the text more readable. To this end, we have standardized and modernized all early modern and Spanish words, including personal and place names (except for some famous texts like the *Nueva corónica*). We leave Indigenous words more or less as they were written at the time, as is standard practice in many newer English-language works: Tenochtitlan instead of Tenochtitlán, Otomi instead of Otomí. This means they are unaccented unless they feature a Spanish component (i.e., "Santa Fe de Bogotá"). When multiple Indigenous spellings exist for a single name or location, we adhere to the most common English and/or Spanish variant: Cusco instead of Cuzco or Qosqo, etc. For pre-conquest names, we use the most accurate variant of Indigenous names (i.e., Motecuzomah) and for post-conquest names, we use the names which members of these families used most to refer to themselves (i.e., Moctezuma). For small hamlets, we adhere to more modern conventions to make consultation easier: Ixtacamaxtitlan instead of Iztacamaxitlán. For Indigenous-derived terms in the present, we use modern Spanish orthography (i.e., Totoró). In general, we have sought to unburden the reading experience somewhat by translating some of the words we use most often into English (e.g., *cacique* to *native lord*). We refer to Indigenous peoples as such, and less often as Natives, to avoid repetition. However, it is worth remembering their legal status as *indios* or Indians. Likewise, we write of Black and Afro-descendant subjects, although they appear most often in the source material as *negros*, *mulatos*, and other terms.

The Radical Spanish Empire

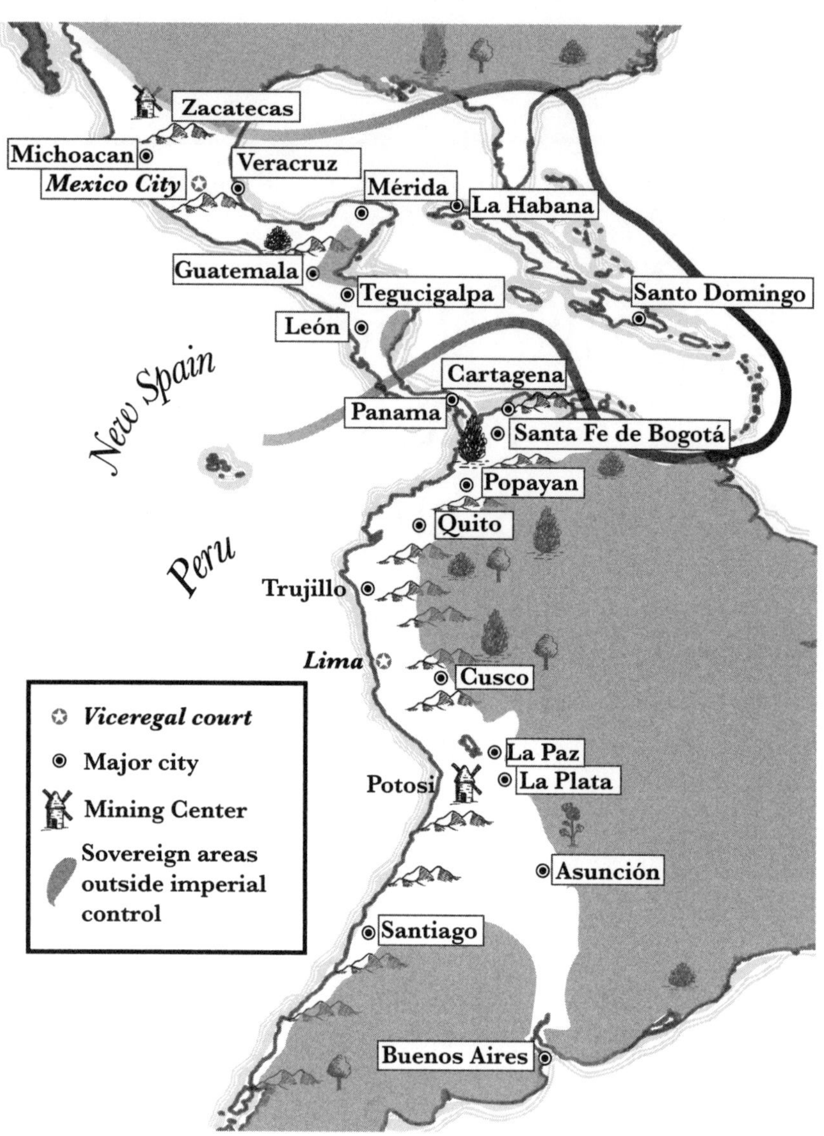

Map 1 Spanish America in the sixteenth century. Regions covered in this study.

INTRODUCTION

A World Upside Down

The world was upside down. The wheels of change whirled. In every quarter, commoners became masters and lords became serfs. New ideas merged with hallowed traditions, and the young declared the downfall of their parents' ways. Peasants freed themselves from their yokes, abandoning their communities. Men and women who were once servants now taunted, abused, and even ran their masters out of town. The once-powerful cursed and lamented. Some went into hiding, fearing the mob. Others reinvented themselves to survive. The story repeated itself, with local variations, for many decades and in every direction.

Lords wept because they knew that the Old World was gone, never to return. A wizened noblewoman urged the young to embrace the vanishing values of bygone times. She waxed,

> When I was growing up there was an infinite number of . . . nobles and rulers! It was like one big palace . . . one could not count the commoners or the slaves; they were like ants . . . But now . . . we are coming to an end and disappearing.[1]

Old dynasties collapsed, and parvenues took their places. This made the nobles' plight even more bitter. A low-ranking official with aristocratic pretensions recalled that the realm had once been ruled by "people of great lineage and caste." Now, commoners were replacing them and infesting society with deceit. There was no question—"the world is upside down."[2]

Those who had been shut out from power were singing a different tune, one of defiance. In one mountain town, a usurper boldly seized the local throne and pronounced his rivals' tyrannical control over for good. He was unlike his long-reigning predecessors—his authority did not derive "from the reign of the ancient people. . . . I displace them. . . . Thus [was] the status of the ancient people; let it be buried forever in the past!"[3]

Commoners were bolder and more mobile than ever before. It was a time of both hope and great fear; even everyday routines were in turmoil. One manic street preacher declared the new dietary and religious fads sweeping the land cosmically disruptive. Those who embraced the new ways "will be destroyed—no one will exist, their lives and their issue will have reached their end."[4] He portended: "Everyone has been transformed. . . . Destruction is imminent!"[5]

The end was near for many indeed. Upheaval, plunder, and confusion consumed cities and towns. Lords schemed as royal palaces burned, some hatching plots against their own former allies and kin. One ruler considering betrayal mused, "Since the world is upside down, let it be all for me."[6] In one theater of this raging conflict, two rebel generals roamed the mountains to bring a new order through terror. Killing the old ruling family down to its last member was not enough: they would destroy their enemy's very memory. They would open the door to a new future—"a new beginning—a new world."[7]

There is something deeply familiar about these cries of hope and despair. The historical record has left abundant traces of them from times when the structure of society violently transformed. Such remarks could have come from many eras; these in particular came from the pens of Indigenous survivors in the 1500s "New World." These authors knew that their societies were collapsing and that long-excluded actors were imagining new orders. They had survived the arrival of the Spaniards—especially in the 1520s and 1530s—accompanied by a handful of friars and royal officials. Their family members had fought against the invaders, joined them, or led them to greater power. Now, they laid down in ink their own reflections on the past decades' horrors and marvels. Some continued to write about these cataclysms into the 1570s, as the pace of Spanish imperial expansion slowed. By then, their society was taking new form, moving from near-total conflict to order.

The old woman's dirge about the aristocracy's collapse comes from a collection of late-1500s Texcocan sermons written by an anonymous Indigenous author likely connected with Franciscan friars in the area. From the Huanuco region of Peru, the ornery official complaining about a deceitful world upside down called himself don Felipe Guaman Poma; his lavishly illustrated petition-jeremiad-chronicle *Nueva corónica* is one of history's greatest artistic treasures. The triumphant convert was a Kakchikel Maya named don Pedro Solís Elías Martín. He described to his family how around 1584, he had dethroned the long-ruling Xajil dynasty and became governor of Tecpan Atitlan.[8] The doomsayer was the commoner Juan Teton, who preached around the Mexico Valley in 1558, warning that air demons (*tzitzimime*) would punish those who embraced the new Christian ways. A group of Nahua artisans in Mexico City recorded his premonitions in their 1560s journal, the *Anales de Juan Bautista.*[9] The nobleman behind the palace scheme was Texcocan lord Tetlepanquetzal, who plotted to betray the Mexica and join the Spanish. His story appears in a seventeenth-century chronicle by part-Indigenous author Fernando de Alva Ixtlilxochitl. The final fragment features elder Quechua Natives' 1542 statements about the great Inca civil war of the early 1530s, when the Inca Atahualpa's "tyrant captains" Chalcochimac and Quisquis sought to defeat rival claimant Huáscar and eradicate his court—just as European disease and Spanish-led armies were arriving to bring down the Inca themselves.[10] All of these writings resoundingly attest to a society in complete upheaval.

Indigenous witnesses left no doubt that commoners and schemers were driving the upheaval, and Spaniards were often no less alarmed. For traditionalists, a great and terrible leveling was at hand. In 1554, Franciscan theologian Alonso de Castro urged Emperor Charles V to reject the antiseigneurial changes for which petitioners had been so effectively agitating. He warned that "it would be the undoing of all order [*policía*] and of the human republic itself. . . . In this manner there will not even be shoemakers left . . . [nor] tailors and carpenters and silversmiths . . . bailiffs and field justices and governors and counts and dukes and kings and clergymen and friars and bishops and popes!"[11] Another friar, the famous Dominican Bartolomé de Las Casas, thought the opposite: it was the hour of justice. He gloated that he had persuaded the king and his ministers to uproot the power of the conquistadors. The royal grants of Indigenous tribute the monarchs had granted to conquistadors, the *encomiendas,* were collapsing thanks to vassals' unrelenting pressure. The "poisonous root of tyranny and captivity" was withering, he declared, and a brand-new universe built on true justice was nigh.[12]

In the highland Andes city of Cusco, Spanish lords faced challenges from friars, Crown officials, Indigenous lords, and upstart commoners. When Crown official Pedro Pacheco arrived to implement royal justice in 1561, the downtrodden gave him a hero's welcome. Tensions flared, and the conquistadors complained: "He has been lording over the envy which arises among . . . the common people of the city—merchants, scribes, artisans, and other salesmen and lazy low-lives."[13] They continued, "Every day these shameless people lose the respect they had for us citizens . . . for we are men of greater honor, valor, and authority than them."[14] The Indigenous lords of Cusco—the *curacas*—expressed similar fears. If the conquistadors did not destroy them, then the commoners would usurp their power. The lords pressed Pacheco: Would they lose privilege and power over their Native communities? Or worse—would they become commoners themselves? Emotions spilled over; lords wept in anger and confusion when a translator gave them the impression they would be "sold like blacks, rams, and hogs."[15] When word got out to these lords' subjects, there erupted "a commotion among the common people of the city in which they publicly proclaimed that they would stand for their liberty."[16]

In the mid-1500s, throughout the centers of Spanish domination in the New World, agitation and questioning of the social order was not the exception but the rule. It was not just a handful of conquistadors, friars, or Native lords who stood to lose power—the very foundations of society were on trial. Nor did this conflict unfurl only in elite spaces; Indigenous and Spanish commoners were an irreverent part of the dispute. They, along with friars, priests, conquistadors, translators, royal ministers, and others, sought to transform society through hundreds of thousands of petitions, lawsuits, and investigations.

The history of the sixteenth-century Indies is not, as many authors once believed, the straightforward conquest of Natives and their cultures by Spanish conquistadors, friars, and officials. It is a convoluted, decades-long drama in which Indigenous individuals and groups joined countless others in jockeying for a place in a society emerging from ruin. Lasting roughly three generations in the core areas of the overseas empire, this radical era saw the structures of Indies society uprooted not just after the conquests but several times thereafter. Everyone and everything was transformed over roughly half a century. Only after this period of deep disturbance did a more stable society of orders begin to emerge, one that would remain in place until at least the early nineteenth century—and arguably much later.

These events were not preordained; the Crown initially encouraged a strongly seigneurial society of orders in the New World. Aristocratic conquistadors who deposed great Native dynasties would sit at its apex, enjoying lifetime governorships and huge semiautonomous realms of their own—not unlike the counts, dukes, and marquises of Spain. In the 1520s and 1530s, this order seemed a sure thing. Yet although conquistadors were poised for greatness, almost all ended up in chains or poverty.

Royal ministers, rattled by the collapse of conquistador power, turned to another plan. Friars had been insisting on creating their own vast theocracies, and Native lords jockeyed for power as well. Yet again, paradoxically, the Crown reversed its support for their projects. Friars' millenarian dreams of ruling great theocratic dominions came crashing down as critics blasted their iron-fisted rule and the Crown rescinded their autonomy. In the friars' stead, ministers often sent bishops to rule. Native lords likewise scrambled to preserve their authority against commoner agitation and officials, but again, a strong seigneurial society failed to materialize. Instead, by the 1570s, a royal administration headed by viceroys, bishops, and inquisitors with almost unlimited jurisdictional power was keeping conquistadors, friars, and Native lords at bay.

How did the Crown's initial plans go so far astray? Why did conquistadors, friars, and Native lords fail to establish their designs? Conquest, atrocities, disease, and the king's distance from the New World all played a role. Yet we argue that it was ultimately vassals themselves who refused these projects and pressed for dramatic transformation. Commoners, women, and a range of other actors deliberately joined a great social melee, denouncing their lords as tyrants, disobeying and questioning authority, and creating their own traditions and truths. Many fought for community changes; others envisioned sweeping regional transformations and total destruction of the current order. Conquistadors and Native lords fell into poverty and ignominy—even the very legitimacy of their dominions collapsed. Paradoxically, the Crown emerged in a stronger position than originally intended, albeit under circumstances only partially of its own making. And when a more stable order finally emerged around 1572, it bore the indelible imprint of subjects' participation.

These struggles continue to shape our world. The legacy of this era is not—as popular culture and historians of the twentieth century have repeatedly proposed—limited to authoritarianism, social exclusion, and dogmatic Catholicism (interspersed with the odd revolt).[17] Its legacies include storied disobedience through the power of paperwork. To this day, Indigenous and commoner movements still use petitions, constitutional reform, and armed agitation to advance their interests. And many of the documents they point to in legitimating their claims were created in and shaped by this era of struggle.

PAPERWORK AND LAWFARE IN THE MAKING OF THE NEW WORLD

But *how* did vassals achieve the epochal overthrow of conquistadors, friars, and Native lords? Our core contention is that the Spanish Crown's system of paperwork justice triggered some four decades of social upheaval, most notably between 1526 and 1572. This paperwork justice was massively bottom up and participatory in nature, enabling vassals of almost all social backgrounds to forcefully challenge the New World's emerging local strongmen. Highly complex factions—slaves, commoners, women, and elites both Spanish and Indigenous—used paperwork to dash the Crown's plans of establishing in Mexico and Peru a seigneurial regime resembling that of Spain. The great leaders of the invasions—Christopher Columbus, Hernán Cortés, and the Pizarro clan—were defeated not on the battlefield or by armed putsch but under avalanches of petitions, lawsuits, audits, and legislative reforms.

As friars and their Native allies began pressing for the establishment of extensive, nearly independent monastic theocracies, vassals again mobilized paperwork to curb their growing power. The tens of thousands of Native lords who ruled in the countryside also saw their influence contained by Spanish authorities, local rivals, and commoner unrest. For nearly five decades, subjects questioned and aggressively undermined these groups' attempts to establish social order.

By the 1570s, then, vassals had trounced conquistadors, friars, and Native lords using royal paperwork. But these victories contained a germ of order. Constant appeals empowered local authorities—especially viceroys but also bishops and inquisitors, who achieved virtually unlimited jurisdictional reach based on petitions and reforms. Further bolstering their legitimacy was a growing social consensus, born from the fatigue of endless lawfare, that obedience was a virtue.

The Crown gradually realized that to achieve social peace, it would have to learn more about the Indies. Kings and ministers had no standing army, no databases, no hard power, and they would never achieve a robust grip over their overseas dominions. Yet they slowly became more capable of asserting royal interests thanks to the surge of paperwork vassals submitted every day. During the radical phase, truth was elusive and doubt ruled supreme. But new truths began to win vassals' acceptance.

Underpinning this emerging regime of truth was a constellation of thousands of local archives kept by vassals, officials, and the Crown that safeguarded the records of subjects' past conflicts. Each struggle had generated truths—statements about winners and losers—that, although utterly distorted and disjointed, were necessary for establishing a new social order. These collections comprised more than just privilege decrees, royal and viceregal edicts, magistrates' sentences, church paperwork, and notarial documents. They also included thousands of works created by Indigenous actors featuring non-European structures and epistemologies. These texts—which often made claims about the nature, culture, and ancient history of the Indies—increasingly became the trenches in which vassals waged political struggles. But their efforts became more and more modest with time. After about 1570, most of Indies society had abandoned its dramatic fight over seigneurialism, monastic theocracy, and Native rule, and its actors struggled instead to personally triumph through mastery of these vast archives.

Paperwork, we argue, was therefore central to both postconquest upheaval and the subsequent emergence of a stable society of orders. Spanish imperial justice was deeply socially unequal by design, but it was also extraordinarily participatory. Subjects could engage the Crown primarily through three channels of paperwork, each with distinct procedures, logics, and outcomes: *gracia, gobierno,* and *justicia.* Subjects petitioned by the thousands for royal and viceregal privileges—lordships, official positions, patents, pardons, and more—and successful vassals received royal decrees in return. This channel was known as *gracia.* Those seeking local, regional, and Indies-wide reforms submitted simple, affordable petitions to various authorities, including kings. This socially inclusive *gobierno* channel enabled countless bottom-up transformations of society. The Crown-appointed magistrates to oversee civil and criminal struggles between parties, creating the slow, convoluted, but also participatory channel of *justicia* litigation. And it periodically dispatched auditors to undertake emergency investigations (*residencias* and *visitas*) that, although formally resembling *justicia,* could create new policies.

Virtually all overviews of sixteenth-century New Spain mine this paperwork for evidence, but none incorporate its structural impact on the era. This omission not only obscures the participation of many thousands of individual Indigenous commoners and elites, Spanish women, enslaved subjects, and others; it also obscures how these actors shaped the empire from within through the triad of *gobierno, gracia,* and *justicia.* By centering paperwork as an actant in the making of the sixteenth-century world, we can appreciate just how foundational the actions of nonelites and non-Spaniards were in the creation of this emerging society. This approach moves beyond particularistic accounts and histories and shifts attention from more extrinsic modes of revolt and resistance to more intrinsic modes of participation and politics.

Hundreds of thousands of sixteenth-century social conflicts were channeled through paperwork conduits. Paperwork reached deep into the countryside, into the very heart of remote Indigenous communities, as well as to the furthest frontiers. This does not mean that Spanish authority always had a forceful, immediate presence on the ground; many magistrates were leagues away from Indigenous communities. In most regions, just a handful of officials were on call. Still, virtually all subjects believed that the struggle for privileges, reform, and justice could only be resolved by a monarch in Europe—or at least by his hand-picked representatives.

This issue, and the generally unsettled nature of postconquest society, transformed paperwork into a raucous, radical affair. In Caroline Castiglione's words, subjects of all backgrounds, including commoners, developed an "adversarial literacy" to deploy at the expense of the powerful.[18] Adversarial paperwork rattled the social order to its core, and contemporaries recognized its power. Alonso de Zorita, an eminent jurist who traveled through much of the New World as a royal auditor, lamented that when savvy commoners discovered paperwork, "they began to rise up against their lords, baptizing their ambition to destroy them" and "become free."[19]

Those who used *gobierno, gracia,* and *justicia* could be destructive, subversive, and boldly disobedient toward local authorities. They used paperwork to challenge the powerful, to resist traditions and create new ones, and to secure social mobility through once-illicit means. We therefore characterize the era's engagement with paperwork as *lawfare,* understanding this term to encompass not just paperwork but also its wider, often-violent social context. *Lawfare* captures the spirit of factional conquest and imposition vassals sought on their rivals. Many actors explicitly intended to use paperwork not merely to undermine a rival's claims but to wage lawfare against them and thereby restructure the entire social order. It was the ubiquity of lawfare, above all things, that gave rise to a radical Spanish Empire.

ENVISIONING A RADICAL SPANISH EMPIRE

Radical movements, whatever name one gives them, have aimed to transform societies around the world many times—from Levelers and Quakers to the Red Brigades and the Taliban, the White Lotus Sect and the Situationist International, the Zealots and the Bolsheviks to uMkhonto weSizwe and the Zapatistas. Some movements were violent interruptions from without: the Mongol conquests of Eurasia, the fall of the Ming dynasty, the imposition of Soviet Communism in Eurasia. In other cases, radical structural reform bursts forth from within: the Reformation, perestroika, feminism, the French Revolution, the Cultural Revolution. No two such moments have ever been identical. In fact, they have been staggeringly diverse: the Haitian Revolution, Wahhabism, liberation theology, the Arab Spring, early Christianity. Some were violent, some peaceful. Sometimes they arose thanks to visionary thinkers, other times due to complex social upswells. Some were deeply conservative; others promised total newness. Some came from the haves, some from the have-nots. Comparing them is not easy, and movements themselves were cleaved by all sorts of internal contradictions. But those who experienced them knew that they were experiencing a world upside down.

How can we tell the story of a society that five hundred years ago was teeming with people agitating for the deposition of the powerful and total societal reconstruction? We have opted for a sociology that foregrounds *radicalism*. Subjects at the time did not, to be sure, rally under the term. Yet the word *radical*—from the Latin *radix*, or root—is implicit in the writings of many Indigenous contemporaries and Spaniards. Some, like Las Casas, sought to destroy the poisonous root, or *raíz*, that was conquistadors' seigneurial power. Others, like Castro, rushed to defend order, the fragile tree growing from conquistador lordship. For Native lords, disorder spelled disaster—for commoners, an unlikely glimmer of hope. Each group envisioned the problem situationally and perspectivally, meaning there was no shared definition of the upheaval. Nonetheless, everyone agreed that a man-made, largely intentional restructuring of society was happening on an unprecedented scale, for better or worse. Elites complained of disobedient vassals, conservatives bemoaned the collapse of status and decorum, and agitators celebrated the defeat of unjust systems of oppression. It was the pervasiveness of these views and structural changes more than the monarchs' occasional approval of the movements that truly made it a *radical* Spanish Empire.

This book makes the case that the Spanish-Indigenous conquests of the 1500s New World unleashed a deeply radical period spanning roughly from Hernán Cortés's 1526 deposition as governor of Mexico to the Peruvian viceroy's execution of the last sovereign Inca in 1572. It was one of the longest profoundly radical periods in recorded history anywhere. For many readers, the concept of the *radical* may call to mind those who have fought to change systems over the past two centuries: Marxists, hippies, preppers, feminists, abolitionists, anarchists, tree huggers, fundamentalists, accelerationists. For those interested in the early modern era, *radical* especially brings to mind the bold commoner movements that sprang up between the onset of the English Civil War around 1642 and the Restoration in 1660. Christopher Hill's classic 1972 *World Upside Down*, for instance, understands radicalism as emerging in the world of English civil war—a world of uprootedness, commoner dissent and disobedience toward elites, brash petitioning, skepticism toward the existing regime of truth, and profound intellectual experimentation.[20]

Not everyone embraces transporting the term *radical* into the early modern era. Some have questioned whether early modern radicals are figments of our imagination—especially since the concept of political radicalism arose only in the early 1800s.[21] Margaret Jacob, for instance, cautions that by overusing the term, we make "everything and everybody into a radical," thereby "rendering the category largely meaningless."[22]

There is danger in painting everything as radical, without a doubt. But neologisms are not always bad. We must simply use them judiciously—refusing, for example, to map radical phenomena onto modern concepts of *Left* and *Right.* Doing away with the concept for the early modern era (and all other eras before 1800) also carries great risk, for it cleaves human history in two parts—one before 1800, in which subjects were not capable of true political action, and one after 1800, when modern people finally began to think and act with clear eyes and minds about transforming the direction of their societies.[23]

Even if we accept that we can speak of radicals before 1800, we face another devilish problem: How do we employ a term with so many contradictory meanings? The field of radical studies is vast, and every scholar provides his or her own definition. For some, reformists need not apply; a radical must be an outsider, an utter fundamentalist, a recluse, a revolutionary. Others urge a more nuanced approach, situating radicalism within a historical context. They see radical thought and action as situational—fierce dissatisfaction and action against any established order, whatever it might be. For these scholars, a given individual's radicalism is often tied up with conservatism and pragmatism. There are no pure radicals, nor are there pure radicalisms. James Colin Davis suggests that it is more fruitful to write of "radical moments" that emerge in specific contexts than to painstakingly vet the credentials of specific individuals.[24] For us, *radical* is neither an unadulterated nor unchanging quality of a person or era. It is a dynamic in which actors confront and critique society with the intent of fundamentally overturning some or all of its foundations in order to create a new one.[25] As Craig Calhoun states, "radicalism is not best understood as a stable ideological position. . . . The question is whether [radicals'] social situations, aspirations, and self-understandings put them deeply at odds with prevailing conditions and patterns of change."[26]

We can now offer our preliminary definition of *radicalism.* Individuals and groups partake in radicalism when they act to undermine and replace existing social structures, challenging social arrangements and elites, questioning dogma, and mobilizing actively against injustice.[27] We are interested not in identifying specific radical people or quantifying *how* radical they were but rather in describing a radical society more broadly—in this case, a multigenerational, continent-spanning radical era in which vassals everywhere disobeyed their lords and strongly questioned and acted against structures of power. Crucially, we are concerned with resistance against local elites, not the Crown. It was the former who enacted virtually all everyday violence and directly oversaw society's apparatuses of labor extraction. Opposing these lords, not the Crown, was the priority for vassals seeking to reshape society's fundamental structures.

Resistance is a category we skirt for analytical reasons. Many tellings of the Latin American past crowd many sorts of actions under the banner of *resistance,* from vast armed upheavals to litigation to everyday foot-dragging.[28] We are not interested in cataloging all the strategies that subjects used to struggle against injustice. For our purposes, we have instead opted to keep paperwork—and the social world of rowdy lawfare that surrounded it—conceptually distinct from resistance. This helps us hone in on the specifics of paperwork and lawfare and underscore their unique importance in shaping this century. In the process of communicating with one another through paperwork, rulers and ruled managed to create substantial structural change—including transformations which no parties fully grasped at the time.

Rebellion, revolt, and *revolution,* too, are terms adjacent to our concerns. Alongside *resistance,* there is a strong argument to be made that these terms are useful for understanding this period. Yet they too invite conceptual and chronological problems. Rebellions and revolts were common in the 1500s, but not all of them were radical. Many, in fact, aimed to remove a figure of authority without transforming society. *Revolution* invites similar ambiguity. Scholars and nationalists in Latin America have long traced a story arc from domination to freedom, monarchy to revolutionary liberation. In nineteenth- and twentieth-century nationalist accounts, the sixteenth century abounds with revolutionary figures who openly defied the Crown, expressed proto-nationalist sentiments, and deserve recognition as fathers of the nation *avant la lettre.* We have no interest in tracing the origins of a proto-nationalist revolutionary spirit; *revolution* risks wrapping this story into other narratives of national resistance. Lastly, these concepts all direct attention to resistance *extrinsic* to the empire.

We see radicalism as having deeply shaped the society that arose in the 1570s mainly from within, not without. It did not so much oppose the emerging viceregal society of orders as it came to constitute it.[29] And finally, for the sake of simplicity, we avoid engaging with the idea of *modernity*—a term perhaps more disputed and opaque than any other. Surely, one can make the case that the Spanish Empire was a crucial part of modernity's rise, however one defines it, but this is an argument for another time. For us, radicalism implies fundamental resistance to existing structures—a stance that belongs to no era in particular. And this radicalism was, for several turbulent decades, intrinsic to Indies society. It is this reality that has encouraged us refer to the *radical Spanish Empire*.

A final consideration encompasses both time and space. *Where* was the radical Spanish Empire, and *when*? Our *where* focuses primarily on the greatest Indigenous population centers: central Mexico, Michoacan, Oaxaca, the Yucatan, highland Guatemala, and the Andes from Muisca to Aymara territory. We consider the Caribbean from 1492 until the 1520s, but after its gradual demographic marginalization beginning in the 1530s, we shift attention to the Indies' new cores. Moreover, we have incorporated some frontier areas such as northern Mexico and various regions of present-day Colombia. We believe that the patterns we describe are generally valid throughout the Indies, but we also expect that their specific expressions were highly contingent and heterogenous. Local studies exploring our model will hopefully refine our narrative. Lastly, we do not consider the Canaries, the Atlantic islands whose European conquest predated the New World by nearly two centuries, although future studies might fruitfully reveal how those events shaped this story.[30]

Our chronology is also more heuristic than rigid. The transition from a society of disorder to a society of orders did not abruptly begin in 1526 with the paperwork deposition of Hernán Cortés or end in 1572 with the Peruvian viceroy's execution of the Inca. Radical lawfare began in the 1490s in the Caribbean with the deposition of Columbus and continued in frontier regions for decades after the 1570s. A society of orders, moreover, did not suddenly emerge in 1572. Rather, it was in the late 1560s and early 1570s that the Crown and its allies on the ground managed to disempower all autonomous and semiautonomous Indies groups. During this period, just as importantly, archives became unmistakably more robust and impactful. Though these phenomena justify 1572 as an approximate turning point, every region has its own complex chronology. Mexico tended to change faster than Peru, for example. Moreover, royal jurisdiction only became firmly established over areas like Santa Fe (today Colombia) and Guatemalan Verapaz in the early 1600s. Many frontiers remained highly unstable and did not develop local social hierarchies until much later, if at all. Still, the most populous regions of the Indies did follow this general trend.

FOUR METANARRATIVES AGAINST THE RADICAL SPANISH EMPIRE

Since the 1960s and especially the 1990s, growing interest in social history and subaltern agency in Latin America has stimulated thousands of excellent studies, almost all about local cases, actors, documents, and regions. From tens of thousands of books and articles in many languages arises the potential to craft an agency-rich approach to the era. And yet, no study has recognized the existence of a radical sixteenth-century society fundamentally cocreated through subjects' engagement with paperwork. We see this gap largely as the result of several long-standing metanarratives, which constitute obstacles we must address before overviewing the historiography.

The roots of agency-poor accounts of the era run deep—in fact, back to the sixteenth century itself. Books printed during and after the radical era crafted myths that conspired against this richer understanding of the region's past. Conquistadors like Hernán Cortés published bestselling accounts that aggrandized their own almost mythical heroism. The Dominican friar Bartolomé de Las Casas, waging fierce lawfare against conquistadors, sought to establish monastic theocracy by taking his denunciations of abuses to the press. He trafficked in stories about powerful but wicked Spaniards tormenting helpless Indigenous victims. Centuries of anti-Spanish polemics ensued, and many resonate today. Widely read Crown chroniclers like Antonio de Herrera explained away sixteenth-century turmoil, describing grueling conflicts and civil wars as the result of a tremendously powerful monarchy gradually imposing its will over the New World.

So were born several myths: the myth of a few Spanish conquistadors who easily overpowered Indigenous societies, of a few friars who miraculously converted millions, of an assertive Crown that ruled by fiat and gradually created an obedient, submissive society. These were, of course, propagandistic works of long-gone times. But they left an enduring imprint.

By the twentieth century, these agency-poor narratives had evolved substantially. The Spanish Empire had collapsed, Latin American nations had painfully emerged, uneven economic development produced winners and losers, a global conflict between Left and Right raged. Many intellectual and political traditions emerged in response to these problems, and their adherents retooled old agency-poor narratives into new, similarly limited accounts.

Four of these metanarratives in particular interest us. The first—the liberal narrative—has been arguably the most prevalent in global intellectual circles over the past two centuries.[31] For its adherents, mankind's development is a long but linear story about the spread of liberty, material progress, democracy, and egalitarian universalism.[32] A genealogy of brilliance travels from Greece to Rome to Italy and France and then to northern Europe and especially Britain, helped along by various freethinking geniuses. These great men and their followers propagate bold new ideas of freedom, liberty, rights, reason, science, toleration, democracy, and so forth, shaping the world through market economies, parliaments, the printing press, Protestantism, the Republic of Letters, and the public sphere.[33] In this narrative, the Spanish Empire stands for feudal backwardness, authoritarianism, and dogma. Sometimes it is a foil; more often it is an absence. Many scholars have critiqued this metanarrative, but its latent power has proven hard to shake.[34] Its assumptions have lived a long life in the historiographies on the Age of Revolution, nation-state formation, and authoritarianism, which traffic a belief that the colonial era was ahistorically flat, nonparticipatory, and prepolitical. Only when subalterns violently rejected empire and embraced national liberal institutions could they begin to shape society—or so the story has tended to go.[35]

The second narrative provides, at first glance, the opposite tale. This is the narrative of decoloniality. Its tradition offers a sophisticated leftist critique of the colonial past, drawing from and reforming older Marxist and Christian reform movements. Its proponents reject modernization-oriented projects typical of the twentieth century, which devastated Indigenous cultures, destroyed nature, and oppressed workers. Decolonialists search for a fairer world free from the universalizing pretenses of the West—especially regarding language, culture, and thought. They thus flip liberals' story of progress. The early modern era was not the dawn of freedom and prosperity but a time of worldwide socioeconomic, epistemic, cultural, and racial oppression. Decolonialists denounce liberals for ignoring the centrality of colonial Latin America in the origin of modernity, arguing that Europeans' exploitation of people and resources there kickstarted the modern world.

Yet decolonialists actually preserve the liberal metanarrative in inverted form. If liberal scholars portray colonial Latin America as a foil of progress, as modernity's other, decolonial scholars proclaim the region to be the mainspring of world history's horrors.[36] Latin America becomes more than a failure of freedom and democracy—it is both the dark side of the Renaissance and the dark side of modernity, where seeds of racism, global capitalism, authoritarianism, fascism, concentration camps, and the Holocaust were first planted.[37] According to this narrative, the Spanish conquests and what followed marked both the beginning of global history and the end of New World politics, especially Indigenous politics. In other ways, however, liberal and decolonial narratives overlap almost perfectly. Both envision a dark Latin America in contrast to a brighter Europe and see a passive, ahistorical, apolitical rest dominated by an active, historical West.

The third metanarrative, the *culturalist-civilizationalist* mode, is more diffuse but similarly influential. Its adherents center culture rather than individuals and their politics as the object of study. Here, Latin America's history unfurls as cultures and civilizations interact and transform,[38] resulting in Indigenous culture's catastrophic decline.[39] This perspective has understandably been popular with decolonial scholars (among others).[40] Many see this civilizational clash as giving rise to a vigorous new Latin American civilization marked by mixing, or *mestizaje*.[41] In this tale, Latin America is not a deficient Europe; it is a new, hybrid civilization, different or even superior to its "pure" cultural ancestors.[42]

This cluster of civilizationalist visions has survived and thrived thanks largely to its long-standing appeal to nationalist, pan-Hispanic, and nativist groups. More recently, scholars have denounced civilizationalism's sometimes insidious racial and nativist underpinnings, which tend to imply or even encourage the gradual erasure of Indigenous and Afro-descendant subjects into a mixed national whole. Scholars have also lamented the resilience of culturalist and civilizationalist essentialisms.[43] These visions of cultural-civilizational encounter, decline, and hybridity therefore often diverge. Yet they coincide in directing attention away from the robust, creative Indigenous and nonelite politics that shaped the 1500s.[44] Ironically, interest in Indigenous culture often has meant erasure of Indigenous politics and history.

A fourth metanarrative, that of Hispanism, deserves careful attention because it has produced massive works of scholarship that have often gone unnoticed in Anglo-American circles. Hispanist interpretations posit that Spanish imperialism was a noble, civilizing, inclusive enterprise, in contrast with the rapacious and discriminatory British. This vision rests on a comparative sociology of race and citizenship.[45] Spain, we are told, embraced racial mixing, allowing manumission of slaves through self-purchase and giving political rights to both Indigenous and free Black subjects. Like Rome, it made citizens of erstwhile "barbarians."[46] Britain did not.[47] This vision, which originated in the eighteenth and nineteenth centuries, appealed particularly to defenders of "good" Spanish and Latin American slavery versus the "bad" slavery of the US antebellum South, where Black people had no rights.[48] Where expansionist *yanquis* insulted Hispanics as racial mongrels, Latin American patriots embraced racial and cultural mixing as a virtue.[49]

Ever since, Hispanism has gained a foothold in Latin America's historiographical imagination, producing dense and important scholarship often ignored up north.[50] Yet for all its redeeming qualities, Hispanist historiography relies on teleological models of empire and epistemological assumptions of harmony.[51] Like many royal chroniclers, Hispanists see the Crown at the helm of a glorious imperial and Christian culture.[52] More so than the other metanarratives, Hispanism's emphasis on civilizing harmonization obscures the region's history of violence, slavery, and discrimination.[53] It offers an inspiring story of integration and collaboration alongside top-down, civilizationalist, and apologist histories protagonized by heroic conquistadors, missionaries, and rulers. Here, the empire was crafted by the benevolent kings of Spain and their vassals as a gift to thankful Natives.[54] In such an account, Indigenous politics is impossible.

Few serious academics today are outspoken Hispanists, but Hispanism's legacy is powerful in archives, museums, politics, and public debate; decades of research continue to cast a long shadow.

That is not to say that we reject these traditions whole cloth. How actors make choices and mobilize politically to shape society over time are structuralist questions of agency shaped by liberal values.[55] We share with decolonial scholars a conviction that Latin America is integral to global history and that this account must center slavery, discrimination, and the destruction of culture. Culture and cultural change are key to our understanding of the past as well. And although we reject Hispanism's underlying premises and goals, it remains true that Iberian institutions and mores could be highly responsive to vassals and often enabled nonwhite actors and communities to become important to the empire's operations.[56]

We believe, however, that these metanarratives share two important commonalities that must be overcome before we can tell our story. The first is agency-poor sociology. These narratives generally deny the impact of Indigenous individuals' and groups' complexity and their power to deliberately and structurally impact society. In liberal and Hispanist currents, Europe and Europeans are the sole motors of historical development. In the decolonial vision, Europeans are perhaps even more powerful, undertaking genocide, epistemicide, and ecocide while faceless Indigenous actors shrink or flee to the mountains. Even the culturalist-civilizationalist narrative, which takes Indigenous culture seriously as an agent of historical change, elides the political strategies of Native groups and individuals.[57]

A second tendency common to these metanarratives is excessive concern with placing broad, presentist moral judgments on the Spanish Empire and its actors. The empire is a glorious achievement (for Hispanists), a cautionary tale about arrogance and oppression (for liberals and decolonialists), or a cauldron in which civilizations' vices and virtues melt into something morally new (for culturalist-civilizationalists concerned with hybridity and national character). Scholars and their narratives often take sides in centuries-old debates about the goodness or badness of the empire, in debates that emerged in the sixteenth century itself. Hispanists have crafted what critics call the Pink or White Legend—a rosy, apologetic vision.[58] Other groups adhere to the Black Legend, in which the Spanish are among the cruelest and most illiberal, dogmatic, and backward of all Europeans.

Ultimately, moralizing and denying Indigenous politics reinforce each other. Moralizing creates images of good or bad Spaniards; the idea that Natives largely lack agency amplifies and reveals outsiders' power and worth. Likewise, the erasure of Native politics results in a misguided sense of overpowerful Spaniards. As Steve J. Stern noted over three decades ago,

> the entire Black Legend debate—the dialectic of denunciation of destructive exploitation and abuse on the one side, the celebration of paternalist protectionism and internal Hispanic debate on the other—reduces the Conquest to a story of European villains and heroes. Amerindians recede into the background of Black Legend history.[59]

Both the Pink and Black Legends, then, are incompatible with a vision of participatory radical politics. How can we approach this violent century without erring on one side or the other?

First, in the pages that follow, we decline to portray Spanish elites as more powerful than they were. They were neither heroic nor villainous supermen. The Spaniards were highly fragmented as a group, their socially diverse constituents wracked by human frailty and fierce competition.[60] Conquistadors were violent and fearsome, yes, but also few and highly vulnerable. Friars, likewise, were deeply influential but few in number (and those like Las Casas were not as exceptional and influential as the scholarship often claims). The Crown was distant, understaffed, uninformed, and lacked a monopoly over violence; a highly effective regime of Spanish-led administrative domination never took hold in the vast Native countryside. Given the circumstances, it makes sense that the Spanish-dominated administration was interested in dialoguing with non-Spaniards, commoners, and women. And although Indigenous lords and commoners were hit hard by violence and disease, they remained the demographic majority into the 1600s and beyond; they did not simply resign themselves to fatalism or everyday resistance.

This book makes evident (as others have long argued) that the viceregal period was extremely fraught—especially for women as well as Indigenous and Afro-descendant individuals and groups. Yet violence and oppression do not preclude politics. Many actors knowingly embraced local and regional programs of disobedience against their lords, resorting to lawfare to unsettle the social structures they found oppressive. It is between the Pink and Black Legends, then, that we discover this universe of sixteenth-century politics—and with it, survivors' art of the possible.[61]

REDISCOVERING POLITICS IN THE SIXTEENTH-CENTURY NEW WORLD

While the legacies of these four metanarratives long stood in the way of new narratives about the sixteenth century, changes have been underway for decades. Indeed, many scholars have challenged these traditions and pointed in boldly different directions. Since the 1960s, scholars around the world have become increasingly interested in the participation of actors beyond the usual roster of wealthy white men. As Lynn M. Thomas has noted, many new works aim to critique and expand existing accounts by discovering the influence of understudied actors.[62]

Scholars of Latin America's past have undertaken careful archival and codicological studies of New World society, offering reasons to doubt the metanarratives. Already in 1971, Lewis Hanke pleaded amid a heated debate about the Black Legend for historians to call "a moratorium on the striking off of generalizations and judgments and to enter the archives for further research."[63] This is precisely what occurred; researchers have turned up countless cases of Indigenous lords, Native commoners, Spanish women, Afro-descendants, and others negotiating oppression, achieving social mobility, and shaping society.

Broader reflections on long-term New World transformations, however, have appeared infrequently since the 1990s. Perhaps the last such work was John Elliot's liberal-leaning 2006 *Empires of the Atlantic*

World.[64] This work, sweeping and erudite, nonetheless repeats old, top-down visions of Spanish America's conquest and divergence from the freedom-loving, autonomous peoples of the British colonies. In Elliott's imagination, the Anglo-American state was liberal and market driven, "the result of a multitude of individuals and local decisions, rather than of a centrally directed imperial strategy."[65] Elliot assumes that the Spanish American state sprung from neoscholastic theory, top down. According to Elliot, "[Spain's American empire] represented a conscious, coherent and at least in theory centrally controlled attempt to incorporate and integrate the newly discovered lands."[66] Other works of like ambition tell a remarkably similar story.[67] They leave a stark dichotomy: the British Empire was shaped by the politics of the many, the Spanish Empire by the politics of the few.

However, several new historiographies offer tools for assembling a different story about this period. Four revisionist directions in particular interest us: the New Conquest History, the New Conversion History, the New Administrative History, and the New Jurisdictional History. This book draws deeply from these perspectives, combining them with archival research to weave what we call the *radical narrative.*

The conquest is the logical place to start. Well into the twentieth century, scholars told the story of the conquest as an almost miraculous Spanish victory—a handful of plucky adventurers overthrowing millions-strong Indigenous societies. Since the 1970s and especially the 1990s, a revisionist school—the New Conquest History—has reformulated almost the entirety of this story. Using a wide range of sources (often archival and in Indigenous languages), these scholars have reframed the Spanish invasions, revealing the pervasive, shrewd local and regional politics of Indigenous actors.[68] Scholars now speak of coconquest, recognizing the political contributions of Indigenous protagonists such as Malintzin, Ixtlilxochitl II, and many others. They have shown this period as one of complex, dynamic societies rife with intrigue, using one another strategically to further their own interests. This emphasis on Indigenous politics has proven nothing short of revolutionary, yet its very success raises questions about later events. Did Indigenous centrality end after the conquests? Or might we similarly reframe social processes in later decades?

Just as the New Conquest History reveals that Indigenous actors co-directed the conquests, what we might call the New Conversion History is showing that Natives were not simply subjected to a spiritual conquest led by a handful of friars.[69] In fact, they had their own reasons to find Christ.[70] Scholars have parsed why certain individuals and groups converted, paying careful attention not just to Native culture but to ever-shifting local Indigenous contexts. The so-called military and spiritual conquests, two cornerstones of the myths of European protagonism and Indigenous passivity, are thus transforming before our eyes into stories about Indigenous politics.[71]

Attention to the vast landscape of early viceregal society has also shifted dramatically. After the invasions and baptisms, the traditional story goes, the Crown took over—as Fred Bonner puts it, power was "wrested from the conquistadors and transferred to the bureaucrats."[72] Between the 1570s and 1600s, a Crown-and-church-dominated capitalist-mercantile order crushed the conquistadors' and friars' seigneurial designs.[73] Yet this story of victory is improbable. How did the Crown's limited, uninformed, underfunded, unarmed forces seize the upper hand from distant Europe? How did royal officials convince vassals to cast aside disobedience and embrace order?

Our book recruits two directions for rethinking the emergence of viceregal society with the Crown at its apex: the New Administrative History and the New Jurisdictional History. The New Administrative History offers a rebuttal to liberal and decolonial understandings of the royal administration as a state apparatus that ruled unchallenged over passive subjects.[74] Beginning in the 1980s and 1990s, groundbreaking studies have suggested that Spanish, Indigenous, and other vassals were profoundly litigious, challenging each other and officials in court.[75] Subjects also communicated directly with monarchs and their ministers; indeed, monarchs governed largely through dialogue with vassals of every status. The Crown and its officials were forced by distance and limited resources to take a passive and responsive stance when ruling; they issued legislation, orders, and judicial sentences only when prompted from below.[76] While Spaniards dominated this system overall, Indigenous groups litigated and petitioned to great effect.[77] They did so not only before kings and viceroys but also before the pope, bishops, and other ecclesiastical institutions.[78] To a lesser but still important extent, Afro-descendant groups and individuals embraced similar efforts, sometimes before the king (especially for martial bravery) and often before bishops.[79] The result was a vibrant, bottom-up space of communication in which vassals petitioned their superiors for changes minor and major.

The emerging New Jurisdictional History, a sibling of the New Administrative History, also offers a wealth of insight about the postconquest milieu. For decades, scholars described the Crown's authority as descending in a neat hierarchy of local authorities to the community level. Yet the reality was far different. Instead, historians argue, kings and their ministers delegated authority to countless individuals and groups on the ground without always establishing clear territorial or even jurisdictional borders between groups, creating a stupefying amount of administrative-corporate ambiguity and conflict. To describe this Crown-delegated, overlapping style, scholars in the past two decades have proposed that the empire was a *jurisdictional* state. According to this vision, the postconquest struggle was not a sociologically tidy battle between Crown, conquistadors, and friars. Instead, the Crown created a true administrative melee by delegating vague, overlapping powers to innumerable local actors.[80] Both explicitly and implicitly, this vision of a polyjurisdictional empire is becoming mainstream among historians.[81]

Jurisdictional politics was the foremost theater of political struggle and nonelite participation in imperial rule. Martin Nesvig has stressed that in early Michoacan, for example, "internal dissent, political rivalry, and violent opposition . . . all characterized the corporations of Christianization."[82] Subjects' and officials' aggressive jurisdictional sparring sometimes exploded from litigation to lawfare to direct warfare between factions—and these fissures invited Indigenous actors into the fray. As Lauren Benton observes, Indigenous actors were able to craft "strategies to exploit the jurisdictional complexity of colonial legal orders."[83] Countless regional and microhistorical perspectives have moved out from behind the once-dominant vision of despotic Crown and defiant subjects, revealing the many ways in which groups struggled for the right to rule over their subjects and themselves at the expense of their competitors.

Seen together, bottom-up legal dialogues and polyjurisdictionalism reveal not just the Crown's delegated, hyperfragmented power but an abundance of nonelite actors engaging in these struggles. Scholars now follow the higher-ranking, middling, and humble actors who navigated officials' overlapping, competing, and contradictory jurisdictional spheres to achieve their goals—often at the expense of powerful rivals and royal officials themselves.[84]

Indigenous actors now appear in much greater focus. Works on Indigenous leaders' postconquest strategies of survival and upward mobility have a long pedigree; indeed, this subfield was among the first to attribute political agency to non-Spaniards.[85] Highly educated Indigenous writers pursued their interests by mastering Spanish and other Old World languages and penning ambitious reports, histories, lawsuits, and polemics.[86] The ensuing politics of legal communication is also now a vibrant subfield. As Yanna Yannakakis has noted, we cannot understand these multilingual, multiactor, polyjurisdictional struggles without acknowledging the involvement of translators, legal agents, and other intermediaries (who were often not Spaniards).[87]

The visibility of commoners' roles has increased substantially in new research, too. Recently, scholars have begun to acknowledge that Indigenous peasants—both as allies and as rivals of other Indigenous groups—imprinted their own designs on viceregal society.[88] Alongside jurisdictional conflict and bottom-up paperwork, scholars are noting that Spaniards did not monopolize imperial administration. At the community level, Indigenous elites and officials (and later, Afro-descendants) retained a measure of jurisdiction and power over local government. Indigenous elites and commoners—struggling to survive and advance during extreme hardship—threw themselves into the jurisdictional melee. Their most stable corporate representation came in the form of electoral municipal bodies, the *cabildos de indios.*[89] In isolated cases in the 1500s, and especially in later centuries, Indigenous groups also founded guilds and religious brotherhoods with their own internal jurisdictions and administrations.[90]

A gradual recognition of the contributions of elite Indigenous women to familial, dynastic, and community politics has recently taken off as well.[91] Spanish women, especially nuns and elite relatives of conquistadors and officials, were active in both family and regional administrative politics—albeit almost always as subordinates.[92]

More careful explorations of church officials' tenures reveal them to also have been responsive to nonelites—often siding with Spanish, Indigenous, and Afro-descendant women against their parents, husbands, slave masters, and other tormentors.[93] These accounts tell of litigants, petitioners, and witnesses manipulating the overlapping administrative venues of the Spanish Empire (for examples, see images in Chap. 4). Even the dreaded Inquisition was not only a dogmatic royal tool demanding subjects' submission but also a resource for individuals of many social groups to wage local feuds.[94] As Jorge Traslosheros argues, "the Indigenous were very engaged with the Inquisition, as references in certain trials, as witnesses, as victims, or even as plaintiffs."[95]

The task ahead, then, is to make sense of the social transformations of the 1500s with these groups and phenomena at their center. To this end, our agency-rich account enters into dialogue with much broader revisions of human history. Our interest in agency is tied to the New Social History's post-1960s interest in the impacts of everyday peoples' politics as well as in broader historiography on early modern radicalism.[96] We emphasize the importance of Indigenous politics, pushing in the direction of Native history as well. Our model dovetails with the central thrust of *The Dawn of Everything* by David Graeber and David Wengrow through shared insistence that mankind's progression—including Indigenous history—has been far more structurally and intellectually inventive than liberal thinkers have supposed.[97]

And yet our approach, paradoxically, also presents European administrative practices that already existed by 1491 as inherently dynamic and responsive to new situations. We do not envision Iberia as a highly consolidated medieval civilization incapable of dynamism. Rather, we follow the thesis that Matthew Gabriele and David M. Perry put forth in *The Bright Ages*—namely, that the medieval era refers not to the absence of change but to the opposite. The scholastic and practical inheritances that first arrived with Columbus and his men were often dogmatic, but a dynamic tradition of vassal-ruler communication allowed for creative knowledge production and fierce dissent.[98] This world of medieval dissent and debate merged with tensions within Indigenous society that predated and outlasted the conquests.

Lastly, we should note that throughout this book, we strongly reject the liberal and leftist vision of the Spanish Empire as a foil for the early modern northern European (and especially British) experience. We advocate for critically reevaluating any sociology that establishes the New World as apolitical. Thus, we see this book alongside classic works such as Hill's *World Turned Upside Down*, E. P. Thomson's *The Making of the English Working Class*, and Charles Tilly's *The Contentious French*.[99] We are not arguing that the Spanish New World looked like Britain in this period. What we offer is a stand-alone sociology of change over time tailored to the era, its categories, and its subjects' own designs. To be sure, the picture that emerges troubles the old Spanish-British dichotomy so dear to the metanarratives we challenge. But we leave other scholars to the task of working out this study's implications for British and other European exceptionalisms.

It is clear that in studies of radical traditions, the Spanish Empire is too often either explicitly rejected or simply omitted, while British and similar cases receive pride of place.[100] Without a new narrative and historical sociology, the story of Indies radicalism cannot be told.

THE ARC OF THE RADICAL COUNTERNARRATIVE

Once we have accepted the centrality of participatory paperwork—mainly through *gobierno*, *gracia*, and *justicia* channels—to these events, an otherwise difficult-to-see world of radicalism reveals itself. The archives teem with the petitions, lawsuits, and testimonies of not only Spanish elites but also many others who fueled chaotic social disintegration and gradual recomposition. This lawfare was central to the development of conquests and conversions and the unplanned failure of seigneurialism. It was also important to the gradual expansion of royal authority and the creation of a more stable social order.

The protagonists of this story include preconquest Indigenous societies—especially their leaders, ruling dynasties, ritual specialists, local lords, and serfs—and the conquistadors and their auxiliaries, not just Spanish men but those of Afro-descendant and other Old World backgrounds too. The Native combatants who called themselves *indios conquistadores,* who supported and even directed Spaniards, play important roles as well—continuing for decades after the invasions. In the countryside, friars, Indigenous Christians, Native city governments, and innumerable commoners appear, as do urban Indigenous figures, elite and otherwise. Crown officialssurface, with all their powers and frailties, and local royal and ecclesiastical representatives do too—especially viceroys, bishops, inquisitors, and their many subalterns (including scribes, notaries, and other paper pushers).

In researching this story, we did find that certain social groups—while sometimes important to the work of radical lawfare—tended to act within larger Spanish or Indigenous factions rather than independently as their own discrete groups. For this reason, we do not highlight their contributions within factional struggle as often as those of other groups. Women, for example, often leveraged participatory paperwork—but generally not as women in a collective sense. Rather, they appear in this story mainly as kin or servants of noble Spanish and Indigenous families, as merchants, or as members of Indigenous communities. Collectivities fronted by men thus often represented women's interests. Afro-descendants were in a similar case. Before the late 1560s, Afro-descendants acted largely as laborers or as free or enslaved aides to powerful cliques—and tended therefore to act within Spanish factions. Individual black-skinned Spanish conquistadors and other elites did make important contributions but typically presented themselves in nonracialized terms or as Spaniards. Outspoken groups of self-described Black vassals began engaging regularly in lawfare in the 1570s and 1580s, albeit during a phase in which core areas were coalescing into a society of orders.

Merchants and miners, likewise, consolidated their influence and litigated but had a more subdued impact prior to the 1570s. We also do not treat an important set of Crown officials, the high magistrates, or *oidores*, as a discrete group. These judges often served lifetime appointments in the New World, meaning that their social bonds and interests were interwoven with others'. Lastly, we do not focus on the *criollos*, who are important to many scholars' narratives of change over time. These sons and daughters of Spaniards born in the New World were closely tied to the conquistador faction during this century, although a distinct self-identity began to diverge by the 1580s. While all these groups shaped the emerging society, their influence was simply less coherent and more subtle than that of other collectives, like, for instance, Native lords or commoners.

In this story, we understand paperwork itself as a powerful actant.[101] Initially, paperwork enabled vassal-Crown communication that significantly weakened or outright destroyed the authority of powerful seigneurial individuals and groups. But it was also a snare. Bottom-up dialogue with the Crown was intoxicating. Even though the king and ministers were distant and nearly powerless to enforce on-the-ground outcomes, vassals became heavily invested in royal responses. They sought them out, waited for them (often for years), contested unfavorable decisions, and assembled collections of exchanges for posterity. As a result, subjects consented to royal power to a considerable degree.

This book thus offers an alternative history of both the disintegration of the New World social order and the establishment of a new one. We aim to provide not just a political or religious account of the era but a novel structural explanation. The conquests were not relatively straightforward military-administrative-ecclesiastical actions that produced a colonial society. Nor did a powerful Crown simply assert its will over the conquistadors. The power of participatory paperwork, leveraged by commoners and elites alike, was essential to the restructuring of the social order.

Such paperwork was also extraordinarily important to destabilizing seigneurial labor patterns and initiating a new market economy—changes generally attributed to the Crown's retraction of grants of Native tribute and labor (*encomiendas*), Indigenous demographic collapse, and discoveries of vast mines.[102] In other words, we frame paperwork as a *system of communication* deeply consequential to these sixteenth-century upheavals. Disease, labor relations, language, and preconquest Iberian and Indigenous cultural patterns played their roles, but only paper-based lawfare explains why and how certain groups won, others lost, and the post-1570s social landscape took form the way it did.

Our history of paperwork lawfare resembles histories of the bottom-up politics that print culture made possible in northern Europe. Such histories have shown how the circulation of hundreds of millions of books and ephemeral print triggered factionalism, religious wars, confessionalism, and waves of skeptical doubt that reorganized polities from the bottom up.[103] They credit print with encouraging techniques of reading, collecting, and organizing information that led to the "Scientific Revolution."[104] And they trace print's role in the rise of new forms of sociability and exchange, including newspapers, salons, and coffee houses, where communities of writers and readers began to create a political public sphere.[105] There are striking resemblances with the surge of radical political factionalism and skepticism in the sixteenth-century Spanish Empire. Neither the political public sphere nor the vicarious community of writers and readers that begot nations, we argue, were born with print culture.

Centering communication and knowledge production moves us away from materialist labor and economic history and into the vast literature on writing, semiotics, and epistemology. Here, however, we do not merely insist on the centrality of Spanish versus Indigenous styles of communication. For many civilizationalists and decolonialists, the 1500s were a paradigmatic clash of literate and nonliterate civilizations in which Western writing (and print) conquered Native orality and pictographic expression.[106] While rejecting this thesis, as we do, other scholars have explored how the power of writing—its contents, symbolism, processes, and particpants—profoundly shaped the social order. They have revealed that Indigenous and nonelite subjects invited themselves into the Lettered City and carried its lessons into a vast lettered countryside—a Lettered Mountain, so to speak.[107] Like them, we insist that vassals creatively used alphabetic writing as they waged lawfare, but we underscore that reducing these actors' politics to civilizational struggle risks obscuring exactly what they were hoping to achieve. Many vassals built and inhabited this lettered dominion (both the city and the mountain). They did so in spite of widespread illiteracy, the challenge of the alphabet, and the abuses of intermediaries (themselves indispensable agents in this process).[108] The speed of this transition into textualization has few parallels in history; in the Latin West, for example, the twelfth- and thirteenth-century penetration of writing into everyday life was gradual and painstaking.[109] In the Indies' radical era, despite ongoing illiteracy, textuality dramatically shaped how groups interacted with each other within mere years or decades.

Emblematic of this relationship between social transformation and paperwork is the *ladino,* a socio-legal category of human difference often ignored in accounts of this era.[110] Scholars have tended (partially correctly) to define *ladinos* as non-Spanish actors who became Christians and adopted Spanish language and dress, but this definition downplays the category's broader and more subversive meanings. Many contemporaries—conquistadors, friars, Native lords, Spanish officials—complained of Indigenous and Black *ladino* subjects who were tirelessly mobile, linguistically nimble, socially insubordinate, and savvy to the extreme regarding paperwork.[111] They learned Spanish or large Indigenous languages like Quechua when necessary; paramount for these diffuse actors was self-transformation through paper pushing and public performance of self-proclaimed status.[112] Many maneuvered for personal gain, while others, like Guaman Poma de Ayala, sought vast, deep change throughout the empire.[113] And they often pushed others to learn the ways of disobedience, especially through paperwork. As one bishop warned from Quito in the early 1560s, "*ladino* Indians" and only disrupted the preconquest structures of Native communities but also "taught them insolence."[114] Two decades later, priest Bartolomé Álvarez fumed, "They wish to master legal knowledge to become pettifoggers" and thereby act "for towards their designs and damage ours."[115]

For this reason, we often foreground *ladinization* in this book. We do not see it merely as adopting colonial Spanish practices and abandoning traditional languages and lifeways or engaging in the creation of a stable new culture.[116] Ladinization was not *mestizaje,* a racial-civilizational ideology that preached harmony, integration, and state-amenable diversity during the national period. In fact, it was very often not acculturation but a type of radical politics by another name. The *ladino* was a savvy veteran of lawfare, neither a warrior nor a polite supplicant but something in between. He or she was the prototypical subject of the radical Spanish Empire's immense discord, internal conflict, and creative adaptation.

Constant lawfare not only enabled the triumph of a new social order but also shaped vassals' subjectivities, memories, and ideas of the past. It impacted the emergence of ethno-legal categories even as subjects shaped them back.[117] Categories like *Indian* and *Native tradition* were rhetorical weapons of lawfare. Communities and individuals during the radical era created collections of documents to defend their interests, often in the form of accounts of preconquest antiquity; these emerging textual communities created ideas of preconquest stability since time immemorial (*desde tiempo inmemorial*).[118] In subsequent centuries, vassals—and historians—would revisit these claims, reading past their politics to construct new accounts of New World antiquity. Archives also documented vassals' genealogies. In Iberia and increasingly in the post-1570s Indies, vassals struggling over status, community belonging, and access to positions of power grounded their arguments in genealogies stored in archives. This strategy led to piecemeal policies in which subjects and officials labeled others in racialized terms—as *mestizos, mulatos,* and others.[119] In response to discrimination, subjects who had been labeled by rivals with these terms sometimes formed discrete racialized communities to fight back.[120] In this sense, impossible categories that described nonexistent groups became, thanks to archival practices, textual communities themselves.[121] Lawfare and archives not only arose from conflict; they also shaped these struggles, becoming reified within the most fundamental features of the emerging society's hierarchy.

Archives were, therefore, powerful actants. Over time, as hundreds of thousands of petitions and lawsuits piled up, communication fundamentally changed. Each year, actors—individuals, families, factions, corporations, cities, provinces—would assemble the outcomes of their paperwork struggles into little archives. And these grew into colossal collections over years or decades. The process was largely bottom up and organic: subjects knew these documents were valuable and therefore treasured them. Archives recorded past dialogues, which remained deeply useful in battles about status, justice, and land. They also safeguarded communities' stories about collectives, determined the nature of racialization, and gave past resolutions permanence. Archives came to constitute the truths of the emerging order—truths that were cocreated, forged in lawfare, fragmented, internally and mutually contradictory, but held be truths nonetheless. Vassals did not merely accept a regime of top-down, alien dogma; both officials and subjects struggled together toward these truths. In the process, they formed a new social order with lasting epistemological underpinnings. Of course, this process was deeply unequal and always tied to European epistemologies in some way. But the extent to which many factions and subjects cocreated it is hard to understate.

We argue that the archive did not rule out social mobility and epistemological creativity. In the radical period, charisma and the ability to summon witnesses secured claims to lands and vassals but also disorder and extreme factionalism over truth making. Archives brought stability and greater epistemological uniformity, without eliminating creativity and social mobility as social climbing persisted through falsification. Counterfeiting flourished.

We argue, therefore, that the Indies' system of communication transformed over time, with important structural consequences. The dialogue gradually changed from rather limited Crown-vassal correspondence before the 1520s to a communication free-for-all involving many officials and subjects in the 1570s. After that point, archives increasingly shaped the ongoing and robust interchange. This shift in the role of the archive, which was initially nearly imperceptible, came to constitute one of the most fundamental divisions between the radical period and the society of orders that followed.

Henceforth, vassal politics ran less through impassioned petitions than through mastery of documentary collections. Far from ending politics, archives shaped how vassals engaged with writing and justice after the 1560s. The radical phase, characterized by fierce antiseigneurial lawfare and generalized disobedience, gave way to a society of orders in which paperwork actually increased in volume (albeit not in structural impact). Lawfare also persisted, but subjects less often succeeded in using it to uproot social structures, instead aiming at bringing specific individuals to justice through an elaborate epistemology of carefully documented and cited past events and established legal principles. Previously, lawfare had featured rowdy assemblages of witnesses, bold statements about atrocities, and claims about the Indies supported by nothing but the author's allegations. Now, lawyers and other legal agents helped litigants and petitioners cite previous royal decrees, notarial documents, genealogies, Indigenous codices, and other types of works to make their arguments. Individual cases exploded in size, sometimes forcing Spanish officials to create streamlined paperwork (*justicia sumaria*) for impoverished Natives. The truth became more citational, and readers combed carefully through previous texts for arguments in their favor. Glossing, close reading, indexing, and retrieval became art forms, all of which made the intermediaries involved in mastering paperwork, and especially archives, increasingly central.[122] Indigenous people and other non-Spanish actors often sought informal training not just in paperwork but in archivization, contributing to society's ladinization.

That is not to say the king and his ministers had no power or that their power remained inert as decades advanced. The Crown simply had no effective recourse to violence to force subjects to do their bidding; force lay instead in the hands of conquistadors and Native lords. Kings and their inner circle also had virtually no direct experience with matters concerning the Indies, leading many vassals to refer to them as blind.[123] Indeed, both their early attempts to sponsor a seigneurial conquistador-dominated society and their theocratic about-face reveal the pliability of royal officials' designs.

Yet even from their unenviable position, rulers managed to pragmatically expand, defend, and even shape the New World. They came to enjoy a monopoly, rarely challenged by vassals, on distributing privileges and official appointments, adjudicating or delegating justice, and issuing both local and sweeping legislation. And while vassals constantly insisted that they had better eyewitness understanding of the Indies than monarchs and subjects pioneered effective use of archives far before the Crown, by the 1560s rulers had begun to claw back considerable influence. During this decade, the imposing inquisitor and auditor don Juan de Ovando y Godoy insisted that the Council of the Indies become more robust. As president of the council, he launched a project of reforming the institution, arranging the contents of its vast, disorganized archives to reinforce royal assertiveness. These reforms meant that by the 1560s, ministers and monarchs had new, if limited, powers to order society according to their vision.

The reforms came at a challenging but opportune moment. By the 1560s, European wars were becoming more expensive and global, forcing the Crown to seek revenue wherever possible. Indigenous tribute was difficult to collect due not only to disease and violence but also to commoners' flight and lawfare. Antiseigneurial movements had freed many vassals from their communities, creating a large workforce that no longer toiled as a traditional obligation but exchanged labor for cash (or its equivalent). The prodigious silver mines of Mexico and Peru, a major source of Crown income, encouraged entrepreneurial ranching and agricultural projects deep into the frontier. Where labor was short or expensive, wealthier subjects began to purchase thousands of enslaved victims, mostly from the Atlantic world.

This situation offered Crown officials great opportunities. Vassals and local authorities had managed to kneecap conquistador and monastic power, and by 1572, no major lordly dominions remained. In the following centuries, Crown-appointed viceroys, not conquistadors' descendants, would prove central to Indies administration. Friars' theocratic power had also become an object of subjects' complaints, helping Crown-allied bishops position themselves as defenders of the poor and miserable. Native commoners often abandoned their weakened lords, creating new communities or moving to bustling urban and mining centers.

In the late 1560s, the former inquisitor President Ovando oversaw the establishment of the Holy Inquisition in Peru and Mexico. The inquisitors, however, played an often-different role from viceroys and bishops.

Whereas the latter two had largely opposed the formation of near-autonomous conquistador and monastic domains, inquisitors prioritized responding to accusations of disobedience in Indies society. Petitioners were also behind these actions, of course, but in the process inaugurated an era of diminished radicalism in which officials much more systematically punished disobedience. What we call the *royal trinity* had emerged from the bottom up: viceroy, bishops, and inquisitors. Their power would last for centuries and ensure that the Crown enjoyed a vast jurisdiction. The dramatic bookend to the radical phase was a Spanish-Indigenous alliance's defeat of the sovereign Inca of Vilcabamba in 1572, which concluded with Viceroy Francisco de Toledo's infamous execution of the last Inca sovereign, Tupac Amaru. By 1572, then, Crown officials—mainly viceroys, bishops, and inquisitors—had managed to route the Indies' most powerful autonomous and semiautonomous seigneurial forces despite considerable weakness.

Our structural argument relies therefore on changes in the nature of paperwork, allowing for the agency of systems of communication.[124] Ultimately, we believe that therein lies the difference between the politics of the Indies on the one hand and Spain and the Latin West on the other. There, paperwork and politics followed similar patterns; in Castile, paperwork politics was also conducted through the channels of rewards (*gracia*), reform (*gobierno*), and litigation and auditing (*justicia*). There and in nearby polities, a dynamic but stable social order also resulted from bottom-up lawfare and archivalization.[125] This process took centuries to unfold, and paperwork's role was important but far subtler and more gradual. In the Indies, meanwhile, mere decades of turmoil resulted in the emergence of a new order.

The outcomes of lawfare were different too. In 1500s Europe, seigneurialism remained robust. In Spain, for instance, Castille featured a relatively stable array of powerful lordships and semi-independent communities. Aragon, Cataluña, and Navarra had constitutional pacts with the Castilian monarchs unlike anything in the Indies.[126] In Andalucía, balkanized seigneurial lordship remained the norm until the nineteenth century.[127] The kingdom of Granada did share patterns with the Indies, as the former comprised lands incorporated through violence and treaties of suzerainty with Islamic polities rent by factionalism within.[128] In Granada like in the Indies, challenges to the Crown's seigneurial lordship were ultimately eliminated—in the Granadan case, through physical expulsion of Islamic communities. And like in the Indies, the Crown in Granada gained control over the appointment of bishops and clergy.[129] But in Granada, once the Crown-delegated seigneurial lordship to entrepreneurial Christian feudal lords, these lords were never removed through bottom-up lawfare. In the Indies, by contrast, the Crown adapted to bottom-up lawfare, gradually and inadvertently establishing virtually universal jurisdictional powers by 1572. The rise of centralized power thus diverged quite dramatically; only later in Europe would rulers reach similar authority. Even the type of authority the Crown achieved was different. Consolidation in the Indies was largely unrelated to military pressure from the outside, as it was in Europe. In the New World, monarchical absolutism was the result of collective efforts against those truly in power, for those who possessed the ability to use violence were the conquistadors, friars, and Native lords.

The consolidation of the Crown did not mean that it became all-powerful in the Indies. On the contrary, its ability to enforce a coherent vision on its subjects remained rudimentary. Yet its position had indeed changed. Lawfare had empowered viceroys, bishops, and inquisitors at the expense of local cliques. And through the manipulation of archives, royal officials and vassals had largely settled on certain fundamental truths. These repositories played an essential role in the generation of consensus where disagreement had once been epidemic. What remained for the Crown, then, was to celebrate the demise of disorder.

This project constituted a subtle fourth conquest: the conquest of historiography. When royal chronicler Antonio de Herrera's monumental *General History* came out in 1601, he described a top-down, foreordained conquest by the Crown. He did so by relying on the council's post-1560s project of expropriating friars' and conquistadors' radical archives, which had fueled lawfare in previous decades. He cannibalized the archives to knowingly erase much of this conflict and instate a story of conquistadors, friars, and royal officials acting in succession to cement the king's might in the New World. He thus established the narrative of Crown conquest.[130] John Elliot's vision of a mighty Spanish Crown engineering Indies society by *fiat* is vintage Herrera. Yet Herrera, unlike Elliot, knew that he had twisted the archive, reading against the archival grain to insist on royal power and social order in the face of evidence.

We argue, on the other hand, that to discover a radical narrative, one must very often read *along* the grain. We do so across numerous local and central archives in Spain, Europe, Latin America, and the United States. The paperwork channels of *gobierno, gracia,* and *justicia* in royal viceregal and local archives do not hide vassals' politics. Indeed, it is easy to find in these archives a melee of commoners and elites, Indigenous and Spanish, men and women.

At the same time, we have had to grapple with the sheer size of these archives. We have consulted well over a million pages of royal, viceregal, ecclesiastical, Inquisition, High Court, municipal, and notarial documents. We have painstakingly traced the connections between documents and their outcomes, for instance linking petitions to the royal decrees they prompted and phrased and following the impact these measures had on society. This work has required not just mining text for historical material but understanding the agency of paperwork and procedure in their own right. And we have endeavored to make sense of Indies-wide trends as a whole, discerning from this vast sample and from regional complexities the changing patterns and structures of politics and communication.

Our centering of politics demanded that we wrestle with a long-standing culturalist and decolonialist tradition: the decontextualization of Indigenous sources. For decades, ethnohistorians have produced sophisticated commentaries on postconquest Native codices and other works. The majority have delved into the intricacies of their non-European epistemologies, placing considerably less emphasis on the politics of these works. In fact, this tendency toward decontextualization and depoliticization of Indigenous texts has deep roots, going back at least as far as the efforts of don Lorenzo de Boturini in the 1730s.[131] Ethnohistorians in his wake have also endeavored to catalog, preserve, and translate these sources—providing a wealth of invaluable materials for our study.[132] Their painstaking efforts have been crucial to incorporating robust non-Spanish material into this book. The task at hand, then, consists of reconnecting Indigenous sources with the lawfare through which many were born, rethinking these cultural artifacts as political resources in their day.[133]

This book risks, in its sweeping ambition, to suffocate local detail and exceptions. We have sought above all to respect contingency, individual and group politics, contradictions (even within individuals), and a wide diversity of outcomes. These phenomena are part and parcel of our model. For this reason, we deliberately provide sweeping overviews *and* denser microhistorical explorations of the processes we describe. It is from these many granular archival cases, not from sweeping theories, that we have built our counternarrative.

* * *

The book is divided into five chapters. Chapter 1 examines the systems of political communication between Crown and vassals that triggered waves of radical, antityrannical, bottom-up lawfare targeting conquistadors, friars, and Indigenous lords. It also shows how a weak Crown emerged with the monopoly on mediating power and new stable social orders organized around viceroys, bishops, inquisitors, and an ethos of obedience. Chapter 2 explores how slavery-related paperwork and antiseigneurialism transformed the northern Mexican frontier into a *ladino* society and global commercial hub built largely on wage labor. New frontier social orders emerged, with former Indigenous commoners and slaves reinventing themselves as Christian crusaders heroically leading military, spiritual, and Crown conquests. Archives triggered this transition and so too did widespread counterfeiting. Chapter 3 discusses bottom-up *gracia* petitions in radical polities rent by factionalism, describing how competitive paper-driven knowledge enabled massive violence while encouraging vassals to create countless novel works featuring non-Iberian epistemologies. *Gracia* simultaneously encouraged the conquests and helped invent new radical traditions for millions of Indies vassals. Chapter 4 explores the culture of vernacular skepticism that swept the sixteenth-century

Indies, enabling disobedience on a massive scale, as well as the various paper technologies that allowed contemporaries piecemeal solutions to generalized doubt. Finally, Chapter 5 underscores the impact of archives in the creation of a new society of orders. It also shows how new forms of Crown knowledge helped officials wrestle power away from vassals and administer an empire besieged by bankruptcy, piracy, jurisdictional weakness, radical doubt, and ignorance.

CHAPTER 1

The Empire That Wasn't

Lawfare and the Fall of Indies Seigneurialism

In 1535, don Vasco de Quiroga wrote to the king from Michoacan, painting a bleak picture of the province and of Mexico in general. The brutal warlord-official Nuño de Guzmán had executed the last Irecha ruler of the Tarascans, Tangaxoan Tzintzicha, after a sham trial in 1529. Four years later, Quiroga arrived with a royal appointment to investigate a land plagued by abuses. He initially took major strides. By 1537 he was bishop, and he wanted to use his power to create a Christian utopia. But his roughly 170-page 1535 audit report to the Crown identified a daunting obstacle for his radical plans: the scourges of tyranny past and present. Before the conquests, Native peoples had lived like slaves under the yokes of Moctezuma, Tangaxoan, and their ilk. Now Michoacán's commoners groaned under the tyrannies of Spaniards and Indigenous lords.

Yet there was reason for the New World's oppressed to be hopeful. It was the role of royal investigators, bishops, and their allies to detyrannize the land.[1] Quiroga reported great success in helping commoners "animate and exert themselves"; they were now "requesting their justice and freedoms, through their painting-complaints. . . . This is an incredible thing for those who have not witnessed it."[2] Already as a High Court magistrate in Mexico-Tenochtitlan, Quiroga and four elder Nahua statesmen had freed innumerable commoners from servitude and slavery, working "at night and at day, and during any hour."[3] One witness said he had seen "a great number of Indian men and women, requesting and defending, in such a quantity that the house was full, or at least the room . . . where he was listening and working and dispatching, and not before a scribe."[4] Many commoners proved their innocence by presenting paintings; some simply testified orally in Nahuatl and Otomi.[5] Among others, Cristobalejo, a Black translator, helped Quiroga navigate this Babel.[6] It was a utopia of oral, painted, and written justice from the bottom up.

Yet Quiroga's bold rhetoric caught up with him. His own audit critiqued him for failing to provide receipts for the petitions and responses he issued. As bishop, his acrimonious disputes with the Augustinians caught the attention of the Crown. A Franciscan investigator, Mena, reported to the king in the late 1550s with a less-than-favorable impression of Quiroga's fiefdom. Two decades after the utopia's groundbreaking ceremony in Michoacan, conquistadors were operating with impunity. The Franciscan investigator complained that "among all the provinces" in Mexico, royal officials "must know about this realm of Michoacan, because this is the most tyrannized of them all." Despite Quiroga's earlier denunciations of Indigenous lords' abuse of commoners, Mena had choice words for the bishop's great ally, the son of the last Irecha, don Antonio Huitzimengari. Don Antonio was a tyrannical *ladino* with too much power for his own good: "If only God had willed him never to have studied. . . . Today he is completely surrounded by lost Spaniards who, once out of earshot, call him a King." Don Antonio had established his own fiefdom, in a sense. He "commits great tyrannies, charging unbearable tribute, [is] a lover of spending greatly on food, clothing, and horses. . . . [and is] prejudicial in the extreme with the honesty of the Indian women." The friar proposed exiling don Antonio to Spain. Quiroga, too, appears in Mena's report less a crusader for an apostolic utopia than a tyrant himself. Mena accused him of neglecting conversion and focusing on material splendors, boiling at Michoacan's "Babylon of a church" and complaining of the cruel servitude of commoners constructing the massive temple.[7]

Quiroga had reshaped Mexico's social relations and decried his enemies as tyrants; now, subjects accused him and his allies of the same. Yet he had overseen a transformation that had occurred all over the Indies. Tyrannical Indigenous sovereigns, conquistadors, and friars lost much of their sovereign power over the province to royal officials and bishops (and in this case, their Native allies). Bishops like Quiroga—as well as viceroys and Inquisitors—managed to channel lawfare to expand their power. By the time Quiroga died in 1565, broad royal jurisdictional authority was markedly on the rise throughout the Indies—yet this expanded authority had not emerged as a top-down royal plan. Innumerable bottom-up challenges denouncing the Indies powerful as tyrants had empowered Quiroga to act and jolted the Crown from its seigneurialist plans, causing a major course correction that reshaped Indies society and global history.

Since 1492, the conquerors of the New World had dreamed of creating an entrenched society of orders with themselves at the apex. Would-be lords looked to Europe and its elaborate tapestry of blue-blooded estates, in which aristocrats had considerable autonomy from rulers and great power over their vassals. The most populous regions of the Indies initially seemed primed for seigneurial order. The Moctezuma and Inca dynasties had ruled through intricate familial-administrative connections over ethnically diverse communities. After the defeat of the great Indigenous nobilities—especially the extensive Moctezuma and Inca families, who lost virtually all of their power, Christian invaders divided up the jurisdictional spoils. The formidable European Trastámara and Habsburg dynasties eagerly ratified their powers, laying the foundations for a seigneurial society of orders between the 1490s and 1530s. The Columbus, Cortés, and Pizarro dynasties won from the kings wide-ranging privileges to rule over their Native and Spanish vassals as semi-independent lords. A mix of urban priests and rural friars—Franciscans, Dominicans, and Augustinians—would arrive to convert pagans and ensure a mass of commoners to obediently fulfill duties. Local Crown officials, in this vision, would share some of this power.

Some four decades later, around 1572, the Indies bore little resemblance to this seigneurial blueprint. The scions of the Columbus, Cortés, and Pizarro dynasties lived in exile in Madrid. There, they litigated against the king to recover the huge aristocratic dominions he had confiscated from them. Many minor conquistadors saw their grants of Indigenous tribute reduced to tiny allotments, and all lost direct jurisdiction over Natives. The once-mighty Moctezuma and Inca also found themselves litigating and petitioning before a foreign lord. The Inca family ruptured—loyal Christians in Cusco, sovereign lords fighting the Habsburgs in Vilcabamba until their defeat in 1572. Even loyalists found themselves divided and often impoverished, petitioning and litigating to preserve oddments of their once-vast authority.

The collapse of these seigneurial powers allowed a peculiar phenomenon: the proliferation of friars' semiautonomous dominions. As Indigenous and Spanish lordships collapsed, several thousand friars, lacking any organized military power, maneuvered through strategic alliances with Indigenous elites to establish realms of their own, both *de facto* and *de jure.* These theocratic jurisdictions promised new apostolic beginnings in the New World—or, in their critics' words, autonomous fiefdoms where friars' abuse ran rampant. Throughout the New World, thousands of savvy Indigenous lords, free of Native dynasties and Spanish warlord-masters, might suddenly rise to almost undisputed community power. Commoners, meanwhile, suffered greatly but tenaciously pressed forward to wrest opportunities from this disorder. Some, playing their cards just right, rose into the ranks of lesser or middling nobility. Others struggled against nobles and abusive Spaniards by variously seizing power in their towns, creating whole new communities, and litigating and petitioning relentlessly to change deep social structures.

For some forty years after the conquistadors arrived seeking a feudal order, then, a society of orders did not take root. Instead, a radically disobedient world was born. Conquistadors unleashed violence and plague, weakening their power. Churchmen tore at the fabric of Indigenous communities with new religious teachings. But it was especially the third conquest, that of the Crown's royal officials and bishops over the conquistadors and friars, that paradoxically prevented a robust feudal order from emerging. Instead of an ordered realm, a radically disobedient and dynamic world was born—and the medium through which it arose was not primarily the sword but the pen.

This outcome is deeply paradoxical; the Crown had certainly not planned for it. In the opening decades of the conquests, monarchs and a small handful of ministers had actually encouraged aspiring aristocrats to rule the New World. Well into the 1530s, they actively encouraged the formation of a conqueror-seigneurial society. Yet in 1572, the landscape was a far cry from these initial designs. Representatives of the Crown had direct jurisdiction over once-nearly autonomous seigneuries. Viceregal officers, inquisitors, and bishops wrested back considerable powers of punishment and administration from once-independent friar theocracies and rural Indigenous lordships.[8] The newly arrived royalist inquisitors in particular asserted broad power over many vassals independently of district. Inquisitors weakened the friars' claims to rule the more remote Indies provinces and, most importantly, made a point of responding to bottom-up accusations of disobedience against the social order. Unlike Spain, where seigneurialism was the norm, in the Indies, an utterly novel viceregal-episcopal-inquisitorial trinity held the upper hand against the once-powerful dominions of conquistadors, friars, and Indigenous lords. But this trinity was more accountable to the Crown and its vassals; bishops could be recalled to Spain, and viceroys and inquisitors experienced bruising audits (which summoned testimonies from every social group). And we must not confuse this royal triumph with the end of bottom-up communication. In fact, this royalist trinity greatly increased opportunities to petition, litigate, and testify by opening new venues and streamlining complaints. The efficacy through which the royalists established a society of orders came from their broad jurisdictions, their ability to create consensus among social sectors through a balance of dialogue and punishment, and their dedication to ending disorder, which by the 1570s had exhausted not only seigneurial groups but many vassals as well.

How did this third conquest happen? Scholars have largely understood it as a contest of wits and muscle between the Crown and conquistadors in which the former gradually defeated the latter through sheer force and resilience.[9] In this vision, the Crown had always opposed seigneurialism. Yet we argue the opposite: very evidently, kings and ministers had initially favored seigneurialism, later sponsoring the power of both friars and Native lords when it failed. Explaining the third conquest, then, requires tracing how the Crown abandoned its original blueprint. This transformation, we argue, can only be understood as the result of massively participatory and contingent bottom-up lawfare. Indeed, officials merely harnessed the lawfare vassals brought before them—especially punishing waves of *gobierno* petitions, *justicia* litigation, and *visita* denunciations. And these subjects made their radical goals clear: they sought to bring down the Indies powerful. Often, subjects organized against local strongmen-administrators, staging paperwork riots that combined overlapping forms of lawfare to powerful effect. In other cases, these actors sought to overthrow not only individuals but also whole social structures—conquistadors' feudal order, friars' theocracies, Native lords' dominions.

The result was a deep, structural transformation of both Indies administration and society itself. Vassals debilitated preconquest social bonds—as did the countless enslaved petitioners who appeared before Quiroga. They challenged the authority of conquistadors, friars, and surviving Native lords to compel their respect and labor. Not only Spaniards but also Indigenous elites and commoners and a smaller contingency of Afro-descendants participated in challenging lords, often ladinizing themselves as they engaged with lawfare and social disruption. Deep social disruption followed, driven by massive internal migration, schismatic communities, new elites, adventurous frontiersmen, and entrepreneurial wage laborers who flocked to mining towns and cities. The weakening of bonded labor and the rise of a large wage-earning population unbound by the traditional social order provided muscle for emergent silver extraction projects. These efforts, located in traditionally less-populous areas and desolate environments—think Zacatecas and Potosi—had forged, as John Tutino has noted, "a new deeply commercial society" by around 1600. The new society linked Europe, the New World, and China into a single mercantile sphere—all without any prefigured "grand design."[10] John Elliot's Spanish Empire, which he argues was prearranged by theologians and jurists in Salamanca, bankrolled by endless silver deposits, and patrolled by absolutist officials, is an illusion. Its origins lay instead in paperwork-based antityranny movements that cracked the foundations of seigneurialism, undid traditional social bonds, redrew Crown blueprints, and set the stage for the emergence of a very different type of society from what existed in Spain and the Latin West.

Paperwork, then, transformed Indies society dramatically. There were countless concepts and actors at play within these struggles, but we argue that the crucial concept of *tyranny* was particularly central. Quiroga's crusade to detyrannize Mexico was not a one-off; numerous vernacular antityranny efforts—sometimes solitary petitions, often large and sustained paperwork revolts—drove social upheaval. By invoking tyranny, vassals managed to convince the Crown that the Indies powerful—conquistadors, friars, Native lords—must lose their dominions.

Scholars have largely overlooked the massive significance of this antityranny lawfare. Many have traced the story of antityranny with little to no mention of a Spanish tradition. Some have mentioned Spanish actors as tyrants themselves or have argued that the Spanish, unlike the British radicals of the 1600s, lacked a truly radical tradition of antityranny.[11] There is no small irony here. More than a few early modern scholars who denounced tyranny were actually twisting the words of a major actor in the radical era—the anticonquistador friar Bartolomé de Las Casas—to denounce Spain as tyrannical in general.[12] A considerable number, however, have noted that two key figures—Las Casas and anti-Inca viceroy Francisco de Toledo—made the category of *antityranny* a centerpiece of their political projects.[13] Toledo (in)famously used antityranny to justify executing the Inca. When scholars invoke both cases, however, tyranny appears as a matter of elites and an exception in a system of obedience toward authority.

Only in passing have historians noted that the term *tyranny* was not the monopoly of authors like Las Casas and officials like Viceroy Toledo but was widespread in Indies intellectual circles.[14] As we will argue, antityranny was far from the exclusive domain of a few friars or administrators. It was a cornerstone of vernacular thought and action among all Indies social groups—and its role in countless paperwork revolts explains why a society of orders failed to arise after the conquests. The consequences of these revolts shook Indies society to its core for decades and determined the shape of the society of orders that gradually emerged from their wake.

By revealing the crucial importance of antityranny lawfare in the Spanish Empire's radical sixteenth-century phase, this chapter reframes the prevailing story of tyranny in the early modern era. It was not primarily an intellectual and socially exclusive phenomenon but rather a strongly vernacular and inclusive one. The Cambridge School has framed early modern thinking on tyranny as essential to the era's transformations but centers Machiavelli's treatises and the Salamanca School's theories of natural law and sovereignty rather than everyday thought and action.[15] This vision relegates antityranny to high politics, intellectual circles, and the medium of print.

Emphasis on top-down discourses of rulership has overlooked the fact that legitimacy implied a practice of petitioning that in Spain went well beyond scholastic rationalization of tyrannicide.[16] It also involved vernacular, manuscript, and administrative ideas about rule—especially practices of communication between monarchs and vassals via petitioning for reform, grace, and justice. In this way, the radical phase shared with the English unrest of the seventeenth century a concern with overthrowing tyrants. Yet it diverged in at least three important ways. First, while some radical agitators in England blasted monarchy and Parliament as tyranny, radicals in the Indies generally aimed to overturn not distant, army-less, largely passive rulers but conquistadors, friars, and Native lords.[17] Second, while radicals in England often deployed their polemics in the form of printed broadsheets, the fury of antityranny politics in the Indies was almost entirely a manuscript affair. Third, Indies vassals' efforts to overturn those they called *tyrants* succeeded to an extraordinary degree considering that they often only had paperwork on their side. Their foes—especially conquistadors and Native lords—had the ability to muster more violence than their rivals, the Crown included.

Ultimately, then, this chapter aims to establish how antityranny lawfare fostered a society of disorder for roughly five decades after the conquest—as well as how the emergence of the administrative trinity of viceroys, bishops, and inquisitors by the 1570s began to reinforce a developing society of orders. Afterward, paperwork revolts and intermittent antityranny efforts would continue, but mainly targeting individual officials and powerful figures, not social structures.

VASSALS AGAINST TYRANNY

During the radical phase, vassals vilified the powerful with countless terms in petitions, lawsuits, and denunciations. But one accusation stands out as particularly fateful: tyranny (*tiranía*). It was largely this concept (and its cognates) that enabled ordinary vassals to disrupt the Indies' emerging social orders between 1521 and 1571. Subjects' and officials' clashes with powerful rival groups and jurisdictions, we argue, were a series of antityranny movements.

The power of the term *tyrant* (*tirano*) derived from another concept: its sibling *señorío,* or *lordly jurisdiction,* one of the master legal-administrative concepts of the Spanish society of orders. Those possessing lordship, "lesser lords, *duques* [dukes], *condes* [counts], *marqueses* [marquises], and other *señores* . . . hold authority over vassals and subjects."[18] Lordly jurisdiction was on Spanish warlords' minds when they conquered the New World; it was what Indigenous dynasties petitioned to recover. And when friars tried to dominate the provinces, they were seeking something akin to lordship, couching their jurisdictional ambitions in corporatist and spiritual terms. Monarchs, of course, had lordly jurisdiction—and both they and their vassals sought when possible to honor those who possessed this important privilege. These rulers were informally bound by honor and law to respect the existence of *señoríos.* If they tampered with jurisdiction for cynical reasons, they risked legitimating outright revolt.

Once a king granted a vassal lordship by act of royal grace, the title generally became the recipient's family patrimony for all time. However, there was a major catch: if a *señor* committed an array of misdeeds, he could fall into the category of *tirano,* or tyrant. A monarch could not depose a *señor* without cause—but could legitimately depose a tyrant. As Robert Chamberlain states,

> A tyrant is the direct opposite of a *señor natural,* both with regard to the mode by which he acquires power and the methods by which he governs. Consequently, if one who rightfully achieved dominion and exercised

> authority as a *señor natural* were to govern contrary to divine, natural, and human law, justice, and reason, and thus to act in contradiction of his supposedly inherently superior nature, he would thereby lose his title.[19]

Thus, the power of the Indies' fragile social structures—comprised initially of many *señoríos*—was threatened by the major legal concept of tyranny, *tiranía.*[20] Through paperwork, vassals of all social backgrounds could resist their oppressors by insisting that the Crown retract power from Indies strongmen.

Indeed, monarchs had to listen to vassals' complaints lest they became tyrants themselves. As one jurist noted, all just kings listen to their vassals with great enthusiasm, "giving them gracious audiences for their complaints; [whereas] the tyrant, seeks to keep them in suspense, hiding from them as if they were enemies."[21] Monarchs learned to take this threat seriously. After Burgundian King Charles imposed an unpopular group of foreign courtiers on Castile in 1517, many cities revolted between 1520 and 1521, so the ruler moved to create opportunities for redress and paperwork control. Historians have long misread the monarch's defeat of the rebels as the doom of proto-democratic liberal parliamentarianism and the victory of absolutism. As historian Aurelio Espinosa has shown, virtually the opposite was true. The king and his counselors ratified a new path: bottom-up communication through councils and courts.[22] Listening in justice was, after all, the antithesis of tyranny. This vassal-lord dialogue crisscrossed the globe in the sixteenth century and enabled subjects to simultaneously conquer the New World and denounce bad government wherever it might arise. When bloody conquests put local authoritarians and abusive strongmen atop the New World social and administrative hierarchy, subjects' paperwork revolts mobilized antityranny protests to great effect.

THE DESTRUCTION OF THE NEW WORLD'S SOCIAL ORDERS

Strange and violent times came to Cemanahuac in the year Ce-Acatl, One Reed. The Tlaxcalteca stood ready for war against the massive Mexica confederation, which surrounded them on every side. The Mexica lords and vassals answered to the sprawling Motecuzomah dynasty. In a bizarre turn of events, the Tlaxcalteca did not fall to Motecuzomah in the west. They fell to another group: men from the east who rode large deer, were clad in metal sheets, and leashed huge, frenzied war-dogs. Many coastal peoples had joined them, sensing that these outsiders had the potential to turn the world upside down.

The Tlaxcalteca snatched victory from the jaws of defeat. They quickly made the unusual warriors allies in their struggle for survival against Mexica expansion. The aristocratic *teteuhctin* leadership, headed by Lord Maxixcatzin, Lord Xicotencatl the Elder, and Lord Xicotencatl the Younger, mustered food, logistics, and massive armies. They guided the foreigners in the direction of old enemies. Soon this alliance slaughtered the aristocracy and warriors of Tlaxcala's powerful enemy Chololla, spreading panic throughout Cemanahuac.

The emboldened Tlaxcalteca drew their new partners to the Mexica heartland. Nearing the bank of the Mexica lake stronghold of Tenochtitlan, the *teuhctlin* lords of the realm of Chalca invited these forces to food and shelter. Chalca elites seem to have had two plans. The first was to eliminate certain dynastic pretenders in nearby Amaquemecan. The second, much more ambitious, was to muster a force powerful enough to strike a grievous blow against what one Amaquemecan chronicler from the region called "Moctezuma's tyranny."[23]

The latter scheme bore fruit almost immediately. The growing alliance swept into the capital of Tenochtitlan, where a strange truce took hold. The newcomers, sensing they were surrounded, broke this tense peace with a major massacre of Mexica elite. The Mexica's supreme lord, *hueytlatoani* Motecuzomah Xocoyotzin, died in the ensuing violence, as did thousands of warriors under his command. The nearly impregnable Mexica capital of Tenochtitlan was in flames. A century-old social order and its meticulous aristocratic and warrior hierarchies began to disintegrate.

Mexica forces did repulse the intruders, killing hundreds of them and thousands of their allies. Yet the strangers and their local allies rebounded. Help came from the Mexicas' traditional confederates in Texcoco. There, elites harbored deep resentment toward their Mexica allies' power. The captain of the invaders promised to resurrect the city's old aristocracies, descended from the philosopher-king Nezahualcoyotl. The invaders replaced the successor to Motecuzomah Xocoyotzin, Cacamatzin, a Mexica loyalist, with another claimant, Coanacoch.[24] A year later, the alliance, bolstered by Coanacoch's warriors and many others, entered Tenochtitlan triumphant.

To the west, the Irecha lords of the great realm of the Irechequa Tzintzuntzani heard from Mexica ambassadors of strangers clad in metal riding deer and refused military aid to their sworn enemies: "May they kill the Mexicans," lord Irecha Zuangua responded.[25] When the foreigners arrived, Zuangua's successor surrendered in hopes of leaving his realm unharmed. As we have seen, the realm—which later became Michoacan—did not manage to escape an unhappy fate.

The Tlaxcalteca, Tetzocoans, Mexica, and Irecha forces then headed south with the foreign captains for further conquests. In the 1520s, they marched into Mixtec, Zapotec, and Maya territories as far as what is today Honduras, exploiting local differences and reshuffling dynasties every step of the way.[26] In Quauhtimallan, the expanding Kaqhikels initially courted these visitors, channeling their might against their enemies the K'iches.[27] Southern conquests were manned by Nahuas of Huejotzingo, Tarascans, numerous Maya groups, and the Tepehuan, Guachichil, Zacatec, Guamares, Xinca, and Lenca, among others. Each offered the invaders thousands of troops after meeting defeat.[28] Simultaneously, the Mexica and other Nahuas were busy subduing the Yucatec Maya in the 1520s and 1530s, also under the foreigners' leadership.[29]

The newcomers set out once again, this time into the South Sea. They took with them many allies from previous conquests, who suffered enormously in the freezing Andes mountains.[30] Small groups of foreigners soon arrived at the northern frontiers of a great dominion—Tihuantinsuyo, subject to the Sapa Inca overlords of Cusco. This Inca dynasty was by far the largest the newcomers had encountered. However, they arrived as the realm was deep in a civil war between heirs of Huayna Capac. Primary claimant Huascar, the Hurin dynasty lord of Cusco based in the south with aristocratic and priestly support, faced the militaristic Atao Huallpa of the Hanan dynasty and his rebels in the north.[31]

The strangers and their allies proceeded as they had in Anahuac: by forging alliances with disgruntled local elites seeking to overthrow their overlords. They found friends in the small Chimu province, a realm crushed by the Inca half a century before. Chimu's local lords were eager to fight their rivals—as were the Tallanes, Huayacuntos, Huancas, Huailas, Huamachucos, and Ñampaellecs, among others.[32] The Cañari, the Chachapoyas, and resentful Inca *yana* slave-soldiers were chief among these allies, offering thousands of warriors.[33]

The foreigners and their swollen armies once again triumphed. After defeating Huascar and killing most of his court, Atao Huallpa was captured by the invading forces. The royal prisoner hastily ordered the execution of his rival, Huascar. Tihuantinsuyo's great Inca sovereigns were defeated: by their own hand and by the expanding might of the anti-Inca coalition.

Many of the Inca *palla* royalty, their finest generals, and their servants rushed to support this confederation. They were soon fighting alongside the newcomers and their former subjects, united now against the northern Muisca.[34] Thousands of Cañari warriors, their erstwhile rivals, joined them.[35] A war was subsiding between the *sihipkua* lord of Tenza, the lord of Icabuco, the lord Ramiriquiri of Tunja, and his brother Quiminza against the *sihipkua* Eucaneme.[36] The Muisca *sihipkua* lords of Chia, Suba, and Guatavita, fresh from these and other conflicts, saw an opportunity to settle old scores. They angled to harness the newcomers' heterogeneous armies against their Muisca enemies within as well as against the Panches, old rivals beyond their traditional sphere of control.[37] Other Inca elites assisted the invading coalition in one of their most precarious outposts, in the southern province of Chile.[38] Around the same time and under similar circumstances, outsiders defeated the Guarani Carios, who then led them against the rival Guaycuru of the Cacho plains.[39]

PLAGUE AND CIVIL WAR: INDIGENOUS DYNASTS IN DISARRAY

In most of the populous parts of Cemanahuac and Tihuantinsuyo and far beyond, great lords fell to these strange coalitions. Yet a new society of orders stubbornly refused to appear for complex reasons. One major factor was disease. Unbeknownst to any of the actors of the conquests, Old World maladies began to devastate New World allies, enemies, and even those they had not yet encountered.

Plague spread through Anahuac and beyond. It devastated central Mexico; perhaps 40 percent of all Mexica died between 1520 and 1521.[40] Elite families were not spared. Motecuzomah's successor and nephew, Cuitláhuac, the Mexica's *hueytlatoani* overlord, perished almost immediately after his election along with "dozens of links in the chain of command."[41] The disease spread rapidly. In highland Quauhtemallan (today Guatemala), one Kakchikel Maya recalled, "After our fathers and grandfathers succumbed, half of the people fled to the fields. The gods and vultures devoured the bodies. . . . So it was that we became orphans, oh, my sons!"[42] Disease often moved in advance of the invaders. Sometime between 1480 and 1500, an epidemic scourged the population of the Yucatan with "pestilent fevers that lasted twenty-four hours, and once they ended, [the victims] swelled up and were filled with worms."[43] When plague struck the Irecha court at Tzintzuntzan, it took High Priest Petamuti, the *cazonzi* ruler Zuangua, and countless other nobles.[44] In the Andes, the Inca overlord *sapa inca* Huayna Capac died, as did general Mihacnacamayta, governors Apu Hilaquito and Auqui Tupac, the Inca's sister Mama Coca, and even the Inca heir Ninan Coyuche.[45] Almost immediately, some two hundred thousand passed away throughout the Quito region.[46] Demographic collapse also brought civil war. In Tihuantinsuyo, the Inca's death unchained a fateful civil war between heirs.[47] Precisely as the strange northern armies arrived, the feuding Inca claimants were clashing on the battlefield, and Tihuantinsuyo's valleys were littered with the corpses of tens of thousands of fallen soldiers.[48]

Disease and war begot social conflict after the conquests, with cycles of bloody retribution erupting following invasion and plague. The Maya house of Xiu embarked on a pilgrimage to the sacred Chichen Izta *cenote* lake in the late 1530s, where they were massacred by rival Cocom lords in retaliation for a massacre a hundred years before. This violence ignited fresh civil war.[49] Furious that certain Mexica had aided the invaders, Tenochtitlan leadership persecuted and killed traitors in their midst, including some of the sons of Moctezuma.[50] Muisca captains persecuted turncoat supporters of the newcomers and often put them to death—as did the *sihipkua* overlord Ubiama when he killed his rival Bojaca.[51]

The old order, already devastated by conquest, saw its foundations teeter in ways unthinkable just years before. Local elites struggled to maintain authority. Maya lords fell into "this unsettled state of affairs" as they "sometimes saw their authority increase, but at other times diminish and even disappear altogether."[52] Old alliances and rivalries also transformed. In coastal Tierra Firme, "previously inimical groups had joined by marriage, alliance, and confederation" due to demographic desolation.[53]

The iron-armed, deer-riding strangers seized the moment and began murdering the courtiers of disease-stricken polities. Paranoid and fearful, warlords employed massacres, hostage taking, and public executions to bring reluctant communities to either support or defer to them.[54] They murdered thousands of unarmed residents and nobles of Cholollan.[55] One captain massacred another eight thousand or so Mexica nobles, military commanders, and war veterans in Tenochtitlan during the Toxcatl festival.[56] The war for Mexico killed thousands more.[57] When another three invading captains met the Inca Atao Huallpa in Cajamarca in 1532, in grave fear of ambush, they engineered a pretense of the ruler's disobedience, attacked his courtiers, and killed perhaps three thousand of Tihuantinsuyo's aristocracy and their wives, elderly, and servants.[58]

Even many of the invaders' aristocratic allies perished. The invasion of Tenochtitlan was fatal for anti-Mexica forces, including Tlaxcalteca and Huexotzincan nobles.[59] Similarly disastrous were the deaths of lords of the houses of Azcapotzalco, Tenochtitlan, Tlacopan, and Tlatelolco during the campaign to Quauhtimallan and beyond.[60] The captain responsible for the massacres in Tenochtitlan later boasted that in Quetzaltenango, "We killed and imprisoned many people, many of whom were captains and lords and distinguished people."[61]

Dynastic lords sometimes attempted to regroup and resist, but this too could prove fatal. Perhaps one hundred thousand Cuscos fell attempting to recover their capital, including the Inca's brother Tisu Yupanqui, the solar priest and general Vila Oma, and the great generals Quisu Yupanqui,

Illa Tupac, Titu Cusi Hualpa, Allin Songo, and Yuncacallo.[62] The Muisca war effort against the trespassers had some success but claimed the life of the ruler Sacresazipa; many other local leaders would follow.[63] The Kaqchikels, who had allied with the disruptive warbands for six months, rebelled, only to see their lords Oxib-Queh and Beleheb-Tzii executed and their new Lord Behele Qat die while forced to pan for gold in a river like a commoner.[64]

Of these larger dynasties, only one would remain sovereign—a branch of the Inca that headed for the Andes' rainforest mountains and ruled from Vilcabamba. In 1572, a new coalition of invaders and local rivals would defeat it. Throughout virtually all of the New World, then, overlords, courts, aristocracies, and communities collapsed. They left behind a power vacuum the conquerors could hardly fill.

THE CHRISTIANS AND THEIR ALLIES

The invaders, mostly Castilian Christians, seemed to be in a strong position to dominate Indies politics after the wars and epidemics. They spoke variants of the same language, were mostly from western and southern Iberia, and marched under the banner of the Trinity. After 1516, they were all vassals of the Holy Roman Empire, a wealthy, extensive, multicultural military superpower. Moreover, these fighters—middling to moderately prominent nobles but also military men, notaries, artisans, musicians, and merchants—all sought privileges from the Habsburg monarchs.[65] For these men, the promise of *gracia* privileges, such as tax exemptions, social privileges, pensions, and lordly jurisdiction, was an obsession (see Chapter 3). Captain-entrepreneurs with the ambition of becoming lords negotiated contracts, or *capitulaciones*, with Crown authorities—most often ministers of the Royal Council of Castile or, after 1524, the Royal Council of the Indies.[66] They invariably included a promise to the king that the invaders would pay 20 percent of their profits to the royal treasury and attempt to convert the Natives. In return, the king would delegate by his powers of extraordinary *gracia* faculties to the conquerors, making them seigneurial lords and enabling them to temporarily appoint justice officials, adjudicate litigation (except cases of capital punishment), and issue edicts. These contracts would theoretically bind conquistadors to the Spanish system of justice, ensuring not only that rivals would respect their jurisdiction but also that captains would treat investors, participants, and Native peoples they had conquered and fought alongside as well as possible.[67]

In the early years, powerful captains did win lordly jurisdiction. Some had nearly boundless powers within their dominions. The monarchs' *Capitulaciones de Santa Fe* had granted Columbus unlimited dynastic authority over the entire Indies as viceroy and admiral; in 1536–1537, his dynasty also received lordship over the Marquisate of Jamaica and the Duchy of Veragua (albeit in exchange for formally relinquishing claims to total Indies power).[68] In 1529, Cortés had petitioned for and received the Marquisate of the Valley, a sprawling checkerboard of Mexico's most populous and fertile Indigenous dominions. He gained criminal and civil jurisdiction over a huge number of subjects: according to one official in 1523, the tally stood at 1.5 million Native vassals.[69] Francisco Pizarro petitioned successfully in 1537 for the creation of his own marquisate.[70] Well into the late 1530s, the Crown also assented to creating marquisates for Hernando de Soto, Pedro de Alvarado, Diego de Almagro, and Pedro de Mendoza, but their premature deaths (from fever, war, assassination, and perhaps syphilis, respectively) doomed these seigneuries.[71] In this way, substantial parts of the Indies' central regions began to resemble the Spanish society of orders, a complex constellation of aristocratic jurisdictions ruled by powerful local lords.

These warlord-aristocrats often also directly ruled the rest of the Indies. Columbus did so as viceroy of the Indies. By 1522, Cortés was governor of New Spain and second only to the king in control over the region's *gracia* functions; he and his successor conquistador-governors each distributed Native tribute at the onset of their rule.[72] In Peru the situation was more unstable, as the Pizarros and rival supporters of Almagro fought over the privilege to rule and reward.[73] In 1540s New Granada, conquistador-governors and royal investigators struggled as well, distributing and redistributing tribute allotments to waves of increasingly exasperated conquistadors.[74]

The conquerors excluded from lordly jurisdiction and governance had limited access to power. Many saw in municipal governance a modest source of honor. One of the first actions conquerors undertook was to officially establish settlements, small jurisdictional areas where they could exact criminal and civil justice and draft their own local legislation.[75] Christian cities quickly dotted much of the circum-Caribbean, Mesoamerica, the Andes, and parts of the River Plate. In the peripheries were smaller cities as well as lesser towns (*villas*) and mining settlements. Scholars have counted some 399 of these by the first third of the 1600s, including over 170 cities with municipal governments.[76] The proliferation of city councils would add to an increasingly elaborate—and unstable—jurisdictional patchwork.

THE WEAKNESSES OF THE CONQUISTADORS

For a brief period, this feudal-municipal society of orders seemed possible. It would be overseen by conquistadors, a hodgepodge of governorships, hundreds of cities, and several hundred lesser conquistador dynasties. However, the intruders faced serious structural challenges. Conquests had extremely high mortality rates. Over half of the conquistadors lost their lives before they could enjoy their spoils.[77] One invasion in the 1490s on Hispaniola ended with over 50 percent of the conquistadors dead of disease and starvation.[78] Over 60 percent of New Spain's two thousand conquistadors perished in the years 1519–1521.[79] Historians have only been able to identify 660 survivors of some 1,930 who arrived to conquer Tierra Firme.[80] In one expedition headed by Gonzalo Jiménez de Quesada, 600 men heading from the coast into the mountains dwindled to a mere 173.[81] Remote, sparsely populated areas were even more dangerous. Captain Francisco de Montejo's Yucatan expedition led a third of his forces to their deaths, largely due to starvation; only the arrival of local ally Lord Naum Pat saved the remaining members.[82] Pánfilo Narváez's invasion of Florida in 1528 began with six hundred men. Four survived.[83]

Death came for powerful captains too. In 1517, Captain Hernández de Córdoba died of wounds received on the battlefield against Maya forces.[84] One of New Spain's foremost military figures, Captain Pedro Alvarado, died in 1541 during the Mixton War, crushed by his horse while retreating from victorious Caxcan forces.[85] Though there were few Spanish mortalities in the Cusco siege, Captain Juan Pizarro met his end there with a stone to the head.

Perhaps the greatest enemies of the conquistadors, however, were their own peers. Lesser conquistadors' municipal governments often confronted each other. Many founders of Spanish cities negotiated directly with Indigenous rulers, carving out vague new jurisdictions against warlords' *capitulaciones*.[86] In response, competing governors and city councils would occasionally go on the offensive, resulting in arrests, fatalities, and deep mutual distrust.[87] Major warlords also bickered about the limits of their vaguely worded contracts.[88] In Costa Rica and Nicaragua, conquistador-governors sparred over *capitulaciones* in 1539, nearly leading to serious bloodshed.[89] Too impatient to wait for years-long royal mediation, the forces of Peruvian captain Diego de Almagro and the Pizarros reached for their swords. Thousands of Christians fought to the death in the Andes.[90]

The Christians' clannish and regionalist biases, hidden just beneath the surface of their shared culture, put their entire enterprises in danger.[91] Most conquerors were from Spain, but their cliques included Basques, Portuguese, Aragonese, Flemings, High Germans, Saxons, Italians, small numbers of Frenchmen, Corsicans, and Albanians, along with free and enslaved Africans and their descendants.[92] Constant rivalries, biases, and misunderstandings threatened the fragile order. The Swabian captain Philipp von Hutten wrote from Tierra Firme during the turbulent early 1540s, when Spaniards and Germans were in open warfare, "I am more fearful of war with the Christians than with the Indians."[93]

These disputes allowed sovereign Native groups to strike back. Lord Pocorosa in today's Panama managed to kill ninety Christians in a 1515 uprising.[94] The first Mexica insurgency, the Noche Triste, struck down six to nine hundred Christians and countless Indigenous allies.[95] Some two hundred Spaniards under siege by Manco Inga's army in Cusco in 1536–1537 were left haggard and physically broken; another two hundred perished trying to lift the siege.[96] In the ensuing Inca resistance, one to two thousand conquistadors perished over a fifteen-year period.[97]

The invaders unleashed bloody reprisals. Authorities burned alive 460 lords and lesser nobility from Huasteca in 1523 for their revolt.[98] Captain Alvarado's campaign abuses soured his alliances with the Kaqchiquel, whom he assailed mercilessly after they defeated him in the city of Iximché.[99] Francisco Pizarro's men mutilated hundreds of Inca royalty during Manco Inca's great siege.[100] The Maya revolted in the 1540s, destroying anything and anyone Christian, but lost by 1547; many were enslaved.[101] Captains in Muisca territories, like Lázaro Fonte and Martín Pujol, waged unrelenting war against sovereign groups, killing several dozen local lords and thousands of commoners.[102] These massacres caused mayhem that severely weakened the structural might of the conquerors.

Just years after their world-renowned exploits, the Christians were physically depleted, rife with factionalism, and barely capable of maintaining dominion over their restless subjects. They and their Indigenous allies had put the Indies' greatest dynasties and settlements to the sword, yet there were few guarantees that the invaders would live to see their lordly ambitions come to fruition. Many would be lucky to escape with their lives.

ASSAILING CONQUISTADOR JURISDICTION

Conquistadors emerged from conflicts in a haze of violence and illegality, yet they always understood the importance of proving through paperwork that they were good and heroic men (and more rarely, women). In thousands of petitions, they sought to remind the king and his officials that they had won for the monarchy a whole hemisphere of vassals and future Christians. Yet questions lingered—had they proceeded legally and according to their *capitulaciones*? God would surely not judge the kings kindly if they tolerated breaches of justice. The great captains especially needed to show receipts for their upright deeds, for their lordly jurisdictions depended on royal approval.

Many proclaimed their exploits to be a victory against tyranny. For the would-be Christian lords of the Indies, these battles were a glorious liberation of commoners and subjugated peoples. Cortés's second major report to the Crown provided rudimentary justification of the conquest of

Mexica dominions on the basis of the "force and tyranny" through which Moctezuma took Natives' "sons to kill and sacrifice to his idols. And they told me many other complaints of him," he added.[103] He later elaborated that the conquests were legitimate, for "to make war on enemies and with a good conscience, it is required that enemies be either rebels or tyrants."[104] In 1533, a drumhead court comprised of Pizarro, a Crown lawyer, and several others collected testimony from some ten Native witnesses and found Atao Huallpa guilty of five major crimes, including "opprobrious tyranny" against his own people.[105] They executed him shortly thereafter.

Warlords played with fire by portraying themselves as heroes battling tyrants, liberating the oppressed, and spreading the Gospel. And Crown officials in Europe had no direct knowledge of what was happening in the Indies. They relied on subjects' incoming reports, many of which were penned by the invaders themselves. Yet occasionally letters might reach them from unhappy subjects—tax collectors, friars, priests, shortchanged conquistadors, and others—reporting that serious crimes were afoot.

These reports were generally not enough for monarchs to strip conquerors of their lordly jurisdictions. They needed much more proof, from many more vassals. In response to particularly grave allegations, the Crown thus commissioned two types of audits—emergency investigations, or *visitas,* as well as periodical posttenure *residencia* inquiries. In the most serious cases, lordship itself hung in the balance. These investigations were massive paperwork undertakings. Some cases took years, and almost all became staggeringly complex. Investigators invited anyone of any status to bring both public and secret claims against the official under scrutiny. Countless Indigenous witnesses came forth to auditors to accuse major conquistador-governors of harrowing tortures and murders, and rival Spaniards accused their administration of unfair distribution of Native labor grants.[106] Women added their complaints, often shedding light on conquistador-captains' most intimate abuses. These atrocities, and subjects' repeated allegations that conquistadors might rise up in tyranny against the Crown, permeate royal officials' accusations against early conquistador-governors and their allies.[107] In response to vassals' complaints, Crown investigators heaped well over one hundred thousand pages of audit paperwork on just twenty-one of the most powerful early Indies conquistadors.[108]

Audits thus escalated into popular revolts—and these were not rare. They happened many hundreds of times, from the very early years of the conquests. Columbus tried every means to prevent his rivals from writing to the Crown, but there was no hiding his extreme cruelty. By 1494, he had alienated many of his own soldiers, military commanders, royal accountants, and friars.[109] Witnesses accused him of hanging rebellious Spaniards and mutilating defiant Indigenous vassals.[110] He nearly starved to death the Hermandad, a brotherhood of lowborn horsemen that, according one fifteenth-century chronicler, acted as a royal force against the "tyrants and robbers" who plagued the peninsula.[111] By 1495, the Crown had already commissioned the first Indies audit against him, and many on the island, including Indigenous vassals, testified to his cruelty.[112] Once the Crown heard reports from its royal accountant Jimeno de Briviesca and accounts of a revolt around 1499, it dispatched a second audit.[113] One chronicler recalled that the rebel leader Francisco de Roldán had hurled against the Columbus clan "terrible complaints, calling them tyrants and cruel men . . . with a thirst for Castilian blood."[114] What happened in this second audit established a pattern for future conquistador-governors.

Investigator Francisco de Bobadilla relied on the testimonies of Native lords, poor Spaniards, and others and revealed rapes, extrajudicial maiming and executions, fraud, and other wrongdoings. The Crown stripped Columbus of jurisdiction and his dynasty's claims to perpetual legislative authority. Bobadilla, now governor, sent him to Spain in chains.[115] In 1504, Columbus complained to his friend in court, doña Juana de la Torre, that there was "nobody too vile to think of affronting me"—he could have stolen the altar of Saint Peter and given it to the Moors and those in Spain would not hate him less.[116] But he was not hated only on the peninsula. He was also "very afflicted, waged war upon, by the bad Christians and Indians of the island."[117] It was a bottom-up war of paper.

Battered by the accusations of local settlers, Columbus's dynasty began to lose its almost unlimited seigneurial powers. These powers not only had included jurisdiction over the entire Indies but also were permanent for him and his entire family, provided major economic benefits, and won him a seat with Castilian grandees.[118] The admiral's lawyer complained that he had been "destroyed" due to "the envies and maliciousness" of hostile petitioners.[119] His son Diego did not break from his father's ways. One prosecutor's report from 1524 stated that among other abuses, Diego had refused to listen to petitions and lawsuits with the High Court, claiming that "as viceroy and as Admiral neither he nor his lieutenants have superiors."[120] He, too, saw his jurisdiction dramatically limited; after his disastrous administration, the Crown gradually restricted his family's privileges.[121] This experience taught kings and ministers to be wary of giving seigneurial titles too freely.

Cortés experienced a similar fate. He had alienated the governor of Cuba during the conquest and struggled mightily against local conquistador rivals. Competing 1522 complaints prompted the emperor to order a 1524 audit, which transpired only in 1526.[122] Yet two auditors fell ill (some accused Cortés of having had them poisoned).[123] Battered by his rivals' petitions to the Crown, Cortés lost the governorship in 1526.[124] When a proper audit finally arrived in 1529, his enemies and victims sprung on their chance. Among many charges was that of "disobeying and rising up in tyranny."[125] More than a few enemies testified that Cortés had shown signs of "not obeying His Majesty and becoming a tyrant."[126] Cortés' status and wealth were consumed by lawfare. By 1529, he faced some eighty-six suits, including denunciations of unpaid bills by carptenters, gunners, mapmakers, and horse keepers.[127] By the time he permanently moved to Spain in 1540 to protect his lordship and titles from denunciations of all kinds, Cortés juggled some thirty large lawsuits and countersuits that kept him constantly in debt, at the mercy of Genovese bankers, and embroiled in conflict not only with the Crown but even with his own legal representatives.[128] His biographer and acquiantance, Francisco López de Gómara, concluded in his 1552 *The Conquest of Mexico* that Cortés was "embroiled in more lawsuits than it befitted his estate."[129]

In the trials surrounding his 1529 audit, vassals alleged that the famous strongman's wickedness was everywhere on display. He had tortured Native leaders, massacred commoners, poisoned rivals, uttered blasphemies, and murdered his wife, Catalina Suárez Marcayda, in cold blood.[130] Hundreds testified against him; one witness alone offered nearly five hundred pages of statements.[131] Many witnesses, including guests at his home, alleged that Cortés had strangled his wife in 1522 after a fight. Women played a central role in the testimonies against Cortés. Catalina's personal assistants, Juana López, Ana Rodríguez, Violante Rodríguez, María de Vera, and María Hernández, personally testified that she had not died from natural causes. The victim's mother, María, would continue this lawsuit against Cortés for years. Cortés himself would unsuccessfully attempt to persuade the king not to listen to these commoner women, who were "of low status and manners [*de baja suerte e manera*]."[132]

His attempts were to no avail. Judges, it turns out, were very interested in what these commoner women had to say. The defendant later complained very bitterly to the emperor that he was being destroyed through paperwork. He wrote that when he returned to New Spain from the peninsula in 1530, the high judges had prevented Indigenous servants from feeding his dependents and retinue while he was under investigation. Some two hundred of his household, including his own mother and first legitimate son, had allegedly starved to death.[133] He never recovered the governorship. One of the world's most powerful men lost against a paperwork onslaught, like Columbus before him.

These conquistador-governor downfalls repeated like clockwork. Mexico's first president, Nuño de Guzmán, would also be its last conquistador-governor. He lost his powers in 1530 after friars' and other rivals' complaints triggered an investigation into his bloody deeds.[134] He was replaced by a high court comprised of royal officials.[135] Licenciate Alonso de Maldonado similarly investigated conquistador Pedro de Alvarado in the late 1530s and took control of Guatemala in 1543, cementing the political downfall of the Alvarado clan.[136] In 1549, a high judge of Guatemala investigated and impeached the Yucatan's last conquistador-governor, Francisco de Montejo.[137] In Peru between 1544 and 1546, against the backdrop of civil war, Licenciate Miguel Díez de Armendáriz investigated and replaced Santa Fe's conquistador-governors.[138] Anywhere in the Indies, vassals' animus toward tyrannical conquistador-governors could arise at any moment and permanently curtail their administrative power.[139] The pattern was everywhere the same: royal appointments of strongmen, tensions with vassals, bottom-up petitions alleging tyranny, audits, denunciations, and finally, monarchs' depositions. Lawfare proved to be a very powerful tool for conquistadors' enemies; nearly every warlord fell against it.

THE FALL OF CONQUISTADOR MARQUISATES AND CONQUISTADOR LORDSHIPS

Strongmen were losing their right to govern the New World, and they would soon lose even their seigneurial privileges. Their most disastrous setback took place in Peru and reverberated far and wide. Likely aware of the difficulties facing Cortés and the Columbus dynasty, Governor Francisco Pizarro and Governor Diego de Almagro, the two most prominent warlords, each attempted to secure his status by corrupting the Council of the Indies' ministers.[140] Almagro sought to marry his half-Indigenous son to the daughter of the council president. This plan fell through for unclear reasons, but another minister eagerly offered his daughter's hand.[141] Almagro said that he could not have married into a better clique in Spain; he was happier than if he had married his son to "a duke or *infanta*"—that is, to a member of the innermost circle of the monarchal family and finest seigneurial lords of Spain.[142] Not to be outdone, the Pizarros hurried to curry favor from the family members of other council ministers, some of whom had rushed to Peru seeking reward.[143] At the peak of his power, Hernando Pizarro allegedly boasted that "if I could see Hell before me and the open heavens on one side, and the King before me," he would triumph over any challenge—as long as the president of the council continued to support him.[144]

These intrigues suddenly began to unravel. Doña Natalia, the minister's daughter betrothed to Almagro's son, died unexpectedly.[145] Worse still, the Pizarros had Diego de Almagro executed, leaving only his son Diego the Younger (whose mother was a Native lord herself) to resist them. Now the usual stream of petitions and denunciations was following both families. Diego accused the Pizarros of defrauding the Crown 800,000 pesos, ruling with "absolute power," and committing "great rapes and acts of incest, adulteries and corruptions of virgin and married women" worse than anything ever seen in human history.[146] By early 1540, Hernando Pizarro was in jail. Peru's fragile, feuding aristocracies prepared for years of merciless legal conflict.

As this trial slowly proceeded, another front against the conquistadors opened—this time in Mexico. The Dominican Domingo Betanzos had scandalized his order and many others by claiming that Natives were sub-human beasts of burden. In response, the bishop of Tlaxcala, the president of Mexico, and two Dominicans sought to elicit official statements against Betanzos from the Crown and the papacy.[147] One of these friars was Bartolomé de Las Casas. In early 1542, he convinced the Castilian parliament and the emperor that abuses against Indigenous vassals were endemic.[148] Auditors now came for the council itself. Between July 1542 and February 1543, the Council of the Indies ceased to operate while under royal investigation. Officials found several ministers guilty of corruption.[149] The famous Junta of Valladolid debated major imperial reforms, many of which Las Casas and his allies in court themselves proposed. Between the council audit and the junta, the emperor's attention was fixed on these problems perhaps for the first time.

Las Casas and many ministers exploited the moment to deal a blow to the very structure of conquistador power. After the junta, the faction in favor of seigneurial privilege for conquistadors lost decisively.[150] The resulting 1542 New Laws are emblematic of the Crown's gradual asphyxiation of conquistadors' dominions. Now, conquistadors would have trouble usurping the wills of the council: the laws not only barred the council from having ties to the Indies but also ordered new, powerful officials to the Indies, banned officials from collecting Native tribute, and placed major restrictions on anti-Indigenous abuses. Most scandalously, the laws determined that conquistadors could not pass feudal holdings on to their descendants without express royal approval.[151] Gradually, the conquistadors' patrimonies would wither away.

Connected events in Mexico soon undid the last great marquisate—that of Hernán Cortés. Traveling to Spain to improve his reputation, Cortés received the title of marquis in 1529. The audits against him and groundswell of subjects' accusations prevented him from ruling his estates in person.[152] His estates did survive past the 1540s, but he complained to his father that the Crown had him mired in a legal "purgatory," crushing him under royal investigation even as the emperor showered him with privileges.[153] After losing his governorship, Cortés used his remaining wealth to invest in expanding the empire's global dominions. But by the 1540s, he was deep in debt and pawning possessions off to the Florentine merchant and lender Giacomo Botti.[154]

His family inherited this purgatory. In the 1560s, Cortés's son don Martín returned to Mexico, hoping to start anew. Yet he found himself consumed by the factional intrigues of bitter conquistadors, Crown officials, friars, and others. As he prepared to travel from Europe to Mexico in 1562, tensions ran high. Conquistadors were increasingly desperate and impoverished, and some reportedly muttering that "in this land the King is not a lord, but a tyrant."[155] There was no viceroy at that moment, but many assumed that his replacement would totally abolish conquistador lordships. As conflicts multiplied, an unspecified woman approached the interim rulers of New Spain, the High Court magistrates. She warned that a conquistador uprising was brewing. Indeed, one collaborator soon confessed in great detail, naming don Martín as a member of a vast conspiracy planning to kill Crown officials and pledge allegiance to France.

The magistrates quickly executed several ringleaders and sent don Martín back to Spain in chains, where he received a traitor's welcome. He defended himself between bouts of grueling torture, promising he was beloved by Native commoners and had been framed by an alliance of Crown officials, friars, and priests—all corrupt perverts and rapists.[156] But it was to no avail. What ultimately crushed him was not the backbreaking torture but the avalanche of paperwork—at least six thousand pages of denunciations, testimonies, and judicial maneuverings.[157] Already in 1567, the High Court abolished his marquisate, once the greatest in the New World.[158] Now, he had few chances of recovering it.

Don Martín thus joined the Pizarros in Madrid as an aristocrat in exile, part of a melancholy crew of courtiers seeking a comeback. Hernando Pizarro litigated in Madrid against the Crown and dozens of rivals for several decades. Despite Hernando's litigiousness, council ministers did not hide their hatred of him.[159] In the 1570s, the incoming Peruvian viceroy confiscated his final possessions.[160] The Columbus dynasty, meanwhile, collapsed. After it failed to generate an heir in 1578, many litigants attempted the family's revival. Here, dirty tricks abounded. Ministers believed that the primary claimant, the Third Marchioness of Guadalest, doña María Ruiz de Liori Colón y Cardona, had attempted to corrupt the case by infiltrating the council.[161] Those seeking seigneurial power were to be kept from the Indies at all costs. In the 1560s and 1570s, Crown-lord relations were at their nadir. The New World's many radical antiseigneurial factions had won the day over the marquises; virtually all of these dominions were either abolished or rendered utterly worthless.

THE TYRANNY OF THE *ENCOMIENDA*

As early as the 1490s, the bruising petitions and audits that vassals used to bring the great conquistador-governors and aristocrats to heel had already begun placing special emphasis on an important concept: *tyranny*. These claims initially singled out specific wrongdoers rather than larger groups or social structures. Gradually, however, they transformed into broad attacks on all *encomenderos* and even on *encomiendas* themselves. The critique of a whole system of hierarchy and labor thus became commonplace.

This radical opposition to *encomienda* emerged slowly. In the 1510s, a small but vocal faction of friars warned that the Crown had granted *encomenderos* too much authority over their vassals.[162] Petitioners—sometimes tax collectors and often friars—led the attack. Already in 1511, according to Las Casas, one Dominican had denounced the "cruelty and tyranny in which you [Spaniards] employ with these innocent peoples. . . . With what authority have you undertaken such detestable wars[?]"[163] The Franciscan friar Luis de Villalpando warned the council that its ministers were responsible for allowing "that every encomendero should be an absolute king . . . without the Indians knowing of any other king or justice, only these lords."[164] Crown officials were deeply unsure of how to proceed, although some were persuaded that this was a systemic problem, not an individual one. In 1555, Las Casas wrote to a colleague that "one person of the Council told me, horrified, of what one currently sees and hears of these tyrannies."[165] Ministers saw that not just seigneurial lords but also *encomiendas* themselves represented a structural problem that demanded a robust response.

Yet seigneurial lords and their allies did not surrender without a fight—of both pen and sword. The Crown initially received a deluge of counterpetitions from Indies conquistadors, especially in response to the 1542–1543 New Laws. Livid letters flooded in. By 1545, word had reached the council that these policies had triggered further civil war.[166] Gonzalo Pizarro and the Crown's new viceroy, Blasco Núñez Vela, faced off about implementation. Their debate began diplomatically, but after a series of misunderstandings, they confronted each other on the battlefield. The Pizarro clan had the viceroy decapitated.[167] Soon, thousands of Spaniards were waging war throughout the Andes. In Nicaragua, the New Laws so infuriated conquistador-governor don Rodrigo de Contreras that he and some Peruvian conquistador-rebels faced off against Bishop Antonio de Valdivieso, a close associate of Las Casas. The Crown successfully sued Contreras for abuses, but once news of his punishments arrived in Nicaragua, his wife, doña María, and sons Pedro and Hernando hatched a murderous plan. Hernando assassinated the bishop, declared himself Prince of Cusco and Captain of Liberty, and briefly seized control of Panama; royalist residents soon defeated him.[168]

This bloodshed shocked the Crown to its core. Dead viceroys, assassinated bishops, thousands of infuriated conquistadors ready to denounce the king as a tyrant—what had gone wrong? What should be done about the conquistadors, who were evidently a dangerous collective? These questions dominated a 1545 junta. Proseigneurial ministers pushed for a return to the pre–New Laws status quo, giving conquistadors civil (but not criminal) jurisdiction in their seigneurial holdings (*feudos*).[169] Opponents sought the reconstitution of conquistador lordships as mere pensions rather than permanent holdings.[170] The emperor urged "temperance" but also suggested that ministers make plans to reinvade Peru to crush the rebels if necessary.[171]

The council suspended many of the New Laws' policies. Nonetheless, its ministers continued to seek solutions less apparent to their adversaries.

Rather than risk further violence, council ministers intended to proceed, according to their own internal records, "in a manner so that no one understands."[172] This statement marked a turning point in the Crown's policy beginning in the late 1540s—it would no longer grant excessive power to conquistadors, instead carefully and subtly starving them of power. In 1556, ministers and the Crown revisited the issue and decided that conquistadors must lose their "civil and criminal jurisdiction, both superior and inferior," and leave it in the hands of Indigenous lords.[173] As the president of Peru suggested, they must be diminished "little by little, and one by one."[174] This process would be driven by the paperwork challenges of friars, Indigenous lords, commoners, and local officials.[175] The Crown was becoming more deliberate about merging vassals' anti-seigneurial lawfare with its own corresponding agenda.

Evidently, however, the Crown was not subtle enough. Officials in Peru were badly outmatched by the mighty Pizarro clan, the scions of which more or less openly threatened that if they did not receive lifetime control over the region, they would declare a new sovereign realm.[176] The Crown sent a priest, President Pedro de la Gasca, to gather dispersed royalists and entice rebels to betray the Pizarros by promising pardons, lordly privileges, and pensions. The royalists—motivated by nothing but royal promises—defeated Gonzalo Pizarro in 1548 with little struggle and promptly executed him and his commanders. This execution did not quell discontent. After la Gasca redistributed the spoils and issued 215 allotments of Native tribute to various protagonists, many were still left out. One complained, "Is it possible for the world to be upside down?"[177] Peru's Spaniards continued to seethe.

What happened next largely cemented conquistadors' reputations as tyrants. A broad group of lesser conquistadors helped speed their own downfall by reaching for their swords.[178] Among other destabilizing revolts in Peru was an effort led by the rebel nobleman don Sebastián del Castillo in 1553–1554, which ended in his execution and won him the epithet "the Tyrant" (*el tirano*). Similarly, Captain Lope de Aguirre declared himself king during his Amazon expedition in the 1560s, killed many of his own men, and slaughtered an entire town of Spaniards on the island of Margarita before royal forces beheaded him.[179] For this, he was also known to subsequent generations as "the Tyrant." A tyrant named Rodrigo Méndez led 350 men to take the city of Panama but failed when vassals seeking royal privileges rushed to stop him.[180] After royalists defeated each of these tyrants, their vacant *encomiendas* passed into Crown hands. Ten to thirty years after the Christians' first forays, then, conquistador-governors and estate holders lost not only the privileges that had enabled them to issue legislation, distribute *encomiendas* to loyal aides, and fulfill other *gracia* and *gobierno* functions but also saw the *encomienda* itself weakened almost beyond recognition. The conquistador lordship, which Las Casas called a "poisonous root of tyranny and captivity," was withering.[181]

THE DOWNFALL OF CONQUISTADOR GOVERNORSHIPS AND ESTATES

Conquerors' great crisis worsened as the Crown increasingly revoked their privileges of administration and replaced them with loyalist officials. As powerful conquistadors collapsed under the weight of audits and lesser warlords disgraced themselves through civil wars and rebellions, monarchs began to appoint reliable and experienced officials to rule the Indies in their stead. The Crown spurned don Diego Colón by counterbalancing his rule with a new magistracy, the *Audiencia,* or High Court, in 1511. The Crown gradually delegated *justicia* adjudication to various such high courts—in Mexico (1526), Santo Domingo (1528), Panama (1538), Lima (1542), Nueva Galicia (Michoacan; 1548), Santa Fe de Bogotá (1549), Charcas (1559–1568), Quito (1563), and the Philippines (1574). Initially, these judiciaries controlled not only litigation but also matters of government, military, and grace, opening up new venues for bottom-up paperwork.

The Crown appointed both magistrates and officials with strong administrative and military faculties. Monarchs soon assigned these governors legislative-executive powers to various provinces. After Diego died in 1526, a joint junta consisting of a high court and a governor ruled from 1527 to 1583; after 1583, the governor took over administrative powers. Other provinces received governors earlier: Panama in 1543, Guatemala in 1561, New Granada in 1571, Chile in 1568.[182] Viceroys, superior even to governors and high judges, would further cement Crown power. Although the first viceroy of Peru had met his death at the hands of the Pizarros' men, the tide had turned by the 1550s. Viceroys now commanded considerable respect from vassals thanks to their distribution of *gracia* privileges and eagerness to listen to *gobierno* petitions.

The two uppermost echelons of conquistador power, the conquistador governorships and major *mayorazgo* estates, had succumbed by 1570. The third stratum of conquistador power, that of minor *encomienda* estates, did not suffer quite as dramatic a fall—in fact, it persisted in a weakened form through the entire sixteenth century (and in some cases beyond). Nonetheless, the council and its viceroys began to deprive even lesser conqueror-rulers of not only these grants but also virtually all jurisdictional faculties. Gradually but inexorably, the Crown punished "cases and crimes . . . revolutions [and] scandals" within conquistador lordships.[183] Vassals' lawsuits, especially from friars and Natives, along with viceroys' redistributions of tribute after demographic collapse, sapped smaller lords of their power to govern their commoners as they saw fit.[184] Lawsuit by lawsuit, petition by petition, the Crown gained turf with minimal recourse to violence. Conquistadors had become mere pensioners.

No officials were more threatening to conquistadors than viceroys. Unlike other officials, viceroys could distribute privileges in the name of the king—including *encomiendas.* New Spain's first viceroys not only undercut conquistador jurisdiction but also aggressively appropriated vacant tribute titles and distributed these privileges to loyalists. With every change of viceroy in Mexico and Peru, conquerors lost more tribute grants.[185] Royal officials increasingly took over grants of Indigenous labor, forcing New World elites and communities to seek not feudal tribute grants but temporary labor allotments, or *repartimientos,* which allocated Indigenous work to short-term projects.[186] This shift drove many vassals to compete through *gracia* petitioning before the viceroys and kings. Historian José-Juan López Portillo notes that the ensuing "voluntary—rather than coercive or mercenary—mobilization . . . was an enviable accomplishment by contemporary standards in Europe or anywhere in the Americas."[187] The powerful but limited conduits of petitioning of the early postconquest years had been flung open.

There was little the conquistadors could do. According to royal officials, in 1566 various disgruntled conquistadors had been planning to kill all royal officials within reach and rally the people around "liberty, liberty, against the violence and tyranny of the King don Philip."[188] Viceroys had no army. They should have been defenseless against these men, who were the true bearers of violence. And yet many subjects sensed that now was their moment to win royal privileges. The movement was betrayed. Afterward, many subjects approached the viceroys and monarchs requesting rewards for having thwarted it. Notably, a group of some seventy self-described *mulato* vassals led by the shoemaker Juan Bautista produced a *gracia* petition insisting on their pivotal assistance to royal officials in arresting Cortés and his men.[189] They, too, sustained the radical dismemberment of conquistador power. With the judicial defeat of the Pizarros in the 1570s, the New World's last major aristocratic dominions had fallen and passed entirely into royal control.[190]

INDIGENOUS DYNASTIES ON THE PAPER BATTLEFIELD

During these years, Indigenous elites went through a period of utter uncertainty. More than a few wound up as commoners; a friar named Juan de Salmerón warned the Crown in 1583 that he needed to help the Nahua lords, for "many of them have become the servants and serfs of the very same Indians whom their ancestors had lorded over."[191] Alongside conquistadors, the New World's former ruling dynasties—battered by disease, Christian and Indigenous-led massacres, civil wars, and invasions of neighboring polities—struggled mightily to recover what had been theirs.

For the Indies' defeated sovereigns, the Motecuzomah, the Uachusecha, the Inca, and other large ruling dynasties, disaster came swiftly. They had once commanded extensive settlements, armies, and family estates; now their authority hung by a thread. The Moctezumas, as they were now called, lost their supreme *tlatoaque* powers in Tenochtitlan as early as 1525, when Cortés appointed a Mexica loyalist from outside the family to govern the Indigenous side of the city.[192] For a mere eight years, the Purepecha sovereigns maintained power under Spanish suzerainty. However, the conquistador-governors repeatedly arrested their Irecha ruler, the *cazonztin* don Francisco Tangaxoan. After his vassal Quaranque accused him of attempting to kill Spanish president Nuño de Guzmán during a joint attack on sovereign Indigenous groups, authorities quickly tried, tortured, and executed him.[193] The Inca divided into two rival groups during the 1530s: one branch continued to assert independence against the Spanish, while the other became a prominent but subordinate aristocracy within Cusco, bereft of formal ruling powers. Except for the part of the Inca line that fled to Vilcabamba and resisted, then, all major dynasties became aristocracies with little or no jurisdiction.

The many spheres of Spanish paperwork proved perilous for Indigenous dynasts. Upstarts from within lower aristocratic rungs angled to usurp their power. Some tried to outsmart their superiors in court. For instance, don Andrés de Tapia Motelchiuhtzin was a prominent Mexica service elite who befriended Cortés and in 1525 became the governor of the defeated Tenochtitlan–Mexico City. His appointment marked the end of the Moctezumas as governors.[194]

The Moctezumas had lost Mexico, but perhaps they could maintain and even expand their jurisdiction over their old patrimonial fiefdoms. This was the plan of don Pedro Moctezuma, who was, according to Spaniards, the sole legitimate heir of Motecuzomah. He battled to retain one of the Mexica's original kingdoms, Tula, claiming that his ancestors had ruled it indirectly.[195] Tula would constitute don Pedro's estate, underpinning his seigneurial aspirations. Yet don Pedro's enemies fought back using the participative and ruthless Spanish bureaucracy. Don Pedro insisted that his mother, doña María Miahuaxochitl, had been governess of Tula, but the town's local elites and commoners resisted him fiercely in court. Don Pedro lost his governorship of Tula sometime in the 1530s due to unspecified crimes. In the late 1530s, his enemies in the town—led by one Francisco Aztlatl and his elite and Otomi commoner allies in the Indigenous municipality—alleged that he had lost his legal claim to the estate.[196] Aztlatl and his clique refused to allow don Pedro and his mother to collect tribute in Tula, exiled her to Mexico City, and demolished the dynasty's ancestral houses.[197]

A bureaucratic morass began to consume the dynasty's primary heir. The viceroy dispatched an Indigenous investigator from Tlaxcala, who conducted an investigation (in Latin) that determined that don Pedro had exaggerated his claims to authority over Tula. The defendant responded that the investigator's mediocre efforts betrayed the Tlaxcalan's anti-Mexica bias, and he presented paperwork counterattacks to the Mexican viceroy. Simultaneously, he petitioned the emperor in person but received only 1,000 pesos in yearly rent—a small sum that could scarcely keep his large household afloat. Accusing Tula elites and commoners of intransigence and usurpation, the dynast continued to submit petitions, proofs, and witness testimonies supporting his dynasty's claims well into the 1550s. Don Pedro won tribute from six of the town's twenty-one districts, but by the 1550s, Tula commoners were so incensed by his incessant challenges that they contemplated rising up and killing him. By the 1560s, the self-declared "great lord" (*gran señor*) complained that he was in debt due to legal battles and experiencing difficulty collecting tribute.[198] The commoners and elites of Tula had defeated and nearly bankrupted the once-great dynasty in court—even destroying its ancestral home.

Like the Moctezumas, the ruling Irecha dynasty, or *uacusecha*, of the Irechequa Tzintzuntzani also survived. Once the *cazonzi* rulers of the realm of the Tarascans, they now faced the dilution of their power by conquistadors, friars, bishops, and Indigenous commoners eager to challenge them in court.[199] They maintained a somewhat strong grip on community affairs at least until 1577. At that point, the head of an illegitimate branch of the ruling Huitzimengari branch, don Constantino Bravo Huitzimengari, took on the role of governor through savvy intrigue in the Indigenous municipal council.[200] Though weakened, this family managed to petition viceroys and the Crown successfully for ongoing privileges, including yearly pensions. Members of the Huitzimengari branch of the dynasty survived well into the final decades of the seventeenth century, while other branches endured as pensioners into the late 1700s.[201]

The Inca dynasts who survived the Cusco civil wars, Christian conquests, and Spanish civil wars faced many uncertain paths. This family was simultaneously more adroit at keeping its ruling power and more ill fated than the lords of Anahuac and the Irechequa Tzintzuntzani. It was also better off, in a sense, because one branch managed to resist Spaniards and their Indigenous allies for almost four decades, entrenched in the rainforest stronghold of Vilcabamba. The split began early. One of the sovereign Huayna Capac's sons was Paullu Topa Inca, who became an essential ally of Diego de Almagro and the Pizarros; the other was Manco, who resisted the Spaniards as the Inca sovereign of Vilcabamba.[202] Paullu engendered numerous Inca elites who, despite never governing Tihuantinsuyo, again, held the title of Inca lords.[203] Dozens of members of this Inca branch and scions of several other royal families received generous tribute grants during the 1500s and seem to have been more successful at maintaining them than many Spaniards.[204]

That leaves the sovereign branch of the Incas. Local Peruvian officials, hoping to entice the Sapa Inca of Vilcabamba into Christian society as *señores,* promised Manco Capac's son Sayri Tupac what amounted to an extensive autonomous *mayorazgo* in 1548.[205] Over a decade of tense debates and ongoing warfare, the Inca negotiated a realm for himself that included Yucay, a fertile and populous area with special significance to the Inca.[206] By 1558, the Inca had returned to Cusco and seem poised to finally win the Indies' second-largest realm, a marquisate in all but name. However, in 1561 Sayri Tupac was fatally poisoned—supposedly by a vengeful Cañari commoner. Without a male heir old enough to inherit, decades of litigation began.[207] The great estate of Yucay would remain a dream of Peru's would-be *señores.* A vast network of Inca claimants scrambled to win royal officials' support and inherit not only Sayri Tupac's lands but also the royal privileges Paullu had won in the 1540s.[208] Many saw their fortunes decline as lesser lords and even commoners began to usurp the family name and openly contest Inca privileges in court.[209]

The inner circles of the Indies' greatest dynasties thus lost many of their jurisdictions and struggled to lay stake to patrimonial estates, leaving one path for them and their fellow elites: to largely abandon claims to authority but preserve formal titles and other aristocratic privileges. The Crown and viceroys welcomed this changing priority. In 1530s Mexico, for example, the high nobility petitioned the viceroy for the novel Tecle Lord (*caballero tecle*) privilege, cementing recipients' status at the uppermost stratum of Native nobility.[210] Others traveled to Europe to win royal privileges. One such case is illustrated by the efforts of don Hernando de

Tapia, son of don Andrés de Tapia Motelchiuhtzin. Don Hernando petitioned voraciously in the 1530s for a number of Spanish privileges and even secured the Vatican's title of Knight of the Golden Spur. His children fared well, and his lineage lasted into the 1700s.[211] However, he never laid serious claims to recover his father's lordly jurisdiction. The sovereigns who managed to survive became pensioners petitioning the viceroy and his faraway superior, the Spanish king.

MONASTIC THEOCRACIES AND INDIGENOUS CONVERSION

Lawfare defeated the marquises and conquistador-governors and hobbled the *encomienda.* Even council ministers, once in favor of rewarding warlords with seigneurial power, soured after reading so many petitions, lawsuits, and audits. Indigenous dynasts, too, became mired in paperwork to preserve their dwindling estates and authority. A major power vacuum opened up in the countryside. Christians struggled to govern and convert these expanses—and few were better suited for this task than the mendicant orders. Council ministers and royal officials had long stated that friars were better suited than venal priests and bishops for the task of converting Indigenous pagans.[212] Conquistador-governors had also initially welcomed friars' arrival, as had Native lords and communities seeking protection from their subjugators.[213] Officials therefore often sponsored friars, especially Franciscans, Dominicans, and Augustinians, providing them generous allocations of Indigenous labor and tribute. Thousands heeded the apostolic call. By the 1580s, there were around fifteen hundred mendicants in central Mexico and another thirty-five hundred or so throughout the rest of the Indies.[214] The largest orders, the Dominicans, Augustinians, and Franciscans, were particularly eager and capable of evangelization, sending Spanish-born friars to extremely remote corners of the Indies. In central Mexico alone, friars erected 277 monastery-towns.[215]

Few contemporaries anticipated that a relatively small group of unarmed preachers would eventually claim jurisdiction over much of the New World. And yet, they managed to establish hundreds of theocratic jurisdictions, dominating the countryside alongside indisposed conquistadors and Native lords.[216] Indeed, they directly competed with these rival groups in cooperation with their own Native allies.

We have already seen that friars often aggressively pursued the weakening of conquistador power. Initially, they had defended the warlords. But many mendicants bristled at the warlords' indifference to spiritual conquest and intimidating proceedings in everyday disputes. Others agreed with vassals' widespread impression that conquistadors (as one said about Cortés) "had no more conscience than a dog."[217] Some friars were their staunch allies, of course, but many preached a message of Christian opposition that they would soon make the basis of their own might.

The friars' *de facto* seigneurial world was different from that of the conquistadors. It was not a clan but a religious order that sought to rule. Friars' radical idioms were also idiosyncratic: when they expressed radical opposition to conquistadors and expressed their own vision of Indies rule, they did so in a certain register. The 1530s crisis in Mexico, which pitted a large group of Franciscans against Cortés and his allies, is a case in point. In 1539 Tlaxcala, central Mexico, the Archangel Saint Michael and the armies of Spain and New Spain outdid the stalemated saints Santiago and Hippolytus, at last defeating the Moors in Jerusalem. This Christian victory took place in an opulent Nahuatl drama organized by Franciscan friars and their Indigenous allies. The play's message rings strange today but was at the time audaciously obvious: the friar-Indigenous alliance was on the verge of crushing Spanish conquistadors' power in the New World. This victory would lead to a new Jerusalem, an apostolic theocracy unlike anything attempted in Christendom since the Last Supper. The story of this production verged on the scandalous. Tlaxcalan actors played two great Christian armies, those of Spain and New Spain. These Native crusaders besieged the devil's troops—the Moors and Jews—to recover captive Jerusalem. They were helped by the two saints who had accompanied the conquistadors in the destruction of the Mexica realm: Spain's Muslim-killing patron saint, Santiago, and Mexico's then-patron of conquest, Saint Hippolytus. But neither mighty Santiago nor Hippolytus proved strong enough. Only when the Archangel Michael appeared did the Christians turn the tables. Resistance was futile—not even the devil could withstand Michael. The Muslims and Jews rushed to surrender, accepting mass baptisms.

The Franciscans' celebration of the authority of Michael over Santiago and Hippolytus was a strong message in and of itself. The conquistadors' saints were inferior in power to the archangel, who would ultimately defeat Satan himself on Judgment Day. Whereas the Franciscans had helped the conquistadors conquer land, their protector Michael had arrived in Mexico to save mankind's souls from the devil once and for all. Even more radical and obvious were the names the Franciscan and Indigenous performers chose for the leaders of the enemies of Christendom: Sultan Hernán Cortés of Babylon and the Moorish Captain General don Pedro de Alvarado. These Moorish tyrants—the two greatest captains of the Spanish conquest—held Jerusalem prisoner until they surrendered to the archangel, the Franciscans, and the Tlaxcalan armies of Christ. And so, the greatest struggle of human history—of Christians against the devil—was won that day in Tlaxcala.

This depiction of Spanish-Native spiritual conquest was a call to arms for the Tlaxcalan audience. Indigenous vassals could overthrow their conquerors. Infidel elites' feudal domains would fall to a true apostolic theocracy unlike anything the Old World had ever seen.

Theocratic separatism often boosted ambitious Indigenous groups while draining once-powerful communities of lands and labor force. It also fueled countless lawsuits between Indigenous towns.[218] The orders, enjoying broad royal and local support after the conquests, strengthened their positions by petitioning furiously for viceregal and royal privileges and reforms. They often did so by encouraging Indigenous subjects to petition in their stead, helping their allies from behind the scenes.

The emboldened friars' rule over Jerusalem was anything but mild and meek. The differences between friar and conquistador soon blurred—not only spatially but also jurisdictionally. Emperor Charles V, at Hernán Cortés's behest, had initially petitioned the papacy to allow friars to claim extraordinary jurisdictional powers normally reserved to bishops or even the pope.[219] These efforts prompted the Curia to issue the 1522 rescript *Exponi nobis*, which gave friars who were physically distant from bishops almost absolute "ecclesiastical and civil authority."[220] In the 1520s, they even elected Mexico's earliest bishops—a sign of their might in the Indies' urban centers.[221] But that was not all. According to *Exponi,* friars in areas far from or without bishops could take on episcopal power.[222] This provision seemed innocent enough, but according to the medieval bull *in Coenae domini,* friars with papal commissions could excommunicate anyone who used "force or violence" to usurp ecclesiastical power or property as well as anyone who opposed papal rescripts.[223] These bulls gave friars powers far beyond their usual duties of confirmation, penitence, communion, marriage, last rites, and Christian doctrine.[224] They could now discipline and punish their Spanish and Indigenous rivals just like local feudal lords. They became *de facto* civil, religious, and even inquisitorial authorities. With good reason, historian Henry Kamen has observed that the Indies became dotted with "virtually independent republics in which the missionaries [were] the state."[225] Cortés surely had not imagined that the friars would repay his efforts by casting him as diabolical captain of the infidels only years later.

This spiritual conquest, led by friars and their allies, was in many cases wildly successful. Where conquistadors failed to carve out massive feudal dominions, friars triumphed. Notably, Dominicans royal officials petitioned diligently to oversee the vast sovereign Indigenous Verapaz region in the province of Guatemala. The High Court of Mexico, seeking to diminish the infamously abusive conquistador-governor Pedro de Alvarado, negotiated with the Dominicans and granted them the *Capitulaciones of Tezulutlan* to pacify the province. The Dominicans proceeded to intertwine their power with strong local elites like the Q'eqchi' lords don Juan Apo Batz and Juan Matalbatz, who solidified their power by overseeing new religious brotherhoods.[226]

The region of Verapaz became a monastic fortress from which few petitions could escape to local or royal officials. The agonistic dynamics through which vassals used paperwork to topple the powerful did not apply here. Wary of interlopers, friars and Native lords forbade the entry of outside Spaniards or their associates into the area. In the process of harmonizing Verapaz's two power groups and preventing jurisdictional conflict, the Dominicans stopped virtually any complaint about abuses from leaking out.[227] Verapaz was, for all intents and purposes, a monastic lordship of the most absolute sort, won without the violence of the conquistadors.[228]

In some ways, the friars thus acted as an anti-Spanish bulwark, shielding Native communities from further disruption. They helped fuel radical movements by providing an influential alternative to conquistador segneurialism and actively petitioning against abusive warlords. But they did not merely protect Natives; they also unsettled Indigenous society. As friars cemented their jurisdictional might, they presented a direct threat to Indigenous elites. Before the conquests, many noblemen and noblewomen participated actively in sponsoring temple construction, divination, communications with deities, and other acts. Competing Indigenous dynasties had long destroyed one another's temples and deities, constructing their own on the ruins. Friars now presented conquest as absolute and final: non-Catholic practices had to be eradicated.[229] The relatively lenient conquistadors were not the main culprits of this traumatic Christianization—here, friars and their newly converted allies took the lead, inflicting "perhaps the greatest destruction on Native society" of all.[230] And because much of this destruction and upheaval occurred in friar enclaves, few vassals initially managed to break the parchment curtain and reveal the nature of the situation.

FRIARS AS TYRANTS

When word reached Indies officials and the Crown, however, they repeatedly discovered that theocracy could be every bit as fearsome as conquistador rule. Throughout the Indies, friars' growing power led their erstwhile allies and vassals to denounce them as abusive. Like the conquistadors, mendicants coerced commoner labor with great building projects, harsh personal servitude, and enormous tributes.[231] Already in 1531, the Crown responded to unspecified reports that Mexico's Dominican order had compelled Natives to build "sumptuous" monasteries, causing laborers great harm.[232]

Soon the friars' authority became intolerable to vassals. Friars cited papal bulls to excommunicate royal officials.[233] They punished illicit Indigenous beliefs and practices, usurping royal powers. Some illegally lashed and otherwise physically punished Natives, while others harassed Indigenous officials appointed by Crown delegates. Friars everywhere punished Indigenous subjects for what they considered to be sodomy.[234] They even took vassals' lives—a gross violation of royal authority. Officials fretted that mendicants were extrajudicially executing Indigenous idolaters, even lords.[235] The elites of Cuauhtinchan remembered that in the late 1520s, a friar had extrajudicially executed an elite named don Thomás Uillacapitz for child sacrifice, remarking that "when they killed him, there was still no justice."[236] The Nahuas of Huejotzingo recalled in 1560 that when the "Tlaxcalans pushed out and rejected the fathers" immediately following the conquest, "many of the high nobles were burned, and some hanged."[237] These were not isolated events.[238]

Soon the structure of theocracy fell under wide scrutiny. In the 1540s, the head commissary of the Franciscans of Guatemala noted that his order had been accused of "wanting to make ourselves kings and popes." He defended their use of arrests against Native vassals by stating that "it is necessary with them to have the hammer of punishment and the nail of fear."[239] A conquistador-official alliance headed by Mexico City alderman Juan Velázquez de Salazar complained in 1552 that the orders' "ambition to rule is extremely great."[240] A royal treasury official reported from Cartagena in 1552 that friars were forcing sons of lords to grind corn, humiliating them and costing them the respect of commoners; friars had also seized bailiffs' rods and were illegitimately enforcing justice.[241] One anonymous 1589 petition complained that certain friars had been abusing Natives and smashing their officials' rods of justice in symbolic acts of disobedience against both local and royal authority.[242] The High Court of Guatemala caught wind in 1585 that the Dominicans of Chiapas "have the Indians in great servitude, and they [the Indians] have never known another spiritual or temporal superior."[243] Similarly, the archbishop of Mexico complained of friars smashing Indigenous rods of justice, forcing Natives to build opulent monasteries, and keeping them under "tyranny and cruel subjection."[244] Friars sometimes saw their own mission as inherently antiepiscopal. As one wrote in a private letter to Las Casas in 1555, it was his duty and pride to resist the powerful, especially the bishops.

He boasted, "I don't care a straw, for in fact, it is my glory, to be on bad terms with tyrants."[245]

Absolute monastic theocracy most famously reared its head in the 1550s and 1560s Yucatan. This region was not unlike Dominican Verapaz. There, the friars—in this case, Franciscans—held near-total *de facto* control over the Mayan countryside. However, unlike in Verapaz, the Franciscans lacked explicit royal grants of *de jure* power, and petitioners managed to alert the Crown of abuse. Though the Franciscans had styled themselves as the protectors of Indians against conquistador abuse, Diego de Landa and his small group of Franciscans overpowered all other regional factions and became just as cruel (with certain Native factions' support). When the friars heard from two Maya Christians that they had discovered widespread idolatry and human sacrifice, they overplayed their hand. They used a legal loophole, invoking the bulls *Exponi* and *Coena* to claim the power to operate as bishops, which gave them inquisitorial and civil jurisdiction over Natives. The Franciscans and their allies tortured thousands of Mayans, leading to hundreds of deaths and dozens of suicides. No rival group was bold enough to stop them. Even their Maya allies were revolted.[246]

Friars also wielded their power against Spaniards. In 1556, Francisco Hernández, a Spanish resident of Valladolid, Yucatan, denounced friars for grievous abuses against Indigenous vassals. Yet in the process, he allegedly blurted out in front of many Indigenous Christians that "the friars . . . do not preach any truth, all was lies; that which they preached was not of God but the Devil, and that he felt pity [for the Indians] that they were the friars' slaves."[247] The friars had a justice officer arrest him for blasphemy.[248] Hernández loudly complained that it was a gross abuse of power.

Little wonder, then, that friars appeared often in petitions and *visitas* as usurpers and tyrants themselves. The very term that proIndigenous Dominicans like Las Casas had used to devastating effect against conquistadors was now being turned against them. In 1563, Diego Rodríguez, appointed protector of the Indians of Guatemala and the Yucatan, accused the friars of abuses "never before heard of in the Indies" and warned that these atrocities owed to the fact that the region's social factions were all under the Franciscans' thumbs.[249] Even one of the Franciscans of the Yucatan expressed disbelief at his peers' "many tyrannies and cruelties and tribulations and thefts."[250]

Natives denounced friars' misdeeds before viceroys, governors, and investigators. These high-ranking officials agreed that if the orders usurped Crown power to mete out justice, they too might become tyrants, leaving the Natives "lost and destroyed."[251] Many groups, including *encomenderos,* royal officials, Indigenous commoners and elites, Spanish settlers, and even priests and bishops, sought to limit friars' power through petitioning and litigation.[252] In 1562, the viceroy of Peru noted "the complains which Indians bring forth every day against friars . . . their excesses, the imprisonments, the missions full of clamping tables [*cepos*] and prisons."[253] He concluded that "there is no lord, not even the most powerful, as powerful as they are over the Indians."[254] The radical era was unkind to powerful tyrants. These mendicants' stars would soon come crashing down to earth.

NATIVE LORDS NAVIGATE MILITARY AND SPIRITUAL CONQUESTS

Rural Indigenous lords were, alongside conquistadors and friars, the most important authority figures in the Indies countryside. They were also the most numerous, although many had died—and would continue to die—from diseases and violence. Survivors now faced decades of struggles with Spanish imperial paperwork, on which their power became utterly dependent. Almost every issue imaginable seemed to force them to petition and litigate. For instance, in 1551, the Mexican viceroy complained that there was no overarching system for determining who was to be a Native lord; their destinies were defined by numerous inconsistent authorities.

> Some succeed in their charges through the inheritance of their fathers and grandfathers, others by election, and others because Moctezuma appointed them . . . others because it has happened that encomenderos would appoint them and remove them as they found convenient, and others were appointed by friars.[255]

These changes wrought substantial harm to Indigenous rulers. A moment of considerable peril was the creation of *encomiendas.*[256] Many high lords' formal status faded after the conquistadors' distribution of tribute duties. By the 1560s in the Yucatan, the powerful *halach uinic* overlords and their *cúuchcabal* courtiers had "disappeared altogether from the Indigenous political landscape," partly due to the *encomiendas*' simplification of Native political structures into the lordship-governorship, the lesser lordship also called the *batabil.*[257] In the Muisca realm, *zipa* and *zape* high lords and *sihipkua* lords became mere lords (*caciques*), even as the once-subordinate *tyba* captains became lords themselves.[258] Similarly, in northern Peru the *hatun curaca* high lords lost their power over lesser *curacas,* as did the *hunu* overlords of Quito.[259]

In many cases, *encomienda* distribution undercut large families that had ruled collectively, as conquistador-governors appointed a single Native lord and headman over an *encomienda.* Early New Spain alone contained over fifteen hundred communities, or *altepeme,* all of which were subsumed in one way or another into the *encomiendas.*[260] And after epidemics struck, the *encomiendas* often folded several towns into one, merging multiple *altepeme* ruling dynasties into a single lordship held by a head of family who possessed continued but limited jurisdiction, a Crown salary, and responsibilities to raise taxes for his Spanish superior.[261] The *encomienda* thus drastically upset preconquest aristocratic lineages, replacing joint rule with lords who were variously lesser captains, former high lords, or figureheads of once larger dynasties.

Friars' and Native Christians' persecution of unbelievers presented another danger. A convoluted, multisided spiritual conquest had begun, splitting Indigenous communities into factions. For a brief but violent time, friars' new Indigenous converts rebelled against their non-Christian parents, seeking a clean break from the past. It was no accident, for "early friars often lavished their attentions on children, especially elite children, pitting them against their elders and thereby further undermining lines of authority."[262] In one Nahua account, young Christian Natives stoned a local Indigenous priest to death; in Tlaxcala, Lord Acxotecatl Cocomitzin responded to these gangs' destruction by killing his son and his son's mother.[263]

Rural lords who survived these bloody purges virtually always became Christian and strategically adopted certain aspects of the Spanish culture of the *señor.* One Indigenous account shows the importance of this transformation. The *batab* lord Ah Nakuk Pech, of ancient Maxtunil lineage, left a written testimony from sometime after 1553 about "when the tribute was given to the captains of the Spaniards."[264] He stated that his vassals paid *encomendero* with local goods and in turn "received coats and caps and shoes and rosaries and hats, and we were greatly celebrated."[265] In this way, "we principal chiefs were made *hidalgos* by the captains. . . . Power was given to us through God and the king who governed."[266] Religious conversion followed. The *batab* recalled, "When the water entered into my head, when I received the baptism, I was called don Pablo Pech."[267]

Yet a labyrinth of Christian norms and paperwork traps still awaited don Pablo and other lords. Friars, bishops, priests, and royal officials imposed marriage practices on Indigenous aristocracies and lesser nobilities, targeting polygamy and marriage with family members. These practices had been essential components of elite life and cross-polity alliance making before the conquests. Beginning in 1520s New Spain and 1530s Peru, priests and friars pushed for monogamous marriage and strongly discouraged incest, both tasks that they largely achieved by the 1550s.[268] The Christian prohibition of elite Indigenous polygamy shrank ruling families, impeded alliances with large dynasties, and reduced the power of prominent Native women.[269]

These norms made paperwork a perilous maze. Rivals sought to wage lawfare against lords by framing them as bad Christians—especially as idolatrous and otherwise immoral. The historiography has generally painted a picture of inquisitions as unilateral vehicles of Christian authoritarianism, yet beneath the surface of persecution of ritual specialists, local intrigues were often at play. In 1539, Bishop Zumárraga famously burned don Carlos Chichimecateuctli, a Tetzcoca noble, at the stake for idolatry. However, don Carlos's accusers were largely members of a rival noble faction seeking to prevent don Carlos from seizing power. Don Carlos had tried to rape his brother's widow, as was his lordly prerogative. In response, notes Bradley Benton, his rivals embarked on a "distinctly colonial strategy by engaging the Inquisition against him."[270]

Commoners often posed a threat to Native lords; their testimonies could be particularly damning. For instance, the *pilguanes* (commoners) of Iguala testified against their lord don Juan in 1545, accusing him of various attempted rapes.[271] In the 1560s in Tarascan lands, commoners in Zinapecuaro accused their lord don Alonso Huapean of over five hundred crimes in an extensive lawsuit in the Purepecha language.[272] Accusations of sexual immorality often came from lords' own homes. Commoner domestics, including women, could use the episcopal and monastic inquisitions to denounce elite Indigenous rivals. For instance, a lawsuit against don Juan of Matlatlan featured Yzmulanga, one of his twenty consorts. Similarly, the slaves of the elite don Cristobal used intimate knowledge of his home to report his supposed idolatry.[273]

Lords were everywhere under legal assault. One friar noted, with some exasperation, that "there is never a want of accusations" of Natives against their lords.[274] The chaos of the early *encomienda* distributions, the rise of new jurisdictional spaces, the ambiguity of inheritance rules in succession cases, and other issues led lords to petition and litigate by the thousands—very often in self-defense from their own communities and kin.[275] This weakness encouraged local lords to ostentatiously embrace friars and reassure their communities of their upright Christian standing. Many undertook anti-idolatry efforts themselves, as the Tlaxcalans did in the 1540s.[276]

NATIVE LORDS AS TYRANTS

Rural Native lords, perhaps more than any other social group, had to deftly navigate all sorts of challenges to cling to power during this period. Yet some might win back considerable autonomy and even great power through the fall of Indigenous sovereigns, the decline of the most powerful Spaniards, and the vacillating power of friars. In 1583, the Andean lords don Felipe Caquia and don Pedro Hilapai of Guancane described Inca tribute as abusive but impossible to resist "due to the great fear which we had of him due to his tyranny."[277] Now, some communities breathed easier. By 1556, the king and his ministers had openly agreed that conquistadors must lose power over Native communities and that Native lords must recover their jurisdiction. However, the council's policy had a catch: Spanish authorities could constantly audit Indigenous lords and replace them if necessary.[278]

These lords began to experience not only the turmoil of constant seigneurial upheavals and collapses but also direct pressure from rivals and commoner subjects through lawfare. The king and his ministers, who in the 1550s evinced sympathy for Indigenous lords, had turned against them by the late 1560s in response to many reports arriving from the Indies.[279] The reasons were the same as with conquistadors and friars: complaints about growing authority and abuses. Friars in Mexico complained that bishops, who diluted their powers of punishment, were prompting Native lords to not only disobey the friars' orders but also openly return to polygamy and other un-Christian practices.[280]

Local officials had already begun to allege Native lords' tyranny by the late 1540s, welcoming petitions against them from commoners, rival elites, and Spaniards of many stripes.[281] The Crown responded by forbidding Peru's Indigenous lords from tyrannically taxing subjects in 1552.[282] A steady stream of complaints persisted. In 1560s Peru, Crown agents still decried Indigenous lords as tyrants who abused commoners without pity.[283] One high judge of New Spain similarly wrote the Crown with concern in 1560 that Native lords were to collect commoners' tributes, but only if these were not "tyrannically imposed."[284]

It was not just officials who warned about Indigenous lords. The conquistador Pedro de Avedaño reported to the Peruvian viceroy sometime in the 1560s that many Native lords in remote areas had actually gained substantial power after the fall of the Incas. With the Inca gone, "the lords of the entire realm have come to tyrannize the natives. . . . With the arrival of the Spanish and the lack of Inca government they seized matters and pre-eminences that were the Inca's, with civil and criminal jurisdiction that they never had."[285] Others suggested that many Native lords' preconquest authority remained unchanged. One petitioner wrote from Mexico in 1562 that "these natives are very fatigued by their governors and principals, because they rob them and live in the same tyranny which they had employed during their years as infidels."[286]

Native lords faced substantial threats from their own commoners. For example, in 1572, one don Pedro won royal privilege to act as Native lord over the Muisca community of Cuitiva. However, when a royal official traveled to Cuitiva, he found that the commoners had accused don Pedro of tyranny and usurpation and instead appointed the child Tirguanicipa as their leader. The official supported this move, costing don Pedro his position.[287]

These paperwork rebellions repeated frequently throughout the Indies, unsettling local elites and fanning division within Indigenous communities.[288] Ministers and Indies officials listened with great care, often deciding to divorce abusive Native lords' families from hereditary jurisdiction forever. As viceroys' power increased, lords hoping to continue exercising local rule had to petition for privilege to act as Indigenous governor.[289] To make matters worse, lords had to evade the legal efforts of rivals who knew that the rules of the game were still fluid.[290]

OPPORTUNITIES FOR INDIGENOUS COMMONERS AND LOWER NOBILITY

Indigenous commoners suffered greatly during the conquests. Some nonetheless found opportunities to improve their lot amid these jurisdictional revolutions. As the Mexican High Court sought to stabilize the royal administration, for example, its Spanish magistrates and their noble Indigenous consultants attracted countless Indigenous commoners. Many were slaves seeking freedom. Witnesses recalled that chief magistrate Vasco de Quiroga and his assistants answered every day "a great number of Indian men and women, requesting and defending, in such a quantity that the house was full, or at least the room . . . where he was listening and working and dispatching, and not before a scribe."[291] He freed thousands despite the protests of many lords.[292]

Commoners might also seek friars' protection against local conquistadors and Native lords, accelerating the downfall of religious specialists. Some allied with friars to avoid tribute, for instance. Others persuaded friars to appoint them to positions of authority, making them *de facto* elites. One High Court official complained in 1565 that in Chiapas, Dominicans were taking commoners and "making many of them noblemen."[293] With commoners made into lords, who would pay tribute? Friars did indeed offer their Indigenous allies—both commoners and elites—enticing reasons to convert and join theocratic communities. In 1540s Mexico, friars, whose power remained considerable, frequently appointed Indigenous lords with viceroys' approval.[294] Friars, priests, and cathedral councils offered young Natives positions through which to boost their social status.[295] In central Mexico, elite Indigenous men could enroll in friars' schools like the Colegio de Santa Cruz and the Colegio de Tlatelolco.[296] Others could negotiate for positions of prestige, including the role of money-collecting fiscales (alms gatherer and financial steward, or mayordomos) and *cantores* (choir singer) among others.[297] In the friar-dominated Yucatan of the 1550s and 1560s, friars appointed Indigenous *guardianes,* or religious leaders, to oversee Christianization, alms collection, and other activities.[298] Yucatec elites could attend Christian schools and preserve their written traditions, become religious *fiscales,* or become municipal officers—governors, mayors (*alcaldes*), aldermen (*regidores*), and *mayordomos* (keepers of community finances).[299]

Viceroys further jostled preconquest hierarchies by introducing another sphere of Indigenous jurisdiction to counterbalance that of Native lords and Native governors: the Indigenous municipal system, which officials in Mexico began implementing as early as the 1530s.[300] Municipalities offered new positions of power for Natives as lifetime or appointed council members (*regidores*), elected *alcaldes* (subordinate judicial officers), and notaries. Municipal officers raised and managed community funds and had police and tax-collecting duties. These city councils incorporated an uneasy compromise between commoners and lower-elite officials. The introduction of municipalities often resulted in the displacement of lords' dynastic power; instead, lower elites and male commoners became able to determine their communities' property, financial, labor, and justice affairs.[301] Crown authorities often determined who the presiding cabildo leaders, or *gobernadores de indios,* would be, and a range of Spaniards meddled in election politics, further confusing claims of popular will.[302] Overall, however, Indigenous municipalities served as checks against the power of Native lords, usurping their administrative, financial, tributary, and judicial powers.[303] These institutions also allowed social mobility, as Natives without aristocratic pedigrees might become tribute-exempt dons through municipal participation, especially if they became *alcaldes,* or governors, with substantial jurisdictional oversight over local communities.[304]

Indigenous municipalities were important sources of community administration as well. They raised funds to petition viceroys and the Crown for collective privileges, and some of their officials were involved in collecting tithes and alms for the church.[305] They had jurisdiction to resolve judicial disputes and minor criminal cases, collect tribute, and give, rent, and appropriate land.[306] Indian municipalities produced thousands of documents, including "petitions, cabildo minutes, land rental and land sale documents, wills, and many others."[307]

Municipalities often produced their own *acta* policies in response to petitions. In and around the Valley of Mexico, the Nahua had by the 1540s and 1550s formed idiosyncratic versions of these institutions, in which elites with pre-Hispanic pedigrees deliberated, accepted petitions, and issued Nahuatl-language *actas* of their own.[308] In Oaxaca, the majority of communities had municipal governments by the 1550s, and in the Yucatan, local Spanish officials sought to implement them by the 1550s (though this implementation became systematic only after 1580).[309] Very few municipal books survive: the most famous and complete are those of Tlaxcala, which begin in 1547.[310] It is clear, however, that municipalities encouraged *gobierno* and *gracia* petitioning not only through *actas* but also by raising funds for petitioning and litigating before viceroys and even the Crown.[311]

The praxes of Native municipalities in the Viceroyalty of Peru are more difficult to discern. As historian José Carlos de la Puente has noted, Peru's early Native municipalities "have not received the same attention as their Mesoamerican counterparts. . . . The reality is that we know very little about how [these councils] worked in practice."[312] However, one in Cusco had similar roles to the Native municipalities of Mesoamerica, namely, holding elections, punishing local wrongdoers, issuing local legislation, or *actas,* assisting the church, and allowing descendants of the Inca and mobile commoners (*yanaconas*) alike to become voting aldermen.[313] In less densely populated areas of Peru, such as the Muisca territories in New Granada, Natives did not establish municipalities during this period, leaving local jurisdiction in the hands of elites and Crown-appointed officials.[314] In some areas of the empire, then, commoners and lower lords had greater access to formal decision-making than in others.

COMMONERS AND COUNTERFEIT LORDS IN IXTACAMAXTITLAN

The implications of these jurisdictional changes within Indigenous communities were enormous. They opened doors to all sorts of conflict—often led by commoners against erstwhile Native lords. Though access to paperwork was not homogeneous, it could trigger immense struggle even in small communities distant from Spanish centers.

A crude drawing from the small Nahua town of San Juan, in central Mexico, tells one such story. The image's rawness is fitting, for it depicts a raw event. We see a group of Indigenous commoners forcing their way into a church, bloodying two Native lords, and hurling stones and verbal abuse at a Spanish Franciscan friar. Indigenous lords lie humiliated on the ground, brilliant red blood gushing from their noses and mouths. The image serves as a poignant reminder of the violence and brutality that often accompanied such conflicts.

The conflict took place in 1564 in Ixtacamaxtitlan, in the province of Puebla, central Mexico. There, in a region of mild, green valleys and dramatic mountains and plateaus, lived several thousand Nahuas. Their town had long linked bustling Lake Texcoco to the ocean and was a strategic Mexica position against nearby Tlaxcala. Although Cortés swept through without bloodshed in 1519, he appointed the abusive conquistador Bartolomé Herrera as lord of the town. Seeking to avoid Herrera, some villagers left hilly Ixtacamaxtitlan for the valley's merchant corridor. Two communities thus formed—the older, more populous San Francisco in the hills and the small but growing San Juan in the valley. Decades of uncertainty followed; disease decimated both towns, and Spanish administrators split Ixtacamaxtitlan into two equal entities by replacing Herrera with one conquistador lord for each town.[315] Then, the Franciscans began arriving to missionize—their initial preference for San Francisco confirmed its Native lords' conviction that San Juan belonged to them.[316] Yet suddenly, the social order reversed: in 1561 the Franciscans took up permanent residence in San Juan, finding it more accessible and easier to minister to. The Mexican viceroy ordered San Francisco to render San Juan administrative and spiritual obeisance.[317]

The traditional lords of San Francisco would become tribute-paying commoners, and the parvenus of San Juan would rule over them. This situation could not stand. San Francisco's rulers and commoners attempted to keep San Juan's lords out at all costs, refusing their entry and arresting their farmers. In 1564, the powder keg exploded, and San Francisco's former lords, now commoners, fought back against San Juan's former commoners, now lords.

That year, San Juan's representatives came before a Spanish field justice with a hair-raising report. For three years, the Indigenous towns of San Juan and San Francisco had been almost at war. Now, San Francisco's commoners were declaring themselves absolute lords of the region, arresting and stealing from San Juan's residents with impunity.[318] San Juan witness don Mateo de Olmos attested that "these are commoners who have made themselves into lords."[319] Martín Quezpal, a San Juan commoner, added that for three years, San Juan's inhabitants had been "up in arms and confederated, and they do not wish to obey their elders and regional seat [*cabecera*] as they had in antiquity." The ringleaders promised peasants that they "did not have to obey anything, for they are to become their own lords and leaders."[320] So it was everywhere in the empire—social order was turning upside down, and commoners were now lords.

At first, cooler heads prevailed. But the lords of San Juan could only take so much. On a Sunday morning in February 1564, the elite Indigenous officials of San Juan and a Franciscan friar named Sebastián de Ribero headed to San Francisco to round up villagers to hear mass. To their great surprise, they encountered a priest named Juan de Blandianes, sent by the bishop of Tlaxcala. The leaders of San Francisco had fooled the priest, convincing him there were no friars in the town. Clearly, it was a ruse to encourage the bishop to place San Francisco under his care at the expense of the Franciscans—and, by proxy, the leaders of San Juan. The Franciscan and his San Juan allies carried on, rounding up the San Francisco villagers in the town square. The San Juan elites, standing in the market plaza, ordered certain San Francisco commoners to help the priest they had deceived to carry his possessions back to Tlaxcala.[321]

Then, hell broke loose. San Juan witnesses recalled that San Francisco commoners poured into the plaza, thundering, "Come out, for now is the time to take revenge on our enemies, who have fallen into our hands after so many days of waiting."[322] Men and women let out their loudest war cries, swinging fists and hurling rocks at the San Juan intruders. The priest found himself in the marketplace melee, where commoners flung dirt in his face.[323] But the San Franciscans saved most vitriol for their Indigenous rivals, whom they threatened to kill, crying out "*Ma miqui, ma miqui!*"—Nahuatl for "die, die!"[324] The San Juan Indigenous authorities and the Franciscan sought refuge in the church, but this did not stop the multitude, which smashed down the ramshackle building's walls, windows, and doors and stormed inside. The Franciscan attempted to use soft words, but the crowd pelted him with rocks, spat on him, and said that "they would kill him because he was no friar but a devil."[325] Lookouts alerted the San Francisco throng of an approaching Spaniard down the road—and quickly dragged several San Juan officials into the rugged mountains. They strung up the bloodied officials by their wrists and suspended them by wooden beams for four days before releasing them.[326]

The would-be elites of San Juan drew up their raw denunciations of San Francisco violence. But San Francisco also had its day in court. Its accused rebel ringleader and self-proclaimed governor don Alexandre Vázquez claimed he was an "ignorant Indian who has not been able to pursue justice."[327] His legal agent, Augustín Pinto, presented the Spanish high magistrates in Mexico City a rousing legal manifesto defending his clients' claims. San Francisco was not a community of upstart commoners, he argued. The real upstarts were the tricksters of San Juan. His clients could prove through ancient codices that San Francisco's leaders had ruled Ixtacamaxtitlan for six to seven centuries; it was the San Juan subjects who were breakaway commoners, not them. Moreover, their independence had been confirmed by previous conquistadors, the Cholula mediator, and the friars.[328]

Figure 1.1 Evidence from litigation between the towns of San Juan and San Francisco Ixtacamaxtitlan depicting a violent dispute over jurisdiction. At the top left, the commoners and lords of San Juan violently abuse those of San Francisco. The top right features the commoners and lords of San Juan abusing the friar and lords of San Francisco. The bottom left shows San Francisco victims fleeing to the church, which the mob breaks into. The top left depicts the San Juan mob binding its victims, the bottom right, dragging them to a mountain and stringing them up by their wrists. Footprints lead the viewer's eyes through the narrative, from top right to bottom left, then top left to bottom right. Gallica / Bibliothèque nationale de France, Manuscrits—Mexicain 75, no folios.

The 1564 case then went cold. But in 1583–1587, another lawsuit brought by San Juan showed that San Francisco's elites had once again invited a priest, refused to submit to their neighbors, and expelled rivals' Indigenous authorities. San Juan's commoner elites ultimately triumphed and subordinated older San Francisco, perhaps because this town's population was simply growing much faster due to merchant and cattle-ranching traffic. It was a Pyrrhic victory: by the early 1600s, the outsiders had largely overpowered San Juan.[329] In fact, it was the more isolated San Francisco that retained its Indigenous government.

VICEROYS AND THEIR SUBALTERNS IN THE COUNTRYSIDE

Waves of paperwork revolts had prompted the Crown to limit the power of conquistadors, friars, and Indigenous lords. Seigneurialism was virtually absent from the Indies by 1572; only Dominican Verapaz and a few small seigneurial holdings (like the Columbus' struggling governorship of Jamaica) remained.[330] Over time, these struggles began to encourage new patterns of authority and, ultimately, a new society of orders. As monarchs appointed officials to subdue towering figures, those agents' power steadily grew. By the 1560s, viceroys and bishops were close to achieving both *de jure* and *de facto* lordship overconquistadors, friars, and Indigenous lords. After the Inquisition arrived in the Indies in the late 1560s and early 1570s, the viceregal-episcopal-inquisitorial trinity would congeal. This administrative trinity did not reach anything resembling total power, nor did its officials reject dialogue and paperwork once they became established. However, through them, the Crown achieved an intricate but remarkably broad set of jurisdictional powers over would-be strongmen. With this jurisdictional victory behind them, these officials would collaborate with allied subjects to create a more obedient, stable, and formally hierarchical society.

Following the conquests and mission projects, the Crown had little direct oversight over rural spaces. Viceroys' growing authority enabled them to make progress in the countryside already by the 1550s. Slowly but surely, local conflicts and complaints led the Crown to invest viceroys with considerable power over vast regions. These officials did not merely govern by waiting for subjects' grievances. When they received complaints, they often appointed direct representatives to investigate distant problems, even where friars and Native lords were most powerful. Viceroys could send Spanish and Native auditors into the countryside to "mete out justice in all matters."[331] Each audit was an opportunity for vassals to disobey their local lords, as viceroys often commanded auditors specifically seek out the testimonies of the poor. Like Crown-ordered audits, these visits were moments in which vassals, especially Indigenous subjects, could petition vehemently for new policies and judicial outcomes; visits were the origin of many viceregal ordinances.[332] At least twenty-four of these audits took place in the sixteenth century, the earliest dating from the mid-1530s.[333]

Audits sought to target abuses in general, making them broad and resource intensive. Viceroys also could respond to reports with more focused inspections by Spanish and especially Indigenous commissioners to solve local conflicts—usually land disputes, tribute investigations, public works, conflicts of jurisdiction, investigations of officials, and inquiries into local crimes.[334] During the turbulent 1540s and 1550s, the viceroys of New Spain issued dozens of commissions every year.[335] On at least three thousand occasions, viceregal commissioners headed out from the court and sought to remedy a range of injustices. In the process, these officials oversaw a massive distribution of administrative, gracious, executive, and judicial authority throughout some of New Spain's most distant regions.[336]

General and targeted audits were dangerous for Indigenous lords. Commoners and rival elites might target them for slights real or imagined. After many of these audits, viceroys replaced abusive lords with loyalists to act as impartial outsiders, often Natives of considerable status from nearby towns. A number of these outsiders had commoner support; of the two hundred who won Mexican viceregal commissions to take over community affairs, many had the explicit support of peasants.[337]

Viceroys did not always send commissioners as an ad hoc response. They also appointed an increasingly powerful group of full-time, salaried Spanish field justices (*corregidores* and *alcaldes mayores*). Since 1530,

Mexican viceroys relied strongly on *corregidores,* who had policing, judicial, and financial responsibility over *encomiendas,* mission towns, and Indigenous communities.[338] By 1545, there were already roughly one hundred of these officials throughout Mexico.[339] To centralize royal authority further and likely to offer subjects the option to appeal *corregidor* power, in the 1540s the Mexican viceroy introduced the *alcalde mayor,* who was to adjudicate and enforce edicts in the most strategically and demographically important Indies towns.[340] Both types of field justices had the power to create policies at the town level, which Spanish and Native municipalities could not resist.[341]

For many Indigenous subjects, these field justices were both undeniably useful and rather fearsome. From commoners' perspectives, they were critical in curbing conquistadors', friars', and Native lords' impunity. By the 1560s, Mexico's friars were (on paper, at least) no longer to physically punish Natives or others and were instead to refer them to these viceregal subalterns.[342] In response to 1550s complaints by reformist friars in Peru, viceroys moved to install field justices in strategic Indigenous communities to counterbalance the power of Indigenous lords over commoners.[343] These lords protested vociferously before Peruvian authorities, to no avail.[344] By the mid-1500s and especially after the 1570s, the viceroys had deployed a constellation of officials who could resist conquistador-lords, theocratic friars, and locally powerful Native lords in the countryside. This was the consummation of viceregal jurisdiction in more populous rural areas but not the beginning of a muscular, omnipresent, interventionist government apparatus.

BISHOPS' NEW SPIRITUAL CONQUEST

Viceroys were powerful in their courts and could recover royal authority in the countryside. However, this jurisdiction was nowhere near universal, partly because the viceroys were not ecclesiastical officials. It was the bishops who would act as the Crown's most reliable sentinels against monastic tyranny and usurpation in religious matters. The king and ministers had the power to appoint bishops but initially distrusted them and even allowed them to be elected by friars in Mexico.

With the 1537 appointment of Quiroga as bishop in Michoacan, the Crown began to take a more active role in appointing prelates. As friars' zeal caused friction in Indies society and petitioners warned the Crown of abuses within their theocratic dominions, rulers' attitudes began to change. Mexican conquistador Pedro de Ahumada had written the council in 1560 that the friars "do not wish to be priests, nor allow the appointment of priests, nor do they obey their prelates. . . . Each one, in the place where he resides, wishes to be bishop, and pope, and king."[345] Yet Crown-appointed bishops had broad faculties they could directly use to end this tyrannical usurpation. Particularly useful were their extraordinary powers to dispense ecclesiastical grace,[346] which enabled them to remove friars and appoint priests in their stead. When friars died or orders caused trouble, bishops would often choose to expand their jurisdiction over those towns. As Archbishop Alonso de Montúfar plainly counseled the king in 1556, placing "eight or ten priests where there are currently one or two friars, their empire would cease."[347]

Michoacan was ground zero in these conflicts. The Crown's embrace of episcopal authority yielded results there early in the 1550s, which for some offered a model for recovering rural jurisdiction throughout the Indies.[348] Archbishop Montúfar railed that friars acted like Crown officials and prelates, taxing Native commoners and building massive monasteries the likes of which were unseen in Spain. The orders had created a "tyranny and cruel subjection of the Indians, their persons, and their possessions" and would stop at nothing less than "supreme control over all the Indians, more than if they were their own vassals."[349] The 1563 Council of Trent further empowered bishops to move against the orders.[350]

In many Indies regions, the friars were finally on the defensive.[351] In the 1560s and 1570s, the struggle spread to Peru; for example, in Quito, the bishop clashed acrimoniously with the friars and their allies but largely prevailed.[352] Friars did not passively surrender their authority. Armed conflict could—and did—erupt between them and the bishops, often interspersed with furious litigation. Throughout New Spain, there were cases of missionaries sacking churches in protest of bishops' jurisdiction, as well as priests vandalizing or even torching monasteries. Indigenous elites often found themselves dragged violently into the fray.[353] This was most famously the case in Michoacan, where a decades-long conflict began with the bishop's arrival in 1538 and his moves against local Franciscans and Augustinians. But bishops ultimately used bureaucracy to achieve the upper hand. Episcopal notaries eagerly collected information about friars' abuses, including orders' illegal executions of Indigenous religious specialists, and bishops themselves rarely shied away from excommunicating their rivals.[354] The High Court of Quito complained in 1579 that the city's bishop and his colleague in Popayan would "pursue the friars and exile them and excommunicate them."[355]

These clashes generated reams of petitions, lawsuits, and audits, and friars rarely came out on top. Bishops could not only appoint priests by decree to weaken friars' grip but also conduct *visitas* of ecclesiastical dominions, giving them substantial bureaucratic power over the orders. Indeed, their investigative jurisdictions formally applied to the entire Christian sphere, including hospitals, brotherhoods, religious schools, monasteries, nunneries, and Indigenous towns.[356] In response to many petitions, including those of Indigenous vassals, bishops could punish local abusers and draft ordinances. Throughout most of the core Indies regions, friars were in retreat by the 1570s.

The friars' piecemeal but unmistakable loss of *de facto* jurisdiction against viceroys and bishops had major implications for Native vassals. Already by the mid-1510s, bishops had limited civil jurisdiction over Indigenous conflicts. Bishops held the title of Protector of Indians, which the Council of Castile created in 1516 for Las Casas. This position was initially vague but allowed bishops vast civil and juridical powers over Indigenous affairs and the power to delegate protectors in their stead.[357] In late 1520s Mexico, Archbishop Juan de Zumárraga used the title to listen to innumerable Indigenous complaints and muscle rival high judges. The latter, however, petitioned the Crown and won a 1531 royal decree that limited bishops by stipulating that protectors could delegate episcopal protectors only with high judges' approval.[358] Bishop-protectors had no juridical or legislative powers but had coercive faculties—they could force Natives to attend mass, jail vassals, issue fines, and even investigate royal officials operating in their parishes.[359] Yet especially in regions with bishoprics but weak royal control, bishops were, at least in terms of local enforcement and Indigenous affairs, often "superior to civil authorities."[360] The Peruvian Archbishop Jerónimo de Loaysa, for example, used his powers during 1540s *visita* investigations through the Andean countryside, responding to Indigenous petitions on the way.[361] This meant that in New Spain until the 1550s, Natives often petitioned these officials before going to friars or even royal officials.

Compounding bishops' power over Natives was the episcopal Inquisition. Starting in the 1510s, bishops had the ability to prosecute Spanish and Indigenous heretical statements and actions.[362] Ecclesiastical trials could stain the honor of the guilty, making them dreaded theaters of downward mobility for Natives and others. Episcopal inquisitions periodically persecuted Indigenous vassals, especially elites. They tended to socially humiliate and demote those found guilty but could also have the accused tortured or even executed.[363] Indigenous Christians worked as subalterns within episcopal inquisitions—especially in remote Andean regions where priests were rare.[364] These inquisitions offered positions of upward and downward mobility, not unlike those in friars' dominions.

The rising powers of bishops threatened friars' broad jurisdictions, but the Crown generally took care to avoid delegitimizing either group. The Crown wanted both friars and prelates to maintain peace and win vassals' respect. Constant struggles against the orders might cause more harm than good. For instance, friars complained during a series of 1570s conflicts in New Granada that High Judge Cepeda's investigations had so humiliated them that one Native commoner, sick of a friar's arbitrary abuse, felt it acceptable to violently smear him with dung and dirt.[365]

As a result, friars clung to some degree of power against the secular clergy through clever and diligent petitioning. The groups had arrived at a stalemate by the 1570s. The orders' sophisticated and well-coordinated defense in this struggle involved, among other strategies, using their procurators in the royal court to outmaneuver the clergy. One priest complained to the council in 1577 that "the friars send procurators with each Armada," and thus the "the honor of the habit of Saint Peter [was] . . . discarded in the Indies."[366] Indeed, friars unsuccessfully but ingeniously attempted in the 1560s to 1580s to convince the Crown that they themselves should appoint bishops over Indigenous communities and thereby create what some historians have called "Indian cathedral cities."[367] And even if bishops defeated friars in certain provinces, the orders might simply push further into the frontier.

The bishops curtailed many monastic usurpations of royal power. In the most central regions, they played a crucial role in penetrating friars' theocracies. However, truly far-reaching *de facto* and *de jure* episcopal sway in the countryside took decades, even centuries, to take root. For instance, Guatemala's bishops won consistent oversight over Verapaz starting in 1607 but would only definitively claim ecclesiastical jurisdiction over most of rural Mexico by the 1700s.[368] Still, their presence was essential for bringing down friar dominions. This created further structural turmoil, litigation, and social readjustment. Native elites and commoners once again had to confront these changes and strategize accordingly—sometimes using the new figures as resources for radical projects.

THE INQUISITION, BETWEEN DISOBEDIENCE, TYRANNY, AND ORDER

Completing the royal trinity that achieved jurisdiction by the 1570s was the Holy Tribunal of the Inquisition. An extensive network of theologian-judges tasked with uprooting un-Christian beliefs among the faithful, the bishop inquisitor had already existed in the Indiesbut it was not yet an autonomous royal institution. Las Casas proposed installing a formal inquisitorial body in the Indies in 1516.[369] However, it was only after the great imperial reforms of the late 1560s—in the context of Inquisitor Juan de Ovando's investigations and reforms of the Council of the Indies, the great 1566–1567 revolt in Mexico, and an increase of pirate attacks—that the Crown decided to create a formal overseas branch.[370] Ministers knew of the abuses of bishop-inquisitors in 1530s Mexico and those of the Franciscans in the 1560s Yucatan. So in 1569, they specifically stipulated that the Inquisition had no jurisdiction over Native vassals, who they argued were not yet firm in the Christian faith.

Inquisitors thus arrived in Peru in 1570 and Mexico in 1571. These theologian-judges were to persecute heretical statements and actions, stripping bishops of these powers on arrival.[371] They were rarely more than three per major city but brought with them a large staff of attorneys, secretaries, and others. These included dozens of unsalaried assistants or *comisarios,* who undertook and oversaw local Inquisition actions, and many *familiares,* who spied on the population, collected reports alleging heresy, and enforced inquisitors' commands.[372] Although the Inquisition had a reputation as the ultimate vehicle of state repression, at the time many vassals understood it to be yet another resource, another forum to petition against the powerful. Inquisition Spanish, Indigenous, and Afro-descendant women of all social backgrounds often appealed to inquisitors, denouncing slave masters, churchmen, local rivals, and others.[373]

Inquisitors were eager to intervene against physically abusive husbands and slave masters.[374] To receive help from the Inquisition, witnesses had to allege that abusers had committed crimes against the faith. When a violent husband and *encomendero* in Chiapas thundered to his terrified wife, "Do you not know that I am as good as God before you?" she accused him of blasphemy.[375] In 1572 Honduras, doña Inés Barba de Ballezillo accused her wealthy merchant husband, Pedro de Torres, of whipping her and his male and female slaves every day, declaring, "By God and Holy Mary, I shall make you pay!"[376] Inquisitors exiled him to Mexico City. In Peru, Black slaves—men and women—accused their master Blas de Ávila of blasphemy while whipping them.[377] Other Afro-descendants followed suit.[378] Indigenous men and women subjected to the same treatment resorted to similar tactics against their masters.[379]

Many accused priests and friars of spiritual crimes and sexual abuses.[380] Read in isolation, these allegations might seem like one-off cases. Yet contemporaries perceived women's actions as part of local intrigues against church officials. Priest Ochoa de Lejalda accused Indigenous women who claimed he had propositioned them of participating in the "machination" of elite Spanish and Indigenous enemies.[381] In 1589, the bishop-inquisitor in the Yucatan heard numerous such accusations against priest Andrés Mexía. The defendant rejoined that the Maya women who had accused him were related to the powerful Pol family, whose scions were punishing him for having ordered local Natives to clear a road through their property. Still, the bishop believed the teenage women who accused Mexía, exiled him for two years, and banned him from delivering sacraments.[382]

The Inquisition eroded seigneurialism further. In Spain, the Inquisition could proceed against anyone, including elites, and had jurisdiction in any lordly or monastic domain.[383] It was the same in the New World—and here, the friars' jurisdictions were most threatened. Although they still fought for autonomy against the Crown and bishops, they generally lost against the Inquisition. In 1569, one bishop accused Spaniards in general and friars in particular of "great license and liberty" and celebrated the soon-to-arrive Inquisition as the perfect tool to weed out insubordinacy from this "new land."[384] And it showed results. When a Dominican friar intruded on episcopal jurisdiction in 1580, Bishop Lucas de Paz of Chiapas accused him before the Inquisition of "manifest Lutheranism" and summoned various Native and *mulata* women to enumerate friars' usurpations.[385] Another Crown official complained before the Holy Office in Itzapa that local friars required discipline, lamenting their lust for "usurping the jurisdiction of others," which he equated to "heresy."[386] During a violent 1574 church-friar struggle in Teutl, Guadalajara, Augustinian friar Juan de Amézqueta responded to the bishop's excommunication by saying he "would wipe his ass with it."[387] Another Augustinian flatly denied the bishop's authority. Inquisitors led both to prison tied to the tail of a horse and tried them for rebellion, offenses to episcopal authority, and violently entering a temple under church jurisdiction.[388] It is little wonder that in 1578, the Augustinians of Tlaxcala complained that the Inquisition had damaged the order's power and reputation.[389] All remaining organized resistance to royal jurisdiction from the friars was coming down.

The inquisitors' goal was not to totally eradicate the friars—just to curb their ambition to transform society and rule their own dominions. As one inquisitor dryly noted in 1599, it was a priority to ensure that "the friars . . . obey their superiors."[390] The Inquisition, wary that the Inquisitors themselves might incite subjects to disobey friars, sometimes stepped in to protect friars. When the Dominicans of Huanuco, Peru, butted heads with a local field justice, he warned that the Inquisition would finish them. After all, they "had burned over a thousand friars."[391] The Holy Office exiled him to Spain. The Inquisition also helped friars discipline their own orders.[392] Friars obviously recognized that the Inquisition was mainly harmful to them but eked out small victories nonetheless.[393] For example, they could use the institution to curtail disobedience from Spanish elites and merchants who had challenged them in the past. One friar wrote from New Spain in 1571 that God had sent the Inquisition to tame the Spaniards of these "new lands," whose wild behaviors had caused Natives to lose faith.[394] Four years later, a friar similarly complained from Tabasco that Christianity was in crisis, for Spaniards' unruliness was sapping Native respect for the church.[395] The orders lost much power, but at least fewer vassals insulted them openly on the streets.

With inquisitors prepared to punish anyone who inflamed social conflict, public displays of defiance became markedly less common and less radical. Indeed, for all the opportunities inquisitors offered vassals seeking to humble the powerful, none could have mistakenly believed that these authorities were sympathetic to disorder. Fostering obedience was, indeed, the whole point of the Holy Office. Its administrators explicitly sought to put an end to the New World's grave problems of "disobedience and defiance."[396] Undoubtedly, the Crown sponsored the Inquisition to defend the Indies against internal social fragmentation and outside heretical threats. Authorities understood the Holy Office as the antidote to the Indies' decades-long social unrest; many celebrated that the "people born in this land"—the New World's Spaniards, *mestizos,* and *mulatos*—would finally get a taste of rigorous spiritual discipline.[397] They hoped a measure of spiritual order would come to a land riven by decades of turmoil.

CHECKS AGAINST THE MONARCHICAL TRINITY

The viceroys, bishops, and inquisitors sat atop the emerging Indies social order, where they would remain for centuries. Yet they had many conflicts to sort out. What would happen when their powers became too broad? How would they resolve conflicts between themselves? These problems persisted. Viceroys in particular attracted attention and criticism from other authorities and vassals. The Crown was keenly aware that their powers were dangerously broad. It sought to ensure that they had limited tenures, in theory preventing them from growing tentacle-like connections to Indies elites. Bottom-up paperwork kept them, and all royal officials, on perpetual high alert. Dramatic reports to the Crown alleging official abuse often resulted in audits culminating in financial punishment and demotions.[398] Indeed, viceroys and other high officials were subject in many ways to the same paperwork revolts that had toppled the conquistador-governors.[399] These investigations resulted in charges, demotions, and dismissals. In rare, extreme situations, they could result in trials and even executions. For instance, in the mid-1540s, overzealous governor Juan de Carvajal executed the German conquistadors of Venezuela Philip von Hutten, Bartolomeo Wesler, and others for insulting him. A royal investigator soon had Carvajal dragged by a horse to the gallows.[400]

Vassals also accused high-ranking officials of tyranny. The city council of Guatemala accused High Judge Cerrato of tyranny in 1551, for instance, complaining of his nepotism and unilateral implementation of royal decrees.[401] Viceroys, governors, and field justices experienced similar scrutiny. King Philip II and the council were well aware of officials' potential to overreach, but their only solution was to make clear that investigators themselves might receive punishment. The king wrote in 1584, "Just as it is fair to punish the investigated . . . the same applies . . . to the investigators."[402] These denunciations rarely resulted in major institutional changes, as they had in decades past.

Bishops also had certain resources that they could leverage against abusive officials. These included the power to issue special *mandamiento* edicts excommunicating high-raking royal officials. Bishop Zumárraga did so in 1520s Mexico in retribution for royal officials' hostility toward his ally Cortés.[403] In 1533, the bishop of Santo Domingo excommunicated a high judge.[404] When the governor of Tucumán, Francisco de Aguirre, declared in public in the late 1550s that "excommunications were terrible for little men, but not for me," the bishop of la Plata and his theologians moved ferociously against him. Using these powers, the bishop took Aguirre to trial, sentencing him to lashes, two years of jail, holding a candle in church, and a large fee for his "ignorant propositions."[405] The bishop of Cartagena reported to the Crown in 1563 that the city treasurer was a tyrant who had been duly excommunicated for abuses against Natives.[406]

Although bishops were not subjected to audits, their broad power also had limitations. The Crown could curtail their power in response to vassals' petitions—and it did so periodically. Some local institutions could thwart them; the cathedral council, the urban seat of bishops' bureaucratic power, was one such force. As bishops consolidated their jurisdictions, they sought to build cathedrals and institute cathedral councils. The latter institutions were staffed by canons and headed by deans, who were virtually all Spaniards appointed by bishops and, by the 1560s, by the council.[407] Cathedral councils gathered, debated by vote, and (less often) answered petitions, producing *actas* that decided the cathedral's administration, governed the cathedral's finances and dependent colleges and hospitals, managed its ecclesiastical jail, and coordinated petitions to the Crown and pope.[408] Like bishops, deans and canons could collectively excommunicate vassals.[409] These councils shared a number of ill-defined powers with bishops—they had ecclesiastical jurisdiction and often pursued lawsuits against competing bishoprics and religious orders, alleging usurpation.[410]

The greatest power canons possessed was to collectively revoke a bishop's jurisdiction altogether. They flexed this power in 1592 against the bishop of Michoacan, who called it a "rebellion and schism never before seen in such a new land."[411] Indeed, bishop–cathedral council conflicts were endemic in sixteenth-century Michoacan. In Peru, conflicts could also flare up, as they did in 1559 La Paz. There, a prelate ordered the local cathedral council investigated, only to be surprised by violent resistance. The canons reached for weapons, barricaded themselves in the church, and refused entry.[412] The bishop's *visitador* lamented, "They would die before consenting to being investigated."[413]

The royal Inquisition too encroached on bishops' turf in the late 1560s and 1570s. Henceforth, crimes of heterodoxy would largely fall to inquisitors, not bishops. Its agents had power over viceroys and other high-ranking officials as well. Not only did inquisitors strip many jurisdictional attributes from bishops, they also claimed, through royal privileges, the power to investigate any royal official, including high judges and viceroys.[414] They could even excommunicate officials, as they did with the viceroy of Peru in 1588; he had to plead various other religious officials to be allowed back into the church.[415]

Inquisitors' subalterns proved just as problematic as viceroys' field justices. Their broad immunity to other venues of royal justice sparked countless complaints and lawsuits.[416] Already in 1572, the viceroy of Mexico complained that inquisitors' agents were abusing the population and treating Natives "like slaves"; by 1573, Lima's High Court was complaining of their serious abuses and usurpations of royal power. The viceroy moved firmly to prevent them from overextending their great powers, but struggles over inquisitorial jurisdiction would continue well into the 1600s.[417] The solution, as for all powerful institutions, was to subject inquisitors to periodic, bruising audits that invited the denunciations of all sectors of society. As with audits against viceroys, subalterns, and others, inquisitors had to survive a melee of denunciations as rowdy and factionalist as Indies vassals could muster.[418] But the audits of viceroys and inquisitors were different from those the Crown had appointed against conquistador-lords. The latter had resulted in the abolition of conquistador governorships and helped ensure the downfall of postconquest seigneuries. Now, the audits of royal officials tended to focus on individual wrongdoing alone. Officials might receive fines and even prison sentences, but their institutions did not fundamentally change. A society of orders was taking form.

CONCLUSIONS

In the summer of 1572, a multiethnic force comprising 250 Spaniards, 1,500 Cusco Natives, and about 500 Cañaris marched into the Andes rainforests and seized the sovereign Inca, Tupac Amaru.[419] Viceroy Toledo ordered him executed, accusing him of tyranny and alleging his illegitimate claim to the Inca line, abuses against royal vassals, and treason. He also accused the Inca dynasty itself of being founded on illegitimate premises: idolatry, sodomy, incest, and tyrannical conquest of many free Indigenous communities.[420] Toledo then proceeded to undertake sweeping investigations throughout the Andes and beyond, tirelessly listening to Spanish and Native petitioners' ideas to create a new society of orders. While his reputation as an iron-fisted absolutist is largely fiction, he undeniably played a major role in ushering in a postradical era.

Many historians have written of a conquest by the Crown, and indeed, by the 1570s this story seems plausible. But the king and his ministers had not arrived at the viceroy-bishop-inquisitor trinity through a deliberate plan. In fact, they had initially envisioned a very different order, one of strong conquistador seigneurialism and weak royal jurisdiction. As these lords suffered one massive paperwork revolt after the other, they lost virtually all their power and influence. The great duchies and marquisates that had dotted the Iberian Peninsula did not take root in the Indies. The lordships of the Columbus, Cortés, and Pizarro dynasties—the only ones that survived long enough to attempt real control—quickly collapsed among accusations of tyranny. Friars and Native lords followed similar trajectories. Subjects mobilized against these tyrannies with volleys of petitions, litigation, and witness statements, both intentionally and inadvertently creating a roughly five-decade era of disorder.

Paperwork politics was utterly central to these events. It allowed vassals to guide the king and ministers far from the society they had initially envisioned. The rise of viceroys, bishops, and inquisitors was similarly not preordained, contrary to what many historians have argued. The Crown did not really conquer the Indies so much as it dialogued incessantly with vassals—whose radical endeavors and constant lawfare created openings for these officials to step in. Strangely, the radical era ended in something of a success for the Crown, as vassals ultimately elevated its power over local seigneurialism. Perhaps most remarkably, vassals and the Crown achieved this victory over conquistadors and Native lords despite the latter's violent hold over Indies society.

The 1570s marked the establishment of stable, wide-reaching Crown jurisdiction over the New World. But although the era that followed was less turbulent, it had its own politics. Paperwork continued to play a major role in this postradical phase. The new viceregal-episcopal-inquisitorial trinity sought obedience and stability but did not achieve this end entirely. Indeed, new struggles occurred between viceroys, bishops, and inquisitors as they recruited factions of vassals to come to their aid.

Mexico's famous Tumult of 1624 is a case in point, illustrating both what had changed and what had stayed the same. In the viceregal capital, the viceroy clashed spectacularly with the archbishop and High Court, triggering a massive revolt comprising all social groups. The viceroy had alienated the High Court judges by wading into *justicia* cases, excluding them from urgent decision-making sessions, and appointing extraordinary justice officers. He had also enraged the archbishop by challenging ecclesiastical immunity and ignoring churchmen's subsequent petitions for redress. The viceroy's camp took to fining, arresting, and exiling the archbishop's men, accusing them of sedition. When the archbishop put all churchmen on strike, many responded by arming themselves against royal officials. A large multiethnic crowd fumed at the viceroy's interference in the great plaza of the capital. On January 15, 1624, some twenty to forty thousand stormed the viceregal palace, crying out against his tyranny.[421] The viceroy slipped into a costume and blended into the crowd, shouting "Hurry up! They are toppling that traitor!"[422]

Predictably, this riot—which began with paperwork—ended with extensive denunciations and audits. But the details ultimately mattered little. The king, seeking a return to order and obedience, pardoned all participants in 1627.[423] Keeping the peace was the priority; reforming the system was not. Evidently, paperwork riots and antityranny movements had gone nowhere, even after the emergence of a stable society of orders. There were many other episodes like this, major and minor, in subsequent centuries. What had changed from the radical era was both participants' thirst for structural change and the Crown's interest in major institutional and social experimentation. Individuals might be tyrants in this new order, but power structures—such as the office of the viceroy—were to be modified as little as possible. A viceroy might be tyrannical, but the system was not.

CHAPTER 2

Guns, Horses, and Paperwork

Antislavery and the Making of the Ladino *Borderlands*

On October 6, 1550, Judge Miguel Contreras Ladrón de Guevara sent two Indigenous interpreters from Mistlan—Nahuatl-speaking Alonso and Otomi-speaking Pedro—into the borderlands. They were to order the surrender of the runaway community of Zacatlan in the Mexican Bajío. There, he reported that the barbarous Chichimecs had amassed one hundred rebels, including six Africans. For nearly ten years they had been raiding near Guachinango, wreaking havoc on cattle ranches and tenements built among silver-rich bluffs. Hundreds of Indigenous slaves from all over the Chichimec frontier and Africa had been hauled to Guachinango to mine silver and tend horses and cattle. The maroons of Zacatlan were getting in the way. Judge Contreras brought armies, mostly Indigenous allies, to the fight. But he also brought paperwork. He had to document and follow procedure before engaging the rebels, including reading them warnings and drawing notarized paperwork and questionnaires to assess not only their guilt—to mete out justice—but also their knowledge. Were they becoming "people very knowledgeable and savvy" (*personas muy sabias y entendidas*)?[1] Judge Contreras was worried that the rebels were already mastering legalese and paperwork. The borderlands of Mexico had Native warriors armed with not only guns and horses—like the Comanche and others immortalized in the Western imagination in the 1800s—but also legal know-how. A *ladino* society of guns, horses, and paperwork was emerging in the Native borderlands.

One astute frontier *ladino* who would go on to appear before the Council of the Indies and admonish the king was don Francisco Tenamaztle. An Indigenous slave turned maroon, Tenamaztle used paperwork to gain lands and vassals. On July 1, 1555, this Chichimec subject personally approached council ministers in Valladolid. Tenamaztle, who required an interpreter, handed in a document introducing himself as the lord of the kingdom of Jalisco.[2] Coached by friar Bartolomé de Las Casas, Tenamaztle offered a dismal history of the conquest by the tyrant Nuño de Guzmán, who, after having wreaked havoc in Michoacan and Panuco, had entered Jalisco in the early 1530s to establish a kingdom called New Galicia. Tenamaztle recalled acquiescing to the authority of Nuño, welcoming the Franciscans, receiving baptism, and taking a wife. Despite this friendly reception, Nuño raided communities to obtain slaves for mining gold from the region's rivers. Nuño killed and tortured Indigenous lords who refused to submit to the new conquistador-tribute regime. This warlord was a "great tyrant, destroyer and oppressor of the Mexican peoples" who had destroyed Tenamaztle's own "lordship and republic."[3] So Tenamaztle had fled into the cliffs of Jalisco. After nine long years of exile and survival, he had reached out to a man in a high place: the bishop of New Galicia. A meeting with the viceroy was in the works, but the High Court had objected and ordered Tenamaztle sent in chains to Spain to face trial. With the assistance of Las Casas, Tenamaztle concocted a powerful denunciation—both of ongoing tyranny in the borderlands and having been deprived of the lordship that was justly his. In just twenty years, Tenamaztle had become the "very knowledgeable and savvy" person Judge Contreras had most feared. He was now a *ladino.*

Tenamaztle had *savoir faire,* but he still faced an uphill climb in demonstrating his innocence and making claims to lordship. He added to his petition a sworn interrogation of three witnesses, two Franciscans and one

Spanish veteran of the Mixton War (1540–1542), Antonio Botiller.[4] Only Botiller confirmed that he had met Tenamaztle personally, albeit briefly, the day Tenamaztle had surrendered and come down from his cliff fortress in Nochistlan to Viceroy Mendoza. Botiller did confirm that Tenamaztle was the leader of an extensive maroon society of some 20,000 Chichimecs and others.[5] He argued that Tenamaztle had voluntarily surrendered to the viceroy's armies of some 1,200 Spaniards (700 horsemen, 300 harquebusiers, and 200 crossbowmen) and 50,000 armed Natives.[6] Riding a horse, Tenamaztle had accompanied Viceroy Mendoza to the neighboring fortified cliffs of the Mixton, the stronghold of another maroon community of 30,000.[7] Tenamaztle had then given the viceroy the slip.

Council ministers, facing Tenamaztle's *gracia* petition for restitution, struggled to evaluate his credibility. Was don Francisco Tenamaztle really the dynastic king of New Galicia, as he and Las Casas argued, entitled to land, vassals, and pensions? Other documentation arriving from Mexico described him as anything but a lord. Viceroy Velasco answered the question in no uncertain terms: Tenamaztle was a commoner, the leader of a maroon community in the Mixton War.[8] The trial ended when our quick-witted protagonist succumbed to disease in Valladolid in 1556.

The story of Tenamaztle, the commoner turned ruler in the northern borderlands, takes us into unexplored historiographical areas. Within one generation, the Chichimec Tenamaztle had become a *ladino* so adept at negotiating paperwork that he had managed to change his status from slave to original Indigenous emperor of the entire kingdom of Nueva Galicia. The alliance of Tenamaztle and Bartolomé de Las Casas reveals how Native actors could use factionalism within the empire to theorize their lordship in spite of conquest—in this case, by triangulating episcopal-monastic alliances and embracing Christianity and paperwork. In the radical Spanish empire, top-down efforts to evangelize and control were far from the only forces that drove ladinization; conversion and paperwork also worked in the service of rebellion, social mobility, and disobedience.

The story of the radical Spanish Empire is not just that of cores but also that of borderlands. In the previous chapter, we focused on the Mexica, Inca, and populous areas that have often been the subjects of colonial

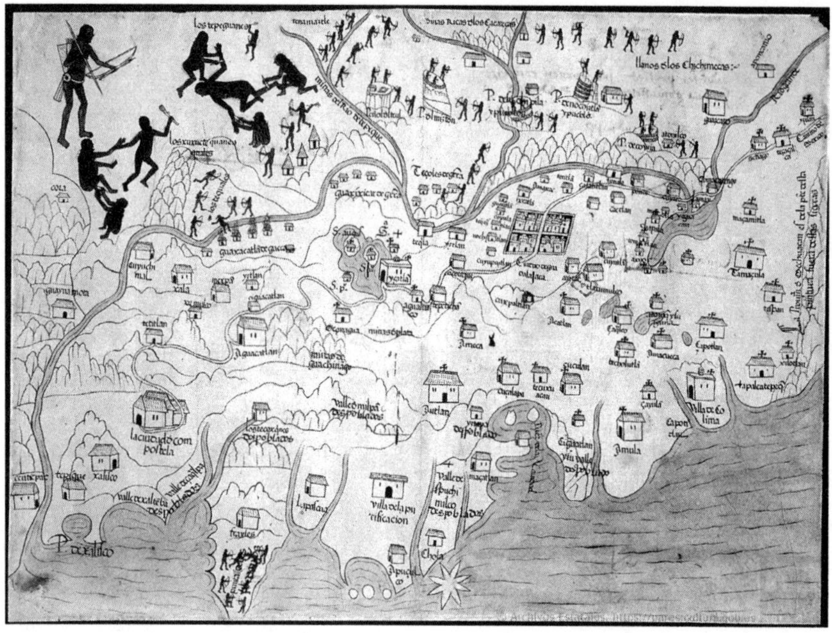

Figure 2.1 Circa 1550 map of the Kingdom of New Galicia and cliff rebels, describing the Mixton War of 1540–1542. The map identifies Tenamaztle's troops to the left of the cliff maroon communities of Mixton and Nochistlan. Several other cliff communities are visible across the rivers on the upper half (east) of the map. To the upper left, Chichimec rebel communities flay captives for cannibal consumption. Dozens of Indigenous Christian settlements are located in the lower (western) half. Ministerio de Cultura y Deporte, Spain, AGI, Mapas y Planos, México 560.

historiography. Here, we focus on areas scholars often define as frontiers or borderlands. The story of these regions is allegedly one of independent Indigenous polities fending off Europeans and each other through captivity and warfare. But the case of Nueva Galicia reveals something else: namely, societies so radically transformed by bottom-up Indigenous agency that within a generation or two, they became vital cores of the Spanish Empire rather than borderlands. In fact, Nueva Galicia became a center of the emerging global economy (along with other regions, most notably Potosi).

How this was possible cannot be understood without recognizing paperwork's seminal role in both unsettling and settling the region's society. Many frontiersmen like Tenamaztle engaged in a heady mix of rebellion and paperwork, but eventually settled into dozens of municipal republics.

Map 2.1 Map of central Mexico, the Bajío, and the Chichimec frontier. The map enumerates most of the places covered in this chapter.

The region's significance then began to dramatically change. Gradually, the northern Mexican borderlands and many other frontier areas became core economic regions of the empire. Discovering, provisioning, and laboring in the region's great silver mines, frontiersmen transformed the global economy, catalyzing major transformations in the world order from Europe to China and beyond.

This chapter concentrates on seemingly minor forms of paperwork mostly available to Indigenous captives and slaves rather than the vast paper-driven public dialogues that led to the cyclical collapse of seigneurial lordship (see Chapter 1). That said, the decline of seigneurial power also played a major role in these regions, because it allowed commoners to move more freely across the land. The radical dynamics of bottom-up lawfare created conditions for the transformation of seigneurial economies of tribute into mercantile economies of commoner free labor—a phenomenon that since Marx's *Capital* has been associated with seventeenth- and eighteenth-century England.[9] The sixteenth- and seventeenth-century mining cities of the Indies received tens of thousands of deracinated commoners, attracted by the social mobility of new internal frontiers. Although liberal narratives frame the story of capitalism as an intrinsically European phenomenon, we argue that Indigenous politics played a significant role in the construction of crucial regional nodes of the global commercial order. Native peoples were not passive victims of Spanish colonialism and its erasure-bent regimes of systematic labor and territorial dispossession, as many decolonialists have argued. Their societies were thus far from US American and other similar variants of "settler colonialism."[10]

Other models are necessary to explain what happened in these areas. We agree with John Tutino that it was in the Mexican Bajío that less aristocratic forms of production took hold, great economic dynamism occurred, and the Spanish peso became the world currency.[11] Similar phenomena occurred in Potosi.[12] In the 1980s, scholars like Carlos Assadourian and Steve Stern presented the rise of free labor markets in the Spanish Indies as the result of the regional decline of Indigenous and conquistador seigneuries.[13] Tutino, however, introduced Indigenous politics as the driving force of this process.

Our model shows that paperwork was the vehicle through which Tutino's Indigenous politics worked. Frontier society became an imperial core through the interconnected roles of radical agitation and disruption, bottom-up paperwork, and ladinization. Frontier paperwork battles involved procedures beyond the audits used by bishops, inquisitors, *audiencias*, field justices, viceroys, and governors. These forms of paperwork included the *requerimiento* (a text Christians read aloud before conquering sovereign peoples), procedures on slave branding, and ad hoc ordinances around military campaigns that enabled contesting arrests and gaining freedom. Gradually, *ladino* subjects learned to create new communities using various tactics, including negotiation with Spanish officials. These communities dot the region to this day. We also seek, therefore, to develop the concept of ladinization as an alternative to common categories of analysis such as *mestizaje*, or hybridity (ubiquitous in civilizationalist literature).

In the sixteenth century, novel Indigenous societies began to emerge out of the endless recycling of legal emancipation, maroonage, war, and again legal emancipation. Many of these societies incorporated dozens of ethnic groups. Ethnogenesis through bottom-up paperwork significantly shifted the geopolitical balance of the Indies—and ultimately, the world. In places like the Bajío, Potosi, and the Pacific and Atlantic lowlands, new economies of scale arose around mining, cattle ranching, and agricultural production.[14] We concentrate on one area in particular that proved central to the economic reorganization of the continent and the Atlantic and Pacific economies: Nueva Galicia. We leave out Potosi, whose emergence as the economic engine of a global empire has been relatively well studied.[15]

This chapter complements growing literature on how Atlantic African slaves in Iberian Africa and the Iberian Americas creatively used tribunals to contest their enslavement, purchase freedom, prevent their families from being dispersed, and denounce masters for rape or abuse.[16] Less well known is the way in which Indigenous slaves used tribunals to gain freedom. Nancy Van Deusen has studied the case of Indigenous slaves who were taken to Spain and used tribunals to gain emancipation in the wake of 1542 New Laws.[17] Our aim, in turn, is to move toward more comprehensive and less fragmented understandings of how Indigenous slaves used paperwork in the pursuit of freedom—and in the process, to elucidate the transformative social power of this paperwork. We argue that the radical era witnessed continent-wide use of courts by Indigenous slaves, especially in frontier regions. Endemic factionalism pushed the Crown to create special audits and paperwork for these borderlands. The discourse of legitimate rulership (see Chapter 1) forced the Crown to encourage all vassals to participate in paperwork audits and denounce the mighty, as Tenamaztle did.

In this society, violence and bottom-up paperwork created totally new social forms. Commoners—Indigenous slaves or deracinated individuals working at conquistador-lords' patrimonial lands or mining sites—deserted en masse. Rebels raided mines and Spanish landholdings (*estancias*), battling the armies of royalist Indigenous lords and Spanish militias stationed in garrisons (*presidios*). These garrisons enslaved more people, to be sure, but they also created tribunals for captives to press claims of freedom. Access to tribunals changed over time. The unintended consequence of a weak Crown was the constant issuing of new, contradictory edicts to settle factional petitioning and favor auditing. Edicts haphazardly multiplied: the laws of Burgos (1512) introduced the reading of *requerimiento* suzerainty contracts to communities prior to raids; the Mexican antislavery laws of 1529–1530 sought to limit Indigenous slave markets; and the New Laws of 1542 aimed at structurally diminishing the power of seigneurial lords—including by undermining slavery. In the northern Mexican frontier, post-1542 conflict and captivity continued but created peculiar forms of warfare in which even the smallest privateering parties, by law, had to be led by *letrados,* lawyer-captains deeply conversant in edicts, statutes, and paperwork.[18] Such practices would culminate with Juan de Oñate's late sixteenth-century Zacatecan expedition to China via the Rio Grande, the Plains, and California that left thousands of pages of painstaking documentation of viceregal contracts, suzerainty treaties, petitions, litigation (there were multiple trials against Natives and among Spaniards), and every participant involved (horses, cattle, sheep, seeds, axes, knifes, viceroys, secretaries, notaries, council magistrates, half-Indigenous privateers, friars, captives, Zuni, and Pueblos).[19]

Frontier paperwork audits allowed tens of thousands to escape enslavement and establish themselves in new settlements. Nomads, deracinated commoners, freedmen, runaways, and maroon communities became adept at staking up claims to freedom, status, and property via paperwork. They thereby created new Christian communities throughout the frontier.

As the society of orders took place (often considerably later than in core regions), collective acknowledgment of the radical origins of these many collectives faded. Communities created by maroons, slaves, Indigenous conquistadors, part-Indigenous miners, and deracinated commoners increasingly appeared as noble and even Spanish. As these settlements negotiated political and territorial rights with local authorities, they crafted Catholic narratives of miracles and Indigenous aristocratic agency. Runaway communities became settlements of Indigenous conquistadors led by Christian heroes who had domesticated neighboring savages. These invented traditions would have broader repercussions throughout Mexico and beyond. The so-called Creole religious tradition of the Spanish American baroque in the Mexican Bajío originated largely in the political agency of Indigenous peoples.[20] We argue, therefore, that it is best to understand many aspects of Indies society as the work of not Spanish-born *criollos* but Indigenous *ladinos.*[21] Contrary to Hispanist myth, much of the empire was as *ladino* as it was Spanish.

How, then, should we think about these crucial borderlands societies? In some ways, the ethnogenesis we explore resembles that of Atlantic Africans in African ports and slave ships.[22] The model of ethnogenesis of Atlantic Africans first articulated in the 1980s by Sidney Mintz and Richard Price better captures the phenomena we describe than *mestizaje* does.[23] It too was a world of slaves, freedmen, runaways, rebels, new languages, and new cultural practices. Yet in other ways, models of Atlantic ethnogenesis and creolization differ from our case. Frontier Indigenous ethnogenesis in the radical era was conditioned by subjects' legal know-how and strategic adaptation to paperwork, which enabled the transition of deracinated commoners and slaves into honorable Christian frontiersmen. Framing this world as an expression of cultural hybridity or *mestizaje* obscures this savvy. Nor was it a creolized plantation or urban society in which denizens lived in the shadows of their white masters. Rather, it was a unique form of frontier expansion that combined violence and paperwork, dominated by Indigenous *ladino* subjects and ladinized ways of thinking.

SLAVERY AND EMANCIPATION BEFORE THE NEW LAWS

Beginning in 1492, the Caribbean and Atlantic coast of Tierra Firme, from Guyana to Panama, witnessed massive enslavement of Natives. The Bahamas became a net exporter of Lucayo slaves to be divers in the oyster riffs of Margarita and Cubaya.[24] Many others were sold in Europe. It is difficult to overestimate the scale of the early Indigenous slave trade.

The archival evidence on Indigenous slavery—or lack thereof—often resulted from factionalism. If a warlord or official invested in the trade managed to avoid audits through political know-how or sheer violence, there would be no paperwork and therefore no written evidence. The early politics of postconquest Mexico was deeply informed by all parties involved in Indigenous slavery, including slaves themselves. The more factionalism there was, the more slaves—but also the more audits.

Spaniards procured slaves in two forms, one via *guerra* (warfare) and another via *rescate* (trade). Rescate was possible because captivity was a widespread for of interethnic violence.[25] The mounting scale of the slave trade triggered countless petitions and a maze of policies, including royal decrees, ordinances, and edicts (*mandamientos*), seeking to regulate captivity. For every royal order banning an aspect of the trade and ordering the release of slaves, new laws by the Crown, governors, and viceroys acknowledged requests by town councils to let Indigenous slavery and captivity stand and expand.[26] The laws of Burgos of 1512, for example, made the reading of suzerainty treaties a *requerimiento.* To justify captivity raids, privateers now had to document that they had offered communities recognition of local hierarchies and authorities in exchange for explicit acknowledgment of the spiritual and temporal sovereignty of the Spanish Crown. As delegates of the sovereign, privateers could legally demand logistical support from local communities. When these locals resisted, privateers could launch slaving raids that contemporaries regarded as considered morally just—but they had to record these procedures.[27]

Conquistador violence in the Indies generated additional paperwork and audits. Beginning with the infamous 1512 *requerimiento,* every frontier raiding campaign (*entrada*) had to document that sovereign Natives understood their two choices—either surrender and declare vassalage or resist and face enslavement or death in just war.[28] For captivity to be legal, its slavers had to document their transactions. Slaves had documentation branded upon their bodies and faces: *R* for a slave purchased (*rescatado*) in commercial transactions with enslaving Indigenous sovereign polities and *G* for a slave captured in war (*guerra*). Crown officials had the monopoly over the iron brands to secure both rights and royal taxes. Warlords had to brand captives before notaries and witnesses, demonstrating compliance with royal decrees and local edicts.

With the expansion of conquest from the Caribbean to the mainland, the enterprise of enslavement dramatically expanded. Tens of thousands of victims were removed and resettled even before Cortés landed in Mexico. Conflicts over unregulated slavery had raged since Columbus began his conquests.[29] While our focus here is on central and northern Mexico, the Caribbean context was connected to events on the mainland. By the 1520s, settlers were abandoning the Caribbean Isles in droves, heading to Mexico and other emerging dominions. Many of those who remained threw themselves into slaving ventures. Discontented royal officials complained against their superiors in the High Court of Santo Domingo, leading to a broad royal audit that uncovered a slapdash administration. Officials kept disorganized archives with opaque bookkeeping and even missing volumes.[30] Island residents repeatedly complained that slavers were smuggling human contraband throughout the region, prompting waves of investigations.[31]

A recurring complaint was that Native peoples were being illegitimately enslaved in the coastal Panuco region of Mexico before being shipped to the Caribbean. By the late 1520s and early 1530s, slavers traded them for horses bred on the Caribbean Isles. Slavery was central to the triangular conflict pitting the most powerful conquistadors of Mexico, Nuño de Guzmán and Cortés, against each other and the Crown. The Crown had appointed law student Nuño de Guzmán to audit Cortés. But as Nuño's power expanded and petitioners began reporting his many abuses, the Crown soured on him.[32] Nuño became governor of Panuco as part of a coordinated campaign by the Crown to diminish Cortés's power in 1526. The campaign included another appointee, the general auditor Luis Ponce de León, charged with investigating Cortés in Mexico City. But this auditor was evidently poisoned in 1526, just weeks after arrival. When Nuño arrived in Mexico in 1527, he managed to remove Cortés's allies' access to Panuco slave labor; as governor of Panuco, he cut Cortés's supply of slaves. The Crown was impressed and appointed him president of the first Mexican High Court in 1528. In this capacity, he was to audit Cortés and allies. When Nuño embarked on the conquest of the Chichimec North, he brought with him many of his rival's Spanish and Indigenous allies. He forced conquistadors and Native lords to muster fifteen thousand Indigenous soldiers—eight thousand from Huejotzingo,

Tenochitlan, Tlateloco, Texcoco, and Tlaxcala and seven thousand from Michoacan.[33]

Nuño soon fell victim to the same paperwork he had used against Cortés. The Franciscan friars, important new factional players in central Mexico, firmly sided with Cortés against Nuño. The Crown abolished Nuño's High Court and, in 1530, sent another auditor and new judges to replace it. To destroy Nuño, the Franciscans focused on his role as a slaver in Panuco. The same year the Crown abolished the High Court, it also issued a ban on Indigenous slave trade in Panuco and the Indies at large. The second High Court quickly seized Nuño's property in Panuco and Mexico City as collateral for the treasury funds Nuño had taken to organize the conquest of Nueva Galicia.

The story of Nuño's rise and fall is exemplary. It shows that a man who introduced regulations to Cortés's unregulated slave trade produced enough documentation to be held accountable. The more factionalism and paperwork, the more power the Crown held to control the rise of rival lords. Cortés enslaved Natives with minimal oversight until 1526, but after 1527, proceduralization of enslavement took form.

The case of Judge Juan Cortés de Matienzo illustrates this transformation. In 1529, he headed to Panuco to investigate how slavers had captured victims under Cortés and Nuño. Matienzo discovered that he could not document the trade under Cortés and could therefore level no charges. The ten witnesses Matienzo deposed stated that Cortés's allies went through the province's conquistador dominions and Indigenous markets, each ally buying one hundred to one hundred fifty slaves. They would branded thousands of slaves and sent them to Mexico City to be distributed among Cortés's followers to work in mines.[34] Others went to the Caribbean Islands to be traded for horses. Under Cortés, one horse allegedly purchased one hundred Panuco slaves.[35] Cortés's regime had left no documentation.

Under pressure by the threat of audits by rival factions, Nuño instituted several ordinances to document enslavement. After ridding Panuco of Cortés's faction and assigning his followers Indigenous tribute, Nuño decreed that no conquistador-lord could employ Native slaves as serfs or personal dependents (*naborías*).[36] He also banned Panuco's settlers from transporting slaves to Mexico City. Nuño's scribes issued dozens of slaving licenses, preventing frontiersmen from purchasing more than thirty slaves per license. During his audit, Matienzo collected all the licenses Nuño had issued between April 30, 1527, and September 13, 1529.[37] These receipts document the ubiquity of a sprawling Indigenous slave market. Moreover, they reveal that many buyers procured their victims from Native communities. For instance, Huasteca communities in Panuco sold thousands of slaves to Nuño and his men.

Nuño believed these measures would regularize enslavement, clearing his conscience and the king's. Now every enslaved Native would be deposed before a notary and a Huastec translator to establish his or her status and origin.[38] Then Nuño instituted a "fair" price, which in fact was considerably inflated.[39] He increased the price of slaves in Indigenous markets to improve Panuco's economy because the region lacked mineral wealth. With these prices, a Caribbean horse could now buy only fifteen slaves, not one hundred, as it had under Cortés.[40]

This documentation proved dangerous for Nuño. He made a bitter enemy in the new bishop-elect of Mexico, Juan de Zumárraga. The bishop, a supporter of Cortés, had access to Matienzo's 1529 audit. He was thus able to provide detailed accounting of the Panuco–Caribbean slave trade. Zumárraga proved that from 1527 to 1529, Nuño had authorized some ten thousand slaves shipped in thirty-one separate vessels.[41] Nuño did not deny it. He had personally exported a third of the ten thousand slaves to create cattle ranches and accumulate dozens of horses to be used in the conquest of Nueva Galicia. Nuño considered that until Panuco could develop its own agricultural and cattle resources, the province's future depended solely on this trade. He presented his policy of shipping slaves to the Caribbean instead of central Mexico as a way of protecting lives, for the removal of lowlanders to the cold central Mexico lands had proven to be a death sentence. Nuño also argued that he had reformed the trade, providing hearings for the wrongfully enslaved. He followed procedure and paperwork to the letter, freeing falsely held captives as a matter of policy.[42]

Nuño's fate rested in his receipts. The 1537 audit of his tenure as governor of Panuco from 1527 to 1533 featured many accusations, for which he sat in a Mexico City prison. One charge focused on his practices of enslavement. Had he allowed enslaved individuals to contest their status? The auditor, Juan Álvarez de Castañeda, concluded that he had freed numerous slaves wrongfully purchased and branded. Nuño's actions had elicited bitter complaints from many individuals. Judge Castañeda documented the cases of Diego Anaya, Diego González, and Pedro González de Truxillo, whose slaves Nuño had freed. Judge Castañeda also cited the case of Menzía, a Native woman Pedro González de Trujillo had wrongfully branded. The evidence showed that the accusation that Nuño had created no bottom-up paperwork venues for wrongfully held captives to plead freedom was false. Judge Castañeda absolved Nuño of this charge.[43]

Castañeda's audit included the 1528 letter Nuño wrote to his second-in-command in Panuco, Juan Pérez de Jijón. In the letter, Nuño ordered Pérez to stick to the rules. Nuño's ordinances were clear. As representative of the Crown, Pérez had sole control over the branding of slaves and thus was to interview victims using an interpreter. Any conquistador seeking to purchase a slave had to appear with his respective Native lord and establish that his captive was not a commoner. If the victim alleged freedom, Pérez was to investigate whether he or she was being rightfully sold.[44] In addition to this ordinance, Nuño followed the 1530 royal decree ordering a census of all new slaves taken after the prohibition to ship slaves to the Antilles. Moreover, Nuño issued his own policies that made it illegal for transient Spaniards to move freely through Indigenous communities, for he believed transients were responsible for trafficking slaves. Travelers in Panuco thus would need licenses. The governor forbade Native lords from gifting commoners to Spaniards, who would often brand and enslave them.[45] Nuño, who had attended law school, understood what he was doing. Every move he made he documented carefully, one enslavement at a time.

Factions embraced, reformed, and attacked enslavement of Indigenous subjects to further their own politics. High Judge (and later bishop) Vasco de Quiroga saw fighting slavery as key to carving out space for royal and episcopal power. The Crown instructed Mexico's High Court and bishops to enforce a broad regulation of enslavement in 1529 and again barred the enslavement of Natives through a 1530 royal decree, mandating that none could be enslaved through the procedures introduced by the laws of Burgos of 1512, just-war *requerimiento,* or via Indigenous markets.[46] This new policy ordered authorities to compile a written census identifying each slave and master, with documented proof that the captured had been seized through just war or rightful purchase. The Crown expected high judges and bishops to report any problems with enforcement.

Quiroga's 1536 posttenure audit shows that anonymous whistleblowers had charged him with liberating thousands of slaves from Native lords without any documentation—thereby badly disrupting Indigenous society. Assisted by Mexica elders, including don Diego Tlalilotoque, don Juan Mesquatlaylotlan, and don Pedro, he had employed summary justice to free countless unjustly enslaved men and women.[47] According to Quiroga, Native traditions had allowed commoners to sell themselves until they could repay their debts. Famine, debt, and hardship could cause vulnerable individuals to offer themselves or their children to slavery under Indigenous customary law.[48] Quiroga used his power to "reeducate" Native lords, also making it easier for Indigenous slaves to win their freedom. For Quiroga, Spaniards were twisting Natives' loose understanding of slavery as rental labor into permanent bondage. He henceforth made it more difficult for Spaniards to acquire slaves in markets. Spanish witnesses loudly complained that these practices limited the supply of slaves to work in mines and therefore badly diminished royal rents.[49]

Such bottom-up paperwork audits transformed Indigenous customs. One should not underestimate the impact of Quiroga's itinerant Indigenous courts on central Mexico. In 1531, the community of Huejotzingo documented in detail all the tribute it had paid the Crown as part of a trial Cortés brought against Nuño. The conquistador had accused the governor of illegally taking communities' tribute from him.[50] The codex of Huejotzingo of 1531 painstakingly enumerates all the resources the community invested in Nuño's expedition to Nueva Galicia in 1529–1530. It includes the gold coins the lord of Huejotzingo, don Tomé, spent to buy a horse to lead some 320 Huejotzingo warriors into battle. The community used woven blankets and slaves as currency in addition to actual gold coins to purchase feathers and gold for don Tomé's army banner: a colorful, golden-feathered Virgin Mary. Strikingly, the community included images of eight enslaved men and twelve enslaved women of at least three different ethnicities whom the lords of Huejotzingo sold to assemble this precious banner.[51] Native lords had faith that conquests in the north would repay their investments. In documenting the campaign to conquer Nueva Galicia, Nuño repeatedly complained that the Indigenous armies he brought along would raid Native towns to get captives. Much of the violence that was attributed to Nuño came in fact from his Indigenous allies, he stressed, and he had no control over them.[52]

Yet if Huejotzingo had thousands of slaves as currency to barter in 1531, it had only four by 1558. The 1558 *Matricula de tributos de Huejotzingo* (at the French National Library) documents the family structure of every

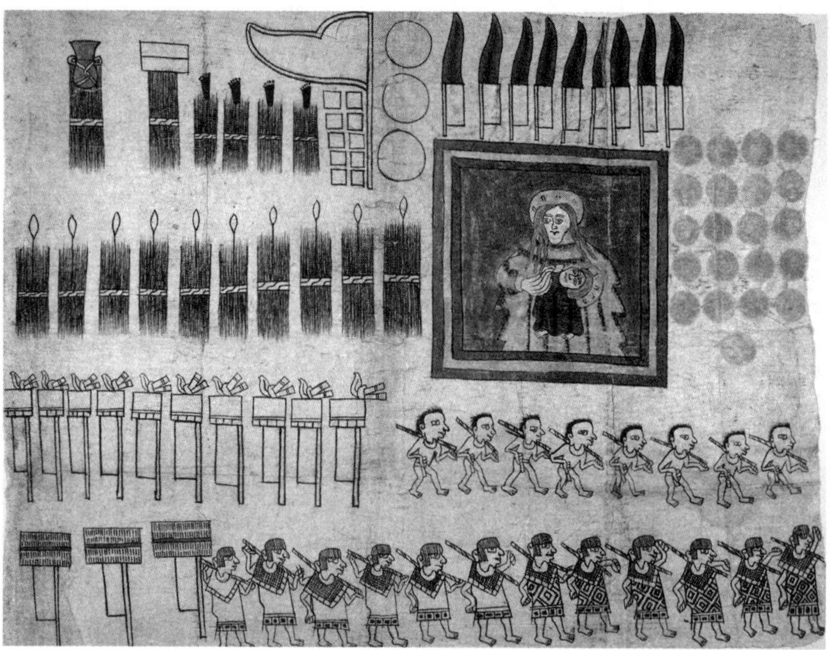

Figure 2.2 Indigenous accounting page enumerating coins and slaves used to pay for feathers and gold to embroider a battle pendant of the Virgin. Codex Huejotzingo, 1531. Harkness Collection, Library of Congress.

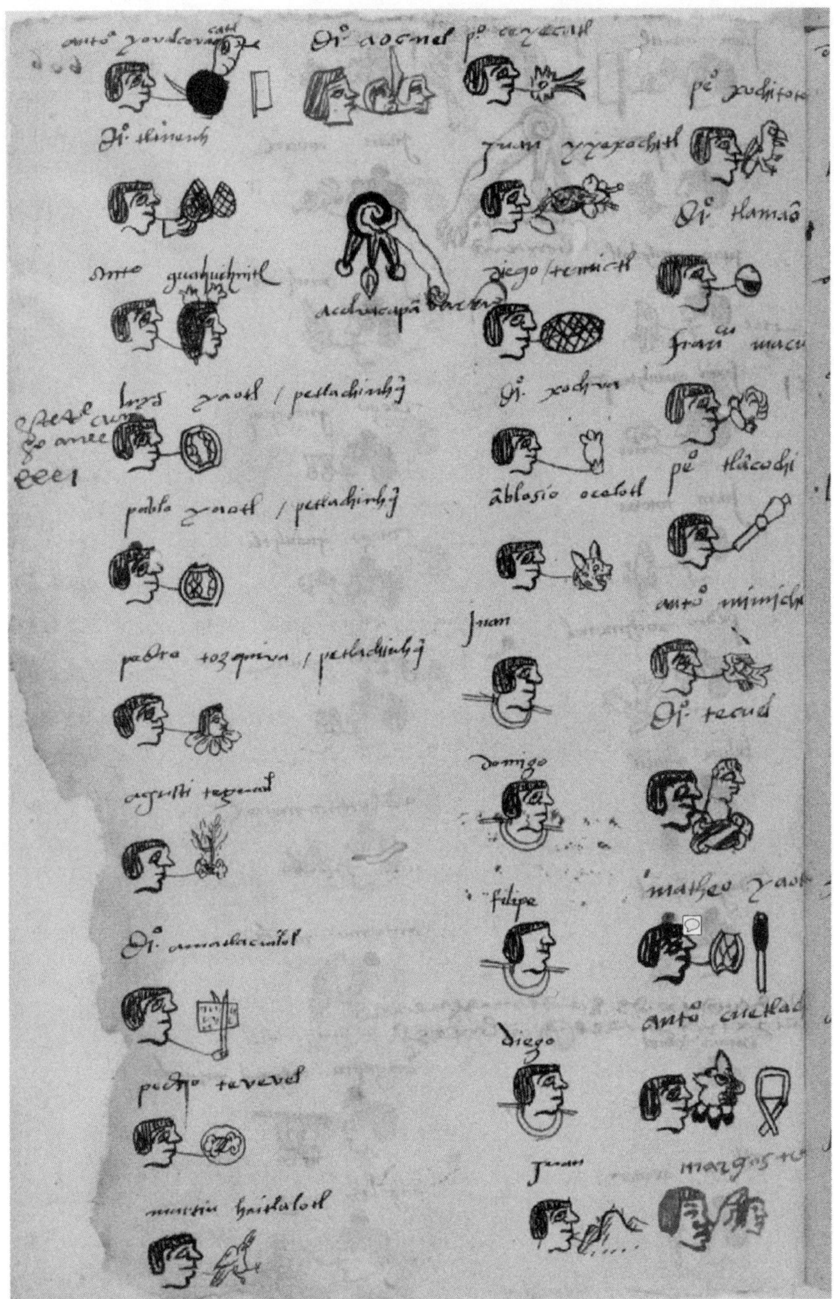

Figure 2.3 Tributary roll with four slaves in the neighborhood of Acolhuacan. The only quarter in the entire 1,146 pages of the 1558 *Matrícula de tributos de Huejotzingo* with slaves. Gallica / Bibliothèque nationale de France, Mexicain 387, 606v.

household, neighborhood by neighborhood, town by town, in painstaking detail. In the entire 1146-page volume, there is a tangential record of only four slaves. They appear in a list along with the name of hundreds if not thousands of tributary commoners, rendered in two scripts, alphabetic and logographic. The four slaves, represented wearing slave collars, do not have Nahua names: they are identified as Juan, Domingo, Felipe, and Diego.

Between the 1530s and 1540s, a major effort to restructure slavery was indeed underway in Mexico. The year after Nuño issued his 1533 ordinances to curb the Panuco slave trade, Mexico High Court judges—including Quiroga—summoned the justice (*corregidor*) of Texcoco, Rodrigo Gómez, to address a denunciation. The Franciscan abbot claimed that Gómez was illegally holding slaves in his houses in Texcoco and Mexico. Franciscan pressure forced the High Court to investigate Gómez's practices as both conquistador and official. In doing so, it uncovered a vast underground market of slaves in Texcoco.

It all began in early 1534, when Gómez, as conquistador of Atucupa, had the young Native lord don Antonio imprisoned. Gómez had don Antonio shackled in the local monastery of Texcoco for eight months. Gómez explained to the resident Franciscan friar Juan de Alamada that don Antonio was a tyrant who had abused his authority, arbitrarily killing nine men in his community on pagan altars. The friar acquiesced but soon grew suspicious of this story, as Gómez ordered another lord, this time in Huejutla, jailed for allegedly having killed and sacrificed one of Gómez's own slaves. Was Gómez accusing Native lords of sacrifice to enslave their dependents? Was he using the Franciscans for his dirty deeds? Fray Alamada wrote his superior Fray Luis de Fuensalida and the Franciscan bishop Zumárraga, asking them to contact the High Court and immediately initiate an investigation.[53]

In the first week of November 1534, the High Court had don Antonio unshackled, asking him to testify before a Franciscan and a Native, Alonsico, as interpreters. Don Antonio denied having had killed anyone and accused Gómez of having taken one of his slaves. The young lord then suggested that Gómez had dozens of slaves imprisoned in his Texcoco house.[54] A commoner, Lorenzo, testified that four months earlier,

Gómez had ordered the Indigenous sheriffs (*alguaciles*) of Texcoco to secure seamstresses and feather workers for Gómez's own urban workshop. They had complied. These men and women, however, had been kept from visiting their spouses and children; the commoners were upset.[55] The judges had sufficient evidence. When Texcoco sheriffs visited Gómez's house, his brother surrendered three imprisoned commoner women.

On November 11, commoners Ana, Juana, and Isabel offered sworn testimony before the interpreter Álvaro de Zamora. All three told the same story and added further detail. Gómez had a network of Native women slave catchers working as intermediaries. While visiting the market of Texcoco, two of them—Isabela and Angelina—had approached the women, promising them jobs as feather workers (*amantecas*) at Gómez's house. Isabela offered each woman the same deal: five blankets (as currency) for every feathered and embroidered pillow. When the three commoners entered Gómez's house, his mother-in-law locked them up, feeding them nothing but six measly tortillas per day. The workers could not leave, and when they tried, Gómez locked them in stocks. The imprisoned commoners complained that Gómez had not allowed them to attend mass, not even on Sundays. The three women testified that Gómez had some twenty other branded slave women in his house doing feathered embroidery work as well.[56]

The same day, the High Court ordered their scrivener, Antonio de Turcios, to visit Gómez in his Mexico City house. There, he found Gómez prostrated in bed. The judges demanded he explain his prison. Gómez argued that they were idolaters who had captured commoners to sacrifice. The magistrates demanded to see the paperwork of the idolatry trials. Gómez promised to comply as soon as his health improved.[57] Immediately the judges had officials raid Gómez's Texcoco house to look for the twenty slaves and two Native intermediaries, Isabela and Angelina. Sheriff Santillana testified that he found only two imprisoned women. The other slaves had disappeared.[58]

The two women they found in the house, both named María, offered sworn testimony on November 17. They repeated the story told by the previous three women about their entrapment. María I offered more detailed testimony on the main intermediary Indigenous peddler, Isabela. She argued that Isabela was from Calpulapan, not Texcoco, and visited markets there and in Tlaxcala looking for branded runaway slaves, specifically women. María II testified that Gómez's mother-in-law had killed her child. Both women testified that Gómez had ordered all his slaves moved to his Mexico City house, along with his mother-in-law, the overseer.[59]

With this testimony, the High Court ordered the scribe Ceynos to visit Gómez's Mexico City house. There, he found nine slaves: two Magdalenas, three Marías, little Beatrizica, Isabel, Anica, and Angelina.[60] The testimony of all nine slaves was consistent. Most had been branded in the past and had escaped their previous masters. Some had simply been abandoned. Most had taken up residence in Texcoco, where they had married and established families. They were all pious, God-fearing Christians.[61] Gómez himself acknowledged the abuse, conceding that at least one Otomi woman he had enslaved had died jumping off his walled house to freedom.[62] But Gómez protested that he had the king's permission and had legitimately procured these slaves. The judges ordered Gómez produce this decree within six days, along with the paperwork of the idolatry trials that had landed so many lords in prison. Gómez could not produce either.[63] On April 3, 1536, Gómez was found guilty and imprisoned. His sentence was reduced to house arrest given that he was bedridden and physically impaired.[64] The enslaved Native commoners and imprisoned lords were released.

Gómez's story reveals vast underground slaver networks throughout central Mexico. Officials tried to locate the remaining slaves, but some never appeared. It seemed that they had been taken by the Indigenous intermediary Isabela to her own house in Texcoco. The slave Angelina, who had accompanied Isabela to Indigenous markets looking for runaway slaves, suggested that seven of the missing slaves belonged to Isabela, not Gómez.[65] The story also shows how easy it was for commoners to become deracinated personal servants or slaves. The first six rescued Natives were not runaways but Texcocan commoners Isabela had targeted in Indigenous markets. Gómez's conflict with the Indigenous lords in his jurisdiction—and particularly in his conquistador dominion—was triggered by his desire to steal slaves from Native lords. Paperwork audits, triggered by lord-friar-conquistador factionalism, created opportunities for deracinated commoners and slaves to gain freedom.

EMANCIPATION AND ETHNOGENESIS AFTER THE NEW LAWS OF 1542

In central Mexico, the institution of slavery transformed and diminished within two generations. Factionalism within powerful Mexico parties politicized slavery, transforming it into a liability for major figures such as Cortés and Nuño but also local elites like Gómez. The climax of antislavery efforts came with the New Laws of 1542 (see Chapter 1). These had their origins largely in Peru, as powerful conquistadors attempted to bribe well-connected court women and otherwise influence council ministers. Soon, the emperor himself was directing an investigation into their plans for limitless power. During the ensuing scandal, Las Casas joined the fray and successfully pressed for more oversight on Indigenous enslavement, especially by conquistadors.[66]

The New Laws undermined the possibility of perpetuity of seigneurial lordship in the Indies; conquistadors' Native tribute grants began reverting to the Crown within one to two generations, making it impossible for feudal lords to establish Indies estates. Slavery and personal servitude—*servicio personal*—were largely abolished. The uproar over the New Laws and Peruvian civil wars shattered the Crown's vision of loyal conquistadors, enabling the rise of friar theocracies as a counterexperiment. The aftermath of these laws was massive structural change that powerfully impacted the development of Mexico's frontier societies.[67]

Struggles in Panuco, central Mexico, and Peru sent shockwaves through Indies society. Factional struggles mainly undermined conquistadors' and Native lords' access to slaves. And factionalism inside Indigenous communities often played just as important a role as conquistador strife and competition. In central Mexico, Indigenous slavery had greatly expanded and then collapsed. Deracinated commoners sought out lives in many communities, not least among them the so-called Chichimec or barbarian borderlands of Guadalajara, Queretaro, Zacatecas, and Durango.

Within a few decades, the postconquest Indigenous cores of Anahuac and Tihuantinsuyo became economically subordinate to the emerging commercial engines in *ladino* borderlands founded by former communities of slaves and deracinated commoners (often called *naborias, yanaconas,* or *forasteros*). This chapter focuses on northern Mexico, although similar processes of radical deracination and commercial development unfurled in coastal Guatemala, Potosi, and beyond.

The case of the pluri-ethnic, mid-sixteenth-century Tarascan community of Cuitzeo in Michoacan is emblematic of these radical changes. This community in the eastern lowlands had long paid tribute to the Irecha lords of Michoacan.[68] In 1490, the Irecha authorized the establishment of a neighborhood of Matlaxincas and Otomies in Cuitzeo known as Huetamo, setting up ethnic tension in the years to come. Cuitzeo was valuable because it produced not only tropical staples like cotton, salt, and chiles but also gold. In 1524, the community was assigned to Gonzalo Ruiz, an ally of Cortés. There is no record of what the community paid conquistador-lords during these years, but it was most likely gold and labor in the mines. In 1533, however, Quiroga's High Court stripped Gonzalo Ruiz of his lordship and placed the community under direct Crown control. Cuitzeo now had to pay tribute to royal officials in bundles of blankets: three hundred every two months (fifteen bundles of twenty each). The Otomi neighborhood of Huetamo was responsible for forty of the three hundred units (two bundles of twenty each).[69]

Ruiz made his comeback, but the timing could scarcely have been worse. He recovered his tribute allotment in 1541 and the next year had the Otomi and Tarascan-Nahua Native lords sign two separate contracts before the High Court and the viceroy. These adjusted the original tribute to include a variety of commodities and personal service. Cuitzeo commoners not only owed blankets and other goods but also had to send crews every two months to work in their lord's mines and landholdings. Cuitzeo's community kept a record of the contract in two separate codices, Codex Huetamo and Codex Cuitzeo, documenting the 1542 Otomi and Tarascan tribute arrangements, respectively.[70]

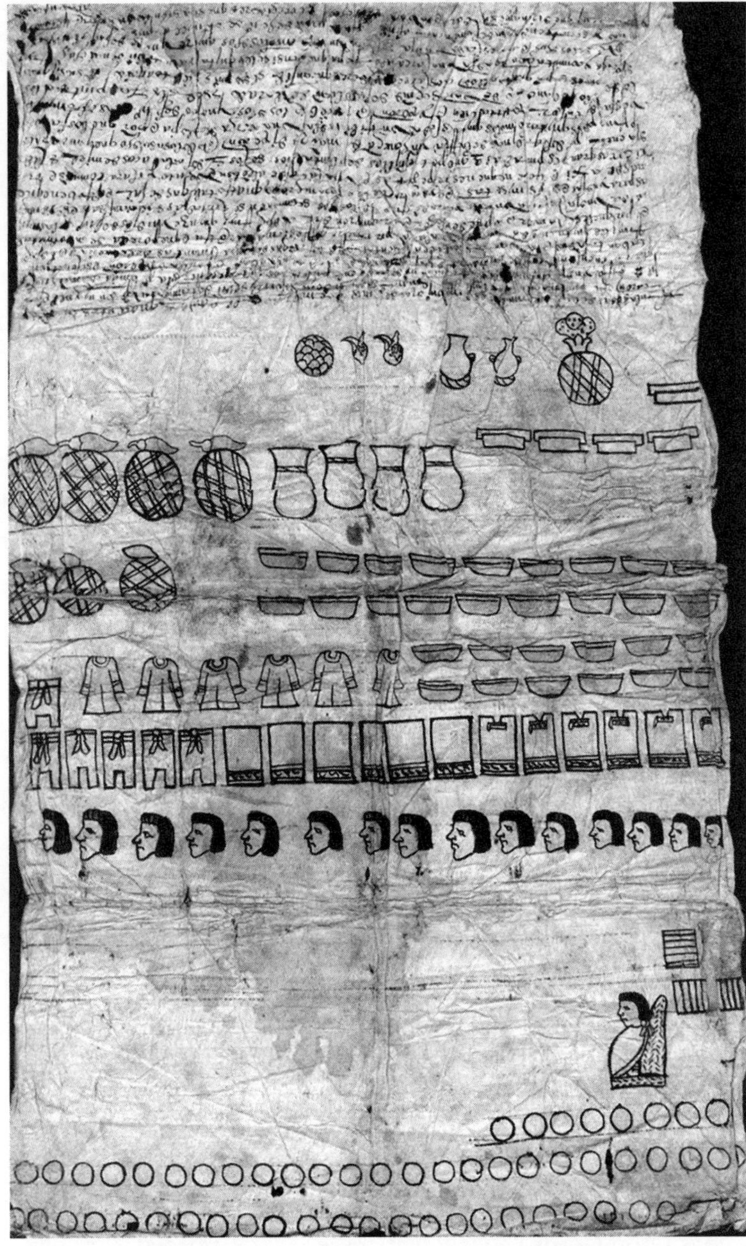

Figure 2.4 Archive of two Otomi neighborhood contracts in Cuitzeo, divided into three sections. The upper third includes Spanish glosses with scribes' signatures. The middle third depicts a contract with a seigneurial lord that includes woven pants, shirts, clay vessels, blankets, bags of salt and honey, and bushels of chiles, cotton, corn, and plantain, in addition to work crews of fifteen commoners. The lower third documents tribute for the Crown—mostly cash and a few bundles of blankets. Universidad Iberoamericana, Biblioteca Francisco Xavier Clavijero, Códice Huetamo.

The following year, news arrived of the New Laws. Furious negotiations began in Mexico. But the conquistadors' enemies pressed forward. In 1549, the High Court barred paying tribute with *servicio personal,* and the two communities stopped sending crews to Ruiz. The conquistador, however, kept tabs claiming the unpaid personal service as debt. Tensions built. The conquistador and two Native lords went to Mexico to settle the dispute, agreeing to commute the debt in exchange for additional tribute in staples. The new contract was added to the Cuitzeo document in Spanish glosses.

The High Court did not approve this arrangement, and tensions in Cuitzeo became unbearable. They exploded in 1553, when Ruiz's part-Indigenous son took over. He cracked down hard on the Otomi neighborhood, assaulting and beating Huetamo's Native lord. Ruiz apparently went to a field justice, Alonso Ortíz de Zúñiga, who sold Otomi commoners' land publicly. Zúñiga flogged and exiled Otomi lords and sent their commoners to the mines as slaves.[71]

The arc of frontier justice bent slowly. Ten years later, auditor-judge don Antonio Rengel investigated Zúñiga's tenure. Rengel enlisted an Otomi interpreter, Pablo de Alvarado, and scribe, Miguel López. Seventeen Otomi commoners and lords appeared to bear witness to Zúñiga's abuse. Each of the Otomi sought to document Zúñiga's actions. Their documents listed in painstaking detail every item each Otomi had lost in 1553 to public auction. Seventeen Otomies turned in pictographic paperwork documenting everything Zúñiga had auctioned off, including lands and household items. Litigants argued that Zúñiga had flogged a few, sent many into exile, and condemned a handful to slave work in mines. Some of the Otomi also leveled accusations of theft against a Tarascan lord of Cuitzeo, don Diego Oaxaque. Otomi lords had lost mattresses, lands, printed Christian catechisms, rosaries, precious stones, bushels of corn, combs, scissors, axes, needles—in short, virtually all their belongings and homes.[72] Francisco Cuini, for example, documented the loss of land, food staples, cash, and household items including exotic birds, feathers, ceramic dishes, scissors, reams of paper, and a printed catechism. Through his interpreter, he denounced the Tarascan don Diego for stealing a bracelet of precious stones.

Cuini, who had been flogged and exiled, argued that don Diego could be seen in Cuitzeo carrying the bracelet around.[73] There were also records of lowly commoners who lost more than just belongings. Andres Cuiatzi, for example, turned in a pictographic list of the property he had lost, including a few coins, a shirt, land, and twenty bushels of corn. Cuiatzi testified that Zúñiga had sent him as a slave to work in nearby mines.[74] Rangel's 1563 audit offered an opportunity for both Otomi lords and slaves—who used their own forms of recordkeeping to plead their cases—to seek justice.

The story of Cuitzeo indicates that latent conflict within Indigenous communities—often with ethnic undertones that had been simmering for centuries before the conquest—drove factionalism and paperwork. The New Laws, themselves borne of factionalism and petitioning, gradually transformed social relations throughout Mexico and beyond. There were hundreds of Cuitzeos in postconquest Tarascan and Nahua communities, as conquest, ethnic conflict, and other conflicts expelled thousands. Take the case of Zempoala, well known for producing in 1580 one of the most emblematic maps of Nahua pictography and cartography.[75]

The map is organized around the Nahua pictogram of Zempoala, a green mountain with deer and cacti topped by a human female head. Yet the map does not document Native tradition so much as massive social upheaval. It depicts the wholesale resettlement of communities from mountains to lower valleys as new aqueducts, pumps, canals, and wells rendered dry lands available to settlement and agriculture.[76] Zempoala appears on the map as a Crown possession, not a conquistador dominion. There is a new center, far from the original one by the large green mountain, around a resettlement (*reducción*) of at least four different Nahua communities. A large Franciscan monastery appears as a political and commercial hub around which four Nahua lords congregate: don Juan, don Pablo, don Francisco, and don Diego. Various large and small red rectangular boxes separate the holdings of communities from those of lords. Most of these Native lords appear clad in white, seated on Indigenous mats signifying their jurisdictional authority. Three rectangle-bounded communities, however, have Otomi lords, dressed with furs. The mountain of Zempoala, symbolic center of the composition, features two Otomi

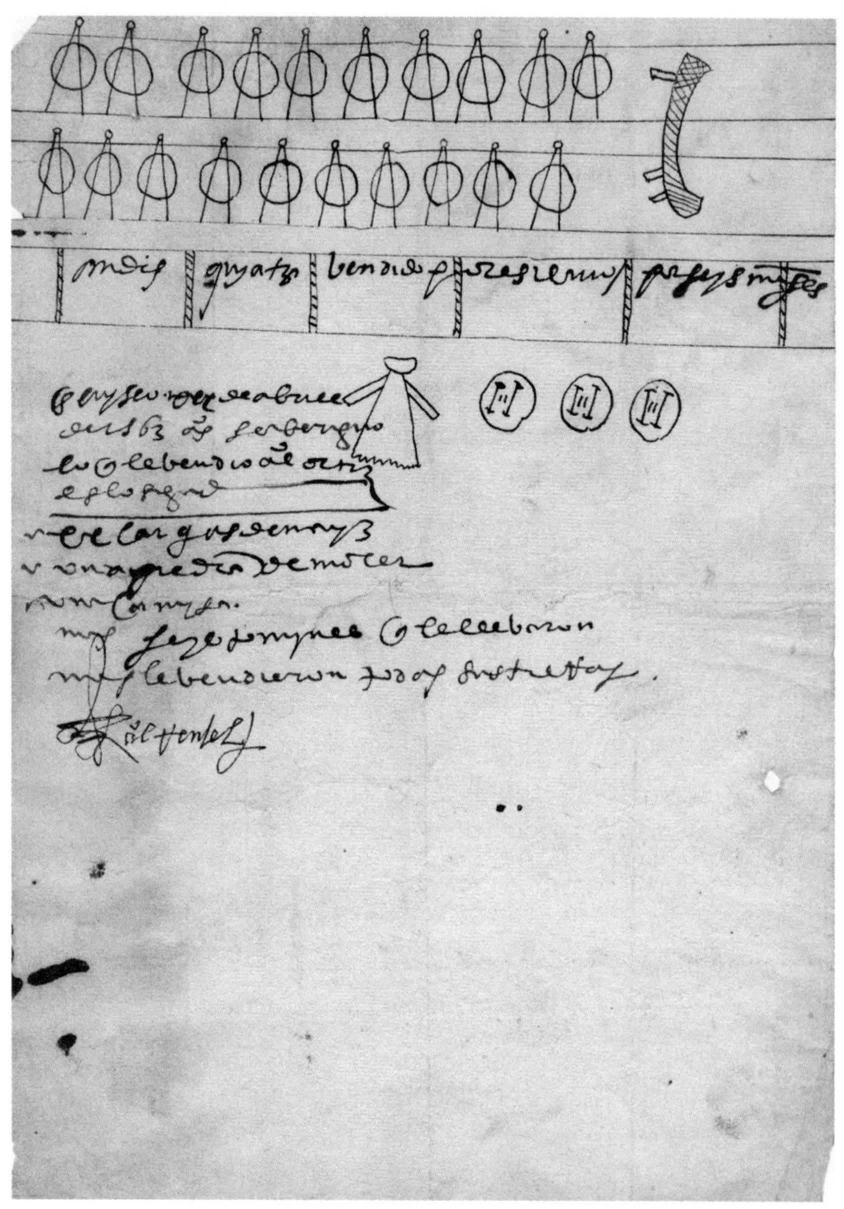

Figure 2.5 Codex titled *Códice de las denuncias de indígenas de Cuitzeo (Michoacán) contra el juez Alonso Ortiz de Zúñiga* (1563). This documents the petition of slave Andres Cuiatzi before High Judge Rengel. The images of coins and clothing at the top were drawn by a slave, while the legal notes below were written by a scribe. Private collection. Photo by Juan Batalla Rosado reprinted with permission.

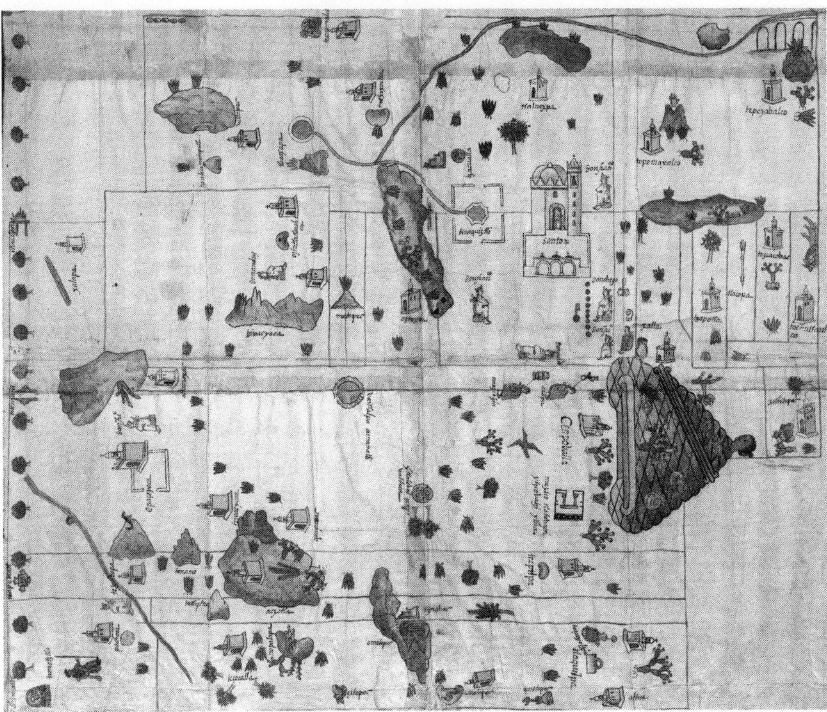

Figure 2.6 Map of Zempoala in 1580 showing the distribution of rulers of different ethnicities across the landscape. There is evidence of new aqueducts and water pumps as well as towns of resettlement. Reproduction courtesy of the University of Texas Libraries, The University of Texas at Austin.

lords sitting right at the boundary of two horizontal red rectangles. A third Otomi lord presides over a tiny vertical rectangle. The map shows processes of ethnic territorialization: the Otomi appear inhabiting small, poor, marginal landholdings, no longer in mixed communities as slaves. Most likely this map represents the anonymous author's factionalist interests, but the story it tells was true in many places. Decades of radical turmoil and lawfare were reshuffling the ethnic boundaries of the empire.

The New Laws of 1542 that allowed Tenamaztle to surface also produced novel mechanisms of social mobility and ethnogenesis on the Chichimec frontier.[77] Along frontiers where permanent war raged, Crown officials' concerns over conquistadors' unaccountable behavior led to oversight by judges, governors, and field justices during military campaigns. To launch a campaign, the viceroy or High Court usually summoned advising committees (juntas) of lawyers, magistrates, theologians, and settlers to determine whether the campaign followed the rules of just war. If it did, these authorities obliged notaries and judges document warlords' every move.[78] Following the New Laws, Crown authorities did not allow ranchers, conquistadors, and miners to organize campaigns into Chichimec frontier on their own. Raided Spanish communities would send petitions along with notarized testimonies of the attacks to High Court judges and viceroys, demanding counterraids. The authorities, in turn, would send captain-judges to organize counterraiding parties of thirty to forty horsemen and hundreds of Indigenous allies. *Audiencias* would also authorize field justices and military officials to lead local forces in mining towns, where they kept paper files for every rebel killed or captured.[79]

Frontier audits were thus ubiquitous. Guachinango, for example, was a new mining frontier that since 1546 had witnessed the arrival of dozens of prospectors; they had established claims over nearly 210 rock outcrops (*vetas*) or mining sites by August 7, 1550, when the town produced a census as part of a year-long (1550), kingdom-wide audit by judge Hernando Martínez de la Marcha of the High Court of Nueva Galicia.[80] When La Marcha visited the mining settlement, Guachinango hosted nearly thirty mining compounds with furnaces and mills to operate with fire and amalgamation. Each compound included the housing buildings of the main miner to whose rock outcrops pools of Indigenous labor from neighboring communities had been assigned by officials (through labor allocations, or *repartimientos*). These lead miners had compounds in which families and followers often had their own mills and furnaces. Compounds also had housing for enslaved laborers, who were largely Indigenous. There were a few of African origin. Mining compounds mixed at least three different types of laborers: deracinated commoners from conquistador dominions, Indigenous slaves, and African slaves. La Marcha did not produce a census of slaves but counted slave housing compounds, of which he listed 145. Miner compounds had as few as one quarter for slaves and as many as fourteen, creating a clear hierarchy of miners and wealth. It is fair to assume that Guachinango hosted no less than five hundred slaves but perhaps closer to fifteen hundred, if one assumes that each quarter sheltered four to ten slaves.[81] When La Marcha entered such mining settlements and towns during his year-long audit of the kingdom, he documented each locale, including the boundaries of Spanish landholdings and Indigenous communities, local authorities' administration, Native and conquistador-lords' treatment of commoners, accounting of shared commoner goods, elaborations of local ordinances, and hearings of local petitions. Spaniards and Native participants in these audits produced mountains of documentation, including maps and codices.[82]

La Marcha's was an itinerant court that probed the legitimacy of subjects' enslavement through oral testimony and summary justice. His duty was to enforce the 1542 New Laws to the letter. Often, the only available evidence was the testimony of slaves themselves, filtered through part-Indigenous interpreters, and the bodily scars of the royal brand. La Marcha distrusted these markings, suspecting that royal accountants who oversaw brandings were in the pockets of enslavers. In every town he visited, he would examine cases of enslaved Natives and deracinated commoners (*naborías*) who served local lords.[83] He left no documentation of how many slaves and deracinated commoners he ultimately set free, but clearly his audits gave the opportunity to tens of thousands to present documentation and witnesses. Given that these audits took place only eight years after the New Laws that outlawed most forms of Indigenous slavery, it is likely that a considerable number achieved freedom.

In addition to dispatching itinerant court audits for the enslaved, high courts often regulated Christian raids against nomadic communities and runaway rebels. These processes, unlike summary justice–based arrangements, produced extensive bottom-up paperwork. Two months after La Marcha visited Guachinango, where he freed an unspecified number of Indigenous slaves, another judge from the High Court of Nueva Galicia, Miguel Contreras Ladrón de Guevara, arrived in town. His charge was to persuade the maroon community of Zacatlan, very near Guachinango, to surrender and delegate their labor to conquistadors. As judge, Contreras had to follow the infamous *requerimiento* procedure, which by 1550 demanded at least three notarized visits to rebel strongholds to depose witnesses and document attempts to convince rebels to surrender. He could not just attack and enslave them; he had to offer them an alternative—namely, to surrender and return to their towns—and get it all on paper. In the process, they acquired new military practices, including the use of arquebuses and warfare on horseback.

Contreras's main concern was to bring the multiethnic Chichimec alliance to its knees. For Contreras, the rebels were not nomads in northern Mexico, as the historiography has it. They were outsiders (*forasteros*), fugitives, and runaway slaves from nearby mines and tribute-paying Indigenous communities who were breaking down corporate town identities and linguistic barriers, mixing with African slaves, and acquiring new technologies of war. The community, formed five years prior, was indeed multiethnic and sheltered an unspecified number of maroons, including five Black men and one woman.[84]

Far away from Christian doctrine and lordly rule, these ethnic and linguistic mixed maroons were becoming a new people: the Chichimecs. All over Nueva Galicia, judge-captains like Contreras sought to destroy these peoples, who were attacking mines and convoys on roads, raiding *estancias*, and rounding up captives, cattle, and horses. Captain-judges like Contreras were not alone; they had Indigenous allies backing them. Local Indigenous lords sought to end Chichimec commoner-slave (*macehual-naboria*) alliances, which deeply threatened local ethnic identities and social orders, including gender roles. Many of these communities participated in wars demanding ransom of Indigenous slaves. Native lords assisted conquistadors like Nuño Beltrán de Guzmán, who subjugated Nueva Galicia in the 1530s, and Viceroy Antonio de Mendoza, who sought to put down the great Mixton rebellion. Tenamaztle's *gracia* petition to the Crown—for recognition of his nobility and service in frontier warfare—included testimonies of the alleged participation of up to fifty thousand Natives in Mendoza's armies. These were the armies that conquered Tenamaztle's Nochistlan cliff-citadel twenty thousand strong. The boundary between Indigenous lords, conquistadors, and commoners like Tenamaztle was not always clear.

Even outright warfare against the multiethnic Chichimecs featured paperwork. Contreras sent two Indigenous interpreters to Zacatlan to talk to the maroons on October 6, 1550, as part of the rigorous procedure, which was to include reams of notarial paperwork, sworn witnesses, scribes, and strict procedural steps.[85] The Natives came from the conquistador-tribute towns of two of the leading miners of Guachinago, Álvaro Bracamonte (who owned thirteen slave quarters in his compound) and Francisco de Estrada (who owned seven). These Natives were Alonso and Pedro, interpreters from the community of Mistlan. The two had to translate the many languages of the rebels to communicate the message of High Judge Contreras in at least two languages, Nahuatl and Otomi. When debriefed, Alonso and Pedro testified that the community's African maroon men and women had urged the rebels to kill the interpreters.[86] The leader of the community, Francisco, blocked them from doing so. But Alfredo and Pedro also warned that the rebels would rather fight and die than surrender. To the rebels, working hard labor in mines for conquistadors was tantamount to slavery.

Twelve days later, Judge Contreras sent several conquistador-miners—Francisco de Estrada, Alonso Álvarez, Diego López de Ayala, and Martín de Rentería—along with don Juan, the Native lord of Acatitlán, an interpreter named Pedro, and a nameless commoner from Cuyutlan.[87] The presence of the Native lord was important because he had been visiting Zacatlan for years, trying to convince his runaway commoners to return. Estrada, Álvarez, López, and Rentería had also skin in the game—namely, that many of the rebels had escaped conquistador dominions. For the second time, conquistadors, Native lords, and interpreters conveyed to the rebels the same message: return peacefully to conquistadors' and Native lords' dominions or face slavery or death.

On return to Guachinango, the witnesses provided additional information about the maroons. They insisted that several *ladino* interpreters, particularly Fernando and a nameless woman interpreter (*nahuatlata*), exerted great influence among the rebels.[88] The miner-conquistador Álvarez spoke in Nahuatl personally with Fernando. Álvarez conveyed the message of Judge Contreras's *requerimiento,* and Fernando forcefully refused. After a scuffle with a group of rebel women yelling insults, laughing, and taunting them as cowards, don Juan, Pedro the interpreter, and the commoner scaled the cliffs and entered the community to speak to the rebels.[89] Then, they disappeared. Indigenous commoners who had accompanied don Juan returned to the conquistador-miner party of Estrada and Álvarez, lamenting that the Christian Natives had been murdered by the rebels. The conquistadors immediately returned to safety in Guachinango. The day after, however, don Juan, Pedro, and the commoner showed up unharmed. The Africans had imprisoned them, urging the community to kill them. Francisco, the community's Native leader, had refused, and a group of unnamed Indigenous merchants visiting the site had untied don Juan, Pedro, and the commoner, setting them free.[90]

After this second round of *requerimiento* warning the Natives to surrender or else, Judge Contreras summoned as many miner-conquistador informants as possible to create a thorough legal foundation for the final step. Contreras put together a questionnaire. Had the maroon community had been warned by previous judge-auditors to surrender? Had Guachinango residents known Judge Contreras had "required" the maroons twice already and had therefore complied with the law? Had rebels engaged in idolatry and threatened to harm neighboring Christian Indigenous communities? Had these maroons welcomed African slaves who would rob and assault passersby? Had the maroons ever attacked the mines of Tepezuatlán, killing and capturing slaves and Africans and murdering Spaniards and allied Native troops who had come to the miners' rescue? Did the very existence of Zacatlan have a larger geopolitical impact in the region? Had the rebels acquired greater knowledge of Spanish military technologies, becoming "people very knowledgeable and learned" (*personas muy sabias y entendidas*)? Had the expansion of their agricultural fields at the bottom of the cliffs made them a beacon for other commoners to escape and thus an imminent threat to the entire region?[91]

Cliff-maroon communities were endlessly reconstituted as commoners either fled or were recaptured and fled again. The evidence shows that Chichimec ethnogenesis was the product of the integration of commoners of many Indigenous communities with African slaves. Maroons in Zacatlan came from at least eight different conquistador dominions and Spanish landholdings: Xalancingo, Guaonecotlan, Aguacatlan,

Guajacatlan, Acatitlan, Quitlan, Cuyutlan, and Guaynamota. Its leaders were *ladinos,* hispanized commoners, most likely former slaves whose knowledge of Spanish and military tactics had helped them achieve leadership positions.[92]

On November 5, Judge Contreras took his armies of conquistador-miner and Indigenous militias, along with numerous notaries and scribes, to Zacatlan. This multiethnic coalition had deep ties. Spanish conquistador-miners were often linked through business and even marriage to Indigenous lords' families. Some of leading conquistador-miners of Guachinango were sons of the first-generation conquistadors who had conquered Nueva Galicia. They also shared enemies. Indigenous nobles in Nueva Galicia supported the conquistadors rather than the maroons, who were challenging traditional patterns of lordship by encouraging peasants to flee their lords and elevating women, commoners, and Africans to important community roles.

The documentary record does not describe a battle; Contreras and his forces evidently managed to reach the top of the cliff. Two secretaries recorded how he and his translators addressed the Chichimec maroons. With him were two notary scribes, a group of conquistador-miners, a Nahuatl translator from Guachinango named Gonzalo, and the Franciscan Francisco Lorenzo. They read the *requerimiento* in Spanish to the maroons, the Native lord, the *ladino* interpreters, and the six Africans.[93] Interpreter Gonzalo immediately translated the *requerimiento* into Nahuatl. The maroon community's own Nahuatl interpreter, Fernando, replied. He rejected the terms. The maroons kept silent on the sidelines. After a pause lasting much of the day, Judge Contreras again had the *requerimiento* read to the rebels. Fernando rejected the terms of settlement again as the maroons reached for their weapons. The judge did not give up. He ordered Gonzalo read the document a third time. Finally, Fray Francisco Lorenzo, holding up a large crucifix, addressed the crowd in Nahuatl, pleading with them to give up. The maroon leadership once again rejected the *requerimiento.* After carefully documenting on paper his last attempt, Contreras ordered allied Native and Spanish militias to take the maroons prisoner, including women and children. Anyone who resisted could be killed.[94]

It seems that the African maroons, the *ladino* interpreters, and Native lord Francisco fled as Tenamaztle had fled before, into the cliffs of Nochistlan.[95] All that is left from Contreras's report is the paperwork of one recaptured maroon, the Otomi commoner Tenuiz. For the trial of this only documented prisoner, Contreras followed the procedure of *requerimiento* and just war. Without this record, he himself could be removed, fined, or tried by another auditor during his posttenure audit. Indeed, his *requerimiento* paperwork only survives in his 1557 posttenure audit. And sure enough, he was charged with murdering Chichimec prisoners without due process.

Clearly Contreras was not negligent when it came to his captive, the commoner Tenuiz. The paperwork of his fateful trial survives. Contreras summoned three interpreters: the Nahua Alonso from Mistlan, the Otomi Pedro from Acatitlan, and the Spanish Martín Pérez. They translated the captive's every word into three languages. Judge Contreras chose Diego López de Ayala to vouch for the accuracy of Alonso's Nahuatl translations.[96] López de Ayala was a family member of the leading conquistador-miner of Guachinango, José López, whose property included seven slave quarters.[97] As a fluent speaker of Nahuatl, Diego appears everywhere in Contreras's documentation. López de Ayala had accompanied the conquistador-miner Álvarez, himself a fluent speaker of Nahuatl, in the second *requirimiento* visit to the cliffs of Zacatlan.[98] An expert translator, López de Ayala had provided detailed answers to Contreras's many questions about the history of the maroon community of Zacatlan.[99] In addition to Alonso and López de Ayala, three other conquistador-miners appear in the documentation as Nahuatl translators.[100]

Tenuiz testified that he had lived as a maroon in Zacatlan for five years. He had originally been a subject of the conquistador Bracamonte and had fled his Indigenous landholding of Amatlan. Tenuiz was familiar with what it took to avoid death when giving testimony. Most of his testimony is suspect, as he denied full responsibility for his actions. For one, he declared that he was not a maroon leader but a lowly commoner, one of seventy.[101] He presented himself as clueless member of a group of children, women, and commoners who deeply feared the African maroons, the Native lord

Francisco, and twenty “war Indians” (*indios de guerra*) who ran the community through fear.[102] He admitted, however, to helping defend Zacatlan against Spanish-Indigenous warbands.[103] He had also been part of a scouting expedition seeking to capture and kill three conquistador-miners—Álvarez, Estrada, and López de Ayala. Worse, Tenuiz confirmed that he had participated in the assault of the mining town of Tepezuacan years prior, burning Bracamonte's houses and killing commoners, Indigenous slaves, and Africans. Tenuiz had committed these crimes out of fear, he insisted.

Judge Contreras's sentence was swift. It was read by Pedro in Otomi and Nahuatl and by Alonso in Nahuatl and Spanish. Tenuiz was given the opportunity to be baptized, which he accepted. He was then was flogged and hanged from a tree on the Zacatlan cliffs. His body was left to rot; anyone who removed it would be summarily executed. As Contreras had failed to capture most of the maroons, he sought to leave a message: the decomposing body of a rebel.

The maroon communities in the Chichimec frontier, including those that hosted Tenamaztle in Nochistlan and Tenuiz in Zacatlan, gathered refugees and runaway slaves, including Africans, from distant areas—so did towns established during the Chichimec wars from 1530 to the mid-1590s. As conquistadors moved into the Chichimec frontier with Tarascan, Otomi, and Nahua allies, the settlers identified several enemies in the mining region of Nueva Galicia, including Huachichil, Zacatecan, Cazcan, Guamar, and Chichimec regional groups. And as more ore outcrops were discovered, miners brought thousands of Indigenous slaves acquired at Indigenous markets into the mines. The local Indigenous nations, living in temporary tenements and as itinerant hunting communities, resisted by raiding mines and encouraging slaves to escape into cliff-maroon communities. Indigenous raiding and maroonage triggered highly regulated counterraids commissioned to judge-warriors by viceroys and *audiencias*.

By the 1560s, semblances of a stable Christian society were appearing throughout the Chichimec frontier. Violence and illegal enslavement persisted, but the region was now dotted with growing *ladino* communities. Sometime in 1561, the king received unspecified reports of continuing problems with enslavement relating to none other than

Viceroy Luis de Velasco's brother Francisco and son-in-law Diego de Ibarra. They had allegedly undertaken cruel, unjustified raids against Chichimec towns.[104] The viceroy ordered Mexico magistrate Luis de Villanueva to head to Zacatecas and investigate. After interrogating numerous witnesses who complained bitterly about economic losses due to Chichimec raids in the Zacatecas mines, Villanueva cleared Francisco and Diego of any wrongdoing. According to witnesses, Francisco had come to Zacatecas via Queretaro with horses and soldiers. But instead of capturing slaves, as the viceroy's enemies had established, Francisco had used his private fortune to offer the Chichimec clothing and tribute, encouraging these communities to settle. Francisco had spent 4,000 ducats in an encounter with the Chichimecs outside San Miguel.[105] All witnesses concurred that Francisco and Diego had not personally profited through the illegal traffic of slaves.

This investigation reveals a great deal about frontier settler society. The region, of ever-greater importance thanks to the abundance of its mines, had been created from at least four different migration diasporas: the movement of slaves and deracinated commoners into mining towns; the resettlement of supporting allied Natives who had accompanied Spaniards in military campaigns and chose to stay; the resettlement of armed Chichimec communities who negotiated peace with *mestizo* judge-captains in exchange for clothing, goods, seeds, and tools to create agrarian settlements; and the recognition of former runaway slave communities.

For example, some fifty settlers established the town of San Miguel in 1555 to serve as an outpost between Queretaro and the Zacatecas mines. The core of the settlement, however, consisted of communities of Tarascan, Nahua, and Otomi subjects, along with pacified Guamars.[106] In 1560, the town of San Luis Jilotepec, to the north of San Miguel on the road of Zacatecas, had four hundred married Otomi Natives originally from Jilotepec.[107] Durango was established in the 1560s by Tarascan, Zacatecan, Chichimec, and Nahua Natives summoned by judge-captains in the mines of San Martín to fight rebel Hucahichiles and Zacatec-Chichimecs.[108]

Mexica vassals left detailed alphabetic records of their participation in the 1561 pacification campaigns led by Pedro de Ahumada around San

Martín, which ultimately created Durango. The documentation reveals the deals Tarascans and Mexica struck with recruiters to capture their own slaves, up to three per warrior. Tarascan and Mexica recruits bitterly complained that Spaniards stole their captives and distributed them among themselves.[109] Yet earlier in the same account, Mexica volunteers described how after one captured Chichimec was tortured and killed by Natives, Spaniards took another captive away to establish his guilt in a trial. Killing the captive without documentation or trial could have brought charges against the expedition's judge-captain.[110] Factionalism within warbands thus led to frontier paperwork and the emancipation of enslaved Chichimecs.

The final pacification of the Chichimec frontier happened in the early 1590s, as Captain Miguel Caldera—part Chichimec himself—struck deals with rebels from Guadalajara to Queretaro, Zacatecas, and Durango. He persuaded them to lay down their weapons in exchange for commodities, agricultural tools, and legal recognition of commons.[111] Michoacan, Guadalajara, and Jalisco, along with the new mines of Zacatecas, Durango, and Sombrerete, went from being a war zone to the economic core of Mexico in three generations.

ARCHIVES AND A NEW SOCIETY OF ORDERS

This peace made the gradual emergence of a society of orders possible. A crucial moment in the transformation came around 1600, with a major campaign of land redistribution and town foundation. Judge-congregator Juan Graniel de Chávez traveled in the hinterlands of Queretaro in late February 1603 with reform in mind. Accompanied by two scribes and a translator-enforcer named Luis del Castillo, he would congregate Chichimec and Otomi tenements and offer commoners land. Judge Chávez approached many shantytowns—Savanilla, Santa María Laguelilpa, Apapataro, Santa María Tlalquelilpa, San Francisco, Santa María Magdalena, San Juanico, and Guaymilpa—and promised commoners private and shared lands in the new community of La Cañada. They would also receive aqueducts and orchards. After careful consideration, all communities accepted his invitation. They moved, carrying wooden planks from their former tenements. Every event was recorded on paper—the Natives signed the documents before witnesses.[112]

Judge Graniel also moved against abusive lords in the area. He discovered five deracinated Chichimec commoners enslaved by the Spaniard Diego Porras. Now free, they congregated in La Cañada too. La Cañada was to be Indigenous only. Judge Graniel ordered the destruction of plots and houses belonging to several Spanish and part-Spanish vassals along the creek. Francisco Guerrero, the tailor Bartolomé Ximénez, Diego Martínez, and a few others lost their crops of corn and chile. The commoners of Guaymilpa tore the houses of the tailor apart, recycling the wood to build new abodes. Initiatives similar to Graniel's were underway everywhere in Mexico in 1603, as auditors moved across the land to regularize land titles for Indigenous commoners.[113]

As a new, stable social order began to emerge, enterprising former runaway slaves became lords. One of the witnesses who testified to the veracity of Judge Graniel's paperwork was don Nicolás de San Luis, a member of the Indigenous council of Queretaro.[114] His social status was that of high-ranking commoner, but he was not particularly distinguished. His status would eventually change, as by the mid-to-late seventeenth century, the Otomi of La Cañada would reshape the persona of don Nicolás into a cultural conquistador, a viceroy-vanquisher of hundreds of thousands of barbarian Chichimecs all over the Bajío. As we will see, numerous collections of forged documents allegedly issued by don Nicolás de San Luis across the Mexican Bajío attest to these transformations.

Yet the history of Otomi commoners turned lords began much earlier than the mid-seventeenth century. The case of one Otomi refugee named Cunni exemplifies how paperwork could be used to establish huge land claims and a privileged place in the emerging society. Cunni was an Otomi merchant-commoner who traded throughout the Chichimec frontier. Before the conquests, he would trade woven maguey blankets and salt with nomad Chichimecs in exchange for arrows, bows, and jaguar, mountain lion, and hare pelts. He would then carry these back to Mexica Tenochtitlan to be sold. Cunni, however, decided to flee northward as soon as Hernán Cortés arrived. Thirty other Otomi followed him, and they found refuge deep in Chichimec territory in a creek near what would become Queretaro.

Cunni's story would change dramatically by the 1580s. In the 1582 *Relación de Querétaro*, penned by the scribe Francisco Ramos de Cárdenas, Cunni appears as a pious noble hero who singlehandedly transformed the frontier from disorderly Chichimec badlands into orderly Christian republics. Cunni's son, don Diego de Tapia, was the informant for the compiler of the *Relación*. Ramos de Cárdenas tells us that the refugee Cunni shepherded his Chichimec and Otomi community to prosperity. In the ravine, they grew cotton, tomatoes, corn, and beans. Then, a conquistador from neighboring Michoacan, Hernando Pérez de Bocanegra, established a landholding near Cunni's ravine with deracinated members of his conquistador dominion. Cunni and the Spaniard soon became friends; Cunni accepted Pérez de Bocanegra's lordship and had his multiethnic community serve as sharecroppers. The Chichimec revolted, seeking to kill all Otomis. Yet Cunni persuaded them to desist by showering them with goods. Pérez de Bocanegra and Cunni then invited one friar to evangelize. Soon after, Queretaro was born.[115]

This story's importance grew over time. Cunni's origins mattered a great deal to the bishops of Michoacan and Mexico, mired in a bitter jurisdictional dispute since 1547. Both prelates claimed jurisdiction over the area and its tithes. Between 1547 and 1585, no fewer than six thousand pages accumulated before Mexico's high judges, including dozens of testimonies by Cunni himself, his wife (Magdalena Jupio), friars, tithe collectors, accountants, ranchers hailing from as far away as Flanders, and Chichimec and Otomi lords and commoners, among many others. Mexico's bishop ultimately won, as consensus emerged that Querétaro's founding father Cunni had hailed from central Mexico, not Michoacan. Although the founder Pérez de Bocanegra had hailed from Michoacan, it was Cunni's origins that mattered. By tracing Cunni's migration to the Valley of Mexico, bishops settled a jurisdictional battle over bishopric boundaries.[116]

Cunni was also reinventing himself, from Otomi merchant to Christian lord. He accepted baptism and took the name Hernando de Tapia.

Hernando understood well how to frame his services to the Crown. He petitioned the king for privileges, prompting a 1569 inquiry into his claims of having civilized the frontier. Still, not one of the three witnesses Hernando presented was willing to vouch for any of his grandiose Chichimec civilizing claims.[117] The story of Cunni-turned-don-Hernando-Tapia is typical of this period and frontier. Tapia was not universally celebrated as a civilizing hero, as it turns out. His rivals accused him of routinely abusing the Chichimecs. On November 10, 1551, Viceroy Velasco ordered an audit on Tapia. The Chichimec reported Tapia as a tyrant. It appears that Viceroy Velasco temporarily removed him as governor of Queretaro and replaced him with an itinerant Indigenous lord, don Augustín Jiménez, a noble from the town of Tecayuca.[118] But don Hernando returned. Sometime between 1560 and 1576, don Hernando was removed again by orders of the *alcalde* mayor don Geronimo de Mercado Sotomayor.[119] In 1564, Viceroy Velasco had the Chichimec commoners of Jurico protected from don Hernando's deceptive and abusive practices, as don Hernando got their lands stolen.[120] But Tapia fought to keep Queretaro firmly under his control—and clearly succeeded, for his son don Diego was governor by 1582.

By 1603, don Hernando appears not as a tyrant but as a hero. In the recollections of five witnesses, he was not just pacifying warlike Chichimecs but founding towns, handing out lands, and converting entire communities to Christianity.[121] This is the model of hero the Otomi would also project onto don Nicolás de San Luis. Don Hernando's long-standing acumen with trade and increasing wealth certainly helped him win many allies. He had aqueducts built in Queretaro, and agriculture grew tenfold. He began using his immense resources to help the Franciscans construct monasteries and convert the region, donating a ranch with nine thousand sheep to the Franciscan-directed Hospital of Indians in Queretaro.[122] His son don Diego inherited three plots of land of nearly one hundred square kilometers (almost twice the area of the Island of Manhattan).[123] Don Hernando had five children recognized as legitimate, four with women married to other Otomi lords.[124] All four of his daughters died heirless, thus folding all of Hernando's land back into don Diego's hands. Viceroy Luis Suárez de Mendoza formally made don Diego a Native lord in 1581.[125]

During the 1603–1604 general audit that established titles and boundaries, don Diego secured titles for his father's land and much more. Witnesses claimed he had obtained new lands from Chichimec commoners by unclear means.[126] Perhaps the commoners had abandoned these lots as they had resettled into congregations.

Don Diego left the Native lordship to his daughter, Luisa, who had entered a convent he had founded: the Religiosas de Santa Clara de la Cruz, one of the wealthiest religious institutions in the whole viceroyalty. Because Luisa, a devout nun, never had children, the convent was left with all the Tapia family holdings. The greatest Creole savant of his generation, Carlos Sigüenza y Góngora, later maintained that this nunnery was one of the most important religious institutions in the entire viceroyalty. Sigüenza's Creole *Glorias* would have been unthinkable without the agency and religious creativity of the Tapias.[127] It seems fitting that Sigüenza also lavished numerous grand titles on don Diego: Capitan General of the Chichimecs, Conquistador of the Valleys of San Francisco and de los Bledos, and Discoverer of the Mines of Tangamanga (San Luis Potosí), Los Pozos, Escanela, Tonatico, and Guazquiluco. In these titles lies a story about the foundation of a society of orders initiated by Indigenous conquistadors and discoverers descended from commoners and slaves. And indeed, globalization triggered by colonial mining economies of scale would have been unthinkable without Otomi lords like don Nicolás, don Hernando, and don Diego.

In 1717, Fray Joseph Díez, guardian of the Colegio Apostólico de la Santísima Cruz of Queretaro, transcribed from Otomi a document allegedly issued in 1502. It narrated a story of conquest on the Chichimec frontier by the Otomi lord Nicolás de San Luis. Díez's manuscript, *Origen de la santísima cruz,* now lies in the Franciscans' archive in Rome.[128] In it, Don Nicolás appears not merely as an Indigenous conquistador-crusader battling arrow-wielding Chichimec with cavalry, muskets, and cannons; he is also a spiritual conquistador, bringing civilization to idolatrous, nomadic, cannibal Chichimec savages.

The document Díez transcribed and sent to Rome was one of dozens of widely circulating manuscripts concerning Indigenous towns throughout the Bajío.[129] According to them, the imperial society of orders had been created by and was composed of Native lords—not mainly Spaniards, as is still commonly assumed.[130] These counterfeited documents transformed don Nicolás de San Luis and his Otomi army captains into officials as powerful as viceroys. The idolized Otomi ancestor led armies to confront hundreds of thousands of Chichimecs with supernatural help from the apostle Santiago and God himself. Next, he and others like him allegedly issued charters to settle barbarians into republican life, complete with municipalities, elections, town justices, and archives. Like a good viceroy, don Nicolás established land titles and administrative boundaries. He and his subalterns baptized and converted millions with the help of only one friar. In exchange for his services, don Nicolás de San Luis received from the monarch coats of arms, membership in esteemed military orders, and noble titles. This outsized, forged Otomi lord, who had likely once been a deracinated commoner, was transformed into the creator of the region's Christian, republican society of orders. And he was not alone—there are collections of decrees and town foundations issued by other alleged Otomi conquistadors: don Alonso Pérez, don Juan de la Cruz Zamora, don Diego de la Cruz Martínez, don Gaspar de Reyes Alfaro, and don Pedro Salvador de Cortés.[131]

The ancestors of those savage Chichimecs allegedly conquered by don Nicolás created their own forgeries of sixteenth-century decrees, edicts, pictographic annals, and coats of arms. The Franciscan Joseph Díaz de la Vega's *Memoria piadosas de la nación indiana* (1782), for example, includes copies of several royal decrees and edicts issued on behalf of Chichimec lord don Juan Bautista Valerio de la Cruz. These documents were supposedly issued by Philip II, his son Prince don Luis, and the viceroys Luis de Velasco, Martín Enríquez, and Lorenzo Suárez de Mendoza from 1550 to 1583.[132] They indicate that Juan Bautista received at least three different coats of arms and was an appointed member of the Military Order of Santiago. One 1559 document by Luis de Velasco allegedly appointed Juan Bautista as capitan general of the Chichimecs in the entire kingdom of Nueva Galicia, parts of Michoacan (Celaya), and a few areas of central Mexico, giving him the authority to lead armies and punish enemies and

Figure 2.7 Don Nicolás appears in the habit of the Order of Santiago. He holds the ensign of imperial sovereignty, presiding as a powerful conquistador-ruler. At center right, in the background, he appears in full armor on horseback, charging against large Chichimec armies. Above him are a cross and the apostle Saint James. The text is based on Fray Francisco Javier de Santa Gertrudis's *Cruz de piedra: Imán de la devoción* (1722). It maintains that the battle took place on July 23, 1531. Underneath don Nicolás's helmet, incomplete text suggests that the image was painted by a "professor of surgery" in 1807. Museo Regional de Querétaro, INAH.

disobedient vassals alike. Velasco also appears to have granted Juan Bautista the right to wear all-white gowns, a gold eagle pendant, and swords. He was a perfect Christian crusader.

All these royal decrees and viceregal edicts were in fact seventeenth-century forgeries that the good friar Díaz de la Vega was willing to accept as fact. By the seventeenth century, Juan Bautista's Chichimec family had created a massive archive to defend their elite status. It included the *Codex Jilotepec,* a forgery seeking to imitate sixteenth-century Mexica pictographic annals.[133] The codex focuses on pre-Christian lordship on the Chichimec frontier, where lords are warrior-heroes endowed with mighty powers who force communities into nomadic existence. Lords come and go; they are elected and deposed for their tyrannical behavior. Most of the codex, however, is devoted to Juan Bautista. He appears as a newly elected, legitimate lord surrounded by a city council, judges, and officers of the peace. The codex celebrates Juan Bautista for providing the militias that, along with the friars, pacified the frontier without Spanish participation. Juan Bautista appears financing every significant construction created in the new town of Jilotepec, including the Church of the Immaculate Conception. The codex ends with the passing of the devout Juan Bautista in 1589, surrounded by choirs of friars and commoners singing his praises. The last page presents the document as a certification of unspecified rewards of merit issued by the Crown. All rewards should be given to his four legitimate heirs.[134] The codex is both a *gracia* petition and a will.

The conflicts that engulfed Indigenous societies in the mid-sixteenth century changed dramatically as a new polity of social orders emerged in the seventeenth century. If sixteenth-century Otomi communities left archives of radical paperwork, their counterparts in the seventeenth century left counterfeited archives of Otomi lords establishing stable new hierarchies and social orders.[135] The very communities that arose due to sixteenth-century deracination, violence, and slavery began to produce documents to gain the lasting admiration and alliance of Franciscan missionaries. Using paperwork, archives, and savvy alliances, these *ladino* commoners endeavored to create stable and permanent hierarchies. And by the 1600s and 1700s, the so-called Spanish Creole religious history of the Bajío was repurposing these Indigenous narratives of agency and religious conquest to consecrate its own services to the empire.

Other Otomi areas created counterfeits that were far more credible than those of Otomi and Chichimec nobilities around Queretaro and that fool scholars to this day. Successful Otomi merchants purchased archives from struggling Mexican lords. These downwardly mobile aristocrats pawned to Otomi muleteers their most valuable possessions—namely, collections of titles, wills, coats of arms, and decrees (*cédulas*). The more archives the Otomi commoners acquired, the more room they had to forge credible counterfeiting claims to nobility, tributaries, and lands. Forgers like Joseph de Morales, the *mestizo* Roque García, and his son Diego García combined titles from struggling *cacique* families in Tenochtitlan, Tlalteloco, and Axacuba to churn out enough documentation to invent their own lordships.[136] By the late seventeenth century, tribunals admitted dozens of counterfeited *cédulas* and wills as facts, including García's counterfeited codices *Cozcatzin* and *Azcatitlan*. These muleteers moved across the Bajío and the central Valley of Mexico, peddling corn and selling forgeries. To struggling communities fending off Spanish landholdings, they offered decrees, titles, and maps. To aspiring *caciques*, they offered wills and decrees.

CONCLUSIONS

Don Hernando de Tapia-Cunni and don Francisco de Tenamaztle were two of many *ladinos* who mastered the art of borderland paperwork. Tenamaztle died before he could see his imagined borderland empire of Jalisco come to fruition. But the Otomi don Hernando succeeded where Tenamaztle had failed. His mastery of paperwork was such that he managed to accumulate an actual mercantile kingdom around Queretaro. Don Hernando and his heirs, don Diego and Abbess Luisa, created one of the most important and wealthiest religious institutions of the entire viceroyalty. Along with figures like don Nicolás de San Luis, they transformed the commercial and religious landscape of the entire Bajío. It was they and their commoner communities who really conquered the borderlands for Christ and the Crown.

Paperwork made these transformations possible. Engendered by competing sovereignties, mechanisms to audit the power of rising tyrants gave voice to commoners and slaves seeking to escape captivity. These changes reorganized the empire on a continental scale. We have focused on silver-rich northern Mexico, although many other regions—notably Peru's Potosi—followed similar patterns. In the borderlands, pioneers created societies based on cities, mines, and agricultural landholdings that emerged within two generations. They were often not European but Native, part-Native, or (less often) African maroons, commoners, and slaves who came together to form new multiethnic Christian republics.

Before and especially after the New Laws of 1542, frontier struggles and enslavement became closely intertwined with administrative procedures. Many Christian attempts to conquer frontier regions featured meticulous paperwork, as officials sought to avoid rivals' accusations and charges of abuse during audits. Meanwhile, subjects seeking freedom became *ladinos*, masters of paperwork, using the new procedures to their advantage. Efforts to resist multiethnic Christian warbands led to the formation of multiethnic alliances and the creation of peoples who shared knowledge of Spanish and paperwork procedure. Ethnically mixed commoner towns emerged in the borderlands; these new societies ultimately enabled economies of silver mining to emerge, making early modern globalization possible. *Ladino* societies were created by Indigenous commoners of all kinds whose lives were as impacted by paperwork as by guns.

The Spanish imperial borderlands were far from irrelevant to global commerce, as liberals have implied by striking them from metanarratives of early modern world economic takeoff. Nor were they primarily places of European violence, extermination, and erasure, as adherents to the decolonial metanarrative have staked. Civilizationalist frontier sociologies have emphasized ethnogenesis, focusing on *mestizaje* as biological and cultural recombination. Hispanist narratives, lastly, have reinvented these spaces as regions in which an inclusive Spanish civilization marched against barbarian peoples. All of these narratives obscure that these areas were largely shaped through the agency of Indigenous slaves and commoners who moved to the margins of the empire to flee oppression or gain freedom, only to become incorporated as key players. Shrewd *ladino* actors contributed to horizontal agrarian, labor, and social patterns organized more along wage labor and mobility than ties to powerful local lords.

Yet after the 1600s, as lasting peace and a thriving commercial society arose, once-radical *ladino* societies reimagined their radical past within Christian narratives of spiritual and military conquest. Their societies were of Indigenous conquistadors led by Christian heroes with ancient lineages. These memories were the deliberate reworkings of commoners, fictions to help them establish new aristocratic objectives and distance themselves from the dangerous radical traditions and dubious social origins of yesteryear. By the late 1600s and 1700s, Indies-born Spaniards repurposed these myths to construct a local Catholic patriotism essential to Mexican high society's idea of its place in the empire and world. The frontier had been deradicalized.

CHAPTER 3

The Conquest of Everything

Gracia *Paperwork and New World Knowledge*

In 1545, a man named Gualpa found himself in dire straits. He was far from his Chumbivilcas home, living as an uprooted *yanacona* servant entangled in conquistadors' civil wars. Before the conquests, he had worn a dignified feather headdress given to him by Inca Huayna Capac as a marker of his elite status. Now he wore a Spanish commoner's hat and survived at the mercy of a violent gang of Spaniards and Portuguese treasure-seekers. Gualpa tried to please them by leading them to a remote sacred burial site, or *huaca,* to loot. At the peak of a great hill, a gust of wind knocked Gualpa to the ground. When he came to his senses, he saw before him the unmistakable shimmer of silver. Gualpa and his fellow *yanacona* Chalco celebrated their lucky break. They had uncovered the legendary silver veins of Potosi, a mountain with mineral riches that would transform the empire and globe from Europe to China and beyond. Gualpa later received baptism and became don Diego Gualpa—and in late 1572, on his deathbed, told his story before several witnesses, including the elderly don Diego Conde Gualpa Inca and Francisco Hacha. A priest, Rodrigo de la Fuente, recorded the discoverer's tale: his illustrious genealogy, his fall into servitude, his discovery, and his descent into obscurity. His son don Juan was determined to make something of his father's deeds before he passed. Don Juan approached Viceroy don Francisco de Toledo that year with a petition, stressing this "great service."[1] Toledo was reportedly very sympathetic and dispatched a priest to determine the truth. In 1578, the council granted to Juan and his family a royal decree ordering local officials to reward them.[2] Ministers knew that silver was streaming into Europe and Ming China, at last cementing the commerce that had spurred Christopher Columbus to sail east in 1492. Don Diego's service to the monarchy, they acknowledged, had transformed Spain's place in the world.

As silver-hungry European pirates ravaged the coasts of the Spanish Empire in the 1570s, another family began building its case. Spaniard José de Orozco y Gamarra personally helped repel invaders. Later, he married Atahualpa's descendant doña Ana Acarpa Coya. Their son don Bartolomé Inca y Orozco would assist him in building novel mining contraptions, which they described in a book encoded in a cyphered script. Around 1605, the Inca traveled to Madrid and submitted the encrypted book to the council, which then forwarded it to the royal master cryptographer, Luis Valle de la Cerda. The brilliant cryptographer was not merely impressed. Hoping to astonish King Philip III during his own petition for privileges, he decoded segments of the inventors' text and marveled at this cyphered invention's "exquisite and novel design, created with a great excess of ingenuity."[3] Don Bartolomé did not hesitate to seize the moment at court to expand his own privilege; he, too, won a royal pension.[4]

In 1569, one don Francisco de la Cueva submitted to the council six copies of a roughly four-hundred-page privilege petition—totaling almost twenty-five hundred pages. The heavy file told of his relatives' violent exploits. Don Francisco's relative, a great warlord, had undertaken "the conquest and pacification of New Spain . . . through the industry, personal efforts, and great prudence which were unleashed upon its natives."[5] Forty witnesses confirmed this destruction, merciless counterinsurgency, and desolation. This relative was don Pedro de Alvarado, one of the most ruthless and violent of all the conquistadors. Don Francisco de la Cueva was petitioning on behalf of his wife, doña Leonor de la Cueva—don Pedro's daughter with Tecuelhuetzin Xicotencatl, the daughter of Tlaxcalan nobleman and warrior Xicotencatl II Axayacatl. Numerous relatives of doña Leonor, like the great Tlaxcalan statesman don Julian de Castilla, testified to don Pedro's deeds. Don Julian also noted, with some trepidation, that don Pedro had married Tecuelhuetzin not according to Spanish custom but by the laws of the Tlaxcalans—an awkward detail, since Tecuelhuetzin would remain by don Pedro's side even after he remarried, twice, to Catholic women. But underscoring this fact was not in the interests of don Francisco or doña Leonor. In any case, the gambit worked, and the council awarded doña Leonor Indigenous tribute.[6]

One petition at a time, vassals' quests to secure royal and viceregal privileges for themselves transformed the Indies, the empire, and the world. At the center of this chapter are sixteenth-century vassals' strategies to obtain royal privileges—efforts that always orbited around *gracia* paperwork. Centered in the royal and viceregal courts, this channel brought subjects into dialogue with monarchs and viceroys, spurring thousands to undertake explorations, conquests, and mass violence. These invasions very often inflicted lasting damage on Indigenous societies' creations—for example, destroying archives and non-Christian sources—and also demanded vassals communicate through a distinctly European, alphabetic format. In this way, *gracia* embodies not just invasion but a broader semiotic conflict between Western and Indigenous knowledge.

And yet, *gracia* paperwork's wider universe paradoxically inspired men and women to write about the New World, explore its nature, describe its ancient history and current Indigenous customs. In fact, *gracia* prompted a bottom-up deluge of knowledge creation that remains fundamental to our understanding of the entire hemisphere. Nor were *gracia*'s consequences exclusively destructive of non-European epistemologies. *Gracia* spurred hundreds of postconquest works, which were related to this channel but nonetheless used conventions that did not exist in Europe at the time. And while conquest was considered a masculine and Christian undertaking, *gracia* was an inherently participatory conduit. Many of those engaging in *gracia* were Spanish peasants or Indigenous elites and commoners. A smaller but not insignificant group were women, Afro-descendants, and others.

We contend that *gracia* must anchor any understanding of how the radical Spanish Empire came to be, how its politics functioned, and what purposes knowledge production served. Experts have often acknowledged *gracia*'s importance in the conquests and the establishment of the empire. Still, they have downplayed this channel's impact on postconquest society by eliding its role as a resource for bottom-up politics and motor of knowledge production. They have dismembered and isolated its various parts, segmenting into separate fields of inquiry what was once a single, integrated paperwork apparatus. Researchers often separate formal *gracia* dossiers—the *relaciones de méritos y servicios*—from the worlds of *gobierno* and *justicia* on the one hand and hundreds of Indigenous codices and other works on the other. By reuniting these genres, we recover a fuller sense of the era's possibilities for political agency and a clearer vision of how the radical era emerged and evolved.

This world of paperwork politics and manuscript-driven knowledge production has remained largely misunderstood and invisible. In most versions of the enduring liberal narrative, for example, it was the printing press and the book that overturned medieval, monkish, and static manuscript culture. For some, entrepreneurial knowledge, often in print, unleashed the dynamic phenomena that characterized the early modern era—European expansion, diversity of thought, natural discoveries, social mobility, and ultimately, globalization and capitalism. In this telling, the drivers of change were seventeenth-century print-based projects of scientific conquest spearheaded by elite Protestant men.[7] Another variant emphasizes an epistolary network of freethinking antiquarians, the Republic of Letters, which crisscrossed between polities and fostered the key liberal values of civility and toleration that later morphed into the Enlightenment.[8] Yet in the Spanish Empire, a far more consequential milieu of knowledge production had by this time profoundly transformed societies across the globe. By around 1600, the world had been transformed and reinterpreted through the medium of *gracia*—by the Catholic, monarchist likes of Christopher Columbus, don Diego Gualpa, the Inca y Orozcos, and doña Leonora de la Cueva.

Decolonial scholars, on the other hand, have argued that print culture transformed the New World into an epistemological monoculture with European elites at the top; cultural civilizationalists have similarly traced print, books, and the alphabet's triumph over Native codices and epistemologies as a precondition of modernity's twisted birth.[9] Codices become divorced from the politics that created them, as Dana Leibsohn notes: "Too many still circulate as iconographic reservoirs and signifiers of indigeneity cut loose from local aspirations."[10] We argue that *gracia*—a vast universe of manuscripts, not print—drove politics and action at once incredibly violent and creative, participatory and elitist. It was key to the creation of what scholars today call *early modernity*, enabling globalization and largely determining how politics and lawfare could be waged.

The invisibility of this radicalism is partly due to the appearance of *gracia* paperwork. On the surface, these documents—masculine, boastful, steeped in the language of privilege and social superiority—seem an odd resource for unsettling a social order. The formal core of *gracia* paperwork are *relaciones*, which primarily consist of the *probanza de méritos y servicios*. Such petitions generally feature a cover letter (also called a *relación*) and proof (or *probanza*) consisting of notarized witness statements proving royal service to the Crown and society. Vassals stressed their merits (*méritos*) and services (*servicios*), requesting minor and major privileges ranging from tax exemptions to mechanical patents to massive pensions to official positions—and even seigneurial dominions.[11] In response to successful requests, the council would draft a royal decree establishing a privilege, which the king would ratify.

Don Diego de Figueroa reveals that these cases could be deceptively creative. His files consist mainly of three dossiers from 1577, 1580, and 1591. These feature notarized documents presented before the Quito High Court and later, the council. The first dossier features sixteen questions and five witnesses, the second five questions and three witnesses, and the final eight questions for three witnesses. A dozen-odd notarial transcripts, powers of attorney, and council officials' scribblings complete the case. At some eighty pages long and featuring nineteen different documents, this *gracia* request is typical, if rather short.[12]

So far, so dreary—but what appears to be a tedious string of Spanish notarial bromides written by an aging elite man is, on closer inspection, far more interesting. Don Diego claimed to be from the sovereign Indigenous house of Cajamarca, Peru, conquered recently by the Inca. His grandfather had often broken bread with the Inca Huayna Capac, and although his kin had fought the Spanish, they soon supported the Crown by turning against the tyrant Pizarros, distinguishing themselves as exemplary royalist vassals in Quito. Don Diego lived as an impeccable Christian, a grammarian and musician, and an upstanding official of Natives in Quito (*alcalde mayor de indios*). He "helps and defends" the Natives "with their needs, helping them write petitions about land disputes . . . and other matters, without pay."[13] He battled bandits, Native rebels, and British pirates at his own expense. Council ministers were understandably impressed. They issued him *gracia* privileges: the *alcalde* position in perpetuity, a large pension, and substantial Indigenous tribute.[14]

Despite its conservative appearance, don Diego's case belies a world of rapid social change and factionalism that bred radicalism. *Gracia* was an established paperwork genre with Iberian roots.[15] Its *probanzas* were characterized by a certain conservative formulism, featuring droning appeals to royal authority. Some scholars have suggested that these proofs represent a tool of the colonial state to control vassals' innermost sense of self.[16] Others have seen these documents as contributing to a discourse of racialized status, which is true to a considerable extent.[17] Yet behind these formulas lay not only conformity and hierarchy but also radicalism and dramatic social mobility. Of course, thousands of Spanish conquistadors—almost all white men—submitted petitions after their invasions. Their descendants, many pensioners or priests, followed suit.[18] So did many officials.[19] But researchers are increasingly finding other types of petitioners in the archives too. They include not only conquistadors' and officials' wives, daughters, and other female relatives, whose petitions constitute perhaps 5 percent of the total submitted to the council.[20] At various levels of the royal administration, Indigenous and part-Indigenous subjects submitted many such dossiers.[21] A smaller number of Afro-descendant conquistadors also created *relaciones*, while toward the end of the century, enslaved and manumitted subjects might insist on their services to the Crown.[22] Scholars have been slower, however, to note the sheer diversity of deeds vassals insisted counted as service to the Crown. For example, many dossiers describe not just navigation, conquest, and imperial defense but botanical discoveries, mineralogical finds such as those of don Diego Gualpa, mechanical inventions like those of José de Orozco and his Inca son don Bartolomé, official service like that of don Diego de Figueroa, and the creation of great writings and works of art—to name only a few avenues.[23] Studying *gracia*'s formal characteristics, then, reveals not only the actors but also the range of themes covered in these texts.

We argue for including an even broader understanding of this channel in the universe of paperwork politics. After all, a vassal might be a petitioner of *gracia* and of *gobierno,* might litigate, and could participate in audits. If we consider not just *gracia* but the wider world of privilege, a much broader panorama of radical social change reveals itself—with *gracia* at the core. In fact, this dynamic channel was a driver not only of knowledge production but also of globalization, spatial mobility, and rich invented tradition. After Gaulpa serendipitously found silver, Potosi's landscape became dotted with multitudes of llama dung-fueled Indigenous furnaces. The outline of a great cosmopolitan city deep in the Andes began to emerge. The mills, aqueducts, artificial lakes, mercury-copper-salt-iron amalgams—in short, the knowledge that powered the city—grew as the result of thousands of bottom-up initiatives.[24] Privilege seeking, competition, and factionalism helped trigger this innovation. The radical Spanish Empire was not directed by neoscholastic, top-down theories of state. Order came unintendedly out of millions of paperwork actions that, in pursuit of honor and factional politics, created the first truly global commercial order and the first society organized along the needs of this trade. Moreover, many vassals seeking social advancement enthusiastically embraced travel across the globe and toward the court, expecting the largely passive Crown to handsomely reward their exploits.

This is not a simplistic story of Europe's rise to total global domination, however. It is true that centering *gracia* does not necessarily move us far from European epistemologies. We remain bound by certain paperwork formalisms, Western conventions, and, of course, alphabetic writing. Yet *gracia* and its wider social contexts encouraged vassals to create works featuring Indigenous epistemologies—such as pictographic codices (*pinturas*), pictographic maps (*pinturas* or *mapas*), large wall codices (*lienzos*), and corded knots. While fewer than twenty preconquest manuscripts survive, Indigenous vassals created thousands during the radical era—hundreds of which still exist today.[25] These works were intrinsically political. Indigenous survivors of the conquests faced a dual, interconnected struggle: to certify elite status before the Crown and to cement legitimacy at home. Commoners were everywhere questioning tradition and privilege; elites needed to assertively shore up their status. Conversely, lesser elites and commoners challenged old aristocracies, often producing proof of their own bloodlines—sometimes entirely out of thin air. These struggles were fundamentally debates about privilege and the structure of society more generally. They were inextricable from the radical era itself. And these agendas required the creation of Indigenous works—especially maps, histories, and genealogies—on an industrial scale. This chapter thus breaks the traditional historiographical boundary separating the *relaciones de méritos* and Indigenous works, especially codices, to understand the postconquest era.[26] Codices and other Indigenous sources, we argue, often belonged to the single logic and social praxis of *gracia*.

Breaking down these genre barriers brings into focus a radical invention of tradition in which vassals forced major social changes and attempted social mobility. In the 1500s, privilege seeking generated a written tradition of hundreds of thousands of pages in which vassals produced new knowledge. Explorers and conquistadors created stories of their deeds, passing them down across centuries. Indigenous and part-Indigenous families and communities established ancient genealogies that reached back centuries before the conquests. Friars, officials, Indigenous commoners, and others generated a vast manuscript canon describing everything from marriage practices to cosmovisions to the politics of Native sovereigns. Since they were part of fierce factional struggles, these visions were mutually contradictory and agonistic. Their adherents all sought to establish their pretensions as natural and just, proclaiming to defend the social order even as they destroyed it.

But can something be *traditional* and *radical* at once? Scholars such as Craig Calhoun have long made the case that northern European and US American radical movements, especially those with commoner bases, did not always articulate major challenges to the social order by advocating for utter destruction of tradition. Rather, they mobilized tradition to their ends. While such invocations have rubbed many late modern radicals the wrong way, Calhoun demonstrates that a "radicalism of tradition . . . [has] been at the center of most modern social revolutions."[27] In the sixteenth-century New World, this phenomenon was surely more dramatic; society had been so uprooted by violence, disease, and lawfare that we see vassals cocreating tradition on the fly. A great number of Indies traditions, then, were radical—figments of ruthless Indigenous and Spanish lawfare. This was no sleepy manuscript world, nor was it mere epistemicide against Native lifeways.[28] What many scholars have studied as culture was, we insist, also radical politics. Even tradition was partisan.

Ultimately, we reject the culturalist perspective that Indigenous documents' radicality rests in their hybridity or *mestizo* epistemologies. When scholars look at an Indigenous map from the 1560s, for instance, many remark on the decline of Indigenous pictorial skill, the superimposition of alphabetic writing, or the *mestizo* combination of conventions. Yet we argue that the social importance of these texts did not inherently lay in their formal contents. Such Indigenous cartography served radical purposes when it assisted sectarian factionalism to undermine dominant social structures. The same map could have later been deployed in service of a new society of orders.[29] The radicalism of *gracia* petitioning was unrelated to the epistemological alterity of the document. Radicalism lies neither in epistemic plurality nor in epistemic destruction alone. Both plurality and destruction matter inasmuch as they are deployed to question or support social orders. Many Indigenous works emerged in creative Indigenous milieus, where increasingly ladinized subjects channeled the power of epistemological pluralism to maximize their social mobility.

Gracia was, then, a vibrant manuscript milieu, a motor of imperial expansion, conquest, and discovery, and a profoundly participatory and epistemologically diverse driver of knowledge production. Although its formalisms and rhetoric celebrated social hierarchy, it was a central tool for vassals engaging in radical politics. The result was an extensive written patrimony throughout the New World, which subsequent generations would—and still do—cite when seeking to understand the region and leverage the authority of the past in contemporary politics.

We must never forget that violence was inseparable from this creation. Indeed, we understand *gracia* to constitute vassals' conquest of everything—the transformation of any deed, violent or peaceful, the pursuit of any knowledge, the elaboration of any argument—into privilege paperwork with which to win royal favor and defeat competitors. *Gracia* thrived, moreover, not only in the context of Crown patronage but also in a world where disease and violence had fragmented society into countless unstable factions. For this reason, *gracia* in the Indies was actually more participatory, epistemologically diverse, and abundant than it had been in newly conquered Spanish Granada or the Canaries. There, too, subjects used paperwork in their struggle to survive and increase their status. However, even a superficial survey reveals that the Indies' more numerous, rattled, and politically active lordships, communities, and entrepreneur-conquerors set the region apart from the rest of the empire.[30]

This channel was not only a tool for creating disruption. As innumerable petitions piled up in local Spanish and Indigenous archives, they came to constitute the Indies' bedrock truths. The fact that so many vassals had cocreated these works gave them legitimacy, and certain broad consensuses about the past spread throughout the Indies. Providing the foundations of a new regime of truth and status, *gracia* gradually transformed from a violent, disruptive force to a cornerstone of the society of orders that gained ground beginning around 1572. Vassals' subsequent political struggles would focus on the implications of these traditions and the texts that describe them, much as British citizens debate the Magna Carta and US Americans debate passages in the Constitution. *Gracia* continues, through its archival and social legacy, to shape New World politics in the present.

PRIVILEGE AND THE BIRTH OF AN EMPIRE

The overseas empire would never have been born without *gracia*. Indeed, we might say its founding document was one such privilege. On April

17, 1492, Columbus received the famous *Capitulaciones de Santa Fe,* the contract-privilege that established his lifelong seigneurial power over the Indies.[31] Explorer-conquerors always had such documents on their minds, prompting them to carefully record their exploits (and exaggerate them if need be).[32] Early travel reports offered European readers—mainly royal officials—a general overview of Indies inhabitants and nature. The reporters' main ambition was not glory in the Republic of Letters but the transformation of accounts of service into centuries of dynastic might.

This world of textual production was initially quite formulaic. Only high-ranking captains and navigators submitted reports; sailors generally did not. Ships had an authoritarian structure and narrow opportunities for social mobility—as did early conquistadors' warbands, which were dominated by their captains. These captains, however, wrote prolifically. Cortés, a trained notary, had perhaps the keenest sense of how to construct a reputation using the complementary worlds of public and secret writing. He painstakingly documented thousands of minuscule events as he led his small warband into Cemanahuac.[33] On one fateful and especially clever occasion, Cortés fabricated Moctezuma's capitulation of his entire empire in notarial detail, a falsehood the conquistador disseminated throughout Europe using both manuscript petitions to the Crown and the printing press—a public relations coup that pressured ministers to grant him the title of marquis.[34] Subsequent strongmen repeated Cortés's playbook, writing detailed accounts of Indies societies, battles, and geography and spreading stories of their own deeds both through public relations and paperwork proceduralism. Old World readers discovered vast overseas expanses largely through writings that served to secure their authors *gracia* privileges. Indeed, such descriptions were key to an emerging awareness of events in Spain, the New World, and beyond; the first early modern ideas of the Indies and the globe were deeply tied to this paperwork.[35]

The conquests of the 1520s onward dramatically opened the doors to petitioners. Now, writers were Spaniards of many social backgrounds, as well as a smaller number of Afro-descendants, Portuguese, and others—including a handful of women.[36] For a conquistador to receive any kind of reward, especially Indigenous labor but even entry into the ranks of the Spanish grandees, he would need to certify his exploits. He would need to have a notary produce a *probanza* featuring the testimonial declarations of eyewitness peers.[37] These texts guaranteed to a faraway king, or at least a viceroy, that the individual's claims had some sort of wider social credibility.

Even the most traditional *gracia* petitions and their *probanzas* fostered extensive textual production. Petitions could be quite descriptive. Each candidate would provide a relatively thorough biography, including the claimant's immediate ancestry and deeds during the conquest. As one historian notes, "one cannot escape feeling that a great many conquistadores were perfectly capable of writing excellent full-length chronicles."[38] These stories had enormous power. They were part of the lifeblood of Iberian and Indies nobility itself, a textual font of aristocratic and administrative social capital. By the 1520s and 1530s, then, *gracia* paperwork was beginning to encourage not just reports and simple petitions but reams of supporting evidence. The importance of these statements increased with their staggering volume; they reached viceregal and royal desks by the thousands in the sixteenth century.[39]

It was not long before Indigenous men and some women began to submit their own *probanzas* summarizing their services to the Crown during the conquests.[40] These works guaranteed that textual production would not remain in the hands of Spanish navigators, captains, or soldiers—and neither would privilege. Many Native conquistadors stressed an entire community's contribution—especially those of Nahua and Mexica groups that followed Spanish captains south into Guatemala and beyond.[41] Maya elites followed suit, stressing their ancestors' assistance to conquistadors.[42] In Peru, Indigenous *probanzas* were largely the same but generally included testimonies about not only initial conquests but also subsequent decades of sieges and civil wars.[43] And while Quechua elites, especially the Inca, dominated this process, major Aymara lords participated as well.[44] These efforts generally hewed close to Spanish paperwork conventions but told a dramatically different insider's story of the conquests—in which Natives were the protagonists.

Gracia paperwork began to encourage Indigenous candidates to demonstrate truth claims using non-European epistemologies. For example, don Felipe de Paucar of Jauja's dossier included not only the typical witness statements that he had helped Pizarro but also a *Report of the Indians Which I, Guacra Paucar, Gave the Marquis Francisco Pizarro.* This extensive 1558 text includes hundreds of entries listing in painstaking detail specific contributions to Pizarro: potatoes (2,386 bales, or *hanegas*), ropes (112), and Native men and women (2,930, of which 138 men and 232 women died), for instance. Remarkably, this report was not based on the usual European systems of proof—witnesses, receipts, written statements. It was based on the corded mnemonic system of the *quipu,* which Andean communities have long used but the exact epistemological workings of which continue to befuddle European scholars today.[45] *Gracia* evidence, then, needed not appear only in European formats.

The violence and antiseigneurial movements of this period encouraged both winners and losers to write, for *gracia* provided defeated lords with a pathway back into the empire. One sovereign—the Inca Tuti Cusi Yupanqui, who ruled over the unconquered stronghold of Vilcabamba—submitted his own notarized historical account in 1570 to the president of Peru. He recounted the 1530s and 1540s conquests and subsequent conflict with the Spanish from a decidedly non-Spanish perspective as part of his self-declared efforts to "negotiate with the King." On returning to Madrid, the president was to give "the following history to the monarch . . . advising His Majesty that I am the . . . firstborn and the son with the right of succession—of the many children left by my father Manco Inca Yupanqui."[46] Privilege and its paperwork thus encouraged and structured not only conquest and imperial expansion but also claimants' certification, reputation building, and even capitulation.

GRACIA AND THE CONQUEST OF KNOWLEDGE

The main conquests and wars had died down by the 1540s and 1550s, and opportunities for Spanish and Indigenous vassals to stress their armed service were diminishing. Where would all these rough-and-tumble men (and a few rough-and-tumble women) turn to next? There was no single answer. Some took to crafting guides on how to conduct frontier warfare. Captain Bernardo de Vargas Machuca, one exceptionally violent and ambitious frontier soldier, produced not only a slew of *gracia* documentation of his exploits but also several military manuals. These included his famed *Indian Militia and Description of the Indies* (1599), which he claimed to have written while "in the midst of the gulf of my ambitions"—in sovereign Native lands far outside of Spanish control.[47] His services earned him the positions of castellan of Portobelo and governor of Margarita.[48] In 1584, another frontier soldier, Baltasar de Obregón, provided a lesser known but very similar book-length manuscript of "advice and warnings . . . regarding war among Indians." He framed the text as one of his lineage's overall military contributions: "My successors, fathers, and grandparents, were occupied in serving Your Majesty in conquering, populating, and pacifying your kingdom . . . in whose obligation I have imitated in the conquests of New Biscay, California, Cibola, and New Mexico." He continued, "I have occupied myself in the service of God and Your Majesty with a chronicle, commentary, and reports of the ancient and modern discoveries of the greater part of the Indies." His intention was to convince the king to give him a prestigious military position on the frontlines.[49]

Knowledge creation needed not concern warfare alone. There were plenty of other things to conquer for the monarchy—nature, for instance. Experts on the natural world could seek to demonstrate how their knowledge benefited the Crown. *Gracia's* open-ended emphasis on royal service encouraged innumerable conquests of the soil, shore, winds, and plant and animal life. As conquests waned, interest in the natural world increased—especially in the New World's inner regions. Some scholars have pinpointed the 1530s as the beginning of Spain's inquisitorial war on natural knowledge.[50] The council's royal decree registers show that in reality, a diametrically opposite process had begun. Hundreds of innovations and discoveries received ministers' patents in the 1530s and 1540s.[51] The manuscript world of *gracia* paperwork was proving itself a flexible tool for vassals and rulers alike.

No subgroup of natural conquests was more important than mineral ones. Enterprising vassals who had discovered mines or devised new mining contraptions could use the same petition-and-response system that had rewarded Columbus and Cortés. Invention and conquest went hand in hand—and few enterprises expanded the Spanish Empire's borders quite like the search for new mines. In 1596, Captain Simón de Silva stated that he had always "served His Royal Person on every occasion . . . with arms and horses as well as slaves and dependents, subjecting rebel Indians, and conquering, discovering, and populating many new towns." He also claimed to have "discovered many minerals, of gold, silver, and mercury, and other metals, which has resulted in, results, and will result in many years of great profits for the royal treasury." He complained that he had not yet received royal support, which was especially unjust because he had used his own funds to "discover a certain invention and artifice of a new processing system for metals with mercury."[52] Silva's complaint illustrates the royal mechanism that motivated vassals' conquests and discovery: many risked their own energy and capital only to request royal aid years or decades later.[53]

All sorts of vassals won privileges for transformative technologies. In 1550, the German Gaspar Lomán won a twelve-year viceregal patent for his invention to "redeem the metals . . . which are extracted from the mines."[54] In 1553, the viceroy issued one Pedro de Saldana a three-year monopoly for a silver-mining invention, "one of the first invented in this land."[55] Many more patents appear in viceroys' privilege registers, or *libros de mercedes.*[56] The Crown issued patents protecting successful vassals' "important secret," "experiment," "new art and engine," or "industry and invention," usually for ten years.[57] By the 1570s, royal decree registers were teeming with mining patents.[58] In some remote but economically thriving areas, like Potosi, city councils also issued patents for mining inventions.[59] Expert discoverers could sometimes aspire to even greater rewards than conquistadors. In 1580, Bartolomé de Medina and Antonio de la Cadena wrote from Mexico that they had created "the first invention of extracting silver from metals through mercury" and asked for 2,000 pesos of yearly rent—more than many veterans of the Peruvian invasions requested.[60] The parallels do not stop there; patent holders often persuaded viceregal officials to grant them Indigenous labor, just like conquistadors.

Indigenous miners appeared in the viceregal and royal registers around the same time Europeans did. Native groups sought royal and viceregal licenses for mines as early as the 1530s. For instance, the Native lords and leaders of Santiago Tecalco, don Salvador and don Martín de Santiago, won a royal decree in 1537 giving them exclusive use of a white jasper mine.[61] Others set out to discover new mines. In 1552, the Mexican viceroy issued an edict allowing Baltasar de Ávila, a Native elite from Molango, to "discover mines and work them" without being harassed by Spaniards.[62] Other individuals and communities in Mexico followed suit.[63] Though the vast Peruvian viceregal records are missing, we know many Native subjects sought rewards for mining discoveries using *probanzas*—as with the ailing don Diego Gualpa, responsible for uncovering the great Potosi.[64]

Indigenous commoners also stood to gain important privileges by discovering mines. It helped that they often knew the lay of the land. In 1575, the viceroy ordered a Spanish field justice to ensure rewards reached the Indigenous geo-prospectors of Xilitla, Tanchipan, and Tanquian, who "had news of many metals of silver and gold and other things."[65] This official was to ensure that "if an elite discovers [a vein,] he should be promoted to governor and his community shall be tribute-free, and if the discoverer is a commoner, he will be henceforth an elite and will be free of tribute."[66] Discovery paperwork became a crucial avenue of social ascent, freeing many peasants from traditional community bonds.

Not every region was rich in mines. No matter—there was plenty more nature to conquer. Flora was an obvious source of interest. In the 1520s and 1530s, the Crown began sporadically granting multiyear monopolies on spice and dye production to various subjects.[67] This meant that vassals often documented their importation of Old World crops to the Indies. For instance, in 1562, doña Beatriz de Salcedo—considered by many to be a Morisca, or descendant of Iberian Muslims—petitioned the High Court of Lima and the council with one such *probanza.* She stated that she had been among the first Spanish women to settle in Peru, had "helped much in the conquest, curing many of the sick," and quite notably "was the first woman to plant wheat in this realm," which the "Spaniards . . . and many of the natives" relied on to survive.[68] Others sought Crown help to substitute Old World plants; in the 1580s, Esteban Ferrofino sought a royal license to exclusively grow and extract oil from the *esnabo* plant.[69]

New World botanical knowledge thus became a common theme in *gracia* paperwork. Pedro de Ledesma won royal cultivation rights to a "certain tree and leaf that in the Mexican tongue is called Xuiquilitl and

Cuauxiquilitl," which yielded a blue dye he claimed could substitute indigo.[70] In 1585, one Rodrigo de Torres Navarra's *probanza* certified that he had served the Crown by overcoming the Andes' perpetual wood shortage by using an Indigenous plant called *hicho* (today *stipa ichu*), resulting in massive benefits to the Huancavelica mercury mines.[71] Spaniards' claims to Indigenous knowledge could also lead to conflict. Conquistadors pushed to the brink by their declining power occasionally took an interest in botany—as was the case with Martín de Ayala, one of the first to submit the northern Yucatan to Crown rule. He began experimenting with a dyewood called *palo campeche,* surely with the help of Mayan acquaintances, in the 1540s. Ayala had few choices, as a Maya revolt had deprived him of tribute. He first traveled to Mexico City, where he brought master dye makers before the High Court and viceroy to demonstrate the dye's perfection and its adhesion to silk and other fabrics.[72] The Yucatan entrepreneur persuaded the Crown that he was *palo*'s inventor. It was to be a short victory. In the 1570s, Procurator Juan Arébalo de Loayza, the legal agent of Mérida, complained that *palo campeche* was not Ayala's discovery—it had long been a product freely harvested by Natives and Spaniards for decades. The governor ruled this monopoly unjust to Spaniards and Natives, and when Ayala's son petitioned to renew the privilege, the council rejected his request.[73]

Even the ocean floor was not safe from conquest. Juan Galvarro won a 1548 patent for a coral-excavating device,[74] and by the 1560s, with the gradual regularization of the Indies fleet, inventors had devised deep-sea diving suits to retrieve "anything under the water—silver, gold, or pearls."[75] Discovery involved expanding not only across the globe but also downward into the earth, the forests, the bottom of the sea. All of these new ventures demanded a vast participatory paper trail.

GRACIA AND THE SPIRITUAL CONQUEST

The conquest of souls generated similar enthusiasm—and violently productive *gracia* documents. Many conquerors boasted in their *probanzas* of destroying Indigenous temples, as did Indigenous petitioners. In a 1556 Latin petition, Xaltocan elite Nahua don Pablo Nazareo, the rector of the

College of Santa Cruz, wrote alongside his fellows don Juan de Axayaca (the brother of Moctezuma), don Juan's wife, doña Francisca, and don Juan's daughter doña María. Don Pablo boasted of how he had helped the Franciscans destroy countless pagan idols in the Mexican countryside, insisting that he and his fellows receive more royal privileges considering their service and connections to Moctezuma.[76] Similarly, the Mayan lord don Pablo Paxbolun of Acalan-Tixchel petitioned in 1564 that he, "with the zeal of serving God our Lord and Your Highness, has always busied himself in helping to bring our holy Catholic faith to the forest Indians."[77] He stressed the miseries and hardships of his spiritual conquest and his success in winning peoples' surrender and destroying idols. Friars supported these petitions, as did Juan de Salmerón, urging in 1583 that "the descendants of those kings and lords" deserved royal aid, "especially those who have helped the Spaniards and the conversion to the faith and the destruction of idolatry."[78]

Well-documented anti-idolatry campaigns often secured social status, both within and beyond the formal bonds of *gracia* paperwork. The Azcapotzalco intellectual don Antonio Valeriano embodied this strategy. Born in the early 1520s, as a teenager he joined the Franciscan College of Santa Cruz. By the 1540s, he was the famous Friar Bernardino de Sahagún's best pupil and collaborator. He helped Sahagún interview elderly Nahuas for the *Universal History* and was himself crucial in framing and sourcing this work. He was also an assistant to extirpation efforts, through which friars' auxiliaries could better defend themselves, their families, and their societies. Valeriano, for instance, petitioned the king on behalf of his Native Azcapotzalco in 1561 for a series of reforms and privileges. These included defending Azcapotzalco, which the Azcapotzalcans claimed in a long Latin disquisition had been the throne of ancient lords for 1,525 years, owning vast lands and even ruling over the Mexica. Now, Azcapotzalco was besieged by friars' and officials' tributary demands and the tyranny of Tlacuba (*tyrannide potius tlacubanenses*) and other communities encroaching on their natural resources.[79] The petitioners also asked for a royal privilege to fund a new university in Azcapozalco, for "it is patent that through mastery of letters, the hearts of Christians, in antiquity swayed by the winds of gentility, become firm in the faith."[80] It is not clear whether the Crown responded, although in 1565, ministers issued (surely in response to a similar request) a coat of arms for the city.[81] In a way, Azcapozalco's prodigal son, Valeriano, did restore ancient rule over the Mexica for a while: in 1570, he became governor-judge of Indigenous Mexico itself and received the king's praise in 1579 for his evangelization efforts.[82] He repaid the Franciscans, interceding for them in a conflict about the location of the nuns of Santa Clara in 1575, and founded the chapel of Saint Joseph of the Natives in 1589.[83] Don Antonio was not just a brilliant thinker—he was a dexterous master of imperial paperwork.

The conquering spirit was not always as strong with churchmen. Priests and friars did not engage with the council as often in the world of *gracia*. Priests occasionally submitted accounts of their services to the Crown, hoping to receive plum positions and climb the church hierarchy. They emphasized their piety, linguistic abilities, and dedication to uprooting un-Christian practices in Spanish and Indigenous communities.[84] These churchmen did not submit nearly as many *gracia* dossiers as conquistadors and other subjects, likely because they addressed bishops directly.[85] Friars generally administered their own internal selection process for candidates. Still, they might seek general royal and viceregal support by researching Indigenous practices—especially with the intention of demonstrating to the Crown how they were uprooting idolatry. For example, sometime in the early 1560s, the Augustinians of Huamacucho produced a report to the king rich with information on Indigenous rites and ceremonies.[86] The text made little secret that the authors intended to furnish knowledge gathered during their major extirpation efforts—thousands of idols destroyed—and were submitting a report to stress the importance of the order's work in Peru. It outlined the deeds and institutional history of the Augustinians in their first decade in the viceroyalty but also included lengthy descriptions of how they discovered "all the secrets and origins of the [Indigenous] gods and many superstitions and lies," including the structure of the priesthood and the deities Ataguju, Sugadcavra, and Vaumgavrad, which locals had worshipped "since time immemorial."[87] The Augustinians' report—a thinly veiled request for royal support in exchange for services—thus documented non-Christian beliefs in order to prove to the king what they destroyed.

The spiritual conquest was not restricted to *gracia*. Christian onslaughts also relied on inquisitorial *justicia* trials, *visitas*, extirpators' manuals, and *gobierno* petitions. These paperwork practices formed part of the wider world of privilege seeking in three ways. First, they had direct negative impacts on many Indigenous elites' standing before the Crown—especially those involved in forbidden rituals. Second, they formed the social-bureaucratic gauntlet Indigenous privilege seekers had to navigate. Finally, they determined the shape of Spanish authority and jurisdiction itself. All of these practices impacted the shape of *gracia* and social status in the Indies more generally.

What transpired in the first years of spiritual conquest after the invasions is largely unknown. Neither the warlords nor the Franciscan friars who came to Mexico in 1524 documented their deeds as they happened. Rather, both concocted *post hoc* accounts to defend their actions when lawfare between them and their rivals erupted. And although conquistador captains quickly descended into bloody rivalry against one another, the first Franciscans stayed neutral—and quiet. Without other mendicant orders in Mexico, they did not have competitors. No jurisdictional conflict meant little to no paperwork—and no paperwork meant little to no oversight. This unchallenged monastic power was therefore an ill omen for Native elites and communities. Looking at Tlaxcala, historians Justyna Olko and Agnieszka Brylak have called the period of 1526–1536 the "Franciscan Terror."[88] Yet jurisdictional sparring flung open the door on this terror. By the mid-1530s, the Franciscans were in open conflict with conquistadors; Augustinians, Dominicans, and others were now competing with and denouncing them, too. When the Crown passed inquisitory powers from mendicants to bishops in 1535, Franciscan friar and bishop Juan de Zumárraga's fierce anti-idolatry policies fell under public and royal scrutiny. It is no coincidence that he proceeded by meticulously documenting his extirpations.[89]

Beginning in the late 1530s, the spiritual conquest's interplay with privilege and non-European epistemologies became clearer. Friars and their Native allies had been battling Indigenous elite priesthoods. Indigenous converts often attempted to use paperwork to elevate themselves at the expense of their rivals, setting ritual specialists on the run in the process. Zumárraga's paperwork makes this manipulation of episcopal inquisition clear. We see Native factions sparring and elite and commoner accusers flocking to Spanish courts, forcing bishops to reckon with unfamiliar concepts, evidence, and intrigues. In 1536, Zumárraga acted against Natives Tacatetl and Tanixtetl based on accusations by an illiterate Spaniard named Lorenzo Suárez, whose Otomi acquaintances had heard reports that locals were carrying out sacrificial bleedings among a temple of "many branches, papers, maguey thorns, and copal, and daggers, and clothing for idols, and feathers, and an herb called *yautle* and incenses and censers," along with "pots of pulque, and food, and cacao." The rite's *tacatlecle* priest, the "great pope" who transformed himself into a jaguar, administered rites according to an anti-Christian calendrical cycle and hid numerous idols in a cave. The trial concluded with several Natives humiliated, whipped, and forced to live in reclusion inside a monastery.[90]

Much more famous is the 1539 burning of Texcocan elite don Carlos Ometochtli Chichimecatecuhtli, which as historian Bradley Benton notes was less an "epic battle between local Native leader and evil inquisitor" than an eruption of Native politics.[91] Don Carlos had attempted with intense ambition to become Texcoco's ruler. His efforts to rape and marry the sitting ruler don Pedro Tetlahuehuetzquititzin's sister doña María ended, however, in disaster. A host of Indigenous women, including his own wife, denounced him as a sexual predator. The bishop's inquisition, eager for additional reports, received word from commoners of Chiconautla that he was not just a lecher but an idolater and dogmatizer against monastic authority. The bishop's agents subsequently searched don Carlos's house and found idols.[92] Don Carlos's legal defense failed to summon a single witness in his favor—it seems he had alienated the entire Texcoco community. His case collapsed, and the bishop had him burned alive.

This case's heavy-handed proceedings earned Bishop Zumárraga a harsh reprimand from the Crown, and council ministers demanded he show a paper trail. Although Zumárraga and others would continue persecuting non-Christian beliefs, the dawn of a more careful and less draconian era of extirpation was upon Mexico.[93] This shift led, on the one hand, to increasing paperwork to ensure officials' proper proceedings. Many trials generated documents in central Mexico, Oaxaca, and beyond that reconstructed elements of non-Spanish belief systems to prove or disprove allegations of defendants' anti-Christian behaviors.[94] These proceedings nonetheless continued to determine whether Indigenous lords could navigate perilous situations or turn them to their advantage, ultimately shaping who received *gracia* and who did not.

For Indigenous elites to survive monastic and episcopal inquisitions and trials, they needed to completely restructure their relationships with their own communities and the supernatural. Their path to privilege required they stay in good standing with their subjects—a difficult task when Spanish officials and their allies regarded certain core practices of authority as un-Christian. Many lords had pacted with their subjects and established authority through feasting, drinking, and offerings. While the exact meaning of each ceremony changed with time and place, for many local lords, these gatherings remained indispensable sources of legitimacy.

But the spiritual conquests and their paperwork were making these gatherings dangerous. Many vassals accused Native lords of hosting *borracheras*, or drunken festivities, especially during secular authorities' *visitas*.[95] In the Mixe town of Amatepec, two rivals, Native governor Luis de Velasco and his adversary don Baltazar López Cantoi, had been litigating incessantly between 1577 and 1589. According to don Luis, his opponent had marched off to create a new town with a group of commoners, promising followers that he would revitalize their preconquest ways. Witnesses alleged that don Baltazar had extorted money from commoners in various ways to pay for his litigation and for *borracheras* that featured ceremonial fighting so fierce one woman died of her wounds. Don Baltazar's new town site was not only "an ancient place of sacrifice," Native rivals insisted, but also the site "where his grandfather used to sacrifice" and was buried.[96] In other words, it is likely that don Baltazar had come from an established lineage of lord-priests, explaining his antipathy toward don Luis, who as governor was the viceroy's appointee. Whatever don Luis's original source of legitimacy, he cultivated the right friends—in Mexico City and with the commoners of his town, who were more than happy to stress that Baltazar had attempted to usurp the "lands of the commons."[97] The Crown ordered don Baltazar cease in his attempts to divide the community and submit to don Luis.

Preconquest authority had never distinguished sharply between the spiritual and the lordly. The Amatepec case hints that this overlap could be dangerous when lawfare overcame a community—and it happened elsewhere as well. In 1569, for instance, an exasperated Franciscan friar petitioned the High Court of New Granada to report *borracheras* in nearby Suba and Tima. A Spanish field justice was to investigate and punish those involved. One witness, the part-Native Diego Cardoso, described a shadow hierarchy of Native officials who would secretly pact "not to forget their sanctuaries and sacrifices, and their offerings, bringing to memory the Indian ancestors who were lords and rich men."[98] Other Native witnesses went on to describe in substantial detail how the *mohanes,* or priests, structured their hierarchies, procured human sacrifices, and practiced their *borracheras.*[99] Ritual experts needed to tread carefully; anyone in their community could manipulate paperwork to further damage traditional hierarchies.

Secular authorities, whose power and reach grew especially in the second half of the 1500s, could join friars, bishops, and priests in persecuting adherents of non-Christian views. Conquistadors had been almost entirely indifferent to these abuses. Until the 1530s and 1540s, royal officials conducted surveys of rural Indigenous spaces with relatively little regard to Native lords' Christianity. In a 1549 Atico *visita,* Lord Chincha Pulca informed officials about tribute arrangements after swearing "in his law upon the sun and by the moon."[100] This toleration changed as Spanish authority set deeper roots. Just over a decade later, the Peruvian viceroy's investigators seemed prepared to punish lords for moral laxity. A 1562 Huanuco *visita* seeking to increase Indigenous tribute output simultaneously investigated whether lords were properly motivating commoners to work and explored Inca systems to compel peasant cooperation and good government by Native elites.[101]

Secular *visitadores*' increasing concerns with morality threatened lords' rule and generated considerable textual production about non-Christian beliefs, often supplied by communities themselves. In a 1561 tax audit in the rural outskirts of Cartagena, for instance, the bishop and several royal associates requested local Natives discuss "their public spiritual and temporal reformation" as well as "the succession customs which the lords [*caciques*] had."[102] These inquiries—directed partly against local Native priests and polygamist lords—yielded long lists of residents, both baptized and "infidels."[103] Similarly, Santa Fe officials conducting *visitas* in 1593 found Natives like the Muisca don Pedro Guyamuche responsible for aiding or at least not preventing widespread idolatry and brought criminal charges against him. His defense attorneys managed to fend off various harsh punishments as he was not abetting "ancient rites and ceremonies"—which the investigation described in substantial detail to charge him and his peers. Don Pedro was simply old and negligent, his lawyer claimed. The High Judges therefore softened their initial verdict and found him guilty of perjury but not idolatry.[104]

Indigenous authorities knew they were gambling with centuries of good social standing by engaging in non-Catholic practices. Anyone could accuse them now. The savviest among them moved to performatively insist on their piety. One strategy was to adapt European methods of documentation and administration to prove oneself. For instance, in 1543, Tlaxcalan governor don Valeriano Castañeda issued a Nahuatl edict using the Latin alphabet to Field Justice (*alguacil*) Feliciano Tizamitl allowing him to proceed against not only sinners but also those "practicing the old idolatry, the eating of the earth, the laying down of straw, rain divination."[105] The Franciscan Terror was still fresh in their minds—and the Tlaxcalans would preserve their good standing in the eyes of the Crown by documenting their conversion down to the last receipt.

Just as previous conquerors had described their deeds in exhaustive detail, spiritual crusaders began to chronicle their exploits. They had good reason to do so, for even men of God sometimes needed to defend their privileges before their rulers. But there were other reasons too. Idolatry trials' non-European, non-Christian elements challenged inquisitors to systematically record what they were hearing from Indigenous witnesses.

What was true, and what was false, in these countless complaints? With social privileges on the line, there was always a good chance accusers were inventing claims whole cloth.

By the 1530s, the problem of veracity regarding un-Christian practices had reached a massive scale. This conundrum opened another venue for good vassals to provide their services to God and the king: research into pagan rituals and beliefs. To conquer paganism and defeat Native ritual specialists, Christians could investigate their worlds just as others recounted the conquests or uncovered the secrets of nature.

In 1533, on the commands of New Spain's Franciscan order and the president of Mexico, Sebastián Ramírez de Fuenleal (also bishop of Santo Domingo), Friar Andrés de Olmos began to interview elders, read preconquest documents, and assemble a text to describe practices to be "refuted" as well as to preserve Nahua society's more positive aspects, which some feared were vanishing.[106] Olmos had acted as an inquisitorial assistant during the heyday of Bishop Zumárraga's campaigns to extirpate idolatry.[107] By about 1540, he had finished his now-lost *Treatise on Mexican Antiquity (Tratado de antigüedades mexicanos)*, which featured major sections on Nahua religion, history, calendrical beliefs, society, and language.[108] Scholars agree that this work influenced what is today called the Magliabecchiano Group, a large cluster of texts produced by Spanish-Native cooperation describing Mexica beliefs.[109] Yet scholars have been slow to note that Olmos's and the Magliabechiano documents almost certainly served as para-inquisitorial texts. They fixated on knowledge of deities, calendrical rituals, and belief systems essential for inquisitors seeking evidence of Indigenous wrongdoing. The role that these and other para-inquisitorial texts played in aiding extirpation was sometimes more explicit. The famous Franciscan Sahagún, who alongside Olmos had collaborated with Bishop Zumárraga in the 1530s in Mexican anti-idolatry trials, coproduced with Indigenous assistants various works that explored Nahua practices in order to surgically uproot non-Christian beliefs.[110] His magnum opus, *The Universal History of the Things of New Spain*, was one such text. His superior Friar Francisco Toral ordered him to produce an extirpation manual to accompany other evangelizers into the field. Although

Sahagún's work also covered other topics relating to Indigenous societies, he explicitly described it as "medicine" for Mexico's "spiritual disease"—no doctor should cure a patient without knowledge of the malady.[111]

Sahagún's knowledge, building on Olmos's and others' works, was unquestionably useful in an inquisitorial context. Yet the *Universal History* was so sophisticated and complete it could also prove dangerous outside of inquisitorial court, since it described in encyclopedic detail many aspects of Nahua life and belief. On April 22, 1577, the council wrote the viceroy of Mexico that its ministers had been informed of Sahagún's work and feared that it might circulate and inadvertently spread "superstitions and the way of life which these Indians had."[112] Bishop don Pedro Moya de Contreras protested in a March 30, 1578, letter to the council stating that Sahagún's books should stay in Mexico and be "visible so that the Inquisition can have notice of a rite when it deals with the guilt of the Indians."[113] And while Sahagún may have complied with the Crown's request, his manuscripts and other para-inquisitorial texts on Indigenous rites and antiquity circulated into the 1600s and beyond.[114]

The churchmen who assembled this paperwork understood themselves as conquistadors of the spiritual and petitioned the Crown accordingly. The Inquisition and other Christian institutions continued to compile information on rites and customs even after 1571, when the Crown forbade them from prosecuting Natives.[115] In 1592, for example, the Augustinian Juan de Vivero suggested in a petition to the Crown that it sponsor works to "understand their [natives'] rites and ceremonies, and make a book of them, and give them to priests, so they can understand and denounce them."[116] As Vivero noted, priests were essential ears and eyes for bishops and other extirpators. Churchmen also produced texts that gathered massive amounts of information on the Indies' past and its peoples' customs. For instance, in Peru, the clergyman Lope de Atienza submitted a long report to the viceroy in 1575 that he hoped would circulate among the priesthood. In his own words, "this small booklet . . . clearly pulls entirely towards one end, although its contents and topics are each different." It was to act as Deuteronomy had for the Israelites—in other words, it would help the priesthood "keep its commandments, and for the good government of its peoples."[117] Atienza provided a trove of knowledge, from a royal genealogy of the Inca to descriptions of Native lords' styles of rule, language, burial practices, clothing, diet, family relations, and other customs, followed by reasons why these traits made priests' work so challenging. The conquest of the Indigenous soul required its own special paperwork.

GRACIA AND THE CONQUEST OF THE PAST

Military and spiritual conquests generated a considerable amount of paperwork directly and indirectly related to *gracia*. But as important as the conquest of lands and souls might be, the Indies had a pressing problem. Every vassal, it seemed, now claimed to be a great conquistador or an Indigenous lord. In an era of radical social upheaval, every commoner claimed to be a king, and whole communities were tearing themselves apart, alleging their ancient independence. The past had grown wild. For contemporaries, charting the treacherous frontier of the past was as great a service to the Crown as any. Privilege seekers thus often merged history writing with their efforts of discovery, conquest, invention, and conversion.

Captain Pedro Sarmiento is a case in point. His 1572 *gracia* petition recounted his many conquests to the king. He had first discovered the Solomon Islands and then overcome the sovereign Inca stronghold of Chuquichaca with "mathematical instruments in one hand, [and] arms in the other."[118] During his conquests, he had roamed Peru, taking its latitudinal and longitudinal coordinates to create "a most particular description of this realm" and "all the most notable, historical, and describable [aspects of these lands]."[119] But he also turned to the past. After the Peruvian viceroy ordered him to create a genealogy of the Inca, he approached forty-two Inca elders and wrote the *History of the Incas*. This endeavor, he claimed, "was no minor service but in fact was greater than all the rest."[120] Here began a new struggle: "contention with all the historiographers."[121] And all of it was "at his own cost."[122] By 1581, he had cited his achievements and reputation to seek Indigenous tribute and request governorship of the Strait of Magellan—which he received.[123] In his telling, conquest of the past was the greatest feat of all.

For many others, especially Native lords, mastering history meant reconquering (and sometimes expanding) preconquest social status. The martial and spiritual conquests had threatened countless Indigenous noblemen and commoners. Now peasants and second-rate elites were making all sorts of claims through paperwork, and lineages needed to counterattack with their own textual production. Vassals saw it as the moment to confirm, tweak, or perhaps outright invent their privileges. During the formative viceregal period, conflicts unleashed a flood of petitions, lawsuits, genealogies, treatises, and extended investigations into the particulars and overarching frameworks of privilege. Native privilege seekers created their own highly partisan New World histories, often richly non-European in epistemology. In these disorderly circumstances, ancient history—or rather, claims to ancient genealogies—transformed through *gracia* into crucial social capital. Quests for the strongest claims to uninterrupted possession of lordship prompted Indigenous elites to stretch their investigations into past centuries—into "time immemorial."[124]

For Native lords, the past was the raw material of social status itself. Major Indigenous houses were thus motivated by the logics of *gracia* to produce deep genealogical claims, some of which strategically emulated the stories of Spain's most powerful aristocrats. All European monarchs traced their spiritual and political lineages to biblical times.[125] The Habsburgs were particularly fond of sponsoring genealogies that linked them to King David (as part of their claim to Jerusalem), to Jesus of the House of David, and to Rome by way of Saint Peter and therefore the Holy Roman Empire itself.[126] The dynasty's scholars also yoked its bloodline to the Roman emperor Augustus and Greek heroes like Hector and Aeneas.[127]

The Moctezumas and Incas were among the most adept at staking their authority from time immemorial. Several Moctezumas made masterful use of texts to ensure their survival through the viceregal period and to the present. Doña Isabel Moctezuma, daughter of Moctezuma, her Spanish husband, Juan Cano, and their progeny were early and diligent researchers of pre-Hispanic Mexica history. Beginning in the 1530s, this branch of the family repeatedly petitioned the Mexican High Court and council for royal rewards, largely on the grounds of the Mexica dynasty's complex preconquest history.[128] The Moctezuma-Canos compiled extensive texts about the conquest and preconquest society, including descriptions of rites, land claims, and "the genealogy and lineage of those who have lorded over and lived in these parts."[129] They submitted petitions in the 1540s to recover their patrimony, offering hundreds of pages of testimony by elder Natives from throughout New Spain. These documents painstakingly described the dynasty's numerous dominions and Isabel's status as the daughter of Moctezuma's primary wife according to Mexica custom.[130] But perhaps the most complex of the Moctezumas' postconquest productions are the *Relation of the Genealogy and Lineage of the Lords* and *Origin of the Mexicans,* prepared circa 1530 by anonymous friars close to Cano and Isabel working on their sons' behalf. These works reach back to the rise of the Mexica, providing centuries of dynastic and political history.[131] Among other things, these and other works served the family as it struggled in court against commoners and elites of their preconquest estate of Tula. They thus illustrate how *gracia* efforts could help lords litigate against their disobedient subjects.

The Moctezuma-Cano case illustrates the paradox of *gracia*'s simultaneous destructive and creative drives. At least one branch of their genealogical investigation was undertaken by friars who openly admitted that "we have destroyed and burned . . . everything ceremony-related [*ceremoniatico*] and suspicious." Yet because don Juan and doña Isabel had petitioned the bishop to appoint friars to undertake this research, these friars had to attempt to decode "the origin of these peoples . . . which they have written in their books by means of figures and characters, and there is variation and many infinite errors and tricks . . . of the devil."[132] The friars begrudgingly undertook research on these texts, supplementing it with elders' testimonies to explore the mytho-historical migrations of the Mexicas' ancestors.

Genealogical struggles motivated similar Peruvian alliances. Juan de Betanzos, an experienced translator between Spanish and Quechua, married the Inca Atahualpa's former wife, Cuxirimay Ocllo, and had her christened doña Angelina Yupanqui. However, the fate of the Yupanqui branch was up in the air in the 1540s. Viceroy Mendoza, who had arrived in Peru from Mexico and knew the importance of histories for governance, commissioned Betanzos to write a history of Peru and the Inca in 1551. Betanzos finished it in 1557. Scholars today celebrate his *Narrative of the Incas* as a uniquely informed window into Inca ruling ideology. And despite his official capacity, Betanzos and doña Angelica bear an uncanny resemblance to Cano and doña Isabel. Like Cano, Betanzos was a commoner Spaniard vastly beneath his Indigenous wife's station. His distinction came from his linguistic abilities and close connection to the Inca world, which allowed him to use his history as an opportunity to both endear himself to Peru's viceroys and reconstruct his wife's claim to the Inca throne.[133] History writing lifted Betanzos's fortunes and prevented doña Angelina from losing everything in the process.

Spanish-Indigenous dynasties descending from the great preconquest lineages led the charge into the New World past. They crafted descriptions replete with unfamiliar timelines, non-Spanish practices, and un-Christian beliefs. Yet these *gracia* petitioners tended to arrange alphabetic, carefully curated accounts for Spanish eyes. Entirely Native lineages alleging similar pedigrees offered more epistemologically divergent accounts. In 1569, twenty-two Incas described before Cusco officials the military exploits of past sovereign Incas. The claimants, represented by don Andrés Topa Yupanqui, don Cristobal Pisac Topa, don García Cayo Topa, and don García Pilco Topa, were to use this *probanza ad perpetua* in a petition before the king.[134] One of the sources confirming their royal descent, they argued, was their collection of *quipu* knotted cords, which replaced typical European archival parchments and papers. Similarly, high-elite Natives' *gracia*-driven quests to claim the oldest possible genealogies sometimes led them centuries before even the rule of the Mexica and Inca. The so-called *Codex mexicanus* of the final third of the 1500s underpinned the judicial claims of less-powerful descendants of Itzcoatl and Huitzilihuitl, early rulers of Tenochtitlan, representing their deep-rooted legitimacy through Nahua calendrical-migratory conventions.[135]

The fallen houses of Anahuac and Tihuantinsuyo were not the only ones to sponsor genealogical defenses of their privilege before Spanish authorities. Local rulers—now styled as *caciques*—did as well, in dizzying numbers. Native lords' claims exhibit spectacular variety and epistemological creativity. The documents they commissioned not only reach far into mythical-heroic and historical preconquest times but also strategically use as many non-Spanish conventions as possible to persuade officials that claims faithfully reflect customs derived from the ancient past.[136] These sources are among the most creative of the era—and indeed, of human history.

The works produced by Native elites in larger cities are a case in point. The city of Texcoco experienced a fraught century of lordly disputes that generated considerable documentation. After the episcopal Inquisition burned its would-be ruler don Carlos, a power vacuum opened. Claimants battled for the city's aristocratic titles and governorships, land, and royal pensions. Don Antonio Pimentel Tlahuitoltzin, don Carlos's half brother and heir to preconquest dynasts Nezahualcoyotl and Nezahualpilli, did everything in his power to secure his privileges. He oversaw the creation of numerous works on the Indigenous past and present, including the *Codex Xolotl*, the *Mapa Quinatzin*, and the *Mapa Tlotzin*.[137] The 1540s *Xolotl* is a fig-bark cartographic-genealogical map. It traces 316 Texcocan genealogies' arrivals to and deeds in the Mexico Valley Basin in a glyphic, nonlinear representation ideal for Nahuas to read aloud.[138] This work roots Texcocan legitimacy in the ancient mythical hero Xolotl and validates the rule of a noble family—likely the ruling Pimentel clan.[139]

Other communities were similarly prolific (see Figure 3.1). Tlaxcala, which had every reason to tout its merits during and before the conquest, produced the most genealogies. Over thirty Tlaxcalan genealogies survive from the mid-1500s to the early 1600s.[140] Local dynasties and the city itself deployed them to secure major privileges.[141] In the words of historian Delia Cosentino, "in their genealogies, the Tlaxcalans found a powerful instrument to . . . negotiate their social and political positions in a changing world." As elsewhere, nobles used these works not only to boost their privileges but also to protect themselves against challenges from commoners and rivals.[142]

Sources in Michoacan do not attest to quite the same vibrant genealogical production as central Mexico. However, when the viceroy appointed Franciscan friar Jerónimo de Alcalá to provide a report on the

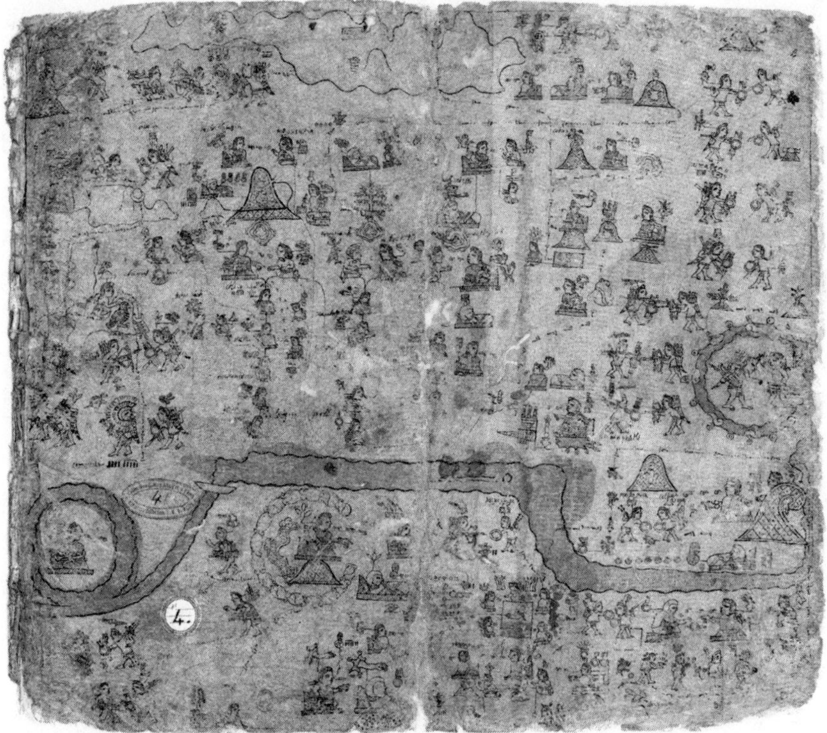

Figure 3.1 The fig-bark Xolotl map, Texcoco, circa early 1540s. This work depicts 316 Texcoca genealogies and how kin groups arrived to the Mexico Valley Basin, represented in elaborate Nahua pictographic conventions by mountains surrounding a stylized river. Gallica / Bibliothèque nationale de France, Manuscrits: Mexicain 4–10.

region's customs in 1539, hoping to render it easier to govern, one don Pedro Cuiniarangari seized the moment. Though he was of priestly and not royal Unanacaze lineage, don Pedro had already risen to the post of *cacique* through military service to the Crown, and he now used the viceroy's order to legitimate himself.[143] It was a critical moment—nine years before, President Nuño de Guzmán had executed the last ruler of Michoacan, Tangaxuan, allowing don Pedro, his enemy and Guzmán's ally, to take power. This conflict spurred the *Relación de Michoacán,* an extensive illustrated work comprising royal genealogy, *relación de méritos,* and a general description of the region.[144]

Even small territory elites could produce reams of privilege paperwork. The Indigenous Cortés-Alvarado clan sought to prove the sovereignty of its community of Tlapa-Tlachinollan with a flurry of glyphic codices telling of ancient migration, human sacrifice, and preconquest intrigues among neighbors and with and against the Mexica.[145] These postconquest documents served local Native lords in a number of succession, tributary, and land disputes before Spanish officials that fundamentally pivoted over claims of privilege and inheritance.[146] Texts were often quite bold in their inclusion of events before Christianization, centering the feats of godlike heroic ancestors. Local Mixtec Ihuitlan lords used the circa 1540 *Lienzo de Tlapiltepec* genealogy to trace their lineage back to the Toltec lords of the Palace of the Eagle and the region's two founders, Lord 13 Vulture and Lady 8 Death, in the thirteenth century. It validated their local jurisdiction, which the Mexica had unjustly taken from them.[147] Muisca engagements were simpler but still significant. During a late 1580s lawsuit between the New Granada High Court and conquistador Diego Rincón over the extent of one local Muisca lord's inherited jurisdiction, the royal protector of the Indians sought to prompt witnesses to delve into the times "before the Spanish arrived to this land . . . ten, twenty, thirty, forty, fifty years before."[148] One subordinate lord, or *capitán,* of Sogamoso, don Miguel Piramarca, responded that while he did not know how to count, he had heard from his parents and grandparents that "the said lord had and possessed" this patrimony "since God awoke the world."[149] Though Muisca litigation did not generate detailed genealogical lists, it still hinged on the authority of the preconquest and ancient past.

In Peru, similar patterns held regarding lords' genealogical claims, which featured numerous stories of the preconquest Inca. For instance, when a number of feuding lords from Chachapoyas struggled for the title of *cacique* in the 1570s, they produced competing genealogies that described ancestors' important deeds in the decades before the Spanish Indigenous conquest—even ostensibly recalling dialogues by Inca leaders from the 1520s. Seeking a resolution, the feuding lords approached auditor Diego Álvarez. Between 1572 and 1574, he investigated the claims of don Francisco Guaman, don Gómez Tomallaxa, don Alonso Chuquimis, and don Hernando Chuillaxa.[150] They each mustered dozens of Spanish and Indigenous Chachapoya and Chilcho witnesses to testify to their lineage's relationship with the Incas Huayna Capac, Huascar, and Atahualpa, and had them officially notarized.[151] Similarly, in 1570s Charcas, the powerful Aymara lord don Juan Colque Guarache submitted paperwork to local authorities and the council to prove his rightful claim to lordship. In the process, he traced his pedigree to the mid-fifteenth-century sovereign Colque, who had voluntarily joined the Inca and assisted him on numerous military campaigns. Don Juan stressed his and his father's subsequent services to the Spaniards.[152] Others cast the Inca as villains. In a remote area of Quito in the 1610s, doña Bárbara Paytaba Cando litigated for her right to the *cacicazgo* of Angamarca and noted that she was descended from the fifteenth-century sovereign Cachitocando. This lord's son Chunchuncando and grandson Tiban had been taken by the Inca as war captives to Cusco after stiff resistance.[153] For doña Bárbara, the Spanish conquest presented an opportunity to recover her family's authority in Angamarca. For many lords, postconquest paperwork opened up both grave dangers and the chance to contest and defend social privileges.

Polemics over privilege were also tied to the problem of succession; dealing with the inheritance of status was a major headache for officials. In Spanish practice, most *gracia* privileges and property passed from father to eldest son. Spaniards called this principle the *linea recta,* or straight line.[154] Yet the conquests' social and demographic ordeals had brought actors together who did not share a single idea of how to structure society, let alone the rules of privilege. The Crown and its vassals had to create rules for a society of orders, ushering Indigenous lords and conquistador claimants into new social and legal hierarchies. Royal *gracia* grants distributed privileges but did not establish enduring legal frameworks. Therefore, vassals used other channels to define how *gracia* should work in the New World. Petitioners proposed *gobierno* reforms, and *justicia* cases multiplied as disagreements flared. Officials' ability to understand cultural practices was an urgent and socially consequential problem.

These confusions were also textually productive. Claimants flooded local courts with succession-related complaints in the 1540s and 1550s. Preconquest practices of succession were highly heterogeneous and rarely conformed to the straight-line principle, making them puzzling for Indies officials. For example, Mexica, Mixtec, and Inca lords inherited jurisdiction from both mothers and fathers, but only after the approval of a council of elders.[155] When claimants invoked preconquest Indigenous marriage, polygamy, incest, and other issues, they created even greater problems for viceregal administrators.[156] In 1555, the community of *Huejotzingo* complained to the viceroy that "in past times among our peoples . . . the son did not inherit from the parents. . . . Family members gathered in the house, and having given council, picked one from among them, who seemed the most apt to rule said house."[157] The viceroy approved the request, fixing the town's succession practices into royal policy.[158] Indeed, viceroys were often flexible when provided with Indigenous claims to jurisdiction not by *linea recta*. Spanish authorities seeking to resolve succession conflicts therefore accepted Natives' "ancient customs"—*costumbres antiguas*—even when they differed sharply from European legal traditions.[159]

These problems erupted throughout the Indies. In the 1550s, Muisca claimants began litigating before the high courts and (less often) before the council, producing genealogical claims.[160] Unlike those claims in Anahuac and its surroundings, Muisca lords did not make claims about the past before the 1470s. Their debates dipped richly into inheritance customs and preconquest occurrences nonetheless, emphasizing the region's custom of authority passing from the lord to his wife's son.[161] In one famous 1570s case, two part-Spanish men inherited Native lordships through this route, generating conflict between many of the region's powerful factions. The massive ensuing lawsuits hinged largely on these and other Muisca preconquest hereditary "ancient usages," which one of the part-Spanish claimants, don Diego de Torres, argued needed to be upheld to an extent but carefully reformed to avoid association with "diabolical . . . rites and ceremonies."[162] In 1574, don Alonso de Silva, don Diego's close friend and fellow part-Spanish claimant to a Native lordship, made an almost identical claim about the "uses and customs . . . rites and ceremonies" the Muiscas had used to appoint lords in a similar lawsuit against the Crown and a fellow lord, don Miguel Holguín.[163]

Peruvian struggles were equally opaque for officials. For instance, in 1559, Spanish officials in Chillos interviewed lord Amador de Anan Chillo and other leaders on local rules of sucession. They testified that "since the time of the Inca . . . the lord or leader who dies passes his lordship to the son, and if he does not have a son or if the son is not fit to rule, the brother or the nephew inherits."[164] In Charcas, similar debates repeatedly erupted, flooding courts with information on Indigenous succession and genealogy.[165] Don Fernando Ayavire y Velasco alleged in a petition intended to begin a lawsuit that his rival claimant was ineligible for lordship; he invoked the deeply non-European concept of complementary *ayllu,* which anthropologists today call *moieties,* dualistic social divisions within a single community. Don Fernando stressed that he hailed from the correct, superior Anan moiety of the Caranga Aymaras and his rival from the inferior and illegitimate Urin. This cultural argument did not prevent don Fernando from using Castilian legal concepts, for he also accused his rival of being a bastard ineligible by *linea recta.*[166] Clearly, these actors were not merely insisting on tradition. They were prepared to strategically shift their arguments and logics to triumph.

PRIVILEGE, TAXES, AND TRIBUTE

Gracia paperwork impacted the entire social structure of the Indies, mediating a massive struggle over who got what. And if succession was a struggle over *who,* the great debates over tribute were a matter of *how* and *how much.* Spanish officials immediately understood that tribute collection and redistribution could not operate according to Iberian rules alone. But whether Indigenous commoners' tribute should be individual or collective, case by case or universal, paid to officials, conquistador-lords, Native elites, Indigenous governors, priests, friars, or others—and in what proportion—bedeviled officials. Equally puzzling was how to redistribute labor and wealth. The power of the royal administration, the status of privilege bearers, and the lives of Native elites and commoners hung in the balance.

Indies commoners had to pay taxes—theoretically, they would tithe and pay the Crown roughly 20 percent of their earnings, the so-called royal fifth.[167] Initially, most paid their conquistador-lord's agents. But for decades, officials were uncertain about how such arrangements should work.

Moreover, both Spanish and Indigenous conquistadors petitioned constantly for tax exemptions. The Mexica and Tlaxcalans, for instance, fought to maintain their tax-exempt status through countless *gracia* petitions. But paperwork about tribute did not stay within the narrow confines of the *probanza* genre. Indies subjects also sent *gobierno* reform proposals about taxation to viceroys and the council and litigated when conflicts arose.[168]

And arise they did. Beginning in the late 1520s, a wide-ranging debate about tribute systems served as a battlefield between Indies factions—each attempting to maximize benefits and sap foes' income.[169] As scholars have noted, these debates generated "substantial information" about preconquest practices in New Spain.[170] Officials often emulated preconquest practices to improve taxation. By the early to mid-1520s, Cortés and other conquistadors were already investigating Moctezuma's tribute arrangements. Royal officials complained that Cortés's depiction of the system concealed his interests.[171] However, his early administration also conserved and relied on preconquest pictographic documents, including the so-called *Tribute Codex* (*Códice de matrícula*), which during Moctezuma's reign had helped Mexica administrators exact massive amounts of tribute from his many subjects.[172] This text featured a long account of Mexica conquests, explaining Moctezuma's complex system and offering clues for how to rebuild it. A mix of Nahua glyphs for place names and tribute items represented this system, and the authors provided Spanish and Nahuatl annotations to help officials understand the contents. This work would be the first of many. By 1530, field justices had received royal instructions to seek out "painting[s] of tributes" and send these pictorial documents to the Crown to establish "the tribute which [natives] gave in Moctezuma's time."[173] Such texts, many in Nahuatl and other languages and in non-European systems of representation, swamped administrators' offices.[174]

Far from resolving the tribute dilemma, these piecemeal texts and reforms posed major interpretative challenges for officials. By the 1530s, officials had begun seeking a more consolidated, coherent tribute system. Mexico's High Court complained to the Crown in 1531 that tribute collection was hampered by rampant conflicts, fraud, and deception.[175]

The Crown responded by sponsoring a broader program of information gathering. The following year, the empress decreed that the High Court should appoint officials to again investigate "what they gave in Moctezuma's time" and by this route "reach the truth."[176] Officials soon envisioned a new typology of tribute payers. Following up on this decree, New Spain's president, Sebastián Ramírez de Fuenleal, noted in a November 3, 1532, petition to the council that "in those lands there are many types of subjects" because of both the complex conquest and the arrangements in the "time of Moctezuma."[177] He believed that understanding the transformations the Mexica had wrought in the previous five decades—that is, beginning around 1480—was key to restoring order.

The Crown's conflict with the conquistadors unsettled tributary rules again in the 1540s. The 1542 New Laws ordered officials to formalize Indigenous tribute and ensure that conquistador-lords tax them "less than they used to pay in the time of the native lords."[178] A major step in this direction was Viceroy Antonio de Mendoza's mid-1540s *Matrícula de tributos,* an extensive illustrated history of the Mexica and elaborate glyphic-alphabetic tabulation of tribute. It was partially based on Moctezuma's own documents.[179] Its perspective, however, was largely that of the workshop of Nahua commoners that supplied its many pages of glyphic illustrations and descriptions of preconquest life, death, and taxes.[180] Commoners may not have had many claims to privilege, but that does not mean they did not play a powerful role in shaping how it functioned.

Tribute collection's rules were a shifting political battlefield. As commoner complaints rose against Indigenous lords, in 1552 the Crown sent further questionnaires on preconquest tribute throughout Mexico. These royal orders suggest that vassals had reported Native lords "tyrannically" overtaxing commoners, prompting the Crown to order New Spain's High Court to investigate tribute practices "since antiquity."[181] In 1553, the Crown decreed that the viceroy and High Court should "inform yourselves and know from the old and ancient natives, under oath . . . how tribute was paid in time of their infidelity," a process that would involve consulting "any paintings or tablets or other method of counting."[182] Friars were to undertake this research. A substantial number responded in 1554 reporting interviews with elderly Natives.[183] Perhaps as part of the same inquiry, Franciscan friar Juan de San Román submitted a major report on the taxes Mexica and Tarascan rulers collected "in times of the infidelity."[184] High Judge Alonso de Zorita credited the same 1553 decree as the inspiration for his lengthy treatise on preconquest tribute systems from Guatemala to Michoacan, *Summary Relation of the Lords*, which he offered as a gift to King Philip years later.[185]

Mexican officials' efforts began to bear fruit in the 1560s, and officials gradually assembled a rough framework. Mexico's high judges sent the Crown a two-hundred-page dossier compiled between 1561 and 1562 that included the region's population tallies and statements that Natives around the capital had negotiated ludicrously low tribute rates in the 1540s and 1550s—especially considering that some specialist laborers earned vastly more than they paid.[186] During the 1550s and 1560s, audits had become increasingly common for renegotiating tribute. In the 1550s, auditor Diego Ramírez and a number of Indigenous colleagues had largely determined central Mexican tribute.[187] But perhaps after consulting the 1561–1562 reports, the council dispatched auditor Jerónimo de Valderrama to Mexico; he proceeded to hike tribute and insist that Indigenous lords stop extra tributary collections that punished shoemakers, carpenters, tailors, and painters.[188] Valderrama had come to Mexico to undermine the alliance of Indigenous lords and friars, siding with commoners and bitter conquistador-lords. His audit produced a trove of commoner codices and depicts a number of tax-related abuses. For instance, commoners documented how High Judge Vasco de Puga's wife, doña Francisca Muñiz, assaulted a Native official for failing to bring her good oranges (see Figure 3.2).[189]

Native commoners and elites petitioned, through *pinturas* (paintings) that combined Iberian and Indigenous epistemologies, to reform tribute arrangements and reshape the mechanics of privilege. The Natives of Tepeucila used *pinturas* against conquistador Andrés de Tapia, as did the community of San Juan Teotihuacan against local friars.[190] In one spectacular example, the Natives of Tepetlaoztoc waged decades of lawfare against their abusive Spanish lords. They took conquistador-lord Juan Velásquez de Salazar to trial before the council in the early 1550s,

Figure 3.2 A Nahuatl alphabetic-pictographic codex from the early 1560s depicts Judge Puga's wife, doña Francisca Muñiz (left), abusing an official, Miguel Chichimecatl (center), over a tribute dispute; she did not like the oranges he offered her (right). *Codex Osuna*/ Pintura del gobernador, alcaldes y regidores de México, Biblioteca Nacional de España, VITR/26/8.

providing some 150 pages of illustrations as evidence against him (see Figure 3.3). The litigants recounted their city's history going back to its mytho-historical wanderings, Lord Nezahualcoyotl's foundational order, and various postconquest events and tribute agreements, including one striking image of henchman Gonzalo de Salazar's abuse during tax collection.[191] This image also reveals how communities kept track of tribute payments and actors using both Nahua and Spanish conventions.

Commoners often spearheaded these cases. In 1573, a group of Mexica, Zapotec, Cholultec, and Mixtec petitioners who had conquered and settled in Guatemala submitted hundreds of pages of complaints about tribute payment and arguments for why their services made them exempt.[192] In 1579, the commoners of *Huejotzingo* sued their leaders in court, summoning a decade of elaborate tribute evidence to support their claims.[193] In 1569, the laborers of Xicotepeque sued their town governor don Miguel for overtaxation before the local field justice and managed to exile him.[194] In this way, commoners could define the parameters of Spanish and Indigenous lordly privilege. They often achieved their ends through non-European or only partially European writing conventions.[195]

In Peru, similar patterns of tribute collection and information gathering are visible, including officials' search for preconquest practices,

Figure 3.3 An illustrated and annotated document brought in the early 1550s by the community of Tepetlaoztoc against abusive conquistador-lord Juan Velásquez de Salazar. The illustration presents tax collector Gonzalo de Salazar's henchman Luis de Vaca (right) abusing two elites to extort tribute from them (center right). The goods they surrendered are depicted on the left (gold discs) and bottom right (jewels). Am2006, Drg.13964, Kingsborough Codex, © The Trustees of the British Museum.

factional struggle, and Indigenous contestation. The Pizarros had allocated tribute to their conquistador allies in the 1540s.[196] Royal forces redid these allocations, largely by interviewing Indigenous survivors. The 1543 *visita* of Caquiaviri was based on communities' knotted *quipu* cords.[197] In 1549, officials sought to understand Inca taxation by interviewing not only the lord Chincha Pulca but also Aymara workers.[198] The result provides a substantial glimpse into the workings of Inca tribute payment, products, and logistics networks, along with a demographic count of taxpayers. The fragmentary archive suggests these efforts continued in the turbulent 1550s.[199] For instance, in 1558 a friar and a Spanish field justice completed an in-depth "report and investigation" on the Chincha Valley's preconquest contributions to the Inca and the sovereign's distribution of privileges and exemptions.[200]

Perhaps more than any other official, Field Justice Polo de Ondegardo distinguished himself for his investigations into past and present Inca society. He stated that his 1561 report to the viceroy in response to the 1553 inquest was based on interviews with Cusco's eldest elites, yielding deep historical statements about the origins of Inca rule as well as commoners' payment of tribute using goods, women, and funerary sacrifices.[201] He even collected limited information on the Indigenous communities that had existed before Inca rule.[202] He produced a treatise on tribute in 1571, the *Relación histórica acerca de los Incas y del Cusco,* perhaps the longest of its type in the sixteenth-century Indies. Here, he cited his long experience as a *visitador* and field justice. He suggested that this work could help fuse the best Christian and Inca practices, thereby reducing Indigenous elites' troublesome attraction to litigation.[203]

But Ondegardo's efforts to prevent Indigenous litigation about tribute were in vain. Don Diego Tauli of Surco appeared before President Castro in 1565 in the name of himself and "the other *caciques* and Indians of this realm," complaining that authorities should redo the old headcounts invalidated by demographic collapse and inform themselves about how Indigenous peoples contributed "in the time of the Inca."[204] Castro ordered his officials to investigate. In 1567, the eminent lawyer don Francisco Falcón submitted a petition on behalf of the viceroyalty's Native leaders and commoners to authorities gathered at the Second Episcopal Council of Lima to improve Native lords' jurisdictions, authority, and reputation throughout Peru, attaching a robust analysis of Inca tribute systems.[205] In 1568, Castro responded (likely to a similar set of petitions) that he "had been informed that in the time of the Incas the sons of principal lords considered legitimate within their customs did not pay tribute," which had prompted the complaints of "some principal lords and their sons."[206]

The result of officials' haphazard, conflictive efforts and dialogues was a cocreated array of tax policies that encouraged administrators, friars, and Indigenous elites and commoners to produce countless works. These works drew creatively from both European and non-European systems of knowledge. In turn, officials used the mountains of information on demographics and society in these documents to run the empire, determine who would receive privileges, and decide how this distribution would proceed.[207] The accounts of Indigenous men and women, commoners and elites, were not apolitical but radical and partisan. And their impact was sweeping: the edifice of Indies taxation was cocreated by the sum of all of these actors and their interests.

PRIVILEGE, LAND DEBATES, AND KNOWLEDGE PRODUCTION

Territory—or more specifically, jurisdiction—proved another major headache for officials. The inheriting of status and functioning of tribute were connected to access to commoners and their communities. Yet in the radical era, jurisdictions were utterly unclear. Communities often resisted traditional lords, either refusing them outright or claiming to have an older and more important aristocracy. Interelite competition worsened the problem, as did conquistadors' and friars' meddling.

It is little wonder, then, that this era saw subjects furiously create hundreds of Indigenous maps.[208] Virtually all surviving examples come from Mexico. These works feature Latin alphabetic components but also Mesoamerican glyphic conventions, genealogies, and epic histories. Lordship was intrinsically connected to jurisdiction over land as well as to issues of communal and private property.[209] In virtually all areas of the Indies, Indigenous lords defended their jurisdiction and ownership over land against commoners, rival noblemen, and Spanish-linked outsiders. Maps were crucial proof of their claims, from the Irecha lands of Michoacan to central Mexico, the Mixtec region, Guatemala, the valleys of Santa Fe, and the Andes.[210]

These unsettled years required the defenders of elite and community land to prove their claims.[211] Native lords appeared before Spaniards to conform to a European conception of lordly patrimony, which entailed proving lordship stretching into time immemorial.[212] These claims prompted Indigenous lords to master Spanish justice and produce a vast range of documents to certify their claims. In central Mexico and other areas of New Spain, one common strategy of petitioners seeking land was to request that the viceroy grant them gracious land titles, or *mercedes de tierras.* These requests and resulting viceregal edicts numbered in the many thousands.[213] Indigenous subjects could also seek writs from conquistador-governors, Spanish municipalities, Indigenous city councils, auditors, and other authorities depending on the time and context. The volume of these complaints and petitions was substantial—in the 1590s, for instance, Tecali's male and female leaders and commoners successfully petitioned for parcels of land dozens of times.[214]

Commoners also used maps to fight back against Spanish dispossession. As epidemics battered rural communities, viceroys increasingly granted *gracia* edicts to ranchers, always under the condition (or fiction) that these farmsteads not harm locals. For example, in 1573, the viceroy granted Spaniard Joaquín de Leguizamo a ranch in Almerías, pending the approval of the town's Native commoners. They were to paint a map of the area and confirm with ten Native witnesses that no harm would come of the decision. However, some testified against Leguizamo; his effort seems to have failed.[215] The map, which combines Spanish alphabetic, spatial, and official conventions and Nahua graphic stylizations and topographical conventions, testifies that most of the land was being cultivated by commoners (see Figure 3.4).

Often, maps helped Indigenous petitioners fend off challengers within their own or neighboring communities. Multiplying disputes created a need for lords to commission more *pinturas* depicting preconquest land tenure. For example, in 1591, a governor of Tlaxcala, don Francisco Quimizotli, produced a *pintura* demonstrating "that he inherited [the land] from his parents and grandparents" to fend off "certain persons" who were trying to take his properties.[216] Others created more specific historical-genealogical claims. In don Juan Zumba's legal struggle against the Spaniard Hernando de la Parra, the lord sought to prove through Indigenous testimony that his Quito lands had belonged to his ancestors "since the time of the Inca."[217] This way, he hoped to expel both Spanish and Chachapoyas outsiders.[218]

Some of these cases involved determining who owned land not only before the conquests but in the deep past—before the rise of the Mexica and Inca. For instance, in 1576, the erudite lord don Pablo Nazareo of Xaltocan sought to prove via a *gracia* petition that he deserved his land rights recognized. He appealed to his wide and deep knowledge and culture—but also stressed that he was a "very virtuous and good Christian" who

Figure 3.4 A 1570s map depicting the community of Almerías, testifying that the region was being cultivated by commoners and that Spaniard Joaquín de Leguizamo could therefore not legitimately accept a viceroy's land grant. A large river and lagoon rendered in Nahua pictographic fashion snakes through the middle of various hamlets. AGN-Mx, Mapas, Planos e Ilustraciones, N.1535.

had studied "grammar, rhetoric, logic, philosophy, and natural theology" and had translated several biblical and theological tracts into Nahuatl.[219] Though the viceroy had given him land titles, he argued, certain Spaniards had "entered into his patrimonial lands. . . . using false petitions and proofs."[220] He attached proof of his claims (evidently now lost) in which he demonstrated, among other things, that his ancestors had been in possession of his lordship and lands since "many years before the Mexicans entered into that land."[221]

Indigenous commoners could kneecap their lords by claiming in court that they were usurpers. These conflicts often generated maps as well. In a notable 1596 case in rural Huamanga, the famed don Felipe Guaman Poma joined family members to allege that he had owned certain lands "since Topa Inca Yupanqui, the lord of these realms."[222] He and his colitigants created not only a map documenting his claims to "my lands and orchards" but also produced drawings of his father, don Guaman Malque and don Juan Tingo, who were ostensibly descendants of Inca potentates (Figures 3.5a and 3.5b).[223] Yet as his rivals the Native Chachapoyas peasants demonstrated, Guaman Poma was in reality a commoner, his maps and histories a charade designed to fool Spanish officials.[224]

Don Felipe Guaman Poma (a trial later revealed his real name was Lázaro) had learned how to twist Spanish justice to his benefit as a translator and expert witness in land border disputes. And somewhat like don Antonio Valeriano, he had found that working for churchmen—like the extirpator Cristóbal de Albornoz—was a wise move.[225] His trajectory was quintessentially *ladino*. When the Chachapoyas commoners exposed him in 1600, Lázaro embarked on the production of his sprawling Andean masterpiece, the *Nueva corónica*, which of course doubled as a petition requesting royal recognition of the author's pedigree and deeds as an official and destroyer of non-Christian practices.[226] His work was monstrously complex, an almost encyclopedic overview of the Andean past and present; it remains scholars' primary window into Andean styles of thought. Yet this disgraced commoner echoed Albornoz's own anti-idolatry research. Lázaro/Guaman Poma was providing a service to the Crown and God by delving deep into Inca and pre-Inca practices, government, concepts of time, and ideas of the sacred.[227] The Andean author expressly envisioned the work as being useful to the Crown, for it contained "things very much of the service of Your Majesty": "the descent of the realm's ancient kings . . . their prime ministers, lords, governors . . . their rites and ceremonies, costume and practices . . . and principal mines of gold and silver," among other important pieces of information. Like so many petitioners before him, he also stressed his distinguished pedigree and his parents' service against the tyrant Pizarros.[228] This canonical work is incomprehensible outside the wider context of struggles over privilege.

GRACIA AND PUBLIC REPUTATION

To an extent, council ministers and Indies officials tried to keep *gracia* paperwork in manuscript. *Probanzas* required candidates to demonstrate that their peers agreed with their claims.[229] *Gracia* petitions were therefore semipublic acts, as they required the performance and cultivation of honor.[230] Yet that does not mean that *gracia* paperwork circulated freely.

Figure 3.5a Commoner Lázaro/Guaman Poma de Ayala's paperwork sought to establish his jurisdiction over Chupas, a large rural expanse outside of Huamanga. This is an image of his alleged ancestor, Native lord don Domingo Guaman Malque de Ayala. Prado Tello File, folio 49r, Department of Manuscripts and Rare Books, The Royal Library, Copenhagen.

Once handed in to viceroys or the council, files were placed under lock and key.[231] The same was true of documents in the wider orbit of *gracia*, including officials' audits and receipts. Perhaps as a result, this vibrant world of debates about status has been little studied.

One might question whether the liberal sociological category of "the public" is applicable to the early Indies. But certainly, the idea that a

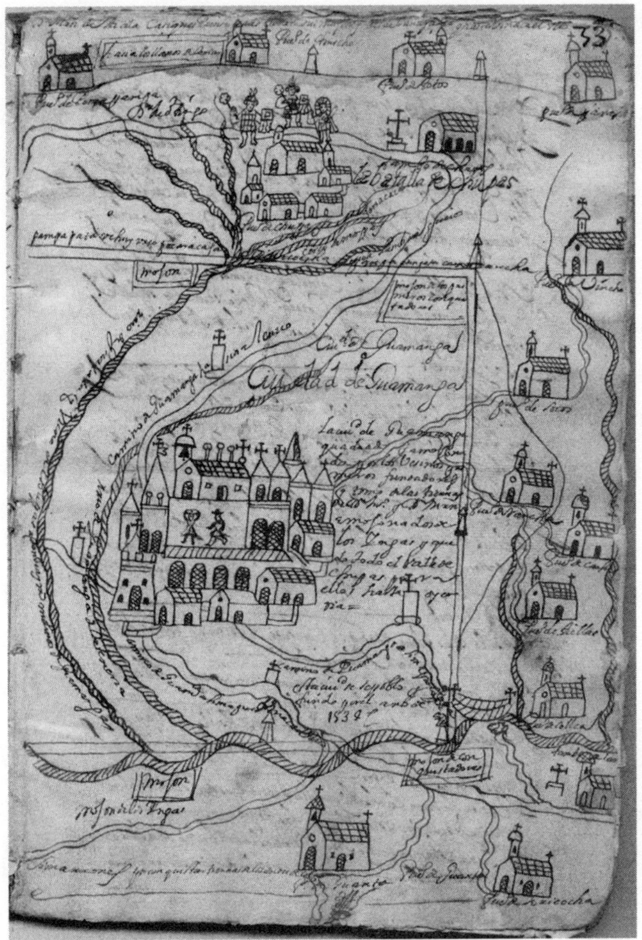

Figure 3.5b A map of Huamanga featuring Chupas (upper part of the map), the rivers of which feed into the city of Huamanga (center). Two rectangles divide this territory: a smaller boundary (*mojón*) made by conquistadors, comprising Huamanga proper, and a larger one comprising Chupas. Prado Tello File, folio 53r, Department of Manuscripts and Rare Books, The Royal Library, Copenhagen.

community could reinforce privileges through demonstrations of public acceptance was widespread. Giuseppe Bono requested the patronage of the king in 1582 partly on the basis that his "secret" wheat inventions could be spread "to all the communities and towns of your realms."[232] Mine-worker Florio Sobrano offered his engineering inventions as "beneficial for owners and the common good and the growth of the royal treasury."[233]

Rather than emphasize the future benefits of a new contraption or discovery, Damián de la Bandera claimed in his 1586 *probanza* to have shared his discoveries with mercury with miners in Potosi for years before his petition—a display of his meritorious republican virtue.[234]

Privileges required a whole world of performance both within and outside the formal *gracia* channel. Spaniards often stressed their privileges publicly through heraldry, which the Crown ratified following *gracia* petitions. Indigenous families and communities also won royal coats of arms this way. They mobilized these insignia and other works to remind their communities of the pecking order. Large-form canvas paintings, *lienzos,* placed particular emphasis on not only military feats but also conversion to Christianity. Some ninety such works survive for central Mexico, all postconquest.[235]

Of particular note are three *lienzos* from the city of Tlaxcala, the town of Analco, Oaxaca, and the Guatemalan town of San Martín Huaquechula, the communities of which created them in the decades after the conquest.[236] Like privilege seekers' *probanzas* and para-grace texts, these *lienzos* stress Indigenous communities' unwavering loyalty to the Crown—even though all three initially battled the Spanish and lost, a fact the *lienzos* elide.[237] Notably, they draw heavily from Nahua pictographic and iconographic traditions and little from alphabetic writing, although they do integrate some Latin text and abundant Christian and Habsburg iconography.[238] Few similar *lienzos* survive, once there were undoubtedly many more.[239] According to Florine Asselbergs, while the social uses of these *lienzos* cannot be fully established, they were likely used for oral retellings in public settings, certainly served as communal and juridical assertions of Native allies' deeds, and could also have been displayed before viceroys and kings.[240]

Even in remote towns, displays of *gracia* were everywhere. Anyone who visited mid-sixteenth-century Coixtlahuaca—be they Spanish official, priest, elite marriage partner, slave, or Indigenous commoner—would have found it hard to miss a massive document hanging from the lord's palace wall. This was the *Lienzo de Tlapiltepec,* a towering 1.5-by 4-meter cloth depicting complex genealogical narratives, likely produced by Mixtec elites of Coixtlahuaca in the mid-1500s.[241] From the vantage of an early or late modern European viewer, it is utterly illegible (see Figure 3.6). It depicts seated individuals with symbolic regalia arranged in various columns and clusters, a tangle of lines, and certain larger icons that suggest landscapes. There is no obvious starting point from which a European could begin to read it, and it has no script (aside from a handful of faint annotations in Chocho, which may have been added long after the 1500s). The spidery configuration of thin intersecting strokes in the Tlapiltepec document defines the whole structure of the genealogical account, which reveals its contents to the viewer through a "language of lines."[242]

It is unlikely that a newly arrived Spanish official—no matter how attuned to European and Mesoamerican genealogical thinking—could have intuitively understood the *Lienzo de Tlapiltepec*'s epistemology. The *lienzo*'s many scenes are divided by red lines, black lines, and footprint paths describing the past of Coixtlahuaca's ruling families.[243] Each connects people to towns and events over five centuries or more. One set of red lines traces relationships between ancestor groups and actors in the more recent past.[244] One binds the protagonist lineage to early conquests and settlements, another to the household of an important elite woman and her progeny. A complex series of black lines show more recent battles, alliances, settlements, and migrations that point to events just before the conquest.[245] Ancestral events on the left side thus reveal connections to historical ones on the right, suggesting that "later historical developments were understood as repetitions or fulfillments of the ancient original semi-mythical one."[246] Whoever kept the *lienzo* would have been able to read substantial information from this work—from the recent past to mythical times, regarding hundreds of nobles and their connections as well as their exploits across hundreds of kilometers of the Mixtec region.[247]

Why would individuals operating within the postconquest, European epistemological grid have created this *lienzo*? Why produce a document illegible to Spanish officials? Bas van Doesburg has outlined some of the social circumstances behind the *lienzo*, exploring the lineage of Lord 11 Vulture and his wife Lady 3 Serpent, both rulers of Coixtlahuaca just

Figure 3.6 The mid-1500s *Lienzo de Tlapiltepec,* a 1.5-by-4-meter narrative canvas *(lienzo)* depicting Mixtec lords' genealogies from the region of Coixtlahuaca. The complex image is crisscrossed by faint red and black lines that form a dynastic-spatial-mytho-historic account. On the left side are mythical events, and on the right side are more recent historical ones. These mirror one another. Together, they tell the story of how Coixtlahuaca's ruling families came to assert jurisdiction over hundreds of kilometers of the Mixtec region. Royal Ontario Museum.

before the conquest.[248] Lord 11 Vulture's claims of ancestral dominance appear rock solid in the *lienzo,* linking his genealogy back to the great houses of Lord 6 Water and Lord 6 Monkey as well as the Toltec lords of Cholula through centuries-old marriages—and even to a mythic past before the eleventh century.[249] Van Doesburg suggests that the *lienzo* was made in the mid-1500s in Lord 11 Vulture's royal palace in Coixtlahuaca and postulates based on strong evidence that two crises were affecting the by-then deceased lord's household.

One crisis we might call external or Spanish—that is, the family's vulnerability before the viceregal administration. Indigenous lords were exposed not only to the dangers of conquest and disease but also to the possibility that a viceroy might suddenly decide to appoint a temporary or permanent replacement for them. These external conflicts were, however, almost always manifestations of dissent and antilord intrigue at the community level. Why might members of the Coixtlahuaca community have been upset by the rule of Lord 11 Vulture's family? A clear reason, glossed over by the *lienzo* but not Mexica documents, is that in 1503, an eighteen-year-old Lord 11 Vulture helped Mexica forces crush a joint Mixtec-Zapotec rebellion in Coixtlahuaca.[250] The *lienzo* completely neglects to mention that Lord 11 Vulture may well have been *made* a ruler by Motecuzomah II or elevated from an obscure branch of the ruling family to the position of undisputed town leader.

The Spaniards' arrival generated an external crisis. During the crucial years of 1521–1550, Lord 11 Vulture's descendants may have struggled to justify their rule before the community. It appears that between 1530 and 1545, the titled rulers were the child don Domingo and his tutor don Diego.[251] Perhaps taking advantage of Coixtlahuaca's weak leadership, sometime around 1535, neighboring town Tequixtepec usurped (likely via the justice system) a number of its commoners and lands. In 1540, don Domingo complained before Spanish officials that these lands had been held "by his ancestors since time immemorial."[252] Other towns attempted similar expansions at Coixtlahuaca's expense, as did Huauhtla in 1552.[253]

To make matters worse, sometime during this period (likely during the late 1520s), another revolt seems to have broken out and been violently suppressed by Spanish officials or their allies, resulting in exile and forced labor in the mines for many from Coixtlahuaca.[254] Don Domingo's family was thus delegitimated from several sides—by his ancestor Lord 11 Vulture's pro-Mexica intrigues, his family's rebellion against certain Spaniards, and humiliating legal setbacks from formerly subordinate towns. In this milieu, there were many reasons for his family to elaborate a massive *lienzo* to display, perhaps in his palace. It would remind his kin of their dynasty's exploits, warn other elites not to attempt usurpation, forewarn commoner insubordination, and perform lordship before Spanish officials. *Gracia* was the most public of private affairs for Indigenous and Spanish subjects alike. It was here, more than in the world of print culture, that the Indies produced much of its most vibrant and consequential knowledge.

THOSE LEFT OUT

Gracia and its wider universe were relatively socially inclusive, enabling Spanish and Indigenous men to request or defend status. Many petitioners were commoners or middling vassals hoping to improve their lot. Moreover, broader discussions about the administration of privilege included input from commoners seeking to contest their noblemen's prerogatives.

Yet for Spanish and Indigenous women and Afro-descendants in general, claiming privilege was far more difficult. Although women did participate in the conquests, few directly requested recognition for their bravery. Those descended from enslaved Africans reckoned with considerable social stigma. Still, a number of dark-skinned conquistadors petitioned the king to request *gracia* privileges.[255] In 1538, Juan Garrido, who called himself a "resident of black color, citizen of this city" of Mexico, petitioned the king. He claimed to have planted Mexico's first wheat.[256] In some regions, Spanish governors might even give Black slaves Native tribute grants for their service.[257] Other Afro-descendants positioned themselves as royalists against insurgent conquistadors. For example, in 1568, the tailor Juan de Llerena petitioned on behalf of Mexico City's six thousand "mulatos" alleging their important "service to Your Majesty" of keeping the city safe during the turmoil of 1566–1567 associated with the Cortés-Ávila conspiracy.[258] In 1568, he requested the foundation of a hospital for non-Spanish and nonIndigenous vassals, for hospitals had been excluding Afro-descendants. Ten years later, citing the same services, he asked that the Crown reduce the tax for "mulatos y mulatas."[259] The Crown ordered the viceroy investigate. This petition presages a window of opportunity for Afro-descendants in the final years of the 1500s—participation as militiamen was a possible means of ascent. Nonetheless, claiming participation in the spiritual conquests or alleging noble ancestry was generally off the table.

One exception was the Afro-descendant leader don Antonio Sebastián de Illescas, who initially struggled against the Crown in remote Esmeraldas, Quito. He, like many others in the region, had been a runaway former slave, but through force and alliances, he came to claim the status of Indigenous lord and governor. With the help of a friar, he stressed in a 1586 letter to the king that he would offer his vassalage to conquer, evangelize, and populate the region in return for a pardon and recognition of his lordship.[260] His efforts succeeded. Don Antonio's rivals, the Afro-Indigenous Arobe family led by Francisco de Arobe, would later claim similar privileges.

These unique Afro-Indigenous lords had tapped into a world of privilege most could only dream of. In 1599, Quito's High Magistrate Juan del Barrio de Sepúlveda sent the new king, Philip III, a magnificent portrait of the Arobes by the Indigenous painter Andrés Sánchez Gallque. Del Barrio wrote:

> Being of the impression that Your Majesty would like to see these barbarians (who have until now proven invincible) in portrait, it would be a most extraordinary thing to send with their letter and report to Your Majesty; they are well-disposed men, agile, and very limber. . . . They are rendered in this portrait in a lifelike manner . . . except in their clothing, which they received after they rendered their peace and obedience."[261]

The high magistrate made no secret of it: the famous portrait was not just a gesture of surrender useful for these Afro-Indigenous lords' future pretensions as a frontier nobility. It was also part of del Barrio's own request for privileges. The next section of the report is a list of "labors of the aforementioned Doctor del Barrio which have been undertaken and which remain to be in service of God and His Majesty . . . which are very notorious and proven in his deeds and other testimonies."[262] Even the painting of Arobe itself, now one of the most famous in Latin American history, was a ploy to win favor in the court, a piece in the game of *gracia*. For its upwardly mobile Indigenous painter, Andrés Sánchez Gallque, this commission increased his social status in Inca and Spanish circles in Quito; little wonder his son later received the title of don.[263]

Yet the cases of Garrido, Llerena, Illescas, and Arobe were rather extraordinary in the 1500s. As Spanish officials attempted to distribute privileges, slave origins and lack of Indigenous or European mobility excluded a large swath of Indies subjects. Women petitioned for *gracia* more often, signing perhaps 6 percent of all *probanzas*.[264] They stood to inherit not just small pensions but considerable privileges, including vast conquistador lordships.[265] Yet they most often claimed these as relatives of men, especially as wives and widows. A certain doña Inés of Lima, widow of Francisco Martín de Alcántara, pleaded in 1543 for the privilege of Indigenous tribute, both on the deeds of her husband and in recognition that she had been "the first married woman who entered those lands and began to populate it."[266] We have already seen that in 1562, doña Beatriz de Salcedo also petitioned from Lima asking for recognition of her husband's deeds and her own agricultural enterprises. Elite Indigenous women similarly petitioned often, seeking to inherit their family's lordship or the privileges for royal service. In some cases, this included the right to directly rule over their communities.[267] Clearly, however, the logics and practitioners of *gracia* strongly favored men and their swaggering achievements.

GRACIA'S TRANSFORMATION IN THE SOCIETY OF ORDERS

In the early 1600s, at virtually the same time that don Bartolomé Inca y Orozco was in Madrid marketing his cyphered inventions to the king, another Inca was also in the court. Don Melchor Carlos Inca arrived with a very different project, which reflected a gradual and subtle but important change in the praxis and epistemology of *gracia* paperwork. He was aiming high: he sought the extremely prestigious Habit of the Order of Santiago. In 1606, he submitted his petition to the Council of Orders. His mother was of Extremadura's low nobility, but he was also the direct grandson of the Inca lord Paullu.[268] This entitled don Melchor to the privileges won by Paullu, inheritor of Huayna Capac and a friend of the Christians during the conquests who had led an army of fifteen thousand against the rebel Manco Inca. Similarly, Paullu's son don Carlos Inca, father of don Melchor, had distinguished himself by fighting against the tyrant conquistador-rebel Fernández Girón.

Royal officials conducted a customary secret investigation throughout Madrid. Numerous prominent Spanish witnesses in the capital agreed that it was "public and widely noted" that don Melchor was legitimate, and because Inca lords had received tribute in antiquity, he made a fitting candidate as a *señor* and member of the order. The dossier also appended a 1600 viceregal investigation into don Melchor's lineage, drawing on Cusco's oldest Native and Spanish witnesses and certified by the president of the Council of the Indies. The file stressed that while Huayna Capac and his partner Iñas Collque had not married according to Spanish custom, they had "lived a married life according to their rites" and celebrated the birth of Paullu and recognized him as their son.[269] It was thus only fair that don Melchor ask for a massive pension of 30,000 pesos a year. The Council of Orders agreed—and don Melchor received the habit.

But don Melchor had played the council. The unpleasant truth is that his grandfather Paullu had not been, after all, the direct descendant of Huayna Capac according to Spanish convention. Paullu was the son not of Huayna Capac's main spouse but of a Yaucu woman; for Spaniards, he might be a bastard or at least an out-of-wedlock son.[270] Perhaps for this reason, don Melchor seems to have continued seeking evidence of his legitimate claim to the Inca title. Following his 1607 victory, feeling his old age and likely planning to help his out-of-wedlock son Juan Melchor in a future struggle over privilege, the solution dawned on him. He needed special proofs, those of the sort people no longer produced in the early 1600s: eyewitness accounts of immediate postconquest society.

Evidently, don Melchor asked a friend in Cusco for a hand.[271] A certain Friar Antonio, perhaps his old ally the Augustinian friar Antonio Martínez, drew up a report on Inca antiquities that supported his claims. Among the documents were enigmatic 1542 statements that Cusco's surviving "old Inca" *quipucamayocs*, the keepers and readers of *quipu* cords, had made before Viceroy Vaca de Castro. The *quipucamayocs* traced their origins, the rise of Tihuantinsuyo, and the events of the conquests, especially stressing the good deeds of Huayna Capac's son don Cristobal Paullu Topa. Scholars today largely agree that this document has elements of forgery, perhaps during or after the 1560s; its internal inconsistencies are too great.[272]

But perhaps more importantly, the basis of Inca claims in the late 1500s and early 1600s were drawn from the authority of *quipu* cords. For as the text notes, "these quipucamayocs had been sorts of historians or accountants."[273] This case therefore reveals how *gracia* epistemology changed as the society of orders took form. In 1550, a beleaguered lord could insist before a Spanish official that he had been appointed lord by Motecuzomah or had resisted the Mexica, and his peers and subjects could support him, providing statements administrators would hold as authoritative. In 1600, however, these ancient Indigenous witnesses had passed. Their children—and more likely their grandchildren—were not eyewitnesses. They could reiterate tellings of what came before, but nothing more. The scarcity of authorities on preconquest antiquity and the conquests made such statements a commodity. Yet struggles for privilege continued to rage in the seventeenth century. Sometimes, documents would have to simply appear. The society of orders demanded it. Don Melchor had documents forged to cleanse his grandfather's lineage, Paullu's, and thus ease his own entry into a military order. As we saw in Chapter 2, the forgery of documents in the Bajio among the Otomi secured many seventeenth-century families of commoners deep genealogies and claims to lordship.

When vassals secured documents from this essential period of radical disruption, they treasured them. Conquistadors, Indigenous lords, Indigenous-Spanish dynasties, and Spanish and Native communities especially venerated them, knowing that in these documents rested access to privilege, tax exceptions, special access to viceregal officials, and everyday prestige.

And so it was that in the society of orders, struggles over privilege became archival struggles. A phase of pure *gracia* creation gave way to a custodial phase. This phase, in turn, taught ambitious subjects to treasure the epistemologies of the radical era even as they increasingly copied, transcribed, and superseded old genealogies, maps, and other sources. When conflicts erupted, the oldest and most epistemologically curious documents were often the most precious.

In 1678, the Mexican High Court heard yet another long-simmering quarrel. This case was between two feuding members of the Guzmán family, a well-established dynasty of Indigenous lords from Coyoacan in the Mexico Valley. One side, led by the self-declared *mestizo* don Juan Hidalgo Cortés Moctezuma y Guzmán, claimed descent from the Mexica as well as the rival Tepanecs' forefather Acolnahuacatliacatel and the Chichimec lord Tztontecomatl and lady Tzompachtli.[274] On the other, their relatives and rivals doña María de Guzmán and Tomás de Parrales claimed the lordship belonged to them, offering similarly powerful arguments.

In some ways, this litigation reveals how little had changed since the mid-sixteenth century. The litigants each had Nahuatl documents, witnesses, emphasis on the differences between succession customs of Spaniards and Natives, illustrations, tribute records, and genealogies reaching deep into the past.[275] The Coyoacan lords' cases echo the sixteenth century but reveal nonetheless an astonishing transformation in communicational styles between the 1550s and 1680s. During the radical phase, claimants to Coyoacan lordship might have presented handfuls of valuable documents—recent witness statements, fresh royal decrees, viceregal edicts, notarial documents like Nahuatl testaments, a smattering of Spanish justices' determinations. But this 1680s lawsuit shows that already by 1600, Native lords' archives had exploded in size and complexity. Both sides mustered over four centuries of Coyoacan history and a maze of postconquest paperwork proof. Though the Coyoacan case only survives in fragmentary form, we know that between 1678 and 1681, Spanish authorities read at least 259 documents. The earliest Spanish source was dated 1537, and the vast majority dated from 1540 to 1580.[276]

Indigenous lords, and indeed nearly every social group in the Indies, voraciously collected archives to wage lawfare. With each passing year, archives grew. Countless documents wound up in these collections: *gobierno* and *gracia* decrees, *justicia* rulings, tribute records, baptismal certificates, notarial writs of every kind, genealogies, personal correspondence, codices, pious donations. The list of archive-hoarding corporations was equally vast: families, brotherhoods, convents, monasteries, bishops, cathedral councils, cities, inquisitors, local officials, royal administrators, and beyond. Virtually everything was at stake in this collection. Property, wealth, and debt—from a few pesos to hundreds of thousands—were in jeopardy. Even more important was social status: family privileges, honor, legitimacy. Often it was both riches and prestige—lordship, pensions, tribute exemptions. These stories were the stuff of power and privilege.

A gradual but profound transformation had taken place in how actors structured their society and debated their place within it. In 1550, striking Indigenous codices, memories of elders, and eyewitness accounts of conquistadors and their victims held great weight. In the 1600s, a petitioner or litigant living in the core of the empire could scarcely hope to triumph by simply producing and presenting such works. Instead, a successful *gracia* or *justicia* case now relied on combining current testimonies with over a century of past sources. In the 1550s, it was typical for conquistadors to formulate stories of their experiences of the conquest; in the 1650s, their descendants merely cited and recounted their ancestors' glorious actions, attaching a parade of favorable decrees and testaments. Indigenous lords continued to elaborate genealogies—some of them wildly epistemologically different from Spanish ones—but more often relied on century-old family accounts, which they pulled out of wooden chests and presented to Spanish and Indigenous authorities. When don Juan Hidalgo presented himself in 1678, he argued that he possessed Coyoacán's lordship thanks to the "privileges and royal decrees of his Majesty the Lord Emperor Charles the Fifth, of Good Memory."[277] The Coyoacan litigants clung to documents from the 1530s and 1540s like their lives depended on them. And in many ways, their lives did.

Rather paradoxically, then, this postradical society of orders rested on the foundations of disorder and radicalism. The texts that vassals had produced in the 1500s became the pillars of a more stable world of privilege. In the 1680s, the Coyoacan litigants were struggling both with each other and with the legacy of the radical phase. In fact, most sources they cited came not from the 1680s but from the period of 1540–1580, when this important city-state's rulers faced their worst crises of legitimacy. Royal decrees, Mexica city council orders, Nahuatl testimonies, tribute lists, Mesoamerican property maps and genealogies, and other sources peppered the case. The texts even told of how the Hidalgo family had weathered the 1567 abolition of the massive marquisate of don Martín Cortés. Coyoacán's rulers had lost administrative control over their governorship when the viceroy had appointed the ambitious outsider don Constantino Huitzimengari, heir of the fallen Irecha lords of Michoacan, in the early 1600s. But the local elites survived, and now the Hidalgos claimed their privileges—in part from having married into don Constantino's family.[278] Though this litigation tells of how the Nahua family closest to the Irecha don Constantino triumphed, it tells yet another story, one in which aristocratic power is everywhere triumphant. By 1593, the Crown had restored the confiscated Marquisate of the Valley to the redeemed Cortés family. As this conquistador clan gradually recovered its jurisdiction over their marquisate and new challengers sought the Native lordship of Coyoacan in 1730, the High Court ordered the privative judges of the Marquisate of the Valley to issue a determination. It was not only Indigenous lords like the Huitzimengari and feuding Guzmáns who had survived but also the Cortés dynasty and others who managed unlikely jurisdictional comebacks. And so the case disappeared deep into the Marquisate of the Valley, where the trail goes cold.

CONCLUSIONS

Ultimately, the story of *gracia* paperwork is a story of Indigenous politics orbiting around royal and viceregal privileges. It is a story that invites us to recognize an alternative sociology of early modern knowledge production. To read along the archival grain is to see how *gracia*'s procedures enabled many vassals to contest social structures and request privileges.[279]

Manuscript culture could drive global conquest, natural discovery, conversion, history writing, and more. In the process, *gracia* paperwork and associated texts spurred a monumental invention of tradition—a veritable conquest of the past. And while the channel of *gracia* was indeed massively violent and elitist, it also featured important epistemic and socially participatory openings. Indigenous politics, in particular, was everywhere in *gracia* paperwork.

As vassals took to paperwork to achieve and contest privilege, they dismembered and reassembled New World society. It was not just violence and disease but also subjects' conflicts over the rules of privilege that devastated traditional societies and thwarted the seigneurialism of conquistadors, friars, and Native lords. In this way, *gracia* constituted the inverse of the antityranny efforts traced in Chapter 1. While antityranny highlighted powerful figures' flaws and demerits, *gracia* highlighted claimants' merits and services to the Crown. Antityranny movements represented vassals' efforts to destroy the privileged; *gracia* did the opposite. Commoners and enslaved Natives could use *gracia* to socially reinvent themselves as lords while conquering and settling the frontier, as so fatefully occurred in the Mexican north. Indeed, the story of globalization can scarcely be separated from privilege paperwork, since it was this system that made such ventures both feasible and socially desirable.[280]

Gracia contributed to both continental disorder and the gradual emergence of a society of orders. It greatly strengthened the vassal-king bond, as the promise of reward generated consent. As Crown-affiliated viceroys, bishops, and inquisitors beat back seigneurialism, they increasingly controlled local distribution of *gracia*, cementing the social order in ways that were elusive during the radical era. But even more powerful was the role of the archive. Individual Spanish and Indigenous families and communities assembled huge collections of *gracia* paperwork. Subjects' struggles for status within the society of orders increasingly depended on control over such compendia, which invariably prized privileges. The descendants of families and corporations that had created these documents came to obsessively care for them. This custodial devotion to old royal decrees and documents was a major source of affection for the monarchs as well.

From countless musty leather chests emanated individual, family, and community consent and a society that embraced shared archival truths.

Subjects in the 1600s and 1700s were in awe of this past. Ironically, over time this era of radical creation became the epoch of heroic conquests and the last window into antiquity and time immemorial. A great radical era, then, was concealed by subjects' constant reinventions of tradition. Curiously, by reinventing *gracia* documents as apolitical reflections of culture and ancient civilizational heroism, many radical activists in the liberal era have managed to appeal to Latin America's timeless traditions. Although we might forget its centrality, *gracia* still shapes our ideas of what radical change looks like in the Americas, often through the guise of tradition. This obscure paperwork channel continues to conquer everything, not least our imaginations.

CHAPTER 4

The Traps of Doubt

Skepticism and Radical Politics in the New World

In 1584, the wizened Chiapanec lord don Juan Atonal clashed with the bishop of Chiapas, Pedro Feria. It was David versus Goliath. The bishop's honor was at stake—as was don Juan's very life. Bishop Feria had been undertaking an ecclesiastical audit of the highland Guatemala communities of Chiapas and Suchiapa when he heard a hair-raising report of apostacy, idolatry, and black magic among Chiapanec elites. A group of Indigenous commoners warned Feria that certain Native men and women had created an unlicensed religious sodality, calling themselves "the twelve Apostles" and "the great Junta." They made the rounds at night, publicly claiming to be able to transform into gods and goddesses, bring rain and storms, and bestow wealth on their followers. The powerful don Juan was their protector, along with his son Cristóbal, who had recently been expelled from Chiapas for incest with his mother-in-law. Bishop Feria had his assistant round up "information from many eyewitnesses, men and women, discovering the gravest things"—sexual crimes, sacrifice, idolatry. Feria fumed that these elites had fabricated their Catholic piety, showing "exterior signs of Christianity [and] . . . that although Juan Atonal is considered by all to be a saint, it has been revealed through these reports that he is a demon."[1]

The bishop had a powerful hand, as few accusations were more serious than idolatry. But don Juan had several aces up his sleeve—including the trump card of doubt. Indeed, even before Feria arrived at Chiapas, he and his son were one step ahead. Although Feria tried to surprise don Juan and don Cristóbal, he found they had skipped town, heading to the Guatemalan High Court to speak with their close friend, the president. Don Juan had also allied himself with the Dominicans, who now stubbornly refused to participate in Bishop Feria's trial. The bishop wrote with surprise that when he warned that he would report these indignities to the Crown, his Dominican rivals responded "with much anger and indignation that he was threatening them with the king, and that if I were to write, they would write too, with just as much truth as I." The High Court intervened. Its attorney, speaking as the voice of the alleged idolaters, "submitted a petition alleging they had been aggrieved with cruel imprisonments." This lawyer doubted the allegations of idolatry. As a result, authorities freed the accused from jail and instructed the local Spanish field justice in Chiapas to defend them.

The bishop despaired that don Juan's clique had "returned happily to their houses, laughing to themselves about ecclesiastical justice." He described how don Juan and some fifteen to twenty of his comrades had entered Chiapas victorious, "having triumphed over Jesus Christ and his faith and his Church and his laws, and the Indians said publicly that everything is a joke, except for the field justice and the King, and that the bishops and friars had tried to fool them with their churches and their laws."[2] Using the justice system, alliance making, and a coy manipulation of doubt, don Juan and his allies had made a mockery of Bishop Feria and the son of God himself.

It was almost impossible to persecute don Juan, the prelate thundered. The Dominicans would support the influential Chiapanec with a story that would make the council question everything about the bishop's account. The High Court's lawyer considered Feria's charges insufficient and the witnesses' story questionable. But Feria did not lose hope, for he heard another story he thought might give him the upper hand. During his countryside audit, he was approached by some eighty to one hundred old Natives, all vassals of don Juan. They brought with them a royal decree in Chiapanec in which the king "admonished me . . . to take care of them and defend them." They requested the bishop punish their lord for fraudulently underreporting some two hundred tributaries and passing the burden to the elderly. The bishop, eager to certify their statements, brought a notary. The bishop sent a 1585 report to the bishops of Mexico, but its outcome is unclear.[3] In 1587, don Juan remained powerful, and Feria died in 1588, suggesting that the Chiapanec emerged triumphant from the dispute.[4]

The struggle between don Juan and the bishop in some ways confirms the liberal and decolonial sociologies of a dogmatic, hierarchical empire, featuring a powerful and intolerant man's accusations of Indigenous sacrifice, idolatry, and apostacy. But there is another story here, for David outsmarted Goliath. His weapons were not foot-dragging, rebellion, or midnight sabbaths—he played by the rules of paperwork. He built alliances with the Dominicans and High Court.[5] He and his allies then cast the powerful prelate's motives and witnesses into question. Feria knew his failure to arrest and possibly execute don Juan had publicly undermined the authority of the church. The Chiapanec lord had used doubt and paperwork to work the system and had prevailed, upending the social hierarchy Bishop Feria sought to impose.

Don Juan's defiance was by no means unique, yet stories of this sort of disobedience and manipulation of doubt have had no place in enduring metanarratives. In the liberal vision, genealogies of skepticism travel straight from ancient Greece to the Reformation, the Enlightenment, and ultimately democratic modernity, propelled by the printing press.[6] According to some, a culture of doubt put England and its colonies on the pathway to freethinking radicalism; everywhere else, authorities cracked down and imposed dogma.[7] Such accounts of European skepticism virtually always avoid considering absolutist Catholic Iberian traditions, let alone New World traditions.[8] The empire, after all, established the Inquisition—and where skepticism did not thrive, tyranny took hold. Decolonial accounts have tended to view the Spanish conquests as the source of a theocratic-capitalist modernity that imposed uncompromising dogma on the New World's many inhabitants.[9] In the civilizational-culturalist account, meanwhile, the struggles of actors like don Juan appear as abstract, depersonalized conflicts between Indigenous tradition and insincere conversion.[10] And lastly, Hispanism largely has emphasized skepticism as a virtue belonging to authors like Miguel de Cervantes—at the expense of those like don Juan the Chiapanec lord. There is little space to acknowledge the centrality of the radical politics of skepticism in this era.

The liberal, decolonial, and culturalist approaches have some merit, of course. After all, Feria argued that don Juan was a false Christian through and through. The story of a powerful, dogmatic man's persecution of a Native community and its leader is plain to see. But it is not the whole story. Don Juan's Catholic allies disagreed with the bishop's charges; theirs was an exemplary, almost saintly man. And everyone involved knew that the deeper truth of don Juan's faith would remain forever elusive, unknown to anyone but himself. Indeed, it was largely irrelevant. Whether one believed that he secretly led a cabal of satanic apostles had more to do with one's factional allegiance than with facts. This was a contest of wits and politics that pitted don Juan's faction against his episcopal and Native foes, not merely a struggle between dogma and insurgent Indigenous resistance.

It was largely through this sort of skeptical subterfuge that many vassals like don Juan engaged in radical politics against the powerful—often successfully. In much scholarship, sixteenth-century Indies society appears as the dogmatic opposite of a skeptical society, as either skepticism's total absence or its dogmatic nemesis. Yet although several influential metanarratives have denied or elided the existence of skepticism in the Indies, questions about the truth were actually a fundamental part of everyday life and the system of Crown paperwork. In fact, doubt was a key ingredient in the making of the radical Spanish Empire. It both arose from and fueled hard-nosed questioning of authority—and, in turn, social transformation.

Maureen Ihrie defines the core elements of skepticism as "prudence, caution, close and careful examination of all things" and characterizes it as a broad philosophy that "questions whether it is possible for man ever to possess or obtain any certain knowledge."[11] Others have defined skepticism more narrowly as a philosophical position rooted in ancient Greek thought—a more narrow understanding that many now question. Scholars have begun asking: was skepticism the special heritage of Europeans, and especially northern European Protestants, who recovered and fulfilled ancient Greek philosophy? Or must we rethink skepticism altogether? Revisionists offer at least four alternative ways of thinking about histories of truth and doubt. The first is universalist: all people, even nonphilosophers, have employed skepticism.[12] The second rejects purism: there are no absolute skeptics, only those who strongly question perception before eventually insisting on a truth.[13] Third, empirical research has revealed many historical cultures of doubt in other societies,[14] including Spain's own intellectual and literary traditions of doubt.[15] For instance, Mercedes García-Arenal has argued that a wide array of epistemological skepticisms existed in Iberian society.[16] Fourth, some scholars have theorized a specific culture of judicial skepticism, noting that early modern administrators' and dissident subjects' quarrels forced them to reckon with the elusive nature of truth.[17] Skepticism need not always concern God's nature; in fact, most scholars agree that proponents of early modern doubt generally remained steadfast in their faith.[18]

Nevertheless, research on participatory administrative-judicial skepticism in the early Spanish New World remains almost entirely *terra incognita*. A select few have noted the promise of this direction. As Leticia Mayer Celis writes, "What happened in that world which began to globalize? The emotions and passions mixed: fear, hatred, disparagement, compassion, but above all, doubt ruled supreme."[19] The skeptical thinking that emerged from this global encounter, she and José Luis Egío have argued, stimulated Spanish Dominicans, Jesuits, and others to develop the methodology of skeptical probabilism, a practical philosophical current that dominated Europe's judicial practices for decades.[20]

Most relevant for our purposes is Arndt Brendecke's work on the Council of the Indies. He argues that the council—and the empire—largely operated through an enduring indifference to the truthfulness of facts; ministers knew that petitions were false and nonetheless answered them. As Brendecke argues, in this premodern world, "manipulation *always* takes place."[21] This situation ensured that vassals could communicate with the Crown in a sort of "permanently politicized" exchange, helping a far-flung monarchy reap the loyalty of its subjects at the expense of facticity.[22]

We argue, similarly, that the sixteenth-century New World's radical circumstances fostered one such culture of doubt; many actors claimed God's unquestionable existence while questioning mankind's ability to grasp virtually any other truth. In the sphere of paperwork, doubts about the truth were particularly pronounced. In fact, contemporaries insisted that this momentous and distressing overseas expansion had created not only administrative-juridical problems but also epistemological challenges that those in Europe could scarcely grasp. At least according to Indies vassals, this era had unleashed problems of epistemological uncertainty unseen in the Old World. For those hoping to subvert the emerging order, uncertainty was a powerful tool to undermine the power of local elites and even question whole social structures. We thereby expand on Brendecke's argument by staking that radicalism proliferated in large part thanks to this culture of doubt, which itself was strongly connected to paperwork. In contrast to Brendecke, however, we discern the crucial division of council and local Indies paperwork into *gobierno*, *gracia*, and *justicia* and clarify exactly which political strategies vassals could employ. We also depart from the social milieu of the Council of the Indies to the New World, where the consequences of radicalism become even more dramatic. We trace concrete measures that officials developed in response to radical doubt, demonstrating that the Crown did not remain crippled by skepticism and indifferent to truth forever.

This chapter argues that a widespread secular and practical vernacular-administrative skepticism permeated Indies paperwork, offering vassals considerable room to question authority. Virtually all contemporaries outwardly professed unwavering faith in the Trinity, but when it came to judicial-administrative affairs, officials recognized how little they knew. Vassals made sure to constantly remind them of their ignorance. In the Indies, officials realized, the truth was fragmented, possessed by no single person or administrative body. Distance from Europe rendered New World realities difficult for vassals to communicate to overseas superiors. Virtually all subjects resorted to forcing complex ideas onto brief, lifeless

Figure 4.1 An ecclesiastical mayordomo (fiscal) is compelled by a priest to turn over ink and paper to stop production of paperwork that could incriminate the priest. Felipe Guaman Poma de Ayala. *El primer nueva corónica y buen gobierno* (1615/1616), p. 636, GKS 2232 4°, Department of Manuscripts and Rare Books, The Royal Library, Copenhagen.

pieces of paper. Many despaired that Indies petitions' materiality, narrative structure, and reliance on inadequate written language smothered the truth. Vassals had to play with words, accusing rivals of impassioned factionalism, twisting legal categories, and resorting to hyperbole to stir officials to action. Hyperbole often painted whole groups, even the entire

Indies, as wicked. Others pushed back against the strategy of hyperbole, urging self-restraint, simplicity, and equal treatment of all subjects. In this struggle, the truth stood no chance; all that was left was uncertainty.[23] Radical questioning of the truth of law and the validity of the society of orders had profound social consequences, as don Juan and his allies so masterfully taught Bishop Feria (see Figure 4.1).

Throughout the chapter, we include images from *Nueva corónica y buen gobierno* (1615) to illustrate Guaman Poma's repeated complains on the utter unreliability of testimonies in the colonial archive As introduced in Chapter 3 and argued in Chapter 5, the *Nueva corónica* was an eleven-hundred-page analysis of the Indigenous politics of deception, manipulation, and triangulation of testimonies that characterized petitioning and paperwork in the sixteenth century. Guaman Poma organized his entire *gracia* and *gobierno* petition on how to reform and secure credibility in a world of total hermeneutical suspicion over identity and truth. We take Guaman Poma to be an extraordinary ethnographic informant on the politics of Andean deception, witness manipulation, and identity counterfeiting. The images we include reveal this unnoticed aspect of his work.

RADICAL DISRUPTION AND STATUS ANXIETY

Doubt in the sixteenth century touched all aspects of Indies life. Among the most important to the structure of society was skepticism about status. *Gracia* petitioning was so participatory and intuitive that virtually anyone could attempt a reinvention. On the peninsula, especially after the establishment of Madrid as the court, countless commoners created new identities for themselves. The rougher characters among them earned the famous moniker of *pícaro* and became the subject of numerous plays.[24] In the Indies, such entrepreneurial reinventions extended not only to the vast, uprooted Spanish population but also to Indigenous subjects. The pillars of the society of orders—claims to aristocracy and lordship—had been shattered. The basis of reconstruction should have been the truth, but who was willing to tell a true story about their origins?

Many feared that officials would not be able to replicate Spain's stable social order in the New World. High Judge Tomás López wrote to a Franciscan colleague in the Yucatan in 1562 that royal privileges elevated the wicked while justice officials punished the virtuous.[25] It was not just a matter of outright malice by Crown officials, he stressed—all writing coming from the New World was distorted. He lamented, "One of the ills of the Indies is that not everything is always well-understood . . . [many] write and certify matters very contrary to how they are."[26] López echoed a theme that applied to officials, friars, conquistadors, and others. An anonymous high-ranking official wrote a similar report, likely in the 1590s, calling New World vassals—especially conquistadors and miners—masters of "pretenses and sophistical reasoning."[27] Commoners and elites alike engaged in duplicitous writing, blurring the distinctions between these social groups.

The widespread culture of distrust owed in large part to the radical defiance conquistadors had shown the Crown from the 1540s to the 1560s. Many groups mobilized paperwork against these tyrants, muddling the integrity of privilege distribution in the process. A hierarchical world had not emerged. Instead, the Indies had become a society of disorder in which the aristocracy and empire itself engaged in deceiving each other. Local Indies officials often tried to defuse the tension by tolerating former rebels, but mutual suspicion still ran deep. A Dominican friar warned in a top-secret report circa 1550 that many Spaniards had two-timed Crown officials, switching from the rebel camp or outright covering up their acts of treason. For instance, Martín de Robles, the man responsible for killing the viceroy and placing his head on a pike, had turned on the insurgents and now lived comfortably as a conquistador-lord. The Dominican urged the Crown not to proceed against everyone all at once but to "dissimulate" and gradually and selectively expel traitors under the pretext of living un-Christian lives.[28] This sort of report taught ministers a hard lesson about Indies governance. They would have to learn to both distrust the conquistadors and mask their own programs. Conquistadors, meanwhile, resented that they had won the New World but not the Crown's faith—and had few qualms about twisting the truth in turn. Dissimulation thus became endemic, in both the court and the Indies.

The Spaniards who arrived after the conquests may not have presented the same societal danger as the conquistadors, but they were no less wily.

In a world of unprecedented, globe-spanning mobility, Europeans could reinvent themselves and their status with considerable ease. Just as traitors could become gentlemen, so too could newly arrived commoners shape-shift into elites. This mobility inspired both earnest denunciations and mordant parodies. One Franciscan noted in the mid-1560s that the identities of so-called Spaniards arriving to Mexico were completely uncertain: "It is not known if they are Spanish, or French, or English, or Greeks or Latins, nor if they are Christians or pagans—rather, anyone can be whatever he pleases."[29] Even living outwardly as a well-known Christian citizen was no guarantee of a man's faith. A 1700 chronicle of Potosi (drawing from earlier Portuguese reports) spun an entertaining tale about one such trickster.[30] In 1562, a certain Captain Zapata discovered a precious vein of silver in Potosi. He became the epitome of a gentleman, known for his "many excellencies and moral virtues" as well as his "very beautiful and grave manner."[31] The city was shocked to discover after his departure that he had been a Greek born in Turkey. After decades of living in Potosi with "a rare secrecy, and dissimulation," he had returned to Istanbul, reverted to Islam, and become "an enemy of God" in the service of the Ottoman sultan.[32]

Some found humor in this disorder. In 1598, a certain Mateo Rosas de Oquendo torched Lima's would-be privilege seekers in a memorable satire. Something about the ocean crossing turned vinegar into wine—and Spain's commoners into Peru's aristocrats.

Que buena fuera la mar	Oh if only the sea were so kind,
Y amiga de gente grave	and such a friend of important folks,
Si lo que haze con los vinos	if what it did to wines,
Hiciera con los linaxes	it also did to lineages,
Que avinagrando ruines	turning the bad ones into vinegar,
Los buenos perfisionase	and perfecting the good;
Mas con contrarios efectos	But see the contrary effects
Los que en estos casos haze	That in this case apply,
Que a los baxos haze nobles	For the lowborn become nobles,
Y a los nobles ganapanes.	And the nobles ruffians.[33]

Once these commoners reached Lima, many began refashioning themselves—including through paperwork. Now, they claimed,

Todos fueron en Castilla	All of them were, in Castile,
Amigos de personaxes;	The friends of great figures,
Su padre fue en un Castillo	His father in a castle
Veinte y seis años alcaide	Twenty-six years a prefect . . .
Luego se van al Virrey,	Then they go to the viceroy,
Que importa mucho el hablalle.	With whom speaking is most important . . .
Maquinan torres de viento,	They dream up windmills;
Conciben mil necedades,	And contrive a thousand fatuities,
Uno pide situaciones,	One requests apportionments,
El otro pide eredades,	The other patrimonies,
El otro repartimientos,	The other Native labor,
Otro pretende casarse;	The other intends to marry;
El uno pide Ariquipa,	One requests Arequipa,
El otro pide los Andes.	The other the whole Andes.[34]

The poet goes on to mock Lima's culture of counterfeit achievements and false identities. He admonishes it and proclaims a Christian solution: to embrace one's lowly origins and the virtues of work. He reminds his readers,

Cosa vil es la nobleza,	A lowly thing is nobility,
Pues tales efectos haze:	For it produces these effects,
Busquemos todos oficios,	Let us all seek out trades,
Que ellos dan las calidades.	For it is these that grant us our qualities.[35]

Rosas de Oquendo boldly rebutted the falsehoods of status and celebrated the value of work—but also called for a return to a society of orders in which everyone would dutifully remain in their place. His poem is as much a denunciation of the radical promise of the New World as an idealization of the society of orders gradually emerging there. Rosas Oquendo resurfaced again in 1621 when one Pedro Mexía de Ovando brought to light in Lima a new publication, *Primera parte de los cuatro libros de la Ovandina,* the first part of a planned, larger, four-part study of all the noble houses in the "kingdoms" of Peru and Mexico that proved explosive. Mexía de Ovando's treatise had been approved by the viceroy himself, the Prince of Esquilache, and one Lima High Court magistrate, don Alonso Bravo de Saravia. The publication was immediately denounced as a grotesque effort of Jewish and Morisco converts to gain public acceptance by manufactured dynastic backgrounds as Rosas Oquendo had warned. The Inquisition rounded up all the copies of *La Ovandina* and initiated an investigation, collecting Limeño broadsides ridiculing the doctored lineages with verses that explicitly drew on Rosas Oquendo.[36]

The verses mocked the attempts of merchant and petty traders to gain distinction through mercenary writers like Mexía Ovando, while promoting a society of counterfeiting, deceit, and thievery:

Las noblezas emprestadas	Nobilities taken out on loan
y en público las sacar,	and then publicly flaunted,
por ladrones se han de dar	for thieves should they be had,
los que las traen hurtadas	those who claim what's stolen.
Válgate el diablo, Ovandón!	The devil take you, Ovando you!
¿Por qué queires que te crea	Why do you demand to be believed
el que tu Ovandina lea	by he who reads your *Ovandina*
si toda ella es invención?	if she is nothing but invention?[37]

Fray Antonio de Peñaranda, one of the two censors commissioned by the Inquisition of Lima to investigate the case, concluded that Mexía de Ovando was politically dangerous as he encouraged *pecheros* (commoners) to promiscuously articulate claims of nobility to escape their station.[38] Censor licenciado Gaspar de Valdespina launched a detailed study of dozens of false assertions and claims of families who had stained lineages. He added that the crime was Mexía Ovando's as well, as the latter charged up to fifty ducats to supply any willing family with false lineages.[39] For both Inquisitors, the scandal resided in the viceregal license that had lent perpetual credence to lies—a brusque critique to a government that could have transmogrified mendacity into sanctioned verities. The book and the censors' reports were sent to Madrid to the Suprema, the highest inquisitorial court, that dismissed the reaction by the Peruvian Inquisitors as exaggerations. For the friars Diego de Barrasa and Francisco Verdugo, Peru needed a system of social estates to order society, and this book clearly encouraged everyone to behave by these values of nobility and service. There was no harm for a society born of disorder for everyone to abide by the ideology of blood hierarchies.[40] It was a pragmatic and transactional understanding of truth making. The Suprema's decision came in too late for *La Ovandina* as no copies survived the 1622 round up. Yet Mexía de Ovando continued to ply his wares in Peru, Mexico, and Santo Domingo without further harassment, offering Crown authorieties new books on economic and political reform.[41]

The New World's turmoil not only gave commoners opportunities to claim ancient noble descent. It also offered extreme cases of self-fashioning. Few stories of early modern mobility are more spectacular than that of Alonso Díaz Ramírez de Guzmán, born to middling citizens of Guizpúzcoa around 1585. After winding up in trouble in Peru for yet another violent outburst, Alonso encountered the bishop of Huamanga and his secretary. Here, Alonso made a stunning confession: *he* was Catalina de Eraso, a *she*.[42] Catalina summarized:

> This is the truth, I am a woman, I was born in such-and-such place, daughter of Mr. and Mrs. so-and-so. . . . I went to such-and-such place, I undressed myself, I clothed myself, I cut my hair, I went hither and thither, I sailed, I ported, I portered, I killed, I wounded, I maimed, I lashed, until I came here in the present moment, at the feet of your Illustrious Lordship.[43]

The shocked bishop asked her: "In the end, is this true?"

"Yes, sir."

He responded, "Please do not be alarmed that your remarkableness unsettles one's expectations." To this, she countered, "Lord, it is so, and if your Illustriousness wishes to free himself of doubt, [I will show] via the experience of matrons, I am still a maiden."

The matrons confirmed her story. She later returned to Spain, where she petitioned the king for her services and won a handsome lifetime pension.[44] This narrative, one of Spain's most celebrated early modern accounts, deals not just with the complexity of self-identity—while Catalina de Eraso was certainly a real person, her autobiography is a devilishly complex mix of truth and fiction.[45]

Transatlantic mobility enabled European actors to adopt new personae easily. Indigenous people did not cross the ocean nearly as often, but that does not mean that they did not reinvent themselves. Native commoners often severed old ties with their lords and left their communities behind. In the early years of conquest, many abandoned their towns after the conquistadors transformed them into *encomiendas*; few tribute payers wanted to live under this heavy-handed rule.[46] Other commoners skipped town to avoid their own lords, which sometimes exacerbated conflicts between Native lords. In 1551, the lords of Fumeque and Chiguachi nearly went to war over some eight hundred commoners who had left the former's dominions, alleging abuses.[47] In other cases, Natives traveled far from their original places of residence. While many conquistador-lords and Native elites petitioned bitterly against their tributaries' migrations, the sparse viceregal officer corps could rarely hope to return them.[48] These cases were not isolated; half of Quito's inhabitants were transient Natives, for instance.[49] In Mexico, deracinated migrants flocked to cities and mining towns in search of wage labor.[50] Often, these commoners received the title of *forastero,* or outsider.[51]

Mobile commoners could further tangle the social order by becoming Native lords. Many were auxiliaries who had followed Spanish allies far beyond their family lands. For example, one don Francisco Hati had once been a tribute-paying goatherd named Francisco Saquinga. But when he wandered from his original community to the Quito town of Latacunga, he became a textile industrialist, moneylender, owner of some twelve thousand sheep, and local Native lord.[52] In petitions and lawsuits, hundreds of individuals labeled "intruder lord" (*cacique intruso*) appear.[53] This was the ladinized New World at its most subversive.

Even the highest echelons of Indigenous nobility were plagued by doubts about status. Many dynasts traveled to Madrid, hoping—as

Spaniards did—that the crossing would transform their status. In 1576, a council official complained that the royal court was full of claimants to Moctezuma's throne and asked for one pretendent's expulsion to Mexico to prevent others from developing similar ambitions.[54] Individuals with Spanish fathers and Indigenous mothers also maneuvered to improve their status, often deliberately obfuscating their family histories. A case in point is the part-Inca humanist scholar Garcilaso de la Vega, author of a translation of Judá Abravanel's *Dialogues of Love,* the famous printed chronicles *The Florida of the Inca* (1605), and parts one (1609) and two (1617) of the *Royal Commentaries of the Incas.* He alleged that he was the son of an Inca noblewoman doña Isabel Palla Chimpu Ocllo and the Spanish conquistador Sebastián Garcilaso de la Vega y Vargas. His lifelong mission consisted of redeeming his father's reputation, tarnished in Peru and at the royal court by involvement with the tyrannical Pizarro clan.[55] Garcilaso also sought to improve the image of his Indigenous family. This dual project drew him into a life of scholarship. In 1596, he completed his father's genealogy whose bloodline he traced "to the Goths."[56] He also published texts stressing his family's worthiness to the Crown, which he hinted should help him improve his standing.[57] His histories, today widely regarded as masterpieces, are full of expert dissimulation and subterfuge regarding his family's troubled past. He openly celebrates himself as an Indigenous wordsmith, ingeniously rewriting Peru's past—and his own—in the process.

STRUGGLING FOR THE TRUTH IN PRIVILEGE AND JUSTICE PAPERWORK

The culture of status inflation was a major concern for vassals, officials, and monarchs. The problem was particularly acute in *gracia* paperwork, the vehicle through which vassals achieved social standing. Lying about one's identity to authorities threatened the empire's mission and ethos of service and reward. Officials took steps early on to safeguard the truthfulness of *gracia* dossiers. By the 1510s, subjects seeking *encomiendas,* pensions, royal offices, and other rewards needed to provide notarized *probanzas* featuring favorable witness testimonies.[58] By 1528, perhaps earlier, the council ordered any would-be privilege seeker to appear before the highest local authority—usually the High Court. Petitioners had to submit dossiers and publicly swear an oath of truthfulness before a notary, after which High Court magistrates would either refuse the candidate or recommend him or her to the king and council.[59] Viceroys later became the go-to officials for many types of privileges.

Crown officials introduced certain epistemological safeguards to *gracia* petitions. They demanded oaths, witness statements, and local authorities' recommendations. These safeguards made *gracia* procedures similar to litigious *justicia* cases. In *gracia*, petitioners provided a one-sided statement of honor and service, complete with proof from upright eyewitnesses. In *justicia*, litigants did the same but inverted the argument: they sought to prove that rivals and their witnesses were dishonorable, untrustworthy, and low born. For magistrates, *justicia* cases were long agonistic and dialectical slogs, but with a major advantage: rival parties themselves uncovered evidence allegedly revealing one another's lies. By contrast, in *gracia*, every candidate appeared perfect, and all witnesses agreed.

Officials vetting *gracia* and *justicia* cases thus faced types of paperwork that converged and diverged. Both types relied heavily on witnesses. One strategy for officials vetting *gracia* and *justicia* cases was to measure the quantity and social status of the witnesses a petitioner or litigant had mustered. Officials tended to give the most weight to elite witnesses and those with privileged eyewitness insights. These witnesses served to persuade officials that petitioners' or litigants' claims had universal acceptance. A successful litigant or petitioner had witnesses prove that each of their claims was "public and notorious."[60] If vassals were going to fabricate claims, they had to muster all of their social capital. Authorities nonetheless found that petitioners and litigants seemed to almost always find witnesses to testify on their behalf. Feuding parties might present diametrically opposed realities, and privilege seekers always appeared extraordinarily meritorious.

This evidentiary problem caused innumerable headaches and further destabilized the already imperiled social order. A circa 1569 petition by Santo Domingo's high judge Doctor Diego de Cáceres denounced these problems. He complained that the entire system of "proofs of who has served Your Majesty . . . is a mockery and a matter built on air."[61] Witnesses tediously and predictably aped privilege seekers' claims, and there was no way to fact-check, for the only person capable of undertaking counterinvestigations was the court's overworked royal attorney. The high judges of Nueva Granada complained extensively in 1579 that much of the problem stemmed from the province's lack of resources for follow-up investigations. The descendants of conquistadors were impoverished and numbered in the thousands, and the court's coffers were depleted. To rigorously determine which applicants were actually worthy of privileges would "require henceforth all of our time . . . otherwise we would not be able to resolve one in a thousand requests." The judges stated that their approach was thus to air on the side of extreme caution, rewarding only the sons of conquistadors with the best, most publicly renowned pedigrees.[62]

One strategy officials embraced was to threaten vassals who lied with gruesome violence. The empire had long-standing laws prohibiting false testimonies. Various classical Roman, Visigothic, and medieval juridical commentaries forbade them.[63] So too did more recent legislation; the eighty-third and final chapter of the 1505 Castilian Laws of Toros established such malicious acts as crimes, especially in the context of court cases.[64] By the mid-sixteenth century, legislation made the punishment clear: extraction of the guilty person's teeth—perhaps in reference to the oral nature of the crime.[65]

Despite officials' obvious difficulties in determining guilt, some did occasionally catch vassals in the act of lying before notaries under oath. In 1538, the residents of Santo Domingo Diego de Cieza and María Álvarez won a decree prompting the High Court to prosecute subjects who had provided false statements against them.[66] In 1546, Licenciado Pedro de la Gasca of Peru was to apprehend two criminals who had uttered falsities against Captain Bartolomé Pérez.[67] When Quito authorities sentenced two Spaniards to the crime, they fled Quito for Spain before local justices could extract their teeth.[68] Wrongdoers also faced imprisonment and exile. When the governor of Tierra Firme accused one Francisco de

Sepúlveda of false testimony, the council ruled that the perpetrator was to return to the court in Spain in chains to explain his actions.[69] Nicolás de Lescano of Mexico City was sentenced to exile in 1584 for having allegedly presented false testimony, but he sought to be pardoned "for having given a false testimony . . . without harm to third parties, and inadvertently and with ignorance and no sort of malice." The council was unforgiving; it wrote that "what they ask has no grounds."[70]

Litigation featured unique epistemological tools not available in *gobierno* and *gracia* cases. In *justicia,* litigants waged battle against one another's credibility. Attacking the reputation of rivals and their witnesses was an art and a specific praxis: the proof of flaws, or *prueba de tachas.*[71] Castilian decrees spelled out most of the rules for *pruebas.* For witnesses to provide valid testimony, they had to be individuals in good social standing. Conversely, those in bad social standing were considered *tachado,* flawed.[72] By the mid-1560s, there was a stable series of guidelines for court cases, in which litigants could begin the *prueba* midway through. Determining who was flawed was also an art. Magistrates generally voided the testimonies of those who were closely related by friendship, dependence, or family bonds to the litigants. Likewise, sworn enemies of feuding parties and anyone who testified under coercion or bribery could not participate, nor could those under the age of sixteen. Criminal records invalidated testimonies—including for people who had lied in previous cases under oath or litigated incessantly. Then there was a long list of criminals and low-lives whose word counted for little: those of ill repute, forgers, gamblers, thieves, pimps, seducers of nuns, rapists, diviners and spellcasters, the excommunicated, murderers, poisoners, abortionists, traitors, heretics, and apostates. The extremely poor, the mad, cross-dressers, and hermaphrodites were also not permitted, in theory, to provide statements before judges in civil and criminal cases.[73]

This list suggests that those without honor counted for less, as did those who had weak volitions and could be easily induced to testify, like gamblers or the mad. Those who had been threatened to say something specific could not be heeded. But in other cases, even those in high-standing might be *tachado.* Few strategies were as ubiquitous as alleging that a rival elite witness was blind with rage.[74] The powerful Marquis don Martín Cortés complained that he was hounded by enemies in 1563, noting "the enmity and palpable hatred that many in this land have had, and have, for me."[75] One royal decree won by a high judge in Guatemala in 1563 stated that his enemy High Judge Echegoyen had gathered against him "a sinister and untrue report . . . bribing [his] servants with promises of great quantities."[76]

Church officials felt the heat too, especially during their posttenure audit cases. Bishop of Mexico Juan de Zumárraga discovered as much sometime in the 1530s, during his struggle with High Judge Diego Delgadillo. When the bishop's rival publicly summoned witnesses to the High Court to testify, he caught wind of the "thirty or forty allegations" against him, which, "truthfully, having heard and read them, gave me horror and dread." The man was clearly "blind with passion," Zumárraga warned.[77] Friar Miguel de Talavera wrote in 1587 about certain malicious witnesses against Zumárraga during his audit, likening them to "rabid wolves . . . [who] not being able to personally catch their prey, have endeavored to darken" the archbishop's reputation with "false witnesses [paid] with bribes, promises and threats."[78] When Friar Domingo de Santo Tomás passed through Cusco in the early 1560s, he complained that the city's leading residents "held a petition" they intended to send to the king "in which they raised a thousand false testimonies against me."[79]

Sometimes the bureaucratic blood sport of *tachas* took on unique New World characteristics, consisting of blasting whole groups—women, Native lords, *mestizos*, the enslaved—through comparison with internal and external enemies of the empire. The president of Guatemala García de Valverde wrote to the council during the posttenure audit of High Judge Auxatia about a certain don Diego de Herrera, who "having forgotten his conscience . . . put forth the most ugly and grave statements one can imagine. . . . In each statement he placed three or four witnesses, mestizos, wenches [*mujerzuelas*], enemies of mine, low and lost people."[80] An anonymous, undated petition would defend a certain official of testimonies against him by calling them "vile and delinquent witnesses . . . slaves . . . and recently arrived African slaves [*bozales*] . . . and Moors."[81]

The New Granada scribe Francisco Velázquez would be both the victim of such pejoratives and an offender himself. His enemy Licenciado Monzón accused him of having grandparents "burned . . . for being relapsed Jews" in various false testimonies. He shot back that one of the witnesses was a *mestizo.*[82] The *prueba de tachas* reveals the encroaching of Indies categories of human difference into lawsuits—and that many litigants could manipulate prejudices to bring enemies to their knees.

Commoners also had to defend themselves from rivals, including powerful officials, through *tachas.* The soldier Juan Troyano wrote in 1572 from the Yucatan that he had petitioned to "serve, deal, and inform, and manifest the falsity and betrayal" of the lies of certain officials, "men so haughty, masked, avaricious, immoderate, and disguised that they live by lies."[83] *Tachas* were thus a quintessential part of lawfare.

Many vassals harangued, even slandered, each other. Virtually every group was in some way insulted in *justicia* cases. But the constant juridical abuse of women, Natives, slaves, commoners, and others does not mean that they did not appear as witnesses. Rather, magistrates overseeing civil and criminal cases—along with investigators conducting post-tenure audit lawsuits, the *visitas* and *residencias*—paradoxically accepted litigants' denunciations of flawed witnesses while listening to these very same individuals. Moreover, auditors were expected to both secretly and openly seek out the testimonies of the poor, women, and slaves in order to evaluate the tenure of officials.[84] Ecclesiastical courts, including the Inquisition, thirsted for the witness testimonies of women, Natives, slaves, and others. These nonelite witnesses could, after all, play crucial roles in documenting the wrongdoings of Christians.

In 1575, Franciscan friars in the Tabasco community of Zavatanes filed one such inquisitorial lawsuit. The order was struggling acrimoniously with a secular official, Juan Garzón, when the friars took the oath of Native commoner Pedro López. He recalled how, after the Franciscans had issued an excommunication edict against Garzón during a jurisdictional dispute, Garzón had mockingly said his punishment "was meaningless, and he would tear it to pieces." He said that the Franciscan Pedro Lorenzo who had issued the order "was nobody, his job consists of saying mass and praying. . . . A father, a father, a father, you trust him merely out of obedience."[85] The friars believed López's testimony, attacking Garzón as having uttered "words more Lutheran than Christian."[86] Two days later, Garzón and his men confronted the friars in public, tearing the edict to shreds before the church doors; the friars exclaimed, "Oh God! We are in England . . . showing no more respect than the Arabs do."[87] To make matters worse, Garzón had his own proof in hand when he committed this sacrilege. The Franciscans stammered that, in plain sight of the astonished Native commoners, "the lieutenant began to read me a certain document full of false testimonies."[88] The friars countered Garzón by soliciting Pedro López's testimony and the accounts of several others. They then sent the file the bishop, begging him to act.[89] These conflicts thus prompted furious, discriminatory language even as they drew as many actors as possible into the melee. Who was right and who was wrong might hang on the testimonies of the least powerful, like commoner Pedro López.

Indigenous commoners wielded such depositions to powerful effect. Sometimes commoners were instrumental in bringing down their lords. The Xajil Chronicle, for instance, recorded that one Spanish field justice undergoing an audit sought to invalidate *caciques*' statements while pressuring Native townspeople to testify falsely on his behalf.[90] In other cases, commoners brought Spanish authorities to their knees with hostile allegations The priest Bartolomé Álvarez complained about the power Indigenous subjects mustered against churchmen, lamenting that "the Indians testify and provide information against priests. . . . They have accused many of being *putos* [male whores], in such a manner that before the archbishop of Lima [Gerónimo de] Loaysa they, having accused a cleric and presented their information. . . . The cleric died of shame."[91] (See Figure 4.2.)

A whole social praxis involving elite and commoner litigants alike sprung up. In the fog of lawfare, the practice of alliance building was ubiquitous, driving further skepticism. Vassals learned to defend themselves in court and bolster their chances of winning privilege petitions by assembling complex alliances. Castilians had long complained that their society was rife with extensive social rivalries centered around kin,

Figure 4.2 An Indigenous woman is accused by a priest of adultery and turns to an Indigenous council (*cabildo*) with a petition to the bishop accusing the priest of misdeeds. The image represents the manipulation of tribunals by petitioners. Felipe Guaman Poma de Ayala. *El primer nueva corónica y buen gobierno* (1615/1616), p. 668, GKS 2232 4°, Department of Manuscripts and Rare Books, The Royal Library, Copenhagen.

friendship, and patronage networks—*bandos*.[92] Joining blue-blooded rivals were countless other rivalries—between clergymen and royal officials, for example.[93] Factions often cut across class categories, bringing elites into direct conflict and social actors into erratic and variable alliances with and against one another.[94] Indies society was rife with extensive, fluid, socially heterogeneous factions. Don Juan Atonal in Chiapas joined forces with men and women in his community, the Dominicans, and the Spanish governor and High Court to thwart the bishop. Likewise, the Franciscans of Zavatanes allied themselves with both the bishop and local Indigenous commoners. The governor of Santo Domingo, Alonso de Zuazo, complained in 1518 of the "factions and cliques" between Columbus's family and the local conquistadors "that have existed until now, that have totally destroyed the land."[95] One official wrote in 1559 that "in almost all of the provinces of the Indies there have been two factions among the Spaniards: one of the conquistadors and another of the friars."[96]

Yet such groups often suffered internal cleavages. The conquistadors were divided by factions: priest Luis Sánchez stated in 1566 that in both Mexico and Peru, they battled "a hundred by a hundred, and a thousand by a thousand, until they finish themselves."[97] Officials feuded with one another too. The bishop of Tlaxcala complained that conflicts within the High Court of Mexico had formed deep divisions that harmed society in general. With officials feuding, "the commoners divide themselves into factions . . . and finally everything falls into a [terrible] state."[98] In 1562, the Franciscan friar Francisco de Bustamante fumed that the local justice officials had cast on New Spain a "dreary fog . . . [of] a thousand lies and affinities . . . passions and factions."[99] These social alliances deeply troubled officials as they attempted to sort truth from fiction, especially in vassals' *gracia* and *justicia* dossiers. Judges were suspicious of collusion, and litigants' lawyers diligently sought to invalidate testimonies that they argued revealed not the truth but extreme partisanship (see Figure 4.3).

By the 1570s, commoners' and Indigenous subjects' testimonies, along with factional and jurisdictional struggles, had rendered Cusco into a most dangerous place. There, all reputations could be shattered and all social estates easily brought down. The connected cases of Pedro de

Figure 4.3 The alliance of an Indigenous lord and a priest against a field justice (*corregidor*) through manipulation of testimony. This is a temporary alliance, as the priest turns against the Indigenous lord and demands bribes. Felipe Guaman Poma de Ayala. *El primer nueva corónica y buen gobierno* (1615/1616), p. 602, GKS 2232 4°, Department of Manuscripts and Rare Books, The Royal Library, Copenhagen.

Quiroga and Cristóbal de Albornoz are illustrative of the dangers of the sixteenth-century transactional and pragmatic understandings of truth making. Pedro de Quiroga, appointed to the cathedral chapter of Cusco in 1568, was named commissioner of the new Inquisition in Peru after having served Viceroy Toledo as auditor the bishopric of Arequipa.[100] In 1573 this appointment elicited the rage of the new bishop of Cusco, Sebastián Lartaún, who claimed total authority over inquisitorial powers. Lartaún commissioned two members of the cathedral chapter, Cristóbal de Albornoz and Luis de Armas, to investigate Quiroga for financial corruption and to have therefore the commissioner and an independent Inquisition removed. However, it was the testimony of an anonymous Indigenous female commoner that allowed Albornoz and Armas to seize and imprison Quiroga, for the Indigenous woman had accused Quiroga of physical assault, leaving open the possibility of sexual malfeasance. The investigation also revealed that Quiroga's affair with the Inca princess, doña Angelina Yupanqui, had been observed by her Indigenous servant. Quiroga was soon released as these testimonies could not be verified. He thereafter immediately began an inquisitorial investigation into Albornoz and Armas. Quiroga produced an anonymous witness that accused Albornoz of Lutheran heresies by offering mass without having previously cleansed himself through prayers. Quiroga also managed to prove that Albornoz had counterfeited his identity, falsely claiming to having a law degree in canon law from the University of Valladolid.[101] Quiroga himself would later be accused of forging his own identity as canon to secure his position in the cathedral chapter and as Inquisition commissioner. Quiroga, allegedly, was a friar who therefore was banned by law from occupying such clerical positions in cathedral chapters and inquisitions.[102]

Historians know Albornoz for his role in identifying an Indigenous religious revival in the province of Huamanga, the so-called Taki Onkoy. It is now clear, however, that Albornoz used *gracia* petitions to apply for higher offices in the cathedral chapter of Cusco, eliciting misleading testimonies on alleged religious threats, the record upon which historians have sought to reconstruct the Taki Onkoy. Albornoz was seeking to punish Indigenous communities in Huamanga after they had denounced him for graft and abuse.[103] We know that many campaigns against Indigenous idolatry in Peru were prompted by clerics either accused by Indigenous communities of malfeasance or by efforts to bolster the cleric's vitae when applying for promotion within the Church. Paperwork and testimonies were systematically deployed to destroy enemies and rivals.[104]

These are the experiences that prompted Pedro de Quiroga to write his unpublished *Coloquios de la Verdad* (*Colloquys on Truth*) in Cusco. Quiroga's *Coloquios* seek to capture the status of truth making in Peru compared to Spain by having three characters—a newly arrived and naive colonist (Justino), an old encomendero-turned-hermit (Barchilón), and the former Inca elite (Tito)—mediate on the social mobility and testimonies in Peru. Quiroga describes the conquest as an epochally transformative event that should have created a society of orders but that had turned Peru into a monstrosity in which no one respected authority or social estates. A chastened Barchilón warns Justino not to expect anyone to respect secrecy, hierarchies, and friendships. Barchilón presents Peru as a society contradictorily obsessed with both honor and equality: "Unlike men in Castile, the spirits of men here are self-conceited and made for equality; they would not put up with anything else."[105] Barchilón cautions Justino not to trust Indigenous commoners, otherwise his secrets would be made public: "Pay attention to what you say . . . for men here pay careful attention to your mouth and will count your words and would then reveal them to everyone."[106] Barchilón sees Indigenous women as the worst—sexually promiscuous and quick to entrap and corrupt newcomers into their practices of deceit. Justino, Barchilón insists, should avoid potential enemies even among the seemingly powerless, "because in this land a mosquito can harm even the most powerful. From the day you arrive in this land assume you are surrounded by visible and invisible enemies."[107]

Quiroga used Tito the Inca to convey a message of elite Indigenous despair. The former Inca appears changing masters after the conquest, becoming in time a *ladino*, and eventually moving to Spain where he learned to admire the stability and hierarchies of Spain. Tito, however, chooses to return to Peru to become a deracinated commoner who witnesses the destruction of all Inca hierarchies and the rise of once-marginal peasants into new local lords, a collection of petty local tyrants abusing Indigenous community to death. *Colloquys on Truth* is a despairing meditation on the triumph of once-empowered commoners, whose testimonies and values had rendered impossible a society of orders, leading to the collapse of both Inca and European societies of orders.

The ubiquity of factionalism and deceit drove radical politics and radical doubt. Lawfare consumed the truth itself. Many worried that witnesses were incapable of being truthful in their privilege and litigation paperwork; they brought their biases, their frailties, and a whole world of subterfuge to court. Yet suspicion did not fall on petitioners' and allies' statements alone.

Even official intermediaries who were supposed to vouchsafe the truth could become the objects of scorn and suspicion. Notaries were meant to ensure the veracity of documents, and vassals uttered all sworn statements in front of them.[108] Yet they often had intrigues in the communities within which they were embedded and could be involved in substantial distortions of their own truth statements.[109] The governor and leaders of Tlaxcala complained sometime in 1583 or 1584 that a local sheriff had gone to prison in Mexico City due to his scribe Pedro Núñez's "testimonies and things they have uttered contrary to the truth" and for bringing "induced" witnesses before the local authorities. Authorities caught Núñez and barred him from returning within thirty Spanish leagues of Mexico City, at which point he planned to move to Tlaxcala—something the Tlaxcalans refused to allow.[110]

Translators too were objects of suspicion. The fact that most subjects in the empire did not speak Spanish complicated not only notarial testimonies but also the entire edifice of royal justice paperwork. Bishop Zumárraga complained of late 1520s Mexico that President Nuño de Guzmán's schemes featured a wicked Spanish royal interpreter, García del Pilar. This unscrupulous individual manipulated all those around him, especially Natives. The bishop thundered, "I certify to Your Majesty truthfully that it is the opinion of all those who desire to serve God . . . that [Pilar's] tongue should be pulled out and severed, so that he could no longer use it to speak the great wickednesses and robberies which he invents every day."[111] Profound anxiety among Natives and Spaniards regarding interpreters' fealty was endemic throughout the Indies.[112]

As early as the 1510s, subjects were also complaining to the Crown about lawyers and procurators.[113] In 1580, for example, the City Council of Lima accused a procurator of secretly inserting text into its petition to benefit his clique.[114] Throughout the 1500s, there were ubiquitous accusations of lawyers tormenting litigants—especially Native ones—by engineering never-ending lawsuits.[115] In one case, the Indigenous communities of Achachalintla, Mecatlan, Cohauytlan, and various others complained about the malpractice of "interpreters and scribes and procurators and others"; the Crown responded with a 1582 decree barring these officials from the region.[116] While the council and king explicitly denounced this problem, including in the 1542–1543 New Laws, complaints were endemic.[117]

Many vassals pined for a time before paperwork. Some imagined the Inca to have ruled without such agents, who in the present "destroyed the realm."[118] The great Andean chronicler Guaman Poma would depict the Inca in such a light: during the rule of the Inca Tupac Yupanqui, "there were no murderers nor litigation nor lying nor petitions nor *proculadrones* [procu-liars]."[119] These statements recall Cervantes's Don Quixote, who rhapsodizes to a group of rather confused goatherds that in the Golden Age, there were no judges and therefore no "fraud, deceit, or malice."[120] Now, in "this Iron Age," judges accept bribes, enchanters magically change the appearances of physical objects, and virtuous knights do not receive their due.[121]

Administrative-judicial skepticism echoed from the Andes and the Yucatan to the royal court. The most heated debates happened in the Indies, where jurisdictional conflicts and outright civil war had engendered a broad malaise. Many subjects held out hope that the distant Crown could more objectively reflect on the truth—the fatherly monarchs and their upright ministers steering the empire toward justice and good administration. Perhaps the epistemological problems of passion, factionalism, flawed witnesses, and greedy intermediaries that plagued the New World would not emerge within the monarch's own circles. Or was the court another theater of intrigue? In the late 1520s, and especially in the 1530s to 1540s, powerful conquistador lobbies attempted to co-opt council ministers and even royal secretaries. Flush with plundered Mexica and Inca treasure and exquisite tribute items, these warlords attempted to secure themselves against local enemies by reshaping the court in their image. Cortés, of course, was the first to arrive, lavishing court women with Mexica loot.[122] After him followed agents of the two great Peruvian cliques, the Almagros and Pizarros, with even greater hauls. The conquistadors sought to merge their factions with ministers' and royal secretaries' families through friendship or marriage—all of this unbeknownst to the monarch.[123]

These connections with the court were perilous for all involved. Ministers entangled their official duties of upholding royal justice and administration with personal designs. And their Indies connections were growing dangerous. In Peru, warlord Diego de Almagro faced off against the Pizarro clan, with both sides attempting to wed their kin to council ministers' families.[124] The clashing conquistadors brought disgrace on their whole enterprise when the Pizarros executed Diego amid vassals' petitions to the Crown alleging vast conquistador fraud and abuses.[125] Soon, the feuding gangs hired lawyers in the court and traded allegations that various ministers were "suspicious" or partial.[126] A network of illicit connections revealed itself. One minister's wife, doña Mencía de Esquivel, alerted ministers from other councils that Pizarro had attempted to bribe her.[127] Her report reached the emperor and likely prompted the famous audit of the Council of the Indies in 1542. After this long, bruising inspection, investigators found numerous ministers guilty of corrupting imperial justice. Doubt had seized the emperor and driven his expurgation of conquistadors from the council.

Friars' dreams of theocratic dominion stood to gain from this skeptical environment. With Las Casas simultaneously battling to weaken conquistadors, the emperor decided to limit their might and socially distance council ministers from powerful vassals in the famous 1542 New Laws.[128] The sovereign had learned a difficult lesson: not only his trusted ministers but also his royal secretaries and their wives were constantly being wooed by conquistadors' gifts.[129] He would warn the prince in a secret 1543 letter that even his closest officials could embroil themselves in "passions, partialities, and quasi-factions."[130] He also warned his son Philip of "the voices of women" and noted that his own secretary had involved himself in "passions" due to his wife's links to conquistadors and others.[131]

This skeptical stance not only helped secure the downfall of the conquistador lordships but also deeply impacted Philip's rule. As king, Philip would repeatedly favor efforts to distance ministers from vassals. A spate of scandals in the 1560s to 1590s underscored this problem. Once Madrid became the court in 1561, subjects from every corner of the world flocked there in search of privilege and success in lawsuits. The court was expensive, and council bureaucracy could be slow, spurring a resurgence of bribery attempts—often through well-connected women. An early audit led by the powerful investigator don Juan de Ovando collected the testimonies of many Indies travelers, whose allegations shocked officials. In 1567, one Licenciate Ramírez told Ovando that a wealthy Peruvian claimed to have so thoroughly bribed ministers that "all that was left for him was to sleep with them. . . . He swore to God that if he wished, he could marry anyone in the Council."[132] Tellingly, conquistadors were no longer the ringleaders of this corruption; it was mainly merchants and disgraced officials in Madrid driving the subterfuge.

In response to this crisis, the king made Ovando president of the council. Ovando soon issued the 1571 *Ordinances*, which systematically commanded ministers keep distance from vassals.[133] His successor, Hernando de Vega y Fonseca, insisted in 1585 that these ordinances be printed and distributed to ministers, reminding them to be "clean" (*limpios*) especially when making ecclesiastical appointments in the Indies.[134] Evidently, something was again afoot. The following year, the royal secretary reported that a secret committee was seeking to prevent "that women negotiate with ministers."[135] Wealthy New World actors were often at the root of the problem. Some sought privileges, while others had been exiled for bad government and were attempting to clear their names in Madrid. The secretary fretted that these *Indianos* were "most dangerous" and believed they wished to corrupt ministers.[136] After a new audit, the king realized that even President Vega supported some of these troublemakers and was "very partial in defending those under investigation."[137] Other findings suggested ministers were not infrequently biased (*aficionados*).[138] What to do about this recurring problem? The Crown's inner circle of monarchs and secretaries acted by exiling certain women, punishing select officials, and doubling down on an ethos of impartiality.[139]

These and other incidents taught the monarchs the corrupting dangers of social proximity to the Indies. They therefore hesitated to appoint ministers who had had direct social experiences in the New World. This hesitancy had major consequences, for now the Crown ruled almost entirely by paper communication. Only a handful of ministers had seen Santo Domingo, Mexico, Guatemala, and Santa Fe de Bogotá with their own eyes.[140] Rulers also discovered that sending ministers to the Indies could end in disaster. For instance, in the late 1550s, King Philip II dispatched Spanish commissaries to negotiate with the Peruvian conquistadors about their waning power.[141] These officials soon waded into local disputes, and unhappy vassals accused them of factionalism and corruption.[142] Their return as trusty ministers was out of the question.

The monarchs gradually learned a hard lesson through countless disputes, Indies petitions, and court whistleblowers' reports: ministers must be socially distanced from the New World as much as possible. This created a sort of red line. Kings expected Indies officials to wade into patrimonialism and intrigues, invariably becoming biased and impassioned themselves. Ministers in court would be more ignorant of the New World and therefore more impartial. Indeed, council ministers would develop enough suspicion toward their overseas colleagues to investigate them after their tenure, scrutinize their claims about New World realities, and arduously defend petitioners' right to denounce them. High-ranking officials would have to persuade council officials of their virtue, truthfulness, and impartiality using the same rhetorical strategies all other petitioners employed. While many insisted that the truth statements of women, the poor, Natives, and others were invalid, the Crown was not certain that its most powerful conquistadors and ministers were any more truthful. This royal suspicion toward local officials opened doors for commoners and other nonofficials to continue participating in imperial rule through petitions, witness statements, and denunciations.

GOBIERNO PETITIONS AND THE TRUTH

Sixteenth-century actors—from humble commoners to powerful ministers—came to associate *gracia* and *justicia* with corruption, malice, and untruth. Both channels of paperwork were expensive, required witness statements, and passed through local officials. These practices theoretically curbed falsehoods, but contemporaries believed the paperwork that resulted was completely infected with factionalism and bias. In *gobierno* paperwork, petitioners found a very different type of resource with its own epistemological advantages and disadvantages. These documents were cheap to produce, and vassals could send them directly to the Crown (even anonymously) without witness statements, notarial certifications, or local officials' approval. This streamlined channel thus posed special difficulties, forcing vassals and Crown officials to ponder the elusiveness of truth in arguably more profound ways.

The Crown's openness to receiving vassals' *gobierno* petitions was enormously beneficial for both parties. Monarchs legitimated their rule in large part through this dialogue. No substantial spy or police networks were necessary in this arrangement; kings and officials could expect subjects to propose changes, report problems, and accuse others, forming what Arndt Brendecke calls a "vigilant triangle" of bottom-up surveillance and denunciation.[143] It was also imperative that these reports be truthful, for *gobierno* petitions formed the basis for virtually all administrative and legislative royal decrees and viceregal edicts. They established general and particular rules, orders, and clarifications on military matters, administrative issues, religious problems, and so on.

Here was a considerable problem: vast tracts of law had an unsteady basis in the truth. As conquistador Juan de Avendaño complained, "kings and their councils cannot remedy [their realms] nor things come to perfection" if reports were false.[144] Many vassals warned that this system of communication was infested with evidentiary problems the Crown was ill equipped to evaluate. And the problems were many indeed. Bernardo

Ramírez de Vargas wrote from Guadalajara that "sometimes because of the variety of opinions" subjects sent to the council, "there comes to be so much confusion that none of these can be given credit."[145] These problems were serious for *gracia*, which underpinned all privileges, and for *justicia*'s many adjudications of civil and criminal wrongs. But if *gobierno* reports were false, bedrock rules of Indies society were compromised.

The first epistemological problem of *gobierno* was distance. The monarchs' and council's physical and social separation from Indies vassals—largely a consequence of conquistadors' efforts to dominate ministers in the 1520s to 1540s—paradoxically made petitioning less biased but also less informed. Ideally, the king would see his people and bring justice to his realm. As Friar Miguel de Talavera wrote, "only the presence of Your Majesty exiles and destroys all the evils of the realm and conserves it in much peace, tranquility, and development."[146] Just as in the parables of Solomon, "the King, who sits upon the throne of justice, with a single gaze dissipates all evil."[147] Yet King Philip was no Solomon. The king simply could not see the Indies from his seat in Spain.[148] And considering ministers' dalliances with Indies subjects, it was perhaps better to preserve his distance.

With a faraway king, was justice possible? Advocates of radical change seized this problem to encourage royal skepticism and thereby increase their own authority. In 1552, Las Casas warned that the High Courts were "as distant as Rome to Valladolid, and another more than Belgrade to Seville, and Your Majesty three or four thousand leagues of ocean away." With a faraway and uninformed king, he wondered, "by what remedy will the aggrieved Indians reach justice?"[149] In 1566, Las Casas's acolyte, the priest Luis Suárez, wrote from Peru that "there are so many lands in the Indies, and so remote from Spain, so many provinces so different from each other, and they bear no resemblance of those here."[150] Vassals characterized royal justice as blind. One Augustinian warned that "your royal council governs very blindly . . . because they do not have, nor can they have, knowledge [*conosçimyento*] . . . of what is convenient for those parts."[151] High Judge Licenciado Jerónimo de Orozco faulted the council for certain decrees but conceded to them that they had only erred "for not having seen them with their eyes ... for otherwise, forcibly, they must determine many things ... blindly."[152] After all, the issues of the province "can barely be understood" without being there in person.[153]

Could the king make petitions his eyes? Friar Talavera elaborated that with an absent monarch, vassals "must sink" into the court "all the letters [*cartas*] that are the only [things] with which one can negotiate with Your Majesty."[154] High Judge Juan de Salmerón similarly wrote from Mexico in 1530 that the court could not "know the things" of the Indies "save by means of petitions [*relaciones*]" because "the land is so distant or because one cannot know the things of it" without first-person knowledge.[155]

The king was certainly aware of the epistemological problems petitions presented. For example, ministers forwarded King Philip II the 1558 petition of the high judge of Santa Fe, Francisco Briceño. This official complained that the king should appoint three high judges from the Indies to serve as council ministers, so that they could come to "know ... the diseases" of the Indies. After all, "the shepherd who does not know the flock ... is not a good shepherd." It was an obstacle, he warned, that "those of the Council of the Indies" learned everything "by report [*relaçion*]."[156] King Philip recorded considering the document's arguments, but he did not embrace the recommendation.

The king needed eyes, and commoners and other Indies petitioners offered theirs. An anonymous 1525 supplicant stated that only he could "see with clear eyes and give Your Lordship clear news."[157] Some of these claims verged on the absurd. One subject from Peru described himself as an oracle of the truth. Another claimed his reports were a panacea so powerful that the discovery of the immortality-granting philosopher's stone would pale in comparison.[158] Friar Alonso Portero said that his petition would provide the king and council "some light with which you may learn about and penetrate the darkness into which this realm has fallen."[159] The president of Charcas referred to his petition as a "clear and disabused mirror" of the ecclesiastical issues of the Indies.[160]

Vassals often pressed a more sophisticated argument: they were not as eminent as Crown officials but had the advantage of superior perspective. They were eyewitnesses of Indies reality, so they could better take in its staggering diversity and terrible problems. One friar, Pedro Juárez de Escobar, offered a particularly vivid set of metaphors. He praised the council's ministers as brilliant men but stressed that they were "great giants" standing in "low and profound valleys." The vassal, on the other hand, was like "a dwarf or a pigmy . . . on the peak of a mountain," gifted not with the height of social status but with the best vantage point.[161] He concluded with a similar metaphor: "A short-sighted man can better see an object he has before him, than an eagle or a lynx if they are far away."[162]

Many emphasized the importance of not only eyesight but also experience. In 1587, the famous friar Gerónimo de Mendieta urged the king to accept his proposals in part because he had been an "eyewitness for more than thirty-three years."[163] The official Sancho López de Agurto wrote from Mexico that "in these parts there is no person so ancient in affairs as I."[164] Indies veterans claimed to possess the ability to transmit the truth thanks to experiential evidence. This power could easily belong to commoners, too. The Spanish miner Baltazar de Bañuelos, for instance, wrote from Zacatecas in 1584 that the king should remember "the concrete experience [*experiencia cierta*] we who live in the New World have."[165]

Matters were not so simple, of course. Council ministers had reason to believe that subjects who had lived for many years in the Indies might actually have accumulated biases and motives to distort the truth. It was vassals' factions and passions that had nearly corrupted the council. Insiders were untrustworthy and outsiders trustworthy—not the other way around. During his investigations into Indies defenses and transport, the Italian engineer Bautista Antonelli rebutted that in the Indies, "there are very few persons to whom one can give credit, because everyone pulls towards their interests, not to the service of Your Majesty nor to the common good."[166] His subsequent struggles with entrenched local veterans of Indies life reveal that sometimes the outsider, not the insider, could best describe the New World to distant administrators. The council ultimately sided with Antonelli every time.

If neither insiders nor outsiders inherently told the truth, who might? Petitioners often framed the issue in terms of sin versus moral purity. With a pure and pious heart, a subject could honestly report to officials without the biases of greed or wrath. Friars emphasized that they were free of these deadly sins—unlike merchants, conquistadors, and other crass devotees of worldly pleasures and passions. Friar Pedro Durán wrote, "I am not moved by vengeance nor by passion nor by any other interest, only by the love of God."[167] The Augustinian Francisco de Ortega wrote that as a "poor friar, neither passion nor affinity nor particular interest are to move me, only zeal for the common good and the service of God our Lord and His Majesty." He went on to argue that "because of the religious habit I wear I am more obligated than a *secular* [priest or prelate] to say and deal in the truth."[168] One Gerónimo de Villacarillo wrote from Peru that "all of Your Majesty's vassals have the obligation to advise thee . . . though all these may have the obligation, even more [obligated] are the Friars to whose number I belong."[169] In very similar terms, a group of Franciscans wrote that they had a

> Christian obligation, all of us, to give testimony of the truth, for if not, for lack of providing it, this truth itself might perish, and afflict the entire republic, and in particular we friars have in these parts [the responsibility] to give Your Highness that testimony, for the distance is so far . . . and so diverse the reports (*nuevas*) . . . according to the variety of opinions and interests that move each person, and because we in this affair cannot be moved by anything other than by the zeal of the truth, we have for this cause the audacity to say how we feel.[170]

Alas, trusting friars was not so straightforward. Their rivals undermined their testimonies, observing that they could be as biased as any other group and were deeply implicated in all sorts of jurisdictional struggles and even plots to subvert Crown rule. Official Francisco Briceño advised in 1558 that "Your Majesty not believe a thing that a rich man or a Dominican friar says about the things that would be appropriate for Peru."[171] Moreover, opponents accused mendicants of being so rustic that their moral advantage was irrelevant. The Yucatan Protector of the Indians Diego Rodríguez Vivanco proclaimed that many friars were uneducated "idiots," little different from lowborn commoners.[172] Not even friars could be trusted (see Figure 4.4).

Figure 4.4 Two priests swap parish appointments to exact vengeance on complaining Indigenous parishioners. The image represents a case of priest-led politics leading to unreliable testimony. Felipe Guaman Poma de Ayala. *El primer nueva corónica y buen gobierno* (1615/1616), p. 584, GKS 2232 4°, Department of Manuscripts and Rare Books, The Royal Library, Copenhagen.

The problem of truth in this paperwork regime went further than good versus evil—nor did issues always stem from vassals' social biases and cliques. Epistemological problems connected with paperwork itself destabilized society. These issues produced an evidentiary gulf that even the best vassal and wisest ruler could not overcome. Indeed, vassals often warned that ministers and kings lacking experience had virtually no prospect of understanding the Indies, no matter how good the information arriving to them might be. Their permanent and incurable ignorance stemmed from a lack of sensory experience. The petitions and books of Gonzalo Fernández de Oviedo strongly press this case. He warned the Crown in 1523 of how Tierra Firme had been "lost and destroyed and robbed" by conquistadors like Captain Pedrarias, all "hidden and obscured from your Majesty and his Council."[173] His rhetoric about suspicion and truth appears in greater detail in his printed works. His *Natural hystoria* (1526) and *General y natural hystoria* (1547) echo many petitioners' claims about the importance of their knowledge, the flaws of other accounts, and the difficulties of expressing Indies realities. Some in Spain might disagree with his accounts, but after all, "just as the blind man cannot determine colors, so can he who is absent not testify to these matters, as could he who has seen them."[174]

And yet Oviedo only addressed half of the problem. He was optimistic that writing could transmit important truths, but not all were so sure. Some vassals offered sophisticated critiques of the intrinsic limitations of paper and language. Petitioners reflected on subtler and deeper problems that made the truth elusive in the Indies. To rule by petitions, many argued, was to capitulate not only to authors' biases but also to the narrative structure of writing itself.

Gobierno petitions' narratives, and Indies writing in general, forced the question, Could reports ever capture reality? Or were paper and words simply insufficient? Vassals answered often in the positive—the king could provide justice for his subjects by listening to them on paper. Many others, however, urged the Crown to consider that the situation was more complex. The minister who sought to understand the Indies through writing, insisted Briceño, resembled the reader "who reads a book of chivalric romance." Ministers learned of the Indies through fantasy narratives as alien from truth as any story of knights and giants. King Philip reflected on the letter and remarked that "in some of these things I think he is not without reason."[175]

Perhaps language itself was an obstacle to the truth. One friar bemoaned the limits of description of any sort, writing to the Crown that "there is no human tongue" that could capture the suffering of his peers in the religious orders at the hands of their various enemies.[176] Another mendicant complained that the Crown's policies on Native tribute were so harsh that "with no words can we ponder" the impending harm of these measures.[177] In 1580, the archbishop and president of New Granada sent the Crown a joint petition to complain about an investigator in the province, claiming that "it is impossible to say or exhort through any words . . . the confusions that have resulted" from his actions.[178] In an undated letter from Mexico, Friar Melchor de San José wrote the king that Natives' idolatrous practices and other Indies problems were "a matter more to sit and weep over than to explain with words."[179]

Few subjects completely abandoned the prospect that petitions, words, and language could achieve reforms. Yet many continued to be vexed by this problem—especially because officials lacked the time to read everything, forcing vassals to abbreviate complex circumstances. The high judges of Charcas stated that "these provinces, like all the others in the world, require information seen through one's eyes," complaining that the province's problems "require a very large and particular account [*relación*]."[180] Petitions could not veraciously transmit subjects' lived experiences to the council. The president of Charcas similarly complained that Viceroy Toledo's tyrannical actions in the province, along with countless other issues, made it so that "writing a thorough letter [*relaçion*]" was "almost impossible . . . because the matters that have arisen are almost infinite. . . . It would be necessary to write a very prolix writing and even this would not suffice due to the difficulty that there is in expressing it all."[181] An abridged truth was an imperfect truth.

Vassals expressed similar concerns about how to briefly explain matters of complexity and alterity. The conquistador Gerónimo López began a letter by lamenting that "the things that happen here are very great, and many, and severe, [and] for me to tell them, there would be the need for a great quantity of paper."[182] More marginal subjects also expressed these concerns. The Natives of New Spain collectively wrote in 1556 that "we could not without very extensive papers write the grievances that we receive" from rural justice officials.[183] The half-Spanish, half-Indigenous lord don Diego de Torres addressed the king in person, telling him that "if I had to provide an account to your Majesty about how every particular thing has happened and occurs in detriment of those miserable Indians, I would have to write a book of great volume . . . [an] infinite history."[184]

The king and his ministers therefore received only abbreviated glimpses into Indies reality. Friar Pedro Suárez de Escobar explained the dilemma very well. On the one hand, if he wrote at length, "I'd fear not being heard," but if he wrote little, his proposals would "not be sufficient in what they say." He stated that the twenty-four sections of his petition were "so brief that they can be called the extracts and sum of a great book and tome . . . dealing with the good management of the secular and ecclesiastical estates."[185] Two Spanish vassals, Pedro de Torres and Captain Juan Maldonado, expressed exasperation that "there have been so many damages and acts of violence [*fuerças y violençias*] that occur every day that no paper would suffice to write and express to Your Majesty."[186]

The king was just a man—this, too, posed a problem. Vassals often despaired that their lord could not possibly inform himself on the Indies completely because he was physically incapable of reading and absorbing such materials. Bishop Zumárraga complained from Mexico in the 1530s that he "would have given a much more longer [account] but for fatiguing the ears and breast of His Majesty with this long conflict and lamentable story."[187] The Natives of Chiapas collectively lamented that they could not personally inform the king due to their great distance from Madrid, bemoaning that "we can also not manifest [our problems] through writing as they are so many and so great that it would be sorely irritating to Your Majesty."[188] Sometime early in King Charles V's reign, Friar Pedro de Córdova said that as "problems here are difficult to believe because of the greatness of their evils," he would petition; however, to write them all would be "much prolixity . . . a long matter, and the pious ears of Your Highness would not be capable of them."[189] And tire the king these vassals did. This was especially true as the empire grew to include the massive realms of Mexico and Peru. Philip II wrote to his secretary that "I really don't know what" these petitioners "think of me, other than I must be made of iron or stone. . . . I'm so tired they will soon find out that I'm human like everyone else."[190]

Vassals were conscious of this fact—to the point that they shortened their letters—but the vast machine of the empire ran on paper, and so ruler and ruled wrote on regardless. Subjects often mentioned that their problems were so pressing that though they took the Crown's time into consideration, they had to write regardless. In 1554, Friar Tomás de la Torre said the gravity of his reports "did not allow him to write briefly or to speak in parables."[191] The conquistador Pedro de Ahumada wrote in 1560 that he had hesitated to write the king because though the Indies were in great need of reform, "I wished to not send [my letters], seeing as they were so many."[192] Another subject wrote that he was "determined to not tire Your Majesty" but wrote nonetheless.[193] The priest Luis Suárez said, "Your Lordship forgive me if I have been longwinded, which is not convenient for a person so busy [but] the nature of the issue absolves me."[194] A group of Franciscans wrote from Chile that the gravity of their report gave them "license to exceed the brevity of style that one tends to have in writing Your Majesty."[195] Yet by abbreviating their writings, vassals knew they were creating knowledge that was imperfect at best.

Writing vast *gobierno* treatises was no panacea. Could the inhabitants of the Indies, chained to a brief and lifeless paper medium, harness intense rhetoric to communicate their vivid and terrible experiences? Perhaps with a brief, forceful, and rousing delivery of the problem, they could shock the Crown.[196]

Rhetorical eloquence, or lack thereof, presented both a solution and a problem. Subjects fretted that they lacked the power to harness the language to transmit Indies realities. One anonymous petitioner—perhaps Hernán Cortés—wrote a brief letter to the king in the 1520s that though there were "things that would be good for Your Celsitude to know . . . I will tell them in summary as best as I can, for to say them as they happened, I know not how."[197] When Gómez de Cervantes warned of impending pirate attacks, he added, "Oh, who could or would deserve to put his lips on one of Your Majesty's royal ears to say what my quill refuses."[198] The New Granada–based Spanish soldier Juan Ruíz Clavijo stated in 1573, "I wish I had the ability . . . to signify to Your Highness the great persecution that many of your vassals suffer in this realm."[199] The problems of this faraway, different land were too great for men of such limited eloquence.

Many petitioners carefully phrased their letters for maximum impact, although this strategy came at a cost: runaway hyperbole. Hyperbole, both refined and crude, seemed essential to vassals. The two anonymous Dominicans who wrote Charles V in the 1520s warned that "the destruction and dissipation" of Santo Domingo was worsening by the hour and that "it is a great decline and affront for Spain. . . . God [has] given them lands so wide and rich . . . and so quickly . . . turned them to desert."[200] Friar Juan de Bélmez wrote that when "men fall mute instead of pleading remedies for this realm," wicked officials run rampant and "the rocks weep blood of compassion and pain."[201] Another friar, Gil González de Nicolás, pleaded the council to heed his suggestions "by the entrails of mercy of Our Lord God."[202] In 1552, Las Casas aptly claimed, after decades of apocalyptic warnings about Spanish rule in the Indies, that he so often suffered from seeing Natives' plight that "God seems to have given me the vocation of forever weeping over others' pain."[203]

Friars were not the only friends of vivid prose, of course. The Mexico-born intellectual Gómez de Cervantes stated that he wrote a long petition because the friars and priests had implored him "with tears of no less than blood flowing from the heart asking me to write Your Royal Majesty."[204] The governor of the Philippines exclaimed that the province had "so much to remedy" that one could only "weep [on] its consummation and ruin."[205] The governor of Cuba nearly blurted out a blasphemy when he begged the king's personal secretary Juan de Ibarra to send money to the High Court because the treasury was completely depleted: "I can only believe that the Devil will remedy this, for God no longer makes miracles, and especially not for men like me." He continued, "For the love of God, or for love of my not losing myself, Your Mercy, persuade His Majesty to provide me with money."[206]

Vassals also fretted about the king's purity of heart—another reason to write brief, hyperbolic texts. Could the king even handle the perfect truth if it was so shocking? Some suggested that they had refrained from offering a full account of what they had seen because the story would revolt and shock the king's heart. The priest Luis Suárez insisted that if he divulged the reality of the Indies, "Your Lordship would order me to be silent, because ears so Christian could not hear crimes so grave as Spaniards have committed and today commit to the Indians."[207] They thus resorted to insinuating evils too great to communicate through paper.

Hyperbole and insinuation only worsened the climate of distrust. Petitioners' exaggerations in *gobierno* petitions had the deleterious effect of casting entire groups as incapable of telling the truth. The bishop of Cusco wrote in 1539 that "the avarice of the Spaniards here is so great and unruly" that they were little different from "so many wolves."[208] He warned that the Crown should never trust anyone who disagreed with his proposals, "such true propositions . . . that whosoever may speak against them, must not be heeded."[209] After describing in explicit detail numerous conquistadors' murders of Native men and women in the Yucatan, Friar Luis de Villalpando stated in 1550,

> I write this with great bitterness of heart, seeing how without remedy these miserable [Indians] are. . . . The cause of all this is that as the King is uninformed, wishes not to be lord of these miserable Indians, but to make every encomendero an absolute ruler.[210]

He continued, "Everything here is backwards. . . . I beg that God forgive those who inform Your Highness so poorly!"[211] As these statements reveal, partisan conflict could quickly spread to generalizations—even about large collectives. In a way, the *tachas* had metastasized to exclude not only specific witnesses but also whole groups and social structures.

Gobierno petitions' spiraling hyperbole often put the entire Indies on trial. When the Franciscans of New Granada reported their struggles with a local governor, they bemoaned "the malice of the people . . . of this most wicked soil."[212] Las Casas stated that the conquest had left "the Catholic faith . . . defamed" and that the empire was pure "viciousness. . . . It has been the greatest loss and vainglory to ever befall any prince or king nor any province or realm ever in the world."[213] And this dismal picture often came from the highest echelons of local government. High-ranking officials frequently blamed inhabitants of the Indies of absolute moral deficiency. The Charcas royal attorney stated in 1561 that "in no other part of the world are there so many sins to punish in this kingdom."[214] Viceroy Toledo wrote in 1572 that Peru was a "kingdom of greed" and that his reforms were like "sticking hands into its wounds."[215] He argued that the situation was much worse than any petition had suggested to the council. There was no easy way to govern "such strange worlds," nor was "it possible [for the Council] to understand" its problems "through the letters of such a corrupted people." Never in his long career, he said, had he encountered such a wicked and lax society.[216] Similarly, the president of Guatemala wrote against enemies who sought to misinform the council in 1554 that "the truth is that the people of the Indies are very loose and very wild."[217]

Hyperbole begat suspicion and cynicism, but others urged the Crown to doubt these allegations. Was the New World so utterly corrupt that nobody there was to be trusted? The High Court of Guatemala pushed back in 1551, pleading for nuance. The judges said,

> Your Highness shall be persuaded to believe that here there are good and bad people, and people or truth and people of untruth. . . . Let us pitch away the opinion common here that there is no good person, nor a single soul to trust, that the people of the Indies are absolutely wicked, thieving, full of evils. . . . [Here] there are also people of honor and who have God and their consciences in account.[218]

A primary reason for these simplistic impressions of the Indies, they suggested, was the unstable *gobierno* system. With desperate vassals sending "so many complaints and so many petitions" to the council, the entire region was suspect.[219] Incessant lawfare had generated deep distrust between subjects, fueling negative characterizations of the Indies as a whole. The Guatemala magistrates urged ministers not to surrender to these disenchanted and pessimistic visions.

Grappling with problems of distance, expertise, and language, petitioners also relied on the practice of crafting and reworking fundamental Indies social and legal categories. Labeling others was an indispensable strategy, and vassals' abuse of categorization generated further reflections on the truth. Officials and subjects alike saw the utterly artificial and political nature of such categories. A case in point was the term *Indian*. Much hinged on how petitioners and litigants framed this legal construct; life-or-death issues like tribute, labor, slavery, and self-government were contingent on officials' understandings of Indio-ness. Vassals expressed exasperation at the ways others portrayed Natives before officials, changing characterizations to serve their own purposes. In 1518, High Judge Zuazo of Santo Domingo complained to an important adviser to King Charles that many Spaniards had misled the Crown into believing certain islands had no Indigenous populations. They had peddled false claims that these islands "were barren, in order to depopulate them and kill as many Indians as lived there."[220] By manipulating categories and their meanings, vassals legitimated horrible injustices, he warned.

Others complained about subjects' strategically inconsistent descriptions of Natives. For example, Indies-born conquistador Pedro de Ahumada scoffed at friars' deliberately contradictory characterizations. He reported that these mendicants "make these Natives poor-little-me's [*pobrecitos*] and miserable men [*miserables*], and then other times say that they are dogs and devils. . . . Other times that they are able and good Christians, and then that they are incapable and . . . wicked and ungrateful." These characterizations changed with the "particular interests and opinions" of each friar writing to the council.[221]

Officials certainly knew that vassals were playing malicious games by categorizing whole swaths of humanity. The outgoing viceroy of Mexico gave his successor Luis de Velasco a piece of advice: while some vassals would tell him that "the Indians are simple and humble and that neither malice nor arrogance reign within them . . . others to the contrary, [saying] that they are very rich and that they are vagabonds." Accounts hinged on the biases and secret agendas of each subject. The only solution to this problem was to "not believe the ones nor the others, but rather, simply deal with them as you would with any other nation."[222] Through suspicion, Velasco would discover the true nature of the Native vassal: he was a man like any other.

Similarly, an unsigned petition from one of Peru's late sixteenth-century viceroys—perhaps Velasco himself, who accepted the position in 1596—told council ministers that they were clueless about the character of Natives and how to best benefit them. He stated that some vassals emphasized their "ignorance and simplicity," while others insisted on their "malice . . . saying they know well how to defend themselves and complain acutely." Some claimed Natives' "poverty" and others the value of "what they win and earn." He concluded that "the Kings and their Councils" had been "fooled . . . with the accounts of charity and others of manipulations, always respecting the pretensions and passions" of each petitioner.[223] These factions' letters had profoundly distorted what the council believed about millions of Indigenous subjects. The problems of truth finding in the Indies unsettled the stability of even the most basic legal categories. In the New World, one had to approach categories of human difference with great distrust, for they were the product of innumerable secret agendas.

Vassals and officials struggled over whether to suspect Indigenous subjects and how to represent the truth itself—and Indigenous epistemologies repeatedly wound up at the center of these struggles. Many litigants also adopted strongly skeptical epistemologies when Indigenous parties presented *pinturas* or códices. These works often featured a mix of non-European epistemologies, special representations, and glyphs, and might also include alphabetic annotation in Spanish or Nahuatl. According to contemporaries, there were two major problems that these documents presented, prompting doubt among all parties involved. First was that the meanings of any arguments represented in the glyphs needed to be interpreted correctly before authorities. With the special epistemological expertise, there was always room for experts to enjoy unckecked powers of deception. To counter these powers, interpretations had to be offered in front of other competent witnesses, with an audience if possible. Second, the translator had to faithfully represent the litigants' arguments, refraining from twisting any contents to suit his own interests. To safeguard against malicious interpreters, translations had to be delivered in front of other linguistically competent witnesses.

In the milieu of lawfare, however, the question of the validity of Indigenous codices often triggered debates about Indigenous veracity—and their spirited rebuttals. Spaniards frustrated with Indigenous opponents could therefore allege that Native testimonies and documentation were inherently not to be trusted. For instance, in the early 1530s a large group of Indigenous elites claiming to represent "the natives of New Spain" blasted the High Court for questioning their ability to make truthful claims.[224] These elites had previously represented tribute rolls and paintings that proved the magistrates' abuses before the King. But according to the magistrates, this effort was a ruse and the documents were worthless. The whole charade had been engineered by the Franciscans and the Cortés clan, who were defending themselves from the High Court and President Nuño de Guzmán's uncompromising lawfare. To triumph in this dispute, friars and conquistador-lords would variously bribe and beat Natives to "paint whatever they ordered."[225] Due to these never-ending intrigues, argued one magistrate, one should not trust anything Indigenous litigants said or presented in court. He protested that they were "infidel Indians, enemies of our Catholic faith . . . poor, vile, lowly, idolaters and sodomites, drunkards, [who] eat human flesh and are very great liars."[226] But the Indigenous elites angrily protested this defamation, defending their honor and the truth of their testimonies and paintings.[227] And their point evidently stuck. While many feuding parties might contest the veracity of *pinturas* and Indigenous testimonies, they continued to form a key part of imperial paperwork for centuries.[228] After all, the same actors who questioned codices and Indigenous testimonies were suspect too. Everyone and everything must be doubted – even doubt itself.

SKEPTICISM AND ROYAL LAW IN ADMINISTRATIVE-JURIDICAL PRACTICE

This vernacular-administrative skepticism did not remain in the Indies. It traveled, like many petitions and voyagers, straight to the imperial capital. Vassals bombarded kings, viceroys, and other officials with competing, incomplete truths—all while tirelessly reminding their superiors of the epistemic problems inherent in *gobierno*, *gracia*, and *justicia*. These contradictions and incomplete truths fostered a rich culture of skepticism at the royal court. Three broad spheres of official reflection on the truth wove further skepticism and fluidity into its ethos and administration, building on crises that emerged from vassals' attempts to co-opt the Council of the Indies. The first sphere of reflection was the mirror of princes genre, which—in response to both the Indies and broader imperial problems—urged monarchs to distrust ministers and even monarchs themselves. The second was the concept of royal decrees as fluid and imperfect. The casuistic methodology of probabilism, so influential in 1600s Europe, arose in Spain thanks partly to these New World debates. In the hands of local Indies authorities, probabilism imbued the administration with an enduringly nondogmatic stance. Lastly, the council's post-1570s improvement of royal archives helped rulers become more consistent and assertive, reinforcing the flexible but stable society of orders.

The expansion of the Spanish Empire and the Habsburgs' creation of Europe's great courts shaped a robust tradition of giving advice to princes. Here, skepticism was also robust. Not all of these forms of princely advice owed to New World events, of course. Likely with an eye on Europe, Erasmus of Rotterdam had already dedicated his 1516 printed work *Education of a Christian* to the young Prince Charles V. It contained advice about how the youthful ruler should approach the truth for the benefit of the realm. Erasmus argued that the king should be the realm's most suspicious man. He stated that "the prince . . . must be the most discerning" of all, followed by his ministers.[229] On the one hand, he should welcome the counsel of "wise men" as his "hands and eyes" and take great care in defending poor and middling subjects by listening to their pleas.[230] On the other, he should guard himself against falsehood. Falsehood took at least two forms. The first was simple error, for the populace often embraced "false opinions, just like those people trussed up in Plato's cave, who regarded the empty shadows of things as the things themselves."[231] The second was the depravity and secret interests of courtiers and ministers, who could give wicked advice and conceal "rival interests" through false information—or even worse, flattery.[232] Erasmus warned that "the most pernicious flatterers of all are those who operate with apparent frankness but . . . contrive to urge you on."[233] The closer to power the official was, the more Charles was to distrust him.

To avoid the traps of ignorance and bias, Charles would have to take several steps. One was to constantly listen to differing viewpoints. Erasmus recounted a story about Alexander the Great, who "had the custom of covering one ear with his hand while hearing cases, saying that he was keeping it free for the other party."[234] Charles was to be "entirely free from all gross passions," seeking always the common good.[235] Most importantly, however, he was to have "the best possible intentions" when "avoiding or removing evils," for his own upright behavior and benevolence would win vassals' honesty and teach them moral rectitude by example.[236]

Catalan scholar Furió Ceriol's 1559 *El consejo, y consejeros del príncipe* (The Council, and Counselors of the Prince) provided advice to Philip and his Spanish ministers and was perhaps the most elaborate treatise on the topic available to the public until the end of the century. Ceriol's vision was for the king to sit above all and suspect all, for good governance springs not from a mediocre ruler whose ministers can easily fool him but from a critical and scrupulous monarch.[237] His ministers were to avoid all *bandos* and reject any opportunity for favoritism toward vassals; only by favoring the whole body of the republic could the doctor-counselor provide a lasting cure.[238] There were to be thus two councils—the king's own mental faculties, "the institution of the Prince," and then those of the councils. The prince was to keep himself distanced from the possible traps of incoming letters and ministers' advice while seeking to employ only the most morally upright, dispassionate, altruistic counselors.

The last sixteenth-century mirror of princes to deal with the matter of suspicion was the Portuguese lawyer Martín de Carvallo Villasboas' *Espeio de principes y ministros*, circa 1598. Carvallo had been a lawyer in Milan and wrote mainly with the Council of State in mind.[239] However, his book also laid bare one analysis of how the king and ministers were to calibrate the petition-and-response system toward the truth in general. As the master value for the ruler, he stressed prudence, without which governance was impossible.[240] But how could one achieve prudence? For one, the king was to control any "passions or joys that deprive man of the rest and quietude" necessary for deep thought.[241] Another strategy was, of course, to consume vassals' reports whenever possible: "Happy is that Prince who procures to listen every hour personally and through ministers. . . . He will thus not only know what happens in his State, but will do good by God . . . and with his Vassals."[242] However, there was one major problem. These two approaches needed a third—that of experience. A greenhorn artist might use his great intellect and envision a beautiful portrait, but his trembling hand would ruin the image.[243] Carvallo warned that "in arms, art, letters, and other things, experience perfects all."[244]

Carvallo did not think that a prince alone could acquire prudence and its components of dispassionate reasoning, responsiveness, and experience.[245] He needed ministers who were also free of sin and lacking personal vendettas and biases, irresolution, and laziness.[246] The prince would avoid candidates with these defects, appointing ministers who were both educated and experienced and could work fast while thinking subtly and "penetrating in difficulties" of statecraft.[247] However, Carvallo was perhaps more naive than the king and many Indies vassals. He suggested that the power of writing could accurately describe the world. He stressed that "the most prudent and faithful counselor of the Prince is the book, because books, without fear, without adulation, without passion, and without [the quest for] rewards, tell the Prince faithfully everything he wishes to know."[248] By reading, the prince could acquire, more than prudence, facts themselves: "Reading one can penetrate the Star, and everything upon the terrestrial globe, no matter how remote it is from this hemisphere."[249] Using reading and critical thought (*operación del entendimiento*), books could transport before the prince every people, every custom, every fact. Carvallo rhapsodized: "Reading . . . you will see the Pope, the Emperor, the Theologian . . . Hell, the sailor, the Turk . . . the barbarian's dress and habit, and those of the polished. . . . Reading you see, hear, and read."[250]

This was a more optimistic interpretation of the relationship between writing and reality than most Indies vassals and ministers, and even monarchs, expressed in their own writings. Others paused to reflect on the difficulties of finding the truth in a courtly context, in which rulers analyzed the world through abstracted images, papers, and words. One minister of the Council of Castile, Bishop don Pedro de Navarra, wrote in his 1560s work *Dialogues of the Difference between Speaking and Writing* that speech and text were different like "a live flame" to "a painted fire."[251] Cervantes conjures a similar image in *Don Quixote*. The titular protagonist scoffs at Crown knowledge, saying that while courtiers might encounter "painted enemies," true fellow knights-errant meet them "in their real body." Whereas ministers look at maps, Don Quixote and his adventurous ilk "measured the whole of the earth in our own feet."[252]

A strong current of gendered ideas coursed through this advice literature—surely a response to the general crisis of trust in Madrid. By the 1590s, tirades against women's influence in imperial administration had become much more common in mirrors of princes. Jesuit Pedro de Ribadeneyra (1527–1611) counseled the prince in his *Treaty of Religion and Virtues* to beware "the lightness and liberties of women."[253] The prince was to carefully patrol an increasingly effeminate society that had declined due to "communications with foreign nations, the excess of gold and silver and stones and spices, and presents that have arrived from the Indies."[254] The Franciscan Juan de Santa María (1551–1622) similarly warned in his 1616 *Tratado de republica* that "no judge open his chest to passion."[255] One had to avoid effeminate weakness to ensure that all received justice: to "free the oppressed, the orphan, the aggrieved widow, [and] send them the light of God."[256]

By the 1540s, Emperor Charles had become deeply suspicious of Indies conquistadors and other actors. King Philip also possessed a highly developed vision for how to apply skepticism to statecraft. He cautioned his son on his deathbed in 1598 to avoid passion and take care to gather as many reports as possible. He stated that the truth, or the next best thing, would gradually emerge through intelligent readings of documents. By reading vassals' letters against the grain, one could discover "important secrets." If the issue still did not reveal its nature, the prince would have to collect further information and with a "variety of these reports [achieve] a more copious cognition of the things of the world." Armed with texts and the counsel of experienced men, "one seizes better from the plausible [*verisimilar*] the truth."[257]

Echoing Ceriol's advice, the ailing monarch instructed his son to create two spheres of decision-making: a "council on the inside of the breast of the Prince, and an external one in the Councils" staffed by trusted and experienced ministers.[258] Neither was to be superior. They were to remain autonomous but in communication, ensuring that the ruler would not make rash decisions but also preventing a small clique of ministers from seizing the reins of government entirely.[259] The king thus expressed on the eve of his 1598 death his hermeneutics of suspicion and his faith that the solution to imperfect information was to procure ever more reports from his innumerable vassals.

Monarchs' constant thirst for subjects' reports—which they themselves could not read without ministers' assistance—imbued decrees with flexibility. Kings could not easily patrol every petition's truth claims, nor could they grasp most Indies realities. What if the king had been misinformed by a malicious petition? What if its author misunderstood Indies circumstances? What if a petitioner mischaracterized a group of vassals—like the Natives or the conquistadors—for secret, wicked ends? These were matters of utmost concern, from monarchs down to commoners. In recognition of this problem, both the Crown and its local officials frequently sought to mitigate enforcement of decrees. The Crown included a clause within royal decrees stating "I have been informed"—*yo he sido informado*—not only to avoid suggesting local meddling but to declare "that the king made his decision in awareness of the circumstances on-site" and not with perfect information.[260] The Crown acknowledged that the evidentiary basis of its policies was imperfect, potentially compromised by petitions' many epistemic problems.[261] In fact, the entire edifice of monarchical decrees was based on a skeptical epistemology.

The Crown's acknowledgment that its decisions could be flawed opened important avenues for vassals to contest edicts. The main legitimate recourse for vassals dissatisfied with a royal decree was to submit a counterpetition, which subjects often called a *súplica.* This supplication entailed a special bureaucratic process of its own. The aggrieved individual or group would appear at the High Court before the Crown notary. The counterpetition would begin with the aggrieved individual or group's explanation for not obeying the decree.[262] For example, on August 27, 1560, the council issued a decree reprimanding the archbishops and bishops of the Indies for excommunicating and fining vassals left and right for minor offenses.[263] The prelates were no longer to excommunicate for trivial matters. On January 15, 1561, the viceroy and High Court summoned Archbishop Montúfar of Mexico City to explain himself. He protested that "the decree was won with the truth having been silenced . . . with a *siniestra relación,* and His Majesty was not informed truthfully." The policy should not be enforced until "His Majesty and his Royal Council could be informed," especially because enforcement of the edict in this new land might sow "lascivious wickednesses and the gravest offenses to God." This case epitomizes two common beliefs: that decrees might be based on *siniestras relaciones* and that they were invalid if subjects could provide a superior account of the facts.

Officials and vassals in the Indies made self-serving interpretation of royal decrees into an artform. They combined these readings with *súplicas* to endlessly twist edicts, which often led the Crown to chastise its vassals for the malicious tactic (*malicia*) of delayed interpretation. For example, King Philip II expressed his displeasure in 1592, citing the viceroy of Mexico's November 17, 1591, report, that certain justice officials had a "bad interpretation of one of my decrees" and should implement it immediately, without *súplica* or delay.[264] Altogether, the legal truths that emerged from the petition-and-response system did not always generate an authoritative, final truth statement. Indeed, these documents often perpetuated suspicion even more, all while expanding vassals' political arsenals. As a result, while decrees remained very important, local actors struggled to interpret and implement them.

The vast number of royal decrees also generated further skepticism among officials. In 1612, the viceroy of Peru wrote to his successor in 1614, he had struggled to interpret the king's volition between so many contradictory and piecemeal documents. He explained that two "friends" had assisted him in this task: Discretion (*recato*) and Suspicion (*sospecha*). Petitioners and litigants might try to fool him by presenting a decree that established a certain rule. But after diligent searching, he might find that the king had later contradicted and negated it. So a viceroy seeking to avoid manipulation by vassals was to refrain from deciding a matter until he had a deeper understanding of his archive and of the royal intent. Moreover, he should be equally cautious when listening to legal advice from courtiers, for Peru was full of "those who would endeavor to fool you."[265] Thus, skeptical reflection on the nature of truth came to permeate the everyday practices of ruling the New World.

A radically disrupted society, runaway factionalism, bottom-up petitioning, and responsive legislation—these phenomena produced intellectual earthquakes in Spain and around the world. On the one hand, vassals submitted hundreds of thousands of *gobierno* proposals to the king, hoping to receive a favorable answer. On the other, fierce local debates could not always await the monarch's response. One common solution in such cases, especially by the 1540s, was for officials to consult with theologians and jurists about the best local solution to take in light of royal decrees and other sources of law. These experts offered dialectical local interpretations as temporary but morally legitimate replacements for an authority's decision. And this literature formed a major new tradition of skeptical jurisprudence: the methodology of probabilism, a doctrine of truth finding that guides jurists and theologians who face casuistic problems through a specific series of skeptical dialectics to reach any outcome that will probably avoid sin (even if other options seem safer or more probable). Human beings could select any resolution likely and therefore morally licit—and leave perfect knowledge to God. This method is inherently skeptical, framing total certainty as impossible for mere mortals.

Probabilism has multiple historical genealogies, one of which is strongly connected to important Salamanca Dominicans' struggles against conquistadors in the Indies. Most scholars have argued that probabilism and its concomitant intellectual revolution began with Dominican Bartolomé de Medina's 1577 treatise *Prima secundae parties.*[266] However, others note that the story reaches back further, particularly to the Indies. Medina's teacher was the Dominican Francisco de Vitoria, who famously decried the illegality of the New World conquests. Some Salamanca students of Vitoria, like Alonso de la Veracruz, taught theology and philosophy in Mexico. La Veracruz's work on the problem of the morality of Indigenous Purepecha inheritance rules informed his widely read marriage treatise, the 1556 *Speculum coniugiorum.*[267] Others from this school headed to Native missions as far as Chile, where they debated the legitimacy of Indigenous enslavement.[268] Yet another colleague of Medina's, and a major proponent of probabilism, was Tomás de Mercado. He formulated moral approaches to commercial problems that arose as Seville merchants went to the New World in search of social mobility and noble status.[269]

Most scholars believe that monarchs adopted this probabilistic casuistry when legislating.[270] However, it seems probabilism also owed much to Indies realities. Egía's work suggests that the distinct methodology of probabilism emerged in the mid-1500s largely as a global Dominican response to decades of Indies lawfare. Probabilism thus owes more to the Spanish Empire's system of *gobierno, gracia,* and *justicia,* as well as to Dominicans' responses to the radical circumstances of the early New World, than the other way around. This system of skeptical thought did not stay in the Indies or Spain. From Salamanca, the probabilist tradition spread across Europe, especially through Jesuit writings and curricula; it became overwhelmingly popular throughout the continent between the 1580s and the 1650s.[271]

Yet probabilistic casuistry was not an easy fix for the Indies' many problems. It was a slow and nondefinitive approach. Moreover, it could contribute to vassals' mischief, as they debated whether to implement royal decrees. This problem, and the informational frailty of decrees based on petitions in general, spurred the Crown to make important changes. By the late 1550s and 1560s, ministers realized that they had drafted decrees almost entirely in response to petitions and that these decrees were thus disorganized, confusing, and even contradictory. Incoming *gobierno* petitions especially continued to puzzle ministers. President Ovando was dismayed when he took control of the council, noting past ministers' neglect of archives and information.[272] He urged compilations and indices of decrees and commissioned fact-finding projects but especially began collecting key petitions to constitute new factual databases.[273] The Crown managed to establish a considerably better grasp of military and financial issues by the 1570s and 1580s. By the 1590s, it had several dozen geographical and thematic collections in its archives.[274] This paperwork revolution was deeply connected to custodial practices, as new archives allowed ministers to put certain dubious claims to the test. It also enabled ministers to envision the New World much more synoptically than before. The resulting royal assertiveness set the stage, paradoxically, for a seventeenth-century showdown between forceful Crown ministers and local vassals relying on casuistry and counterpetitioning to shape royal law.

Of course, nothing functioned by royal fiat alone. As we shall see, vassals clamored for novel paperwork solutions to prevent runaway deceit. Already in 1565, Franciscan friar Jerónimo de Mendieta suggested to Ovando that the Mexican administration create a vast database on all vassals to prevent their constant movement from town to town.[275] Local officials were busy creating their own databases. After the 1570s, the Inquisition greatly increased the number of investigations against vassals who had married multiple times or had claimed assumed identities.[276] The commoner Lázaro—turned don Guaman Poma de Ayala through paperwork service—proposed in his *Nueva corónica* (1615) a system of archival identification that dwarfed anything the Franciscan Mendieta might have conceived. Under Guaman Poma's direction, Native lords should be capable of proving their identities through royal decrees to prevent lying commoners from usurping social status and becoming false lords.[277] Each type of Native official would possess a *título* or identity paper, from the highest Inca to the lowest enforcer.[278] He even advocated that all travelers always carry identity papers in roads and inns to identify themselves by lineage. Anyone without papers would lose their goods and be tried.[279]

The Crown never achieved the kind of substantial grip on the truth that would enable it to act unilaterally. Ministers, viceroys, magistrates, and inquisitors still relied on petitions, denunciations, and biased reports.

However, administrators were far less passive than they had been just decades before. They had gradually devised novel solutions to temper skepticism. These resources reinforced on-the-ground transformations of local power in favor of viceroys, bishops, and inquisitors. Commoners slowly lost power to make claims over the truth, and ministers incrementally solidified their grip over their dominions. For many vassals, this was a relief: a society was emerging in which fraudsters lost the upper hand and doubt no longer tyrannized all.

CONCLUSIONS

The history of the New World is indeed one of Spaniards smashing idols and burning heretics. But it is also a history of women and men like don Juan Atonal and his followers. Yes, he was accused by a powerful bishop of heinous crimes, including idolatry and apostacy. But he had doubt on his side, and he used it as a key to escape the traps of faith. He and his Dominican allies knew that everyone wrote "with as much truth" as their rivals. It was through this acknowledgment and clever manipulation of the empire's jurisdictional fissures and traditions of uncertainty that don Juan and his peers walked triumphantly out of jail and back into community life.[280] Indeed, it was Bishop Feria who found himself ensnared in the traps of doubt.

Doubt has many histories. Identifying this endemic skepticism in the creation of the sixteenth-century Spanish New World is essential to understanding its society. Countless non-Spanish, nonelite actors participated in a thriving, tormented culture of sophisticated questioning. Moreover, this churn of vernacular-administrative skepticism moved upward into the highest echelons of the imperial administration—as well as outward across Europe. It forced vassals to reckon with new methodologies of casuistic probabilism, bolstering the Salamanca Dominicans' influential theorizations. It also prompted the Crown to experiment with more assertive styles of rule and invited reflections on how paperwork might create a society of orders. Vernacular skepticism shaped statecraft and philosophy at least as much as the other way around.

This rich and consequential culture of vernacular skepticism was created from below, not just by rulers, theologians, or philosophers. Elites and commoners—women and men of all backgrounds—engaged skeptically with *gracia, justicia,* and *gobierno* paperwork. Indeed, their doubt was an essential ingredient in the unsettling of the New World. Even as inquisitors and other officials persecuted vassals with heterodox religious views, the world of paperwork justice opened to subjects vast new panoramas of reflection on the nature of the real. The paper-based, agonistic, and participatory administration of justice and governance directed vassals' skepticism inward—toward the written word, language, and the medium of paper—and outward toward society in general.

Indeed, though the justice system was permeated by religious values, many mores operated in the service not of dogma but of doubt. The Old Testament itself justifies this approach, argued vassals. Warning about Indigenous commoners who testified falsely against priests, Bartolomé Álvarez cited Jeremiah 18:18, in which the people conspire against the prophet:

> Come and let us devise devices against Jeremiah; for the law shall not perish from the priest, nor counsel from the wise, nor the word from the prophet. Come, and let us smite him with the tongue, and let us not give heed to any of his words.[281]

While some Spanish and Indigenous vassals were certainly aware of ancient Greek academic skepticism, other ancient skeptical schools, and debates in the present, these traditions were less influential than everyday experience and ubiquitous sources like the Bible. The vernacular world of paperwork struggle was a font of skepticism regardless of whether petitioners cited Greek philosophy. In a world with so many petitioners and litigants, doubt was part of everyday life. Vassals' assurances that they were telling the truth and invocations of God's omniscience during oath swearing proved feeble bulwarks against rivals' suspicions of their *tachas, bandos,* malice, and passions and the limits of justice across distance.

Even the royal conscience, a deeply personal relation between the Maker and the monarch, spurred rather than stifled skepticism—and prevented rulers' decrees from being the final word.

Doubt was therefore a fundamental force in shaping the empire. Neither the priesthood nor the Inquisition stifled judicial-administrative skepticism, as Álvarez knew all too well. The participatory nature of *gobierno, gracia,* and *justicia* made a monopoly on the truth nigh impossible. Vassals therefore reflected on the truth constantly, regarding it as another weapon in the great bureaucratic battlefield. Their endemic disobedience leaned explicitly on the elusive nature of truth in law. Keeping the *gobierno* channel open in particular generated constant jurisdictional conflict between conquistadors, friars, Natives, officials, and others. An anonymous 1590s report noted that Council President Juan de Ovando had observed that this open communication caused

> disarray and liberty, with all the estates biting others and each other, and [causing] in the Royal Council much confusion because the reports of this very new land are so various, contrary, and biased.[282]

It is little wonder that by the 1570s, many vassals and officials were tired of this skeptical system of administration. Indeed, doubt helps explain how and why a new social order arose. Officials assembled the administration in response to a multitude of skeptical concerns. Ovando's reforms attempted to create an archive of legal and descriptive facts for the empire, and with them, a more orderly and active Crown. The final decades of the century saw, for the first time, great efforts to envision the legal order as a coherent whole.

A new society of orders did gradually emerge, with kings, viceroys, bishops, and inquisitors taking increasingly assertive roles in ascertaining and determining the truth. The council, local officials, and Indies subjects alike experimented with ways to limit extreme factionalism, uncertainty, and ultimately, disorder. Their increasing decisiveness would be essential for making society more cohesive. But another force, intimately connected to the problem of truth, played perhaps an even greater role in stabilizing society. Vassals tended to pragmatically embrace documents as true as long as officials, intermediaries, and subjects had created them through correct procedures. The sum of these documents was the archive, or more precisely, the archives: an interconnected array of thousands of local collections belonging to vassals and officials. These repositories grew both from the bottom up, and—to a lesser extent—from the top down through limited royal initiatives. They succeeded in cementing a more stable regime of truth, which shored up a society once utterly consumed by skepticism. It is to the archive's conquest of the Indies, and the Crown's conquest of the archives, that we now turn.

CHAPTER 5

The Conquest of Archives

From Society of Disorder to Society of Orders

Don Diego de Torres left Nueva Granada for Spain in 1577, after five years of petitioning and litigating before the High Court.[1] He was one of thousands of *genízaros,* half-Indigenous rangers, who in the mid-1500s were expanding the limits of the empire. Although he was an experienced frontiersman and one of the best pikemen in the region, he failed to become a conquistador-pensioner.[2] Next, he tried his hand at being an Indigenous lord.[3] Things now turned sour. Don Diego did have some compelling arguments on his behalf. His mother, Catalina de Moyachoque, had been a prominent Muisca, the oldest sister of the lord of Turmeque. Don Diego, meanwhile, had received a Dominican education, and was well-traveled and prepared for lawfare. To claim lordship over Turmeque, he demanded the baptism of countless Muiscas; here, the spiritual conquest had not yet come to pass.[4] Despite his claims, he could summon no Native witnesses on his behalf. Without them, he was no Indigenous lord.[5] So he set sail for Spain, hoping to persuade a council with ministers who had no idea about Nueva Granada politics or customs.

In Madrid, don Diego made some inroads with his smooth talking. He had promised to help many Native lords in Nueva Granada petition the Crown, carrying their letters across the sea. Along his way to Spain—during which he survived a shipwreck—he met friends of council ministers. It did not hurt that he brought with him hundreds of emeralds.[6] At the royal court, he drummed up enough witness support to persuade ministers to an extent—they requested confirmation from Nueva Granada authorities. Meanwhile, he performed his lordship and successfully petitioned for royal stipends for life and the prestigious position of royal stablemaster in Madrid.[7]

The part-Muisca swashbuckler's plans evidently clashed with the archives. He then attempted to master them himself. The council's visionary president, Juan de Ovando, was reforming the institution, transforming heaps of documents into sprawling archives which would at last help the king and ministers understand the Indies. No longer would the Crown be swamped and exhausted by the radical era's tens of thousands of royal decrees, innumerable court sentences, and heaps of lawsuits and petitions.[8] Of interest to don Diego was one of Ovando's new manuscript compilations of legislation on Indigenous matters: the Book of the Republic of Indians.[9] With this volume in hand, don Diego began to act as the legal representative of many Indigenous lords from Nueva Granada.[10] He also positioned himself as a champion of the spiritual conquest, which friars had failed to impose on the province. In 1578, don Diego argued in a rare face-to-face meeting with the king that without friars, the conquistadors ruled supreme; unbaptized Natives toiled as slaves in households, mines, textile mills, and fields.[11] And perhaps most cunningly, don Diego persuaded his monarch to audit the royal officials and archives of Nueva Granada. In 1580, he sailed back to his homeland with royal auditor Juan Bautista de Monsón by his side.

In Nueva Granada, word of a paperwork reckoning spread panic. Conquistador-pensioners and officials heard of the *genízaro*'s advance; rumors that he was joining British pirates and runaway enslaved communities prompted one major city, Tunja, to cancel Corpus Christi celebrations and order the confiscation of part-Indigenous subjects' weapons.[12] Monsón also soon generated pandemonium with his audit in the capital of Santa Fe. An informant claimed that one High Court magistrate had been a sodomite—so the accused dispatched this tipster, stuffing his severed penis into a wound in his abdomen. Monsón quickly caught the murderer, who now implicated other judges and the archbishop in sodomitical acts and other crimes. The investigator soon realized that he was powerless against local factions, which accused him of illegally marrying his son to the young daughter of a conquistador.[13] The audit became a battle over control of communication and archives: both camps raided rivals' couriers and archives and openly manipulated testimonies. As vassals began plastering the city with scandalous broadsides and accusations of sodomy, the rest of the High Court executed the allegedly sodomitical magistrate. Monsón now jailed two of the avenging magistrates. This move only worsened the situation. Both sides mobilized armed bands of part-Native and Black vassals, who raided prisons and insulted and mistreated all Crown authorities equally.[14] Monsón's enemies imprisoned him, dragging him through his own palace to his cell. In 1581 the king commissioned a new magistrate, Cristóbal de Azueta, to mediate. No sooner had he arrived than his own slave had poisoned him, and he died during intercourse with his young lover.[15] The case collapsed.

Only the arrival of yet another auditor, don Juan Prieto de Orellana, solved the crisis. He took a different strategy, allying himself with Indigenous commoners. He issued them countless land titles and moved the labor market away from servile relations to wage labor, sapping conquistador power. These aspiring lords would henceforth be mere pensioners. Prieto de Orellana also shored up royal authority by empowering field justices (*corregidores*), weakening conquistadors and Native lords alike.[16]

Monsón and don Diego sailed back to Spain in disgrace. The auditor had become the audited. Many years later, Monsón was found guilty by the council for having forced witnesses. His investigation had collected no fewer than twenty thousand pages of documentation; now their veracity was utterly compromised.[17] Don Diego, meanwhile, lamented bitterly that Prieto de Orellana's new order was even more entrenched than what came before. Factionalism and struggles over seigneurial lordship gave way to nearly absolute Crown jurisdiction and authority. The winners of this audit would be the lasting victors of Nueva Granada society, the archives piling up with documents confirming the winners' stories.

These texts became the truths on which to a new social order was built. New Granada would experience no further rapid and profound structural reforms. Don Diego died amid his litigation for the lordship of Turmeque; years later, his Spanish widow collected a pension in his name.[18] His only social advances had come from his ability to act as an archival broker in Madrid for other Native subjects. Friendships with the Incas of Quito, for instance, had helped him obtain large holdings in Quito.[19]

Otherwise, don Diego's ambitions had been blocked by his radical vision. By the 1560s and especially the 1580s, the Indies' radical era was coming to a close. By this time, the Crown, many vassals and the trinity of viceregal, episcopal, and inquisitorial authorities had become thoroughly persuaded that extensive royal jurisdiction was the antidote to seigneurialism. Obedience was a cardinal virtue, not furious systemic critique. The would-be Native lord had managed to encourage the fateful audits of the 1580s, which reshaped Nueva Granada, instating royal power over seigneurial forces. This new arrangement left little room for a man who sought to create a new friar-lord alliance in Turmeque and beyond.

Vassals' and officials' embrace of obedience and royal absolutism were not the only forces driving these changes throughout the Indies. Another motor of this epochal social transformation was the archive. Don Diego's story illuminates how local and imperial archives transformed the ruler-vassal bond, changing the nature of communication and serving as an increasingly important site of paperwork struggle. President Ovando's mission to order the Indies ran through the archive—as did Diego's dreams of social mobility, Monsón's audits, and Prieto de Orellana's commoner alliances. These repositories came to enjoy wide legitimacy. Gradually but almost irreversibly, everyone turned to archives for the truth—a shift that forever transformed ruler-ruled communication and society.

Archives shifted the logic of society and the shape of politics. Their constant expansion and growing importance in Indies struggles transformed how paperwork and lawfare functioned. Archives featured heaps of past decisions of *gobierno, gracia,* and *justicia* and everyday documents like contracts and wills. Subjects carefully clung to all scraps of paper from the radical phase, for these could become useful resources in future struggles. And their paperwork battles became longer, slower, more formal, more erudite affairs. Petitions became lengthier, sometimes growing into interminable *arbitrios* or treatises. Lawsuits cited more legal sources, including royal decrees. Petitioners and litigants had once been experts in mobilizing witnesses to create ambitious truths and even in sending bold but unsubstantiated petitions to the Crown. As archives became more important, these vassals increasingly shifted their strategies. They became experts on precedent, glossers of unclear phrases, collectors of quotes. Archival brokers' fortunes soared. Those without archives, on the other hand, suffered.

As these behemoth collections piled high, they captured and cemented countless cocreated truths. Whereas the truth in the radical era had been wild, spontaneous, and highly pliable, archives gradually tethered it to new styles of communication and more demanding standards of proof. Lawfare had been conducted by all as an unrestrained social battle in which truth was asserted through mobs of witnesses and farfetched assertions, leading to paralyzing doubt. Yet this doubt prompted subjects to cling to previous decisions as truths when waging new struggles. The interlocked constellation of family, local, and royal archives therefore proved a powerful tool—not just for struggling subjects but for the establishment of a widely shared truth and ultimately, a society of orders.

The outcomes of vassals' paperwork politics also shifted. As we saw in Chapter 1, efforts to topple tyrant lords and reform whole social structures diminished by the 1560s and especially the 1570s to 1580s. Attention moved to individual corrupt officials, and cases became more pedantic and lawyerly. This growing pedantism also affected everyday struggles; all vassals, including non-Spanish *ladinos*, had to adapt careful strategies around mastery of archives and legal categories. Subjects not only scrutinized rivals' every blemish but also delved into their genealogies—little wonder don Diego's rivals blasted him as *mestizo*, part-Indigenous and therefore allegedly untrustworthy. Categories like *mestizo* would proliferate as genealogical experts mined archives to trace family histories many generations back.[20] Indeed, the roots of the infamous racialized categories we call the caste system are found in this agonistic style of factional struggle, which existed by the 1540s but exploded in frequency after the 1570s. One might even argue that the proliferation of these racialized categories was little more than the sublimation of radical-era factionalism into a new era of fastidious hierarchical struggle.

As individuals felt themselves discriminated against by the haphazard policies of the radical era and the increasingly punctillious rules of the post-1570s phase, they organized themselves more and more around textual communities. Joanne Rappaport has shown, for instance, that viceregal social groups began to base their collective identities, politics, ideas of the past, and everyday life, around their archives.[21] In Mexico, Peru, and beyond, the result of archivalization was the rise of self-described communities of *mestizos, mulatos, negros,* and most notably, the *Nación Indiana,* an Indies-wide Indigenous lobby. All of these emerging identities were based on local and royal archives.

This archival morass sometimes attracted vassals' denunciations—*it is all corrupt*—but for the most part, paperwork collections enjoyed broad consensus. Self-described *mestizos* used archives when combating friars; friars used archives when rebutting. All sides reached to the archives in waging this new type of entrenched lawfare. In this way, the struggles of the radical era—and the categories they forged—would define society for centuries to come.

These repositories did much of the work of conquest that many historians have attributed to the Crown in the late sixteenth century. The emergence of broad royal jurisdiction and a society of orders had more to do with vassals' creation of many radical archives than with boots on the ground. And because archives were cocreated from the bottom-up, they legitimized this emerging order more than force alone ever could.

The consummation of the society of orders also came to rest on a fourth conquest, building on those of the sword, the cross, and the archives: the conquest of historiography. We have argued throughout this book that these three conquests were in reality characterized by bottom-up alliances of elites and commoners, men and women, and Indigenous and Spanish actors (among others). This historiographical conquest was more markedly top down. Previously, vassals' factional scholarship blasted their rivals. Conquistadors, friars, and Indigenous authors blasted each other before their readers. But by the late 1500s weary vassals and Crown historians wrote histories cleansed of the century's messy, radical dynamics. Some began to completely sanitize and omit traces of the radical.

By the 1570s, royal historians had caught on and carried this strategy forward. They acquired and retooled once-radical archives to tell a story purged of royal weakness and Indies conflict. The Crown's deradicalized vision told of a fantastic, even mythologized empire in which catastrophic upheavals and bottom-up lawfare had never existed. The Indies' rulers had slowly but inevitably imposed themselves over the New World, patiently bringing their master plans to fruition just as they had envisioned since 1492. This vision remains central to many metanarratives today. It explicitly reinforces the liberal vision of an overbearing Spanish state and the decolonial vision of the postconquest end of Indigenous politics and history. Hispanists cite these often heavily propagandistic accounts to depict the empire as driven by admirable values of Christian charity and civilization to the benefit of Native vassals. The historiographical conquest thus conquered radicalism itself, scrubbing it from the record.

These transformations were crucial for the emergence of the society of orders—and its politics as well. Culturalist scholarship has emphasized that after the Counter-Reformation and especially in the 1600s, a baroque ethos captured the Indies. This was a conservative culture of hierarchical corporatism, ornamental extravagance, *mestizaje,* and an embrace of aesthetic and social contradiction.[22] Here, the visual world—clothing, art, music, festivals, even the placement of pillows—played an outsized role in ritually staging an elaborate hierarchy. Even if there is some truth to this vision, we insist upon tracing this new era's evolving political patterns rather than insisting mainly upon culture. We prefer the dichotomy of radical disordering and ordering to Renaissance versus baroque. Crucially, placing emphasis upon politics helps underscore that though lawfare changed, struggles continued. The centrality of Indigenous commoners, elites, and women changed, and in some ways diminished, but never disappeared—far from it. This era's politics continued under other guises. Moreover, the increasing presence of Afro-descendant actors and their politics introduced new political struggles even as a society of orders consolidated.

This book and this chapter make claims about how and why sixteenth-century politics changed. These are also methodological claims. We insist that archival politics played an essential role in the transition from radical to orderly society, but also that these repositories never constituted an exclusive register of elite voices, European categories, and imperial reason. Instead of proclaiming the need to read archives against the grain, we underscore the need to also read them along the grain—largely because, in fact, these repositories burst with the (mediated) voices of subalterns. Reading along the grain, we argue, does not only turn up evidence of white anxieties and Europeans' instrumental reason.[23] To the contrary, we insist on viceregal archives' polyvocality and political relevance for many actors. Here we follow historians of antebellum slavery Lesly Harris and Daina Ramey Berry, who have urged scholars to dig deeper into the archive rather than proclaiming their sterility and thus forcing scholars to resort to critical figuration when reconstructing subaltern voices.[24] To discover the wider world of non-Spanish actors who shaped and embodied the empire, we need to understand that archives are largely registers of dialogue between rulers and ruled (albeit always under asymmetrical circumstances). Archives feature petitions, denunciations, testaments, and other fragments cocreated by often-ignored actors. But these non-elite actors themselves used archives as they struggled to shape their lives and society around them. It is often the historiography itself which has argued for the sterility of archival research; it is this claim of sterility, more than anything, that we must read against the grain.

Reading the archive along the grain and against this historiography yields striking results. In this chapter, we demonstrate that growing Crown power and major social transformations resulted initially from bottom-up initiatives. Just as the other conquests were largely cocreated affairs, so too were the efforts of vassals and administrators to rebuild society using archives. Some of these initiatives were triggered by don Diego de Torres's petitioning in Nueva Granada, but others are initiatives that most historians see as top-down impositions, particularly those of Investigator

Valderrama in Mexico and Viceroy Toledo in Peru. We demonstrate the vast involvement of Indigenous commoners in Valderrama's reforms, which served as a blueprint for Toledo's and Prieto de Orellana's reforms (among others). Even President Ovando's investigation of the council was largely the result of bottom-up maneuvering unleashed by Martín de Cortés's conspiracy and the agitation of Indigenous-friar alliances.

Our insistence on following the flows of the archive has also brought us to a bottom-up account of the origins of most *casta* (racial) terms in the Indies. These terms, we argue, did not come from prefigured and inevitable Hispanic racial traditions rooted in medieval and Reconquista prejudices or from the logic of capitalism as it transplanted itself into the Indies' tropical soil. Rather, they emerged from factional petitioning, often featuring Indigenous and part-Indigenous politics. As lawfare caused seigneurial regimes to collapse and paperwork invited an agonistic melee, the regime of *tachas* increasingly featured racialized terms of disparagement. Some vassals underwent withering scrutiny from rivals, resulting in fractional and genealogical regimes of categorization (from *mestizos* to *tercerones* and *cuarterones*, for example). Such struggles manifested themselves increasingly as vassals fought over coveted positions—access to municipal office, universities, canonries, and so forth.

Paradoxically, the opposite also occurred: other vassals disappeared into Indigenous and Spanish groups. Many headed to the frontiers or into traditional Native communities, where factionalism was less multipolar and social competition less fierce. There, as we saw in Chapter 2, they often managed to become dark-skinned Indigenous Spaniards in the archives. Others became not Spanish but Indigenous, as don Diego de Torres and the chronicler Diego Muñoz Camargo hoped to become. Crucially, these three regimes of categorization—fractional, hispanizing, and indigenizing—rested on archival fictions and strategies, and mined documents that vassals had created during the radical phase.[25]

While the univocality and exclusivity of archives—along with their utility to imperial designs—has been greatly overstated, there is a story of domination and power here, too. Archives conquered the Indies, we argue. These collections of documents achieved this by transforming communication. They enabled Crown officials to modestly yet significantly expand their assertive power by controlling the archives in turn. But even more importantly, archives conquered the New World by stabilizing and slowing down social conflict.

Here, we offer a new historical sociology of communication to explain the dialectical dynamics of disorder, order, and politics in early modern history. The liberal metanarrative of the history of the printed book has argued that several factors motivated the bottom-up social chaos wrought by print in the Reformation: wars of religion, skeptical crises, the political revolution of the English Civil War. Print, in turn, helped a reordering of society, as authors and administrators sought to combat chaos and instroduce the stabilizing institutions of experimentation and empiricism, commercial exchange, and polite sociability. In this liberal story, these print-driven reforms created the public sphere, birthing the modern nation as a broad imagined community. We offer, on the other hand, a sociology based on manuscript-based, petition-driven, bottom-up systems of political communication. In the Indies, the system of petition and response generated decades of social disorder, which encouraged (but did not preordain) the rise of viceroys, bishops, and inquisitors (Chapter 1); new global markets based on the emancipation of captives and the mobility of commoners liberated from seigneurial lordships (Chapter 2); a faction-driven revolution of creative and violent epistemological plurality (Chapter 3); and sweeping waves of debilitating social doubt (Chapter 4).

The archives played another role: that of stabilizing society. They encouraged actors to struggle against each other before officials by presenting a battery of documents that all actors agreed could potentially be truthful. They tended less to create inventive new texts (as they did more often in the radical phase) than to collect, preserve, strategically deploy, and reinterpret old documents. This archive was both a resource and a snare. It helped vassals amass victories and further their politics. However, it also limited the concepts and creativity that had been virtually limitless in the radical era. And soon the Crown discovered that the archive—a vast, dispersed, and complex whole—could be tamed and made useful. This chapter modifies Arndt Brendecke's provocative analysis that the Spanish imperial petition-and-response system made no concrete use of Indies knowledge, rendering archives as simple repositories of unserviceable political communication. Rather, we argue that the first full-fledged version of the overseas European information state is to be found in 1570s Madrid, in the Council of the Indies.[26] Unfortunately, historiography on early modern information states has tended to overlook the Spanish Indies' case entirely, although ministers pioneered overseas rule by archive.[27]

Crown officials' late 1560s turn toward archival collection was key to their vision of creating order—and this vision required secrecy. Scholars have long noted the council's obsession with secrecy in the late sixteenth century; we argue that it was not just ministers' fear of foreign powers but their desire for Indies obedience and social peace that drove Ovando's foundational reforms.[28] Radical skepticism and factionalism had to be brought under control, so the Crown began to confiscate feuding factions' radical archives in both the Indies and Spain.

In the process, council ministers increasingly discovered the New World, seeing this vast dominion as a coherent system and organizing archives to reveal and remedy the empire's critical weaknesses. Meanwhile, the reforms of investigators Valderrama, Toledo, Prieto y Orellana, and others created a more enduring basis for society, through which more petitioners than ever could approach the Crown. However, their stabilization of a regime of archival truth reduced social mobility for many *ladinos,* who had thrived on documentary invention and reinvention.

A subtle fourth conquest was underway. Royal chroniclers learned from Indies historians to silence the region's stories of tyranny and radicalism. With the publication of Antonio de Herrera's 1601 and 1615 *magna opera,* the Crown finally managed to offer readers the illusion of a smooth series of conquests: invasion, conversion, and royal control. This way, the Crown symbolically finalized the conquest of the archives with its own conquest of historiography. The story Herrera told gradually gained traction and remains largely intact centuries later, making his the longest lasting of all the conquests. He and many other subsequent scholars have ensured the erasure of Indies politics, and especially Indigenous and radical politics, from this turbulent century.

RADICAL REFORM, REVOLT, AND CRISIS IN 1560S MEXICO

When Investigator Jerónimo de Valderrama and marquis Hernán Cortés' heir don Martín Cortés arrived in Mexico in early 1563, few could have anticipated the consequences of their actions. These two men—who desired to shore up an orderly society at last—created unprecedented turmoil. They set off processes that empowered Indigenous commoners and thereby cost friars and Native lords considerable power over their communities. They also decimated conquistador power, driving seigneurial power in the Indies to its 1567 nadir.

In the 1560s, archives were emerging everywhere, as lawfare generated heaps on heaps of paperwork. Every faction had its own collection. Valderrama's arrival further encouraged commoners to assemble archives and petition to defeat the seigneurial tyranny of friar and lords from Oaxaca to central Mexico. Don Martín's presence, on the other hand, triggered events that led to the ultimate defeat of conquistadors as a powerful faction. These events in Mexico helped the Crown realize that the empire was a passive victim of lawfare. Valderrama's *ad hoc* strategies to defeat seigneurial lordships through broad bottom-up alliances taught the council the importance of centralized archives, while the great reformer of the Council of Indies, President Juan de Ovando, learned from Valderrama the importance of moving against friar theocracies and tyrannical Indigenous lords. In the wake of Valderrama's visit, the council created an archive of tens of thousands of royal edicts on the evolving and contested powers of friars and bishops in the Indies since the 1490s. Ovando used this code on "Spiritual Power and Patronato Real" to justify a monopoly of church authority in the hands of newly empowered Crown functionaries—namely, bishops and inquisitors. Ovando thereafter sent viceroys to Mexico and Peru to complete Valderrama's bottom-up reforms and consolidate the Crown's monopoly over all seigneurial power without recourse to armed violence. These investigators, in turn, experimented with commoner alliances, weakened seigneurial lords, and reshaped the Indies for centuries to come. Central to their approach was conquering once-radical archives for Crown interests.

As a royal minister and treasurer, don Jerónimo de Valderrama was on a mission to increase Crown income after the empire's recent bankruptcy. He set out to increase tribute revenues, securing the flow of silver and uprooting nepotism in viceroy and high magistrate circles. Yet his main target was the friars' seigneurial power. Although the exact circumstances that prompted Valderrama's investigation are unclear, the fierce clash with the Mexican archbishop—who alleged in 1561 that friars were acting as "absolute lords and shepherds"—surely shaped his mission.[29] Franciscan Landa's massacres in the Yucatan likely also played a role. But how could Valderrama combat such powerful theocracies? He had no recourse to force and had lost nearly his entire clique of twenty-one dependents in a shipwreck, along with all his belongings.[30] The investigator complained that he had almost no reliable allies.[31] Within his first year, he dismissed three scribes whom he suspected of being easily bribed and perhaps even spying on him.[32] He only trusted one secretary, who had survived the shipwreck with him and promptly seized key archives in Mexico City to prevent rivals from falsifying documents.[33] Valderrama repeatedly warned the council and king not to believe any reports about him.[34] Nothing was as it seemed in Mexico; if Native commoners wrote against him, they had surely been goaded to action by the friars.[35] Even the bishop of Oaxaca alerted the investigator of friars' power to bend the truth. With subjects terrorized, sworn notarized interrogations were useless.[36] It dawned on Valderrama: tyrants had destroyed the truth, rendering the Crown ignorant.[37]

The investigator thus followed the antityranny playbook that had worked so many times before in the Indies. He constantly denounced friars as tyrants and "absolute lords" who acknowledged no superior.[38] Friars had allied themselves with Native lords and now administered their own lordships, collecting tribute, running jails, commanding police forces, building enormous monasteries, and managing sweatshops. They were particularly powerful in Oaxaca and Verapaz (Valderrama could have mentioned the Yucatan as well). With Native lords' consent, the orders controlled tribute gathering and quotas and delivered sermons informing commoners that they owed the Crown no tribute because the conquest was illegal. Everywhere, rebellious friars preached radical messages of disobedience against the Crown. Some sermonized against Valderrama himself, as did Dominican friar Domingo de la Anunciación in a fiery mass before Mexico's authorities.[39]

A distant, uninformed, unarmed monarch could not protect vassals from such tyrants. Valderrama had to build local alliances and collect information on the abuses of friars and Native lords. To make matters worse, he came to suspect that Mexico's viceroy and magistrates were supporting this theocratic model—likely to triangulate against conquistador power. He was correct; radicals like Las Casas had indeed been influencing ministers since the early 1540s.

What made these friars so appealing to Crown officials was their demand that the king and ministers protect the downtrodden. Valderrama's strategy thus featured three crucial components. First, he would ally himself with Native commoners, the downtrodden themselves. Second, he would court conquistadors to win the support of local strongmen. And throughout, he would marshal paperwork to prove this abuse to the council—largely by demanding everyone present and keep documentary collections.

Marquis don Martín Cortés provided Valderrama with essential strategic input. The two had already met in Madrid.[40] Valderrama was up against viceroys, magistrates, Native lords, and friars—a powerful alliance—but don Martín proposed two concrete tactics. First, he advised breaking the alliance between Indigenous lords and friars. Their theocracies kept the commoners in thrall and the Crown from its taxes. To this end, the marquis urged strictly regulating, standardizing, and documenting Indigenous tribute. Lords and friars had long been exacting peasants' contributions off the books, demanding so-called *derramas.* He therefore suggested a radical agrarian reform by which all landless commoners would receive parcels to harvest and tributary rolls would be kept for tributary transparency.[41] No longer would friars and Native lords shelter commoners from Crown oversight and exploit them off the record. Valderrama embraced this proposal. All Mexican income—conquistadors, monasteries, sales tax, tithes—would henceforth form a single, consolidated tributary pool for viceroys to distribute as they saw fit. A vision of royal consolidation was coming from an unexpected quarter—a seigneurial lord.

Second, don Martín proposed weakening the viceroys' power, for these officials had distributed privileges not to the conquests' veterans but to undeserving parvenus. This strategy was a blueprint for a conquistador comeback, yet Valderrama accepted it. The investigator sent the council detailed lists of official appointments, land titles, pensions, and cash illegally taken from the viceregal treasury.[42] Valderrama needed to shore up support through his own patronage networks. For instance, he appointed the marquis's half-Indigenous brother don Martín (son of Hernán and his famous consort doña Marina Malintzin) to the position of sheriff (*alguacil*) of Mexico City. As Mexico's Indigenous vassals angrily protested Valderrama's reforms, this don Martín would prove instrumental in putting the revolt down.[43]

COMMONER POLITICS, RADICAL LAND REFORM, AND REVOLT

On arriving in Mexico in 1563, Valderrama set out to communicate with commoners. He wanted to know how deep the tyrannical roots had spread. He elicited paperwork from numerous towns in central Mexico: Tepeapulco, Cholula, Tula, Uchalcoatengo, Xochimilco, Amecameca, and Coutinho. He found friars controlling municipal politics and siphoning commoner labor for their own purposes and a huge monastic-Indigenous administration. Cholula alone had forty choir members and sixteen trumpeters.[44] He also collected testimonies from Yahuitlan, Cuernavaca, Tehuacan, Teposcolula, Temaculapa, Tlaxiaco, and Achintla in the Mixteca Alta detailing the friars' powerful theocracies. The picture was dismal. Friars appointed Native leaders and local authorities without royal consent, taxed commoners to fund synods, ran complex workshops and textile businesses, and forced Indigenous vassals on their deathbeds to sign away their lands to the orders. They also usurped bishops' jurisdictions. Local witnesses complained that the Franciscan friars in the Mixtec had not only removed St. Peter's Day from annual religious festivities but also replaced it with St. Francis's, foregrounding the power of friars over bishops. Commoners testified that friars had repeatedly told them that neither the Crown nor conquistadors had the right to collect tribute.[45]

The commoners responded eagerly to Valderrama's investigation, providing a wealth of information about friars' abuses. They also used his presence to move against their own lords. Explosive paperwork riots ensued. Commoners in the province of Tepeaca, for example, took aim at Indigenous lords don Diego Ceynos, Diego de Olarte, and Gabriel de los Ángeles. These aggrieved lords appealed to the High Court, hoping to defend their patrimonial lands: Xicotla, Acazinco, Acocaque, Santiago de Chimilco, Santa Margarita Mazapila, Acuzaque, San Pedro Tlalhitic, Santiago Acatlan, and San Nicolás Tamazola. Each lord had hundreds of sharecroppers with whom they had recorded contracts to provide services. Since time immemorial, the lords argued, they had negotiated contracts with commoners in the form of paintings. But while these lords had paintings, so did commoners. The High Court ruled in favor of the lords—these were not commons but rather lords' patrimonial lands that tenants worked but did not own. But the commoners appealed. Using Valderrama's argument, they argued that idolatrous, tyrannical lords had lost sovereignty over their private lands in the wake of the conquest. These lands were now the king's to redistribute at will. The High Judges turned down the appeal as well. In 1571, the lords had the sentences read before the defeated sharecroppers.[46]

Valderrama's investigation often succeeded, however, in restoring property and redistributing land to the benefit of commoners and at the expense of the friar-lord-magistrate alliance. Few documents tell this story like the so-called *Codex Osuna* (see Figure 5.1). Since its late 1800s publication, *Osuna* has enjoyed considerable renown for its documentation of Spanish abuse against Natives. But the story is immensely more complex. It is a testament to and archive of commoner paperwork, through which artisans and landless commoners approached Valderrama with various claims. Among them are complaints about Mexico's most powerful officials, one of the factions the council wished him to audit. It includes, for example, the city council of Tetepango's denunciation of High Court magistrate Vasco de Puga for unpaid wages. On August 27, 1564, commoners

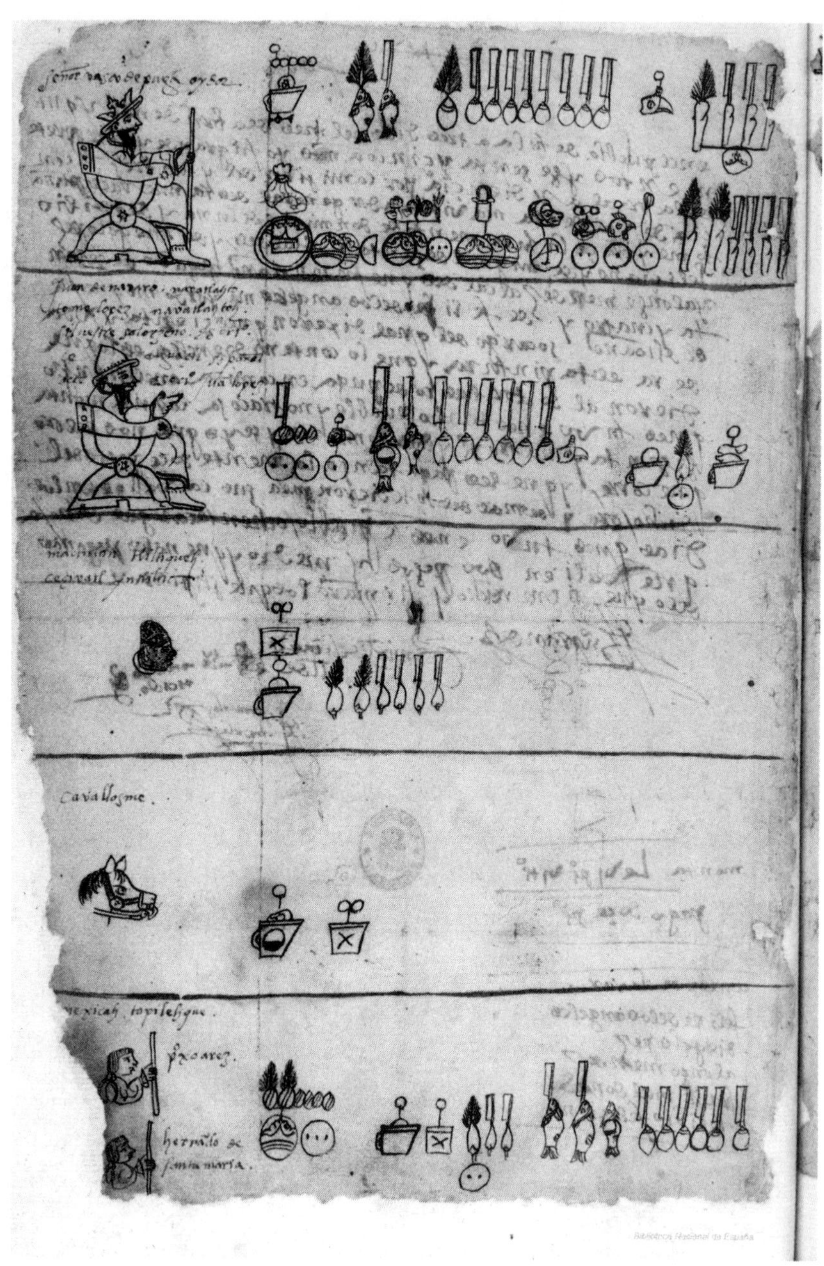

Figure 5.1 This page documents the expenses incurred by Dr. Puga and his Spanish, Black, and Indigenous household after an audit of Native communities. It includes symbols for horses, slaves, and magistrates who visit the communities with an enumeration of each group's payments for foodstuffs (poultry, fish, mutton, chiles, etc.). "Pintura de la comida." *Codex Osuna*. F. 492v-30v, Biblioteca Nacional de España, VITR/26/8.

Diego Flores, Matías de la Cruz, Pedro Claudio, Domingo Vázquez, and Francisco Tlocatl appeared before Valderrama to offer sworn testimony regarding every item consumed by High Judge Puga and his retinue.[47]

More dramatically, Valderrama's new tributary policies energized commoners to demand huge tracts of aristocrats' land. Commoners in Atlixocan each received plots of two hundred or four hundred square meters (*brazas*) from the redistribution of twenty-one square kilometers (two *caballerías*) of the lands of lords of Mexico.[48] Thousands of landless commoners seem to have benefited from this case of radical land reform, forced on the lords by an alliance of commoners and the investigator. *Osuna* casually documents commoners' annexation of an area nearly half the size of the Island of Manhattan.

These radical reforms did not benefit all Indigenous commoners. In Mexico City, many found the reforms not emancipating but threatening. In recognition of the Mexicas' services to the Crown, neither Native lords nor commoners there paid annual tribute. The Indigenous municipality helped assign commoners to public works and services to Crown officials. They also served the local Franciscans. Valderrama was eager to end these messy and untransparent arrangements. Henceforth, all Mexica commoners would simply pay tribute like other Natives. Valderrama's new policy triggered furious responses from the Mexica. To add insult to injury, Mexico City was a trading town, not an agricultural community. Therefore, a tribute of half a bushel of corn per commoner would put inordinate pressure on the landless majority. The news came as the Indigenous municipality struggled with the Spanish city council over dry land recovered from the lake by drought, dikes, and aqueducts. The so-called *Codex Reese,* or Beinecke Map, was typical of the internal documents produced by the Indigenous municipality of Mexico to document this land (see Figure 5.2). Lords assigned commoners tiny parcels to transform into corn-growing lots (*chinampas*) in 1564, likely to help offset the proposed tributary burdens.[49]

The fury of the Mexica commoners vividly appears from their perspective in the Nahuatl *Anales de Juan Bautista.* One important section details political struggles in 1564 and 1565 regarding tribute burdens. Carpenters,

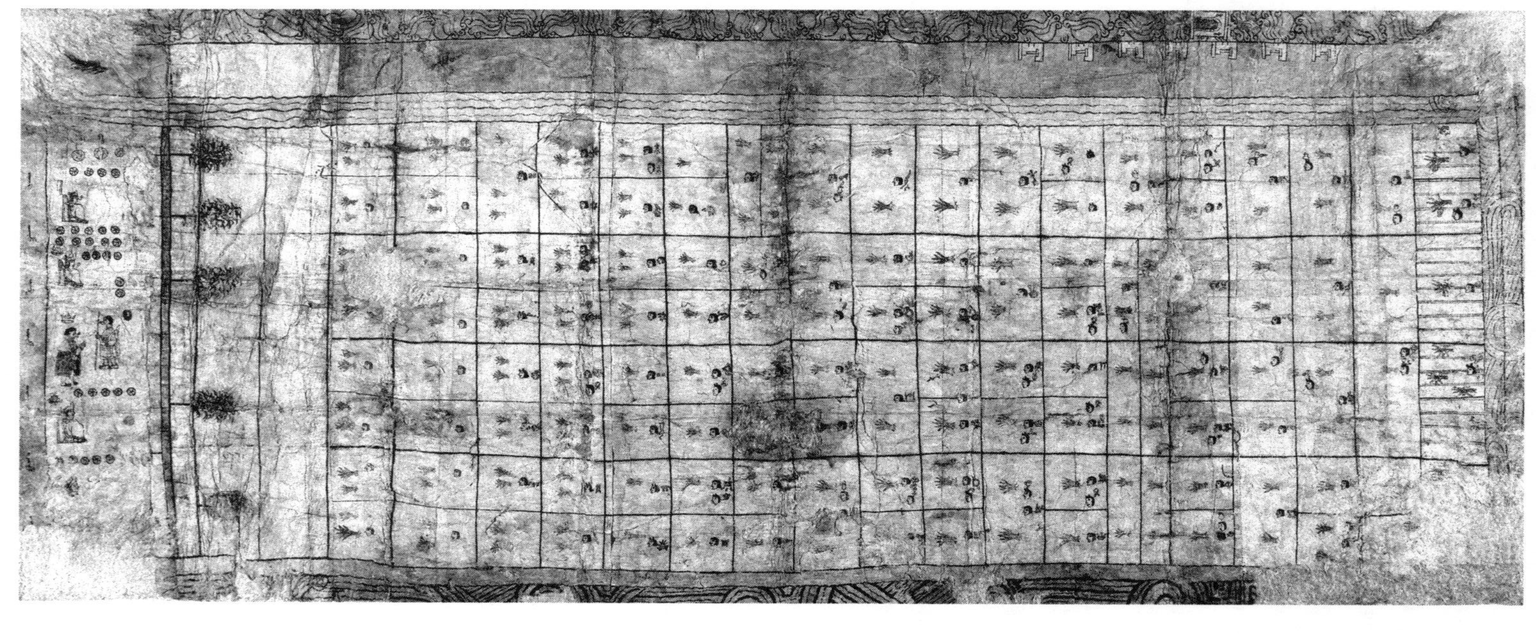

Figure 5.2 A cadastral map of land recovered from the lake of Texcoco. Each plot is labeled with the type of soil and name of a commoner in Indigenous glyphs. To the left, in Indigenous script, is a list of the four lords of Tenochtitlan since the conquest—from 1521 to 1564, when under Luis de Santa María Cipac, last hereditary lord governor of Tenochtitlan, the city witnessed riots triggered by the implementation of Valderrama's new tributary policy. *Codex Reese*, Beinecke Rare Book and Manuscript Library, Yale University.

tailors, and particularly painters sought confirmation that Valderrama's new cash and corn tribute payments would forever end their continuous unregulated labor services both to deliver grass to magistrates and viceroys and to complete public buildings.[50] The annals were mostly written by painters but also by tailors and carpenters who spoke against the Indigenous municipality, the hereditary lord governor don Luis María Cipac, and friars. Painters, carpenters, and stonecutters boycotted friar workshops.[51] Painters created new guilds.[52] Artisans created their own organizations independent from their traditional lords.[53] Valderrama's reforms were inflaming local politics and inflaming radical situations. Friars rushed to stop the exodus, seeking to convince artisans not to abandon in monastic workshops. They promised to send embassies both to the monarch and the Pope to persuade them to halt these tributary reforms.[54]

Throughout the city, commoners sang the sorrowful *tlacahualizcuicatl cuextecayotl*, the Huastecan lamentations.[55] What could be done? One group of friars urged lawfare before both Valderrama and High Court judges.[56] Mexica lords encouraged their subjects to respect "the word of self-sacrifice of the community" and bemoaned that disobedient, unhappy commoners should have "listened to the words of your fathers."[57] But tempers were running high. While some friars pleaded for patience, others denounced Valderrama as a demonic figure who belonged in hell.[58]

In June 1564, Valderrama's official ruling became public. The main author of the *Anales* recalled his conversation with the investigator: "When I heard it, I immediately said . . . It won't be possible, [the commoners] have nothing to pay with. Are they not landless? Can you not see the state they are in?"[59] Besides, the Mexica were unaccustomed to hard labor, he warned. Valderrama agreed; they would pay in pesos and corn, not in labor-heavy deliveries of grass. The exact sentencing was scheduled for July 13, 1564, in the public plaza at two in the afternoon. The Mexica governor declared his commoners would tribute around 1 peso and a basket of corn every four months.[60] The lords profusely apologized to their livid commoners, to no avail. The *Anales*' author recalled that "the people shouted, hitting their mouths. . . . The old women cried and became enraged."[61] The crowd denounced the lords as cowards. Violence erupted.

The mob began vandalizing the walls of flowers decorating the square, and men and women fell from their podiums in the fury and confusion.[62] The Indigenous authorities presented themselves as powerless and reminded the Natives that their ancestors had been conquered.[63] This declaration of powerlessness and defeat further enraged the collective. Violent riots broke out, with men and women vandalizing the plaza. Viceregal officials captured dozens of Natives, many of whom were incarcerated, flogged, and publicly sold as temporary slaves.[64]

The *Anales* document a polity at war within. Many Mexica commoners suffered and rioted, and the once-respected Native lords lost a great deal of their prestige. On the other hand, artisan commoners who made luxury goods (paintings, in this case) clearly benefited from the reforms. Their labor could no longer be tapped by Indigenous lords, friars, and viceregal bureaucracies through coercion or without payment. In fact, the reforms promised them a handsome windfall in the form of transparent cash payments.[65] The *Anales* thus document how Valderrama's investigation overturned the social order. One commoner faction, the artisans, emerged victorious.

Angry commoners also used paperwork to challenge their lords. In the three months leading to the July 1564 rebellion, Indigenous artisans initiated two different legal processes targeting the city's Mexica lords. On March 2, 1564, the bakers Juan Daniel and Toribio Totonoc, the tailor Pedro Macías, and the grass collector Mateo Suárez sued the entire Mexica nobility.[66] Through their lawyer, these commoners summoned five witnesses to testify under oath regarding nineteen different charges. They accused the Mexica nobility, among other things, of rigging municipal elections, abusing commoner labor, accepting bribes, running illegal taverns selling *pulque* (agave wine), and holding court in their homes instead of the palace of the lords without public scrutiny. The plaintifs accused the lords of holding idolatrous dances (*mitotes*), wearing sumptuous feather costumes, and enjoying saunas (*temezcales*) in the nude with clearly religious overtones.[67] Through their attorney, the lords rejected all of the charges. The artisans were lowborn, drunken nobodies.[68] They were incapable of understanding these elites' aristocratic ethos, munificence, and devotion, and should rediscover respect in their natural superiors.[69] The lords' allies testified that they were faithfully married Christians who danced for Catholic celebrations and went to saunas strictly for health reasons.

The second trial against the lords left fewer details but reflects how commoners' archives were becoming key for radical politics. In May 1564, artisans in the mechanical trades led by Toribio Lucas and Pablo Sandoval took the municipality to task for unpaid salaries.[70] The commoners produced detailed archival evidence of quantities of annual service since 1555, the year the Indigenous *cabildo* was investigated by a visiting Native judge, Esteban de Guzmán. They presented his charges as well as detailed records of tribute paid going back nine years. These lords had evidently extracted formidable quantities of unremunerated labor.[71] Commoners also accessed court records going back to around 1558, which held the sworn testimonies of middle-ranked Indigenous managers charged with wrangling laborers and on whom the lords had shifted the blame.[72] Commoners even secured the testimony of rival factions within the traditional hereditary lineages to confirm their charges against the current lords.[73] In so doing, they showed an extraordinary mastery of archives and lawfare.

The lords responded with paperwork and archives of their own. They had kept dozens of orders signed by the viceroy proving that they had the right to mobilize commoners to build and maintain jails, the viceregal palace, churches, and roads.[74] The lords' archive was as good as that of the commoners. These documents, including the *Osuna,* show not only commoner politics but also how Indigenous elites fearful of vassals' challenges responded by assembling and presenting archives of their own.[75]

Valderrama's plan was working. Although his arrival had prompted social unrest, he was making considerable inroads without force. The friars and Native lords were on the defensive, as were important Spanish officials who protected them. The commoners generally embraced Valderrama, although some cursed his name. More efficacious than any single human actor was the logic of the archive itself. Commoners who could muster years-old proofs of their claims had much to gain from a new, transparent labor regime that would break down monastic seigneurialism and Native lords' abuses. As the *Anales* recall, an embassy of commoners approached Valderrama with a painting to prove their lords' abuses. The auditor praised the artisans but also chastised them: "It is very good what you say, [but] you should have depicted these events long ago."[76]

CORTÉS'S CONSPIRACY AND THE DANGERS OF DECEPTION

There remains one major twist in Valderrama's story. Marquis don Martín and his vast network of resentful conquistadors were on the verge of a comeback. His father, Hernán, had created and then nearly destroyed the Cortés dynasty with his disastrous blunders—including the brazen murder of his wife. The marquisate's great estates had been under indirect administration for decades. Now, the most illustrious conquistador-aristocrat in the Indies was returning to claim one of the empire's greatest seigneuries. Valderrama had weakened the friars and royal officials who had kept the conquistadors in check. The time was ripe.

Nonetheless, the marquis snatched defeat from the jaws of victory. During Valderrama's visit, Viceroy Luis de Velasco died. The political void was immediately filled by the marquis and his allies. His prestige among Indigenous commoners rose. Every time he and his wife, doña Ana Ramírez de Arellano, passed their seigneuries in Cuernavaca and Oaxaca, Indigenous commoners lavishly received them.[77] The baptism of their twins was a spectacular public festival.[78] The Valderrama-Cortés alliance promised to reshuffle Mexico's politics even more radically than before, marking a new conquistador-commoner era with friars and Native lords on the ropes.

But the marquis overplayed his hand. Many magistrates still loathed him. The viceroy's son, Luis Velasco II, and his brother, Francisco, challenged the marquis in Mexico City's streets. Rival gangs taunted one another, and even fought openly in the capital's thoroughfares. Valderrama, who had largely protected the marquis from denunciations, left for Spain in 1566.[79] The marquis was exposed.

The High Court and the Velascos now turned violently against their sworn enemy. Secret reports—possibly hatched by officials themselves—warned that the marquis and other conquistadors were planning a coup. They would assassinate Mexico's highest administrators and declare don Martín king. The rebels would also coordinate with undercover agents in Peru, and—with the pope's blessing—declare loyalty to France.

For four months, the High Court launched a massive lawsuit accusing the marquis and his allies of high treason. Authorities tortured many and publicly beheaded the prominent Ávila brothers, who had once acted as the spokespeople of Mexico's conquistador lobby. The marquis and his two brothers, Luis and Martín, were imprisoned and tortured.[80] Anticonquistador factions flooded the courts with denunciations.

The Crown naturally reacted with great concern. A new viceroy, Gastón de Peralta, arrived to mediate, but he too fell into a paperwork snare. Petitioners had him recalled with an avalanche of documents denouncing him as inept and corrupt; he only lasted four months. Then came two council ministers, Alonso Muñoz and Luis de Carrillo, charged with investigating the alleged conspiracy. Soon they had incarcerated nearly ninety of Cortés's followers, executing ten, exiling forty-three, and condemning six to galley slavery. The High Court abolished the marquisate, a move the Crown later upheld. In the aftermath of the conspiracy, Mexico's greatest conquistadors had been crushed. They would never mount a comeback.

The political significance of the events was clear. The marquis's guilt, however, was not. By the time yet another new viceroy, Martín Enríquez de Almansa, took over in late 1568, thousands of pages of investigations of dubious credibility had accumulated in the viceregal and royal courts.[81] According to don Martín, the cases were built on grotesque manipulation of forged evidence, innuendo, and countless legal irregularities of process. No amount of investigation seemed to confirm his involvement. Then again, he could not easily prove his innocence either—and many of his peers were now imprisoned or worse.

More than anything, this lawsuit created the impression that Indies archives and documents were tainted and useless. The trial was riddled with accusations of forged evidence, unreliable witnesses, and blatant disrespect for legal procedure.[82] Valderrama had already warned the Crown about factionalism. He could not do much more than to expand the archive and add voices into the echo chamber of Indies paperwork. The Crown needed to develop new approaches to weighing evidence. And beginning in 1568, it did.

PRESIDENT OVANDO AND THE IMPERIAL INFORMATION STATE

The Mexico crisis played a central role in triggering yet another investigation—this time of the Council of the Indies itself. This investigation, in turn, transformed not only the council but also the empire. As the marquis and other exiles returned to Spain in spring 1567, Mexico remained in turmoil. News flooded in that "one must not fear the Frenchmen nor the Turk but a tyrant" operating from within.[83] The new viceroy had worsened the situation, inflaming already high tensions. One report described local officials barricaded in their palaces, expecting him to help the conquistadors retake Mexico.[84] And everyone understood that if Mexico fell, the Indies would too.

Lawfare forced litigants to the court and ministers to Mexico. The marquis's attorney had recused every Mexican magistrate and alleged a conspiracy by the Velascos; he begged for a council minister to personally investigate.[85] Meanwhile in Madrid, the marquis summoned evidence before none other than his old ally council minister Valderrama and even elicited his testimony—a clear conflict of interest.[86] The king's royal secretary was monitoring the situation already in the summer of 1567.[87] In June 1567, the king sent investigators—including council minister Alonso Muñoz—to Mexico to enforce swift justice.[88] They sent the viceroy back to Madrid for sympathizing with accused rebels.

Now the fateful events of 1541–1542 began to repeat themselves. In the court, powerful rivals battled, as the Almagros and Pizarros had, through lawfare and secret family connections. This time, the struggle pitted the friar-official clique, headed by the Velascos, against the marquis and his men. Had council ministers been bribed by the marquis or the Velascos? Accusations flew. The marchioness—who was managing her husband's lawsuit while he sat under house arrest in Madrid—recused most council officials, accusing them of harboring hatred for their clan.[89] Minister Alonso Muñoz had even told the bishop of Michoacan that he wished to arrest the marquis and "cut off his head in the public plaza," or so the defense attorney argued.[90] This whole Velasco clique was nothing more than "fabricators of the falsehoods raised against the said Marquis."[91] The Velascos responded by recusing Minister Valderrama for being the marquis's good friend and ally.[92] The defiant council attorney, meanwhile, remained completely convinced of the marquis's guilt. Minister Muñoz had uncovered letters in Mexico dated March 1566 and signed by the marquis seemingly instructing his agent to buy weapons and bribe important figures in the court; the council later discovered efforts by the marchioness to coordinate witness statements in advance.[93]

As it had in the early 1540s, the Council of the Indies faced a crisis of credibility. Royal observers hatched a plan for a new investigation.[94] A slow-burning, secret investigation of the council began in Madrid, with Inquisitor Ovando at its helm. Between June 1567 and April 1568, dozens of witnesses complained of the council's ignorance, disorganization, thirst for bribes, and favoritism.[95]

There were other sources of trouble as well. In the early 1540s, Las Casas had inserted himself into the council investigation to stress the tyranny of the conquistadors. The result had been clauses in the 1542–1543 New Laws that triggered radical reform and civil war. Now, this aging firebrand and his colleagues attempted to repeat their success. His allies read a petition aloud in the council that year, slamming the conquistadors and Crown for tyranny.[96] One fervent adherent of Las Casas, Franciscan friar Alonso de Maldonado, caused a stir in 1566 by warning the king and his ministers that they were going to hell for allowing abuses against Indigenous vassals.[97] He urged a doubling down on friar theocracy, in which the king gave special heed to men of faith. Factionalism was destroying not just truth but the social fabric, and now "the Indians are greatly scandalized in the light of the little credit given to the truth."[98] Only monastic rule could restore virtue, morals, and truth and persuade Native commoners of the Crown's Christian zeal. As things stood, ministers were indifferent to conversion and thus "are in a state of eternal damnation."[99] A grand junta of theologians would lay these issues to rest.[100] Again that year, cleric Luis Sánchez of Popayan warned that "everything that arrives from the Indies... informs wrongly" and urged a similar junta of theologians.[101] Evidently, such petitions reached the papacy; its ambassadors began suggesting that the pope was interested in sending a *nuncio*—an investigator—to audit unspecified abuses against the church in the Indies.[102]

The council moved to silence Friar Maldonado, and the Inquisition took him to task in Toledo for warning that the king and his men were damned to hellfire.[103] But in early 1568, the king ratified exactly such a junta—the *Junta Magna.* Its goal, however, was not the establishment of a firmer friar theocracy. Rather, it aimed for a more centralized episcopal order along the lines of the Council of Trent, which had recently concluded in Rome. Cardinal Diego de Espinosa, president of the Council of Castille and general inquisitor, oversaw the proceedings, where decades of complaints and conflicts came to a head. The final manifesto produced demonstrates that the Crown had at last formulated a coherent stance on Indies matters: it wanted clearer hierarchies with viceroys, bishops, and inquisitors atop the pyramid. Viceroys would maintain their broad jurisdiction, distributing Native tribute and privileges on an *ad hoc* basis.[104] Bishops would receive Jesuit assistants; friars would obediently answer to bishops, becoming their "subjects and subordinates."[105] The Inquisition would be established, albeit without jurisdiction over Natives.[106] Borders and tribute levied on Indigenous commoners would be simplified and made "as fixed as possible."[107]

As the junta wrapped up, Investigator Ovando was still collecting information about council wrongdoing. Once he became president in 1571, he moved to solve a number of major informational deficiencies and bring his institution into line with the junta's mission to end disorder. He noted that ministers' disorganized royal decrees had caused much of the chaos. Opaque bookkeeping had also enabled gross corruption. And Oviedo understood that the most effective recipe to counter venality was to legislate social distance between council officials and vassals. Henceforth, all transactions had to be fully documented in writing; the council legislated twenty-five different types of new books to be kept by scribes, secretaries, royal prosecutors (*fiscales*), accountants, cosmographers, and chroniclers.[108] Ovando insisted on the importance of social distance and archives within the council to establish the purity of every transaction.

Ovando bemoaned that ministers lacked sufficient factual knowledge about the Indies. He ordered his subalterns to double down on organizing council papers to establish basic facts about the New World. Officials created a finding aid for some seventeen to eighteen thousand *gobierno* decrees, which had long been in disarray. A later synthesis compiled two thousand foundational policies into one manuscript book, clarifying ecclesiastical, temporal, litigious, Spanish, Indigenous, treasury, and commercial policies. His successors pressed on with this codifying project. Ministers also established new repositories of descriptive facts about the Indies, hoping to help sort out *gobierno, gracia,* and *justicia* cases. Indeed, they often read and fact-checked new petitions, displaying some confidence in Indies affairs thanks to the archives they were mastering.[109] This consultation of archives to produce ordinances would characterize the future society of orders, when Crown ministers, bishops, viceroys, and inquisitors would rely ever more on them. For instance, the council's compilations of the 1570s correspond to bishops' conciliar ordinances of the mid-1580s. Here, episcopal committees transformed the input of clergymen and vassals into enduring church policies.[110]

Archival reforms came just in time for the Crown. Already by the 1550s and increasingly as the century progressed, the Crown struggled against piracy and bankruptcy. A major priority was therefore to revamp the treasury in the Indies to pay for geopolitical battles against Ottoman Islam in the Mediterranean and Lutherans and Calvinists in the Atlantic and the South Sea. By the 1570s, Ovando had helped create special semipermanent committees to tackle this issue. These juntas created their own archives. The Junta of Finance used its information and expertise to sort out the Crown's messy finances and dozens of other major problems.[111] The military-focused Junta of Puerto Rico did the same, surveying Indies reports, rejecting biased and factually incorrect proposals, and coordinating a constellation of forts to repel pirate attacks.[112] These archival reforms demonstrate the considerable power of organized paperwork. In the 1560s, ministers had virtually no clue about the Indies. By the 1590s, having reorganized their holdings, they possessed the Latin West's premier archive for overseas rule. Petitioners lost considerable power as ministers became more knowledgeable, while the empire benefited from officials' clearer understanding of the whole.

Ovando and other officials had an even closer eye on domestic issues. They mainly sought to use this more coherent archive to diminish the endemic social conflict roiling the Indies. He sent out long questionnaires to create "descriptions of the Indies."[113] Every Indies locale and town was to create maps and respond to dozens of questions about New World resources and histories.[114] These orders yielded dozens of community replies known to historians as the *Relaciones geográficas.*[115] Though these documents proved difficult for officials to instrumentalize, some officials did develop technologies to make space, jurisdiction, and conflict easier to manage. Already in 1557, royal cosmographer Alonso de Santa Cruz had lobbied the king to help the council manage bitter factionalism triggered by lack of clear territorial boundaries between lay and ecclesiastical administrative units. Ovando saw in cosmography a solution to some of the factional fighting in the Indies; he therefore promoted the painstaking collection of longitudinal and latitudinal measurements with which to draw accurate maps (see Figure 5.3).[116] Ovando and cosmographer Juan López de Velasco recognized that the violence between Balboa and Pedrarias—as well as Alvarado and Pizarro, among others—had originated from the ambiguity of administrative boundaries in Crown contracts and appointments. Cartographic clarity could save lives, money, and lots of paper.

One consequence of these efforts—drawing accurate maps, collecting information on every locale and region, forming expert committees—was that Crown officials envisioned the Indies as an integrated global system for the first time. Edmundo O'Gorman has argued that America was not discovered but invented as navigators from Columbus to Magellan recognized that a new continent stood between Europe and Asia.[117] Be that as it may, the first true discovery of the New World—understood as a holistic conceptualization of the entire region—transpired in the wake of

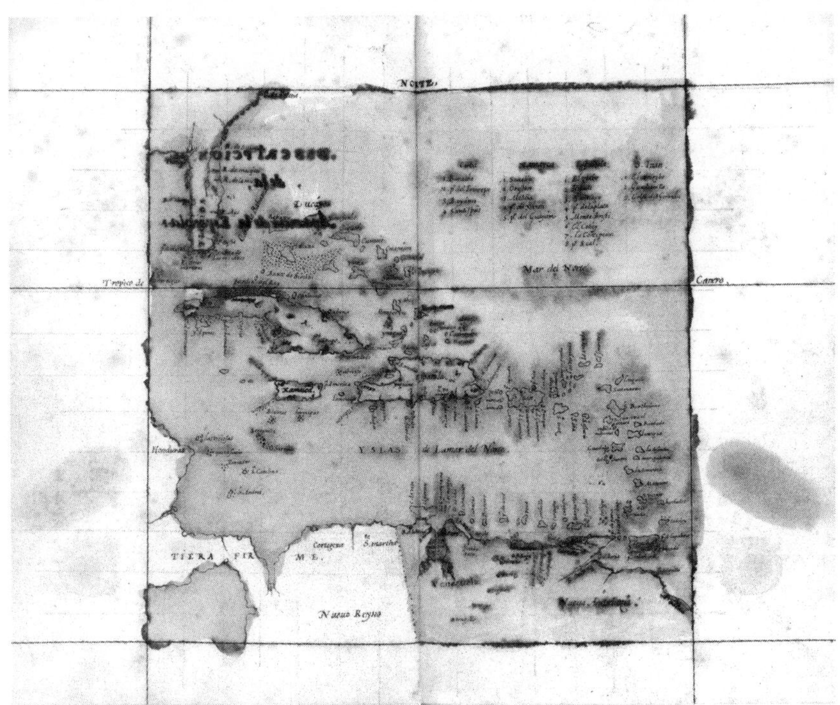

Figure 5.3 Juan López de Velasco, map of the High Court of Hispaniola. John Carter Brown Library, Codex Sp.7. 1575.

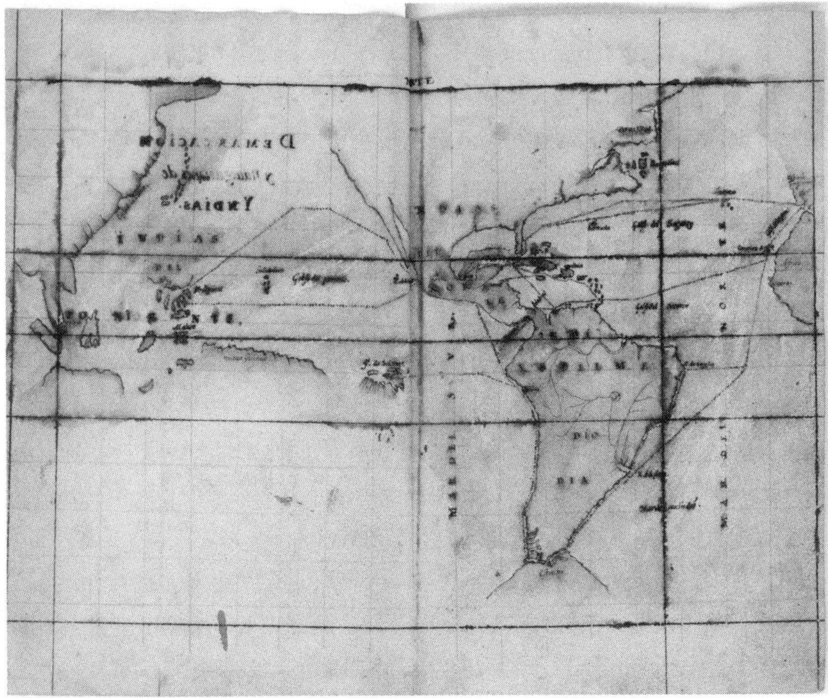

Figure 5.4 Juan López de Velasco, map of North and South America. John Carter Brown Library, Codex Sp.7. 1575.

Ovando's archival reforms. Now ministers could finally see the Indies as a vast machine, and as part of a complex, interlocking imperial apparatus spanning the entire planet (see Figure 5.4).

DISCIPLINING RADICAL ARCHIVES

Archival reforms in Madrid were creating a more vigorous and virtuous council. However, it was impossible for the Crown to consolidate power from a cramped office in Madrid; royal subalterns would need agents on the ground to bring order to the Indies. Few figures in Peru's history have come to represent the institution of order quite like Viceroy Toledo. For good reason, historians consider his long tenure (1569–1581) a watershed for the viceroyalty. His mission was to transform the realm according to the vision laid out in the great 1568 junta. Toledo's 1572 execution of the sovereign Inca of Vilcabamba was controversial then as now and symbolically marks the end of the radical phase. He also sought to map Peru, regularize its messy jurisdictions, reinvigorate its mines, curb friar theocracy and Native lordships, and balance power between Indigenous commoners and lords. Above all, he sought peace and obedience in the Indies' most troubled viceroyalty. To achieve this daunting goal, he deployed both bottom-up paperwork strategies and top-down approaches. While garnishing legitimacy and information from communication with vassals, this viceroy developed imposing theories to combat local disorder. More broadly, Toledo and council officials in Madrid aimed to neutralize not only radicals but also radical archives, through their confiscation or even outright destruction.

In some regards, Toledo was one step ahead of the reforms Ovando brought about after he became President in 1571. When the council's cosmographer requested information on boundaries and natural resources, Toledo reported that he had already appointed his own cosmographer-historian after arriving in Peru in 1570. This expert was Pedro Sarmiento de Gamboa, a typical Renaissance polymath, astrologer, and mapmaker. Gamboa had led various cartographic and military expeditions into the South Sea, including the discovery of the Solomon Islands in 1568 and the fortification of the Strait of Magellan against pirates in 1578.[118] Toledo also commissioned the drawing of administrative boundaries, the collection of natural histories and curiosities, and the investigation and elaboration of Indigenous antiquities.[119]

As Toledo knew, knowledge of the natural world would not only temper jurisdictional conflict; it would also vitalize the Andes's rich mines, swelling the viceregal treasuries and soothing bitter vassals. More silver meant viceroys could distribute more privileges as well. After the conquests, viceroys had mainly used *gracia* to reward conquistadors and Native lords for their military efforts. Toledo, however, dramatically increased support for privileges related to inventors and explorers. Cash rewards, exclusive patents for inventions, and backing for entrepreneurs helped Toledo support production.[120] Potosi became a global industrial hub of silver manufacturing thanks to experimental breakthroughs in amalgamation, water mills, aqueducts, and new ovens.[121] Mercury and silver production increased dramatically in Huamanga and Potosi—so much so that Peru became a major source of wealth for the Crown, helping it avoid bankruptcy and bankrolling its endless global wars.

Peru's endemic factionalism and labor shortages posed a challenge for Toledo. To address these issues, he would need to travel as an auditor throughout the Andes. Leaving his comfortable life in Lima, Toledo embarked on an investigative expedition with an entourage of officials, scribes, translators, theologians, jurists, cosmographers, and physicians. For five years, they trekked across Jauja, Huamanga, Cusco, Lake Titicaca, the High Court of Charcas, Arequipa, and back to Lima. At every stop, countless commoners and lords appeared before him, petitioning and answering his questions. Each stop helped establish clearly defined Indigenous communities, titles of nobility, and local ordinances. The audit yielded dozens of ordinances as well as massive amounts of paperwork, most of which is unfortunately lost. Toledo's mission made powerful use of the communication strategy Valderrama had used roughly a decade before.

Through this fact-finding trip, the viceroy hoped to reconstruct the empire. His mission, like Valderrama's, was a frontal assault on friar theocracy and Indigenous lordship. Toledo was up against the adherents of

Las Casas, who envisioned for Peru a robust semisovereign Native society serviced by friars. In 1562, responding to the empire's bankruptcy, conquistadors had offered the Crown 7,600,000 pesos to keep their lordships. Las Casas had helped organize a network of Native lords—including the Huanca lord don Felipe Guacrapaucar—to propose to improve the offer by 100,000 pesos if they could keep their power intact.[122]

This friar-lord alliance was not the most troublesome Toledo faced. Native lords, especially the sovereign Inca, were a major thorn in his side. The Huancas who petitioned alongside Las Casas were loyalists, having battled tyrant conquistadors from Pizarro to the rebel Girón, and expected the king to honor their service.[123] They were outspoken but not necessarily dangerous. The real problem was the sovereign Inca realm of Vilcabamba, where Dominicans and Augustinians following Las Casas had sought to create another Verapaz on a far greater scale. Las Casas envisioned a peaceful Inca Catholic monarchy in the middle of the Andes, led by an alliance of friars and Inca lords like Titu Cusi. In fact, Titu Cusi and his part-Spanish secretary Martín Pando had the Inca's son baptized and invited two Augustinian friars into sovereign Vilcabamba to create churches and educate Natives. In the late 1560s, using Augustinians as translators and interpreters, Titu Cusi negotiated with President García de Castro and the king for peaceful recognition of an Inca Catholic sovereign state in Vilcabamba as well as large estates and pensions in Cusco.[124] As part of the negotiations, the Augustinians helped Titu Cusi write a history of the origins of Vilcabamba as a polity created with the right to resist.[125]

Even before Toledo left Peru, he had Las Casas and the friar-lord alliance on his mind. On July 13, 1566, the elderly Bartolomé de Las Casas, days before his death, had his petition and two treatises read to the council.[126] His main argument was that the Inca had been lords of the Andes for centuries and remained legitimately sovereign in the present. This reasoning, spread in Madrid and Peru through the agitation of many priests, friars, and Native lords, underpinned a major independent lordship not far from key imperial cities like Cusco, Huamanga, and Huancavelica. Events in Vilcabamba only reinforced the viceroy's conviction that something had to be done.

Toledo sent Spanish ambassadors, whom the Inca summarily executed. What he likely did not know was that in the meantime, the Inca Titu Cusi had died, unchaining a violent conflict inside Vilcabamba. Angelina Quilaco, one of Titu Cusi's wives, had his half-Spanish secretary Martín Pando killed on the spot. She also had the Augustinian friar Diego Ortíz perform mass to resuscitate the deceased Inca. After the friar failed, Quilaco had Ortíz impaled and buried standing on his head.[127] The Vilcabamba Inca likely feared that the arrival of the ambassadors would reveal the bloodbath.

Toledo mobilized hundreds of Cañaris and Chachapoyas and levied Spanish troops as well. They seized Vilcabamba in mid-1572. The killing of the ambassadors provided justification for the conquest; Toledo could now move against the entire edifice of Inca sovereignty. Having captured the new Inca Tupac Amaru, he subjected him to a quick trial, accused him of murder, and executed him. He then rounded up and exiled countless Incas of Cusco who had allegedly supported Tupac Amaru.[128]

Toledo still had to justify his deeds and combat the friars, who would surely denounce him. He had, after all, just destroyed a realm the allies of Las Casas believed was legitimately sovereign. Here, his long-gestating inquiry into Inca tyranny takes center stage. Between 1570 and March 1572, he had collected information to prove Inca tyranny: a set of notarized questions and replies by one hundred Indigenous witnesses in Jauja, Huamanga, and Cusco meant to demonstrate that the Inca had tyrannized Peru long before the Spaniards had arrived.

His approach to eliciting this information diverged from business as usual. Investigators normally proceeded by gathering accusations and carefully compiling evidence about wrongdoing.[129] Many factions would provide input. Toledo, however, simply had to defeat his rivals. While he could not proceed with an agenda comprised of multiple contradictory interests, he had to prove to the king that this defeat was necessary and just. To this end, he articulated a clear theory of why he had unilaterally overridden Inca authority and friar polemics.

His painstaking process of fact gathering implied a juridical reflection. He began by assembling facts—without telling his informants his purpose. Toledo asked one hundred elderly Indigenous lords to remember how their grandparents and great-grandparents had come to power before and after the Inca. From these statements, a consensus emerged. The Incas had only expanded under the leadership of Tupac Yupanqui, Atahualpa's and Huascar's grandfather. The Inca was a very recent empire that had surged within two generations out of the valleys around Cusco, all the way to Quito and Chile. Moreover, Inca sovereigns had appointed lords without regard to lineage. In regions like Jauja and Huamanga and in the vicinity of Cusco, all witnesses acknowledged that their great-grandparents had been appointed by the Inca without respect to lineage or dynastic inheritance. In the Jauca region of Lurinhuacas, Native lords don Alonso Pomaguala, don Felipe Pomacao, don Hernando Apachin, and Alonso Cana delivered very similar answers. Tupac Yupanqui and his son Huayna Capac had arbitrarily appointed local lords at will. From these statements, an image of pre-Inca history emerged. Local communities had been organized in *ayllus,* large extended families, without dynastic lords of any kind.[130] Witnesses did not make it explicit, but for Toledo the message was loud and clear: the Incas were newly arrived tyrants who had ruthlessly and arbitrarily oppressed their people. In fact, under the Spaniards, they were better off.[131]

Toledo now needed to turn these witness statements into a rousing defense of viceregal authority. He was neither an expert theologian nor a jurist, he explained; he was just a lay observer whose mandate was to get the facts straight. In the Indies, Toledo asserted, there was an excessive "diversity of opinions on subjects of so much importance [such as Indigenous tributary, land, and labor policies,] and this has to stop." He went on: "For facts in these kingdoms are [never] clear but forged according to the whim [of factions] . . . to fit any preconceived, desired needs."[132] He would ruthlessly cut through the noise. Here the viceroy looked to the historical expertise of his chronicler Sarmiento de Gamboa, who in 1572 produced *Historia índica* to demonstrate the fairness of crushing Native lords' power.[133]

Arguing that the Inca were illegitimate undid half of the friar-lord alliance. Now Toledo needed to explain why he had trampled the orders and completely disregarded their powerful juridical arguments. Sarmiento de Gamboa and the viceroy's cousin Friar García de Toledo were likely the authors of the anonymous March 1571 "Report of Yucay," a scathing denunciation of Las Casas. In this work, the authors claimed that the devil had used Las Casas to fool kings, ministers, theologians, and indeed, all Christians. But now, Toledo had arrived in the Indies to fulfill God's original plan.[134]

The viceroy's proposal was probably not persuasive. The council would not simply take his word on such things, let alone swallow that the Prince of Darkness had enabled Las Casas to fool them. However, this bold stance seems to have worked for Toledo in Peru. He had managed to overcome powerful local forces with far less disruption than Valderrama, whose alliances had nearly provoked a full-blown civil war.

Toledo also had a powerful ally Valderrama had not counted on: the Inquisition. In early 1570s Lima, the newly arrived inquisitors moved against a vocal critic of the viceroy, Dominican Francisco de la Cruz, the rector of Lima's University of San Marcos. La Cruz had prophesized that the Ottomans would destroy Europe, a new church would arise in the Indies, and he would be its pope.[135] The inquisitors eventually accused him of heresy, disobedience, and treasonous plans—and burned him in 1578.[136] His lengthy and chaotic case reveals how disobedient vassals might wind up in prison for expressing dangerous antiestablishment ideas. He was far from alone. For instance, one priest who accused Toledo of being a "liar and heretic" landed in the Inquisition jail.[137] Radicals now had to tread lightly indeed.

DISCIPLINING ARCHIVES, *LADINOS*, AND FRIARS

The triumph of viceroys, inquisitors, and bishops over unruly friars and Native lords created an explosion of paperwork in Peru and Mexico. Toledo's lengthy investigations generated a slew of ordinances, land titles, privileges, and other documents.[138] Lords acquired clear titles over their patrimonial jurisdictions (*cacicazgos*) and communities over their lands as commons.[139] This was far from the end of Indies politics—Valderrama, Toledo, and other officials had merely inaugurated a new chapter.

Toledo, even more than Valderrama, reshaped the Native countryside, creating hundreds of pueblos of elected municipalities and archives. Scholars have often insisted that Toledo's *reducciones*—land reforms—were a top-down imposition by an autocratic tyrant.[140] Yet the evidence suggests that Toledo's new rules energized commoners to participate in paperwork politics. Now, however, petitions and lawsuits would deal with increasingly local issues rather than sweeping, radical proposals.

Toledo helped establish new bottom-up channels of redress through which commoners could check the power of lords via *quipus* and accounting books. Peasants would keep some eight types of records, including *quipus,* under lock and key in community archives.[141] Field justices and local Indigenous officials would keep transparent records and report regularly about community taxes and other affairs.[142] Parish priests, meanwhile, would keep local paperwork on births, marriages, and deaths.

In the past, paperwork had been a major engine of social disorder. Toledo took care to limit this possibility in future. He appointed special prosecutors for Indigenous litigants, the *protectores de indios,* who would ensure that lords and commoners did not become mired in interminable court cases. This system of summary justice—*justicia sumaria*—was clearly a swing at the powerful and often harmful *ladinos.* It undermined their roles as socially destabilizing pettifoggers. Allied with lawyers and legal agents (often friars), Native lords drained community resources with petty litigation, creating disorder and factionalism. *Ladinos* had singlehandedly created a market of witnesses to rubberstamp any petition, demand, or legal claim.[143] Now, Toledo hoped, this endless lawfare would be no more. He even went a step further, destroying Native archives he regarded as corrupted by *ladino* trickery. In his November 10, 1570, visit to Jauja, for example, he had much of the Native lords' paperwork lit ablaza.[144]

The friars were also on Toledo's list. Throughout the Indies, the Orders had been running a very untransparent administration. Las Casas's Verapaz is a case in point. How this Guatemalan theocracy functioned remains a mystery, for its administrators produced virtually no records. The friars were masters of managing documentation when it suited their interests. For instance, they published archives of papal bulls to confront lay and ecclesiastical bureaucracies, but they systematically culled reports and histories of any misdeeds.[145] Only in an environment of factionalism might vassals report what went on in these dominions. For example, when friars and Native lords in the Yucatan accused the leading families—the Sotuta, Kachunup, Mopila, Sahcaba, Yaxcaba, Usil, and Tiblon—of idolatry and sexual assault, few documents initially reached the outside world.[146] Vilcabamba was no different. But with the growing power of bishops and especially the Inquisition, friars could only avoid oversight with great difficulty. The newly powerful officials kept superb records of everything from major decisions to everyday minutia.

Toledo's epistemological assault on Las Casas and friar theocracies also included outright archival erasure. Just as he burned select Native archives, he moved to prevent the circulation of Las Casas's works. Toledo launched a campaign to collect all copies of Las Casas's treatises and manuscripts in Peru on the grounds that they had spread "so many falsehoods on the facts and so much ignorance on matters of government that it is urgent to collect them."[147] The Inquisition joined in Toledo's campaign, confiscating these works from friars and priests in Lima and beyond.[148] In Peru, officials moved to instill obedience one archive at a time.

In Mexico, royal officials also quickly grasped the importance of dominating archives. Failure to do so opened the door to mayhem. Few cases illustrate this danger quite like that of Juan Suárez de Peralta. The Mexico-born Spaniard had a burning hatred of the marquis don Martín Cortés; his aunt had been Catalina Suárez, Hernán Cortés's first wife, whom Hernán had strangled to death in their bedchamber. The Suárez clan had unsurprisingly joined forces with the Velascos to bring down the marquis by paperwork riot.[149] This family had played a key role in bringing down both marquises, so Suárez de Peralta understood the power of a good archive. He acquired parts of one such collection sometime in the 1550s or 1560s, when papers of Archbishop Juan de Zumárraga, head of the episcopal Inquisition, wound up on the black market. This acquisition proved crucial to Suárez de Peralta's aims: in 1571, the descendants of a Michoacan conquistador summoned the newly arrived Inquisition to report that Suárez de Peralta was extorting them using its secret reports.

Suárez de Peralta threatened to release incriminating details about their father if they did not pay the massive sum of 10,000 ducats.[150]

The Inquisition accused Suárez de Peralta of "breaking the secrecy" of the institution.[151] At virtually the same moment, Inquisitor Pedro Moya de Contreras arrived in Mexico with a mandate to build an immense archive of books containing every record of denunciation, investigation, trial, seized property, prisoner upkeep, salary, employee evaluation, list of learned evaluators and censors, and vote on torture, death, exile, and physical punishment.[152] After a systematic investigation of everyone involved in the dismemberment of the archive of the first apostolic Inquisition (led by bishops), the general inquisitor reincorporated these papers.

Suárez de Peralta had no choice but to flee Mexico in 1579.[153] Once in Seville, he built his reputation as an expert on horses, writing two treatises on horse riding and horse illnesses and cures, one of which was published.[154] The expert horse trainer–veterinarian also gained access to the archives of those involved in the alleged Cortés conspiracy. He decided to write a history of the conspiracy, transcribing the summaries of sentences and trials while waxing lyrical about conquistadors as a misunderstood estate.[155] Suárez de Peralta wrote that until the 1560s, archives were wild and undisciplined. Las Casas, the conquistadors, and others had tirelessly collected documents—licitly or otherwise—and deployed them against their rivals.

In Spain, the Crown's conquest of the archives was also taking place. In the early 1570s, President Ovando sought to tame radical archives and make them useful to the Crown. Royal decrees licensed council agents to gather two such types of collections: those of Las Casas and his allies and those of the conquistadors. Perhaps the largest archive ever to reach the council was that of Bartolomé de Las Casas. He had bequeathed his papers to the Dominican convent of San Gregorio: two mammoth histories and ethnographies, known today as *Historia de las Indias* and *Apologética historia sumaria,* dozens of petitions, reams of documents, and correspondence from his anticonquistador struggles.[156] Ministers confiscated the papers of Friar Bernardino de Sahagún as well. The council secured the archives of conquistador-chroniclers Pedro Cieza de León, Gonzalo Fernández de Oviedo, Francisco de Gómara, Bernal Díaz del Castillo, and Francisco Cervantes de Salazar, among many others.[157] These great radical archives would cause trouble no longer.

This expropriation of historical archives was ultimately meant to discourage conflict. Ovando understood that the New Laws of 1542 had unchained conflict largely because they had been loudly and publicly distributed. Most ordinances Ovando created in the post 1568-audit were not printed. The counterradical movement would not be publicized.[158]

THE CONQUEST OF HISTORIOGRAPHY

From the 1540s until 1566, the perspectives of Las Casas and his allies had been powerful. His radical histories circulated freely in print in the Spanish Empire and beyond. They clashed openly with the chronicles of conquistadors, both reflecting and generating conflict. In Peru, Toledo had personally seen how radical theocratic arguments could greatly aggravate society and even lend legitimacy to rebellion. In Mexico, viceroys had found that conquistadors' own radical visions exposed the kingdom to a clear and present danger. Between 1567 and 1575, the Council of the Indies underwent a dramatic course correction. Radical ideas had outlived their welcome—it was time for social peace.

Secrecy became a key ingredient in the emerging society of orders. As inquisitors, both Ovando and Espinosa understood the value of secrecy. Ovando integrated *secreto* into the very structure and procedures of the council in 1571: twelve of the council's 122 regulations had to do with securing secrecy.[159] The council's rulings creating social distance with vassals already constituted a step in this direction. Secrecy would also help temper radicalism.

Here, the Crown understood the value of a good story. One of the most important responsibilities of the council cosmographer-chronicler was to evaluate Indies histories—at the expense of telling the truth—in pursuit of civil peace. A prime example was the controversy of 1573. That year, council chronicler Juan López de Velasco ordered a massive recall of Diego Fernández's 1571 history on conquistador rebellions in Nicaragua and Peru. Fernández had carefully combed the viceregal archives of

Peru and auditor Pedro de la Gasca, but his statements stirred the pot. As soon as Fernández published his history, Peruvian magistrate Hernando de Santillán y Figueroa presented nearly sixty-four complaints. Among other things, Fernández had accused Santillán of leading a hapless assault on the great tyrant Girón. The author stood his ground, replying to every criticism leveled by Santillán.[160]

Surprisingly, López de Velasco used the power of his office to recommend a total recall of Fernández's books. His reasoning was not based on objectivity but on the unrest that Fernández's account would likely trigger. Settling this dispute, López de Velasco argued, "would do nothing but to stir and bring out many things submerged that are prejudicial to the honor and fame of many people"[161] The function of the chronicler of the Indies was not to identify the truth but to manage factional conflict: "Even if everything is just and truthful, it seems that it is best to consider whether [publication] is convenient to the fidelity to be expected in the future of these provinces." He concluded with a warning: "If declared disloyal . . . these republics and individuals would become discontent and dissatisfied."[162]

This case was not exceptional. Other cases did not involve censuring already published books but rather transforming works before publication. For instance, López de Velasco had Fray Pedro de Aguado's history of the conquest of Tierra Firme (Colombia) and Bernal Díaz del Castillo's history of the conquest of Mexico profoundly edited. Aguado's was purged of mentions of conquistador misdeeds. Neither reworked version was ultimately published.[163]

As council chroniclers excised controversial elements from vassals' histories in order to encourage social harmony, historians engaged in self-censorship. The renowned Inca historian and philologist Garcilaso de la Vega manufactured one of the most enduring accounts of frictionless conquest and Crown foresight. The son of an alleged Inca noblewoman—Isabel Chimpu Ocllo, who in her will never claimed noble Inca descent—and a Spanish conquistador of alleged pure blood nobility, Garcilaso grew up in turbulent Cusco.[164] He left for Spain as a teenager, joining Spanish militias against the Morisco uprisings in Andalucía and petitioning in

Madrid for a decade before the council to restore the honor of his dad, whom the archive repeatedly and undisputably showed had sided with the Pizarros during the *encomenderos*' rebellions against the Crown in the 1540s and early 1550s.[165] Garcilaso kept in touch with loyalist Incas and half-Natives from Peru and hosted *mestizo* vassals implicated in a little-studied 1560s revolt—one that officials warned had sought to link the Vilcabamba Inca to the marquis's clique in Mexico.[166] Garcilaso was persuaded that the part-Indigenous sons of conquistadors had been wronged in the new society of orders.

In Spain, Garcilaso moved to Córdoba, where he collaborated with Jesuit antiquarians. He became close to the bishop of Granada, Pedro de Castro, himself an antiquarian and the son of the investigator and governor of Peru Cristóbal Vaca de Castro, who had given Garcilaso's father one of the richest *encomiendas* in Cusco despite evidence of treasonous behavior.[167] Although this governor had helped put down Diego de Almagro's rebellion between 1542 and 1544, petitioners had accused him of embezzlement, ending his Peruvian career in disgrace. Pedro had spent a fortune restoring his father's reputation, commissioning several histories and epics about the heroics of the corrupt governor.[168] Garcilaso drew near the bishop, learning how to distort and manipulate publications to clear the reputation of those the archive had identified as dishonorable. More importantly, Garcilaso learned from the bishop how to integrate the history of non-Spaniards into the mainstream of universal Spanish history, as Pedro de Castro became a champion of forged documents by *moriscos* on the ancient, apostolic, Christian roots of the Arabic language.[169]

Garcilaso's first published work was a translation of a treatise on Platonic philosophy by an Italian Jew, León Hebreo, titled *La traducción del Indio de los tres diálogos de amor de León Hebreo* (1590). A few years later, he reconstructed Hernando de Soto's expedition to Florida in *La Florida del Inca* (1605). In these two texts, Garcilaso publicly embraced his identity as Indian, an Inca prince, and a skilled interpreter. It was, however, in the *Comentarios reales de los Incas* (1609) that Garcilaso demonstrated the benefits of embracing his *mestizo* self-identity. Emphasizing his *mestizo*-ness, he underscored his ability as a translator-interpreter of things both Spanish and Inca.[170] This project fit well in the new society of orders: *mestizos* would not participate in radical factional conflict but instead serve viceroys, bishops, and inquisitors as frontiersmen, scholars, and priests. The history in the *Comentarios* sanitized many key elements of Peru's past, depicting the Inca as proto-Christian, the conquistadors as noble, and *mestizos* as unwaveringly loyal to the Crown.

This new historiographical climate was both an imposition of the Crown's censors and a strategy of vassals. Emerging narratives reduced the drama of the 1500s to a slow conquest by the Crown and virtuous vassals over a handful of villains, abandoning the uncompromising and fundamentally irreconcilable calls for conquistador or friar supremacy. Many key events had to be sanitized; radicalism was written out of the story.

The project of excising radicalism arguably culminated with the work of the Indies' third royal chronicler, Antonio de Herrera. In 1601, he published a monumental "general history of the actions of the Castilians in the Islands and Tierra Firme of the Ocean Sea" covering five decades of the history of conquest, from 1492 to 1540.[171] Strikingly, in nearly 2,100 pages of text, Herrera managed to expunge virtually all references to Indies tyrants. His book featured numerous descriptions of events that subtly but unmistakably cast a masculine, forceful Crown against inferior antagonists. It masterfully anticipated nineteenth- and twentieth-century accounts, which, under the guise of tedious *histoire évènementielle,* would plot a teleology of Crown supremacy. Herrera's style was entirely deliberate. He had at his fingertips the radical archives of many conquistadors and friars, including Las Casas, and unparalleled access to council papers. In fact, his history retread Bartolomé de Las Casas's mammoth *Historia de las Indias,* a work that contained mountains of paper evidence on conquistadors' tyrannies. Herrera extracted all he could from the friar's archive before eliminating the radicalism of Las Casas's message.

Herrera's *General History* was not a polemical work, but it generated a firestorm nonetheless. The year it was published, the minister of the Council of War Count of Puñonrostro sued him. The minister was the grandson of Pedro Arias Dávila, alias Pedrarias, the infamous first governor of

Panama (1514–1526). Herrera had recounted rather matter-of-factly how Pedrarias had executed his rival Blasco Núñez de Balboa for murder.[172] Puñonrostro took the fight to the public arena, publishing manifestos denouncing the royal chronicler's biases. Herrera had read what was in the archive, however. In the ten-year lawsuit that ensued, the chronicler unleashed his archival arsenal on his foe. Drawing on Las Casas's unpublished scholarship, he represented Pedrarias as the worst tyrant who had ever lived in the Indies. Herrera no longer wrote in soft and noncommittal terms; Puñonrostro's ancestor had been a corrupt, murderous criminal who had enslaved countless thousands in Panama and the wider region. He fed dead Natives' body fat to dogs to train them to hunt and kill more. He held kangaroo courts like that of Balboa, silenced his foes, and had his wives bribe council ministers.[173] He was the very definition of a tyrant.

Puñonrostro retorted with documents from the royal archive of Simancas, demonstrating Pedrarias's outstanding bureaucratic career and nontyrannical behavior.[174] Herrera replied by questioning the reliability of the archival documents Puñonrostro had unearthed. Who would have dared resist a bloodthirsty tyrant such as Pedrarias? The archives Pedrarias produced had been corrupted by tyranny; one could only trust Las Casas and other radicals. Puñonrostro lost, and Herrera won. Herrera's published first three volumes of *General History* were not recalled as Puñonrostro had demanded. The legal fight, however, took a toll. Herrera would not publish the remaining two volumes until a decade later.

Herrera's work represented the culmination of historiography as the foundation of Crown authority. Over the course of the lawsuit, Herrera showed that he was entirely aware of the radical movements of the 1500s. He was also a skeptic of the archive through and through. But in his printed works, he sought to erase Indies radicalism so as to project Crown power in a period when it actually had little. The kings emerged as omniscient agents who had installed their noble visions from the top down. It is this story we often find represented in liberal, decolonial, and Hispanist accounts of the Indies. For writers like Elliot, this top-down authoritarianism represents the key difference between the Spanish and

British empires. Once the council and its chroniclers had conquered the archives, royal and other chroniclers conquered the historiography. This historiographical conquest, it turns out, would last longer than the rest.

ARCHIVES AND THE NEW SOCIAL ORDER

The late 1560s and 1570s were clearly watershed years for the Indies. The great Indies marquises were at their lowest, and the Incas of Vilcabamba were defeated. Bishops' powers were growing. The *Junta Magna* and the great investigations of Valderrama, Ovando, Toledo, and Prieto y Orellana (among others) had crushed the theocracies of friars and the autonomy of local lords. The Inquisition was monitoring disobedience of all sorts almost entirely through denunciations. Officials were rounding up radical treatises and archives, placing them under lock and key. Indigenous commoners had played a major part in this transformation and were now embracing a less radical agenda. As the viceregal, episcopal, and inquisitorial trinity solidified, vassals responded with far less radical forms of bottom-up politics.

Scholars have called the society of orders that began to emerge from this newfound political stability "the baroque." This society remained dynamic and full of regional variation, social mobility, conflict, and intrigue. But the style of communication, conflict, and paperwork changed. The full-on lawfare of the 1530s to 1560s began to shift, with cases growing longer and more orderly. The rhetoric of antityranny became more focused on individuals and small groups than massive structural change. The vocabularies of status and dishonor became more elaborate. Everywhere, money and archives defined status much more than vassals' pure willpower.

One type of conflict in particular represents this changed ethos: the "pillow wars," status-oriented legal battles that important Crown officials waged against one another for perceived insults to their honor during ecclesiastical events. Here, every chair, hat, and cushion mattered. In 1608, struggles erupted between Mexico's councilmen, High Court magistrates, prelates, and inquisitors about which authority should sit on what crushed velvet chair during group meetings.[175] In the mid-1500s, such debates would have seemed unthinkably frilly. By the 1600s, they were a common and essential part of defending one's social preeminence.[176]

It was a time of piety, veneration of saints, and construction of great cathedrals. As bishops became more powerful, cities began to transform in their image. Bishops oversaw the Indies' countless Catholic urban associations. Religious brotherhoods fell under their jurisdiction and approval—but also enabled subjects of any social background or ethnic origin to decide their corporations' own internal policies, which they called *estatutos, ordenanzas,* or *constituciones.*[177] These institutions were sometimes administrated by Natives and Afro-descendant subjects, giving these marginalized groups a limited but consequential opportunity to shape the religious policies of their communities.[178] Women initially had no access to these brotherhoods, however. Even in convents, as Asunción Lavrín has argued, nuns' "rules of governance . . . were ultimately dependent on their male authorities."[179] Only in the 1600s would these sodalities' rising power offer opportunities for non-Spanish women's self-governance.[180]

Another important sign of the emerging society of orders was the Crown's concession of numerous nobiliary titles and lordships to vassals. Only in the early to mid-1600s did the Crown begin to distribute new high-aristocratic titles for New World elites. Although recipients never reached the autonomy they would have had in Spain, they nonetheless achieved semisovereign administrative spheres. Some existed largely on paper: since the 1500s, the Columbus dynasty's claimants had struggled over their Duchy of Veraguas, ultimately ceding its administration in 1558 to the Crown. Yet increasingly large new lordships began to appear. In 1609 and 1614, the king conceded to the descendants of Viceroy Velasco the Marquisate of the Salinas of Río Pisuerga—followed by the County of Santiago of Calimaya in 1616. The Moctezumas won the Duchy of Moctezuma of Tultenco in 1627.[181] In 1614, the last remaining legitimate heir to the Inca, Ana María Lorenza García Sayri Tupac de Loyola y Coya, received the new Marquisate of Santiago of Oropesa.[182] The Cortés clan technically recovered the Marquisate of the Valley in 1574, and the Crown restored some of their civil and penal jurisdiction in 1593. But since they were prohibited from traveling to the New World, they would not reside there until 1629.[183] The Pizarro family at last recovered their old Marquisate of the Conquest in 1630, complete with twenty thousand tribute-paying Indigenous commoners.[184] After the 1630s, the number of nobiliary concessions skyrocketed.[185] The seigneurial hierarchy gradually took hold anew, this time lasting until the fall of the Spanish Empire itself.

As the church strengthened its hand, viceroys cemented themselves as the Indies' supreme dispensers of privilege and government measures. A vibrant court society sprang up. The best positioned vassals were the dependents of kings and viceroys.[186] Of the 149 *caballeros,* or great nobles, of Lima in the early 1600s, only a quarter were conquistadors. The rest were the *caballeros desta ciudad,* "knights of the city" including "viceregal retainers, crown bureaucrats, cathedral prebendaries, city mayors and aldermen," and actual knights.[187] The viceroys had repeatedly redistributed Native tribute and other favors to the detriment of rebellious conquerors, leaving their loyalists in charge of much of the realm's status.[188]

Still, the rise of new seigneuries masked the reality that an economy based on the labor of tribute-paying serfs was obsolete in many regions. Many elites' privileges (including tax exemptions) were vehicles for enrichment on the market. Early after the conquests, conquistadors had found that their duty to feed many dependents cost them over twice the value their Indigenous tribute turned to commerce.[189] The luckiest among them literally struck gold or silver in remote mines—like Diego Maldonado the Rich, who became likely the wealthiest man in Peru and perhaps the world.[190] In New Spain, petitioners with Spanish names won hundreds of viceregal grants (through the same system of *gracia* privilege distribution) to construct millhouses and water mills; several dozen Native individuals and communities did as well.[191] By the 1570s, the first *haciendas,* great agricultural-industrial properties, were beginning to arise in New Spain and Peru.[192] In other areas, large plantation-type operations and textile mills sprang up, often staffed by enslaved subjects. These mines, *haciendas,* plantations, and textile mills would mark Indies history in the centuries to come. While they played a structurally significant role in this new society, their emergence did not jolt the core of Indies society and administration the way the radical era had. It was rather the other way around: the radical era had produced them.

Native lords often sought to preserve their privileges by engaging with the market. Some managed to leverage mercantile changes and achieve considerable wealth. The Peruvian *cacique* of Latacunga, Sancho Hacho, acquired a major textile factory, a mill, a cochineal field, and many guinea pigs in the 1560s.[193] The *cacique* don Diego Tomala of the island of Puna dressed like a Spaniard, carried guns, owned slaves, petitioned the Crown for reward in the 1550s, and won a shield of arms in 1560. His son learned to write, sing, play the organ, and ride horseback.[194] This family earned great wealth providing ships and transportation between Guayaquil and Puna.[195] Tomala's son married a Spaniard and reportedly had a fortune of over 100,000 pesos, a house, and may have owned a large ship in the area.[196]

Nowhere were Indigenous subjects' roles in the viceregal economy so dramatic as Potosi, where misery coexisted with Mammon. As Jane E. Mangan has argued, Potosi itself was the product of "native initiative, collective and individual," including not only wealthy Native men but also many women.[197] The traveling friar Diego de Ocaña marveled that "there are in Potosi many rich Indians, in particular one who is named Mondragón. . . . I found him eating on the ground at a low table . . . and he has all of his wealth before his eyes, and has a room full of silver. . . . I asked him how much he had there, and he responded to me, 'there are three hundred thousand pesos of assayed silver, one hundred and twenty thousand of which he lends to the King every year for the dispatch of the Armada.'"[198] The Inca *pallas,* or noblewomen, of Potosi were so rich, he said, that soldiers sought to have affairs with them to enjoy their wealth.[199] He was astonished by the *pallas*' generous support of the Jesuits, who tapped this wealth to host extraordinary religious processions.[200]

This new economic regime was based on the hard labor of many commoners and, increasingly, the toil of thousands of enslaved individuals. Still, commerce allowed middling and humble Christians an opportunity to rise above their station. Some living among Natives in central New Spain, like Miguel García de la Banda and Sebastián González, amassed thousands of sheep and pigs and married their daughters off well.[201] Afro-descendants, who had no claims to New World lineages and were often descended from slaves, found in the world of business narrow opportunities through which to ascend socially. The part-Portuguese Baltasar

Drago "accumulated a work force of black slaves, and was able to marry his mestizo [*sic* for *mestiza*] daughter, with a dowry of 4,000 pesos, to a Spaniard."[202] Though few Afro-descendant merchant men and women engaged in long-distance trade, many ran small shops, or *pulperías*.[203] The free Black woman Luisa Villalobos arrived in Potosi from Panama and created a thriving pawning and banking network, circulating pesos of slaves to other slaves. Her business included other free Black women in Lima and La Plata in a vast, intracontinental traffic of embroidery, linens, perfumes, European clothing, fine Andean woolens, mercury, and nonminted cones of refined silver (*piñas*) that also included wealthy and poor Indigenous women. Luisa would leave her considerable fortune to the Jesuits in Lima, a niece, and, oddly enough, her former master.[204]

Some Indigenous commoners escaped their tribute responsibilities and, through many different strategies, became *caciques*. They might amass wealth through work and the market, build new social bonds, create fictions of traditional rule, petition claiming to have helped Christian conquistadors win the land, or all of the above—as did the goatherd Francisco Saquinga, who became "rich and hispanicized" and transformed into don Francisco Hati in the 1580s.[205] Becoming *ladino* was largely about paperwork, but it was also about joining the vast world of commerce.

A cash society inherently featured considerable risk, and with it, upward and downward social mobility. By 1600, there were fifteen merchants in Peru who had assets over 300,000 ducats, an astonishing fortune over seven times greater than the income of some marquis in Spain.[206] Yet merchant deals could collapse at any minute. Ships sank or were sacked by pirates; mines collapsed or became exhausted; agents betrayed their deals.[207] For these reasons, miners and other businessmen frequently struggled to pass their wealth on to their descendants.[208] One observer of early seventeenth-century Lima noted that sixty merchants had suffered bankruptcies of over 100,000 pesos.[209]

The line between aristocrat and merchant blurred, creating new anxieties. Merchants often played the part of noblemen, patronizing artistic and religious projects and engaging in "conspicuous consumption [that] transmuted wealth into status."[210] By 1557, the viceroy of Peru noted merchants' growing wealth and power, informing the Crown that "they are many more than the conquistador-trustees [*encomenderos*]. . . . And those who are rich, I do not know if their presence is convenient for the realm."[211] By 1600, merchants' power was unstoppable; they crowded out the sons of conquistadors for positions of honor.[212] By 1602 in Buenos Aires, merchants also dominated over conquistadors.[213] In Tunja, aldermen fumed when a humble artisan who had become wealthy sought to join their ranks; they fended off such pretenders until later in the 1600s.[214] In the early 1600s, Spanish merchants had weak power in the Mexico City municipality, but over the decades, they rose to compete with Indies-born descendants of conquistadors.[215] Louisa Hoberman notes that they increasingly held important advisory and judicial positions in the Mexican viceregal courts.[216] By the 1600s, merchants were everywhere in urban and rural royal office.[217] And after the Crown began raising funds in the 1600s by selling important viceregal offices, merchants, bureaucrats, miners, and commercially inclined conquistadors gained ever-greater economic and political power.[218] Many contemporaries grumbled about these injustices, but in the new society of orders, it was hard to argue against money.

The church itself became permeated with merchant allies and activities after the 1550s. Though they established themselves only in the 1570s, the Jesuits in New Spain were exemplary in their mercantile dealings, befriending commercial magnates, investing wisely, and amassing impressive superrefineries and other industrial projects.[219] All religious groups used a particular legal writ, the testimony (*testamento*), to ensure wealthy Spanish and Indies notables, widows, and others donated to them generously in the form of *capellanías*, or benefices.[220] The Franciscans were infamous for having lesser Indigenous nobility sign away countless pesos in exchange for the well-being of their souls.[221] All elites did participated with gusto; establishing benefices or supporting religious groups ennobled their families, and their shields of arms and paintings graced churches for centuries.[222] Friars and Jesuits began to gain significant power as merchants. Although they rarely had the autonomy of the theocratic friars of the mid-1500s, one prescient petitioner complained in 1599 that "half of New Spain is in the hands of monks and Jesuits."[223]

Everywhere, social struggles became less systemic and more localized. As Indies factions dug deep paperwork trenches, a new regime of labeling arose. Already in the 1550s but especially after the 1570s, thousands of Indigenous communities began to seek the expulsion of outsiders, including part-Spanish and part-Indigenous individuals they labeled *mestizo, mulato,* or *zambo.* And not just Indigenous communities—friars complained to the Crown that bishops had replaced their parishes with illiterates (*idiotas*), Portuguese, *mestizos,* bastards, unruly Spaniards born in the Indies (*criollos*), and others. While municipalities, universities, guilds, and corporations all specified who was an outsider, inquisitors especially encouraged this widespread culture of labeling. They were particularly keen to determine non-Christian and non-Spanish ancestry.

The Inquisition's own internal hiring prohibitions mirrored the new society of orders. In 1604, for example, its officials banned hiring "any butcher, tailor, pastry-confectioner, [or] shoemaker."[224] Vassals responded by reworking old privilege petitions to emphasize their "Old Christian" genealogies, sterling Christian deeds, and impeccable social status. Some bitterly complained that such policies unjustly excluded Indigenous, Afro-descendant, and other sincere Christian subjects from serving God and the king.

A hallmark of the emerging society of orders was a highly complex and dynamic array of communities organized around racialized categories. By the late 1560s, whole groups of people had lost rights and privileges due to factional struggles. Petitioners won discriminatory policies against *mulatos* and *mestizos,* for example. The preferential policies petitioners and local officials cocreated for Spanish and Indigenous vassals forced Black subjects to form separate communities and petition for their own spaces. An increasingly assertive Crown also sought to more aggressively tax vassals, especially Afro-descendants, prompting more new racialized communities.[225] As bishops and friars struggled over individual parishes, trading accusations of appointing unfit candidates, the orders convinced the Crown to ban part-Indigenous contenders.

Mestizos did not form a coherent social group, but in the 1570s and 1580s, part-Indigenous subjects' efforts to prove their worth to the Crown required they come together. They sought to overturn discriminatory policies prompted by friars clashing with bishops. Self-described *mestizos* thus formed an epistolary network spanning from Lima and Cusco to Arequipa and Loja. Their members made a point of being seen publicly as a group, which required that they maintain religious brotherhoods. In this way, the diffuse and imprecise legal category of *mestizo* became part of the architectural, ritual, and social landscape due to post-1570s paperwork struggles. Well into the 1700s, successor movements sought to defend and expand the rights of *mestizos*, always citing the same texts.

Similarly, during the 1600s, Indigenous petitioners increasingly claimed broader self-identity; many, for example, claimed membership to the Indies Nation, or *Nación Indiana*. Their efforts included not just petitions around a series of core 1500s texts but also public spectacles, construction of churches, canonization efforts, and other drives to secure legislative and social reforms.[226]

In this way, archives became a core component of the emerging racialized society. Vassals struggling for rights and prestige used repositories of documents in ways that furthered their politics while simultaneously materializing, engraining, and naturalizing texts' contents and categories.[227] This takeover of the archive was a collective process—starkly uneven, but collective nonetheless. It was the achievement not of boots-on-the-ground violence but of much subtler forms of coercion. And in contrast with the radical period, this regime posed great challenges to commoner and Native social mobility.

ARCHIVES, INDIGENOUS MERCHANTS, AND NEW PAPERWORK

The story of Diego Muñoz Camargo helps to illuminate the dynamics at play in the process of mastering archives—as well as how life in the Indies changed after the 1570s. Camargo was born in 1529 to Spanish father Diego Camargo and a certain Juana de Navarra, who despite her name was a prominent Tlaxcalan noblewoman, a *cacica*.[228] Considering himself both a Spaniard and a full member of Tlaxcalan society, Camargo regularly moved through the Tlaxcalan republic and Spanish imperial administration. His mastery of Spanish and Indigenous archives from the radical era—and his embrace of the increasingly important merchant ethos sweeping the Indies—secured his rise to power and helped bolster the partial sovereignty of Tlaxcala.

Anyone hoping to thrive in this new society still had to be a master of *justicia* litigation, *gracia* privilege seeking, and *gobierno* reforms. Camargo certainly was, petitioning tirelessly for privileges and reforms for both himself and his kin. He insisted to the Crown that he was the eldest legitimate son of "his father the conquistador and settler."[229] He also sought integration into the Tlaxcalan elite by acting as a translator during their embassy to Madrid. Through a series of successful petitions to the king and the Council of the Indies, the second Diego and his allies sought major legislative reforms that would drastically reshape the city's history. Ambassadors proposed a vast array of policies and prompted council ministers to issue at least forty-three royal decrees to establish numerous legislative and administrative measures back in New Spain. For example, officials were to investigate whether the four dynastic lines of Tlaxcala should have administrative and litigious jurisdiction over their subjects. Indigenous *alcaldes* would become the much more prestigious *gobernadores* and have greater power to resolve court cases to reduce High Court litigation; officials would ensure the concentration of dispersed rural Indigenous settlements into towns.[230]

Good archival management was essential to his success. Camargo was a master of archives both Spanish and Indigenous. In 1581, he sent two agents to the "realms of Castile" to bring back proof from the Soria and Valladolid archives that his father and grandparents were low nobility, or *hidalgos*.[231] He also defended the interests of his Native acquaintances and kin through litigation. He helped defend doña María Quetzalahuaxochtzin in court against Justina, the wife of one don Fernando de Salazar; aided doña María Manrique de Lara Maxixcatzin prove before authorities that she was the heiress of her elite father; and acted as a witness when Juan Álvarez and Margarita litigated against Mateo García and Ana Guacaxochitl using Indigenous *pinturas*.[232]

His archival expertise helped him advance in New Spain's educated milieu, ingratiate himself to the king, and cement his Hispano-Indigenous dynasty. He started his *Beginning and Origin of the Dynasty and Realm of Tlaxcala* around 1562. He also wrote a *Natural History,* which he gave to viceroy of Mexico Martín Enríquez in 1577, after receiving a royal request to file a report on the province's plants and animals.[233] In the mid-1580s, he handed King Philip II two of his histories as a magnificent gift.[234] He wrote another manuscript entitled the *Sum and Epilogue of Tlaxcala* between 1588 and 1589. To create his works, he pored over the Bible, Plato, Bede, and Saint Isidore and read the postconquest works of Spaniards Francisco López de Gómara, Cervantes de Salazar, Jerónimo Ruíz de la Mota, and others.[235] He met the great Franciscan friars Motolinía, Bernardo de Sahagún, and Jerónimo de Mendieta, among others, and read the ethnographies they intended to use to extirpate Indigenous idolatry.[236]

In addition to European sources, he drew on preconquest Nahua songs, chronicles, and genealogical codices, as well as other Native sources from the 1550s.[237] He would be handsomely rewarded, successfully winning two royal decrees conferring him royal stipends. One stressed that he had gone above and beyond the traditional services vassals rendered to their rulers: he had "made with much work and study and diligence" a "very great and particular book with all the matters and antiquities" regarding the history of Tlaxcala.[238] The Crown awarded him a 200 peso yearly rent in addition to another 1500 peso rent in recognition of his father's conquests.

Yet Camargo was also a controversial man. In many ways, he embodied the dark side of the new society of orders. Past his stories of belonging to conquistador lineage and Indigenous aristocracy, he was a commercial wheeler-dealer and slave owner. He embraced Castile's quintessential agrarian, mining, and industrial practices, making a fortune selling tens of thousands of sheep in Oaxaca and Tlaxcala, vending bales of wool by the hundreds to merchants, and owning cows, horses, and mares. He was the superintendent of a local slaughterhouse.[239] Over and over, his desire for privilege and status spurred discovery, innovation, and exploitation.

He roamed central Mexico discovering mines, and he co-owned textile factories that produced rags, blankets, wool clothing, and mourning attire.[240] Like many Natives, he traded in cacao, cochineal, and aniseed and proved himself to be an exceptional businessman whose profits reached the thousands of ducats.[241]

With this power and influence, he sponsored various Christian initiatives. He raised funds through the Bull of the Holy Crusade for the Spanish-papal alliance against the Ottomans and other enemies and collected money to finance the Spanish Armada's imminent and ill-fated attack on England.[242] He helped the half-Burgundian architect Luis de Arciniega and the famous Flemish painter Simon Pereyns receive payment for their work in the church in Tlaxcala.[243]

He also had earthly gain in mind. The new cash economy demanded profitable labor, and the Indigenous population was at its nadir. So Camargo did as many others did: he purchased enslaved Black men, women, and infant children, whom slavers were importing in ever-greater numbers. He was apparently no kind master, even sending a relative to chase down a slave named Felipe who had escaped the mines of Nuestra Señora de las Nieves Chiametla.[244] Like any powerful Spaniard in New Spain, he had poorly paid servants—with names like Gaspar, Francisco Ynutli, Matías Tlahuizmeme, and Felipe—to accompany him in his travels.[245] He thus managed to live like a true landed elite. He kept an opulent household, lorded over his servants and slaves, brandished weapons, and enjoyed wine.[246]

Diego was only one step ahead of his many enemies in Tlaxcala. On February 1, 1583, the commoners of Huamantla successfully petitioned the viceroy of Mexico for a provision compelling the field justices of Tlaxcala Pedro de Torres and Antonio Jiménez to issue swift, harsh justice against him.[247] He had committed an unspecified wrong involving collecting excessive tribute and other "crimes and excesses," but the *alcaldes* had merely given him a slap on the wrist. The viceroy ordered that these officials take the case up once more and "punish him with rigor and without remission" according to their findings.

In 1589, a group of elite Tlaxcalans—apparently allied with the same Natives of Huamantla—traveled to Madrid to inform the king and council that they had had enough. They would expel Diego by invoking a ban on part-Spanish individuals—who many at the time called *mestizos,* or "mixed ones"—from the region forever. A Crown decree from June 14, 1589, declared that "from the Indian laborers and lords of the four houses of the province of Tlaxcala of that land, I have been informed that notwithstanding what I have provided and ordered regarding that mestizos not live among Indians . . . Diego Muñoz Camargo and his brothers and other dependents [*deudos*], all mestiços, live in the said province."[248] The decree mentioned their earlier petition to the viceroy and the order that the *alcaldes mayores* expel him and his family from the city's jurisdiction but noted that this order had not been executed. The Crown ordered it done and "that the said mestiços nor others not reside or live among the Indians." The same group once again petitioned successfully on August 3, 1589, alleging that the previous embassy had been a sham, with elite don Antonio de Guevara seeking to further only his own interests and not those of the city. The petitioners were livid that these individuals were taxing commoners so heavily that they were imprisoning them and having them indentured into textile factories. They turned on Diego again, pleading that the viceroy expel him. The council agreed to all of their requests and ordered their officials comply.[249]

This story shows how, as the radical Spanish Empire transitioned into a more stable phase, the nature of bottom-up paperwork changed as well. Vassals had always engaged in agonistic labeling and merciless stereotyping. Diego, for instance, had become a *mestizo* and was therefore to be expelled from Tlaxcala. The Crown had ordered Diego out, but he had a powerful defense against allegations that he was a *mestizo* outsider. In fact, he had protected himself from these and other potential enemies with an impenetrable wall of social bonds and paper testimony. He had dozens of notarial contracts certifying his business dealings, evidence of his work as a translator for important Tlaxcalan community members, favorable mentions in the city council registers, petitions to the viceroy, a successful role in the 1585 Tlaxcalan embassy to Madrid, and even personal appearances before King Philip II with spectacularly illustrated historical gifts. Many powerful Tlaxcalans owed him for more than just legislation; during their stay in Madrid, the city's four ambassadors won important family privileges and prestigious coats of arms.[250] He had built their archives too.

Diego was simply too important for the community to expel. His military and scholarly service won a Crown pension, and the Tlaxcalan elite repaid his efforts by making him part of their innermost circle. In fact, in 1588, the city council gave him a substantial amount of land—a powerful symbolic and economic gesture. They gave another reason for their close relationship: Diego had married Leonor Vázquez, "elite of the house of Maxixcatzin," one of the city's four great dynasties.[251] The two amassed even more houses and lands in Tlaxcala.[252] Through her bloodline, governorship of the city was passed on to Diego and Leonor's son Diego Muñoz Camargo *el mozo* (the Lad). This succession went against many royal decrees—no part-Spanish individual was to hold this Native title—but their local power and the goodwill of the region was too great. Diego *el mozo* would pass in 1634, leaving no heirs, but as late as 1707, local part-Natives José Miguel and José Muñoz Camargo claimed descent from this line of conquistadors and Tlaxcalan elites.[253] The house of Maxixcatzin, on the other hand, endured well after the Mexican Wars of Independence in the early 1800s, having weathered the great storm of the conquest.

The rise of Tlaxcala, Diego Múñoz Camargo, and the Maxixcatzin lineage through privilege petitioning hints at the broader story of the new society of orders. The Tlaxcaltecans navigated adroitly within the viceregal-episcopal-inquisitorial trinity, leaning especially on viceroys' privileges and Christian miracle narratives to defend the city's integrity. Since the 1550s, they had proudly defended their role in the conquests of the Mexica and countless others, including in regions as far north as Texas and as far East as the Philippines. As the power of the secular church expanded, they developed a regional iconography celebrating their conversion, conquests, and miraculous visitations. Chief among these was devotion to Our Lady of Ocotlán, who appeared to the humble Tlaxcalan Juan Diego Bernardino in 1541. This cult, like so many others, would germinate and grow in the 1600s and 1700s.[254] Indeed, throughout the Indies, Indigenous-sponsored cults of the saints became theaters in the struggle for recognition and even survival. Spanish communities, and less often Afro-descendant ones, also began to frame their interests through miracle cults and the cult of the saints—the most famous being the dark-skinned Virgin of Guadalupe. Common stories about sacred events in the 1500s disguised, however, this fundamentally new form of agency in the viceregal world.

There are obvious parallels between the lives of Diego Muñoz Camargo in Tlaxcala and Diego de Torres in Turmeque. Both were ambitious part-Spanish, part-Indigenous men with strong roots in conquistador and Native society. Both traveled to Madrid and petitioned the king, writing about the histories and customs of their mothers' societies, and became archival brokers in a bid to garner support from wary Native contemporaries. And both were labeled as *mestizos* by their enemies. But the differences are also striking. Diego of Tlaxcala succeeded in endearing himself to his mother's society despite local opposition, and his son became a Tlaxcalan lord. He was as apt as a merchant (and slaver) as he was generous as a supporter of church institutions and local Native families, befitting a Mexican society in which order was taking root. Diego of Turmeque, on the other hand, appeared to contemporaries as a dangerous follower of Las Casas. His attempts to insert himself into Muisca politics—and then into the turbulent investigation of Monzón—caused panic during the 1570s, when Nueva Granada was far from settled. The Crown thus refused to let Diego of Turmeque leave Madrid, where he died without a fortune or broad base of social support.

Guaman Poma de Ayala is another towering Indigenous intellectual whose life centered around the archives. Yet he did not benefit from the new society. To the contrary. While the two Diegos led successful projects of reform and managed to cultivate persuasive elite identities on paper, Guaman Poma failed. The scope of the ambitious illustrated treatise he sent to the king, the *Nueva corónica y buen gobierno* (1615), completely exceeded those of both Diegos. Conspicuously, he finished his text around the same time that Herrera's final opus on the Crown's conquest of the New World hit bookstores. Yet Guaman Poma stood out.

On the one hand, Guaman Poma was vastly more creative in his reflections on the power of the archive. On the other, he was far less successful in translating mastery of archives into social mobility. His origins are unknown, but his rivals would persuasively identify him as lowly Lázaro, a simple peasant. He was likely from the Huamanga region and probably acquired familiarity with Spanish through work in the city's hospital for Indigenous commoners. He achieved some mastery over paperwork, moving up in the social hierarchy as he served Spanish officials undertaking land redistribution and registration efforts in the 1590s. At that time, the Indies teemed with local land-boundary conflicts and disputes, a problem that worsened as Spaniards increasingly established large commerce-oriented landholdings (*estancias*) that competed with Indigenous communities. In Huamanga's land audit, Guaman Poma appears in many documents as a lesser lord under the name don Felipe Guaman Poma.

But the archive was not on his side. As he learned in the audit how others staked blood claims to lordship and lands, Guaman Poma took the opportunity to claim titles over lands as an Indigenous lord. Unfortunately for him, these lands were already occupied by the Chachapoya commoners, a group of *yanacona* serfs who after the conquest had settled in Huamanga. Guaman Poma went to the High Court in Lima, where he presented claims to lands and elite blood descent. The Chachapoyas sued him, and a Spanish official confirmed that Guaman Poma was a fraud and perjurer named Lázaro. He was lashed and expelled.[255] Once exiled to the province of Lucanas, Lázaro doubled down in his effort to gain titles and recognition as a lord of blood. He continued to be chased out of Indigenous towns as he made ever more grandiose, absurd claims.

These experiences motivated Lázaro to critique the emerging archive that had prevented him from creating truth out of thin air. Between 1610 and 1615, Lázaro compiled his magnus opus, the *Nueva corónica y buen gobierno* (1615). This chronicle was steeped in paperwork: a *gracia* petition masquerading as history of his ancient lineage bloodlines (*crónica*) and a *gobierno* petition of reform addressed to both Philip III and the pope. His history covered several ages—the era of apostolic Runa simplicity, the Inca era, the conquest, and the new Toledan regime. Lázaro sketched out a lineage that stretched back millennia, making his chronicle a sort of lengthy *gracia probanza.* As the alleged sole legitimate surviving Inca in Peru, Guaman Poma cast his petition as an audit too. Investigation paperwork structured his narrative: the *Corónica* replicated the structure of audits such as those of Valderrama and Toledo. In this work, Guaman Poma depicted himself as an auditor moving throughout the Andes, evaluating every community and officer in the land and listening to commoners' and lords' requests for hundreds of concrete reforms.

The result of his audits was a sustained treatise on epistemology, the equal of any written by Montaigne or Descartes in the seventeenth century. The viceregal archives were powerful—he recognized it over and over throughout his work. But they were based on unprecedented fraud. His reading of the Inca and the conquest pronounced the deception underlying all claims to truth in Spanish and Indigenous archives. In his account, the Inca dynasty was fabricated by the deracinated, lying commoner Manco Capac, who introduced himself as the direct descendant of the sun and stars, born in a cave. Guaman Poma contested the Incas' claims. Instead, he reconstructed a deep history of Adamic and Noahic Andean rulers with lineages uninterrupted for five thousand years, whom Inca usurpers had unjustly removed. He was the only surviving lord of this deep Andean lineage, making him the equivalent of King Philip III, himself descended from Noah. Guaman Poma also claimed descent from Tupac Yupanqui, the first Inca lawgiver to restore pre-Inca legal order and stable social hierarchies. To top off his exaggerated claims, Guaman Poma framed the Spanish conquest as massive act of commoner misdirection, deception, and blatant counterfeit. It was, he argued, the very reason his genealogical lines had been confused and reshuffled. With the conquest, commoners had become lords and lords commoners. Cobblers and peons had become Inca. Genealogically corrupted Jews and *moriscos* had become Spanish lords.

Guaman Poma ended his chronicle with an analysis of the social order inaugurated by Toledo. Going against the emerging historiographical consensus of Herrera and Garcilaso, Guaman Poma presented the new social order as a bottom-up regime in which every group continued to manipulate the truth—including Indigenous women, who used paperwork to denounce husbands, friars, and Indigenous lords, wreaking havoc. He considered Indigenous women who crossed sexual racial boundaries to be whores or worse.[256] The new social order appeared as disorderly, contingent, and illegitimate as the one it had replaced. In Guaman Poma's chronicle, the Crown had no foresight, knowledge, or control. The archive had conquered the New World, yes, but it was a diabolical archive. He offered his book as a new beginning, a new testament to replace the old law. The old archive had to be utterly eliminated; the Indies would be forever misshapen if the king failed to act. Guaman Poma was thus a radical in an era of order. But the archive he despised defeated him. The Chachapoyas had their documents in order, while he did not. They had their lands and became low-ranking lords. The chronicler, meanwhile, lived in poverty and exile.

ARCHIVES AND FORGERY

Guaman Poma was not a competent forger. He could never produce the archival documents he needed to make his case against the Chachapoyas. In his *Nueva corónica*, he resorted to including a made-up letter by his "father" don Martín de Ayala, the lowly commoner turned-almighty-Andean-lord, who conveniently stated all assertions by the author were authoritative and credible.[257] Guaman Poma crafted his clumsy forged letter following *probanzas* of *gracia* written for Cusco Inca witnesses. He had likely obtained these in the early 1600s, while illustrating the history of the Incas of the Mercedarian Friar Martín de Murúa, then a parish priest near Lucanas.[258] Most of Guaman Poma's documentation was not archival. He allegedly drew on the oral testimonies of the few descendants of the Runa (pre-Inca) lineages of the four quarters of the former Inca empire. But these *probanzas* could not pass factual scrutiny. His alleged witnesses were on average 150 years old.[259] For his claims of pre-Inca history to have any credibility, he needed very old non-Inca witnesses from far away provinces, so he simply invented them. Guaman Poma misunderstood the conquest of the archives of the late sixteenth century.

Guaman Poma was not the only early-seventeenth-century commoner-pretender without the documentation to prove his exaggerated claims to Inca blood lineage. Those who succeeded, however, did not do so in the core areas of Peru but in the frontiers, where archives and documentation were not yet as well developed. These regions maintained the epistemological conditions of the radical age, a period in which charisma and the ability to translate political support into witnesses' testimonies alone could secure any commoner lasting status. Take for example the case of Diego Ramírez Carlos who grew up in La Paz and was the exact contemporary of Guaman Poma. Diego was a *mestizo* instrument maker who in 1619 approached the Franciscans to enter the Amazon lowlands of the Moxo Province. He convinced the friar Gregorio Bolívar to support his petition to the viceroy to convert Chuncho Natives and settle their lands. Soon Diego and Fray Bolívar entered Chuncho land, where Diego began to behave like the Inca, wearing an Inca tunic and crown (*tocapu* and *mascapaicha*). Diego explained to the friar that the Chuncho were communities that had fled the Inca highlands and wanted an Inca to convert and live in pueblos. The friar first went along, but by 1626 had turned against Diego's deceit and treason, for the commoner artisan had hijacked the sovereign authority of the king. When caught, Diego claimed to be one of the *mestizo* sons of Melchor Carlos, a *mestizo* himself. The commoner artisan Diego had no papers to prove he was an Inca, yet like Guaman Poma, he had the deep desire to be one. The undocumented Diego, however, did manage to be an Inca among the Chuncho for at least six years, while deceiving the court in Lima with the help of Franciscans.[260]

There is also the case of the counterfeiter Pedro Chamijo, another contemporary of Guaman Poma who was a lowly runaway commoner raised by Jesuits in Cádiz that arrived young in Pisco circa 1620. Chamijo married the daughter of a mulatto muleteer and one Indigenous woman and settled near Huamanga for nearly sixteen years. When his father-in-law died, Pedro took the mules and fled to the Anti (the Amazon "Andes") near Jauja to cohabitate with the daughter of a local lowland lord. Pedro emerged from the tropical forest with a new name, Bohórquez, a cadre of Indigenous lords as witnesses, and maps and paintings to prove that he had found the long-lost Inca state of Paititi. Several expeditions followed and in the last one of 1650, Pedro secured the title of *adelantado* with broad powers to convert the Natives and settle the land. Pedro founded pueblos, issued decrees, and secured support from Indigenous communities.[261]

Dominicans, however, sent reports back to Lima denouncing Pedro for behaving like a conquistador, capturing slaves and raping women. The viceroy sent militias that captured Pedro, who was sent as prisoner to the Araucano frontier to fight wars against the Mapuche.[262] Pedro soon fled to Tucuman where he mingled with ladinos, servants of the city's main Franciscan convent. The ladinos introduced him to one of the lords of Calchaqui, a very lush and large highland valley between Tucuman and Salta that no Spanish had managed to conquer since Almagro first crossed the valley with Paullu in the 1530s on his way to Chile. Pedro convinced the frustrated Jesuits that he could impersonate the Inca and secure them thousands of converts. Pedro also convinced the governor to acknowledge him as a legitimate Inca, the *mestizo* son of Melchor Carlos who had returned from Spain.[263]

With no documentation to prove it, however, Pedro secured the backing of every authority that staged a fifteen-day celebration in the town of London. They gathered hundreds of caciques and *vecinos* in festivals involving theater, poetry, masses, bullfighting, and horse lancing tournaments. Pedro became the Inca on the promise that he would deliver the land for entrepreneurs, miners, and friars. Pedro could not control Indigenous politics and soon everybody's expectations came crushing down as war ensued. Pedro was captured, imprisoned in Lima for seven years, and finally executed. Like Diego, Pedro the commoner impersonator had no archive to prove his claims; yet he developed the means to be declared Inca of Tucuman by all factions.

Guaman Poma's failure helps illuminate an epistemological change that began to gain traction by the 1570s. Until then, vassals generally had to engage in protracted factional conflict by presenting legally valid *probanzas*, and these demanded petitioners securing as many sufficiently authoritative witnesses as possible. Indigenous subjects who had enough charisma to secure communal support in testimonial validation of Indigenous *quipus* and codices generally succeeded. In cases that invoked the ancient past, the older the witnesses, the better. Out of this chaos, however, order slowly emerged. These older witnesses gradually began to disappear. Now, authorities had to judge arguments about the past almost exclusively by drawing upon the pragmatic and transactional version of the truth stored in legally binding documents produced in the radical era. As the archives gained traction in lawfare, the logic of the *probanzas* changed accordingly. Those who wielded seemingly valid-looking archival documents would more easily secure Crown and viceregal rewards and win legal cases. Unsurprisingly, forgery flourished.

Where Guaman Poma failed at forgery many others succeeded. As we described in Chapter 3, don Melchor Carlos Inca protected his application to knighthood in the Order of Santiago by cleansing his grandfather Paullu's vitae from any reputational stains. To improve Paullu's dossier, Melchor Carlos commissioned a forged document that has long bedeviled historians.[264] In Chapter 2, we described generations of Otomies who mastered the art of forgery, providing lords and commoners with the required codices, titles, and royal decrees to secure office and gain upward social mobility. As José Carlos de la Puente has shown, by the mid-seventeenth century, a host of upwardly mobile Indigenous commoners from Jauja, Cajamarca, and Lima began to arrive in Madrid with forged notarial documents to secure titles and privileges for themselves before the Crown. These parvenues also petitioned on behalf of other Indigenous vassals back in Peru and on behalf of the elites of the entire "Indigenous Nation"—the *Nación Indiana*. Through the wealth they acquired through the market, these commoners-turned-lords acquired forged documents and assembled vast networks of Native and Spanish witnesses in Madrid. In so doing, they displaced the traditional Inca elites of Cusco as the true Incas of Peru.[265]

De la Puente offers a detailed study of one such counterfeiter, the ladino commoner Lorenzo Ayun. Trained by Franciscans in Reque, northern coastal Peru, Lorenzo wound up in Madrid in 1645, serving the powerful *creole* friar Buenaventura de Salinas y Córdoba. With the encouragement of the creole friar, Lorenzo assumed the identity of an Andean lord to write *gobierno* petitions (*memoriales*) addressed to the king, attaching Atahualpa to his name add credibility to his petitions and denunciations. Franciscans gave him cover and Lorenzo did meet the king in person in 1646, just like don Diego de Torres did in 1579. In 1646, Lorenzo left for Mexico with Fray Salinas y Córdoba who was charged with the government of all the Franciscans in this viceroyalty of New Spain. When the powerful friar died in 1653, Lorenzo returned to Peru and moved to Jauja to impersonate one Jerónimo Limaylla, the illegitimate son of the recently deceased lord of Lurinhuanca. Limaylla had left for Lima young to be educated by Franciscans and had never returned, for he had died young. Lorenzo knew enough about the early life of Jerónimo and that the sucession of the rich *cacicazgo* of Lurinhuanca was up for grabs. Like the early modern French Martin Guerre, Lorenzo swooped in, claiming to be the long-lost son of the dead lord and thus the true heir to the disputed *cacicazgo*. For some ten years (1655 to 1665), the new don Jerónimo moved between Jauja and Lima, disputing the lordship of the community to two main rivals. Clearly aware that the resurrected don Jerónimo was a forger, some elite factions in Lurinhuanca openly supported Lorenzo. They were impressed by his ladino command of paperwork and, more important, by his proven record: the ability of having once gained the attention of the king himself. With the help of notarized testimonies, Lorenzo built a vast written legal archive of witnesses vouching for his blood nobility status as don Jerónimo. After losing twice to Lurinhuanca rivals, however, Lorenzo returned to Madrid in 1665 as don Jerónimo to appeal. Although he never obtained the much-sought-after lordship, Lorenzo did secure great authority in court. He continued to write *memoriales* as don Jerónimo Limaylla, seeking reform on behalf of the *Nación Indiana*. In practice, Lorenzo became a pan-Andean lord, acting in court as the legal representative of many Indigenous local authorities, the spokesperson of the textual community that was the *Nación Indiana* as late as 1678.[266] These successes, as well as others we have discussed in Chapter 2, were clearly associated to the spread of markets enabled by the collapse of seigneurial regimes.

There are other cases of forgers taking advantage of the authority accrued by archives and the astute use of paperwork by ladinos. Take the case of don Alonso Florencia Inca, a mid-seventeenth-century alleged descendant of Huascar.[267] Don Alonso's brother José, it appears, traveled to Madrid where, using old *gracia* decrees issued by Charles V to his Inca ancestor, Tito Atauchi Inca, he secured a title, a coat of arms, and a plumb office in Potosi as a royal accountant and as field magistrate in Paria, Charcas.[268] Both brothers corresponded with their Inca "aunt" doña Isabela Atahualpa, the great granddaughter of Atahualpa, the Inca who had murdered every member of Huascar's lineage. Doña Isabela was the matriarch of a web of descendants of Atahualpa crowded around San Roque in Quito. She was the hub of a vast network of correspondents connecting Incas in Lima, Cusco, and Quito. Throughout the 1640s and 1650s, Alonso informed doña Isabela of his intention of visiting Quito on his way to Spain to gain rewards. In 1661, the secretary of doña Isabela, Roque Ruiz, had a letter circulate among many Indigenous lords that don Alonso should be coming as an Inca to bring justice to the Natives.[269] Meanwhile don Alonso, descendant of a conquistador and Inca princes (*palla*), secured an appointment as field magistrate (*corregidor*) in Ibarra, to the north of Quito. For years, doña Isabela had prepared the arrival of her nephew, and when don Alonso arrived in mid-December of 1666, he was immediately greeted in Indigenous towns by crowds with baroque public pageants, befitting of an Inca. Don Alonso did not disappoint the crowds, displaying a large genealogical family tree, a six-by-six-foot canvas tracing his lineage back to the "Inca" and an exquisitely dyed vicuña woolen (*cumbi*) that had allegedly once belonged to the Inca.[270] In Ibarra, a Spanish town, he did not bother to perform as Inca but as a Spanish grandee, signing verdicts as Knight of the Royal Collar and Royal Arms, *caballero de la cadena y armas reales*.[271] Don Alonso acted brusquely, often humiliating lower authorities as an autocrat. Complaints quickly spread, and the High Court of Quito ordered an audit that revealed the false titles and the dangerous displays of Inca paraphernalia. High magistrates had don Alonso jailed and sent to Lima for a trial; they also had Roque Ruiz jailed and tortured to reveal a vast network of Indigenous correspondents (with their own postal service) seeking the restitution of an Inca monarch.[272]

It is difficult to ascertain the true scale of forgeries after the 1570s, but the case of one doña María Joaquina Uchu Inca Tupac Yupanqui y Huayna Capac in Mexico from 1789 to 1800 certainly sheds light on how ubiquitous they became. One day in 1789, doña María Joaquina appeared before the new Mexican viceroy, count of Revillagigedo, to request special privileges for her siblings, sons, and spouse.[273] According to numerous repeated, unanswered petitions, doña María Joaquina and her husband the Inquisition notary Juan Sánchez Rojas, had met before with the viceroy no fewer than seventeen times. The couple argued that five previous Peruvian viceroys since 1771 had already provided doña María's family with housing, subsidies, and privileges.[274]

Now, doña María asked Revillagigedo for rewards for her own sons and husband, including thousands of ducats for Sánchez Rojas to travel to Spain to petition the king. According to the many unanswered written petitions by doña María Joaquina and her husband, Revillagigedo responded to all these orally delivered claims with disdain. He demanded archival evidence. His subalterns had been unable to find any evidence that the five previous viceroys had helped the Uchu Inca clan. To overcome this critique, doña María and her husband claimed that previous viceroys simply had tapped into their own personal wealth and had therefore left no archival traces.[275]

Clearly annoyed, Revillagigedo insisted upon proof. Doña María thus began to produce large amounts of primary documents, dating back to three 1544–1546 royal decrees, particularly one from 1545 favoring the heirs of one Gonzalo Uchu Guallpa, Inca son of Huayna Capac, with privileges of all kinds. These included the right to have armed guards and occupy the most distinguished seats in cathedrals and public events—privileges that would best even Peru's viceroys.[276] Revillagigedo found none of this plausible.[277] Doña María persevered and turned in documentation dating back to the mid-seventeenth century that proved her ancestors had successfully used the decrees to secure privileges. She had no original copies of these 1540s decrees, but she did possess copies transcribed by notaries beginning in the mid-seventeenth century. Doña María Joaquina, for example, had documentation of a group, the Uchu of Lambayeque (northern coastal Peru), of very humble origins. Using a series of decrees from 1653 and 1701, the Uchu had changed their status, first by gaining release from encomienda tribute and later by acquiring the privilege of collecting tribute themselves. In 1717, the former Uchu of Lambayeque had moved to Lima, and one of them, Miguel Uchu Inca, used these decrees to obtain permission to visit the king. On the way, he had wound up in Mexico on his way to Spain.[278] This Miguel was doña María Joaquina's father.

All these documents and more eventually secured doña María and her second husband (she remarried one Spanish trader don Agustin de Estrada immediately after Sánchez died in 1794) some rewards in 1797. It was not the viceroy Revillagigedo, however, who acknowledged doña María's petition. The relentless petitioner later secured a 300-peso annual pension from a new viceroy, the duke of Santa Fe.[279] He nevertheless harbored doubts on the veracity of the 1540s decrees, and in 1797 sent doña María's 402-folio dossier back to Spain to have the head archivist of the newly formed Archive of the Indies investigate.

The head archivist replied that he had been unable to find any record of doña María's royal decrees. He had managed to find one decree issued in 1545 on behalf of Paullu, also known as Cristóbal Topa Inca, the ally of Almagro and Pizarro against Manco Inca, and the grandfather of the famous don Melchor Carlos.[280] All the 1540s royal decrees the Uchu of Lambayeque had used to gain privileges and status in Lima in the second half of the seventeenth century appeared false.

But doña María was not the only Uchu Inca of Lambayeque who manipulated the archives. Other members of the commoner family had also moved to Lima around 1700, securing, as her father had, a royal pension. They used not only the same strategies, but many of the same documentation she presented. In the 1760s, one don Domingo Yupanqui, who most likely was one of the brothers of doña María's father, don Miguel, surfaced in Madrid with his two sons. He requested privileges that he slowly and systematically secured by forging baptismal records and changing names to accentuate his alleged Inca descent. Domingo had his son Dionisio Yupanqui accepted into the army officers' corps where Dionisio developed his own distinguished and counterfeited career to become the "Inca" spokesperson during the constitutional debates in Cádiz after 1808.[281]

There is plenty of evidence that in Cusco, as early as the 1560s, forged royal decrees favoring petty Cusco nobles or commoners began to surface.[282] Clearly by the mid-seventeenth century, the use of forged decrees had become an epidemic. It had become a preferred path of commoner vassals seeking social mobility. The nouveau riche, including Indigenous traders, muleteers, retailers, artisans, and militia and guild potentates also frequently resorted to this method.[283]

The 1730s disappearance of the dynasty claiming the Marquisate of Oropesa, the seigneurial estate of the descendants of Manco Inca that had devolved to the Crown with no rightful heirs in the 1730s, triggered a renewed surge in forgery. Suddenly in Cusco a host of archives with suspect documents of all kinds began to be assembled by new claimants, including those of an affluent provincial muleteer named José Gabriel Condorcanqui Noguera. He claimed to be the only legitimate descendant of the last Inca who survived Toledo's assault on the Inca of Vilcabamba in 1572. But officials dismissed his claims and denounced his documentation as false. The spurned don José Gabriel would soon mutate into Tupac Amarau II, and in 1781 would lead the largest peasant rebellion ever witnessed in the mature Spanish Empire.[284]

DEPOLITICIZING THE INDIGENOUS ARCHIVE

Throughout this book, we have insisted on the vigor and consequentiality of Indigenous lords' and commoners' politics. Their engagement with lawfare enabled a total reconstruction of the social order. Yet just as Herrera buried the radical era with his tidy narrative, many scholars have transformed archival evidence of Native politics into a story of cultures and codices. Guaman Poma's story as the commoner Lázaro is unknown, largely because experts have refused to read Indigenous sources historically as political records.

This shift was already at play in the 1500s, with vassals' own insistence on time immemorial. But during the Enlightenment, the Indigenous archives produced in the radical era were completely decontextualized. They became Indigenous bibles and hieratic riddles to be puzzled over and trafficked. This exoticization often literally tore pictographic components of paperwork from their contexts.

Consider the Italian Lorenzo Boturini Benaducci, who traveled through the countryside of central Mexico in the 1730s. On his long trip, he purchased the family archives of struggling lords hit by a wave of disease spreading throughout Tlaxcala and beyond.[285] Boturini used these archives to devise new revolutionary theories about the development of writing and mental faculties. Boturini was a pious man determined to prove that the miracle of the Virgin of Guadalupe happened in Tepeyac and that Juan Diego's rustic robe (*tilma*) was the Virgin's way of communicating with Nahua commoners through pictograms. He collected any Indigenous document that referenced the cult of Tepeyac. The *Anales of Juan Bautista,* through which artisans in Mexico had documented their experiences, made passing references to Guadalupe's chapel. Boturini therefore added it to his collection.

A follower of Italian philosopher Giambattista Vico, Boturini created an Indigenous archive that took all agency out of Indigenous pictography. Everything appeared as Native culture and Catholic prefiguration. In this sense, Boturini was among the first to render radical Indigenous paperwork into changeless, picturesque codices of an alleged authentic Indigenous self.[286] He still stands today for the revolutionary arrival of a new inquisitive modernity, a form of early modern antiquarianism that would rewrite the history of the Americas through the collection and study of Indigenous codices.

These new styles of reading and collecting sources transformed how we think of the Indigenous past—from politics to curio. This was the fate of Guaman Poma's *Corónica,* which reached Spain but seems to have been given away as a gift and ultimately reached the Royal Library of Copenhagen.[287] Litigation and petition also transformed into mere artifacts. The *Codex Osuna* is a case in point. Although it documents the struggle of commoners and lords in 1564–1565 in Mexico City, it first left the viceroyalty as a curiosity, an amusing gift for a duke. This mutiperspectival archive, documenting factionalism within one Indigenous polity, became the *Codex Osuna*—a single, unified document featuring cryptic Mexican hieroglyphs. The heir of the duchy of Osuna himself, Mariano Téllez-Girón y Beaufort de Osuna, had the codex printed as a curio in 1878.[288]

CONCLUSIONS

The Crown never conquered the Indies outright. There was no armed takeover or imposition of an autonomous Weberian State in Mexico or Peru. Rather, the radical phase gave way to an era of social order thanks to a number of changes both gradual and abrupt. By the 1560s, archives had become a site of struggle. Archival collections had always existed in the Indies, but their growing complexity and social heft transformed the nature of vassal-lord dialogue. These repositories encouraged the formation of a pragmatic regime of truth shared by many and helped shore up legitimacy for a society that agreed on the basics of an Indies order. Politics in this more hierarchical period were increasingly shaped by archival epistemologies and practices: curation, citation, glossing, genealogical thinking. These methods led on the one hand to the formation of sophisticated regimes of discrimination, including racial-genealogical categories, and on the other to the consolidation of discriminated vassals into collectives with concrete social practices (as Indians, *mestizos, mulatos,* etc.).

Inasmuch as the Crown managed to eke out an assertive stance in its vast dominions, it did so not through powerful armies but through archival politics. Kings, ministers, and local officials had initially garnered support by distributing and redistributing privileges to different factions. However, with mastery of the archive, they could increasingly aspire to more. They could overcome factionalism, understand the Indies as a whole, and devise limited pathways of assertiveness previously impossible. The Crown belatedly began to curate and utilize its archives in the 1560s and especially the 1570s. President Ovando's reforms created the first proper European overseas information state, which wrested from its own once-disorderly papers the first holistic view of the geography and resources of the New World. Fortifications, fleets, and resources could be shuffled and reshuffled to address piracy attacks without having to rely on misleading partisan petitions. An independent archive liberated the council to save the empire just as internal factionalism, piracy, and bankruptcy threatened to destroy it.

The archives conquered by reinforcing among Indies vassals a set of common values, legal concepts, and especially truths. Each Indies faction sought to force its truths and archives on its rivals, but by the 1570s, it was the Crown that was increasingly disciplining these once-radical archives. In so doing, officials eked out limited assertive power. And their ambitions did not stop there. They determined that they would need to not only crack down on radical factionalism's excesses and dangers but also assault radicalism's very memory.

This understanding led to a fourth, equally significant, conquest: that of historiography. As radical disorder gave way to stable new social orders, communities began to memorialize their pasts differently. The partisan histories of the past gave way to narratives of the Crown's top-down foresight and control. This historiographical conquest is largely responsible for the erasure of a massive Indies archive, including a vibrant sphere of participatory debate that had produced sweeping skeptical doubt, epistemological innovations, and knowledge of all kinds. The historiographical conquest of the late 1500s and early 1600s gave us the narrative of three top-down conquests: military, spiritual, and royal. All of them are historiographical inventions belied by the archives, and all continue to exert great power. To understand Latin America's radical past, we must read against the historiographical grain and along the grain of the archive.

There is no fixed date for the transition between the radical era and the society of orders. What is certain is that sometime around 1572, this society's radicalism peaked and entered a new phase. Archives were largely born of this radical era but now helped order emerge. The occasional radical debate might still appear, and frontier societies remained convulsed. Yet the overall trend toward order was unmistakable.

This world was now what many scholars call "baroque," a social order in which massive and uncompromising debates about structural change lost considerable ground and hierarchy was everywhere becoming more visible and elaborate. Obedience became a cardinal virtue. The Crown, no longer threatened, restored the marquisates it had abolished and created new lordly estates (albeit without the broad powers they had once enjoyed). Strapped for cash, it also began distributing more and more privileges to the highest bidder. And commerce driven by stunning mineral and agricultural wealth continued to shape—many contemporaries would have argued *distort*—all strata of this much more stable society.

More restricted and particular debates replaced broad attacks on social structures. While the volume of paperwork actually expanded, its power to reshape society in new directions decreased. Archival tricksters and *ladinos* who had previously reinvented themselves lost ground as emerging social truths became increasingly codified. More and more vassals squabbled about the trappings of privilege, inventing fractional categories of racialized discrimination. These regimes of human categorization grew more reified as communities of self-described Indians, *mestizos*, and *mulatos* (among others) became social realities. For Indigenous actors looking to forge ahead, mastering writing and Spanish paperwork was not sufficient. Now, assembling and brokering archives was a must. The divergent fates of don Diego of Turmeque, don Diego of Tlaxcala, the Inca Garcilaso, Guaman Poma, doña María Joaquina Uchu Inca Tupac Yupanqui y Huayna Capac, and many others demonstrate how crucial and perilous this transformation might be.

The new social order proved challenging for Indigenous actors, as demographic catastrophe decimated communities and a new mercantile system based on wage labor and slavery grew dominant. Many began denying that Indigenous actors had played any role in creating this long-lasting society. Conquistadors—including some Native ones like the Tapias—celebrated their Christian heroism as proof of their (implicitly and even explicitly Castilian) nobility. Others downplayed Native agency further still. Las Casas had long erased Indigenous politics as part of his patrimonialist and patronizing vision of friar theocracy. Herrera and many other chroniclers erased factionalism from the New World's history—and along with it, commoners' and lords' successful initiatives. They replaced this agonistic story with a simpler one featuring the three conquests: invasion, conversion, and Crown ascendency. Even Native archives came under attack. Europeans like Boturini increasingly appropriated and dismembered Indigenous codices, reducing these radical works to expressions of culture. And when nations emerged in Latin America, liberal and civilizationalist narratives would frame the viceregal era as a prepolitical wilderness.

Indigenous subjects—millions of individuals and communities who had shaped the conquests, conversions, and archives of the New World, discovered and labored in the great silver mines of Potosi and Zacatecas, linked China to Europe, and honed a tradition of antityranny, skepticism, and structural change—largely disappeared from sight. They were framed as conquered peoples, the vanishing vestiges of a bygone traditional world soon to be replaced by modern white settlers or a new *mestizo* society. Yet history has, by and large, proven these narratives wrong. Native peoples pressed on with political projects throughout the seventeenth century straight into the present. They continue to shape world history today, as do the radical Spanish Empire's traditions. Throughout Latin America and beyond, forms of Native radicalism influenced by sixteenth-century events have repeatedly transformed the region, confounding radicals and reactionaries alike.

CONCLUSION

Ladinoamérica's Radicalism in Invisible Ink

The world-renowned Mexican scholar Octavio Paz wrote in 1982 that "a society defines itself not only by its attitude to the future, but also by its attitude concerning the past."[1] In nationalist Mexico, the most common intellectual stance toward the viceregal era has been precisely one of denial. An era that represented colonization and subordination was largely scratched with fury from the record, the rest amended for posterity. Paz was sharply critical of these alterations, for "naturally, this deformation is nothing other than the projection of our own deformities."[2] Yet Paz's vision of the past was scarcely less deformed. He saw Mexico as a rigidly hierarchical society stunted in its intellectual growth, dogmatic to the core, and ruled by a divine king who crushed dissent through religious orthodoxy. This world was a "rich and sensual society, yet devout and superstitious, obedient before royal power, submissive to the mandates of the Church."[3]

Every generation rewrites the past with both black ink and invisible ink, he mused. Some stories must be told loudly, others mouthed silently. Indeed, he wrote in bold the histories of censorship, hierarchy, civilizationalist intolerance, and dogmatic superstition. He left hidden the Indies' rich traditions of debate, antityrannical agitation, social mobility, and skepticism. In short, he—like many Mexicans before him—wrote the history of a radical Spanish Empire in invisible ink.

Scholars today widely regard the sixteenth century as a, if not the, formative era in Latin American history. Few would contest that the arrival of Europeans, Spanish lifeways, and Christianity deeply marked this period, as did strong strains of religious intolerance, epistemicide, Indigenous dispossession, and slavery, among other distressing legacies. Yet the region's unique postconquest social context was shaped by not only conquistadors, friars, and administrators but also Indigenous lords, Native commoners, and women. Five decades of thought and action left a radical legacy: antityrannical movements, new and dynamic paperwork-driven frontier societies, a treasure trove of texts and artifacts used by vassals to disrupt and reconstitute the social order, and a sophisticated culture of doubt.

There are many reasons why Paz could not see the political and skeptical radicalisms of the age we have studied here. The extraordinary creativity and bottom-up paperwork participation of millions has remained invisible to historians since 1600, as Crown-appointed historians like Herrera put together an extraordinarily compelling narrative of the few (conquistadors, friars, and the King) conquering the many. This was the account of an empire that arrived in the Indies fully prefigured, planned and implemented from above by a clique of neoscholastic clerics and one meddlesome king. This was the antithesis of the more bottom-up and democratic colonial British America. Four paradigms have reinforced this foundational historiographical blindness. Liberalism, decolonialism, culturalism, and Hispanism, as we have explained, are largely responsible for rendering invisible the Radical Spanish Empire and its vast, dialogical antityrannical politics. Yet over the past fifty years, scholars have produced a vast corpus of local and microhistorical studies suggesting an empire that offered Indigenous peoples, commoners, women, and slaves multitudes of channels of political participation through the paperwork of *gobierno, gracia,* and *justicia.*

Throughout this book, we have laid great emphasis on the importance of bottom-up communication and the form and functions of petitioning, litigation, and archives as alternative explanations to these otherwise impossible conquests. This has brought us to contest one of the central myths of liberal and decolonial scholarship: the historical model of early-modern print culture. For many scholars, print was the novel medium whose socially explosive appearance—especially in Protestant Northern Europe—set into motion radical change and ultimately modernity itself. This tale has played a powerful role in blinding Paz, and many before and after him. For him, viceregal culture was sensuous but censorial, lacking in dissent. Similarly, many others have read the largely Catholic, heavily redacted corpus of printed works produced in the Empire to reflect a broad rejection of Indigenous epistemologies and Native political participation.

We have offered an alternative sociology to this dubious story of print as the Big Bang of modernity. We have instead centered on manuscript communication based on paperwork-driven, bottom-up systems of political participation. In the Indies, the system of petition and response generated decades of radical social disorder and the rise of viceroys, bishops, and inquisitors (Chapter 1); new global markets based on the emancipation of captives and the mobility of savvy *ladino* commoners liberated from seigneurial lordships (Chapter 2); a privilege-seeking eruption of creative and violent epistemological plurality (Chapter 3); sweeping waves of debilitating social doubt about the relation between paperwork and truth (Chapter 4); the rising power of archives that helped tame radicalism while reconfiguring new social orders from the bottom up and creating pragmatic, widely accepted regimes of truth (Chapter 5).

Rejecting these four narratives and taking particular issue with the myth of print allows us to highlight the massive structural roles played by Indigenous actors. We have firmly insisted on the importance of Native politics in this era. In the past two centuries, many reformist intellectuals and radical groups have attempted to read past the viceregal era—the radical sixteenth century included. One casualty of this choice has been the possibility of studying Indigenous politics. Scholars often call to read against the grain to recover fragmentary Indigenous voices. Yet when we approach the archives along the grain, we discover tens of thousands of long and significant Indigenous petitions, lawsuits, allegations. The Indigenous story after the conquest is not just a vision of the vanquished, but one of deliberate radicalism, mutability, and adaptability. We see the constant richness of imperial subjects' protests, epistemological creativity, and skepticism. Describing the spirit of a vast region is always a risky venture, but one could do worse than to center Latin America's *ladinidad*, its disruptive savviness, not as a disembodied force but as the doing of countless *ladinos* and their radical politics.

Our story of radicalism has also traced the rise of a stable New World society and administration. No army successfully imposed itself over the Indies. In the 1500s, bearers of violence—especially conquistadors and Native lords—emerged badly weakened from the great multifactional contest. Friars, too, failed to establish theocracy. Vassals and officials instead gradually established the power of a royal trinity of viceregal, episcopal, and inquisitorial authorities that shared a much broader jurisdiction than had ever been possible in the rest of the Spanish Empire. These authorities and the Crown continued to rule in a bottom-up fashion while moving against wanton disobedience and factionalism. The runaway accumulation of factional paperwork led to a struggle over archives in which authorities again managed to wrest limited power from their rivals. A world of violent and epistemologically creative paperwork infused with radical skeptical tendencies slowly gave way to one of order and pragmatic archival truths. The society of orders became increasingly visible as the century came to an end, although it remained convulsed by the dynamism of an emerging labor market made possible by decades of antiseigneurial radicalism. As Indigenous-mined silver in new borderland communities reached China in Spanish galleons, early modern commercial globalization took off.

Radicalism was anything but extrinsic to the empire. It was not underground or even unusual. To the contrary, it was—between about 1526 and 1572—intrinsic to Indies history. The sixteenth century's fierce disputes, agonism, bottom-up movements, doubt, and creativity left a social and intellectual legacy in Latin America that sits alongside legacies of violence, dogmatism, and injustice. It was not just a solitary friar like Las Casas but an entire society in uproar.

Radical currents in subsequent centuries were not always brought by promethean European anarchists or communists to thankful New World commoners. Humble and elite Indigenous people, women, various factions of Spaniards, and others cocreated this dissenting tradition. Although Indigenous organizers are often well-versed in more recent European and

Latin American literature and theories on resistance, which largely come from Western-educated European and New World circles, many of the most successful activists have not needed to brush up on nineteenth- and twentieth-century radical manifestos. They have a fully formed lexicon of radicalism that is still relevant in the present. And it is often from rural regions that Spanish American nations—and the world—continue to be shaped in radical new directions. Indeed, Latin America's history can hardly be understood without recognizing the deep roots of this radical tradition.

THE REBIRTH OF THE COUNCIL OF THE INDIES IN COLOMBIA

Many, especially in the Indigenous countryside, have kept the flame of radicalism alive through the nineteenth century and into the present. By the early 1800s, the empire was in tatters and American nations were on the rise. In 1834, Spanish monarchs abolished the Council of the Indies; in 1916, however, the council was reborn—not in Madrid but in rural southern Colombia. Its ministers were not Spanish jurists but elders of the Indigenous municipalities of Loaní and Toy in Tolima.[4] They called themselves the Council of the Indies. They answered to no king, only to God. Their goal was to force the hostile state to recognize their lands and rights and end racist discrimination against Indigenous Colombians. Their call reverberated across ethnic lines. Four years later, other communities joined, adding fifteen hundred signatures in support of this council. They hailed from the towns of Calibío, Totoró, Paniquitá, Chero, Tambaló, Quichaya, Ortega, El Dinde, Guamacas, Pedregal, Yaquirá, and El Caguán. They sent the Colombian government a clear message: "This Council recalls the Supreme Council of the Indies . . . under which all the interests of America were protected. . . . Through it, and by it, our own rights will come to be respected and recognized."[5]

The council appointed as its representative a messianic figure: the tall, muscular, solemn don Manuel Quintín Lame Chantre, a Nasa born near Popayán in 1883 (see Figure C.1).[6] Don Manuel's educational background was extremely humble. He never learned to write well and insisted that

Figure C.1 A 1943 photograph of don Manuel Quintín Lame Chantre, a charismatic Colombian Indigenous leader active in the Tolima region. Photo by Gerardo Reichel-Dolmatoff, reproduced with permission from Archivo Arkhé, Madrid.

his university had been the forests and hillsides. His highly poetic prose reveals deep Indigenous and Catholic leanings, including a background in scholastic philosophy and pedagogy.[7] It had been during his time in Panama under the employ of General Carlos Albán, a conservative scientist and lawyer, that he learned the rudiments of reading and writing.

Gradually, don Manuel found himself forced into political action. Perhaps as early as 1910, he had tried to defend his father's properties from the encroachment of white settlers, who had assassinated his youngest brother. It was payback; don Manuel's father had conservative leanings, and the land invaders were liberal.[8] Don Manuel sought help in the regional capital of Popayán, where he met a politically radical lawyer who introduced him to viceregal documents in the archives that proved his claims to the land. That year, seven Indigenous communities elected him as their representative before the government.[9] By 1924, he claimed to speak for 183,600 Native citizens in 197 communities.[10]

His charisma won him many followers, and his movement treasured colonial archives as a unique source of power. He traveled to Bogotá in 1914, researching in the national archives and telegramming his findings to his allies.[11] In 1915, he announced to his Indigenous peers, "Conforming with the ancient writings which appear upon royal decrees in the history of our country, we will take back our rights."[12] He allegedly proclaimed in 1916 that he would free Indigenous peoples from their slavery and denounced the government as illegitimate, declaring, "I accept no other property titles but those granted by the King of Spain."[13] Indeed, "from history, and from documents, spring my rights."[14] In later years, don Manuel would validate his authority by claiming descent from the Indigenous lord don Juan Tama de Estrella, who appears in the record by 1696 and in 1708 successfully petitioned Spanish authorities for land titles.[15]

For his participation in protests, petitions, and revolts, officials repeatedly jailed and tortured him. Little wonder, for his message was deeply subversive. He declared lawfare and (if need be) armed revolt against tyrannical white landowners and government officials, new Columbuses and conquistadors, who trampled the king's decrees.[16] Don Manuel also preached radical skepticism against oppressors in Tolima and the Colombian government: "Oh beloved people! Oh Indigenous and other poor people—let us snap the chains of tyranny, of humiliation and deceit, let us not be seduced by these lips bathed in sarcasm!"[17] He thus tapped into deep reservoirs of antityranny and doubt about authority. His followers did the same. In 1927, a petition signed by fourteen thousand Indigenous women closely associated with don Manuel declared the state the "apotheosis of tyranny" and urged citizens to be wary of its promises.[18]

What sort of radical was don Manuel? He was a riddle for allies and enemies alike. He explicitly refused to take sides in Colombia's liberal-conservative struggle.[19] His movement was conservative and Catholic but also explicitly anti-elite, anticlerical, and anti-Spanish. He denounced white invaders—conquistadors and landowners—in equal measure.[20] He nonetheless revered the Council of the Indies and the king, mixing respect for law and documents with bursts of armed struggle. He briefly joined the socialists but distanced himself when Moscow's irreligious, centralizing tendencies became more explicit; many of his former allies went on to play major roles in the Communist Party.[21] His conservative and liberal enemies, meanwhile, mocked and feared him as a wild, stupid, and dangerously atavistic force. The hostile press blasted him as a sensual drunk, a part-Black trickster, and a "*ladino*, audacious, and of unsettled character."[22] Yet he remained elusive. Don Manuel fit no archetype easily available to twentieth-century Hispanic thinkers. His radicalism came from a tradition that contemporary politicians and theorists of modernity failed to grasp.

The Indigenous leader's efforts were widely deemed a failure during his time. His successes were initially limited to local land recovery.[23] Colombia would be wracked by decades of catastrophic guerrilla violence, marginalizing don Manuel's followers and the entire movement.[24] He died in relative obscurity in 1967. By the 1970s, however, leftist intellectuals increasingly claimed him as an inspiration. His movement—*lamismo*—inspired an armed movement in his name, which demobilized in 1991, and helped introduce the concept of multiculturalism to the new Colombian constitution that year. Lame influenced the Regional Indigenous Council of Cauca (Consejo Regional Indígena del Cauca), which since 1971 has struggled for Indigenous autonomy and rights under his name.[25] The

Nasa philosopher, former Colombian senator, and *lamista* Jesús Piñacué Achicué, among many others, continues to cite sixteenth-century debates as he cocreates and criticizes the government today.[26]

Many in Colombia used their claims to land against onslaughts of land usurpers, reminding the magistrates that they had a "title which arrived to us from the Spaniards in the colonial period."[27] Since the early 1960s, Colombian authorities have invited petitions from Indigenous, Afro-descendant, and commoner communities to reclaim colonial and precolonial community lands. Thousands of citizens petitioned the state and in just over four decades recovered limited sovereignty over thirty million hectares of land.[28] Local cultural productions celebrated these struggles. For instance, in 1959, a carnival troupe in the Indigenous community of Cañamomo Lomaprieta sang,

que en las manos los tenemos,	For in our hands we have
los títulos del virrey,	the titles of the viceroy
con estos nos presentamos,	with these we present ourselves,
al tribunal superior,	to the Superior Tribunal,
y nosotros les probamos	and with it we certify
que sí tenemos valor.	that we do indeed have valor.[29]

Throughout South America, movements and leaders emerged with similar goals and strategies. Don Santos Marka T'ula, an illiterate Aymará Indigenous lord, was born around 1879 in Qhurawara de Paqasa, highland Bolivia. Early in his life, he discovered sixteenth-century documents that demonstrated his entitlement to the ancient lordship of the Mallku Aymarás. These documents would serve him in a broader Indigenous struggle against abuse and land seizures by Spanish-speaking Bolivians. In 1883, the Bolivian legislature decreed that all Indigenous communities that could not prove possession of their land reaching back to the colonial era would lose their properties. Spanish-speaking outsiders seized parcel after parcel of land for years on end.

Around 1914, a diligent Native legal agent discovered that the territory's owners during the viceregal era had been the Marka T'ula dynasty.

The smoking gun was a 1577 document in the Lima archives signed by Viceroy Toledo during his great land audits of 1569–1581. This manuscript mentioned don Santos's ancestor Carlos Marka T'ula.[30] Yet the government declared the documents to be forgeries, and Spanish-speaking land invaders triumphed that year.[31]

Don Santos, with power of attorney to speak for many local La Paz Indigenous leaders, now roved Bolivia's cities and towns in search of further archives, proof, and justice. His agitation landed him in jail in 1917 and again in 1918. The following year, perfecting his Quechua, he built an even vaster multiethnic alliance of local lords and approached the government in their name. They demanded, as a collective, that the Republic of Bolivia honor the Spanish monarchs' centuries-old agreements with the Indigenous peoples of the Viceroyalty of Peru. They also insisted that government troublemakers had locked the archives and hidden many documents, attempting to thwart the movement.

With the help of Spanish-speaking intermediaries and a wide network of investigators, the claimants amassed copies of viceregal sources reaching back to the 1500s. Lords from the entire region arrived to pray at don Santos's house, offering the dried bones of livestock to the sacred Willkani Lake. These offerings were burned as a sacrifice to dispel any evil forces the sources might contain.

The movement again called on the government to "honor the ancient laws of the Crown of Spain."[32] Fearful of the growing movement, the government jailed don Santos yet again. Then began a radical alignment. Don Santos's fame grew among working-class Indigenous guilds in the capital—the construction workers, embroiderers, tailors, blacksmiths, locksmiths, painters, shippers, and butchers of the Local Labor Federation (Federación Obrera Local). Despite being an illiterate rural community leader, don Santos broke bread with anarchists, who brought to the table another radical tradition.

Unlike Bolivian radicals of his time like Eduardo Leandro Nina Qhispi, however, don Santos did not draw his inspiration from modern European radical movements.[33] His vision, and that of the of hundreds lords he represented, had other roots—the sixteenth-century Spanish Empire.

Marka T'ula's insistence on his lordship and the need for justice drew from the "ancient laws of the Spanish Crown."[34] He admonished the Bolivian Parliament in 1927:

> Cast a glance upon [our documents] and you will see in them the most horrible crimes, by which the Indigenous race finds itself overwhelmed. In antiquity, these abuses did not exist, though we were governed by strangers, and the King had given us guarantees which we see certified in these ancient titles which we possess in this Imperial Villa of Potosí, a royal decree has been issued and attests that in the mines the ancient natives had obtained the legitimacy of our lands.[35]

The Aymará radical was not naively nostalgic for the Spanish Empire. He was keenly aware that sixteenth-century Indigenous movements had won important privileges and other documents through pressure and that the European whites *(q'aras)* had conceded land and liberty to the commoners *(jaqis)* only because they had demanded them.[36] Marka T'ula made common cause with urban Indigenous and working-class radicals. Yet he anchored his legitimacy as a Native lord to the great audits of Viceroy Toledo—the man who came to bring order to Peru. T'ula also explicitly framed his quest to uproot systemic republican abuses as part of a tradition of radicalism reaching back to the sixteenth century, his ancestors, the king of Spain, and Las Casas.[37]

Santos Marka T'ula denounced the inequalities and humiliations of the new liberal order, the architects of which had rigged the system in favor of Spanish-speaking landowners and against Native lords and commoners.[38] He continued to petition the government and sue land invaders, but it was in vain; the government rejected his claims.[39] Although he never learned to read, in 1928 he founded the Bartolomé de Las Casas Center, for underprivileged rural children. Heeding the entreaties of Indigenous women, he also spoke out against the bloody Chaco War between Bolivia and Paraguay (1932–1935).[40] His influential brands of radical communitarianism and pacifism were, however, not influenced by a Bakunin or a Marx. They came from his culture, his everyday experiences, the pained cries of his community, and a deep tradition of paperwork-based dissent with roots in the sixteenth-century Spanish Empire. Just like don Manuel, don Santos was a radical of a different sort.

Like in Colombia, rural Bolivian actors have widely embraced viceregal documents' contents—and even their discourses. Highland Bolivian lord don Santiago Carvajal's personal archive, which features only documents from the twentieth century, still reveals the deep imprint of viceregal legal formulas and forms of redress. Tristan Platt, a personal friend of don Santiago's, has argued based on close readings of these papers that ongoing Indigenous efforts to decolonize Bolivian society and recover community land owe as much to the preconquest Aymará tradition as they do to the "*ancien régime* democracy" of Indigenous municipalities from the sixteenth and seventeenth centuries.[41] Often times, actors pointing to these documents have succeeded in creating local solutions as well as broader legislative, constitutional, and social reforms, as they did in the past.[42]

Mexico's own early twentieth-century history, which witnessed one of the world's most famous radical eras, was strongly colored by this tradition. Emiliano Zapata, who brought Mexican forces to their knees with his famous commoner revolt, swore his radical revolution would one day restore his claims to the Anenecuilco lands and lordship. He had inherited viceregal-era land titles from his uncle, and three months before his 1919 assassination, he swore, "It is for this reason which I fight. . . . My pueblo's papers stand to be guaranteed."[43] Mexico's new revolutionary government would not forget Zapata's demands, and its reform-oriented institutions received thousands of petitions for agrarian transformation from commoners throughout the nation in the 1920s.[44] Many featured colonial documents.[45] As Paz wrote from Mexico City, he worked for a state strongly influenced by Zapata and in a society utterly conditioned by centuries of bottom-up paperwork politics. And radical autonomist movements inspired by Zapata, most famously the Mexican Zapatistas, continue their struggle as of the finalization of this book.

Political movements in the United States, too, have also denied viceregal-era politics while being strongly influenced by them. The Chicano movement, which embraced Aztec nativism, engaged little with the colonial era except to denounce it as a dark age for Indigenous peoples. In this way, its vision was similar to Marxist, anarchist, and other radical movements that had little patience for the *ancien régime*, an era neither primitive nor modern, characterized by pitiless cultural destruction and little else.[46] Yet the codices and other sources many Chicano thinkers drew from for their own radical reimagining of US American society were created (and protected and repurposed) precisely in this era of ostensible absence.[47] And when Chicano activists scoured archives for the foundations of their radical project, creating new artworks and genealogies in the process, they were retracing the steps of don Manuel, don Santos, and thousands of others from the sixteenth century (and beyond).[48]

The sixteenth century's radical imperial tradition remains very much with us today. And everything seems to indicate it will remain with us in the future. A tradition of deliberate, structural disobedience and lawfare did not emerge *ex nihilo* in the twentieth and twenty-first centuries. It did not even reemerge, for it never actually disappeared.

Decades after don Santos Marka T'ula's death in 1939, his son don Gregorio Barco recalled to a group of oral historians that certain unspecified tormentors had once contemplated killing his father while he worked for radical reform. But the would-be murderers saw in him something strange. They marveled,

> He must be no human, he is the one who cries for every man, for all the poor of the whole world. . . . God is within him, it is best not to come close.

Don Gregorio recalled his father's response:

> You can kill me, but my descendants will number thousands upon thousands.[49]

So it is, one might say, with the radical tradition of the sixteenth century. This many-headed tradition of New World radicalism has endured, insusceptible to political repression and indifferent to intellectual neglect. And it seems destined to endure well into the future.

ARCHIVE ABBREVIATIONS
NOTES
ACKNOWLEDGMENTS
INDEX

ARCHIVE ABBREVIATIONS

ADC	Archivo Departamental del Cusco
AGI	Archive of the Indies (Seville)
AGJ	Archivo General de la Justicia, Spain
AGN-Colombia	Archivo General de la Nación (Colombia)
AGN-Mexico	Archivo General de la Nación (Mexico)
AGS	Archivo General de Simancas
AHN	Archivo Histórico de la Nobleza (Toledo)
AHN-M	Archivo Histórico Nacional-Madrid
AHP	Archivo Histórico de Potosí-Casa de la Moneda
ANE	Archivo Nacional del Ecuador
ARAH	Archivo de la Real Academia de la Historia
BFZ	Biblioteca Francisco de Zabálburu
BL	British Library
BNE	Biblioteca Nacional de España
BNF	Bibliotheque Nationale-France
BSLE	Archivo Biblioteca del Monasterio de San Lorenzo de El Escorial
BUS	Biblioteca de la Universidad de Salamanca
HKR	Library of Congress (LOC) Hans P. Kraus Collection
HSA	Hispanic Society of America
IVDJ	Instituto Valencia de Don Juan, Madrid
JCB	John Carter Brown Library

KB	Det Kongelige Bibliotek, Danmarks Nationalbibliotek og Københavns Universitetsbibliotek
LL	Lilly Library
NL	Newberry Library
NLB	Nettie Lee Benson Latin American Collection

NOTES

INTRODUCTION

1. *The Art of Nahuatl Speech: The Bancroft Dialogues,* ed. Frances Karttunen and James Lockhart (Los Angeles: University of California, 1987), 147.
2. KB, Guaman Poma de Ayala, *El primer nueva corónica y buen gobierno*, GKS 2232, 40, 762/776r.
3. Robert M. Hill II, *The Social Uses of Writing among the Colonial Cakchiquel Maya: Nativism, Resistance, and Innovation* (Washington, DC: Smithsonian, 1991), 16.
4. *Anales de Juan Bautista,* ed. Luis Reyes García (Mexico: CIESAS, 2001), 157.
5. *Anales de Juan Bautista,* 159.
6. *The Native Conquistador: Alva Ixtlilxochitl's Account of the Conquest of New Spain,* ed. Amber Brian, Bradley Benton, and Pablo García Loaeza (University Park: Pennsylvania State University Press, 2015), 89.
7. BNE, Mss/2010, 45r.
8. Judith M. Maxwell and Robert M. Hill II, trans. and commentary, *Kaqchikel Chronicles: The Definitive Edition* (Austin: University of Texas, 2006), 517–518.
9. *Anales de Juan Bautista,* 159.
10. BNE, Mss/2010, 45r.
11. IVDJ, E.25, C.40, 141.
12. Carlos Sempat Assadourian, *Transiciones hacia el sistema colonial andino* (Mexico: Colegio de México, 1994), 190.
13. AGI, Lima 110, "Muchos años ha."
14. AGI, Lima 110, "Muchos años ha."
15. AGI, Justicia 434, N.2, R.1, 23v.
16. AGI, Justicia 434, N.2, R.1, 2r.
17. For a discussion of these ideas, see Jeremy Adelman, "Introduction: The Problem of Persistence in Latin American History," in *Colonial Legacies: The Problem of Persistence in Latin American History*, ed. Jeremy Adelman (New York: Routledge, 1999), 1–14; Steve J. Stern, "The Tricks of Time: Colonial Legacies and Historical Sensibilities in Latin America," in Adelman, *Colonial Legacies,* 135–150.
18. Caroline Castiglione, "Adversarial Literacy: How Peasant Politics Influenced Noble Governing of the Roman Countryside during the Early Modern Period," *American Historical Review* 109, no. 3 (2004): 783–804.

19. Alonso de Zorita, *Relación de los señores de la Nueva España,* ed. Germán Vázquez (Madrid: Hnos. Noblejas, 1992), 81.
20. Hill, *World Turned Upside Down.*
21. Richard Greaves, *The Radical Underground in Britain, 1660–1663* (New York: Oxford University Press, 1986), 4.
22. Christopher Hill, *The World Turned Upside Down: Radical Ideas during the English Revolution* (New York: The Viking Press, 1972); Margaret C. Jacob, "How Radical Was the Enlightenment? What Do We Mean by Radical?," *Diametros* 40 (2014): 99–114, here 102.
23. Hobsbawm proposed this sequence of the prepolitical to political; see E. J. Hobsbawm, *Primitive Rebels: Studies in Archaic Forms of Social Movement in the 19th and 20th Centuries* (Manchester: Manchester University Press, 1972). For a critique, see Ramachandra Guha, "The Brilliance and Dogmatism of Hobsbawm," *Economic and Political Weekly* 47, no. 46 (2012): 36–39. For a similar viewpoint to ours about viceregal politics, see Brian P. Owensby, *Empire of Law and Indian Justice in Colonial Mexico* (Stanford: Stanford University Press, 2008), 1–8.
24. James Colin Davis, *Alternative Worlds Imagined, 1500–1700: Essays on Radicalism, Utopianism and Reality* (Cham: Palgrave, 2017), 4. After all, actors before the 1800s did not describe themselves as such; see William H. Brackney, *Historical Dictionary of Radical Christianity* (Lanham: Scarecrow Press, 2012), 5; Timothy Morton and Nigel Smith, "Introduction," in *Radicalism in British Literary Culture, 1650–1830: From Revolution to Revolution,* ed. Timothy Morton and Nigel Smith (Cambridge: Cambridge University Press, 2002), 1–28.
25. Greaves, *Radical Underground in Britain,* 4–5.
26. Craig Calhoun, *The Roots of Radicalism: Tradition, the Public Sphere, and Early 19th Century Social Movements* (Chicago: University of Chicago Press, 2012).
27. These are very loosely adapted from Paul McLaughlin, *Radicalism: A Philosophical Study* (London: Palgrave, 2012), 201–204.
28. On this vagueness, see Jocelyn Hollander and Rachel Einwohner, "Conceptualizing Resistance," *Sociological Forum* 19, no. 4 (2004): 533–554. For a recent work on Indies resistance, see Dana Velasco Murillo and Robert C. Schwaller, eds., *Overlooked Places and Peoples: Indigenous and African Resistance in Colonial Spanish America, 1500–1800* (New York: Routledge, 2024).
29. In the late 1500s, we argue in Chapter 5, a limited return of seigneurialism did take place, but under much more constrained circumstances than the Crown and conquistador-explorers had originally intended.
30. Felipe Fernández-Armesto, *Before Columbus: Exploration and Colonization from the Mediterranean to the Atlantic, 1229–1492* (Philadelphia: University of Pennsylvania Press, 1988).
31. For several key discussions on this vision, see Adelman, "Introduction," 1–14; Mark Thurner, "After Spanish Rule: Writing Another After," in *After Spanish Rule,* ed. Mark Thurner and Andrés Guerrero (Durham: Duke University Press, 2003), 12–57, here 24, 29–30, 40; Alejandro Guzmán Brito, "La crítica póstuma al derecho indiano," in *Derecho y administración pública en las Indias hispánicas,* ed. Feliciano Barrios Pintado (Cuenca: Universidad de Castilla-La Mancha, 2002), 1:843–858.
32. We share most of these values; however, we are deeply critical of the liberal narrative's fable of the past. For an excellent overview of the complexities of defining this term, see Michael Freeden, *Liberalism: A Very Short Introduction* (Oxford: Oxford University Press, 2015), 1–6; Michael Freeden and Javier Fernández-Sebastián, "European Liberal Discourses: Conceptual Affinities and Disparities," in *Search of European Liberalisms,* ed. Michael Freeden, Javier Fernández-Sebastián, and Jörn Leonhard (New York: Berghahn, 2019), 1–36.
33. Roger Hart, "The Great Explanandum," *American Historical Review* 105, no. 2 (2000): 486–493, here 493.
34. This style of writing history has also been broadly criticized. See, among many others, Jeremy Adelman, "An Age of Imperial Revolutions," *American Historical Review* 113, no. 2 (2008):

319–340; Frederick Cooper, *Colonialism in Question: Theory, Knowledge, History* (Berkeley: University of California Press, 2005), 15–32; Marcela Echeverri, *Indian and Slave Royalists in the Age of Revolution: Reform, Revolution, and Royalism in the Northern Andes, 1780–1825* (Cambridge: Cambridge University Press, 2016), 8–11.

35. This narrative allows for actors like don José Gabriel Condorcanqui Noguera to foreshadow liberation.

36. Santiago Castro-Gómez, *Crítica de la razón latinoamericana,* 2nd ed. (Bogotá: Pontificia Universidad. Javeriana, 2011 [1996]), 13.

37. Enrique Dussel, "Europa, modernidad y eurocentrismo: Sistema-mundo y transmodernidad. Debate sobre la geocultura del sistema-mundo," in *Hacia una filosofía política crítica* (Bilbao: Desclee de Brower, 2001); Catherine E. Walsh, ed., *Pensamiento crítico y matriz (de)colonial: Reflexiones latinoamericanas* (Quito: Abya Yala, 2005); Irene Silverblatt, *Modern Inquisitions: Peru and the Colonial Origins of the Civilized World* (Durham, NC: Duke University Press, 2004); Claudio Lomnitz, *Death and the Idea of Mexico* (New York: Zone Books, 2005), 63–97; Aníbal Quijano and Immanuel Wallerstein, "Americanity as a Concept, or the Americas in the Modern World-System," *ISSJ* 134 (1992): 549–557, here 550.

38. See the works of Miguel León-Portilla, including *Toltecáyotl: Aspectos de la cultura náhuatl* (Mexico: FCE, 1980). León-Portilla, James Lockhart, and many others are representatives of the civilizationalist perspective; see also Pedro Carrasco, "La transformación de la cultura indígena durante la colonia," *Historia Mexicana* 25, no. 2 (1975): 175–203.

39. See Tzvetan Todorov, *The Conquest of America: The Question of the Other* (New York: Harper & Row, 1982); Serge Gruzinski, *The Conquest of Mexico* (Cambridge: Polity, 1993), 1–3, 28, 55, 68–69; *The Mestizo Mind,* trans. Deke Dusinberre (New York: Routledge), 2002. For a critical discussion of this enduring tradition, see Stefan Rinke, *Conquistadors and Aztecs: A History of the Fall of Tenochtitlan* (Oxford: Oxford University Press, 2023), 5–6.

40. Walter D. Mignolo, *The Darker Side of the Renaissance: Literacy, Territoriality, & Colonization,* 2nd ed. (Ann Arbor: University of Michigan Press, 1995), 1–7, 71. Another long tradition, that of ethnohistory, has of course been deeply shaped by culturalism; see, among many others, Miguel León Portilla, *The Aztec Image of Self and Society,* with an introduction by J. Jorge Klor de Alva (Salt Lake City: University of Utah Press, 1992).

41. Gloria E. Anzaldúa, *Borderlands/La Frontera: The New Mestiza* (San Francisco: Aunt Lute Books, 1987).

42. Marilyn Grace Miller, *Rise and Fall of the Cosmic Race: The Cult of Mestizaje in Latin America* (Austin: University of Texas Press, 2004).

43. See, among many others, Miller, *Rise and Fall of the Cosmic Race,* 1–9; Federico Navarrete, *México racista: Una denuncia* (Mexico: Grijalbo, 2016); Peter Wade, *Blackness and Race Mixture: The Dynamics of Racial Identity in Colombia* (Baltimore: Johns Hopkins University Press, 1993); Walter Mignolo, *Local Histories/Global Designs* (Princeton: Princeton University Press, 2000), 320. On ideas of *mestizaje* and their lasting power, see Milena Ang and Tania Islas Weinstein, "Introduction," in *Beyond Mestizaje: Contemporary Debates on Race in Mexico,* ed. Tania Islas Weinstein and Milena Ang (Amherst: Amherst College Press, 2024), 1–36, here 1–8, and the other contributions in this volume. For the depolitizicing illusion of culturalism, see Steve J. Stern, *Peru's Indian Peoples and the Challenge of Spanish Conquest,* 2nd ed (Madison: University of Wisconsin Press, 1993), xliv–l. For an effort (in our view incomplete) to transcend tales of syncretism and toward creative responses to cultural contact, see Louise Burkhart, *The Slippery Earth: Nahua-Christian Moral Dialogue in Sixteenth-Century Mexico* (Tucson: University of Arizona Press, 1989), 9.

44. Among others, Kelly S. McDonough has highlighted the contemporary lack of interest in Indigenous intellectuals after conquest; see Kelly S. McDonough, *The Learned Ones: Nahua Intellectuals in Postconquest Mexico* (Tucson: University of Arizona Press, 2014), 3–6; Kelly S. McDonough,

Indigenous Science and Technology: Nahuas and the World around Them (Tucson: University of Arizona Press, 2024), 4–5, 14–15.

45. On Hispanism, see Jorge Cañizares-Esguerra, "De cómo olvidar y recordar en la invención de Latinoamérica y España," *Revista de Occidente* 509 (2023): 22–32. For an influential and well-selling example, see Elvira Roca Barea, *Imperiofobia y leyenda negra* (Madrid: Siruelas, 2022).
46. Antonio Feros, *Speaking of Spain: The Evolution of Race and Nation in the Hispanic World* (Cambridge: Harvard University Press, 2017); Frank Tannenbaum, *Slave and Citizen: The Negro in the Americas* (New York: Knopf, 1947).
47. David A. Lupher, *Romans in a New World: Classical Models in Sixteenth-Century Spanish America* (Ann Arbor: University of Michigan Press, 2003).
48. Ada Ferrer, *Insurgent Cuba: Race, Nation, and Revolution, 1868–1898* (Chapel Hill: University of North Carolina Press, 1999).
49. Cañizares-Esguerra, "De cómo olvidar."
50. We cite here only a few authors whose books we have used throughout. Ricardo Levillier, *Don Francisco De Toledo, supremo organizador del Perú, su vida, su obra (1515–1582)*, 3 vols. (Buenos Aires: Porter Hnos., 1935–1940); José Toribio Medina, *El descubrimiento del océano pacífico: Vasco Núñez de Balboa, Hernando de Magallanes y sus compañeros* (Santiago de Chile: Imprenta universitaria, 1913); Guillermo Lohman Villena, *El Señorío de los marqueses de Santiago de Oropesa en el Perú* (Madrid: s.n., 1948); Guillermo Lohman Villena, *Las minas de Huancavelica en los siglos XVI y XVII* (Sevilla: Escuela de Estudios Hispano-Americanos, 1949); Guillermo Lohman Villena, *El corregidor de indios en el Perú bajo los Austrias* (Madrid: Eds. Cultura Hispánica, 1957); Guillermo Lohman Villena, *El testamento inédito del Inca Sayri Túpac* (Lima: [Tip. Peruana], 1965); Guillermo Lohman Villena, *Juan de Matienzo, autor del Gobierno del Perú* (Sevilla: Consejo Superior de Investigaciones Científicas, Escuela de Estudios Hispano-Americanos, 1966). Each country in Spanish America has one or two distinguished Hispanists, each with an oeuvre as lengthy as Levillier's, Medina's, or Lohman Villena's. Moreover, many Hispanists published volumes of primary sources.
51. In many ways, it is also a civilizationalist approach but distinct from culturalist approaches in its relative lack of engagement with anthropology, sociology, ethnohistory, and similar fields.
52. See for example the extraordinary two volumes on Bartolomé de Las Casas by the foremost Hispanist Manuel Giménez Fernández, *Bartolomé de Las Casas,* 2 vols. (Madrid: CSIC, 1953–1984). There is no mention of Indigenous agency in its nearly two thousand pages.
53. Pedro Cardim, Tamar Herzog, and Gaetano Sabatini, eds., *Polycentric Monarchies: How Did Early Modern Spain and Portugal Achieve and Maintain a Global Hegemony* (Eastbourne: Sussex Academic Press, 2012).
54. See for example the otherwise impressive studies of Carmelo Sáenz Santa María, *El licenciado Don Francisco Marroquín: Primer Obispo de Gatemala (1499–1953)* (Madrid: Ediciones Cultura Hispánica, 1964); Berta Ares Queija, *Tomás López Medel: Trayectoria de un clérigo-oidor ante el nuevo mundo* (Guadalajara: Institución Provincial de Cultura Marqués de Santillana, 1993).
55. Lynn M. Thomas, "Historicising Agency," *Gender & History* 28, no. 2 (2016): 324–339.
56. José Javier Ruiz Ibáñez, *Hispanofilia: Los tiempos de la hegemonía Española,* vols. 1 and 2 (Madrid: FCE, 2022).
57. For an excellent historiography of these developments, see Caroline Cunill, "How to Approach Indigenous Law?," in *The Cambridge History of Latin American Law in a Global Perspective,* ed. Tamar Herzog and Thomas Duve (Cambridge: Cambridge University Press, 2024), 95–140, here 96–111; Caroline Cunill, "La negociación indígena en el Imperio ibérico: Aportes a su discusión metodológica," *Colonial Latin American Historical Review* 21, no. 3 (2012): 391–412, here 395.
58. Miguel Rojas-Mix, *Los cien nombres de América* (San José: Universidad de Costa Rica, 1991), 183.

59. Steve J. Stern, "Paradigms of Conquest: History, Historiography, and Politics," *Journal of Latin American Studies* 24 (1992): 1–34, here 22.
60. Stern, *Peru's Indian Peoples*, li.
61. Wayne Te Brake, *Ordinary People in European Politics*, 1500–1700 (Berkeley: University of California Press, 1998), 5–7.
62. Thomas, "Historicising Agency," 324–339, 325.
63. Lewis Hanke, "A Modest Proposal for a Moratorium on Grand Generalizations," *Hispanic American Historical Review* 51, no. 1 (1971): 112–127, here 112.
64. J. H. Elliott, *Empires of the Atlantic World* (New Haven: Yale University Press, 2006).
65. Elliott, *Empires of the Atlantic*, 407.
66. Elliott, *Empires of the Atlantic*, 409.
67. María Alba Pastor, *Crisis y recomposición social* (Mexico: FCE, 1999). For a subtler but still top-down account, see the textbook Mark A. Burkholder and Lyman L. Johnson, *Colonial Latin America*, 8th ed. (Oxford: Oxford University Press, 2012).
68. The historiography of the New Conquest History goes back to Nathan Wachtel and Sempat Assadourian. For an excellent summary of this current, see Matthew Restall, "The New Conquest History," *History Compass* 10 (2012): 151–160.
69. See the excellent reflections by Louise Burkhart, "Introduction," in *Words & Worlds Turned Around: Indigenous Christianities in Colonial Latin America*, ed. David Tavárez (Boulder: University Press of Colorado, 2017), 4–28.
70. For exemplary research with a thorough recent historiography of this turn, see Ryan Dominic Crewe, "Las políticas de conversión en México después de la conquista," *Historia Mexicana* 68, no. 3 (2019): 943–1000, especially 949; Ryan Dominic Crewe, *The Mexican Mission* (Cambridge: Cambridge University Press, 2019), 7–10; Richard Trexler, "From the Mouth of Babes: Christianization by Children in Sixteenth-Century New Spain," in *Religious Organization and Religious Experience*, ed. J. Davis (London: Academic Press, 1982), 97–114; Patricia Lopes Don, *Bonfires of Culture* (Norman: University of Oklahoma Press, 2010), 7, 11–16; Bradley Benton, *The Lords of Tetzcoco* (Cambridge: Cambridge University Press, 2017), 40–45; Stephanie Wood, "Nahua Christian Warriors in the Mapa de Cuauhtlantzinco," in *Indian Conquistadors: Indigenous Allies in the Conquest of Mesoamerica*, ed. Laura E. Matthew and Michel R. Oudijk (Norman: University of Oklahoma Press, 2007), 254–288; William F. Hanks, *Converting Words: Maya in the Age of the Cross* (Berkeley: University of California Press, 2010); Edward W. Osowski, *Indigenous Miracles: Nahua Authority in Colonial Mexico* (Tucson: University of Arizona Press, 2010); Mark Z. Christensen, *The Teabo Manuscript* (Austin: University of Texas Press, 2016), 4; Nancy M. Farriss, *Maya Society under Colonial Rule: The Collective Enterprise of Survival* (Princeton: Princeton University Press, 1984), 335–343; Mark Christensen. *Nahua and Maya Catholicisms: Texts and Religion in Colonial Central Mexico and Yucatan* (Stanford: Stanford University Press, 2013); Jorge Iván Marín Taborda, *Vivir en policía y a son de campana* (Bogotá: ICANH, 2021). For the central Andes, see Pierre Duviols, *La destrucción de las religiones andinas (conquista y colonia)*, trans. Albor Maruenda (Mexico City: Universidad Autónoma de México, 1977 [1971]), esp. 283–285; Rolena Adorno, "Images of Indios Ladinos in Early Colonial Peru," in *Trans-Atlantic Encounters*, ed. Kenneth J. Andrien and Rolena Adorno (Berkeley: University of California Press, 1991), 232–270; and notably, John Charles, *Allies at Odds* (Albuquerque: University of New Mexico Press, 2010), 3–12; Sean F. McEnroe, *Indigenous Elites of the Colonial Americas* (Albuquerque: University of New Mexico Press, 2020), 111–134; Byron E. Hamann, *Bad Christians, New Spains: Muslims, Catholics, and Native Americans in a Mediterratlantic World* (New York: Routledge, 2020). For two classic expressions of this tradition, see Robert Ricard, *Conquête spirituelle du Mexique* (Paris: Institut d'Ethnologie, 1933); Pedro Borges, *Análisis del conquistador spiritual de América* (Sevilla: EEHA, 1961); Fernando de Armas Medina, *Cristianización del Perú* (1532–1600) (Sevilla: EEHA, 1953).

71. Others have inverted this story. It was all an Indigenous ruse; seemingly faithful converts duplicitously continued to worship old deities masked in Christian guises, keeping their ancient civilizations intact. This version, too, denies the possibility of authentic conversion and essentializes the motivations of Indigenous actors.
72. Fred Bronner, "Elite Formation in Seventeenth-Century Peru," *Boletín de Estudios Latinoamericanos y del Caribe* 24 (1978): 3–26, here 18. This tradition is far too old and diffuse to receive an exhaustive citation; see, among many others, Heraclio Bonilla, "Cómo España gobernó y perdió al mundo," *Revista de Estudios Sociales* 1, no. 5 (2000): no page; J. M. Ots Capdequí, *El estado español en las Indias,* 4th ed. (Mexico: Colegio de México, 1965), 25, 42; Richard Konetzke, *América latina II: La época colonial* (Mexico: Siglo XXI, 1972), 102–104; Leslie Bethell, *Historia de América Latina* (Barcelona: Editorial Crítica, 1990), 1:156, 168–169; Silvio Zavala, *El mundo americano en la época colonial,* 2nd ed. (Mexico: Porrúa, 1990), 1:109, 126, 290; Mark A. Burkholder and D. S. Chandler, *From Impotence to Authority* (Columbia: University of Missouri, 1977), 1–5; Horst Pietschmann, *Staat und Staatliche Entwicklung am Beginn deer Spanischen Kolonisation Amerikas* (Münster: Aschendorffsche Verlagsbuchhandlung, 1980), 12, 22, 51, 106, 173; Francisco Luis Jiménez Abollado, "Una institución indiana: La encomienda," in *Encomenderos y caciques indígenas al norte del Valle de México, siglo XVI,* ed. Francisco Luis Jiménez Abollado (Hidalgo: UAEH, 2009), 15–22, here 18–20; Magdalena Chocano Mena, *La fortaleza docta* (Barcelona: Bellaterra, 2000), 32; José de la Puente Brunke, *Encomienda y encomenderos en el Perú* (Sevilla: Dialpa, 1992), 23, 246; Marcello Carmagnani, *The Other West,* ed. Rosanna Giammanco Frongia (Berkeley: University of California Press, 2011), 30–35; Alan Knight, *Mexico,* vol. 2, *The Colonial Era* (Cambridge: Cambridge University Press, 2002), 17–19; Colin M. MacLachlan and Jaime E. Rodríguez, *The Forging of the Cosmic Race,* expanded ed. (Berkeley: University of California Press, 1990), 96–102. In the telling of D. A. Brading, the Crown responded to the petitions of Las Casas; see D. A. Brading, *The First America* (Cambridge: Cambridge University Press, 1991), 71–73.
73. María Alba Pastor, *Crisis y recomposición social* (Mexico: FCE, 1999); see the classic works of Gisela von Wobeser, *La formación de la hacienda en la época colonial* (Mexico: UNAM, 1989); Sempat Assadourian, *Transiciones*; see also Andre Gunder Frank, *Mexican Agriculture 1521–1630* (Cambridge: Cambridge University Press, 1979), 38–40.
74. *Administración,* or governance, was a widespread term in the 1500s. Here it is not invoked in its twentieth-century sense of a vigorous, socially autonomous state with clear directives but rather in the sense employed at the time, as in a space overseen by ministers; see Sebastián de Covarrubias Orozco, *Tesoro de la lengua castellana* (Madrid: Luis Sánchez, 1611), 15v.
75. For an excellent overview, see Yanna Yannakakis, "Indigenous People and Legal Culture in Spanish America," *History Compass* 11, no. 11 (2013): 931–947, here 934; Richard Kagan, *Lawsuits and Litigants in Castile, 1500–1700* (Chapel Hill: University of North Carolina, 1981); Stern, *Peru's Indian Peoples*; Woodrow Borah, *Justice by Insurance* (Berkeley: University of California Press, 1983); Andrés Lira González, *El amparo colonial y el juicio de amparo mexicano.* Mexico: Fondo de Cultura Económica, 1971; Susan Kellog, *Law and the Transformation of Aztec Culture, 1500–1700* (Norman: University of Oklahoma Press, 1995); see also, among others, Charles R. Cutter, Tomás Mallo, and Daniel Pacheco Fernández, "Indians as Litigants in Colonial Mexico," in *De la ciencia ilustrada a la ciencia romántica,* ed. Alejandro R. Diez Torre (Madrid: Doce Calles, 1995), 21–32; Franklin Pease, "¿Por qué los andinos son acusados de litigiosos?" in *Derechos culturales,* ed. Marco Borgui et al. (Lima: Pontificia Universidad Católica del Perú; Universidad de Friburgo, 1996), 27–37; John Murra, "Litigation over the Rights of 'Natural Lords' in Early Colonial Courts in the Andes," in *Native Traditions in the Postconquest World,* ed. Elizabeth Hill Boone and Thomas Cummins (Washington, DC: Dumbarton Oaks, 1998), 55–62; Jovita Baber, "Native Litigiousness, Cultural Change and the Spanish Legal System in Tlaxcala," *Political and Legal Anthropology Review* 24, no. 2 (2001): 94–106; Martín Monsalve, "Curacas pleitistas

y curas abusivos," in *Elites indígenas en los Andes*, ed. David Patrick Cahill and Blanca Tovías (Quito: Abya-Yala, 2003), 159–174; Andrés Lira, "El indio como litigante en cincuenta años de audiencia, 1531–1580," in *Memoria del X Congreso del Instituto Internacional de Historia del Derecho Indiano* (Mexico: UNAM, 2005), 765–782; Jacques Poloni-Simard, "Los indios ante la justicia," in *Máscaras, tretas y rodeos del discurso colonial en los Andes*, ed. Bernard Lavallé (Lima: IFEA; PUCP, 2005), 177–188; John Charles, "Indigenous Litigants and the Language Policy Debate in Mid-colonial Peru," *Colonial Latin American Review* 16, no. 1 (2007): 23–47; Gabriela Ramos, "Litigios y probanzas de caciques en el Perú colonial temprano," *Fronteras de la Historia* 21, no. 1 (2016): 66–90.

76. Caroline Cunill, "Philip II and Indigenous Access to Royal Justice," *Colonial Latin American Review* 24, no. 4 (2015): 505–524; Richard J. Ross, "Legal Communications and Imperial Governance," in *Cambridge History of Law in America*, vol. I, *Early America (1580–1815)*, ed. Christopher L. Tomlins and Michael Grossberg (Cambridge: Cambridge University Press, 2008), 104–143; Aurelio Espinosa, *The Empire of the Cities* (Leiden: Brill, 2009).

77. Alcira Dueñas, "Indian Colonial Actors in the Lawmaking of the Spanish Empire in Peru," *Ethnohistory* 65, no. 1 (2018): 51–73; Thomas Duve, "El concilio como instancia de autorización: La ordenación sacerdotal de mestizos ante el Tercer Concilio Limense," *Revista de Historia del Derecho* 40 (2010): 1–29; Felipe E. Ruan, "Andean Activism and the Reformulation of Mestizo Agency and Identity in Early Colonial Peru," *Colonial Latin American Review* 21, no. 2 (2012): 209–237; "The Probanza and Shaping a Contesting Mestizo Record in Early Colonial Peru," *Bulletin of Spanish Studies* 94, no. 5 (2017): 843–869; Kelly McDonough, "Indigenous Rememberings and Forgettings: Sixteenth-Century, Nahua Letters and Petitions to the Spanish Crown," *Native American and Indigenous Studies* 5, no. 1 (2018): 69–99; José Carlos de la Puente Luna, *Andean Cosmopolitans* (Austin: University of Texas Press, 2018); José Carlos de la Puente Luna, "A costa de Su Majestad: Indios viajeros y dilemas imperiales en la corte de los Habsburgo," *Allpanchis* 72 (2008): 11–60; Luis Miguel Glave Testino, "Manuscritos reivindicativos de Incas, Caciques, y Defensores de la Población Indígena," *Revista Andes* 4 (2021): 35–59; Luis Miguel Glave Testino, "La formación de una liga indígena en Lima (1722–1732)," *Diálogo Andino: Revista de Historia, Geografía y Cultura Andina* 37 (2011): 5–23; Andrew Laird, "Nahua Humanism and Ethnohistory," *Estudios de Cultura Náhuatl* 52 (2016): 23–74; Miguel A. Valerio, "The Spanish Petition System, Hospital/ity, and the Formation of a Mulato Community in Sixteenth-Century Mexico," *The Americas* 78, no. 3 (2021): 415–437; Nancy van Deusen, *Global Indios: The Indigenous Struggle for Justice in Sixteenth-Century Spain* (Durham: Duke University Press, 2015); María Carolina Jurado, "Fraccionamiento de una encomienda: Una mirada desde el liderazgo indígena. Qaraqara, 1540–1569," *Surandino Monográfico* 2, no. 2 (2012): no pages.

78. Osvaldo Rodolfo Moutin, "The Drafting of the Judicial Order in the Decrees of the Third Mexican Council," *Rechtsgeschichte—Legal History* 24 (2016): 154–170; Osvaldo Rodolfo Moutin, *Legislar en la América hispánica en la temprana edad moderna* (Frankfurt: Max Planck Institute for European Legal History, 2016).

79. Studies on Afro-descendant petitioners and litigants are far more numerous for the 1600s than the 1500s, leaving them beyond the scope of this study. Among others, see José Ramón Jouve Martín, *Esclavos de la ciudad letrada* (Lima: IEP, 2005); Michelle McKinley, *Fractional Freedoms: Slavery, Intimacy, and Legal Mobilization in Colonial Lima, 1600–1700* (Cambridge: Cambridge University Press, 2016); Herman L. Bennett, *Africans in Colonial Mexico: Absolutism, Christianity and Afro-Creole Consciousness, 1570–1640* (Bloomington: Indiana University Press, 2003); Chloe L. Ireton, "Black Africans' Freedom Litigation Suits to Define Just War and Just Slavery in the Early Spanish Empire," *Renaissance Quarterly* 73, no. 4 (2020): 1–43; Yobani Maikel Gonzales Jauregui, "Mujeres afrodescendientes en tribunales del Perú colonial," *D'Cimarrón* 1, no. 1 (2018): 20–36; Yobani Maikel Gonzales Jauregui, "Lima colonial, ciudad negra, siglos

XVI–XVII," *Historia Caribe* 18, no. 43 (2023): 263–295. For royal *gracia*, see Héctor Linares, "'Un Negro de mucho Precio': Seeking Freedom and Honor through Royal Service in Sixteenth-Century Panama," *The Americas* 81, no. 4 (2024): 533–567. For *gobierno*, see Robert Schwaller, "'For Honor and Defence': Race and the Right to Bear Arms in Early Colonial Mexico," *Colonial Latin American Review* 21, no. 2 (2012): 239–266; Valerio, "Spanish Petition System."

80. For a recent overview, see Tamar Herzog, "How to Approach Colonial Law?" in *The Cambridge History of Latin American Law in Global Perspective* (Cambridge: Cambridge University Press, 2024), 141, 146–158. For two predecessors to this turn, see Richard E. Greenleaf, "The Inquisition and the Indians of New Spain: A Study in Jurisdictional Confusion," *The Americas* 22, no. 2 (1965): 138–166; António Manuel Hespanha, *La gracia del derecho* (Madrid: Centro de Estudios Constitucionales, 1993). For four foundational statements, see Lauren Benton, "Jurisdictional Politics in the Spanish Colonial Borderlands," *Law & Social Inquiry* 26, no. 2 (2001): 373–401; Tamar Herzog, "The Meaning of Territory," in *Globality and Multiple Modernities*, ed. Luis Roniger and Carlos Waiman (Brighton: Sussex, 2002), 162–182; Darío Barriera, "Justicia, justicias y jurisdicciones (Ss. XVI-XVII)," *Revista de Historia del Derecho* 31 (2003): 69–95; Carlos Garriga, "Orden jurídico y poder político en el Antiguo Régimen," *Istor: Revista de Historia Internacional* 4, no. 16 (2004): 1–24. See chap. 1 of Darío Barriera, *Historia y justicia* (Buenos Aires: Prometeo, 2019).

81. Elisa Caselli, "Introducción," in *Justicias, agentes, y jurisdicciones*, ed. Elisa Caselli (Mexico: FCE, 2016), 1–24; María Paula Polimene, *Autoridades y prácticas judiciales en el Antiguo Régimen* (Córdoba: Prohistoria Ediciones, 2011); Darío Barriera, *Microanálisis de la construcción de un espacio político: Santa Fe, 1573–1640* (Santa Fe, Argentina: Museo Histórico Provincial, 2013); Tamar Herzog, *Frontiers of Possession* (Cambridge: Harvard University Press, 2015); Karen Graubart, "Learning from the Qadi," *Hispanic American Historical Review* 95, no. 2 (2015): 195–228; Francisco Quijano, "El republicanismo y constitucionalismo de Bartolomé de Las Casas," *Historia Mexicana* 65, no. 1 (2015): 7–64; Francisco Quijano Velasco, *Las repúblicas de la monarquía: Pensamiento constitucionalista y republicano en Nueva España, 1550–1610* (Mexico: UNAM, 2017); Thomas Duve, "Was ist >Multinormativität<?—Einführende Bemerkungen," *Rechtsgeschichte—Legal History* 25 (2017): 88–101; Tamar Herzog, "The Uses and Abuses of Legal Pluralism," *Law and History Review* 41, no. 1 (2023): 1–12; Jorge Díaz Ceballos, "New World Civitas, Contested Jurisdictions, and Inter-cultural Conversation," *Colonial Latin American Review* 27, no. 1 (2018): 30–51. In the past decade, scholars have refined this complex picture of overlapping Spanish imperial jurisdictions by emphasizing polycentricity; see Cardim, Herzog, and Ruiz Ibáñez, *Polycentric Monarchies*. However, this polycentric argument can be overstated.

82. Martin Austin Nesvig, *Promiscuous Power: An Unorthodox History of New Spain* (Austin: University of Texas Press, 2018), 79.

83. Lauren Benton, "Colonial Law and Cultural Difference," *Comparative Studies in Society and History* 41, no. 3 (1999): 563–588, here 564.

84. Nesvig, *Promiscuous Power*, 2–12, 51–58; Nicole von Gremeten, *Violent Delights, Violent Ends: Sex, Race, and Honor in Colonial Cartagena de Indias* (Albuquerque: University of New Mexico, 2013), 5; Juan José Ponce Vázquez, *Islanders and Empire* (Cambridge: Cambridge University Press, 2020).

85. For a recent historiography, see Sara Vicuña Guengerich and Margarita R. Ochoa, "Introducción," in *Cacicas: The Indigenous Women Leaders of Spanish America, 1492–1825*, ed. Margarita R. Ochoa and Sara Vicuña Guengerich (Norman: University of Oklahoma, 2021), 9–44, esp. 11–14; for certain important works in this now-extensive subfield, see María Rostworowski de Diez Canseco, *Curacas y sucesiones: Costa norte* (Lima: Minerva, 1961); María Rostworowski de Diez Canseco, *Señoríos indígenas de Lima y Canta* (Lima: Instituto de Estudios Peruanos, 1978);

Charles Gibson, *The Aztecs under Spanish Rule* (Stanford: Stanford University Press, 1964); Ronald Spores, *The Mixtec Kings and Their People* (Norman: University of Oklahoma Press, 1967); Karen Spalding, *Huarochirí: An Andean Society under Inca and Spanish Rule* (Stanford: Stanford University Press, 1984); Nancy Farriss, *Maya Society under Colonial Rule* (Princeton: Princeton University Press, 1984); Susan Ramírez, "Thoughts on the Consequences of the Shifting Bases of Power of the 'Curaca de los Viejos Antiguos,'" *Hispanic American Historical Review* 67, no. 4 (1987): 575–610; Luis Miguel Glave, *Un curacazgo andino y la sociedad campesina del siglo XVII* (Lima: Insituto de Pastoral Andina, 1989); Robert Haskett, *Indigenous Rulers* (Albuquerque: University of New Mexico Press, 1991); James Lockhart, *The Nahuas after the Conquest* (Stanford: Stanford University Press, 1992); John K. Chance, "Class and Ethnic Identity in Late Colonial Mexico," *Hispanic American Historical Review* 76, no. 3 (1996): 475–502; John K. Chance, "Marriage Alliances among Colonial Mixtec Elites," *Ethnohistory* 56, no. 1 (2009); John K. Chance, "The Predicament of the Late Colonial Mixtec Cacique," *Ethnohistory* 57, no. 3 (2010): 445–466; Scarlett O'Phelan, *Kurakas sin sucesiones* (Cusco: Centro de Estudios Bartolomé de Las Casas, 1997); Kevin Terraciano, *The Mixtecs of Colonial Oaxaca* (Stanford: Stanford University Press, 2001); Margarita Menegus and Rodolfo Aguirre Salvador, eds., *El cacicazgo en Nueva España y Filipinas* (Mexico City: UNAM, 2005); Yanna Yannakakis, *The Art of Being In-Between* (Durham: Duke University Press, 2008); William F. Connell, *After Moctezuma: Indigenous Politics and Self-Government in Mexico City, 1524–1730* (Norman: University of Oklahoma Press, 2011); Peter Villella, *Indigenous Elites and Creole Identity in Colonial Mexico, 1500–1800* (New York: Cambridge University Press, 2016); Benton, *Lords of Tetzcoco.*

86. Among others, see José María Navarro, *Una denuncia profética desde el Perú a mediados del siglo XVIII* (Lima: PUCP, 2001); Kenneth Andrien, *Andean Worlds* (Albuquerque: University of New Mexico Press, 2001); Miguel León-Portilla, *Francisco Tenamaztle* (Mexico City: Diana, 2005); Alcira Dueñas, *Indians and Mestizos in the "Lettered City"* (Boulder: University Press of Colorado, 2010); Roberto Choque Canqui and Luis Miguel Glave, *Mita, caciques y mitayos* (Sucre: ABNB, 2012); McDonough, *The Learned Ones*; Gabriela Ramos and Yanna Yannakakis, eds., *Indigenous Intellectuals* (Durham: Duke University, 2014); Amber Brian, *Alva Ixtlilxochitl's Native Archive* (Nashville: Vanderbilt University Press, 2016); Gonzalo Lamana, *Colonial Indigenous Intellectuals and the Question of Critical Race Theory* (Tucson: University of Arizona, 2019).

87. Yanna Yannakakis, "Native Agency in the Making of Colonial Legal Cultures," *Comparative Studies in Society and History* 57, no. 4 (2015): 1070–1082. For other works on translation, see Caroline Cunill, "Los intérpretes de la Audiencia de México en el siglo XVI," *Historia Mexicana* 68, no. 1 (2018): 7–48; Luis Miguel Glave, "Intermediarios lingüísticos y culturales entre dos mundos," *Allpanchis* 36 (1990): 435–516; Mark Lentz, "Los intérpretes generales de Yucatán: Hombres entre dos mundos," *Estudios de Cultura Maya* 33 (2009): 135–158; John F. Chuchiak, "Maya Scribes, Colonial Literacy, and Maya Petitionary Forms in Colonial Yucatán," in *Text and Context*, ed. Antje Gunsenheimer, Tsubasa Okoshi Harada, and John F. Chuchiak (Bonn: Shaker Verlag, 2009), 159–184; Martin Nesvig, "Spanish Men, Indigenous Language, and Informal Interpreters in Postcontact Mexico," *Ethnohistory* 59, no. 4 (2012): 739–764; Yanna Yannakakis, "Introduction: How Did They Talk to One Another?" *Ethnohistory* 59, no. 4 (2012): 667–674; José Carlos de la Puente Luna, "Indigenous Language Interpreters and the Making of the Spanish Empire," *Colonial Latin American Review* 23, no. 2 (2014): 143–170; Caroline Cunill, "Justicia e interpretación en sociedades plurilingües," *Estudios de Historia Novohispana* 52 (2015): 18–28; Caroline Cunill and Luis Miguel Glave Testino, eds., *Las lenguas indígenas en los tribunales de América Latina* (Bogotá: ICAH, 2019).

88. José Carlos de la Puente Luna, *Andean Cosmopolitans,* 23; De La Puente Luna, "Of Widows, Furrows, and Seed: New Perspectives on Land and the Colonial Andean Commons," *Hispanic American Historical Review* 101, no. 3 (2021): 375–407; for a very early, pathbreaking 1987 vision

of this local conflict, see Bernardo García Martínez, *Los pueblos de la Sierra* (Mexico: Colmex, 2005), 181–223; see also Chance, "Class and Ethnic Identity," 489; Brian P. Owensby, *Empire of Law and Indian Justice in Colonial Mexico* (Stanford: Stanford University Press, 2008), 22–40, 95, 212; Connell, *After Moctezuma,* 126–129, 136–139, 146, 159, 176–177, 183; Renzo Honores, "Una aproximación a la hiperlexia colonial," *Nueva Corónica* 1 (2013): 1–8; Kelly McDonough, "Love Lost: Class Struggle among Indigenous Nobles and Commoners of Seventeenth-Century Tlaxcala," *Mexican Studies/Estudios Mexicanos* 32, no. 1 (2016): 1–28; Nesvig, *Promiscuous Power,* 64; see also the indispensable S. Elizabeth Penry, *The People Are King* (Oxford: Oxford University Press, 2019).

89. For a very early precursor, see Charles Gibson, "Rotation of Alcaldes in the Indian Cabildo of Mexico City," *Hispanic American Historical Review* 33, no. 2 (1953): 212–223; see also Eustaquio Celestino Solís, Armando Valencia R., Constantino Medina Lima, eds., *Actas de cabildo de Tlaxcala, 1547–1567* (AGN-Mexico, 1984); James Lockhart, Frances Berdan, and Arthur J. O. Anderson, *The Tlaxcalan Actas: A Compendium of the Records of the Cabildo of Tlaxcala (1545–1627)* (Salt Lake City: University of Utah Press, 1986), 35–65; Robert S. Haskett, "Indian Town Government in Colonial Cuernavaca: Persistence, Adaptation, and Change," *Hispanic American Historical Review* 67, no. 2 (1987): 203–231, here 203–207; Margarita Menegus Bornemann, *Del señorío indígena a la república de indios: El caso de Toluca, 1500–1600* (Mexico: CNCA, 1994); Rebecca Horn, *Postconquest Coyoacán: Nahua-Spanish Relations in Central Mexico, 1519–1650* (Stanford: Stanford University Press, 1997), 25; Norma Angélica Castillo Palma, *Cholula: Sociedad mestiza en ciudad india* (Itzapalapa: UAM, 2001); Ana Díaz Serrano, "Repúblicas de indios en los reinos de Castilla: (Re)presentación de las periferias americanas en el siglo XVI," In *Comprendere le monarchie iberiche: Risorse materiali e rappresentazioni del potere,* ed. Gaetanos Sabatini (Rome: Edizione Viella, 2010), 343–364; Silvana Elisa Cruz Domínguez, *Nobleza y gobierno indígena de Xilotepec (siglos xv-xviii)* (Mexico: FOEM, 2012), 133; Sergio Quezada, *Maya Lords and Lordship: The Formation of Colonial Society in Yucatán, 1350–1600,* trans. Terry Rugeley (Norman: University of Oklahoma Press, 2014), 80–89; José Carlos de la Puente Luna, "En lengua de indios y en lengua española: Cabildos de naturales y escritura alfabética en el Perú colonial," in *Visiones del pasado: Reflexiones para escribir la historia de los pueblos indígenas de América,* ed. Ana Luisa Izquierdo de la Cueva (Mexico: UNAM, 2016), 51–113, 55n5; S. Elizabeth Penry, "Pleitos coloniales: 'Historizando' las fuentes sobre pueblos de indígenas de los Andes," in *Reducciones la concentración forzada de las poblaciones indígenas en el Virreinato del Perú,* ed. Akira Saito and Claudia Rosas Lauro (Lima: PUCP, 2016), 439–476, here 439, 440, 466; Rossend Rovira Morgado, *San Francisco Padremeh: El temprano cabildo indio y las cuatro parcialidades de México-Tenochtitlan (1549–1599)* (Madrid: CSIC, 2017); Jorge Iván Marín Taborda, *Vivir en policía y a son de campana: El establecimiento de la República de Indios en la provincia de Santafé, 1550–1604* (Bogotá: ICANH, 2022); Karen B. Graubart, *Republics of Difference* (Oxford: Oxford University Press, 2022). There is very little research on sixteenth-century Indigenous religious corporations, which apparently only began to multiply in the late 1500s; see Dorothy Tanck de Estrada, "Los bienes y la organización de las cofradías en los pueblos de indios del México colonial," in *La iglesia y sus bienes,* ed. María del Pilar Martínez López-Cano, Gisela von Wobeser, and Elisa Speckman Guerra (Mexico: UNAM, IIH, 2004), 33–58.

90. Indigenous brotherhoods in the 1500s remain understudied. Rodrigo F. Alfaro Uribe et al., "'Otictlaneuhtique tlali yaxca totlaçonantzin . . . A quien arrendamos la tierra propiedad de Nuestra Señora . . .'" *Letras históricas* 19 (2018): 47–77; José Antonio Cruz Rangel, "Estudio introductorio," in *Entre el cielo y la tierra: Cofradías iberoamericanas durante la Colonia,* ed. Alicia Bazarte Martínez and José Antonio Cruz Rangel (Mexico: INAH, 2023), 31–76, esp. 50; José Antonio Cruz Rangel, "Cofradías indígenas en el obispado de Tlaxcala: Una pasión cruenta (siglox XVI-XVII)," in Martínez and Rangel, *Entre el cielo y la tierra,* 77–138.

91. Vicuña Guengerich and Ochoa, "Introducción," 15–17; see the chapters of this edited volume as well as Josefina Muriel, *Las indias caciques de Corpus Cristi* (Mexico: UNAM, 2001); Karen Graubart, *Indigenous Women and the Formation of Colonial Society in Peru, 1550–1700* (Stanford: Stanford University Press, 2007); Asunción Lavrin, *Conventual Life in Colonial Mexico* (Stanford: Stanford University Press, 2008); Mónica Díaz, *Indigenous Writings from the Convent* (Tuscon: University of Arizona Press, 2013); Sara Vicuña Guengerich, "Capac Women and the Politics of Marriage in Early Colonial Peru," *Colonial Latin American Review* 24, no. 2 (2015): 147–167; Miriam Melton-Villanueva, "Cacicas, Escribanos, and Landholders: Indigenous Women's Late Colonial Mexican Texts, 1703–1832," *Ethnohistory* 65, no. 2 (2018): 297–322; Ronald Spores, "Mixteca Cacicas," in *Indian Women of Early Mexico,* ed. Susan Schroeder, Stephanie Wood, and Robert Haskett (Norman: University of Oklahoma Press, 1997); Robert Haskett, "The Life and Struggle of Doña Josefa María of Tepoztlan," in Schroeder, Wood, and Haskett, *Indian Women of Early Mexico*; Jessica Criales, "Women of Our Nation," *Early American Studies* 17, no. 4 (2019): 414–442.
92. For an overview, see Susan Migden Socolow, *The Women of Colonial Latin America,* 2nd ed. (Cambridge: Cambridge University Press, 2015), 91, 109; for women in viceregal courts, see among others Antonio Rubial García, "Las virreinas novohispanas: Presencias y ausencias," *Estudios de historia novohispana* 50 (2014): 3–44; Alberto Baena Zapatero, "As vice-rainhas e o exercício do poder na Nova Espanha (Séculos xvi e xvii)," *Revista Histórica* 176 (2017): 1–34; Kimberly Gauderman, *Women's Lives in Colonial Quito: Gender, Law, and Economy in Spanish America* (Austin: University of Texas Press, 2010), 7–8, 26; Kimberly Gauderman, "The Authority of Gender: Women's Space and Social Control in Seventeenth-Century Quito," in *New World Orders: Violence, Sanction, and Authority in the Colonial Americas,* ed. John Smolenski and Thomas J. Humphrey (Philadelphia: University of Pennsylvania, 2005), 71–91. Karen Vieira Powers, *Women in the Crucible of Conquest: The Gendered Genesis of Spanish American Society, 1500–1600* (Albuquerque: University of New Mexico Press, 2005), despite denying any post-conquest "place for women in politics or religion" (41), demonstrates the opposite, 74–75, 82, 98, 176–177, 188–191. Kathryn Burns, *Colonial Habits: Convents and the Spiritual Economy of Cuzco, Peru* (Durham: Duke University Press, 1999), 7; Nancy van Deusen, *Embodying the Sacred: Women Mystics in Seventeenth-Century Lima* (Durham: Duke University Press, 2017). For commoner women, see Juan Manuel Ramírez Velázquez, "Women Building the Colonial Archive: Legal Authority, Female Knowledge and Affective Mobility in the Sixteenth-Century Iberian Atlantic World," *Journal of Early Modern History* 13 (2024): 281–300. This list is far from exhaustive.
93. Among many others, see Patricia Seed, *To Honor, Love, and Obey in Colonial Mexico* (Stanford: Stanford University Press, 1988); Bennett, *Africans in Colonial Mexico*; McKinley, *Fractional Freedoms*; Gauderman, "Authority of Gender," 89–91; Germeten, *Violent Delights, Violent Ends,* 16.
94. Gretchen D. Starr-LeBeau, *In the Shadow of the Virgin: Inquisitors, Friars, and* Conversos *in Guadalupe, Spain* (Princeton: Princeton University Press, 2003), 67. For an overview of the post-Franco transformation in Inquisition studies, see Kimberly Lynn Hossain, "Unraveling the Spanish Inquisition: Inquisitorial Studies in the Twenty-First Century," *History Compass* 5, no. 4 (2007): 1280–1293, here 1280–1281; Joan Cameron Bristol, *Christians, Blasphemers, and Witches: Afro-Mexican Ritual Practice in the Seventeenth Century* (Albuquerque: University of New Mexico Press, 2007), 16–18; Hamann, *Bad Christians, New Spains.* Some, however, see both royal directives and local politics at play; see, for instance, Richard L. Kagan, "Politics, Prophecy, and the Inquisition in Late Sixteenth-Century Spain," in *Cultural Encounters: The Impact of the Inquisition in Spain and the New World,* ed. Mary Elizabeth Perry and Anne J. Cruz (Berkeley: University of California Press, 1991), 105–126, here 110. For a recent meditation on

the politics of the historiography of Spanish Inquisition studies, see Gretchen D. Starr-LeBeau, *Seven Myths of the Spanish Inquisition* (Indianapolis: Hackett, 2023).

95. Jorge Traslosheros, "Los indios, la inquisición, y los tribunales eclesiásticos ordinarios en Nueva España," in *Los indios ante los foros de justicia religiosa en la Hispanoamérica virreinal*, ed. Jorge Traslosheros and Ana de Zaballa Beascoechea (Mexico: UNAM, 2010), 47–74, 53.

96. Thomas, "Historicising Agency," 324–339; E. J. Hobsbawm, "Peasants and Politics," *Journal of Peasant Studies* 1, no. 1 (1973): 3–22; R. B. Goheen, "Peasant Politics? Village Community and the Crown in Fifteenth-Century England," *American Historical Review* 96 (February 1991): 42–62. For a book that differs in focus from ours but also sees bottom-up commoner politics as transformative, see Peter Linebaugh and Marcus Rediker, *The Many-Headed Hydra: Sailors, Slaves, Commoners and the Hidden History of the Revolutionary Atlantic* (Boston: Beacon, 2000).

97. David Graeber and David Wengrow, *The Dawn of Everything: A New History of Humanity* (New York: Penguin, 2021).

98. Matthew Gabriele and David M. Perry, *The Bright Ages: A New History of Medieval Europe* (New York: HarperCollins, 2021); Yanay Israeli, "Petition and Response as Social Process: Royal Power, Justice, and the People in Late Medieval Castile (c.1474–1504)," *Past & Present* 262, no. 1 (2024): 3–44.

99. Charles Tilly, *The Contentious French: Four Centuries of Popular Struggle* (Cambridge: Belknap, 1986).

100. Jorge Cañizares-Esguerra, ed., *Entangled Empires: The Anglo-Iberian Atlantic 1500–1830* (Philadelphia: University of Pennsylvania Press, 2019).

101. Here, we follow other scholars while maintaining a more general view of paperwork's consequences. Works implicitly foreground the power of sixteenth-century paperwork; for more explicit reflections, see Joanne Rappaport, *The Politics of Memory: Native Historical Interpretation in the Colombian Andes* (Durham: Duke University Press, 1998); María Elena Martínez, *Genealogical Fictions: Limpieza de Sangre, Religion, and Gender in Colonial Mexico* (Stanford: Stanford University Press, 2008); Luis Glave Testino, *Memoria y memoriales: La creación del programa político de la nación indiana. Siglos XVI–XVIII* (Cusco: Centro Bartolomé de Las Casas, 2024).

102. Knight, *Mexico*, esp. 2:72–73; Enrique Florescano, "La formación de los trabajadores en la época colonial," in *La clase obrera en la historia de México*, ed. Enrique Florescano and Pablo González Casanova (Mexico: Siglo XXI, 1996), 9–124; Sempat Assadourian, *Transiciones*; François Chevalier, *Land and Society in Colonial Mexico: The Great Hacienda*, trans. Alvin Eustis (Berkeley: University of California Press, 1963); Horn, *Postconquest Coyoacán*, 170; Magnus Mörner, "Economic Factors and Stratification in Colonial Spanish America with Special Regard to Elites," *Hispanic American Historical Review* 63, no. 2 (1983): 335–369, 347; Keith A. Davies, *Landowners in Colonial Peru* (Austin: University of Texas Press, 1984), 162–164.

103. Adrian Johns, *The Nature of the Book: Print and Knowledge in the Making* (Chicago: University of Chicago Pres, 1998); Paul Dover, *The Information Revolution in Early-Modern Europe* (Cambridge: Cambridge University Press, 2021).

104. Peter Burke, *A Social History of Knowledge: Form Gutenberg to Diderot* (Cambridge: Cambridge University Press, 2000); Ann M. Blair, *Too Much to Know: Managing Scholarly Information before the Modern Age* (New Haven: Yale University Press, 2010); Randolph C. Head, *Making Archives in Early Modern Europe: Proof, Information, and Political Record-Keeping, 1400–1700* (Cambridge: Cambridge University Press, 2019); Jacob Soll, *The Information Master: Jean Baptiste Colbert's Secret State Intelligence System* (Ann Arbor: University of Michigan Press, 2009); Lorraine Daston and Katherine Park, *Wonders and the Order of Nature* (New York: Zone Books, 1998); Steven Shapin, *The Social History of Truth Civility and Science in Seventeenth-Century England* (Chicago: Chicago University Press, 1994); Harold Cook, *Matters of Exchange: Commerce, Medicine, and Science in the Dutch Golden Age* (New Haven: Yale University Press, 2007).

105. Jürgen Habermas, *Strukturwandel der Öffentlichkeit: Untersuchungen zu einer Kategorie der bürgerlichen Gesellschaft* (Berlin: Luchterhand, 1962); Benedict Anderson, *Imagined Communities: Reflections on the Origin and Spread of Nationalism* (London: Verso, 1983); Michael Warner, *The Letters of the Republic: Publication and the Public Sphere in Eighteenth-Century America* (Cambridge, MA: Harvard University Press, 2009).
106. Among others, see Gruzinski, *Conquest of Mexico*; the works of Mignolo; Todorov, *The Conquest of America.* While most influenced by the metanarratives of Hispanism and liberalism have largely ignored this communication-oriented perspective or have told it in terms of formal educational institutions.
107. Joanne Rappaport and Tom Cummins, *Beyond the Lettered City: Indigenous Literacies in the Andes* (Durham: Duke University Press, 2012), 4–9; Frank Salomon and Mercedes Niño-Murcia, *The Lettered Mountain: A Peruvian Village's Way with Writing* (Durham: Duke University Press, 2011); Frank Salomon, *The Cord Keepers: Khipus and Cultural Life in a Peruvian Village* (Durham: Duke University Press, 2004); Bianca Premo, *The Enlightenment on Trial: Ordinary Litigants and Colonialism in the Spanish Empire* (Oxford: Oxford University Press, 2017), 10–12. For somewhat similar perspectives, which insist on the inclusivity of the world of letters and the importance of manuscripts, see Fernando J. Bouza Álvarez, *Corre manuscrito: Una historia cultural del Siglo de Oro* (Madrid: Marcial Pons, 2002); Teodoro Hampe-Martínez, "The Diffusion of Books and Ideas in Colonial Peru," *Hispanic American Historical Review* 73, no. 2 (1993): 211–234; Pedro M. Guibovich Pérez, "Indios y libros en el virreinato del Perú," in *Sujetos coloniales: escritura, identidad y negociación en Hispanoamérica (siglos XVI–XVIII)* Carlos Fernando Cabanillas Cárdenas, ed. (New York: IDEA, 2017), 71–193. For a broad global view, see Martin Mulsow, *Überreichweiten: Perspektiven einer globalen Ideengeschichte* (Frankfurt am Main: Suhrkamp, 2022).
108. For a discussion of the literature on intermediaries, see Adrian Masters, *We, the King: Creating Royal Legislation in the Sixteenth-Century Spanish New World* (Cambridge: Cambridge University Press, 2023), 47–77.
109. Brian Stock, *The Implications of Literacy: Written Language and Models of Interpretation in the Eleventh and Twelfth Centuries* (Princeton: Princeton University Press, 1983). See also Thomas N. Bisson, *The Crisis of the Twelfth Century: Power, Lordship, and the Origins of European Government* (Princeton: Princeton University Press, 2009); Michael T. Clanchy, *From Memory to Written Record: England 1066–1307* (Chichester: John Wiley & Sons, 2012).
110. For works that explicitly center *ladinos,* see Adorno, "Images of Indios Ladinos," 232–270; Rolena Adorno, "The Indigenous Ethnographer: The 'Indio Ladino' as Historian and Cultural Mediation," in *Implicit Understandings,* ed. Stuart B. Schwartz (Cambridge: Cambridge University Press, 1994), 378–402; Rappaport and Cummins, *Beyond the Lettered City,* 18, 41; Manuel Aguilar Moreno, "The Indio Ladino as a Cultural Mediator in the Colonial Society," *Estudios de Cultura Náhuatl* 33 (2002): 149–184; John Charles, "'More Ladino Than Necessary': Indigenous Litigants and the Language Policy Debate in Mid-colonial Peru," *Colonial Latin American Review* 16, no. 1 (2007): 23–47; Mauricio Alejandro Gómez Gómez, *Del chontal al ladino* (Antioquia: FCSH, 2015); Bennett, *Africans in Colonial Mexico.*
111. For non-Indigenous Black *ladinos,* see Peter Boyd-Bowman, *Léxico hispanoamericano del siglo XVI* (London: Tamesis Books, 1971), 515, 171, 122. For the "infinitely slippery" nature of the category, see Rappaport and Cummins, *Beyond the Lettered City,* 40.
112. Charles, *Allies at Odds,* 197n3.
113. Guaman Poma nonetheless looked down on *ladinos,* likely due to their reputation as usurpers; see Rolena Adorno, *Guaman Poma: Writing and Resistance in Colonial Peru,* 2nd ed. (Austin: University of Texas Press, 2000), xliv–xlv.
114. AGI, Quito 46, N.47, 7v.

115. Charles, *Allies at Odds*, 200n1.
116. This is an etic term not used at the time. Today, the word has connotations alien to the 1500s that we do not embrace—especially deindigenization. For this debate about ladinization as deindigenization and capitalist integration, see Marta Elena Casasús, "Resabios coloniales en América Central," in *Conquista y resistencia en la historia de América*, ed. Pilar García Jordán and Miguel Izard (Barcelona: Universitat de Barcelona, 1991), 319–338, 327n6. For the term's history in Guatemala, where it remains highly salient, see Richard N. Adams, "Ladinización e historia: El caso de Guatemala," *Mesoamérica* 28 (1994): 289–304.
117. Roberto González Echevarría, *Myth and Archive: A Theory of Latin American Narrative* (Cambridge: Cambridge University Press, 2009).
118. Yanna Yannakakis, *Since Time Immemorial: Native Custom and Law in Colonial Mexico* (Durham: Duke University Press, 2023).
119. Discrimination based on descent began early in the Indies, but what Ben Vinson III calls *castagenesis* increased dramatically after the 1560s; see Ben Vinson III, *Before Mestizaje: The Frontiers of Race and Caste in Colonial Mexico* (Cambridge: Cambridge University Press, 2018); Martínez, *Genealogical Fictions.*
120. See, among many others, Valerio, "Spanish Petition System"; Felipe E. Ruan, "Andean Activism and the Reformulation," 209–237; Ruan, "The Probanza and Shaping a Contesting Mestizo Record in Early Colonial Peru," *Bulletin of Spanish Studies* 94, no. 5 (2017): 843–869.
121. Joanne Rappaport, *The Disappearing Mestizo: Configuring Difference in the Colonial New Kingdom of Granada* (Durham: Duke University Press, 2014); Rappaport, *Politics of Memory.*
122. Among others, see Kathryn Burns, "Dentro de la ciudad letrada: La produccion de la escritura pública en el Perú colonial," *Histórica* 29, no. 1 (2005): 43–68; Kathryn Burns, *Into the Archive: Writing and Power in Colonial Peru* (Durham: Duke University Press, 2010); Tamar Herzog, *Mediación, archivos y ejercicio: Los escribanos de Quito (siglo XVII)* (Frankfurt: Klostermann, 1996).
123. Arndt Brendecke, *The Empirical Empire: Spanish Colonial Rule and the Politics of Knowledge* (Berlin: De Gruyter, 2016).
124. There are many models on the sociology of paperwork in early modern empires. We rely on such works as Hilde De Weerdt, *Information, Territory, and Networks: The Crisis and Maintenance of Empire in Song China* (Cambridge: Harvard University Press, 2015); Jonathan Bloom, *Paper before Print: The History and Impact of Paper in the Islamic World* (New Haven: Yale University Press, 2001); Matthew Hull, *Government of Paper: The Materiality of Bureaucracy in Urban Pakistan* (Berkeley: University of California Press, 2012); Miles Ogborn, *Indian Ink: Script and Print in the Making of the East India Company* (Chicago: University of Chicago Press, 2007); C. A. Bayly, *Empire and Information: Intelligence Gathering and Social Communication in India, 1780–1870* (Cambridge: Cambridge University Press, 1996).
125. Michael Clanchy, "Does Writing Construct the State?" *Journal of Historical Sociology* 15, no. 1 (2002): 68–70; Simon Teuscher, *Lords' Rights and Peasant Stories: Writing and the Formation of Tradition in the Later Middle Ages* (Philadelphia: University of Pennsylvania Press, 2007); Randolph Head, *Making Archives in Early Modern Europe: Proof Information, and Political Record Keeping, 1400–1700* (Cambridge: Cambridge University Press, 2019); Markus Friederich, *The Birth of the Archive: A History of Knowledge* (AnnArbor: University of Michigan Press, 2013); Paul Dover, "The Paper of Politics and the Politics of Paper," in *The Information Revolution in Early Modern Europe* (Cambridge: Cambridge University Press, 2021), 91–148; Ben Kafka, *The Demon of Writing: Powers and Failures of Paperwork* (New York: Zone Books, 2012).
126. José Manuel Nieto Soria, *La crisis trastámara en Castilla: El pacto como representación* (Madrid: Silex, 2021).

127. Ruth Pike, *Aristocrats and Traders: Sevillian Society in the Sixteenth Century* (Ithaca: Cornell University Press, 1972); Bartolomé Yun-Casalilla, *La gestión del poder: Corona y economías aristocráticas en Castilla (siglos XVI–XVIII)* (Madrid: Akal, 2002).
128. Leonard Patrick Harvey, *Muslims in Spain, 1500 to 1614* (Chicago: University of Chicago Press, 2005).
129. Benjamin Ehlers, *Between Christians and Moriscos: Juan de Ribera and Religious Reform in Valencia, 1568–1614* (Baltimore: JHU Press, 2006); A. Katie Harris, *From Muslim to Christian Granada: Inventing a City's Past in Early Modern Spain* (Baltimore: JHU Press, 2007).
130. For example, see Antonio de Herrera y Tordesillas, *Historia general de los hechos de los castellanos* (No press, n.d.), D.VIII, L.VI, 182.
131. Lorenzo Boturini Benaducci, *Idea de una nueva historia general* (Madrid: Juan de Zuñiga, 1746).
132. We are deeply indebted to generations of ethnohistorian-translators, including the so-called New Philologists.
133. For a long historiography of seeing (and not seeing) these sources as political, see Chapter 3.

1. THE EMPIRE THAT WASN'T

1. BNE, Mss/7369, 7r.
2. BNE, Mss/7369, 7r–7v.
3. Armando Mauricio Escobar Olmedo, *Vasco de Quiroga, el Oidor* (Ávila: Gran Duque de Alba, 2016), 295.
4. Escobar Olmedo, *Quiroga*, 157.
5. Escobar Olmedo, *Quiroga*, 170.
6. Escobar Olmedo, *Quiroga*, 81, 88.
7. AGI, Patronato 171, N.2, R.12, n/f.
8. An important omission in this chapter is that of the high judges, treated here as allies and peers of the viceroys. This treatment obscures somewhat their complex and often conflictive relationship with viceroys. Moreover, readers should be aware that personal conflicts often overlapped with corporate competition in these disputes, adding substantial contingency.
9. The friars sometimes appear as royal rivals; more often, they appear as royal allies.
10. John Tutino, *The Mexican Heartland: How Communities Shaped Capitalism, a Nation, and World History, 1500–2000* (Princeton: Princeton University Press, 2018), 31.
11. David Wootton, *Divine Right and Democracy* (Middlesex: Penguin, 1986), 18–19; or more cartoonishly, Brian Loveman, *The Constitution of Tyranny: Regimes of Exception in Spanish America* (Pittsburgh: University of Pittsburg Press, 1993), 34–35.
12. Mary Nyquist, *Arbitrary Rule: Slavery, Tyranny, and the Power of Life and Death* (Chicago: Chicago University Press, 2013), 68–71.
13. For Spanish treatise writers, see David M. Lantigua, *Infidels and Empires in a New World Order* (Cambridge: Cambridge University Press, 2020), 292; Bernice Hamilton, *Political Thought in Sixteenth-Century Spain* (Oxford: Clarendon Press, 1963), 47, 62–66; Simona Langella, "Francisco de Vitoria y la cuestión del tiranicidio," School of Salamanca Working Paper Series (Univ.-Bibliothek Frankfurt am Main, 2015), 1–24; Susana Valencia Cárdenas, "Derecho de resistencia en la teoría política," *Diálogos de Derecho y Política* 17 (2015): 28–41; Pablo Font Oporto, "Tipos de tirano y resistencia en Francisco Suárez," *Anales de la Cátedra Francisco Suárez* 51 (2017): 183–207; Pablo Font Oporto, "Suárez, Mariana, y el tiranicidio: Convergencias, divergencias y silencios estratégicos," *Cuadernos Salamantinos de Filosofía* 44 (2017): 11–34; Yamila Eliana Juri, "Poder político, tiranía y bien común en Francisco Suárez," *Isonomía* 50 (2019): 116–133. For Las Casas and Toledo, see Guillermo Lohmann Villena, "Propuestas de solución de juristas y políticos," in *La ética en la conquista de América*, ed. Luciano Pereña et al.

(Madrid: CSIC, 1984), 631–658, esp. 646–652; Pierre Duviols, "Revisionismo histórico y derecho colonial en el siglo XVI," in *Indianidad, etnocidio e indigenismo en América latina* (Mexico: CEMC, 1988), 25–39; Luis Millones-Figueroa, "De señores naturales a tiranos: El concepto politico de los Incas y sus cronistas en el siglo XVI," *Latin American Literary Review* 26, no. 52 (1998): 72–99, here 90; Carmen Beatriz Loza, "'Tyrannie' des Incas et 'naturalisation' des Indiens," *Annales: Histoire, Sciences Sociales* 57, no. 2 (2002): 375–405; Lydia Fossa, "The Inkas as Tyrants: The Construction of a Twisted Representation," *TTR* 181 (2005): 33–54; Richard Parra, *La tiranía del Inca: El Inca Garcilaso y la escritura política en el Perú colonial (1568–1617)* (Lima: Petróleos del Perú, 2015); S. Elizabeth Penry, *The People Are King: The Making of an Indigenous Andean Politics* (Oxford: Oxford University Press, 2019), 42–67; Germán Morong and Víctor Brangier Peñailillo, "Los Incas como ejemplo de sujeción," *Estudios Atacameños* 61 (2019): 5–26; Jeremy Ravi Mumford, "Francisco de Toledo, admirador y émulo de la 'tiranía' inca," *Histórica* 35 (2011 [2012]): 45–67. For some little-regarded critiques of the liberal scholarship's tendency to deny the Spanish tradition of antityranny, see Francisco de Paula Garzón, *Juan de Mariana: Las escuelas liberales* (Madrid: Biblioteca de la ciencia cristiana, 1889); Harald Ernst Braun, *Juan de Mariana and Early Modern Spanish Political Thought* (Hampshire: Ashgate, 2007), 62. For a recent work that nicely covers broader aspects of antityranny, see Molly Borowitz, "Clearing the King's Conscience: Tyranny and Legal Fiction in the New Laws of 1542," *Colonial Latin American Review* 33, no. 2 (2024): 126–149.

14. David Brading, *Orbe indiano: De la monarquía católica a la república criolla, 1492–1867*, trans. Juan José Utrilla (Mexico: FCE [1991] 2017), 15–17, 44, 57, 68, 119–123, 308, 552, 608, 635, 680; J. L. Mirete Navarro, "La filosofía española de los siglos XVI y XVII," *Anales de Derecho* 7 (1985): 131–144, here 137–142.
15. For the quintessential model, see Quentin Skinner, *The Foundations of Modern Political Thought*, 2 vols. (Cambridge: Cambridge University Press, 1978).
16. Braun, *Juan de Mariana*.
17. Markku Peltonen, *The Political Thought of the English Free State, 1649–1653* (Cambridge: Cambridge University Press, 2023), 14, 22, 69; Rachel Foxley, *The Levellers: Radical Political Thought in the English Revolution* (Manchester: Manchester University Press, 1824).
18. Robert S. Chamberlain, "The Concept of the Señor Natural," *Hispanic American Historical Review* 19, no. 2 (1939): 130–37, here 130–131.
19. Chamberlain, "Señor Natural," 134; Millones-Figueroa, "De señores naturales," 90; Loza, "'Tyrannie' des Incas," 381–382.
20. Thomas Aquinas and other scholastics theorized at length on tyranny, implying that usurpers of legitimate power could be toppled by the people and perhaps even killed if given a fair trial; Eustaquio Galán y Gutiérrez, *La filosofía política de Sto. Tomás de Aquino* (Madrid: Revista de Derecho Privado, 1945), 151–190; Langella, "Francisco de Vitoria," 1–8; Alexander Marey, "El rey, el emperador, el tirano," *Cuadernos de Historia del Derecho* 21 (2014): 229–242, esp. 235–240. For a fifteenth-century Castilian text that drew from the *Partidas* and the *Glosa*, see *Tratado de la comunidad* (*Biblioteca de El Escorial MS. &-II-8*), ed. Frank Anthony Ramírez (London: Tamesis, 1988). It defines *tirano* simply as a "prínçipe cruel . . . [quien] usurpa e ocupa la señoría como non deve, e non usando de derecho corronpe e somete la ley a su parte . . . digna cosa es que tales tiranos sean echados de la comunidat," 23–24, 63.
21. Cerdán de Tallada, *Veriloquium en reglas de estado* (Valencia: Juan Cristostomo, 1604), 24v.
22. Aurelio Espinosa, *The Empire of the Cities: Emperor Charles V, the Comunero Revolt, and the Transformation of the Spanish System* (Leiden: Brill, 2009). For an example of this liberal discourse, see Miguel Martínez, *Comuneros: El rayo y la semilla (1520–1521)* (Madrid: Hoja de Lata, 2021).
23. Susan Schroeder, *Chimalpahin & the Kingdoms of Chalco* (Tucson: University of Arizona Press, 1991), 76; Domingo Francisco Chimalpahin Quauhtlehuanitzin, *Chimalpahin's Conquest*, ed.

Susan Schroeder, Anne J. Cruz, Cristián Roa-de-la-Carrera, and David E. Tavárez (Stanford: Stanford University Press, 2010), 177.

24. Bradley Benton, *The Lords of Tetzcoco* (Cambridge: Cambridge University Press, 2017), 14–20, 26–30.

25. Jerónimo de Alcalá, *La relación de Michoacán* (Morelia: Fimax, 1980); Helen Perlstein Pollard, "El gobierno del estado tarasco prehispánico," in *Autoridad y gobierno indígena en Michoacán*, ed. Carlos Paredes Martínez and María Terán (Zamora: Colegio de Michoacán, 2003), 1:49–60, here 50; Helen Perlstein Pollard, "A Model of the Emergence of the Tarascan State," *Ancient Mesoamerica* 19, no. 2 (2008): 217–230.

26. Susan Schroeder, "Introduction: The Genre of Conquest Studies," in *Indian Conquistadors*, ed. Laura E. Matthew and Michel R. Oudijk (Norman: University of Oklahoma Press, 2007), 5–27, here 3.

27. Matthew Restall and Florine Asselbergs, *Invading Guatemala: Spanish, Nahua, and Maya Accounts of the Conquest Wars* (University Park: Penn State, 2007), 7; Laura E. Matthew, "Whose Conquest?," in Matthew and Oudijk, *Indian Conquistadors*, 102–126, here 109.

28. Schroeder, "Introduction," 14–20; Ida Altman, "Conquest, Coercion, and Collaboration," in Matthew and Oudijk, *Indian Conquistadors*, 145–174, here 150, 159–162; W. George Lovell, Christopher H. Lutz, Wendy Kramer, and William R. Swezey, *Spaniards and Indians in Colonial Guatemala* (Norman: University of Oklahoma Press, 2013), 12, 21.

29. John F. Chuchiak IV, "Forgotten Allies: The Origins and Roles of Native Mesoamerican Auxiliaries and Indios Conquistadores in the Conquest of Yucatan," in Matthew and Oudijk, *Indian Conquistadors*, 175–226, here 178, 213–214.

30. Michel R. Oudijk and Matthew Restall, "Mesoamerican Conquistadors in the Sixteenth Century," in Matthew and Oudijk, *Indigenous Conquistadors*, 28–64.

31. Juan José Vega, *Los Incas frente a España* (Lima: Peisa, 1992), 19; Waldemar Espinoza Soriano, "Los chachapoyas y cañares de Chiara (Huamanga), aliados de España," in *Historia, problema y promesa*, ed. Francisco Miró Quesada, Franklin Pease, and David Sobrevilla (Lima: PUCP, 1978), 1:231–253, here 223; Waldemar Espinoza Soriano, "Los señoríos étnicos de Chachapoyas y la alianza hispano-chacha," *Revista Histórica* 30 (1967): 224–333.

32. Vega, *Los Incas*, 26–28, 58–59.

33. Udo Oberem, "Los Cañaris y la conquista española de la Sierra ecuatoriana," *Journal de la Société des Américanistes* 63 (1974): 263–274, here 263; Udo Oberem, *Sancho Hacho: Un cacique mayor del Siglo XVI* (Quito: Abya-Yala, 1993), 34–42.

34. Susana Matallana Peláez, "Yanaconas: Indios conquistadores y colonizadores del Nuevo Reino de Granada," *Revista Fronteras de la Historia* 18, no. 2 (2013): 21–45, 33.

35. Oberem, "Los Cañaris," 263; Espinoza Soriano, "Chachapoyas y cañares," 223; Espinoza Soriano, "Señoríos étnicos," 224–333.

36. Jorge Augusto Gamboa Mendoza, *El cacicazgo muisca en los años posteriores a la Conquista: del Psihipqua al cacique colonial, 1537–1575* (Bogotá: ICANH, 2017), 528, 539.

37. Gamboa Mendoza, *Cacicazgo muisca*, 238; "Los muiscas y la conquista española," in *Los muiscas en los siglos XVI y XVII*, ed. Jorge Augusto Gamboa Mendoza (Bogotá: Universidad de los Andes, 2008), 116–139, here 122–123.

38. Jaime Valenzuela Márquez, "Indígenas andinos en Chile colonial," *Revista de Indias* 70, no. 250 (2010): 749–778.

39. Juan Garavaglia, "The Crises and Transformations of Invaded Societies," in *The Cambridge History of the Native Peoples of the Americas*, ed. Frank Salomon and Stuart B. Schwarz, vol. 3, *South America*, part 2 (Cambridge: Cambridge University Press, 1999), 1–58, here 3–4.

40. Ross Hassig, *Polygamy and the Rise and Demise of the Aztec Empire* (Albuquerque: University of New Mexico Press, 2016), 128.

41. Noble David Cook, *Born to Die: Disease and New World Conquest, 1492–1650* (Cambridge: Cambridge University Press, 1999), 130.
42. Cook, *Born to Die,* 138.
43. Sergio Quezada, *Maya Lords and Lordship,* trans. Terry Rugeley (Norman: University of Oklahoma Press, 2014), 23–24.
44. Rodrigo Martínez Baracs, *Convivencia y utopía: El gobierno indio y español de la "ciudad de Mechuacan,"* 1521–1580 (Mexico: FCE, 2005), 7.
45. Cook, *Born to Die,* 133.
46. Cook, *Born to Die,* 78.
47. Cook, *Born to Die,* 126.
48. Pedro Cieza de León, *The Discovery and Conquest of Peru,* ed. Alexandra Parma Cook and Noble David Cook (Durham: Duke University Press, 1998), 187–189.
49. Inga Clendinnen, *Ambivalent Conquests: Maya and Spaniard In Yucatan, 1517–1570* (Cambridge: Cambridge University Press, 2003), 30, 149.
50. María Castañeda de la Paz, *Conflictos y alianzas en tiempos de cambio* (Mexico: UNAM, 2013), 175; Charles Gibson, "The Aztec Aristocracy in Colonial Mexico," *Comparative Studies in Society and History* 2, no. 2 (1960): 169–196, here 171.
51. Gamboa Mendoza, *Cacicazgo muisca,* 236, 312.
52. Quezada, *Maya Lords,* 24.
53. Cook, *Born to Die,* 83.
54. Felipe Fernández-Armesto and Matthew Restall, *The Conquistadors: A Very Short Introduction* (Oxford: Oxford University Press, 2012), 107.
55. Ross Hassig, "The Collision of Two Worlds," in *The Oxford History of Mexico,* ed. William H. Beezley and Michael C. Meyer (Oxford: Oxford University Press, 2010), 73–108, here 86–88.
56. Hassig, "Collision," 90.
57. Castañeda de la Paz, *Conflictos,* 175; Gibson, "Aztec Aristocracy," 171.
58. Fernández-Armesto and Restall, *Conquistadors,* 173; James Lockhart, *The Men of Cajamarca: A Social and Biographical Study of the First Conquerors of Peru* (Austin: University of Texas Press, 1972), 11.
59. Hassig, "Collision," 92.
60. Castañeda de la Paz, *Conflictos,* 182–183.
61. Restall and Asselbergs, *Invading Guatemala,* 31.
62. Edmundo Guillén Guillén, *El imperio de Tahuantinsuyo* (Lima: BPCA, 1980), 237–243.
63. José Ignacio Avellaneda, *The Conquistadors of the New Kingdom of Granada* (Albuquerque: University of New Mexico Press, 1995), 110.
64. W. George Lovell, Christopher H. Lutz, Wendy Kramer, and William R. Swezey, *"Strange Lands and Different Peoples": Spaniards and Indians in Colonial Guatemala* (Norman: University of Oklahoma Press, 2013), 15, 63.
65. Robert Himmerich y Valencia, *The Encomenderos of New Spain, 1521–1555* (Austin: University of Texas at Austin, 1996 [1991]), 18–34, 267–275; Lockhart, *Cajamarca,* 28–38.
66. This system was a direct extension of earlier Iberian settlement of the Canary Islands; see John E. Kicza, "Patterns in Early Spanish Overseas Expansion," *William and Mary Quarterly* 49, no. 2 (1992): 229–253, 235.
67. This clause, an adaptation of the *Ordenanzas* of November 17, 1526, appears first in 1526 and is common until 1540; see Francisco Morales Padrón, "Las capitulaciones," *Historiografía y Bibliografía Americanista* 17, no. 3 (1973): 197–219, 199.
68. Julio de Atienza, *Títulos nobiliarios hispanoamericanos* (Madrid: Aguilar, 1947), 44–46; AHN, Osuna 2418, D.1; AGI, Santo Domingo 1121, L.2, 79r–80v.

69. Esteban Mira Caballos, *Hernán Cortés: Una biografía para el siglo XXI* (Barcelona: Crítica, 2021), 273, 305; Mercedes Olivera and M. de los Ángeles Romero, "La estructura política de Oaxaca en el siglo XVI," *Revista Mexicana De Sociología* 35, no. 2 (1973): 227–287, here 236; Silvio Zavala, *El servicio personal de los indios en la Nueva España* (Mexico: Colegio de México, 1984), 1:376.
70. Torres Saldamando, "El marquesado del Conquistador Francisco Pizarro," in *Cabildos de Lima* (Paris: Imprimerie P. Dupont, 1900), 2:158–188, here 158–161.
71. Bernardo García Martínez, *El Marquesado del Valle* (Mexico: Colegio de México, 1969), 20–24.
72. José Luis Martínez, *Hernán Cortés* (Mexico: UNAM, 1990), 505.
73. Himmerich y Valencia, *Encomenderos*, 99; James Lockhart, *Spanish Peru, 1532–1560*, 2nd ed. (Madison: University of Wisconsin Press, 1994), 8–16.
74. María Ángeles Eugenio Martínez, *Tributo y trabajo del indio en Nueva Granada* (Seville: EEHA, 1977), 11–17.
75. Lockhart, *Spanish Peru*, 8, 54.
76. B. H. Slicher van Bath, *Hispanoamérica en torno a 1600*, trans. Carlos Lechner (Alicante: Universidad de Alicante, 2009), 43.
77. Fernández-Armesto and Restall, *Conquistadors*, 107.
78. Demetrio Ramos, "Colón y el enfrentamiento de los caballeros," *Revista de Indias* 39 (1979): 9–87, here 54.
79. José-Juan, López-Portillo, *"Another Jerusalem": Political Legitimacy and Courtly Government in the Kingdom of New Spain (1535–1568)* (Leiden: Brill, 2017), 62; Micheal Clodfelter, *Warfare and Armed Conflicts*, 4th ed. (Jefferson: McFarland, 2017), 31. Hassig suggests 865 Spanish and 1000 Tlaxtalan fatalities; see Hassig, "Collision," 92.
80. Avellaneda, *Conquerors*, 56.
81. Avellaneda, *Conquerors*, 168.
82. Clendinnen, *Ambivalent Conquests*, 21.
83. Clodfelter, *Warfare*, 33.
84. Clendinnen, *Ambivalent Conquests*, 13.
85. Pedro Estalante Arce, *Los tlaxcaltecas en Centro América* (San Salvador: CONCULTURA, 2001), 50.
86. Jorge Díaz Ceballos, *Poder compartido: Repúblicas urbanas, monarquía y conversación en Castilla del Oro, 1508–1573* (Madrid: Marcial Pons, 2020) 55–60.
87. Ceballos, *Poder compartido*, 113, 127.
88. Morales Padrón, "Capitulaciones," 199.
89. Jorge Eduardo Arellano, "Proceso de la conquista de Nicaragua," *Nicaragua Indígena* 10, no. 49 (1970): 3–38, here 17.
90. Vega, *Los Incas*, 45.
91. Danielle Py, "El sentimiento partidista presente en el inicio de la conquista del Perú," *Temas de Historia Argentina y Americana* 17 (2010): 159–180, here 162–164.
92. José Ignacio Avellaneda, "The Men of Nikolaus Federmann," *The Americas* 43, no. 4 (1987): 385–394, 387–389; Rosa Ribas, *Testimonios de la conciencia lingüística en textos de viajeros alemanes a América en el siglo XVI* (Kassel: Edition Reichenberger, 2005), 35; Lockhart, *Cajamarca*, 28, 36; Himmerich y Valencia, *Encomenderos*, 18–34, 63, and 267–275. Unfortunately, the precise origins of African conquistador Juan Garrido are unknown; see Ricardo Alegría, *Juan Garrido: El conquistador negro en las Antillas, Florida, México, y California*, 2nd ed. (San Juan: Centro de Estudios Avanzados de Puerto Rico y el Caribe, 2004 [1990]). Others hailed from Spain. One of the key conquistadors of Peru was Miguel Ruiz, whose mother had been enslaved and sold in Seville; see Lockhart, *Cajamarca*, 36; Gamboa Mendoza, "Los muiscas y la conquista," 118–119; Ribas, *Testimonios*, 35; María Justina Sarabia Viejo, "Presencia italiana en la Nueva España y

su conexión sevillana (1520–1575)," in *Presencia italiana en Andalucía, siglos XIV–XVII* (Sevilla: EEHAS, 1989), 427–462, here 430.

93. Philipp von Hutten, *Das Gold der Neuen Welt,* ed. Eberhard Schmitt (Hildburghausen: Verlag Frankenschwelle, 1996), 144.
94. Díaz Ceballos, *Poder compartido,* 61.
95. Hassig, "Collision," 93.
96. Alonso Enríquez de Guzmán, *Libro de la vida y costumbres de don Alonso Enríquez de Guzmán* (Madrid: Atlas, 1960), 150; Clodfelter, *Warfare,* 33.
97. Clodfelter, *Warfare,* 33; Vega, *Los Incas,* 15, 48.
98. López-Portillo, *Jerusalem,* 69.
99. Resatall and Asselbergs, *Invading Guatemala,* 12.
100. Avellaneda, *Conquistadors,* 221.
101. Clendinnen, *Ambivalent Conquests,* 41.
102. Gamboa Mendoza, *Cacicazgo muisca,* 295–301; AGI, Patronato 192, N.1, R.27.
103. Hernán Cortés, *Cartas de relación,* ed. Mario Hernández (Madrid: Historia 16, 1985), 83.
104. José Luis Martínez, ed., *Documentos cortesianos III: 1528–1532* (Mexico: UNAM, 2015), 1:266.
105. Rubén Vargas Ugarte, ed., *Biblioteca peruana,* 12 vols. (Lima: La Prensa, 1935–1957), 3: 120–121; Rafael Varón Gabai, *Francisco Pizarro and his brothers: the illusion of power in sixteenth-century Peru* (Norman: University of Oklahoma Press, 1997), 55–60.
106. Gamboa Mendoza, *Cacicazgo muisca,* 247–253.
107. José Luis Martínez, *Documentos cortesianos II: 1526–1545,* vol. 4, *Juicio de residencia* (Mexico: UNAM, 1991), 28.
108. Our estimated tally of some 100,546 surviving pages comes from José María de la Peña y de la Cámara, *A List of Spanish Residencias in the Archives* [*sic*] *of the Indies, 1516–1775* (Washington, DC: Library of Congress, 1955).
109. Ramos, "Colón," 9–87, 14, 20, 36, 61–71.
110. Juan Pérez de Tudela, "La negociación colombina de las Indias," *Revista de Indias* 14 (1954): 298–357, 343, 346, 344.
111. Ramos, "Colón," 9–87, here 41.
112. Consuelo Varela, *La caída de Cristóbal Colón: El juicio de Bobadilla* (Madrid: Marcial Pons, 2006), 28, 192–193.
113. Varela, *La caída,* 51–53.
114. Antonio Herrera, *Historia general de las Indias Occidentales* (Madrid: Imprenta Real), Década I, Libro IV, 122.
115. Varela, *La caída,* 38, 66–67, 192–193, 122–131, 193.
116. Cristóbal Colón, *Textos y documentos completos; Nuevas cartas,* ed. Juan Gil Fernández and Consuelo Varela Bueno (Madrid: Alianza, 1997), 430.
117. Colón, *Textos,* 437.
118. Luis Arranz Márquez, "La nobleza colombina y sus relaciones con la castellana," *Revista de Indias* 35 (1975): 83–122, 92–97.
119. Antonio Muro Orejón, Florentino Pérez-Embid, and Francisco Morales Padrón, eds., *Pleitos colombinos I: Proceso hasta la sentencia de Sevilla* (1511) (Sevilla: EEH, 1967), lvii.
120. AGI, Patronato 11, N.1, R.4, N.6, 27r–32r.
121. AGI, Patronato 11, N.1, R.1.
122. Martínez, *Documentos II–IV.*
123. Imma Ascione, "Documenti inediti per la storia di Hernán Cortés," in *Burocracia, poder político, y justicia,* ed. Manuel Torres Aguilar and Miguel Pino Abad (Madrid: Dykinson, 2015), 127–156.
124. Martínez, *Cortés,* 458–461.
125. Martínez, *Documentos II,* N.92, 22–30.

126. Mira Caballos, *Cortés*, 264.
127. AGN, Hospital de Jesus, leg 265 (1), exp 12/ caja 467. María del Carmen Martínez Martínez, "Más pleitos que convenía a su estado: las causas de Cortés en la Audiencia de la Nueva España (1529)," in *Miradas sobre Hernán Cortés*, ed. María del Carmen Martínez Martínez and Alicia Mayer (Madrid: Iberoamericana, Veurvert, 2016): 87–118.
128. María del Carmen Martínez Martínez, "Hernán Cortés en España (1540–1547): negocios, pleitos y familia," in *El mundo de los conquistadores*, ed. Martín Ríos Saloma (Mexico: UNAM-Silex Editores, 2015): 577–598, here 590.
129. "Así, tuvo más pleitos que convenia a su estado." Francisco López de Gómara, *La Conquista de Mexico* (Zaragoza: Agustín Millán, 1552), 149v.
130. Martínez, *Cortés*, 376.
131. Martínez, *Cortés*, 580.
132. Martínez, *Cortés*, 573.
133. Martínez, *Cortés*, 623–624.
134. J. I. Israel, *Race, Class, and Politics in Colonial Mexico* (Oxford: Oxford University Press, 1975), 5.
135. José Ignacio Rubio Mañé, *El virreinato*, vol. 1, *Orígenes y jurisdicciones, y denámica social de los virreyes*, 2nd ed. (Mexico: UNAM, 1983), 29.
136. Murdo J. MacLeod, *Spanish Central America: A Socioeconomic History, 1520–1720* (Austin: University of Texas Press, 2008), 390.
137. Sergio Quezada, *Pueblos y caciques yucatecos, 1550–1580* (Mexico: Colegio de México, 1993), 60–67.
138. Eugenio Martínez, *Tributo*, 22–23.
139. Díaz Ceballos, *Poder compartido*, 71–72, 131–132.
140. Mario Castro Arenas, *Panamá y Perú en el siglo XVI* (Panama: Universal Books, 2008), 90–98; Lockhart, *Cajamarca*, 6–15.
141. AGI, Escribanía 1006B, 247v.
142. AGI, Escribanía 1006B, 247v.
143. Varón Gabai, *Francisco Pizarro*, 50–51; AGI, Lima 565, L.1, 192r; AGI, Lima 565, L.2, 12r; AGI, Escribanía 1007B, cxxir, clxxxr.
144. AGI, Patronato 294, N.4, 40v.
145. AGI, Patronato 194, R.45; AGI, Indiferente 737, N.48b.
146. AGI, Escribanía 1007B, xxxii recto–xxxviii recto.
147. Vicente Beltrán de Heredia, "Nuevos datos acerca del P. Bernardino," in *Miscelánea Beltrán de Heredia* (Salamanca: Editorial OPE 1971), 1:469–496; D. A. Brading, *The First America* (Cambridge: Cambridge University Press, 1998 [1991]), 65–67; Lewis Hanke, *La humanidad es una* (Mexico: FCE, 1985), 44–48.
148. Isacio Pérez Fernández, *Cronología documentada* (Bayamón: Universidad Central de Bayamón, 1984), 568, 570; Lawrence A. Clayton, *Bartolomé de Las Casas* (Cambridge: Cambridge University Press, 2012), 271; Manuel Danvila y Collado, ed., *El poder civil en España* (Madrid: Imprenta de Manuel Tello, 1885), 5:313.
149. BSLE: MS V-II-4, N.69, cxc verso; AGI, Patronato 185, R.34; AGI, Indiferente 737, N.53.
150. AGI, Patronato 170, R.47, 2r-v.
151. Las Casas, 1995, doc. XI, *Conclusiones sumarias sobre el Remedio de las Indias*, 121.
152. Mira Caballos, *Cortés*, 273.
153. Martínez, *Cortés*, 471.
154. Martínez, *Cortés*, 905.
155. AHN-Madrid, Diversos—Colecciones 39, N.1.
156. AGI, Patronato 211, R.1, 3r–5r; AGI, Patronato 210, R.1, 59v–64v.
157. The core dossiers of AGI, Patronato 208, 209, and 210 alone feature some fifty-five hundred; others, such as AGI, Patronato 211, R.1, add hundreds more.

158. AGI, Patronato 17, R.3; Brígida von Mentz, *Cuauhnáhuac 1430–1675* (Mexico: Porrúa, 2008), 522.
159. BL, Ms.Add.33983, 348r–349r.
160. Varón Gabai, *Francisco Pizarro,* 125.
161. BL, AM.28349, 142r–v.
162. Steve Stern, "Paradigmas de la conquista: Historia, historiografía y política," in *Los conquistados: 1492 y la población indígena de las Américas* Heraclio Bonilla, ed. (Bogotá: FLACSO, 1992), 25–65, here 34.
163. BNE, Mss/2814, 7r.
164. AHN-Madrid, Diversos-Colecciones 23, N.55, 2r.
165. BNE, Mss/8553, 4r.
166. Lockhart, *Spanish Peru,* 5.
167. José María Vallejo García-Hevia, "La rebelión de los Contreras," in *Sedición, rebelión y quimera en la historia jurídica de Europa,* ed. Enrique Álvarez Cora and Victoria Sandoval Parra (Madrid: Dykinson, 2021), 129–320, here 228.
168. Arellano, "Proceso," 16–20.
169. HKR, Manuscripts N.127, LOC, Hans P. Kraus Collection, Manuscripts N.135.
170. LOC, Hans P. Kraus Collection, Manuscripts N.137. Doctor Beltrán, Minister Gutierre Velázquez, and Gregorio López suggested that conquistadors receive Native tribute "by way of *mayorazgo* based on the tribute of [Indian] towns by way of grants [*encomienda*], not by any other form of vassalage, nor should they receive jurisdiction. . . . All this should be in the [control of] your royal Crown. . . . Income [*rentas*] of tribute should be received by way of officials of your Majesty, not by their own [power]." See also LOC, Hans P. Kraus Collection, Manuscripts N.125.
171. LOC, Hans P. Kraus Collection, Digital ID N.123.
172. AGI, Indiferente 1624, R.5, N.1, 831r.
173. Carlos Sempat Assadourian, *Transiciones hacia el sistema colonial andino* (Mexico: Colegio de México, 1994), 222–223.
174. Sempat Assadourian, *Transiciones,* 182.
175. Sempat Assadourian, *Transiciones,* 182.
176. García-Hevia, "La rebelión de los Contreras," 228–229.
177. Teodoro Hampe Martínez, "Guerras civiles, desestructuración indígena, y transición," in *Historia de América Andina,* ed. Luis Guillermo Lumbreras (Quito: Universidad Andina Simón Bolívar, 1999), 2:71–98, here 79–80.
178. AGI, Patronato 192, N.1, R.27.
179. Fernández-Armesto and Restall, *Conquistadors,* 111.
180. Royal officials reported the actions of *el tirano* Rodrigo Méndez by 1562; see AGI, Panama 33, N.62.
181. Sempat Assadourian, *Transiciones,* 190.
182. José Sánchez-Arcilla Bernal, *Las ordenanzas de las audiencias de Indias* (1511–1821) (Madrid: Dykinson, 1992), 18–22; Fernando Muro Romero, *Las presidencias-gobernaciones en Indias* (*siglo XVI*) (Seville: EEHA, 1975).
183. AGI, Indiferente 1624, R.5, N.1, 832r.
184. AGI, Indiferente 1624, R.5, N.1.
185. Fred Bronner, "Elite Formation in Seventeenth-Century Peru," *Boletín de Estudios Latinoamericanos y del Caribe* 24 (1978): 3–26, here 18.
186. James Lockhart, *Nahuas and Spaniards: Postconquest Central Mexican History and Philology* (Stanford: Stanford University Press, 1991), 18.
187. López-Portillo, *Jerusalem,* 160.
188. AHN-Madrid, Diversos-Colecciones 39, N.1, 41v.
189. AGI, Mexico 98, "Juan de la Peña."

190. Varón Gabai, *Francisco Pizarro,* 125.

191. AGI, Mexico 286, "La obligación."

192. Emma Pérez-Rocha and Rafael Tena, *La nobleza indígena del centro de México después de la conquista* (Mexico: INAH, 2000), 39.

193. Martínez Baracs, *Convivencia,* 138; Armando Mario Escobar Olmedo, ed., *Proceso, tormento y muerte del Cazonci* (Morelia: FAH, 1997), 25–30.

194. Rossend Rovira Morgado, "De valeroso quauhpilli a denostado quauhtlahtoani entre los tenochcas," *Estudios de Cultura Náhuatl* 45 (2013): 157–195, here 185–187.

195. Paulino Castañeda Delgado and Juan Marchena Fernández, *La jerarquía de la iglesia en Indias* (Madrid: MAPFRE, 1992), 181, 190.

196. Анастасия В Калюта, "El arte de acomodarse a dos mundos: La vida de don Pedro de Moctezuma Tlacahuepantli," *Revista Española de Antropología Americana* 41, no. 2 (2011): 471–500, 486.

197. Калюта, "El arte," 490.

198. Калюта, "El arte," 488–494.

199. Martin Austin Nesvig, *Promiscuous Power: An Unorthodox History of New Spain* (Austin: University of Texas Press, 2018), 63–64.

200. Luise M. Enkerlin Pauwells, "La confirmación de las haciendas en la ribera sur del lago de Pátzcuaro," in *Estudios michoacanos IX,* ed. Martín Sánchez Rodríguez and Cecilia A. Bautista (Zamora: Colegio de Michoacán, 2001), 17–50, here 21.

201. Carlos Salvador Paredes Martínez, "La nobleza tarasca: Poder político y conflictos en el Michoacán colonial," *Anuario de Estudios Americanos* 65, no. 1 (2008): 101–117, here 106–107; Enkerlin Pauwells, "Confirmación," 23.

202. Ximena Medinaceli, "Paullu y Manco ¿Una diarquía inca en tiempos de conquista?" *Bulletin de l'Institut français d'études andines* 36, no. 2 (2007): 241–258, here 241–250.

203. Medinaceli, "Paullu," 255.

204. José de la Puente Brunke, *Encomienda y encomenderos en el Perú: Estudio social y político de una institución colonial* (Sevilla: Publicaciones de la Excma. Diputación Provincial de Sevilla, 1992), 32–34.

205. Guillermo Lohmann Villena, "El señorío de los marqueses de Santiago de Oropesa en el Perú," *Anuario de Historia del Derecho Español* 19 (1948–1949): 347–458, here 356–360.

206. Lohmann Villena, "Marqueses," 23.

207. Lohmann Villena, "Marqueses," 355.

208. Elle Dunbar Temple, *La descendencia de Huayna Cápac* (Lima: Universidad Nacional Mayor de San Marcos, 2009), 200–203, 227–233.

209. José Carlos de la Puente and Sara V. Guengerich, "Incas pecheros y caballeros hidalgos: La desintegración del orden incaico y la génesis de la nobleza incaica colonial en el Cuzco del siglo XVI," *Revista andina* 54 (2016): 9–63, here 19–38.

210. Pedro Carrasco, "Documentos sobre el rango de *tecuhtli* entre los nahuas tramontanos," *Tlatocan* 5, no. 2 (1966): 133–160, 139.

211. Pérez-Rocha and Tena, *Nobleza indígena,* 39–40.

212. See, for example, AGI, Patronato 170, R.50; AGI, Patronato 170, R.14.

213. Martínez Baracs, *Convivencia,* 138.

214. Israel, *Race,* 48; Pedro Borges Morán, *El envío de misioneros a América durante la época española* (Salamanca: Universidad Pontificia, 1977), 124, 311, 353.

215. Ryan Dominic Crewe, *The Mexican Mission: Indigenous Reconstruction and Mendicant Enterprise in New Spain, 1521–1600* (Cambridge: Cambridge University Press, 2019), 3.

216. Juan Fernando Cobo Betancourt, *Mestizos heraldos de Dios* (Bogotá: ICAH, 2012), 50, 60, 64–69, 73–74.

217. Martínez, *Cortés,* 566, also 452, 581.

218. Crewe, *Mexican Mission,* 101–106.

219. Alonso Peña Montenegro, *Itinerario para párrocos de indios* (Madrid: Pedro Marín, 1771 [1688]), Libro V, Tratado I, §X, 469–476, §XVIII, 483–484; Stefan Rinke, *Conquistadors and Aztecs: A History of the Fall of Tenochtitlán* (Oxford: Oxford University Press, 2023); Constantino Bayle, "El IV centenario de don Fray Juan de Zumárraga," *Misionalia Hispánica* 5, no. 14 (1948): 209–269, here 216–217; Rafael José Luis Ruiz Esperidón, "El breve *Exponi nobis fecisti* de Adriano VI" (PhD diss., Pontificia Universitas Lateranensis, Vatican City, 1993). The papal rescript *Alias Felicis recordationis* of April 25, 1521, was the first major document to give friars episcopal jurisdiction; the second was the even bolder May 9, 1522, *Exponi nobis fecisti* (194–197), which granted the pope's "onmímoda autoridad . . . que . . . se extienda a todos aquellos actos episcopales . . . para la conversión de aquellos indios" (198). For direct proof of the emperor's petition for *Exponi,* see 220–221, n53. Friars could forgive sins such as polygamy and suspend any preexisting church constitutions due to the *Alias Felicis recordationis*; see 183.

220. Ruiz Esperidón, "*Exponi,*" 327.

221. Ruiz Esperidón, "*Exponi,*" 330.

222. Alberto de la Hera, *Iglesia y corona en la América española* (Madrid: MAPFRE, 1992), 105.

223. Ruiz Esperidón, "*Exponi,*" 183, 362–370.

224. La Hera, *Iglesia,* 107–108.

225. Henry Kamen, "Clerical Violence in a Catholic Society: The Hispanic World 1450–1720," *Studies in Church History* 20 (1983): 201–216, here 208.

226. María Milagros Ciudad Suárez, *Los dominicos, un grupo de poder en Chiapas y Guatemala, siglos XVI y XVII* (Sevilla: EEHA, 1996), 206–210.

227. Ciudad Suárez, *Dominicos,* 197, 200–201.

228. That is not to say that friars established such dominions everywhere and always in the same way. In Santa Fe, for example, they were quite weak, as their first missionaries failed to establish real control over the countryside due to personal failings and poor alliance building with native lords. There was much contingency in these outcomes.

229. The historiography on anti-idolatry efforts is too vast to cite; for Indigenous participation, see, among many others, Castañeda de la Paz, *Conflictos*; Silvana Elisa Cruz Domínguez, *Nobleza y gobierno indígena de Xilotepec (siglos xv–xviii)* (Mexico: FOEM, 2012), 68; Robert S. Haskett, "Indian Town Government in Colonial Cuernavaca," *Hispanic American Historical Review* 67, no. 2 (1987): 203–231, esp. 205, 228–229.

230. Hassig, *Polygamy,* 124.

231. Stern, "Paradigmas," 35.

232. AGI, Mexico 1088, L.1-Bis, 147v–148v.

233. AGI, Santo Domingo 868, L.1, 93r–93v.

234. Israel, *Race,* 7.

235. Crewe, *Mexican Mission,* 108.

236. Constantino Medina Lima, *Libro de los guardianes de Cuahtinchán* (Hidalgo: CIES, 1995), 37.

237. Arthur J. O. Anderson, Francés Berdan, James Lockhart, and Ronald W. Langacker, *Beyond the Codices: The Nahua View of Colonial Mexico* (Berkeley: University of California Press, 1976), 185.

238. Crewe, *Mexican Mission,* 108.

239. ARAH, Colección Muñoz A-113-68, 16r.

240. ARAH, Colección Muñoz A-113-68, 140r.

241. ARAH, Colección Muñoz A-113-68, 161r.

242. AGI, Indiferente 874, "Cunpliendo con la obligacion," 1589.

243. Ciudad Suárez, *Dominicos,* 211.

244. ARAH, Colección Muñoz A-115-70, 14v, 24v, 27r-v.

245. Mariano Cuevas, *Documentos inéditos del siglo XVI* (Mexico: Museo Nacional de Arqueología, 1914), Doc. XLII, 243.
246. Clendinnen, *Ambivalent Conquests,* 61, 76.
247. AGN-Mexico, Inquisición 6, N.4, 338r.
248. AGN-Mexico, Inquisición 6, N.4, 352r.
249. AHN-Madrid, Diversos-Colecciones 24, N.64, 1r.
250. AGI, Escribanía 1009A, N.4, 9v.
251. López-Portillo, *Jerusalem,* 217; AGI, Quito 8, R.8, N.22.
252. Ethelia Ruiz Medrano, *Gobierno y sociedad en Nueva España* (Michoacán: Colegio de Michoacán, 1991), 48–52; Israel, *Race,* 47; Carolina Ponce Hernández, *Innovación y tradición en fray Alonso de la Veracruz* (Mexico: UNAM, 2007), 89–90. For a 1587 Peruvian petition by a friar that reflects these complex rivalries, see AGI, Lima 317, "El provincial y definidores."
253. Sempat Assadourian, *Transiciones,* 232.
254. Sempat Assadourian, *Transiciones,* 232.
255. Ernesto de la Torre Villar and Ramiro Navarro de Anda, *Instrucciones y memorias de los virreyes novohispanos* (Mexico: Porrúa, 1991), 1:108.
256. See, for example, Olivera and Romero, "La estructura política de Oaxaca," 235.
257. Quezada, *Maya Lords,* 44.
258. Gamboa Mendoza, *Cacicazgo muisca,* 268.
259. Guillermo Cock, "Poder y riqueza de un Hatun Curaca," *Historia y Cultura* 17 (1985): 133–155, here 134; Oberem, *Sancho Hacho,* 7.
260. Cruz Domínguez, *Nobleza,* 85.
261. For example, the *altepetl* of Tepeaca saw its *teccali* noble houses become a *cacicazgo* led by a single ruler. Stephen M. Perkins, "Macehuales and the Corporate Solution," *Mexican Studies/Estudios Mexicanos* 21, no. 2 (2005) 277–306, here 282. Perkins describes how, in the case of Tepeaca, the *cacicazgo* flattened numerous royal houses, or *tecalli,* into the possession of a single *cacique,* 281–283. Lockhart, *Nahuas and Spaniards,* 23, notes that this rarely happened in a simple manner in practice; each arrangement was highly local in nature.
262. Susan Kellog, *Law and the Transformation of Aztec Society* (Norman: University of Oklahoma Press, 1995), 206; Crewe, *Mexican Mission,* 69.
263. Justyna Olko and Agnieszka Brylak, "Defending Local Autonomy and Facing Cultural Trauma," *Hispanic American Historical Review* 98, no. 4 (2018): 584–586.
264. "Crónica de Chac Xulub Chen," in *Crónicas mesoamericanas,* ed. Héctor Pérez Martínez (Guatemala: Editorial Galería Guatemala, 2008), 1:45. For a similar account, also Mayan, see Princeton University Library Archive, Garrett-Gates Mesoamerican Manuscripts, no. 101, "Titulos de los señores del Reino del Quichè," 15r–22r.
265. "Chac Xulub," 45.
266. "Chac Xulub," 47.
267. "Chac Xulub," 47.
268. Hassig, *Polygamy,* 122, 127, 139.
269. Hassig, *Polygamy,* 139.
270. Benton, *Lords of Tetzcoco,* 45.
271. Luis González Obregón, ed., *Procesos de indios idólatras y hechiceros* (Mexico: Tipografía Guerrero Hnos, 1912), 201–203.
272. Paredes Martínez, "Nobleza tarasca," 111.
273. González Obregón, *Procesos;* for slave testimonies, see 141–156, and for the rest, 3–8, 25, 55–64, 80–81, 96–97, 144–145, 154–155, 211.
274. González Obregón, *Procesos,* 15.

275. Gerardo Gutiérrez and Baltazar Brito, *El códice Azoyú 2: Política y territorio en el señorío de Tlapa-Tlachinollan, siglos XIV–XVI* (Mexico: INAH, 2014), 30–37; Eduardo de J. Douglas, *In the Palace of Nezahualcoyotl: Painting Manuscripts, Writing the Pre-Hispanic Past in Early Colonial Period Tetzcoco, Mexico* (Austin: University of Texas Press, 2010), 12; see also AGN-Mexico Indios 2–6.2; AGNC, Visitas de Boyacá 5, 467r.
276. Olko and Brylak, "Local Autonomy," 573–574.
277. Sempat Assadourian, *Transiciones,* 149.
278. Sempat Assadourian, *Transiciones,* 222–223. It is likely Las Casas influenced these decisions; see 224.
279. Sempat Assadourian, *Transiciones,* 159–160.
280. Bayle, "El IV centenario de don Fray Juan de Zumárraga," 260.
281. Sempat Assadourian, *Transiciones,* 210.
282. Sempat Assadourian, *Transiciones,* 215.
283. Sempat Assadourian, *Transiciones,* 233.
284. AGI, Mexico 68, R.27, N.91, 154r.
285. ARAH, Colección Muñoz A-92, 11r. For a similar statement, see Franklin Pease, *Curacas, reciprocidad, y riqueza* (Lima: PUCP, 1992), 151.
286. AGI, Mexico 68, R.27, N.91, 196r.
287. AGNC, Encomiendas 15, 173r–174v; Gamboa Mendoza, *Cacicazgo muisca,* 357.
288. According to Gamboa, only viceroys could appoint and demote *caciques*; see *Cacicazgo muisca,* 353.
289. Lockhart, *Nahuas and Spaniards,* 10; Cruz Domínguez, *Nobleza,* 133.
290. John K. Chance, "La hacienda de los Santiago en Tecali, Puebla," *Historia Mexicana* 47, no. 4 (1998): 689–734, 698–699.
291. Escobar Olmedo, *Quiroga,* 157.
292. Escobar Olmedo, *Quiroga,* 157.
293. AGI, Mexico 68, R.27, N.91, 212r.
294. Crewe, *Mexican Mission,* 100.
295. Crewe, *Mexican Mission,* 108–123.
296. Castañeda de la Paz, *Conflictos,* 248; see also the Yucatan's *doctrina* schools in Quezada, *Maya Lords,* 80.
297. Cruz Domínguez, *Nobleza,* 175.
298. Sergio Quezada, *Maya Lords and Lordship: The Formation of Colonial Society in Yucatán, 1350–1600* (Norman: University of Oklahoma Press, 2014), 38–39.
299. Quezada, *Maya Lords,* 80, 89.
300. Rebecca Horn, *Postconquest Coyoacán: Nahua-Spanish Relations in Central Mexico, 1519–1650* (Stanford: Stanford University Press, 1997), 25; Cruz Domínguez, *Nobleza,* 133, Haskett, "Indian Town Government," 203–207.
301. Lockhart, *Nahuas and Spaniards,* 7.
302. Charles Gibson, *The Aztecs under Spanish Rule: A History of the Indians of the Valley of Mexico, 1519–1810* (Stanford: Stanford University Press, 1964), 178–179; for the case of the Yucatan Indian *cabildos*' social structures, Quesada, *Maya Lords,* 76–82, 91, 94, 100–101.
303. Constantino Bayle, "Cabildos de indios en la America espanola," *Missionalia Hispánica* 8 (1951): 5–35, here 11.
304. Haskett, "Indian Town Government," 209.
305. Haskett, "Indian Town Government," 230–231; "Registro de elecciones . . . de la parroquia de San Sebastián," 34r–43v. LL, Latin American Mss., Peru, 1535–1929 Series,- Box 4, LMC 1627, "Registro."
306. Haskett, "Indian Town Government," 208, 222.
307. Haskett, "Indian Town Government," 204.

308. James Lockhart, *The Nahuas after the Conquest: A Social and Cultural History of the Indians of Central Mexico, Sixteenth through Eighteenth Centuries* (Stanford: Stanford University Press, 1992), 31–37.

309. Ronald Spores and Andrew K. Balkansky, *The Mixtecs of Oaxaca: Ancient Times to the Present* (Norman: University of Oklahoma Press, 2013), 168–169; Quesada, *Maya Lords,* 78, 94.

310. For an analysis and summaries of these *actas,* see James Lockhart, Frances Berdan, and Arthur J. O. Anderson, *The Tlaxcalan Actas: A Compendium of the Records of the Cabildo of Tlaxcala (1545–1627)* (Salt Lake City: University of Utah Press, 1986), 35–65. This institution was not extremely prolific, recording only two hundred and six *actas* between 1545 and 1566. In some years, its *regidores* issued as many as thirty-nine (1550) and as few as zero (in 1546 and 1565), but the trend seems to have been sharply negative, with a total of eighty-nine between 1548 and 1550 alone but only sixty between 1551 and 1560 and twenty-nine between 1561 and 1567.

311. Haskett, "Indian Town Government," 224–225. Perhaps the only sixteenth-century municipal register to survive for Peru contains sparse, if fascinating, information beginning in 1590; see LL, Latin American Mss., Peru, 1535–1929 Series,- Box 4, LMC 1627, "Registro."

312. José Carlos de la Puente, "En lengua de indios y en lengua española: Cabildos de naturales y escritura alfabética en el Perú colonial," in *Visiones del pasado,* ed. Ana Luisa Izquierdo de la Cueva (Mexico: UNAM, 2016), 51–113.

313. LL, Latin American Mss., Peru, 1535–1929 Series,- Box 4, LMC 1627, "Registro."

314. Gamboa Mendoza, *Cacicazgo muisca,* 374.

315. Luis Antonio Nava García, "Iztacamaxtitlán en el siglo XVI" (master's thesis, CIESAS: Mérida, 2017), 8–9, 52–60.

316. Nava García, "Iztacamaxtitlán," 73–88.

317. BNF, Mexicain 75, 21r; this petition was won by the Spanish field justice (*corregidor*) in conjunction with the Franciscans (and possibly the lords of San Juan).

318. BNF, Mexicain 75, 3v.

319. BNF, Mexicain 75, 5v.

320. BNF, Mexicain 75, 13r.

321. BNF, Mexicain 75, 40v.

322. BNF, Mexicain 75, 40v.

323. BNF, Mexicain 75, 43v.

324. BNF, Mexicain 75, 4v.

325. BNF, Mexicain 75, 40v.

326. BNF, Mexicain 75, 40v.

327. BNF, Mexicain 75, 25r.

328. BNF, Mexicain 75, 51r–52r.

329. Nava García, "Iztacamaxtitlán," 164.

330. AGI, Santo Domingo 1121, L.2, 79r–80r.

331. Lara Semboloni, *La construcción de la autoridad virreinal en la Nueva España, 1535–1595* (Mexico: Colegio de México, 2014), 97–100.

332. Semboloni, *Autoridad virreinal,* 98.

333. Semboloni, *Autoridad virreinal,* 98.

334. Semboloni, *Autoridad virreinal,* 107.

335. Semboloni, *Autoridad virreinal,* 120.

336. Semboloni, *Autoridad virreinal,* 84–94. Semboloni predicts that 57 percent of viceregal mandamientos are missing. Multiplying her number of commissions (1947) by 1.57, we get 3,057 commissions; see 84. For an example evidencing these commissions in Peru, see ADC, Cabildo del Cuzco, L.01, Cuad.12.

337. AGN-Mexico, General de Parte 2, Exps.809, 899, 962, 1023, 1294; AGN-Mexico, Indios v.1, Exps.259(115r), 304(138r); AGN-Mexico, Indios v.2, Exp.356(86r); AGN-Mexico, Indios v.3, Exps.211(48r), 300(69v), 674(158v), 766(179v), 814(193v), 952(230v); AGN-Mexico, Indios v.4, Exps.16(4v), 29(8r), 48(14v), 76(23r), 78(24r), 92(28r), 93(28), 101(30v), 132(41v), 140(44v), 141(45r), 146(47r), 148(47v), 186(58r), 192(60r), 201(63v), 210(65v), 254(77v), 271(92v), 282(95r), 496(150r), 800(219v), 880(237v), 881(238r); AGN-Mexico, Indios v.5, Exps.159(114r), 160(114v), 174(117v), 230(131v), 862(292v), 884(297v); AGN-Mexico, Indios v.6.1, Exps.24(6r), 88(22r), 111(26v), 116(27v), 148(37r), 311(84v), 363(97r), 390(103v), 393(104v), 400(106r), 413(108v), 415(108v), 447(118v), 494(133v), 499(134v), 500(135r), 507(137r), 545(144v), 548(145r), 600(160r), 641(170v), 646171v), 664(177r), 670(179r), 671(179r), 682(182v), 703(188r), 768-bis(204v), 806(215v), 836(224r), 847(227r), 848(227v), 862(232r), 881(237v), 896(242r), 916(246v), 930(250r), 1029(279r), 1046(283v), 1140(314r), 1164(320v), 1173(323r), 1181(324v), 1182(325r); AGN-Mexico, Indios v.6.2, Exps.4(2r), 218(49r), 311(68v), 321(71r), 322(71v), 400(90r), 511(112v), 627(140v), 689(158v), 809(196v), 837(205r), 839(205v), 851(207v), 937(241v), 948(244v), 1002(261r), 1005(265v), 1010(270r), 1054(286v), 1057(287r), 1079(294r), 1081(294r), 1087(296v), 1089(299r).
338. Guillermo Lohmann Villena, *El corregidor de indios en el Perú bajo los Austrias* (Lima: Pontificia Universidad Católica del Perú, 2001), 38, 268; María Justina Sarabia Viejo, *Don Luis de Velasco, virrey de Nueva España* (Sevilla: EEHA, 1978), 64.
339. Ruiz Medrano, *Gobierno y sociedad*, 144.
340. López-Portillo, *Jerusalem*, 135–138.
341. Lohmann Villena, *Corregidor*, 38, 268.
342. Crewe, *Mexican Mission*, 108.
343. Sempat Assadourian, *Transiciones*, 253–256.
344. Sempat Assadourian, *Transiciones*, 166, 210–211, 245–256.
345. AGI, Mexico 367, "E visto," 11r.
346. Peña Montenegro, *Itinerario*, Libro V, Tratado I, §XVII, 481.
347. ARAH, Colección Muñoz A-115-70, 29v.
348. ARAH, Colección Muñoz A-113-68, 141r.
349. ARAH, Colección Muñoz A-115-70, 24v and 26r.
350. Nicholas A. Robins, *Priest-Indian Conflict in Upper Peru* (New York: Syracuse University Press, 2007), 13.
351. Israel, *Race*, 47.
352. See the decree won by Quito's Bishop Peña against friars, AGI, Quito 211, L.1, 254r-v.
353. Kamen, "Clerical Violence," 208; Nesvig, *Promiscuous Power*, 48–50, 70–75; Crewe, *Mexican Mission*, 199–209.
354. Crewe, *Mexican Mission*, 108.
355. AGI, Quito 8, R.13, N.39.
356. Peña Montenegro, *Itinerario*, Libro V, Tratado II, §§VIII, IX, X, 506–513.
357. Carmen Ruigómez Gómez, *Una política indigenista de los Habsburgo* (Madrid: ECH, 1988), 49, 84.
358. Ruigómez Gómez, *Política indigenista*, 57; Charles Cutter, *The Protector de Indios in Colonial New Mexico, 1659–1821* (Albuquerque: University of New Mexico Press, 1986), 10–12; Bayle, "El IV centenario de don Fray Juan de Zumárraga," 225.
359. Ruigómez Gómez, *Política indigenista*, 58 and 102; Cutter, *Protector*, 13.
360. Ruigómez Gómez, *Política indigenista*, 58.
361. Ruigómez Gómez, *Política indigenista*, 61.
362. Fernando Domínguez Reboiras, "La Inquisición española y los indios," in *Esplendores y miserias de la evangelización de América*, ed. Wulf Oesterreicher and Roland Schmidt-Riese (Göttingen: De Gruyter, 2010), 45–72, here 57.
363. González Obregón, *Procesos*, 43–51, 77, 190.

364. John Charles, *Allies at Odds: The Andean Church and Its Indigenous Agents, 1583–1671* (Albuquerque: University of New Mexico Press, 2010).
365. Gamboa Mendoza, *Cacicazgo muisca,* 525. For a similar case involving disobedient Spanish residents in Mérida, Yucatán, see AGI, Mexico 2999, L.3, 21r-v.
366. AGI, Indiferente 1387, "En las Yndias," November 23, 1577.
367. Rossend Rovira Morgado and Simone Fracas, "From Huey Altepemeh to Civitates Christianae," *Colonial Latin American Review* 27, no. 2 (2018): 178–202.
368. Rodolfo Aguirre Salvador, "El establecimiento de jueces eclesiásticos en las doctrinas de indios," *Historia Crítica* 36 (2008): 14–35.
369. Domínguez Reboiras, "Inquisición," 51. Archbishops again petitioned for the Crown to license the Inquisition in the 1540s; see AGI, Patronato 184, R.40.
370. Lic. Alonso Muñoz wrote the council in January 1568 suggesting that in the context of recent revolts and general blasphemies, the Inquisition would be a great service. He noted that the dean of the Mexico City cathedral council had been a "heretic, traitor, and simoniac" who had counseled the great *encomendero* ringleaders; AGI, Mexico 68, R.27, N.91, 252v–253r and 249r. Throughout the letter, it becomes clear that he had discussed these issues with the council in 1567, as Ovando was beginning his investigation and reforms.
371. Paulino Castañeda Delgado and Pilar Hernández Aparicio, *La Inquisición de Lima,* vol. 1, (1570–1635) (Madrid: Deimos, 1989), 1 and 173–180.
372. Castañeda Delgado and Hernández Aparicio, *Inquisición,* 50–60.
373. Among may others, see AGN-Mexico, Inquisición 116, N.9, 290v–308v.
374. AGN-Mexico, Inquisición 112, N.1; AGN-Mexico, Inquisición 144, N1, 10r.
375. AGN-Mexico, Inquisición 83, N.1, 124v.
376. AGN-Mexico, Inquisición 115, N.8, 230v.
377. AHN-Madrid, Inquisición 1640, Exp.4, 50r.
378. Pilar Gonzalbo Aizpuru, *Mulato Miguel: Entre amigos y demonios* (Mexico: Colegio de Mexico, 2023), 85.
379. AHN-Madrid, Inquisición 1640, Exp.4, 42r and 50v.
380. AGN-Mexico, Inquisición 68, N.1, 34r–38r; AGN-Mexico, Inquisición 68, N.3, 92r; AGN-Mexico, Inquisición 68, N.5, 334r–384r; AGN-Mexico, Inquisición 69, N.1; AGN-Mexico, Inquisición 69, N.2; AHN-Madrid, Inquisición 1640, Exp.4, 21v.
381. AGN-Mexico, Inquisición 124.1, N.1, 74r–75r. See also AGN-Mexico, Inquisición 123, N.3, 141r.
382. AGN-Mexico, Inquisición 69, N.2, 273v–325r.
383. AGN-Mexico, Inquisición 115, N/E, 207v.
384. AGN-Mexico, Inquisición 118, N.2, 63r.
385. AGN-Mexico, Inquisición 130, N.3, 53v, 32r–53r.
386. AGN-Mexico, Inquisición 89, N.40/Exp.38. For a similar case, AGN-Mexico, Inquisición 33 (no Exp.), 168r.
387. AGN-Mexico, Inquisición 78, N.3, 33r.
388. AGN-Mexico, Inquisición 78, N.3, 32r; see also AGN-Mexico, Inquisición 89, N.19.
389. AGN-Mexico, Inquisición 84, N.3, 35v.
390. AGN-Mexico, Inquisición 1599, N.45, 19r.
391. AHN-Madrid, Inquisición 1640, exp.4, 19r. For similar cases, see AGN-Mexico, Inquisición 130, N.1, n/f. For another example, see AGN-Mexico, Inquisición 44, N.1, 8v–47r.
392. AGN-Mexico, Inquisición 81, N.12, 49r; AGN-Mexico, Inquisición 130, N.13, 470r–472v.
393. AGN-Mexico, Inquisición 112, N.1, 185r.
394. AGN-Mexico, Inquisición 114, N.6, 399r.
395. AGN-Mexico, Inquisición 130, N.1, n/f. See also AGN-Mexico, Inquisición 132, N.50, 244r.
396. AGN-Mexico, Inquisición 132, N.13, 110r.
397. AGN-Mexico, Inquisición 132, N.50, 244r.

398. For instance, the Guatemala city council petitioned for a *visita* of the hostile High Judge Abaunza in 1598; see AGI, Guatemala 41, N.88. See also AGI, Guatemala 394, L.4, 41v; AGI, Patronato 180, R.79, 1123r.
399. Silvio Zavala, *El servicio personal de los Indios en la Nueva España: 1550–1575* (Mexico: Colegio De Mexico, 1985), 402.
400. Juan Friede, *Los Welser en la conquista de Venezuela* (Caracas: Juan Bravo, 1961), 400–405.
401. AGI, Guatemala 52.
402. IVDJ, E25, C40, 6.
403. Martínez, *Cortés,* 618.
404. AGI, Patronato 177, N.1, R.14.
405. AGI, Patronato 188, R.15, 4–5.
406. AGI, Santa Fe 228, "El Licenciado Simancas," February 3, 1563.
407. Oscar Mazín Gómez, *El cabildo de la catedral de Valladolid de Michoacán* (Michoacán: Colegio de Michoacán 1996), 101.
408. Mazín Gómez, *Cabildo,* 111–116; Manuel Olmedo Jiménez, *Actas capitulares de la catedral de Lima* (Salamanca: Editorial San Esteban, 1992), 128–150.
409. See, for example, AGI, Panama 236, L.9, 298r–298v.
410. Mazín Gómez, *Cabildo,* 89–104.
411. Mazín Gómez, *Cabildo,* 115.
412. AGI, Patronato 188, R.14, 1r–3v.
413. AGI, Patronato 188, R.14, 3r.
414. Domínguez Reboiras, "Inquisición," 48.
415. Castañeda Delgado and Hernández Aparicio, *Inquisición,* 104.
416. Domínguez Reboiras, "Inquisición," 93–102.
417. AGI, Mexico 19, N.74, 2v; Castañeda Delgado and Hernández Aparicio, *Inquisición,* 100–101, 116–121.
418. Kimberly Lynn, *Between Court and Confessional: The Politics of Spanish Inquisitors* (Cambridge: Cambridge University Press, 2013), 258–260; Juan Ignacio Pulido Serrano, "La Visita General al tribunal de la Inquisición de México en el siglo XVII," *Memoria y Civilización* 21 (2018): 167–189; Vidal Abril Castelló, *Francisco de la Cruz, Inquisición, actas,* vol. 1 (Madrid: CSIC, 1992); Nelson Andrés Roncancio Parra, "La visita de Pedro de Medina Rico a la Inquisición de Cartagena de Indias, siglo XVII," *Fronteras* 4, no. 4 (1999): 253–269.
419. José Miguel Barros, *Pedro Sarmiento de Gamboa* (Santiago: Universitaria, 2006), 62–64.
420. Duviols, "Revisionismo histórico," 26–32.
421. Angela Ballone, *The 1624 Tumult of Mexico in Perspective* (*c. 1620–1650*): *Authority and Conflict Resolution in the Iberian Atlantic* (Leiden: Brill, 2018), 110–154; Gibran Bautista y Lugo, *La ciudad de México en la monarquía de España, 1621–1628* (Mexico: UNAM, 2020); BNE, Mss/18634/59, 3r.
422. BNE, Mss/20066/13, 124r, "echen a ese traydor."
423. Ballone, *Tumult,* 246.

2. GUNS, HORSES, AND PAPERWORK

1. AGI, Justicia 305, 1338r.
2. AGI, Audiencia de Mexico, L.205, N.11, 1r–4r. León-Portilla has studied Tenamaztle from a very different perspective; his is civilizational, ours radical and *ladino.* He transcribes the file. See Miguel León-Portilla, *Francisco Tenamaztle y Bartolomé de Las Casas en lucha por los derechos de los indígenas 1541–1556* (Mexico: Editora Dina, 1995).
3. AGI, Mexico 205, N.11.
4. AGI, Mexico 205, N.11, 1v–8r.

5. AGI, Mexico 205, N.11, "Información hecha ante la justicia ordinario de Valladolid," 5v. On the Mixton War, see Ida Altman, *The War for Mexico's West: Indians and Spaniards in New Galicia, 1524–1550* (Albuquerque: University of New Mexico, 2010).
6. "Información hecha ante la justicia ordinario," 5v.
7. "Información hecha ante la justicia ordinario," 6v.
8. AGI, Mexico 205, N.11, "Que se da provision que el Virrey envie," 14r.
9. Michael Perelman, *The Invention of Capitalism: Classical Political Economy and the Secret History of Primitive Accumulation* (Durham: Duke University Press, 2000); E. P. Thompson, *The Making of the English Working Class*, rev. ed. (New York: Penguin Books, 1968).
10. M. Bianet Castellanos, "Introduction: Settler Colonialism in Latin America," *American Quarterly* 69, no. 4 (2017): 777–781; Samuel Truett, "Settler Colonialism and the Borderlands of Early America," *William and Mary Quarterly* 76, no. 3 (2019): 435–442.
11. John Tutino, *Making a New World* (Durham: Duke University Press, 2011).
12. Jane Mangan, *Trading Roles: Gender, Ethnicity in Colonial Potosí* (Durham: Duke University Press, 2005).
13. Steve J. Stern. "Feudalism, Capitalism, and the World-System in the Perspective of Latin America and the Caribbean: Ever More Solitary," *American Historical Review* 93, no. 4 (1988): 886–897; Carlos Sempat Assadourian, *El sistema de la economía colonial: Mercado interno, regiones y espacio económico* (Lima: Instituto de Estudios Peruanos, 1982).
14. Dona Velasco Murillo, *Urban Indians in a Colonial Silver City* (Stanford: Stanford University Press, 2016); Mangan, *Trading Roles.*
15. Kris Lane, *Potosí: The Silver City That Changed the World* (Berkeley: University of California Press, 2019); Mangan, *Trading Roles.*
16. Michele McKinley, *Fractional Freedoms* (New York: Cambridge University Press, 2016); Alejandro de la Fuente and Ariela J. Gross, *Becoming Free, Becoming Black* (New York: Cambridge University Press, 2020); María Elena Díaz, *From Colonial Cuba to Madrid: Litigating Collective Freedom and Native Rights in the Spanish Empire, 1780–1814* (New York: Cambridge University Press, 2024); Adriana Chira, *Patchwork Freedoms* (New York: Cambridge University Press, 2022).
17. Nancy Van Deusen, *Global Indios* (Durham: Duke University Press, 2015).
18. Nancy Van Deusen, "Why Indigenous Slavery Continued in Spanish America after the New Laws of 1542," *The Americas* 80, no. 3 (2023): 395–432.
19. For a two-volume, abridged selection, transcription, and translation into English of about two hundred documents from Oñate's original expedition—which still await interpretation, since most of the scholarship revolves around the analysis of only one, the trial of Acoma—see George Peter Hammond and Agapito Rey, eds., *Don Juan de Oñate, Colonizer of New Mexico, 1595–1628* (Albuquerque: University of New Mexico Press, 1953).
20. Peter Villella has explored this concept already for central Mexico. See his very important but insufficiently appreciated *Indigenous Elites and Creole Identity in Colonial Mexico, 1500–1800* (New York: Cambridge University Press, 2016).
21. David Brading, *The First America* (Cambridge: Cambridge University Press, 1991).
22. James Sidbury and Jorge Cañizares-Esguerra, "Mapping Ethnogenesis in the Early Modern Atlantic," *William and Mary Quarterly* 68 (2011): 181–208.
23. Sidney W. Mintz and Richard Price, *The Birth of African-American Culture*, rev. ed. (Boston: Beacon, 1992).
24. Carlos Esteban Deive, *La Española y la esclavitud del indio* (Santo Domingo: Fundación García Arevalo, 1995); Morella A. Jiménez, *La esclavitud indígena en Venezuela, siglo XVI* (Caracas: Fuentes para la Historia Clonial de Venezuela, 1986); Erin Woodruff Stone, *Captives of*

Conquest: Slavery in the Early Modern Spanish Caribbean (Philadelphia: University of Pennsylvania Press, 2021); Molly A. Warsh, "Enslaved Pearl Divers in the Sixteenth Century Caribbean," *Slavery and Abolition* 31, no. 3 (2010): 345–362; William L. Sherman, *Forced Native Labor in Sixteenth-Century Central America* (Lincoln: University of Nebraska Press, 1979); Andrés Resendez, *The Other Slavery: The Uncovered Story of Indian Enslavement in America* (Boston: Houghton Mifflin Harcourt, 2016); Rebecca Goetz, "Indian Slavery: An Atlantic and Hemispheric Problem," *History Compass* 14, no. 2 (2016): 59–70.

25. Fernando Santos-Granero, *Vital Enemies: Slavery, Predation, and the Amerindian Political Economy of Life* (Austin: University of Texas Press, 2009); Eugenia Ibarra Rojas, *Pueblos que capturan: Esclavitud indígena al sur de America Central del siglo XVI al XIX* (San José: Universidad de Costa Rica, 2012).
26. For a taste of the back and forth, see Silvio Zavala, *Los esclavos indios en Nueva España* (Mexico: Colegio Nacional Luiz González Obregón, 1967).
27. "'Ordenanzas reales sobre los indios (Las Leyes de 1512–13),' transcripción, estudio y notas de Antonio Muro Orejón," *Anuario de Estudios Americanos* 13 (1956): 417–471; Rafael Altamira, "El texto de las Leyes de Burgos de 1512," *Revista de Historia de América* 4 (1938): 5–79; Rafael Sánchez Domingo, "Las Leyes de Burgos de 1512 y la doctrina jurídica de la conquista," *Rev. Juridica Castilla & Leon* 1, no. 28 (2012): 1–55.
28. James Muldoon, "John Wyclif and the Rights of the Infidels: The Requerimiento Re-examined," *The Americas* 36, no. 3 (1980): 301–316; Paja Faudree, "Reading the Requerimiento Performatively: Speech Acts and the Conquest of the New World," *Colonial Latin American Review* 24, no. 4 (2015): 456–478.
29. For example, see AGI, Justicia 47, N.1.
30. Enrique Otte, "La despoblación de la Española: La crisis de 1528," *Ibero-Amerikanisches Archiv* 10, no. 3 (1984): 241–265.
31. Bethany Aram and Rafael Obando Andrade, "Violencia, esclavitud y encomienda en la conquista de América, 1513–1542," *Historia Social* 87 (2017): 129–48.
32. Donald E. Chapman, *Nuño de Guzmán and the Province of Pánuco in New Spain, 1518–1533* (Glendale, CA: Arthur H. Clark, 1967).
33. Aristarco Regalado, "Los ejércitos de Nuno Betran de Guzmán," *Estudios Militares Mexicanos* 11 (2021): 19–40.
34. AGI, Justicia 234, 380v–479r, summarized in 475v–479r.
35. AGI, Justicia 234, 381v.
36. AGI, Justicia 234, 503v–509v.
37. AGI, Justicia 234, 533v–540v.
38. AGI, Justicia 234, 494r–500v.
39. AGI, Justicia 234, 545r.
40. AGI, Justicia 234, 381r.
41. AGI, Patronato 231, N.4, R.1, 2r.
42. AGI, Patronato 54, N.3, R.2.
43. AGI, Justicia 234, 104v–105r.
44. AGI, Justicia 234, 543r-v.
45. AGI, Justicia 234, 509v–510v.
46. AGI, Mexico 1088, L.1, 15r–23r.
47. Armando Escobar Olmedo, ed., *Don Vasco el Oidor: Juicio de residencia* (Ávila: Institución Gran Duque de Alba, 2016), 339, 340, 342.
48. AGI, Justicia 232, N.1. Transcribed in Escobar Olmedo, *Don Vasco el Oidor,* 81, 86–88, 134, 157, 170, 187, 213, 216, 249–251.
49. *Don Vasco el Oidor,* 213.

50. For a copy of the codex and Cortés's process against the first High Court, see *The Harkness Collection in the Library of Congress, Manuscripts Concerning Mexico: A Guide*, J. Benedict Warren, ed. (Washington, DC: Library of Congress, 1974): 39–209.
51. *The Harkness Collection*, 62–65.
52. Regalado, "Los ejércitos de Nuno Beltran de Guzmán," 25–26.
53. *Don Vasco el Oidor*, 396.
54. *Don Vasco el Oidor*, 397.
55. *Don Vasco el Oidor*, 397–398.
56. *Don Vasco el Oidor*, 398–401.
57. *Don Vasco el Oidor*, 403; see also 411.
58. *Don Vasco el Oidor*, 403.
59. *Don Vasco el Oidor*, 404–405.
60. *Don Vasco el Oidor*, 406–409.
61. *Don Vascoel Oidor* , 409.
62. *Don Vasco el Oidor*, 413.
63. *Don Vascoel Oidor*, 409–410, 412, 413.
64. *Don Vasco el Oidor*, 413–414.
65. *Don Vasco el Oidor*, 408–409, 411.
66. Adrian Masters, "¿Por qué se decretaron las Leyes Nuevas de 1542? Nuevas luces sobre conquistadores peruleros, mujeres palaciegas y Bartolomé de Las Casas en las reformas de Indias," *Revista de Indias* 82, no. 285 (2022): 293–327.
67. José de la Puente Brunke, *Encomienda y encomenderos en el Perú* (Seville: Excma, Diputacíon Provincial De Seville, 1992); Carlos Sempat Assadourian, *Transiciones hacia el sistema colonial andino* (Mexico: Colégio de Mexico, 1994).
68. J. Benedict Warren, *The Conquest of Michoacán* (Norman: University of Oklahoma Press, 1985); C. S. Paredes Martínez, "Poder político y conflictos en el Michoacán colonial," *Anuario de Estudios Americanos* 65, no. 1 (2008): 101–117; Rodrigo Martínez Baracs, *Convivencia y utopía: 1521–1580* (Mexico: FCE, 2005).
69. In postconquest Mexico, blankets were a form of currency along with sandals, cocoa beans, and pesos; see Hans Roskamp, *Los códices de Cuitzeo y Huetamo* (Zamora: El Colegio de Michoacán A. C., 2003).
70. Roskamp, *Los códices de Cuitzeo y Huetamo.*
71. This paragraph on Ruiz and the conflict in Cuitzeo over tribute is based on Hans Roskamp, "Las matrículas de tributos de Cuitzeo y Huetamo, Michoacán, siglo XVI," in *Caminos y mercados de México*, ed. Janet Long Towell and Amalia Attolini Lecón (Mexico: Universidad Nacional Autónoma de México, 2009), 221–238.
72. Juan José Batalla Rosado, "Un nuevo documento pictográfico de 1563," in *Códices del centro de Mexico*, ed. Miguel Ángel Ruz Barrio and Juan José Batalla Rosado (Warszawski: Uniwersytet Warszawski, Wydział, 2013), 397–496.
73. Batalla Rosado, "Un nuevo documento," 450.
74. Batalla Rosado, "Un nuevo documento," 449.
75. Barbara Mundy, *The Mapping of New Spain* (Chicago: University of Chicago, 2000).
76. R. Valadez Vázquez, M. Castañeda de la Paz, and D. Jiménez Badillo, *Zempoala: Historia y paisaje de un corregimiento en el estado de Hidalgo* (Mexico: UNAM, 2021).
77. Philip Wayne Powell, *La guerra chichimeca, 1550–1600* (Mexico: Fondo de Cultura Económica, 1977); Robert H. Jackson, *Conflict and Conversion in Sixteenth Century Central Mexico* (Brill, 2013).
78. For a sampling of the documents produced by several of these juntas over time, see Alberto Carrillo Cázares, ed., *El debate sobre la Guerra Chichimeca 1531–1585*, 2 vols. (Zamora: Colegio de Michoacán y Colegio de San Luis, 2000).

79. AGI, Contaduría 672, R.6, in Philip Wayne Powell, *War and Peace on the North Mexican Frontier: A Documentary Record* (Madrid: Ediciones José Porrua Turanzas, 1971), 1–66. For the use of corn bushels to pay two thousand Tarascans, see 43. The documentation includes the use of cacao beans to pay for the food of the enslaved (45).
80. AGI, Guadalajara 5, R.4, N.10, 31v–37v.
81. AGI, Guadalajara 5, R.4, N.10, 32r–34r.
82. AGI, Guadalajara 5, R.4, N.10, 15v–16r; 17v.
83. AGI, Guadalajara 5, R.4, N.10, 16r, 18r.
84. AGI, Justicia 305, 1323v–1386v.
85. AGI, Justicia 305, 1345v–26r.
86. AGI, Justicia 305, 1327v–1328v.
87. AGI, Justicia 305, 1329r.
88. AGI, Justicia 305, 1332r.
89. AGI, Justicia 305, 1332v.
90. AGI, Justicia 305, 1335v.
91. AGI, Justicia 305, 1338r.
92. AGI, Justicia 305, 1340v, items viii and ix.
93. AGI, Justicia 305, 1371v.
94. AGI, Justicia 305, 1373v.
95. AGI, Justicia 305, 1379r.
96. AGI, Justicia 305, 1379r.
97. AGI, Guadalajara 5, R.4, N.10, 33.
98. AGI, Justicia 305, 1329v.
99. AGI, Justicia 305, 1346v–1351r.
100. AGI, Justicia 305, 1328r.
101. AGI, Justicia 305, 1374r.
102. AGI, Justicia 305, 1378v.
103. AGI, Justicia 305, 1376r.
104. AGI, Patronato 182, R.6, reproduced in Powell, *War and Peace*, 105–142.
105. Powell, *War and Peace*, 110.
106. AGN-Mexico, Mercedes 4, in Powell, *War and Peace*, 67–69.
107. AGN-Mexico, Mercedes 5, in Powell, *War and Peace*, 77–84.
108. "Memorial of the Indians Concerning Their Services, c 1563," in *Nombre de Dios, Durango: Two Documents in Nahuatl Concerning its Foundation*, ed. and trans. with notes and appendices by R. H. Barlow and George T. Smisor (Sacramento: House of Tlaloc, 1943), 2–45.
109. "Memorial," 29–33.
110. "Memorial," 5–7, describes the testimony of the captive after he was taken away from the mob.
111. Philip Wayne Powell, *Mexico's Miguel Caldera: The Taming of America's First Frontier* (1548–1597) (Tucson: University of Arizona Press, 1977).
112. AGN-Mexico, Tierras 417, Exp.1, 164r–193v.
113. María Cristina Torales Pacheco, *Tierras de indios, tierras de españoles: Confirmación y composición de tierras y aguas en la jurisdicción de Cholula (siglos XVI-XVIII)* (Mexico: Universidad Iberoamericana, 2005); Maria Carolina Jurado, "La primera visita y composición de tierras en Charcas a través de la residencia de don Pedro Osores de Ulloa, juez de tierras del siglo," *Indiana* 33, no. 2 (2016): 9–30. For Peru, see José Carlos de la Puente and Victor Salier Ochoa, "La huella del intérprete: Felipe Guamán Poma de Ayala y la primera composición general de tierras en el virreinato del Perú," *Histórica* 30, no. 2 (2006): 7–39.
114. AGN-Mexico, Tierras 417, Exp.1, 127v; 164r–193v.
115. "Relación geográfica de Querétaro (1582)," in *Querétaro en el siglo XVI: fuentes documentales primarias*, ed. David Wright (Queretaro: Dirección de Patrimonio Cultural, 1989), 122–126.

116. AGI, Escribanía 159B, Parts 11–13. Part of the paperwork triggered by conflict of administrative boundaries has been transcribed by Juan Ricardo Jiménez, *Fundación y evangelización del pueblo de Indios de Querétaro y sus sujetos, 1531–1585* (Mexico: UAQ-MapPorrua, 2014).
117. AGN-Mexico, Tierras 417, Exp.1, 111r–119v.
118. "Mandamiento del Virrey Luis de Velasco, Mexico," November 10, 1551, AGN, 1982, 404–406, reproduced in Jiménez, *La república de Indios en Querétaro 1550–1820: Gobierno, elecciones y bienes de comunidad* (México: Universidad Autónoma de Querétaro y Miguel Ángel Porrúa, 2008), 371–373.
119. AGN-Mexico, Tierras 417, Exp.1, 117r.
120. "Mandameinto de amparo a los Chichimecas de Querétaro para que don Hernando de Torres no les tome sus tierras," 31 enero 1564, AGN-Mexico, Mercedes 7, 267 v, reproduced in Wright, *Querétaro en el siglo XVI*, 372–376.
121. AGN-Mexico, Tierras 417, Exp.1, 133v–164r.
122. "Relación Querétaro (1582)," in Wright, *Querétaro en el siglo XVI*, 138–141.
123. AGN-Mexico, Tierras 417, Exp.1, 126 v; 162r–164r. For the colonial land measurement caballerías to square kilometers, see María Teresa Martínez Peñalosa, *Vocabulario de terminos en documentos históricos* (Mexico: AGN, 1984), 19. The file is reproduced in Wright, *Querétaro en el siglo XVI*, 223–367.
124. *Documentos inéditos para la historia de Querétaro* (Querétaro: UAQ, 1990), 8:169–170.
125. For the wills of Magdalena, María, and Beatriz de Tapia, see *Documentos inéditos para la historia de Querétaro* (Querétaro: UAQ, 1984), 2:117–123; 3:143–147; and 3:165–181. On the 1581 *gracia* document giving don Diego a position of native lordship, see AGN-Mexico, Tierras 417, Exp.1, 21r.
126. AGN-Mexico, Tierras 417, Exp.1, 125v–164r.
127. Carlos Sigüenza y Góngora, *Glorias de Querétaro* (México: Viuda Bernardo Calderón, 1680) 8, 35.
128. Archivio Generale dell'Ordine dei Frati Minori, Roma (Fondo M/Missioni, vol. 35, 3r–12v), reproduced in *Origen de la santísima cruz de milagros de la ciudad de Querétaro*, ed. David Charles Wright Carr (Madrid: Iberoamericana/Vervuert, 2017).
129. David Wright, "Visiones indígenas de la conquista del Bajío," *Estudios de Cultura Otopame* 8, no. 1 (2015): 15–57; Isidro Feliz de Espinosa, *Chronica apostolica, y seraphica* (Mexico: Viuda de Hogal, 1746); Francisco Xavier de Espinosa Santa Gertrudis, *Cruz de piedra* (Mexico: Juan F. Ortega y Bonilla, 1722); "Disertacion histórico-apologetica sobre la conversión de la fe de los indios de Querétaro," Archivio Generale dell'Ordine dei Frati Minori, Roma (Fondo M/Missioni, vol. 62, 96r–176v); Pablo de la Purísima Concepción Beaumont, *Crónica de la provincia de los santos apostoles San Pedro y San Pablo de Michoacán* (1771–1780), 3 vols. (Morelia: Balsal, 1985–1987).
130. Valentin Frías, ed., *Opúsculos queretanos, la conquista de Querétaro* (Querétaro: Escuela de Artes Señor de San José, 1906); Vargas Rea ed. *Nicolás de San Luis funda Huimilpa, Querétaro en 1529* (Queretaro: Archivo histórico de Querétaro, 1946); "Nombramiento de capitán a favor del native lord don Nicolás de San Luis," *Boletín del Archivo General de la Nación* 6, no. 2 (1935): 203–206. See also mansucripts 1, 3, 4, 7–9, 14, 16, 17, 22, 23, 29, 31–33, 59, 60, 65, Fondo Chamacuero, Biblioteca Luís González Colegio de Michoacán, "Merced a Nicolás de San Luis, Alonso Peres y otros fundadores del pueblo de San Pedro de Tenango [1523]," AGN-Mexico, Tierras 3032, Exp.19.
131. AGN-Mexico, Tierras 3032, Exp.19; "Gacetas de la crónica e historia de Salamanca," *Guanajuato* 3 (1986): 13–16; "Cédula de Carlos V otorgando título de conquistador de Chichimecas a don Gaspar de Reyes Alfaro" and "Nombramientos y mandamientos de Don Pedro Cortés," in *Archivo parroquial del señor del hospital, Salamanca, Guanajuato*, transcribed by Monserrat García Rendón, in "Orígenes de Salamanca y su parroquia, siglos XVI y XVII" (PhD diss.,

Facultad de Filosofía y Letras, Universidad de Guanajuato, 2006), 145–152; Monserrat García Rendón, *Génesis de una villa y su parroquia, Salamanca, siglos XVI y XVII* (Salamanca: Presidencia Municipal de Salamanca, 2011), 146–160.

132. NL, Ayer MS. 1193 no. 2; AGN-Mexico, Historia 32, 163v–166r.
133. *Códice de Jilotepec (Estado de México): Rescate de una historia* (Zinacantepec: El Colegio Mexiquense, A.C., Gobierno del Estado de México, Instituto Nacional de Antropología e Historia, 2013).
134. *Códice de Jilotepec,* 98–107.
135. "Información que con citación del gobernador de naturales de república dio don Cayetano Ciriaco de Dan Luis de ser descendiente de don Nicolás de San Luis, indio puro y principal de los conquistadores del reino del pubelo de Xilotepeque en cuya provincia vivió [1791, includes cédula de 1548]," in AGN-Mexico, Civil 1779, Exp.2, 1r–17v.
136. See the extraordinary study by María Castañeda de la Paz, *Verdades y mentiras en torno a don Diego de Mendoza Austria Moctezuma* (Mexico: UNAM, 2007). On seventeenth- and eighteenth-century forgers' workshops, see Stephanie Wood, "Pedro Villafranca y Juan Gertrudis Navarrate: Falsificadores de títulos y su vida (Nueva España, siglo XVIII)," in *Lucha por la supervivencia en la América colonial,* ed. David G. Sweet and Gary B. Nash (Mexico: FCE, 1987), 472–485; Stephanie Wood, "Don Diego García de Mendoza Moctezuma: A Techialoyan Mastermind?," *Estudios de Cultura Náhuatl* 19 (1989): 245–268.

3. THE CONQUEST OF EVERYTHING

1. BNE, Mss/3040, 1r.
2. AGI, Charcas 415, L.1, 15r-v.
3. BNE, Mss/994, 3v.
4. AGI, Lima 2, January 16, 1607. For his *probanza,* see AGI, Lima 472.
5. AGI, Patronato 69, R.1, 5v.
6. It is not clear exactly when she received it; see AGI, Guatemala 1, N.4.
7. Vera Keller, *The Interlopers: Early Stuart Projects and the Undisciplining of Knowledge* (Baltimore: Johns Hopkins University, 2023).
8. Among many other texts, see the recent work by Fabien Montcher, *Mercenaries of Knowledge: Vicente Nogueira, the Republic of Letters, and the Making of Late Renaissance Politics* (Cambridge: Cambridge University Press, 2023), which emphasizes the mobile, mercenary side of this republic.
9. Walter D. Mignolo, "Decoloniality and Phenomenology: The Geopolitics of Knowing and Epistemic/Ontological Colonial Differences," *Journal of Speculative Philosophy* 32, no. 3 (2018): 360–387; Walter D. Mignolo, "On the Colonization of Amerindian Languages and Memories," *Comparative Studies in Society and History* 34, no. 2 (1992): 301–330; Walter D. Mignolo, *The Darker Side of the Renaissance: Literacy, Territoriality, and Colonization,* 2nd ed. (Ann Arbor: University of Michigan Press, 2003 [1995]), 204; Luna Nájera, "Contesting the Word: The Crown and the Printing Press in Colonial Spanish America," *Bulletin of Spanish Studies* 89, no. 4 (2012): 575–596; Rolando Vázquez, "Translation as Erasure: Thoughts on Modernity's Epistemic Violence," *Sociology Lens* 24, no. 1 (2011): 27–44, among many others.
10. Dana Leibsohn, *Script and Glyph* (Georgetown: Dumbarton Oaks, 2009), 8.
11. For a recent study of *gracia*'s formal components, see David Tella Ruiz, "Clasificación y estructura de las probanzas de méritos y servicios," *Nuevas de Indias* 5 (2020): 109–139.
12. AGI, Patronato 132, N.2, R.3.
13. AGI, Patronato 132, N.2, R.3.
14. AGI, Quito 211, L.2, 61v–62r, 133r–135v.
15. Salustiano de Dios, *Gracia, merced y patronazgo real* (Madrid: CEC, 1993).

16. Robert Folger argues that "one of the functions or effects of this bureaucratic apparatus [of *gracia*] that emerged in early modern Spain as a result and instrument of colonial expansion was to produce 'standard' subjects who were compliant with the ideology of colonial rule," *Writing as Poaching* (Leiden: Brill, 2011), 13; see also Mauricio Gómez Gómez, "Ficciones de disciplinamiento en las relaciones de méritos de conquistadores veteranos," *Tiempo histórico* 5, no. 9 (2014): 17–36; Gabriel De La Luz-Rodríguez, "Ethnological Hermeneutics for an Early Colonial Encounter on the Island of San Juan: The 1532 *Probanza* of Juan González," *Ethnohistory* 64, no. 2 (2017): 218–239. For a dissenting view that nonetheless lays heavy emphasis on their medieval and seigneurial logic, see Murdo J. MacLeod, "Self-Promotion: The Relaciones de Méritos y Servicios and Their Historical and Political Interpretation," *Colonial Latin American Historical Review* 7, no. 1 (1998): 25–42, here 26–27, 31.
17. María Elena Martínez, *Genealogical Fictions: Limpieza de Sangre, Religion, and Gender in Colonial Mexico* (Stanford: Stanford University Press, 2008), 123–128.
18. For a general description, see Roxana Nakashima and Lía Guillermina Oliveto, "Las informaciones de méritos y servicios," *Revista Electrónica de Fuentes y Archivos* 5 (2014): 120–128; for conquistadors, Robert S. Chamberlain, "Probanza de Méritos y Servicios of Blas González, Conquistador of Yucatan," *Hispanic American Historical Review* 28, no. 4 (1948): 526–536. For the priesthood, John F. Chuchiak IV, "Toward a Regional Definition of Idolatry: Reexamining Idolatry Trials in the 'Relaciones de Méritos' and Their Role in Defining the Concept of 'Idolatría' in Colonial Yucatán, 1570–1780," *Journal of Early Modern History* 6, no. 2 (2002): 140–167, here 145; Hugo Urbano and Gabriela Ramos, *Catolicismo y extirpación de idolatrías: Siglos XVI-XVIII* (Cusco: Centro de Estudios Regionales Andinos Bartolomé de Las Casas, 1993), 25–26; Gabriela Solís Robleda, "Las probanzas de eclesiásticos y el desarrollo de la iglesia secular en Yucatán," *Península* 13, no. 2 (2018): 9–41; for Basques, José Garmendia Arruebarrena, *Méritos, servicios y bienes de los vascos* (San Sebastián: Eusko Ikaskuntza, 1989); Martínez, *Genealogical Fictions*, 123–128. For how the council and king processed these claims, see Arndt Brendecke, *The Empirical Empire: Spanish Colonial Rule and the Politics of Knowledge* (Berlin-Boston, MA: de Gruyter, 2016); José García Marín, *La burocracia castellana bajo los Austrias* (Sevilla: Universidad de Sevilla, 1976); Ernesto Schäfer, *El Consejo Real y Supremo de Indias* (Madrid: Marcial Pons, 2003), 1:6, 127–128.
19. Nino Vallen, *Being the Heart of the World: The Pacific and the Fashioning of the Self in New Spain, 1513–1641* (Cambridge: Cambridge University Press, 2023).
20. Irene Olivares, "Politics of Communication: Writing, Gender, and Royal Authority in the Spanish Empire (1556–1665)" (PhD diss., University of Kansas, 2016), 76; Liliana Pérez Miguel, *'Mujeres ricas y libres': Mujer y poder* (Sevilla: CSIC, 2020), esp. 154–164; Liliana Pérez Miguel, "Viudas y pobres como lo soy yo: Muger marginalidad Perú, s.XVI," in *Nosotros también somos peruanos*, ed. Claudia Rosas Lauro (Lima: PUCP, 2011).
21. Mario Humberto Ruz, "Una probanza de méritos indígenas, Zinacantán, 1621," *Tlalocan* XI (1989): 339–364; Thomas Hillerkuss, "Los méritos y servicios de un maya yucateco principal del siglo XVI," *Estudios de historia novohispana* 13 (1993): 1–39; M. Carolina Jurado, "'Descendientes de los primeros': Las probanzas de méritos y servicios y la genealogía cacical. Audiencia de Charcas, 1574–1719," *Revista de Indias* 74, no. 261 (2014): 387–422, here 416; Caroline Cunill, "The Indigenous Use of the Probanzas de Méritos y Servicios: Its Political Dimension (Yucatán, 16th Century)," *Signos Históricos* 32 (2014): 14–47; Mario Graña, "La verdad asediada: Discursos de y para el poder. Escritura, institucionalización y élites indígenas sur andinas. Charcas. Siglo XVII," *Andes* 12 (2001): 1–13; Ethelia Ruíz Medrano and Perla Valle, "Los colores de la justicia: Códices jurídicos del siglo XVI en la Bibliothèque Nationale de France," *Journal de la Société des Américanistes* 84, no. 2 (1998): 227–241; Kelly S. McDonough, "Technologies of Communication in Transition: Indigenous Orality and Writing in Colonial Mexico," in *Latin American Literature*

in Transition Pre-1492–1800, ed. Rocío Quispe-Agnoli and Amber Brian (Cambridge: Cambridge University Press, 2022), 275–287; Javier Molina Villeta, "Los méritos de doña Marina, la 'más principal conquistadora': Recuperación y revisión de fuentes," *Anuario de estudios americanos* 81, no. 1 (2024): 1–20. For *mestizos*, see Felipe E. Ruan, "The Probanza and Shaping a Contesting Mestizo Record in Early Colonial Peru," *Bulletin of Spanish Studies* 94, no. 5 (2017): 843–869; Shems Kasmi, "Los primeros mestizos del Nuevo Reino de Granada: Hombres y mujeres de fronteras culturales," *Hispanismes* 4 (2022): online.

22. Matthew Restall, "Black Conquistadors: Armed Africans in Early Spanish America," *The Americas* 57, no. 2 (2000): 171–205; Robert Schwaller, "'For Honor and Defence': Race and the Right to Bear Arms in Early Colonial Mexico," *Colonial Latin American Review* 21, no. 2 (2012): 239–266; Leo Garofalo, "Afro-Iberian Subjects: Petitioning the Crown at Home, Serving the Crown Abroad, 1590s–1630s," in *Afro-Latino Voices: Narratives from the Early Modern Ibero-Atlantic World, 1550–1812*, ed. Kathryn Joy McKnight and Leo J. Garofalo (Indianapolis: Hackett, 2009), 52–63; Héctor Linares, "Antón Zape, 'Un Negro de Mucho Precio': Seeking Freedom and Honor through Royal Service in Sixteenth-Century Panama," *The Americas* 81, no. 4(2024): 533-567 ; Marcella Hayes, "We Have Not Been Tributaries: Peru's Black Community, Historical Memory, and Resistance," in *Resistance in the Iberian Worlds from the Fifteenth to the Eighteenth Century: Dissent and Disobedience from Within*, ed. Pablo Sánchez León and Benita Herreros Cleret de Langavant (Cham: Springer Nature Switzerland, 2024), 239–258.

23. Jorge Cañizares Esguerra, "Bartolomé Inga's Mining Technologies: Indians, Science, Cyphered Secrecy, and Modernity in the New World," *History and Technology* 1 (2018): 60–71.

24. Kris Lane, *Potosí: The Silver City That Changed the World* (University California Press, 2021).

25. Martin Jansen and Gabina Aurora Pérez Jiménez, *Codex Bodley: A Painted Chronicle from the Mixtec Highlands, Mexico* (Oxford: Bodleian Library, 2005), 12.

26. Matthew Restall, "The New Conquest History," *History Compass* 10, no. 2 (2012): 151–160, here 155.

27. Craig Jackson Calhoun, *The Roots of Radicalism: Tradition, the Public Sphere, and Early 19th Century Social Movements* (Chicago: University of Chicago Press, 2012), 84.

28. For epistemicide and its world of exclusion, see Bonaventura de Sousa Santos, *Epistemologies of the South: Justice against Epistemicide* (New York: Routledge, 2014), 92, 153, 200–201; Ramón Grosfoguel, "The Structure of Knowledge in Westernized Universities: Epistemic Racism/Sexism and the Four Genocides/Epistemicides of the Long 16th Century," *Human Architecture* 11, no. 1 (2013): 73–90. Arturo Arias outright denies any Indigenous textual participation during the colonial period except for secret Maya texts: "Except for those surviving documents from the three centuries of formal colonialism that the Spaniards did not destroy, or were kept secretly hidden from colonial authorities . . . they were never able to write out their feelings in their own language or in Spanish, until the second half of the twentieth century," in "Violence and Coloniality in Latin America: An Alternative Reading of Subalternization, Racialization and Viscerality," in *Eurocentrism, Racism, and Knowledge: Debates on History and Power in Europe and the Americas*, ed. Marta Araújo and Silvia Maeso (New York: Palgrave Macmillan, 2015), 47–64, here 79; Walter D. Mignolo, "Preface to the 2012 Edition," in *Local Histories/Global Designs: Coloniality, Subaltern Knowledges, and Border Thinking* (Princeton: Princeton University Press, 2000), ix–xxv, here ix–x; Walter D. Mignolo, "Preamble: The Historical Foundation of Modernity/Coloniality and the Emergence of Decolonial Thinking," in *A Companion to Latin American Literature and Culture*, ed. Sara Castro-Klaren (Malden: Blackwell, 2008), 12–32, here 15–17; Linda Martín Alcoff, "Mignolo's Epistemology of Coloniality," *New Centennial Review* 7, no. 3 (2007): 79–101, here 81–84. For "monoculture of the mind," see Walter D. Mignolo, *The Darker Side of Western Modernity: Global Futures, Decolonial Options* (Durham: Duke University Press, 2011), 140, citing Vandana Shiva, *Monocultures of the Mind* (New York: Zed, 1993).

Postcolonialist scholarship, partly influenced by the overall conclusions of these two well-researched issues, argues that European conquest directly sought to stifle textual production in the sixteenth-century Indies by imposing the epistemological yardsticks of Renaissance humanism and alphabetic literacy; see Mignolo, *Darker Side of the Renaissance,* 128, 133, 169, 290–291; Walter D. Mignolo, "Epistemic Disobedience, Independent Thought and De-colonial Freedom," *Theory, Culture & Society* 26, no. 7–8 (2009): 1–23, here 19; Thomas Alan Abercrombie, *Pathways of Memory and Power: Ethnography and History among an Andean People* (Madison: University of Wisconsin Press, 1998), 130–131; Michel-Rolph Trouillot, *Silencing the Past: Power and the Production of History* (Boston: Beacon Press, 1995), 7.

29. Barbara Mundy, *The Mapping of New Spain: Indigenous Cartography and the Maps of the Relaciones Geograficas* (Chicago: University of Chicago Press, 1999), and specially Alex Hidalgo, *Trail of Footprints: A History of Indigenous Maps from Viceregal Mexico* (Austin: University of Texas Press, 2017).
30. Among other works on Arab *gracia* petitions and the *plomos* who invented an ancient Arab Christian history for southern Spain, see the deeply researched Mercedes García-Arenal, "El entorno de los Plomos: Historiografía y linaje," in *Los plomos del Sacromonte: Invención y tesoro,* ed. Manuel Barrios Aguilera (Valencia: Universitat de Valencia, 2006), 51–78; A. Katie Harris, *From Muslim to Christian Granada: Inventing a City's Past in Early Modern Spain* (Baltimore: Johns Hopkins University Press, 2007).
31. Helen Nader and Luciano Formisano, eds., *The Book of Privileges Issued to Christopher Columbus by King Fernando and Queen Isabel* (Berkeley: University of California Press, 1996); AGI, Indiferente 418, L.1, 1r-v.
32. See AGI, Indiferente 418, L.1.
33. José Luis Martínez, *Documentos cortesianos, I, 1518–1528 Secciones I a III* (Mexico: UNAM, 1990).
34. Matthew Restall, *When Montezuma Met Cortés: The True Story of the Meeting That Changed History* (New York: Ecco, 2019).
35. Vallen, *Being the Heart of the World.*
36. Michel R. Oudijk and Matthew Restall, "Mesoamerican Conquistadors in the Sixteenth Century," in *Indian Conquistadors,* ed. Laura E. Matthew and Michel R. Oudijk (Norman: University of Oklahoma Press, 2007), 28–64.
37. MacLeod, "Self-Promotion"; Chuchiak, "Idolatry," 145.
38. Chamberlain, "Probanza de Méritos," 526.
39. MacLeod, "Self-Promotion," 25; J. Benedict Warren, "An Introductory Survey," in *Handbook of Middle American Indians,* ed. Howard J. Cline and John B. Glass, vol. 13, part 2 (Austin: University of Texas Press, 1973 [2015]), 42–137.
40. Cunill, "Indigenous Use."
41. Oudijk and Restall, "Mesoamerican Conquistadors," 34–35. See also the 1552 petition and *probanza* of Francisco *indios cacique* of Xicalango in AGI, Guatemala 111, N.2.
42. Hillerkuss, "Los méritos y servicios," 9–39.
43. Sara Vicuña Guengerich, "Inca Women under Spanish Rule," in *Women's Negotiations and Textual Agency in Latin America, 1500–1799,* ed. Mónica Díaz and Rocío Quispe-Agnoli (London: Routledge, 2017), 106–129; Jurado, "Descendientes," 414; Piedad Costales and Alfredo Costales, *Los señores naturales de la tierra* (Quito: Xerox, 1982), 117–130.
44. Graña, "Verdad asediada."
45. AGI, Lima 205, N.16.
46. Titu Cusi Yupanqui, *History of How the Spaniards Arrived in Peru,* trans. Catherine Julien (Indianapolis: Hackett, 2006), 3–5.
47. AGI, Patronato 227, R.34, 1r.
48. Bernardo de Vargas Machuca, *The Indian Militia and Description of the Indies,* ed. Kris Lane, trans. Timothy F. Johnson (Durham: Duke University Press, 2008), xliii, li-liv.

49. AGI, Patronato 22, R.7.
50. David N. Livingstone, *Putting Science in Its Place: Geographies of Scientific Knowledge* (Chicago: University of Chicago Press, 2003), 99.
51. AGI, Indiferente 423, L.20, 645r–646v.
52. AGI, Indiferente 1414, "El Capitán."
53. AGI, Indiferente 1409, "Enrique Garcés."
54. For example, see in AGN-Mexico's Mercedes and General de Partes the following files: Mercedes 3, Exp.79, 101r; Mercedes 4, 350v–352r; Mercedes 5.1, 244r–247r and 247r–248r; Mercedes 5.2, 443v–444v; Mercedes 8, 169v; General de Partes 1, Exp.932, 221r, Exp.986, 211r (*sic*), Exp.1080, 262v; General de Partes 3, Exp.163, 80v, Exp.174, 81v, Exp.375, 176r, Exp.451, 212v–213r; General de Partes 4, Exp.136, 136v, Exp.332, 96.
55. NL, Ayer MS 1121, 214r-v.
56. AGN-Mexico, Mercedes 3, Exp.679, 265v–266v.
57. For Miguel Jerónimo Pallas's 1554 silver extraction discovery, AGI, Indiferente 425, L.23, 73r–74r. For Juan de Herrera's 1560 device to reduce the amount of sulfur necessary to extract copper, see AGI, Indiferente 425, L.23, 505v–507r.
58. AGI, Indiferente 425, L.24, 105r-v; AGI, Indiferente 426, L.25, 59r–60r, 88r–90r, 178r–179r, L.26, 115v–116v, 240r–240v, L.28, 4r–5r.
59. Gunnar Mendoza Loza, *Catálogo de los recursos documentales sobre la minería en el distrito de la Audiencia de la Plata, 1548–1826* (Sucre: Archivo y Biblioteca Nacionales de Bolivia, 2005), F.444, F.555, F.605, F.606, F.620, F.631, F.632, F.650, F.703, F.723, F.732, F.747, F.751, F.774.
60. AGI, Mexico 104, N.9, 105r. The Crown granted them recommendations for royal office but no pension.
61. AGN-Mexico, Mercedes 6719-026.
62. NL, Ayer MS 1121, 114r. See also AGN-Mexico, Mercedes 4, 199r.
63. AGN-Mexico, General de Partes 1, Exp.435, 95v–96r.
64. BNE, Mss/3040, 1r–6r.
65. AGN-Mexico, General de Partes 1, Exp.435, 95v–96r.
66. AGN-Mexico, General de Partes 1, Exp.435, 96r.
67. By 1524, the emperor's secretary Francisco de los Cobos had already secured a lucrative ten-year monopoly on various Mexican dyes, including cochineal. See AGI, Patronato 246, N.2, R.9. See also Gregorio de Pesquera in 1536 in AGI, Buenos Aires 1, L.1, 78v–83r; three decrees giving Germans and specifically Micer Enrique Ynguer the right to cultivate saffron in Indies in 1537 and 1538, AGI, Mexico 1088, L.3, 144v–145v, 146r–148r.
68. AGI, Lima 1552, "El la ciudad de los Reyes."
69. AGN-Madrid, Diversos Colecciones 25, N.48, 3r; AGI, Mexico 1684, R.2; AGI, Patronato 183, N.1, R.4.
70. AGN-Mexico, Mercedes 5.2, 24r.
71. AGI, Lima 207, N.19. He did not specify which type of reward he sought, however.
72. AGI, Patronato 64, R.7, 50r.
73. AGI, Patronato 64, R.7, 90r–92v.
74. AGI, Indiferente 424, L.21, 146v–148v.
75. AGI, Indiferente 425, L.24, 228r–229r, 230v–232r, 432r, 433v–435v, 435v–437v, 437v, 438r–439r, 439r–440v; Indiferente 426, L.25, 196v–197r, 256r–257r, L.26, 59r, 107v–109v, 110r–110v, 128r–129r, L.28, 134v, 140v, 142r; Mexico 1089, L.5, 66v–67r, 67r–67v; Indiferente 427, L.30, 190r–190v.
76. AGI, Mexico 168, N.120, 358v.
77. AGI, Mexico 97, "Don Pablo Paxbolun," 1564.
78. AGI, Mexico 286, "La obligación."
79. AGI, Mexico 1842, 44r.

80. AGI, Mexico 1842, 45r. The outcome of the petition is unclear.
81. Berenice Alcántaras Rojas, *Antonio Valeriano, gobernante y sabio nahua del siglo XVI* (Mexico: UNAM, 2021), 36.
82. AGI, Mexico 1064, L.2, 7r.
83. Alcántaras Rojas, *Antonio Valeriano*, 39–40.
84. This chapter does not cover linguistic topics; see, among others, the excellent Valeria López Fadul, *The Cradle of Words: Language and Knowledge in the Spanish Empire* (Baltimore: Johns Hopkins University Press, 2025).
85. Chuchiak, "Idolatry," 141–142; these petitions began to reach the Crown mostly after 1570; see 162. See also Solís Robleda, "Las probanzas de eclesiásticos," 9–41; Urbano and Ramos, *Catolicismo y extirpación*, 25–26.
86. *Relación de la religión y ritos del Perú hecha por los padres agustinos*, ed. Lucila Castro de Trelles (Lima: PUCP, 1992), ix-xiii; AGI, Patronato 192, N.2, R.6, 1r.
87. AGI, Patronato 192, N.2, R.6, 3r–3v.
88. Justyna Olko and Agnieszka Brylak, "Defending Local Autonomy and Facing Cultural Trauma," *Hispanic American Historical Review* 98, no. 4 (2018): 573–604, 583.
89. Patricia Lopes Don, "Franciscans, Indian Sorcerers, and the Inquisition in New Spain," *Journal of World History* 17, no. 1 (2006): 27–49, 32–34; Luis González Obregón, ed., *Procesos de indios idólatras y hechiceros* (Mexico: Hermanos Guerrero, 1912).
90. González Obregón, *Procesos*, 1–16.
91. Bradley Benton, *The Lords of Tetzcoco* (Cambridge: Cambridge University Press, 2017), 41.
92. Richard E. Greenleaf, "The Inquisition and the Indians of Colonial Mexico," *The Americas* 50, no. 3 (1994): 351–376; Patricia Lopes Don, "The 1539 Inquisition and Trial of Don Carlos of Texcoco in Early Mexico," *Hispanic American Historical Review* 88, no. 4 (2008): 573–606; Benton, *Lords*, 43–45.
93. Richard E. Greenleaf, "Persistence of Native Values: The Inquisition and the Indians of Colonial Mexico," *The Americas* 50, no. 3 (1994): 351–376, here 359–360.
94. Benton, *Lords*, 44–53; Alfonso Pérez Ortíz, *Conflictos en la Mixteca Alta* (Mexico: Plaza y Valdés, 2003); Patricia Lopes Don, *Bonfires of Culture: Franciscans, Indigenous Leaders, and the Inquisition in Early Mexico, 1524–1540* (Norman: University of Oklahoma Press, 2012).
95. See also Kevin Tarraciano, *The Mixtecs of Colonial Oaxaca* (Stanford: Stanford University Press, 2001), 147 and 271.
96. BNF, Espagnol 460, 5r.
97. BNF, Espagnol 460, 9r.
98. AGN-Colombia, Colonia, Caciques e Indios 27, D.23, 660r.
99. AGN-Colombia, Colonia, Caciques e Indios 27, D.23, 664v.
100. Guillermo Galdós Rodríguez, "Visita a Atico y Caravelí," *Revista del Archivo de la Nación* 4–5 (1977): 55–80, here 77.
101. *Visita de la provincia de León de Huánuco en 1562*, ed. John V. Murra (Huánuco: Universidad Nacional Hermilio Valdizán, 1967), 1:9–33.
102. AGN-Colombia, Colonia—Visitas—Bolívar: Sc.62-8, D.8.
103. AGN-Colombia, Colonia—Visitas—Bolívar: Sc.62-8, D.8, 861r.
104. Camila Aschner Restrepo, "De santuarios, santeros y saqueos," in *Repensando a Policéfalo*, ed. Marta Herrera Ángel, Camila Aschner Restrepo, and Tania Lizarazo Moreno (Bogotá: Editorial Pontificia Universidad Javeriana, 2006), 83–136, here 110–115. See also AGN-Colombia, Visitas—Boyacá: Sc.62, 17, D.6, 1r–88r.
105. Olko and Brylak, "Local Autonomy," 575.
106. Gerónimo De Mendieta, *Historia eclesiástica indiana: obra escrita a fines del siglo XVI* (Mexico: Editorial Porrúa, 1971), 75.

107. Victoria Ríos Castaño, “El tratado de hechicerías y sortilegios (1553),” *Revista de Historia de la Traducción* 8 (2014): 1–9.
108. Judith M. Maxwell and Craig A. Hanson, *Of the Manners of Speaking That the Old Ones Had* (Salt Lake City: University of Utah Press, 1992), 7.
109. Maxwell and Hanson, *Manners*, 6–7. For these documents, see Juan José Batalla Rosado, “El libro escrito europeo del Códice Tudela,” *Itinerario* 9 (2009): 83–115, here 85.
110. Richard E. Greenleaf, “The Mexican Inquisition and the Indians: Sources for the Ethnohistorian,” *The Americas* 34, no. 3 (1978): 315–344, here 324.
111. ARAH, Colección Muñoz, *Historial universal*, A-77-33, 3v.
112. AGI, Patronato 275, R.79.
113. AGI, Patronato 15, R.5.
114. Greenleaf, “Mexican Inquisition,” 1624.
115. Greenleaf, “Mexican Inquisition.” See also, for example, AGI, Santa Fe 17, R.11, N.92 and N.93.
116. AGI, Inquisición 1408, 1592, “Lo que pide con brevedad remedio.”
117. ARAH, Colección Muñoz, A-38-11, 3r.
118. AGI, Lima 270, 466v.
119. AGI, Lima 270, 466v.
120. Pedro Sarmiento de Gamboa, *The History of the Incas*, trans. and ed. Brian S. Bauer and Vania Smith (Austin: University of Texas Press, 2007), 1, 43.
121. AGI, Lima 270, 466v.
122. AGI, Lima 270, 467v.
123. AGI, Patronato 33, N.2, R.1 and N.3, R.9.
124. This was the ancient Roman principle of *prior tempore potior iure*. More often than not, this principle was implicit; however, jurists sometimes cited it explicitly. See, for instance, Flores Diez de Mena, *Recentiorum quaestionum iuris canonici libro tres* (Salamanca: Didaci à Cussio, 1609), 1:92. Petitioners called the era from which legitimacy had sprung *tiempo immemorial*, a form of *prior tempore* argument they used when they had no concrete proof other than witness statements. See Yanna Yannakakis, *Since Time Immemorial* (Durham: Duke University Press, 2023), 141; see also Tamar Herzog, “Colonial Law and ‘Native Costums’: Indigenous Land Rights in Colonial Spanish America,” *The Americas* 69, no. 3 (2013): 303–321, 305–306.
125. Jiménez de Rada’s circa 1243 *Opera* and King Alfonso X’s thirteenth-century *Estoria de España* already asserted that Noah’s son Japhet inherited Europe and that Japhet’s fifth son, Noah, engendered the first men to arrive in Spain, the Celtiberians. For de Rada’s *Opera*, also known as the *Historia de rebus Hispaniae*, see BNE VITR/4/3, 7v; for Alfonso’s *Estoria*, see BNM, Mss/5795, 2r. See also Mateo Bellester Rodríguez, “La estirpe de Tubal,” *Historia y Política* 29 (2013): 219–246, here 227; Richard L. Kagan, “Clio and the Crown,” in *Spain, Europe and the Atlantic: Essays in Honour of John H. Elliott*, ed. Richard L. Kagan and Geoffrey Parker (Cambridge: Cambridge University Press, 2002 [1995]), 73–100, here 77; Jurado, “Descendientes,” 390–405.
126. Victor Mínguez, “El rey de España se sienta en el trono de Salomón,” in *Visiones de la monarquía hispánica*, ed. Víctor Mínguez (Castellón: Universitat Jaume I, 2007), 19–55, here 19.
127. Marie Tanner, *The Last Descendant of Aeneas* (New Haven: Yale University Press, 1993), 104–118.
128. AGI, Patronato 245, R.2, 1r-v.
129. NLB, Rare Books and Manuscripts, JGI-981-XXXI-1, 1r.
130. AGI, Patronato 181, R.8, 57r–63r; Hanns J. Prem, Sabine Dedenbach-Salazar Sáenz, Frauke Sachse, and Frank Seeliger, *Relación de la genealogía y origen de los mexicanos Dos documentos del Libro de Oro* (Norderstedt: Books on Demand. 2015), 73.
131. Prem et al., *Dos documentos*. That these works laid claim to the family’s Tula estate was no coincidence, of course. This region would be the subject of major litigation from the 1550s onward; see AGNM, Tierras 2346, etc.

132. NLB, Rare Books and Manuscripts, JGI-XXXI-1, 1r.
133. Juan de Betanzos, *Narrative of the Incas*, trans. and ed. by Roland Hamilton and Dana Buchanan (Austin: University of Texas Press, 1996).
134. John Howland Rowe, "Probanza de los incas nietos de conquistadores," *Histórica* 9, no. 2 (1985): 193–245, here 196–221. The outcome of this case is uncertain.
135. María Castañeda de la Paz, "El árbol genealógico de la casa real de Tenochtitlán en el 'Códice Mexicanus,'" *Itinerarios* 24 (2016): 123–146, here 125.
136. On these non-Spanish elements, see Justyna Olko, "Remembering the Ancestors," in *Mesoamerican Memory*, ed. Amos Megged and Stephanie Wood (Norman: University of Oklahoma Press, 2012), 51–72.
137. Bradley Benton, "Beyond the Burned Stake," in *Texcoco: Prehispanic and Colonial Perspectives*, ed. Jongsoo Lee and Glen Brokaw (Boulder: University Press of Colorado, 2014), 183–200, here 62; Eduardo de J. Douglas, *In the Palace of Nezahualcoyotl* (Austin: University of Texas Press, 2010), 5–11.
138. de J. Douglas, *Nezahualcoyotl*, 12–15, 19, 114.
139. In this period, don Antonio Pimentel Tlahuiloltzin was the most likely patron; see de J. Douglas, *Nezahualcoyotl*, 19.
140. Delia Cosentino, "Genealogías pictóricas en Tlaxcala colonial," *Relaciones* 105, no. 37 (2006): 205–236, here 206.
141. Cosentino, "Genealogías," 208.
142. Cosentino, "Genealogías," 208, 233.
143. Angélica Jimena Afanador-Pujol, *The Relación de Michoacán* (1539–1541) (Austin: University of Texas Press, 2015), 180.
144. Afanador-Pujol, *Relación*, 180–182; Ida Altman, "Conquest, Coercion, and Collaboration," in Oudijk and Restall, *Indian Conquistadors*, 145–174, here 151.
145. Gerardo Gutiérrez and Baltazar Brito, *El códice Azoyú 2* (Mexico: INAH, 2014), 34–36. The codices are *Codex Azoyú 1* and 2, the *Lienzos* of *Tlapa* and *Chiepetlan 1*, and the *Palimpsest of Veinte Mazorcas*.
146. As historians Gutiérrez and Brito note, scribes and lawyers had become Native lords' "first defensive line" before Spanish judges by the 1520s, and these officials were perhaps responsible for encouraging the lords to produce these works; *Azoyú 2*, 30–37.
147. Bas van Doesburg, "Origin of the Lienzo de Tulancingo," *Ancient Mesoamerica* 11 (2000): 169–183, here 175.
148. AGN-Colombia, Encomiendas 14, 387r.
149. AGN-Colombia, Encomiendas 14, 399v–400r.
150. Waldemar Espinoza Soriano, "Los señoríos étnicos de Chachapoyas y la alianza hispano-chacha," *Revista Histórica* 30 (1967): 224–333, here 225.
151. Espinoza Soriano, "Los señoríos," 226.
152. Graña, "Verdad asediada," 2–3.
153. Yolanda Navas de Pozo, *Angamarca en el siglo xvi* (Quito: Abya-Yala, 1990), 125–126.
154. The *linea recta* or, in Latin, *recta linea*; see BNF, Cartes et plans, GE D-8393 for a 1566 Latin petition by don Pablo Nazareo and doña María Axayaca, "unam et eadem genealogiam in recta linea."
155. Guengerich, "Inca Women," 110; James Lockhart, *The Nahuas after the Conquest* (Stanford: Stanford University Press, 1992), 103; Ronald Spores, "The Genealogy of Tlazultepec: A Sixteenth Century Mixtec Manuscript," *Southwestern Journal of Anthropology* 20, no. 1 (1964): 15–31, here 18.
156. See an anonymous report on the marriage of the Indians of Santo Domingo in AGI, Patronato 18, N.1, R13.
157. Pedro Carrasco, "Documentos sobre el rango de *tecuhtli* entre los nahuas tramontanos," *Tlatocan* 5, no. 2 (1966): 133–160, here 156–157.

158. AGN-Mexico, Mercedes 4, 223v–226v.
159. See, for example, AGNC, Visitas: Boyacá Sc.5, 467r, 467r.
160. José Augusto Gamboa Mendoza, *El cacicazgo muisca en los años posteriores a la conquista: Del* sihipkua *al cacique colonial* (1537–1575) (Bogotá: Instituto Colombiano de Antropología e Historia, 2010), 116, 568.
161. Gamboa Mendoza, *Cacicazgo muisca,* 111.
162. Gamboa Mendoza, *Cacicazgo muisca,* 106–122; AGNC, Encomiendas 21, 412r.
163. AGNC, Caciques 61, 107r, 127r-v, 165r. See also Santiago Muñoz Arbeláez, *Costumbres en disputa* (Bogotá: Ediciones Uniandes, 2015).
164. Cristóbal Landázuri, *Visita y numeración de los pueblos del Valle de los Chillos 1551–1559* (Quito: Marka, 1990), 232. See also Garci Díez de San Miguel, *Visita hecha a la provincia de Chucuito,* ed. Waldemar Espinoza Soriano (Puno: Corporación MERU, 2013), esp. 27–53; Juan González, *Visita de los yndios churumatas* (La Paz: Musef, 1990).
165. Jurado, "Descendientes," 388.
166. Mario Graña Taborelli, "Bastardo, Mañoso, Sagaz y Ladino," *Anuario Archivo y Biblioteca Nacionales de Bolivia* 6 (2000): 541–556, 547–549.
167. AGI, Contaduría 657, 658.
168. AGI, Contratación 4802; see also Andrea Martínez Baracs, "Colonizaciones Tlaxcaltecas," *Historia Mexicana* 43, no. 2 (1993): 195–250.
169. This is implicit in Miguel Ángel González, "El tributo de los indios comunes a sus caciques durante el período hispánico," *Cuadernos de la Facultad de Derecho* 5 (1983): 151–164.
170. José Miranda, *El tributo indígena en la Nueva España durante el siglo XVI* (Mexico: COLMEX, 1952 [1980]), 24.
171. Miranda, *Tributo indígena,* 48–58.
172. Victor M. Castillo Farreras, "Matricula de tributos: Comentarios, paleografia y version," *Historia de Mexico* 2, no. (1974): 231–296.
173. Vasco de Puga, *Provisiones cédulas: Instruciones de su Magestad* (Mexico: Pedro Ocharte, 1563), 52v.
174. Many are scattered throughout AGN-Mexico, Indiferente Virreinal. For representative tribute records, see Cuauhtitlán's potters, BNF, Mexicain 109; BNF, Mexicain 376; BNF, Mexicain 390. For two pictographic proofs of payment, see NLB, Rare Books and Manuscripts, Ms. G-42; INAH, "Códice de tributos de Mizquiahuala," ca. 1570; and for one with a Nahua numeral system, see Tulane Howard-Tilton Memorial Library, "Tribute list for Mizquiahuala." For an internal document of Huexotzinco's Indigenous municipality, INAH, "Códice Tovar de Huexotzingo," 1566–1693; see also Tulane Latin American Library, "Nahuatl fiscal document"; AGI, Mapas y Planos México 664; AGS, Estado 08334, N.21, "Pintura de los tributos," no date (perhaps 1560s).
175. For hundreds of pages of these, see the AGNM's section *Tributos.*
176. AGI, Mexico 1088, L.2, 38r.
177. AGI, Patronato 181, R.27.
178. BNE, Mss/3035, 14v.
179. José Luis de Rojas, *El tributo indígena en la Nueva España en el siglo XVI* (Zamora: Michoacán, 1993), 74.
180. Yannakakis, *Time Immemorial,* 15–18.
181. AGI, Mexico 1089, L.4, 472r.
182. AGI, Indiferente 532, L.1, 124v.
183. AGI, Patronato 181, R.27, 969r; Miranda, *Tributo indígena,* 118–121.
184. BNF, Espagnol 325, 249r.
185. ARAH, Colección Muñoz A-68-26. It remained unpublished in 1586; see Fray Juan Moyano's petition about this text in AGI, Indiferente 1401, "Fray Juan Moyano." This document reveals

that for unknown reasons (which baffled Moyano as well), the council refused not only to allow the book to be printed after having agreed to it but also to hand its drafts back to Moyano.

186. AGI, Patronato 182, R.2
187. AGS, Mapas, Planos y Documentos, XII-35: Estado, Leg. 8334-21.
188. Miranda, *Tributo indígena,* 134; AGI, Patronato 182, R.11.
189. BNE, Vitr/26/8.
190. AGI, Mapas y Planos México 665; INAH, "Códice de San Juan Teotihuacán."
191. British Museum Am2006, Drg.13964. This case was related to *justicia* litigation stretching back to 1529; see AGI, Justicia 151, N.1. See also Perla Valle P., *Memorial de los indios de Tepetlaoztoc* (Mexico: INAH, 1993).
192. Baracs, "Colonizaciones Tlaxcaltecas," 195–250; AGI, Contratación 4802.
193. INAH, "Códice Chavero," ca. 1579.
194. BNF, Mexicain 113.
195. For instance, AGI, Mapas y Planos México 7; AGI, Mapas y Planos México 9.
196. Galdós Rodríguez, "Visita," 55–80.
197. AGI, Justicia 397, 28r–29v.
198. Galdós Rodríguez, "Visita," 77.
199. Silvio Zavala, *El servicio personal de indios en el Perú* (Mexico: Colmex, 1978), 1:27, 62, 78.
200. BUS, Ms.1796-4.
201. AGI, Patronato 188, R.22.
202. AGI, Patronato 188, R.22.
203. BNE, Mss/2821, 1v–14r.
204. BNE, Mss/3043, 13r.
205. BNE, Mss/3042, 224r–229v. See also AGI, Lima 123.
206. AGI, Patronato 189, R.21.
207. John V. Murra, *Visita de los valles de Sonqo* (Madrid: ICI, 1991); José M. Gordillo and Mercedes del Río, *La visita de Tuiquipaya (1573)* (Cochabamba: UMSS, 1993); David J. Robinson, *Collaguas I,* 2nd ed. (Lima: PUCP, 2002 [1977]).
208. Hidalgo, *Trail of Footprints,* 1.
209. Francisco Luis Jiménez Abollado, "Introducción," in *Encomenderos y caciques indígenas al norte del Valle de México, siglo XVI,* ed. Francisco Luis Jiménez Abollado (Hidalgo: UAEH, 2009), 9–14, 16; Marcelo Ramírez Ruiz, "Territorialidad, pintura y paisaje del pueblo de indios," in *Territorialidad y paisaje en el altepetl del siglo XVI,* ed. Federico Fernández Christlieb and Ángel Julián García Zambrano (Mexico: FCE, 2006), 168–230.
210. For the Pátzcuaro area, see Delfina Esmeralda López Sarrelangue, *La nobleza indígena de Pátzcuaro en la época virreinal* (Mexico: UNAM, 1965), esp. 97; for central Mexico, *El cacicazgo en Nueva España y Filipinas,* ed. Margarita Menegus Bornemann and Rodolfo Aguirre Salvador (Mexico: UNAM, 2005); Brígida von Mentz, *Cuauhnáhuac 1430–1675* (Mexico: Porrúa, 2008), 344–357; Mercedes Olivera, *Pillis y macehuales* (Mexico: CIS-INAH, 1978), 198–202; for present-day Cundinamarca, see Gloria Patricia Lopera-Mesa, "Creando posesión vía desposesión," *Fronteras De La Historia* 25, no. 2 (2022): 120–156; Gamboa Mendoza, *Cacicazgo muisca,* 573; For Quito, Herzog, "Colonial Law"; For Peru, Luis Miguel Glave, "Propiedad de la tierra, agricultura, y comercio, 1570–1700," in *Compendio de historia económica del Perú 2,* ed. Carlos Contreras (Lima: IEP, 2020), 313–443, esp. 331–335; Karen B. Graubart, "Heterogeneous Conceptions of Land Use and Tenure in the Lima Valley," *Colonial Latin American Review* 26 (2017): 62–84; Damián A. Gonzales Escudero, "Una aproximación procesal a la defensa de la tierra indigena," *Revista de la Maestría en Derecho Procesal* 7, no. 1 (2017): 71–100, esp. 78–79; Joseph W. Bastien, "Land Litigations in an Andean Ayllu," *Ethnohistory* 26, no. 2 (1979): 101–131.

211. Mundy, *Mapping of New Spain*; see *Mapping Latin America: A Cartographic Reader*, ed. Jordana Dym and Karl Offen (Chicago: University of Chicago Press, 2011), especially Barbara Mundy, "Litigating Land," 56–60.
212. Herzog, "Colonial Law," 305–306.
213. Brian Philip Owensby, *Empire of Law and Indian Justice in Colonial Mexico* (Stanford: Stanford University Press, 2008), 95–96.
214. AGN-Mexico, Indios 5, N.321–337, 340–344, 351–357, 359–360, 362–363, 365–366, 372, 375–378, 398–401, 414–419, 433–437, 443–446, 478.
215. AGN-Mexico, Tierras 2672.2, Exp.18, 390r.
216. AGN-Mexico, Indios 6.2, Exp.362, 81r-v.
217. Landázuri, *Visita*, 280.
218. José Carlos de la Puente Luna, "Felipe Guaman Poma de Ayala y la apropiación de tierras en el Perú colonial," *Bulletin de l'Institut français d'études andines* 37, no. 1 (2008): 123–149, here 139.
219. AGI, Indiferente 1386, "Alonso de Herrera," 1576, n/p.
220. AGI, Indiferente 1386, "Alonso de Herrera," 1576, n/p.
221. AGI, Indiferente 1386, "Alonso de Herrera," 1576, n/p.
222. Private collection of Elías Prado Tello, "Expediente Prado Tello," 59v.
223. Private collection of Elías Prado Tello, "Expediente Prado Tello," 59r.
224. de la Puente Luna, "Guaman Poma," 123–149.
225. Mercedes López-Baralt and Rolena Adorno, *Guaman Poma de Ayala: The Colonial Art of an Andean Author* (New York: Americas Society, 1992), 39.
226. KB, Copenhagen GKS 2232 4°, 1r.
227. Pierre Duviols, "Un inédit de Cristobal de Albornoz," *Journal de la société des américanistes* 56, no. 1 (1967): 7–39, here 39.
228. AGI, Lima 145.
229. The stock phrase vassals employed was *público y notorio*; see Tamar Herzog, *La administración como un fenómeno social* (Madrid: Centro de Estudios Constitucionales 1995), 255–278.
230. Jurado, "Descendientes," 398, 405.
231. Brendecke, *Empirical Empire*; Arndt Brendecke, "Knowledge, Oblivion, and Concealment in Early Modern Spain," in *Archives and Information in the Early Modern World*, ed. Kate Peters, Alexandra Walsham, and Liesbeth Corens (Oxford: Oxford University Press, 2018), 131–149.
232. BL, Add.Ms.28360, 171r.
233. AGI, Indiferente 1415, November 18, 1597.
234. AGI, Charcas 42.
235. Nicholas Johnson, "What Is a Lienzo?" in *The Lienzo of Tlapiltepec*, ed. Arni Brownstone (Norman: University of Oklahoma Press, 2015), 5–33, here 19.
236. For these *lienzos*, see Florine G. L Asselbergs, "The Conquest in Images: Stories of Tlaxcalteca and Quauhquecholteca Conquistadors," in *Indian Conquistadors: Indigenous Allies in the Conquest of Mesoamerica*, ed. Laura E. Matthew and Michel R. Oudijk, (Norman: University of Oklahoma Press, 2007), 65–101.
237. Asselbergs, "Conquest in Images," 72.
238. Asselbergs, "Conquest in Images," 74–88.
239. Asselbergs, "Conquest in Images," 66; Tsubasa Okoshi Harada, "Otra lectura de la 'Memoria de la distribución de los montes, 1557' de los Papeles de los Xiú," in *Los mayas de ayer y hoy*, ed. Alfredo Barrera Rubio and Ruth Gubler (Mérida: Conaculta, INAH, 2006), 2:778–791, here 785.
240. Asselbergs, "Conquest in Images," 91–93; Florine G. L. Asselbergs, *Conquered Conquistadors: The Lienzo de Quauhquechollan, a Nahua Vision of the Conquest of Guatemala* (Boulder: University Press of Colorado, 2008).

241. Bas van Doesburg, "The Lienzo of Tlapiltepec," in Brownstone, *Lienzo of Tlapiltepec*, 35–73, here 35.
242. Nicholas Johnson, "The Language of Lines on the Lienzo of Tlapiltepec," in Brownstone, *Lienzo of Tlapiltepec*, 95–149, here 132, also 99.
243. Johnson, "Language," 97–98.
244. Johnson, "Language," 132–133.
245. Johnson, "Language," 133.
246. Johnson, "Language," 134.
247. Johnson, "Language," 100.
248. van Doesburg, "The Lienzo," 71.
249. van Doesburg, "The Lienzo," 35
250. van Doesburg, "The Lienzo," 60.
251. van Doesburg, "The Lienzo," 62–63.
252. Bas van Doesburg, "El siglo XVI en los lienzos de Coixtlahuaca," *Journal de la Société des Américanistes* 89, no. 2 (2003): 67–96, 72.
253. van Doesburg, "El siglo XVI," 79–81.
254. van Doesburg, "El siglo XVI," 75–79.
255. Matthew Restall, "Black Conquistadors," *The Americas* 57, no. 2 (2000): 171–205.
256. AGI, Mexico 204, 1r.
257. Restall, "Black Conquistadors."
258. AGI, Mexico 98.
259. AGI, Mexico 102.
260. McNight and Garofalo, *Afro-Latino Voices*, 34–36; AGI, Quito 22, N.56, 5r.
261. AGI, Quito 9, R.3, N.21.
262. AGI, Quito 25, N.45, R.33.
263. Susan Verdi Webster, "El arte letrado: Andrés Sánchez Gallque," in *Andrés Sánchez Gallque y los primeros pintores en la Audiencia de Quito* (Quito: CCE, 2014), 23–97, here 38–47.
264. Olivares, "Politics of Communication," 76.
265. For instance, Liliana Pérez Miguel, *Inés Muñoz y las encomenderas en el Perú (s.XVI)* (Seville: Universidad de Sevilla, 2020).
266. AGI, Patronato 192, N.1, R.32.
267. See the edited volume *Cacicas: The Indigenous Women Leaders of Spanish America, 1492–1825*, ed. Margarita Ochoa and Sara Vicuña Guengerich (Norman: University of Okhlahoma Press, 2021), especially the essays by Bradley Benton, Karen B. Graubart, and Chantal Caillavet.
268. AHN-Madrid, Órdenes Militares—Caballeros de Santiago, Exp.4081.
269. AHN-Madrid, Órdenes Militares—Caballeros de Santiago, Exp.4081.
270. Ximena Medinaceli, "Paullu y Manco ¿una diarquía inca en tiempos de conquista?" *Bulletin de l'Institut français d'études andines* 36, no. 2 (2007): 241–258, here 242 and footnote 3. See also Jane E. Mangan, *Transatlantic Obligations: Creating the Bonds of Family in Conquest-Era Peru* (Oxford: Oxford University Press, 2015), 33–37.
271. In 1610, he wrote up his will, citing illness; see AHN-Madrid, Órdenes Militares—Caballeros de Santiago, Exp.4082.
272. Nicanor Domínguez Faura, "Betanzos y los Quipucamayos en la época de Vaca de Castro (Cuzco, 1543)," *Revista andina* 46 (2008): 155–192; Catherine Julien, "Polo de Ondegardo y el 'Discurso sobre la descendencia y gouierno de los ingas,'" *Histórica* 33, no. 2 (2009): 7–28; Nicanor Domínguez Faura, "El licenciado Polo: ¿ fuente del 'Discurso sobre la descendencia y govierno de los ingas'(ms. 1602/1603–1608)?" *Histórica* 34, no. 1 (2010): 131–144.
273. BNE, Mss./2010, 45r.
274. AGN-Mexico, Tierras 1735, Exp.2, Cuad.2, 422r.

275. *Colección de documentos sobre Coyoacán*, ed. Pedro Carrasco and Jesús Monjarás-Ruiz (Mexico: INAH, 1978), 2:139, 194.
276. *Documentos sobre Coyoacán*, 2:239–247. See also Gilda Cubillo Moreno, "Sucesión, herencia y conflicto en el linaje Istolinque," *Diario de Campo* 8 (2012): 8–14.
277. AGN-Mexico, Tierras, V.1735, Exp.2, Cuad.2, 272r.
278. AGN-Mexico, Tierras, V.1735, Exp.2, Cuad.2, 92r/364r.
279. Leibsohn, *Script and Glyph*, 8.
280. Vallen, *Being the Heart of the World.*

4. THE TRAPS OF DOUBT

1. AGI, Patronato 183, N.1, R.11. While don Cristóbal may well have been don Juan's son, it is also possible that this reference to Cristobal in the document is to a don Cristóbal Arias, *cacique* of Zinacantlán; see Amos Megged, "Accommodation and Resistance of Elites in Transition," *Hispanic American Historical Review* 71, no. 3 (1991): 477–500, 482.
2. AGI, Patronato 183, N.1, R.11.
3. Megged, "Accommodation," 495.
4. Dolores Arramoni Calderón, "Don Juan Atonal, Cacique de Chiapa," *Liminar: Estudios Sociales y Humanísticos* 2, no. 2 (2004): 131–142. Curiously, the High Court claimed in 1585 that it had investigated about two hundred unpaid tributes, also reported by elder Indigenous witnesses; however, they in no way implicated don Juan. See AGI, Guatemala 10, R.12, N.116, 3r-v.
5. Megged, "Accommodation," depicts don Juan as a master of the deal and the justice system; in the 1540s, he (or more likely his father) had mediated between freed Indigenous slaves and conquistadors. He had clashed with the Dominicans—they even publicly lashed him—but apparently he (or his son) had pacted with them by the 1580s; see 484 and AGI, Guatemala 110, N.34, 1r–5v.
6. Jonathan Israel, *Radical Enlightenment: Philosophy and the Making of Modernity 1650–1750* (Oxford: Oxford University Press, 2001), 6–7, 15–16, 45, 59. Many make a stop in radical 1600s England; see Melissa M. Caldwell, *Skepticism and Belief in Early Modern England: The Reformation of Moral Value* (London: Routledge, 2017), 9; Brendan Maurice Dooley, *The Social History of Skepticism: Experience and Doubt in Early Modern Culture* (Baltimore: Johns Hopkins University Press, 1999).
7. Paolo Prodi, "Europe in the Age of Reformations: The Modern State and Confessionalization," *Catholic Historical Review* 103, no. 1 (2017): 1–19; Peter Marshal, "Confessionalization, Confessionalism and Confusion in the English Reformation," in *Reforming Reformation*, ed. Thomas Mayer (Farnham: Ashgate, 2012), 43–64; Evan Haefeli, *Accidental Pluralism: America and the Religious Politics of English Expansion, 1497–1662* (Chicago: University of Chicago Press, 2021); Adrian Johns, *The Nature of the Book: Print and Knowledge in the Making* (Chicago: University of Chicago Press, 2000); Israel, *Radical Enlightenment.*
8. For dissenting views, see Mercedes García-Arenal, "Introduction," in *The Quest for Certainty in Early Modern Europe: From Inquisition to Inquiry, 1550–1700*, ed. Barbara Fuchs and Mercedes García-Arenal (Toronto: University of Toronto Press, 2020), 3–26, here 6; for a critique from the side of British history, see Alexandra Walsham, "The Reformation and 'The Disenchantment of the World' Reassessed," *Historical Journal* 51, no. 2 (2008): 497–528; see also the excellent Stefania Tutino, *Shadows of Doubt: Language and Truth in Post-Reformation Catholic Culture* (Oxford: Oxford University Press, 2014). For most scholars, skepticism is either an ancient Greek philosophical tradition or its late-modern descendant in the form of Protestantism, free thinking, atheism, or liberal or radical values in general (often, it is a combination of all these factors). Charles B. Schmitt seeks a reduced definition of skepticism as a tradition of philosophers who followed a specific clique of ancient Greeks; see Charles B. Schmitt, *Cicero*

Scepticus: A Study of the Influence of the Academica *in the Renaissance* (Berlin: Springer-Science, 1972), 6–7. Richard H. Popkin and many others have cast a wider net but still mainly trace a line from ancient Greece to 1400s Italy to 1500s France and finally to the fertile minds of the great British Protestant intellectuals; see Richard H. Popkin, *The History of Scepticism* (New York: Oxford University Press, 2003), 8. Adam Levine's edited volume on early modern skepticism almost entirely omits Spain and other areas of the world as well, save for a mention of the Inquisition as skepticism's enemy or of the Catholic kings' expulsion of Jews from the kingdom; *Early Modern Skepticism and the Origins of Toleration,* ed. Alan Levine (Lanham: Lexington, 1999), 70, 88, 228; see also Victoria Kahn, *Rhetoric, Prudence, and Skepticism in the Renaissance* (Ithaca: Cornell University Press, 1985).

9. Ángel Rama, *La ciudad letrada* (Hanover: Ediciones del Norte, 1984); Magdalena Chocano Mena, *La fortaleza docta* (Barcelona: Bellaterra, 2000); Walter Mignolo, *Desobediencia epistémica* (Buenos Aires: Signo, 2010), 79; José Santos-Herceg, *Conflicto de representaciones* (Mexico: FCE, 2010), 48.

10. Carmen Bernand and Serge Gruzinski, *Historia del nuevo mundo: Del descubrimiento a la conquista, la experiencia europea, 1492–1550* (Mexico: Fondo de cultura económica, 1996), 348. The "idols behind altars" thesis often repeats this view.

11. Maureen Ihrie, *Skepticism in Cervantes* (London: Tamesis Books, 1982), 14.

12. Aryeh Botwinick, *Skepticism* (Philadelphia: Temple University Press, 2010); Henrik Lagerlund, ed., *Rethinking the History of Skepticism: The Missing Medieval Background.* (Leiden: Brill, 2010). For medieval European philosophy, see Gyula Klima, ed., *Intentionality, Cognition, and Mental Representation in Medieval Philosophy* (New York: Fordham University Press, 2015); Han Thomas Adriaenssen, *Representation and Scepticism from Aquinas to Descartes* (Cambridge: Cambridge University Press, 2017).

13. For one of many such statements, see the useful Diego Machuca, "Introduction: Medieval and Renaissance Skepticism," in *Skepticism from Antiquity to the Present,* ed. Diego E. Machuca and Baron Reed (London: Bloomsbury, 2018), 165–175, here 168.

14. For medieval Europe and Muslim Arab thought see Lagerlund, ed., *Rethinking.* For Arab and Persian influences on Europe, see Fatemeh Chehregosha Azinfar, *Atheism in the Medieval Islamic and European World* (Maryland: Ibex, 2008). For vernacular skepticism in Italy, see Dooley, *Social History of Skepticism*; Edward Muir, *The Culture Wars of the Late Renaissance* (Cambridge: Harvard University Press, 2007).

15. Ihrie, *Cervantes*; Barbara Fuchs, *Knowing Fictions: Picaresque Reading in the Early Modern Hispanic World* (Philadelphia: University of Pennsylvania Press, 2021); Francisco Sanches, *That Nothing Is Known,* ed. Elaine Limbrick and Douglas F. S. Thomson (Cambridge: Cambridge University Press, 1988); María Asunción Sánchez Manzano, *El escepticismo humanista de Francisco Sánchez* (Madrid: Dykinson, 2018); Lorenzo Casini, "Self-Knowledge, Sceptisim, and the Quest for a New Method," in *Renaissance Scepticisms,* ed. Gianni Paganini and José R. M. Neto (Dordrecht: Springer, 2009), 33–60; John Christian Laursen, "Pedro de Valencia's Academica and Scepticism in Late Renaissance Spain," in Paganini and Neto, *Renaissance Scepticisms,* 111–124.

16. García-Arenal, "Introduction," 5, 10.

17. For the concept of judicial skepticism, see Brian P. Levack, *Witch-Hunting in Scotland* (New York: Routledge, 2007). The historiography on religious skeptics before the Spanish Inquisition is extensive; see for example, Stuart B. Schwartz, *All Can Be Saved: Religious Tolerance and Salvation in the Iberian Atlantic World* (New Haven: Yale University Press, 2008); Carlo Ginzburg, *The Cheese and the Worms: The Cosmos of a Sixteenth-Century Miller* (Baltimore: Johns Hopkins University Press, 1992). Very few have seen in the world of paperwork justice a culture of skepticism. For exceptions relating to the Inquisition, see Gustav Henningsen, *The Witches' Advocate: Basque Witchcraft and the Spanish Inquisition, 1609–1614* (Reno: University of

Nevada Press, 1980); Constanza Cavallero, "¿Brujas satánicas o príncipes pecadores? Fundamentos 'políticos' del escepticismo demonológico en la temprana modernidad," *Cuadernos de Historia Moderna* 41, no. 1 (2016): 89–107; María Luz López-Terrada, "Conflicting Certainties or Different Truths?" in Fuchs and García-Arenal, *Quest for Certainty,* 80–104; Paul Michael Johnson, "Feeling Certainty, Performing Sincerity," in Fuchs and García-Arenal, *Quest for Certainty,* 50–79; Lu Ann Homza, *Village Infernos and Witches' Advocates: Witch-Hunting in Navarre, 1608–1614* (University Park: Pennsylvania State University Press, 2022); Moshe Sluhovsky, *Believe Not Every Spirit* (Chicago: University of Chicago Press, 2007), esp. 93, 185; James Amelang, "Between Doubt and Discretion," in *Making, Using and Resisting the Law in European History,* ed. Günther Lottes, Eero Medijainen, and Jón Viðar Sigurðsson (Pisa: Ediplus, 2008), 77–92. For the most important reflection on doubt in Spanish New World administrative circles, see Arndt Brendecke, *The Empirical Empire: Spanish Colonial Rule and the Politics of Knowledge* (Berlin: Walter de Gruyter, 2016).

18. Caldwell, *Skepticism and Belief,* 9–14.
19. Leticia Mayer Celis, *Rutas de incertidumbre* (Mexico: FCE, 2015), 11.
20. Mayer Celis, *Incertidumbre*; José Luis Egío, *El siglo de la experiencia* (Madrid: Dykinson, 2023); Víctor Tau Anzoátegui, *Casuismo y sistema* (Madrid: Carlos III University, 2021). For an overview of probabilism without much attention to the Indies context, see Stefania Tutino, *Uncertainty in Post-Reformation Catholicism* (Oxford: Oxford University Press, 2018). For Sor Juana, see Manuel Vargas, "If Aristotle Had Cooked," *Journal of Mexican Philosophy* 1, no. 1 (2022): 13–38. See also Danilo Marcondes, "The Anthropological Argument: The Rediscovery of Ancient Skepticism in Modern Thought," in *Skepticism in the Modern Age,* ed. José R. Maia Neto, Gianni Paganini, and John Christian Laursen (Leiden: Brill, 2009), 37–54.
21. Brendecke, *Empirical Empire,* 282.
22. Brendecke, *Empirical Empire,* here 284; see 282–285.
23. Brendecke, *Empirical Empire,* 4.
24. For the *pícaro* culture, see Barbara Fuchs, *Passing for Spain: Cervantes and the Fiction of Identity* (Champaign: University of Illinois Press, 2003); Fuchs, *Knowing Fictions*; Jeremy Robbins, *The Challenges of Uncertainty* (Lanham: Rowman & Littlefield, 1998).
25. AGI, Escribanía 1009A, N.4, 228r.
26. AGI, Escribanía 1009A, N.4, 228r.
27. AGI, Indiferente 857, n/f.
28. AGI, Patronato 90B, N.1, R.50. He is almost certainly Domingo de San Martín.
29. Joaquín García Icazbalceta, *Cartas de religiosos de Nueva España,* ed. Joaquín García Icazbalceta (Mexico: Antigua Librería Andrade y Morales, 1886), 120.
30. Consuelo Varela, "La villa imperial de Potosí," in *La ciudad americana,* ed. Salvador Bernabéu Albert and Consuelo Varela Bueno (Aranjuez: Doce Calles, 2010), 133–148, here 134.
31. JCB, Ms. Spanish Codex 2, Book IV, Chap.IX, 64v. Bartolomé Arzáns de Orsúa y Vela.
32. JCB, Ms. Spanish Codex 2, Book IV, Chap.IX, 64v. Bartolomé Arzáns de Orsúa y Vela.
33. BNE, Mss/19387, 17r.
34. BNE, Mss/19387, 17v–18r.
35. BNE, Mss/19387, 20v.
36. AHN-Madrid, Inquisicion 1332. A broadside and the report of Gaspar de Valdespina was transcribed and pubished by Antonio Rodríguez Moñino, "Pedro Mexía de Ovando cronista de linajes coloniales: andanzas inquisitoriales de La Ovandina (1621–1626)," *Tierra Firme* 3–4 (1937): 413–437.
37. Rodríguez Moñino, "Pedro Mexía de Ovando," 417.
38. Censura de Fr. Antonio de Peñaranda, Lima, March 6, 1622. AHN-Madrid, Inquisición 1332.

39. Censura de Gaspar de Valdespina, Lima, April 20, 1622. AHN-Madrid, Inquisicion 1332, Reproduced in Rodíguez Moñino, "Pedro Mexía de Ovando," 431–447.
40. Reporte Fray Varrasa y Fray Verdugo, Madrid, September 28, 1623, AHN, Inquisicion 1332, L.5, N.40.
41. BNE, Mss/3183. For a description of this manuscript, see M., Serrano y Sanz, "Un discípulo de Fr. Bartolomé de las Casas, Don Pedro de Mexía de Ovando," *Archivo de Investigaciones Históricas* 1 (1911): 195–212.
42. We use Eraso's preferred pronoun in this story, namely *she.*
43. Catalina de Erauso, *Historia de la Monja Alférez,* ed. Ángel Esteban (Madrid: Cátedra, 2002), 160.
44. Erauso, *Historia,* 169.
45. Ángel Esteban, "Introducción," in Erauso, *Historia,* 9–90, here 9–24.
46. Karen M. Powers, "Resilient Lords and Indian Vagabonds: Wealth, Migration, and the Reproductive Transformation of Quito's Chiefdoms, 1500–1700," *Ethnohistory* 38, no. 3 (1991): 225–249, here 226.
47. José Augusto Gamboa Mendoza, *El cacicazgo muisca en los años posteriores a la Conquista: Del* sihipkua *al cacique colonial* (1537–1575) (Bogotá: Instituto Colombiano de Antropología e Historia, 2010), 560; AGN-Colombia, Encomiendas 30, 287–364 and 1023–1024.
48. Gamboa Mendoza, *Cacicazgo muisca,* 381, 560.
49. Powers, "Resilient Lords," 226.
50. Juan Manuel Pérez Zevallos, "Movimientos de población indígena en Nueva España (siglo xvi)," *Boletín de Antropología Americana* 30 (1994): 169–183, here 172; Jorge Chapa, "The Creation of Wage Labor in a Colonial Society," *Berkeley Journal of Sociology* 23 (1978): 99–128, 106–108.
51. Karen Vieira Powers, "The Battle for Bodies and Souls in the Colonial North Andes," *Hispanic American Historical Review* 75, no. 1 (1995): 31–56, 31; Powers, "Resilient Lords," 228.
52. Powers, "Resilient Lords," 229–233.
53. Powers, "Resilient Lords," 246.
54. AGI, Indiferente 738, N.242, n/f; see also the excellent José Carlos de la Puente Luna, *Andean Cosmopolitans* (Austin: University of Texas Press, 2018).
55. Inca Garcilaso de la Vega, *Historia general* (Cordoba: Viuda de Andrés Barrera, 1616), 186r.
56. BNE, Mss/18109, 3v.
57. BNE, Mss/18109, 11v.
58. AGI, Patronato 50, R.1.
59. This order would appear in many high court ordinances by 1528; for one instance, see AGI, Panama 234, L.3, 127v–128v; see also Gabriel de Monterroso y Alvarado, *Práctica civil, criminal, e instrucción de escribanos* (No press, 1566 [1563]), 16. For more, see Renzo Honores, "Los caciques y las pruebas," in *XI Jornadas Interescuelas/Departamentos de Historia* (Tucumán: Universidad de Tucumán, 2007), no pages.
60. See, for instance, Vitus Huber, *Beute und Conquista* (Frankfurt: Campus, 2020), 322–325, 338; M. Carolina Jurado, "'Descendientes de los primeros': Las probanzas de méritos y servicios y la genealogía cacical," *Revista de Indias* 74, no. 261 (2014): 387–422, here 405.
61. AGI, Patronato 171, N.1, R.13.
62. AGI, Santa Fe 16, R.23, N.93, July 25, 1579.
63. J. A. Alejandre García, "Del delito de falsedad testimonial en el derecho histórico español," *Historia, Instituciones, Documentos* 3 (1976): 9–139, especially 97–107.
64. *Leyes de Toro* (Seville: Casa de Dominico de Robertis, 1552 [1505]), no pages.
65. García, "Del delito," 112–117.
66. AGI, Santo Domingo 868, L.1, 118v, March 3, 1538.
67. AGI, Lima 566, L.5, 207v–208r.

68. AGI, Indiferente 426, L.25, 93v–94v.
69. AGI, Panama 234, L.3, 150v–150r.
70. AGI, Mexico 217, N.14.
71. Monterroso y Alvarado, *Práctica civil.*
72. Sebastián de Covarrubias Orozco, *Tesoro de la lengua castellana* (Madrid: Luis Sánchez, 1611), 37.
73. Monterroso y Alvarado, *Práctica civil,* 12r–19r.
74. AGI, Mexico 367, 1560, "E visto tanta çeguedad," December 31, 1559, 10r–19v. See also AGI, Patronato 184, R.2, 12v; Huber, *Beute,* 12.
75. AGI, Patronato 171, N.1, R.20.
76. AGI, Santo Domingo 899, L.1, 285r-v.
77. AGI, Patronato 180, R.59, 930v–931v.
78. AGI, Mexico 287, "El hábito de mi padre."
79. AGI, Lima 313, "Ihuxpo Nro s.or."
80. AGI, Guatemala 10, R.8, N.83.
81. AGI, Indiferente 857, "Primeramente que tubo."
82. AGI, Indiferente 1400, "Francisco Velázquez."
83. AGI, Mexico 99, "La presente," 1572.
84. Monterroso y Alvarado, *Práctica civil,* 246r.
85. AGN- Mexico, Inquisición 130, 6r.
86. AGN- Mexico, Inquisición 130, 7r–11r.
87. AGN- Mexico, Inquisición 130, 14r.
88. AGN- Mexico, Inquisición 130, 14r.
89. AGN- Mexico, Inquisición 130, 7r.
90. *Kaqchikel Chronicles: The Definitive Edition,* trans. and commentary by Judith M. Maxwell and Robert M. Hill II (Austin: University of Texas, 2006), 421–431.
91. Bartolomé Álvarez, *De las costumbres y conversión de los indios del Perú: Memorial a Felipe II* (1588) (Madrid: Polifemo, 1998), 30–31.
92. Juan Bautista Carpio Dueñas, "Escándalos, alborotos, bandos y parcialidades," in *Estudios en homenaje al profesor Emilio Cabrera* (Córdoba: Universidad de Extremadura, 2015), 79. See also Marie Claude Gerbet, *La noblesse dans le royaume de Castille* (Paris: Publications de la Sorbonne, 1979), 440–444; Lucien Clare and Jacques Heers, eds., *Bandos y querellas dinásticas en España al final de la Edad Media* (Champigny-sur-Marne: Biblioteca Española de Paris, 1991). For a bibliographical list of materials on *bandos* in Castile, see José Ignacio Ortega Cervigón, "Lazos clientelares y bandos nobiliarios conquenses durante el siglo XV," *Espacio tiempo y forma: Serie III, historia medieval* 19 (2006): 211–231, notes 1 and 2.
93. Ortega Cervigón, "Lazos clientelares," 213.
94. Paulino Iradiel, "Formas del poder y de organización de la sociedad," in *Estructuras y formas del poder en la historia,* ed. Reyna Pastor, Ian Kieniewicz, and Eduardo García de Enterría (Salamanca: Universidad de Salamanca, 1991), 23–50, here 42–43. Gerbet, *La noblesse,* shows the same on 440–443.
95. AGI, Patronato 174, R.8, 46v.
96. ARAH, Colección Muñoz A-115, no. 1525, "En casi todas."
97. AGI, Patronato 171, N.1, R.11.
98. AGI, Mexico 343, "Por otra tengo escripto," April 8, 1553.
99. BNF, Espagnol 325, "Algunos días ha," January 1, 1562, 282v.
100. "Libro de la visita general del Virrey don Francisco de Toledo, 1570–1575," *Revista Histórica* 7, no. 2 (1924): 120–123.
101. AHN-Madrid, Inquisición 1032, 40–42v
102. AHN-Madrid, Inquisición 1034, 384r.

103. Gabriela Ramos, "Política eclesiástica y extirpación de idolatrías: discurso y silencios en torno al Taqui Onqoy," *Revista Andina* 10 (1992): 147–169.
104. Antonio Acosta Rodríguez, "El pleito de los indios de San Damián (Huarochiri) contra Francisco de Avila, 1607," *Historiografía y Bibliografía Americanistas* 23 (1979): 3–33; Juan Carlos García, "El juicio contra Francisco de Ávila y el inicio de la extirpación de la idolatría en el Perú," in *Los Indios, el derecho canónico y la justicia eclesiástica en la América virreinal,* ed. Ana de Zaballa Beascoechea (Iberoamericana-Vervuert: Madrid-Frankfurt am Main, 2011), 153–176.
105. "No lo lleves por los términos de Castilla, porque los ánimos de los hombres son acá tan altivos y están hechos a tanta igualdad que no sufrirán otra cosa," in *Libro intitulado Coloquios de la verdad: trata de las causas e inconvenientes que impiden la doctrina e conversión de los indios de los reinos del Pirú [sic], y de los daños, e males, e agravios que padecen,* ed. Pedro de Quiroga (Sevilla: Zarzuela, 1922), 52.
106. "Mira como andas y lo que hablas, . . . y estan colgados los hombres de tu boca, que te contaran las palabras exponiendo luego el entendimiento dellas," Quiroga, *Coloquios de la verdad,* 53.
107. "Ni tengas enemigo por pequeño que sea, porque en esta tierra un mosquito inquieta al hombre mas poderoso della. Vela sobre ti, que desde el dia que metiste el pie en la tierra donde estas andas cercado de enemigos visibles y invisibles," Quiroga, *Coloquios de la verdad,* 53.
108. Kathryn Burns, *Into the Archive: Writing and Power in Colonial Peru* (Durham: Duke University Press, 2010).
109. Burns, *Archive,* 45.
110. AGI, Mexico 1843, "Don Antonyo," 270r, read by the council April 1, 1585.
111. AGI, Patronato 184, R.7, 5v.
112. Yanna Yannakakis, *The Art of Being In-Between* (Durham: Duke University Press, 2008), 18; Mark Lentz, "Los intérpretes generales de Yucatán," *Estudios de Cultura Maya* 33 (2009): 135–158, here 141; Icíar Alonso, Jesús Baigorri, and Gertrudis Payàs, "Nauhuatlatos y familias de intérpretes en el México colonial," *1611—Revista de Historia de la Traducción* 2 (2008): 1–12; Javier Malagón-Barceló, "The Role of the Letrado in the Colonization of America," *The Americas* 18, no. 1 (1961): 1–17.
113. AGI, Indiferente 419, L.6, 592r; AGI, Indiferente 420, L.8, 316v–317r; AGI, Indiferente 416, L.3, 24v.
114. AGI, Lima 108, "Muy poderoso señor," April 4, 1580.
115. AGI, Lima 121, "Vra voluntad," December 1567; AGI, Lima 122, "En estos rreynos," January 1, 1568. See also BNF, Espagnol 325, 258r; BNF, Espagnol 325, "Memoria para el señor contador," 267r.
116. AGI, Mexico 1091, L.10, 57r, 1582.
117. BNM, Mss/3035, 11v.
118. AGI, Lima 121, "Vra voluntad."
119. KB: GKS 2232 40, Don Felipe Guaman Poma de Ayala, *Nueva corónica y buen gobierno,* 307r/309r.
120. Miguel de Cervantes, *History of the Valorous and Witty Knight-Errant,* vol. 1, trans. Thomas Shelton (London: no publisher, 1725), book 2, chapter III, 74.
121. Cervantes, *Knight-Errant,* book III, 225.
122. Bernal Díaz del Castillo, *Historia verdadera de la conquista de la Nueva España,* ed. José Antonio Barbón Rodríguez (Mexico: UNAM, 2005), 725.
123. James Lockhart and Enrique Otte, eds., *Letters and People of the Spanish Indies: Sixteenth Century* (Cambridge: Cambridge University Press, 1976), 175; AHN-Madrid, Diversos-Colecciones 22, N.43.
124. AGI, Escribanía, 1007B, 372r–373v; AGI, Escribanía 1006B, 246r–247v.
125. AGI, Patronato 194, R.45; AGI, Escribanía 1007B, xxxiir–xxxviiir.
126. AGI, Justicia 1162, N.7, R.1; AGI, Patronato 294, N.4, 18v.
127. Real Biblioteca de San Lorenzo del Escorial (BSLE), &-II-7, 459v.

128. AGI, Patronato 170, R.47, 3r.
129. Díaz, *Historia verdadera*, 758.
130. BNM, Mss/10509, 11v.
131. BNE, Mss/10509, 15r–16r.
132. BL, AM-33983, 69v.
133. BNE, Mss.3035, 19r–37v.
134. IVDJ, Colección Altamira, E.23, Caja 36–373.
135. HSA, 7-II-30.
136. IVDJ, Colección Altamira, E.23, C.36-294. See also IVDJ, Colección Altamira, E.23, C.36-296. Two days later, the president again reported on these "most dangerous" vassals, to which the secretary recommended that he "inform yourself very particularly and extrajudicially about what might be, and which leagues [*legas*] and illicit alliances [*monopodios*] and other bad things are afoot here," in IVDJ, Colección Altamira, E.23, C.36-297.
137. BFZ, Colección Altamira, E.170-1, 6r-v.
138. BL, MA-28349, 141v.
139. HSA, 7-II-30.
140. Ernesto Schäfer, *El Consejo Real y Supremo de las Indias* (Madrid: Marcial Pons Historia, 2003), 1:337.
141. Eufemio Lorenzo Sanz, "Los indios de Nueva España y su pugna con las pretensiones encomenderas," in *Estudios sobre política indigenista española en América* (Valladolid: Universidad de Valladolid, 1976), 2:6–13.
142. AGI, Indiferente 1624, 42r–65r.
143. Arndt Brendecke, *Imperio e información: Funciones del saber en el dominio colonial español* (Frankfurt: Iberoamericana, 2012), 259.
144. AGI, Santa Fe 83, N.14.
145. AGI, Guadalajara 31, N.9.
146. AGI, Mexico 287, "El hábito de mi padre." See also AGI, Mexico 364, 303r.
147. AGI, Mexico 287, "El hábito de mi padre."
148. Brendecke, *Imperio e información*, 482–483.
149. AGI, Indiferente 857, "Aunq muchas vezes."
150. AGI, Patronato 171, N.1, R.11.
151. BNF, Espagnol 325, 261r.
152. AGI, Guadalajara 5, R.13, N.23, 181v.
153. AGI, Guadalajara 5, R.13, N.23, 181v.
154. AGI, Mexico 287, "El hábito de mi padre."
155. AGI, Patronato, 184, R.12.
156. AGI, Indiferente 738, N.40, 3r.
157. AGI, Patronato 170, R.26.
158. AGI, Lima 120, "Príncipe el más alto"; AGI, Indiferente 1624, R.5, N.6, 839r-v, "Bien sé que es."
159. AGI, Santa Fe 234, "La causa."
160. AGI, Charcas 16, R.22, N.97.
161. AGI, Patronato 171, N.2, R.1.
162. AGI, Patronato 171, N.2, R.1.
163. AGI, Mexico 287, "Como sea verdad."
164. AHN-Madrid, Diversos-Colecciones 25, N.57, 1r.
165. AGI, Mexico 107, "La experiençia cierta." See also AGI, Lima 121, 51r.
166. AGI, Mexico 257, "Con un navío," February 10, 1590.
167. AGI, Indiferente 1584, "Relación que se da."
168. AGI, Filipinas 82, N.2, "La gracia y consolación," no date, ca. 1572.

169. AGI, Lima 270, "Todos los vasallos," 1574.
170. AHN-Madrid, Diversos-Colecciones 25, N.4.
171. AGI, Indiferente 738, N.40.
172. AHN-Madrid, Diversos-Colecciones 24, N.64.
173. AGI, Patronato 193, R.9, 116r.
174. Gonzalo Fernández de Oviedo, *General y natural hystoria,* formally printed as the *Corónica de las Indias* (Salamanca: Casa de Juan de Junta, 1547), 3r.
175. AGI, Indiferente 738, N.40, 3r.
176. AGI, Indiferente 2987, "Nro. Señor sea."
177. AHN-Madrid, Diversos-Colecciones 24, N.69, 1r.
178. AGI, Santa Fe 226, April 18, 1580.
179. AGI, Mexico 282, "Post quam."
180. AGI, Charcas 16, R.8, N.40.
181. AGI, Charcas 16, R.15, N.52; see also Charcas 16, R. 15, N.52, 8v; Charcas 16, R.16, N.65.
182. AGI, Patronato 183, N.2, R.7.
183. AGI, Patronato 181, R.31, 1052v.
184. AGI, Patronato 231, N.6, R.5, 3r.
185. AGI, Mexico 284, "Gratia." For similar comments, AGI, Patronato 184, R.35, "Lo sucedido."
186. AGI, Santa Fe 86, N.55, 685r.
187. AGI, Patronato 180, R.59; see also AGI, Mexico 285, "Pues."
188. AGI, Mexico 168, N.56, 172r. See also AGI, Indiferente, 1088, L.12, 314r; AGI, Indiferente 1088, L.12; AGI, Indiferente, 738, N.40; AGI, Quito 9, R.1, N.3; AGI, Lima 134, "Los días pasados."
189. AGI, Patronato 171, N.2, R.5.
190. Geoffrey Parker, *Imprudent King: A New Life of Philip II* (New Haven: Yale University Press, 2014), 61.
191. AGI, Guatemala 168.
192. AGI, Mexico 367, 10r.
193. AGI, Santa Fe 226, N.48bis.
194. AGI, Patronato 171, N.1, R.11.
195. AGI, Chile 64, "Por escrevir."
196. For the broader social and curricular worlds of rhetoric, see Stuart McManus, *Empire of Eloquence* (Cambridge: Cambridge University Press, 2021).
197. AHN-Madrid, Diversos-Colecciones 43, N.11, 1r-v.
198. AGI, Mexico 110, "Grande fue."
199. AGI, Santa Fe 83, N.9, 170r.
200. AGI, Patronato 172, R.6.
201. AGI, Santa Fe 233, 1571.
202. AGI, Lima 313, "Uno de los mayores."
203. AGI, Indiferente 1093, "En las Cartas."
204. AGI, Mexico 110, "Grande fue."
205. AGI, Filipinas 18B, R.7, N.70.
206. AGI, Santo Domingo 99, R.18, N.157.
207. AGI, Patronato 171, N.1, R.11.
208. AGI, Patronato 192, N.1, R.19, 8r.
209. AGI, Patronato 192, N.1, R.19, 9v.
210. AHN-Madrid, Diversos-Colecciones 23, N.55, 2r.
211. AHN-Madrid, Diversos-Colecciones 23, N.55, 2r.
212. AGI, Santa Fe 188, "Aunq despues," July 31, 1566.
213. AGI, Indiferente 1093, "Aunque muchas veces."

214. AGI, Charcas 16, R.1, N.1.
215. AGI, Lima 29, 14r.
216. AGI, Lima 29, 22v.
217. AGI, Guatemala 9A, R.20, N.83.
218. AGI, Guatemala 9A, R.18, N.77.
219. AGI, Guatemala 9A, R.18, N.77.
220. AGI, Patronato 174, R.8, 42v.
221. AGI, Mexico 367, 10v–11r.
222. BNE, Mss/3042, 250v.
223. AGI, Indiferente 857, "Memorial de su ex.a," undated.
224. AGI, Justicia 227, N.7, R.3, 15r.
225. AGI, Justicia 227, N.7, R.3, 15r.
226. AGI, Justicia 227, N.7, R.3, 14r.
227. AGI, Justicia 227, N.7, R.3, 17v-18v.
228. See also AGN-Mexico, Hospital de Jesús 293.3, Exp.139; AGN, Hospital de Jesús L.289, Exp.2, 290r, 835r-837v.
229. *Erasmus of Rotterdam: The Education of a Christian Prince*, ed. Lisa Jardine (Cambridge: Cambridge University Press, 2003), 92.
230. *Erasmus*, 28.
231. *Erasmus*, 13.
232. *Erasmus*, 57.
233. *Erasmus*, 57.
234. *Erasmus*, 100.
235. *Erasmus*, 25, 92.
236. *Erasmus*, 28, 50.
237. F. Furió Ceriol, *El consejo, i consejeros del principe* (Anvers: Viuda de Martín Nuncio, 1559), prologue, n/p.
238. Ceriol, *Consejo*, 35r–43v.
239. Miguel Saralegui, "El idealismo político de Martín Carvallo de Villas Boas," *Revista de Estudios Políticos* 168 (2015): 51–76.
240. Martin Carvallo Villas Boas, *Espeio de principes y ministros* (Milan: Pacifico da Ponte, 1598).
241. Carvallo Villas Boas, *Espeio*, 245.
242. Carvallo Villas Boas, *Espeio*, 16.
243. Carvallo Villas Boas, *Espeio*, 238.
244. Carvallo Villas Boas, *Espeio*, 237.
245. Carvallo Villas Boas, *Espeio*, 193–194.
246. Carvallo Villas Boas, *Espeio*, 30.
247. Carvallo Villas Boas, *Espeio*, 16, 30.
248. Carvallo Villas Boas, *Espeio*, 250.
249. Carvallo Villas Boas, *Espeio*, 238.
250. Carvallo Villas Boas, *Espeio*, 249.
251. Pedro de Navarra, *Dialogos della differencia del hablar al escrevir* (Tolosa: Jacobo Colomerio), 7v.
252. Miguel de Cervantes, *El ingenioso hidalgo don Quixote de la Mancha*, part 2, vol. 3 (Madrid: Joaquín Ibarra, 1780), 63–64; Brendecke, *Imperio e información*, 154.
253. Pedro de Ribadeneyra, *Tratado de la religion y virtudes que deue tener el principe christiano* (Madrid: P. Madrigal, 1593), 397.
254. Ribadeneyra, *Tratado*, 510.
255. Juan de Santa María, *Tratado de y policía christiana* (Barcelona: Sebastián de Cormellas, 1616), 45r.

256. Santa María, *Tratado,* 85v.

257. BNM, Mss/10861, 157r-v.

258. BNM, Mss/10861, 161r.

259. BNM, Mss/10861, 161r.

260. Brendecke, *Empirical Empire,* 62–65.

261. Tau Anzoátegui, *Casuismo y sistema*; John Leddy Phelan, "Authority and Flexibility in the Spanish Imperial Bureaucracy," *Administrative Science Quarterly* 5, no. 1 (1960): 47–65.

262. Brendecke, *Empirical Empire,* 66.

263. LOC, Kraus Collection Doc.05500.

264. AGI, Mexico 1064, L.3, 2v.

265. BNE, Mss/19521.

266. *Prima Secundae Parties Summae* (London: Philippi Tinghi Florentini, 1577); José Luis Egío, "The Global Origins of Probabilism," *Studia Histórica, Historia Moderna* 44, no. 1 (2022) 115–151, here 117.

267. Egío, *El siglo,* 50–66; Mayer Celis, *Incertidumbre,* 11.

268. José Luis Egío, "La Escuela de Salamanca en perspectiva iberoamericana," *Nuevas de Indias* 8 (2023): 185–217, 203–210.

269. Tomás de Mercado, *Tratos y contratos de mercaderes discididos y determinados* (Salamanca: Mathias Gast, 1569), 2r.

270. See, for instance, Tau Anzoátegui, *Casuismo y sistema,* 58; Carlos Garriga, "Gobierno y justicia: El gobierno de la justicia," in *La jurisdicción contencioso-administrativa en España: Una historia de sus orígenes,* ed. Manuel Lorente (Madrid: Consejo General del Poder Judicial, 2009), 47–113, here 67.

271. Leticia Mayer Celis, "La corriente moral del probabilismo y su influencia en la génesis de las ideas científicas de probabilidad," *Estatística e Sociedade* 1 (2011): 67–85, here 65–68; Rudolf Schuessler, *The Debate on Probable Opinions in the Scholastic Tradition* (Leiden: Brill, 2019), 17.

272. Adrian Masters, *We, the King: Creating Royal Legislation in the Sixteenth-Century Spanish New World* (New York: Cambridge University Press, 2023), 185.

273. These included improved *gracia* archives; see, for instance, AGI, Indiferente, 528, L.1.

274. Masters, *We the King,* 196–211.

275. García Icazbalceta, *Cartas de religiosos,* 123.

276. Among many others, see Richard E. Boyer, *Lives of the Bigamists* (Albuquerque: University of New Mexico Press, 1995); Richard E. Boyer, *False Mystics: Deviant Orthodoxy in Colonial Mexico* (Lincoln: University of Nebraska Press, 2004).

277. KB, GKS 2232 4º: Guaman Poma, *Nueva corónica y buen gobierno* (1615), 766, 780, 786.

278. Guaman Poma, *Nueva corónica* 457, 755.

279. Guaman Poma, *Nueva corónica,* 546.

280. AGI, Patronato 183, N.1, R.11.

281. Álvarez, *De las costumbres,* 280.

282. AGI, Indiferente 857, n/f.

5. THE CONQUEST OF ARCHIVES

1. See among others AGI, Escribanía 822A–826C; Santa Fe 56A, N.5, N.11-N.12; and Santa Fe 16, among others in Patronato, Indiferente, and Santa Fe; AGN-Colombia, esp. Caciques e Indios, 61 and Encomiendas, 21. For studies on Torres that markedly differ from ours, see Santiago Muñoz-Arbelaez, *The New Kingdom of Granada: The Making and Unmaking of Spain's Atlantic Empire* (Durham: Duke University Press, 2025), chaps. 4–5; Joanne Rappaport, *The Disappearing Mestizo: Configuring Difference in the Colonial New Kingdom of Granada* (Durham: Duke University Press, 2020); Max Deardorff, *A Tale of Two Granadas: Custom, Community, and Citizenship*

in the Spanish Empire, 1568–1668 (Cambridge: Cambridge University Press, 2023); Ulises Rojas, *El cacique de Turmequé y su época* (Boyacá: Imprenta Departamental 1965).

2. Rojas, *El cacique de Turmequé,* 107–108.
3. Lane, ed., *Defending the Conquest: Bernardo de Vargas Machuca's Defense and Discourse of the Western Conquests* (Penn State Press, 2010).
4. Juan Fernando Cobo Betancourt, *The Coming of the Kingdom: The Muisca, Catholic Reform, and Spanish Colonialism in the New Kingdom of Granada* (Cambridge: Cambridge University Press, 2024).
5. Jorge Augusto Gamboa Mendoza, *El cacicazgo muisca en los años posteriores a la Conquista: del Psihipqua al cacique colonial, 1537–1575* (Bogotá: ICANH, 2017), 587–593.
6. Rojas, *El cacique de Turmequé,* 24–26.
7. AGI, Santa Fe 85; AGI, Indiferente 426, L.26, 143r.
8. Adrian Masters, *We, the King: Creating Royal Legislation in the Sixteenth-Century Spanish New World* (New York: Cambridge University Press, 2023).
9. Rojas, *El cacique de Turmequé,* 42–43.
10. For the lord of Tonina, in Rojas, *El cacique de Turmequé,* 106–107; see also 91–92.
11. AGI, Escribanía 824A (Rojas, *El cacique de Turmequé,* 51–52).
12. Rojas, *El cacique de Turmequé,* 117–143. For the increasing surveillance of *genízaros,* see 246–251.
13. Rojas, *El cacique de Turmequé,* 145–197.
14. Rojas, *El cacique de Turmequé,* 171–181.
15. Rojas, *El cacique de Turmequé,* 217–218.
16. See the unstudied AGI, Santa Fe 56A, N.11-N12.
17. Rojas, *El cacique de Turmequé,* 496–499.
18. Rojas, *El cacique de Turmequé,* 501–514.
19. Rojas, *El cacique de Turmequé,* 484–487.
20. María Elena Martínez, *Genealogical Fictions: Limpieza de Sangre, Religion, and Gender in Colonial Mexico* (Stanford: Stanford University Press, 2008).
21. Joanne Rappaport. *The Politics of Memory: Native Historical Interpretation in the Colombian Andes* (Cambridge: Cambridge University Press, 1990).
22. Bolívar Echeverría, *La modernidad de lo barroco* (Mexico: Unám, 1998), 35–45, 62–69; Ángel Rama, *The Lettered City,* trans. John Charles Chasteen (Durham: Duke University Press, 1996), 10–12.
23. Ann Laura Stoler, *Along the Archival Grain: Epistemic Anxieties and Colonial Common Sense* (Princeton: Princeton University Press, 2008).
24. Leslie M. Harris and Daina Ramey Berry, "Introduction to Researching Nineteenth-Century African American History," *Journal of the Civil War Era* 12, no. 4 (2022): 429–447. They respond to the scholarship of Michel-Rolph Trouillot, *Silencing the Past: Power and the Production of History* (Boston: Beacon, 1995); Marisa Fuentes, *Dispossessed Lives: Enslaved Women, Violence, and the Archive* (Philadelphia: University of Pennsylvania Press, 2016); and Saidiya Hartman, "Venus in Two Acts," *Small Axe* 26, no. 12 (2008) 2: 1–14.
25. Martínez, *Genealogical Fictions.*
26. Arndt Brendecke, *The Empirical Empire: Spanish Colonial Rule and the Politics of Knowledge* (Berlin: De Gruyter, 2016).
27. Blair Ann, Paul Duguid, Anja-Silvia Goeing, and Anthony Grafton, eds., *Information: A Historical Companion* (Princeton: Princeton University Press, 2021); Nicholas Popper, *The Specter of the Archive: Political Practice and the Information State in Early Modern Britain* (Chicago: University of Chicago Press, 2024); Jacob Soll, *The Information Master: Jean-Baptiste Colbert's Secret State Intelligence System* (Ann Arbor: University of Michigan Press, 2009).
28. María M. Portuondo, *Secret Science: Spanish Cosmography and the New World* (Baltimore: Johns Hopkins University Press, 2005); Richard Kagan, "Arcana imperii: Mapas, sabiduría, y poder en

la corte de Felipe IV," in *El atlas del Rey Planeta,* ed. Fernando Marías and Felipe Pereda (Madrid: Nerea, 2002), 49–70; Richard Kagan and Xavier Gil, "La luna de España: Mapas, ciencia y poder en la época de los Austrias," *Pedralbes: Revista d'Història Moderna* 25 (2005): 171–190.

29. AGI, Indiferente 2978, "señores y pastores absolutos."
30. AGI, México 92, *Cartas,* 23.
31. AGI, México 68, *Cartas,* 123.
32. AGI, México 92, *Cartas,* 42–43.
33. AGI, México 92, *Cartas,* 32.
34. AGI, México 68, *Cartas,* 120.
35. AGI, México 68, *Cartas,* 122–123.
36. *Cartas,* 265–271; AGI, Patronato 231, N.4, R.11.
37. Carta, 7 February 1564, AGI, México68 (*Cartas,* 115).
38. Carta, 8 June 1564, AGI, México 68 (*Cartas,* 123); Carta, 8 June 1564; AGI, México 92 (*Cartas,* 140), "señores absolutos."
39. Carta, 18 August 1564, AGI México 97 (*Cartas,* 161–162).
40. The agenda is laid out in his letters to the king, particularly Carta del Marqués del Valle, 10 October 1563; AGI, Patronato 171, N 1, R.20 (*Cartas,* 307–325); Carta del Marqués del Valle, 28 February 1564; AGI, Patronato 171, N 1, R.20 (*Cartas,* 330–340).
41. AGI, Patronato 171, N 1, R.20.
42. Relación de algunas personas de las a quien se han proveído corregimientos, 1564, AGI, Patronato 182, R.13 (*Cartas,* 205–217); Relación de algunas personas de las a quien se han proveído tenientazgos, 1564, AGI, Patronato 182, R.13 (*Cartas,* 217–221); Relación de algunas estancias y caballerías que el Virrey Don Luis de Velasco dio as sus pinaguados desde 1551 a 1563, AGI, Patronato 182, R.13 (*Cartas,* 222–229); Relación de algunos deudos y parientes del Virrey don Luis de Velasco, 1564, AGI, Patronato 182, R.13 (*Cartas,* 229–233); Relación de los pesos de oro que el Virrey de Nueva España don Luis de Velasco mando pagar de la caja real a personas, deudos, amigos, y criados suyos contra lo proveído y mandado por SM, 1564, AGI, Patronato182, R.13 (*Cartas,* 234–254).
43. Carta del Marques del Valle, 28 de febrero 1564, AGI, Patronato 171, N.1, R.20 (*Cartas,* 338); *Anales de Juan Bautista,* ed. Luis Reyes García (Mexico: CIESAS, 2001), par.195 and 202; Javier Molina Villeta, "Los dos mundos de Martín Cortés: Un mestizo en el imperio español," *Revista De Indias* 83, no. 289 (2023): 623–651.
44. Memoria de algunas cosas que contienen las ordenanzas, AGI, Patronato 182, R.22 (included in *Cartas del Licenciado Valderrama,* 193–197).
45. Memorial que envio al licenciado Valderrama, 1563, AGI, Mexico 2547 (*Cartas,* 297–302).
46. Memoria de lo que a don Diego Ceynos le daban, 1571, AGI, Mexico 94, Exp.4; Memoria de las cosas que daban a Diego de Olarte, septiembre 1571, AGN-Mexico, Tierras 2676, Exp.11; Memoria de las cosas que a mi, Gabriel de los Angles, me davan, septiembre 1571, AGN-Mexico, Tierras V.60, Exp.2, 44r-55v. All cases are transcribed in *Colección documental de Tepeaca,* Ns.176–178.
47. *Codex Osuna,* BNE, VITR/26/8, 492r/30r.
48. *Codex Osuna,* 464v–2v. According to María Teresa Martinez Peñalosa, *Vocabulario de terminos en documentos históricos* (Mexico: AGN, 1984), 19, one *caballeria* corresponds to 10.4 square kilometers (or some 42,800 hectares).
49. Pablo Escalante Gonzalbo, "On the Margins of Mexico City: What the Beinecke Map Shows," in *Painting a Map of Sixteenth-Century Mexico City: Land, Writing, and Native Rule,* ed. Mary E. Miller and Barbara E. Mundy (New Haven: Yale University Press, 2012), 101–110.
50. *Anales de Juan Bautista,* 22r (par. 171, 205).
51. *Anales,* 37v (par. 261, 255).
52. *Anales,* 47v (par. 313, 287) and 55v (par. 377, 313).

53. *Anales*, 27r (par.197, 221).
54. *Anales*, 32v (par. 223, 231).
55. *Anales*, 17v.
56. *Anales*, 33v (par. 237–238, 243).
57. *Anales*, 20r.
58. *Anales*, 31v (par. 228, 237), 48v (par. 320, 291).
59. *Anales*, 21r.
60. *Anales*, 24v.
61. *Anales*, 25v.
62. *Anales*, 26r.
63. *Anales*, 36r (par. 252, 251), 25v (par. 191, 217).
64. *Anales*, 26–27v (par. 197–200, 221–223).
65. *Anales*, 21r (par. 163, 201).
66. AGN-Mexico, Civil 644, reproduced in *Codice Osuna reproducción facsimilar*, ed. Luis Chávez Orozco (Mexico: EIII, 1947), 32, 38, par. III; 41 pars. VII-VIII.
67. AGN-Mexico Civil 644 (*Codice Osuna*, 13–30).
68. AGN-Mexico Civil 644 (*Codice Osuna*, 33).
69. AGN-Mexico Civil 644 (*Codice Osuna*, 36–37).
70. AGN-Mexico Civil 644 (*Codice Osuna*, 49).
71. AGN-Mexico Civil 644 (*Codice Osuna*, 41–49).
72. AGN-Mexico Civil 644 (*Codice Osuna*, 78–89).
73. AGN-Mexico Civil 644 (*Codice Osuna*, 152–162).
74. AGN-Mexico Civil 644, "Memorial de los gastos" (*Codice Osuna*, 122–148).
75. BNM, MSS.FACS/999, 465/1r-474/12r (*Codice Osuna*, 181–206).
76. "Está muy bien lo que dices hace tiempo lo hubieras contado así," *Anales*, August 17, 1564, JB #222 (p. 230–231).
77. *Anales*, 54r (par. 360–361, 307–309).
78. *Anales*, 5v (par. 28, 149).
79. The literature on the so-called Cortés conspiracy by in large misses the partisan manipulation of evidence throughout, assuming that Cortés indeed sought to lead a separate polity. See Manuel Orozco y Berra, *Noticia histórica de la conjuración del Marqués del Valle*, años 1565 1568 (Mexico: Tipografía de R. Rafael, 1853); Ramón Osorio y Carvajal, *La conjura de Martín Cortés y otros sucesos de la colonia* (Mexico: Secretaria de Obra y Servicios, 1973), 51; Victoria Anne Vincent, "The Avila-Cortés Conspiracy: Creole Aspirations and Royal Interests" (PhD diss., University of Nebraska, 1993); Ethelia Ruiz Medrano and Michel Besson, "Fighting Destiny: Nahua Nobles and Friars in the Sixteenth-Century Revolt of the Encomenderos against the King," in *Negotiation within Domination: New Spain's Indian Pueblos Confront the Spanish State*, ed. Ethelia Ruiz Medrano and Susan Kellogg (Denver: University Press of Colorado, 2010), 45–78. There is one exception to this list—Shirley Cushing Flint, "Treason or Travesty: The Martín Cortés Conspiracy Reexamined," *Sixteenth Century Journal* 39, no. 1 (Spring 2008): 23–44. Cushing Flint makes obvious the partisan manipulation of evidence and concludes that the conspiracy was manufactured in paper.
80. *Anales*, 6r (pts. 30–31, 149–151).
81. The case and other relevant sources are scattered in many repositories and files. See among others AGI, Patronato 74, N.2, R.1; AGI, Patronato 203; AGI, Patronato 205, R.1(1); AGI, Patronato 208, R.5; AGI, Patronato 216, R.1(3); AGI, Patronato 216, R.1(4); AGI, Patronato 217, R.4; AGI, Patronato 218, R.3; AGI, Patronato 220, R.2; AGI, Patronato 220, R.3; AGI, Escribanía 1007B; AHN-M, Diversos 43, Doc.10; AHN-M, Diversos 43, Doc.34; AGS, Cámara de Castilla, Diversos de Castilla, L.6, N.50; LOC, HC-M, 14-HC-M 36.

82. Cushing Flint, "Treason or Travesty."
83. HSA, 9-IV-3.
84. HSA, 9-IV-2.
85. AGI, Patronato 210, R.1, 3r.
86. AGI, Patronato 210, R.1, 114r–119r.
87. HSA, 9-IV-2.
88. AGI, Patronato 208, R.3.
89. HSA, 9-IV-7. For many references to these recusations, see AGI, Patronato 210, R.1, 162r–167v, 188r.
90. BNE, Mss/11592, 259r.
91. BNE, Mss/11592, 258v.
92. AGI, Patronato 210, R.1, 457r.
93. AGI, Patronato 210, R.1, 240r–246v and following (without pagination), "Esta traslado."
94. BNE, Mss/11592, 258v.
95. The Peruvian section of this audit survives in BL, Add 33983; for Nueva Galicia, see AGI, Guadalajara 5.
96. BNF, Espagnol 325, 307r.
97. IVDJ, Envío 25, C.40, Exp.143.
98. AGS, Patronato Leg.22-77.
99. IVDJ, Envío 25, C.40, Exp.140.
100. Memorial de Maldonado a S.M (1565), AGS, Patronato, leg. 22-77; Memorial de Maldonando al Presidente del Consejo de Indias (1565), BNE, Mss/ 20245[9], 1r–8r.
101. AGI, Patronato 171, N.1, R.11; IVDJ, Envío 25 C.40, Exp.91.
102. Luciano Serrano, ed., *Correspondencia diplomática entre España y la Santa Sede* (Madrid: Escuela Española en Roma, 1914), 2:350–351, 390, 472.
103. Carlos Sempat Assadourian, "Fray Alonso de Maldonado: La política indiana, el estado de damnación del Rey Católico y La Inquisición," *Historia Mexicana* 38, no. 4 (1989): 623–661.
104. AGJ, Archivo Reservado: Legajo 7936, 34r.
105. AGJ, Archivo Reservado: Legajo 7936, "Libro de apuntamientos," 9r; see also 3r, 5v, 8v.
106. AGJ, Archivo Reservado: Legajo 7936, "Libro de apuntamientos," 59v–61r.
107. AGJ, Archivo Reservado: Legajo 7936, "Libro de apuntamientos," 25r.
108. We have counted dozens of new books the council had to keep thereafter; the archive grew exponentially as ministers and subalterns struggled to keep up with paperwork of all kinds.
109. Masters, *We, the King,* 185–193.
110. These ecclesiastical councils did not eliminate the well-entrenched factionalism in church petition-response systems of paperwork. Conflict remained, but they did manage to bring order and obedience into deeply fragmented religious republics. The third council created uniform catechisms, doctrine, and sacramental rules for Mexico and Peru in three distinct Indigenous languages: Nahua for Mexico and Quechua and Aymara for Peru. Sabine MacCormack *Religion in the Andes: Vision and Imagination in Early Colonial Peru* (Princeton: Princeton University Press, 1991); Mónica Martini, "Los sínodos de Toribio Alfonso de Mogrovejo (1582–1604)," in *IX Congreso del Instituto Internacional de Historia del Derecho Indiano* (Madrid: Universidad Complutense, 1990), 2:461–488; Osvaldo Rodolfo Moutin, "Legislar en la América hispánica en la temprana edad moderna: Procesos y características de la producción de los decretos del Tercer Concilio Provincial Mexicano (1585)," in *Global Perspectives on Legal History,* ed. Thomas Duve and Stefan Vogenauer, vol. 4 (Frankfurt: Max Planck Institute, 2016); AGI, Lima 126.
111. HSA, 3/1145, 7; RBPR, Papeles tocantes a Indias I-I7S, N.55, 251r.
112. Masters, *We, the King,* 194–204; AGI, Contaduría 7A.
113. BNE, Mss/3017.

114. AGI, Indiferente 1530; BNE, Mss/3035; reproduced in Francisco, De Solano, ed., *Cuestionarios para la formación de las relaciones geográficas de Indias: siglos XVI/XIX*. (Madrid: Editorial CSIC, 1988), 79–86.
115. Barbara Mundy, *The Mapping of New Spain: Indigenous Cartography and the Maps of the Relaciones Geograficas* (Chicago: University of Chicago Press, 1999).
116. "Alonso de Santa Cruz al Rey don Felipe II solicitando ingresar en el Consejo de Indias (28 de Febrero 1557)," and "Memorial de Alonso de Santa Cruz al rey Don Felipe sobre el mismo asunto (1557)," Archivo de Simancas.- Estado.- Legajo 121, fols. 22–24.
117. Edmundo O'Gorman, *The Invention of America* (Bloomington: Indiana University Press, 1961).
118. Amancio Landín Carrasco, *Vida y viajes de Pedro Sarmiento de Gamboa* (Madrid: Instituto Histórico de Marina, 1945); Rose Arciniega, *Pedro Sarmiento de Gamboa, el Ulises de América* (Buenos Aires: Editorial Sudamericana, 1956).
119. "Lima, 18 Abril 1578," in *Gobernantes del Peru: Cartas y papeles siglo XVI*, ed. Roberto Levellier (Madrid: Sucesores de Rivadeneyra,1924), 6:41–42; Catherine Julien, "History and Art in Translation: The Paños and Other Objects Collected by Francisco Toledo," *Colonial Latin American Review* 8, no. (1999): 61–89.
120. Guillermo Lohmann Villena, "Enrique Garcés, descubridor del mercurio en el Perú, poeta y arbitrista," *Anuario de Estudios Americanos* 5 (1948): 439–482.
121. BNE, Mss/3040, 424r–432v, 375r–376r, 51r–52r, 403r–410r; AGI, Charcas L.42.
122. Jeremy Ravi Mumford, "Aristocracy on the Auction Block: Race, Lords, and the Perpetuity Controversy of Sixteenth-Century Peru," in *Imperial Subjects: Race, Ethnicity and Identity in Colonial Latin America*, ed. Andrew B. Fisher and Matthew D. O'Hara (Durham: Duke University Press, 2009), 35–59, here 40–44.
123. AGI, Lima 569, L.11, 112–115v, 123r-v, 141v; Mumford, "Aristocracy on the Auction Block," 51–52.
124. Teófilo Aparicio López, *Fray Diego Ortiz, misionero y mártir del Perú: Un proceso original del siglo XVI* (Valladolid: Estudio Agustiniano, 1989); John Hemming, *The Conquest of the Inca* (New York: Harvest Books, 1970).
125. Edmundo Guillén Guillén, "Documentos inéditos para la historia de los Incas de Vilcabamba: La capitulacion del gobierno español con Titu Cusi Yupanqui," *Historia y Cultura* 10 (1977): 47–93.
126. Isacio Pérez Fernández, *Bartolomé de Las Casas en el Perú: El espíritu lascasiano en la primera evangelización del Imperio Incaico (1531–1573)* (Cusco: Centro de estudios rurales Andinos Bartolomé de Las Casas, 1988), 410–412; BNE, Res/37; BNE, Mss/3226.
127. Declaración de Angelina Llacsa Chuqui, 25 enero 1595, in Archive of the Augustinian Order in Rome (Archivo General de la Curia Agustiniana), reporduced in Teofilo Aparicio López, *Fray Diego Ortiz, misionero y mártir del Perú: Un proceso original del siglo XVI* (Madrid: Estudio Augustiniano,1989).
128. Kerstin Nowack and Catherine J. Julien, "La campaña de Toledo contra los señores naturales andinos: El destierro de los Incas de Vilcabamba y Cuzco," *Historia y Cultura (Lima)* 23 (1999): 15–81.
129. Brendecke, *Empirical Empire*, chap. 5.
130. AGI, Lima 28B, November 20, 1570.
131. Manfredi Merluzzi, *Memoria histórica y gobierno imperial* (Rosario: Prohistoria, 2008), 44.
132. "[Que] cesse tanta variedad de opiniones en cossas de tan grande ymportancia por no estar los hechos destos rreynos claros sino fingirlos cada uno como se le antoja para fundar los derechos que desea con tanta turbacion y confusion de conciencias asi de la Vuestra Magestad como de la de sus Ministros y moradores destas provincias tan escrupulizadas que qualquiera ygnorante ha ossado hasta aquí poner la boca en el cielo. Y ansimismo parece se puede ynferri que los caciques y principales en su genero y manera no dejavan de tributar." Informaciones

que mandó levantar el virrey Toledo (1570–1572) in Roberto Levillier, *Don Francisco de Toledo: Supremo organizador del Peru. Su vida, su obra* (1515–1582), vol. 2, *Sus informaciones sobre los Incas* (Buenos Aires: Espasa Calpe, 1940), 3.

133. Merluzzi, *Memoria histórica,* 45.
134. BNE, Mss/19569.
135. Vidal Abril Castelló and Miguel Abril Stoffels, *Francisco de la Cruz: Inquisición,* actas II, 1 (Madrid: CSIC, 1996), 1169.
136. Abril Castelló and Abril Stoffels, *Francisco de la Cruz,* actas II, 1, 99–103.
137. Abril Castelló and Abril Stoffels, *Francisco de la Cruz,* actas II, 1, 260.
138. On new Indigenous boundary maps in the context of ancient-regime litigation, see Alex Hidalgo, *Trails of Footprints* (Austin: University of Texas Press, 2017).
139. Margarita Menegus, "El cacicazgo en la Nueva España," in *El cacicazgo en Nueva España y Filipinas,* ed. Margarita Menegus Bornemann and Rodolfo Aguirre Salvador (Mexico: UNAM, 2005), 13–69.
140. See, for example, Jeremy Mumford, *Vertical Empire: The General Resettlement of Indians in the Colonial Andes* (Durham: Duke University Press, 2012); Manfredo Merluzzi, *Politica e governo nel Nuovo Mondo: Francisco de Toledo viceré del Perù* (1569–1581) (Rome: Carocci editore, 2003).
141. "Pleitos de Jauja" AGI, Lima 28A, 63Q, transcribed in Monica Medelius and Juan Carlos de la Puente Luna, "Curacas, bienes y quipus en un documento toledano (Jauja 1570)," *Histórica* 28, no. 2 (2004): 35–82. See also De La Puente Luna, *Andean Cosmopolitans: Seeking Justice and Reward at the Spanish Royal Court* (Austin: University of Texas Press, 2018), chap. 2.
142. *Gobernantes del Peru,* 8:304–382.
143. Ordenanzas del virrey Toledo sobre la orden que se ha de guardar en los pleitos de Indios, L Plata, 22 diceimbre 1574, in *Gobernantes del Peru,* 8:258–259.
144. AGI, Lima 28A; De La Puente Luna, *Andean Cosmopolitans,* chap. 2.
145. For a list of some forty privileges from Pius V archived by the Franciscans and published in Mexico at the height of the Cortés conspiracy, see *Tabula privilegiorum, quae sanctissimus Papa pius quintus, concessit fratribus mendicantibus: In bulla confirmatiois et novae, concessionis privilegiorum, ordum mendicatium,* 1567.
146. AGI, Escribanía 1009B; John F. Chuchiak IV, *El castigo y la reprensión: El juzgado del provisorato de indios* (Mexico: UNAM, 2022).
147. "Con tantas falsedades del hecho de las cosas y tantas ygnorancias en materias de gouierno auia tan urgentes causas para recogerlos y hauerlos mandado vedar vuestro real consejo que de la dilación que en esto a auido desde la junta acá no es poco el daño que se a seguido," Carta de el virrey Toledo a SM, Cusco, 24 de Septiembre 1572, in *Gobernantes del Peru,* 442.
148. Pérez Fernández, *Bartolomé de las Casas en el Perú,* 517–532; Yacin Hehrlein, *Mission und Macht: Die politisch-religiöse Konfrontation zwischen dem Dominikanerorden in Peru und dem Vizekönig Francisco de Toledo* (1569–1581) (Mainz: Matthias Grunewald, 1992), 138–160.
149. Francisco Fernández de Castillo, *Doña Catalina Xuárez Marcaida* (Mexico: Imprenta Victoria, 1920).
150. AGN-Mexico, Inquisición 72, Exp.29, 298v.
151. AGN-Mexico, Inquisición 72, Exp.29, 296r; Gabriel Torres Puga, "¿Resguardar el archivo o proteger el secreto? Conservación y destrucción de expedientes inquisitoriales," *Fontes* 9, no. 2 (2018): 98–114.
152. On Moya de Contreras, see Stafford Poole, *Pedro Moya de Contreras,* 2nd ed. (Norman: University of Oklahoma Press, 2011). On the *ordenanzas* of archives of the new Mexican Inquisition, see "Instrucciones del ilustrísimo Señor Cardenal, Inquisidor General, para la fundación de la Inquisición en México," in *Documentos inéditos o muy raros para la historia de México,* ed. Genaro García (Mexico: Porrua, 1982), 103–114.

153. The denunciation led to an investigation of the sale of the archive by its secretary and further investigations; see AGN-Mexico, Inquisición 72, Exp.32; Carta del provisor, Guadalajara, 4 de febrero 1572, AGN-Mx, Inquisición 74, Exp.16.
154. Juan Suárez de Peralta, *Tractado de la cavalleria, de la gineta y brida* (Sevilla: Fernando Díaz, 1580).
155. BNE, Mss/20143; see also Enrique González González, "Nostalgia de la encomienda: Releer el 'Tratado del descubrimiento,' de Juan Suárez de Peralta (1589)," *Historia Mexicana* 59, no. 2 (2009): 533–603.
156. For Las Casas, see AGI, Indiferente 426, L.25, 134r.
157. On the recall of Oviedo's archive by the council in 1563 and 1566, see Klaus Wagner, "Legajos y otras aficiones del inquisidor Andrés Gascó," *Boletín de la Real Academia de la Historia* 176 (1979): 149–185 (especially 160). On Cieza's recall, see Miguel Maticorena Estrada, "Cieza de León en Sevilla y su muerte en 1554: Documentos," *Anuario de Estudios Americanos* 12 (1955): 615–674. On Gómara, see Joaquín Ramírez Cabañas, ed., *Gómara: Historia de la conquista de México* (Mexico: Editorial Pedro Robredo, 1943), 2:311–319. For Bernal Díaz del Castillo's manuscript, see Archivo General de Centroamérica, Guatemala 10, R.2, N.22A (reproduced in José Antonio Barbón Rodríguez, *Historia verdadera de la conquista de Nueva España: Estudio* [Mexico: Colegio de México, 2005], 1060). On the recall of Sahagún's archive, including the Florentine Codex, see George Baudot, *Utopía e historia en México* (Madrid: Espasa Calpe, 1988), 475–483. On Cervantes de Salazar's archive, see "Carta de Juan López de Velasco," Archivo Colegio de las Vizcaínas (Mexico), L.4, 29r–30v (reproduced in *Cartas recibidas de España por Francisco Cervantes de Salazar*, ed. Agustín Millares Carlo [Mexico: José Porrua, 1946], 107–111).
158. *Ordenanzas del Consejo* (Madrid: Francisco Sánchez, 1585); British Museum, 8042, L.17.
159. Ordenanza 11, 13, 22, 38, 40, 65, 68, 69, 70, 85, 96, 98, 122; see BNE, Mss/3035; BNE, Mss/2987.
160. AGI, Patronato 171, N.1. R.19, 1r–26v.
161. "La dicha averiguación, no se podrá hacer sin remover y despertar muchas cosas enconadas y perjudiciales a la honra y fama de muchas personas," Parecer del cronista Juan López de Velasco, sobre la "Historia, que escribió Diego Fernández, de Palencia," ARAH, Colección Muñoz, T.91, 172r.
162. "Cuando se pueda averiguar lo susodicho y sea justo y todo sea verdad, parece que se debe mirar si será en servicio de V. A. y convendría para la fidelidad que se debe esperar en lo porvenir de aquellas provincias, dejar en historia pública y aprobada por V. A., declaradas por desleales ó sospechosas en su real servicio aquellas Repúblicas y personas, quedando como quedaran dello descontentas y quejosas de la clemencia de V. M. por esto, mal dispuestas para lo que adelante se podría ofrecer"; AGI, Patronato 171, N.1. R.19, 1r. See also ARAH, Colección Muñoz, T.91, 172r.
163. Juan Friede, "La censura española y la 'recopilación historial' de Fray Pedro Aguado," *Boletín Cultural y Bibliográfico* (1963): 167–192; José A. Barbón Rodríguez, "Una edición crítica de la 'Historia verdadera de la conquista de la Nueva España,' de Bernal Díaz del Castillo," *Jahrbuch für Geschichte Lateinamerikas* 22 (1985): 1–22.
164. Since first drafting the dedication of his *Tradución del Indio de los tres diálogos del amor* (1590), Garcilaso presented his mother as the granddaughter of Inca Tupac Yupanqui, the daughter of one Inca Huallpa Topac, alleged brother of Huayna Capac. His mother, however, presented herself never as noble Inca woman but as Indigenous commoner, Isabel Suárez, married to lowly Spanish tailor Juan de Pedroche. See her 1571 will in the notarial archives of Cusco found and transcribed by Aurelio Miró Quesada in 1945, "El testamento de la madre del Inca Garcilaso," *Letras (Lima)* 11 (30): 46–56. There is more evidence of noble lineage from his father's dad, which Garcilaso exaggerated throughout.

165. On these efforts, see Aurelio Miró Quesada, *El Inca Garcilaso* (Lima: Pontificia Universidad Católica, 1994).
166. Teodosio Fernández, "El Inca Garcilaso y el 'Motín de los mestizos' (1567)," *Revista de Crítica Literaria Latinoamericana* 43, no. 85 (2017): 115–134; Berta Ares Queija, "El Inca Garcilaso y sus 'parientes' mestizos," in *Humanismo, mestizaje y escritura en los "Comentarios reales,"* ed. Carmen de Mora (Madrid: Vervuert/Iberoamericana, 2010), 15–29.
167. On the connections between Vaca Castro and Garcilaso's dad, see John Grier Varner, *El Inca: The Life and Times of Garcilaso de la Vega* (Austin: University of Texas Press, 1968), 47–50.
168. José Cárdenas Bunsen, "Correspondencia privada e historia pública: Las relaciones intelectuales de Pedro de Castro, Antonio de Herrera y el Inca Garcilaso," *Colonial Latin American Review* 23, no. 3 (2014): 413–438.
169. José Alejandro Cárdenas Bunsen, *La aparición de los libros plúmbeos y los modos de escribir la historia: De Pedro de Castro al Inca Garcilaso de la Vega* (Madrid: Iberoamericana Editorial Vervuert, 2018).
170. José Antonio Mazzoti, *Encontrando un Inca* (Salem: Axiara Editions, 2016).
171. Antonio de Herrera, *Historia general de los hechos de los castellanos en las Islas i Tierra Firme del Mar Océano en cuatro décadas desde el año de 1492 a 1531*, 2 vols. (Madrid: Imprenta Real, 1601); Antonio de Herrera, *Historia general de los hechos de los castellanos en las Islas i Tierra Firme del Mar Océano en una década desde el al año de 1531 a 1540* (Madrid: Imprenta Real, 1615). The delayed publication of the third volume resulted from Herrera's participation in court plots to have prime minister (*valido*) Duke de Lerma removed, which led to Herrera's temporary downfall. On Herrera as a court historian, see Richard Kagan, *Clio and the Crown: The Politics of History in Medieval and Early Modern Spain* (Baltimore: John Hopkins University Press, 2009), 135–200.
172. Herrera, *Historia general*, I, Dec.II, L.II, Chap.XXII, 71.
173. There are several studies of the Puñonrostro-Herrera debate, but Bethany Aram's is by far the best. Her mastery of the archives involving Balboa and Pedrarias, the cause of the debate, is unparalleled. See Bethany Aram, "From the Courts to the Court: History, Literature, and Litigation in the Spanish Atlantic World," *Colonial Latin American Review* 21, no. 3 (2012): 343–364; see also AGI, Escribanía 1012A; AGI, Patronato 170, R.19, N.30; AGI, Patronato 170, R.19, N.14; AGI, Patronato 170, R.19, N.19; AGI, Indiferente 752. For changes in early 1600s history writing, see the excellent Amorina Villarreal Brasca, *El duque de Lerma: Política y gestión para América en la monarquía de Felipe III* (Valencia: Albatross, 2024).
174. The primary documents are at the AGI and the Puñonrosto family archives. See for example, The Count of Puñonrostro, September 11, 1602, and Antonio de Herrera to the king, September 16, 1602, AGI, Escribanía 1012A; Memorial of Antonio de Herrera, June 10, 1602, AGI, Patronato 170, R.19, N.30; Memorial of Antonio de Herrera [undated], AGI, Patronato 170, R.19, N.14; 4 Declaration of Antonio de Herrera [undated], AGI, Patronato 170, R.19, N.19; Lo que parece en las pretensiones del coronista Antonio de Herrera, July 17, 1615, AGI, Indiferente 752. All the documentation of AGI, Patronato 170, R.19 has been transcribed in *Colección de documentos inéditos relativos al descubrimiento, conquista, y organización de América y Oceanía* (Madrid: Imp. de M. Bernaldo de Quirós, 1882), 37:75–321.
175. AHN-Madrid, Inquisición L.1050, 94v; 339r.
176. AGI, Quito 10, R.9, N.114; AGI, Quito 10, R.7, N.60; AGI, Panamá 15, R.9, N.98; AGI, Panamá 16, R.3, N.43; AGI, Panamá 16, R.8, N.98; AGI, Quito 212, L.5, 1r; AGI, Charcas 419, L.5, 38v–39r.
177. The conceptual lines between these three types of institutions could be quite hazy. See Juan Cordero Rivera, "Asociacionismo popular: Gremios, cofradías, hermandades y hospitales," in *La vida cotidiana en la Edad Media*, ed. José Ignacio de la Iglesia Duarte (Nájera: Instituto de Estudios Riojanos, 1997), 387–400; Carmen Mena, "Las Hermandades de Sevilla y su proyección

americana," in *Estrategias de poder en América Latina*, ed. Pilar García Jordán (Barcelona: Universitat de Barcelona, 2000), 129–150, here 134.

178. *Recopilación de leyes de los reynos de las Indias* (Madrid: Julián de Paredes, 1681), book 1, title IV, law 25, 20r.
179. Asunción Lavrín, *Brides of Christ: Conventual Life in Colonial Mexico* (Stanford: Stanford University Press, 2008), 9.
180. Marcella Hayes, "Women Leaders of Black Lay Confraternities in Seventeenth-Century Lima," *The Americas* 79, no. 4 (2022): 559–586.
181. AGI, Indiferente 451, L.A11, 6v–7r.
182. Guillermo Lohmann Villena, "El señorío de los marqueses de Santiago de Oropesa en el Perú," *Anuario de Historia del Derecho Español* 19 (1948–1949): 347–458, 353–360.
183. Gisela von Wobeser, "El gobierno en el marquesado del Valle de Oaxaca," in *El gobierno provincial de la Nueva España, 1570–1787*, ed. Woodrow Borah (Mexico: UNAM, 2002), 188.
184. AHN-Madrid, Diversos 35, N.16; AHN-Madrid, Diversos 35, N.21; AGI, Patronato 91, R.3.
185. Stuart Schwartz, "La nobleza del nuevo mundo: Movilidad y aspiraciones sociales en la conquista y colonización de la América hispánica," *Revista de historia* 8 (1979): 7–20, here 14.
186. Fred Bronner, "Elite Formation in Seventeenth-Century Peru," *Boletín de Estudios Latinoamericanos y del Caribe* 24 (1978): 3–26, here 3.
187. Bronner, "Elite Formation," 16.
188. Bronner, "Elite Formation," 19.
189. James Lockhart, *Spanish Peru, 1532–1560: A Social History* (Madison: University of Wisconsin Press, 1994).
190. Lockhart, *Spanish Peru*, 24; José Antonio del Busto Duthurburu, "Maldonado el Rico, señor de los Andahuaylas," *Revista histórica* 26 (1962): 113–146.
191. AGN-Mexico, Mercedes 2, 371r; Mercedes 3, 199r, 371r; Mercedes 4, 27v, 303r; Mercedes 5, 170v, 293r; Mercedes 7, 228v, 358r; Vol.8, 50v, 80v; Vol.9, 22r, 198r; Vol.10, 18r, 207v; Vol.11, 279r; Vol.16, 162v; Vol.17, 78v, 87r, 163v; Vol.18, 70r, 75r, 75r, 163v, 165v, 204r, 215r, 326r; Vol.20, 47r, 52v.
192. Rebecca Horn, *Postconquest Coyoacán: Nahua-Spanish Relations in Central Mexico, 1519–1650* (Stanford: Stanford University Press, 1997), 170; Magnus Mörner, "Economic Factors and Stratification in Colonial Spanish America," *Hispanic American Historical Review* 63, no. 2 (1983): 335–369, 347; Keith A. Davies, *Landowners in Colonial Peru* (Austin: University of Texas Press, 1984), 162–164.
193. Udo Oberem, *Sancho Hacho: Un cacique mayor del Siglo XVI* (Quito: Abya-Yala, 1993), 30–32.
194. Adam Szasdi, "Don Diego Tomalá, cacique de la isla de la Puna," *Estudios sobre Política Indigenista Española en América* III (1977): 157–182, here 158–164.
195. Szasdi, "Don Diego Tomalá," 166.
196. Szasdi, "Don Diego Tomalá," 157–182, 172–174. For a similar case, see the *cacique* of Chatapotó, don Baltasar Saman, who similarly complained that British pirates had robbed him of 14,000 ducats; see AGI, Quito 24, N.24.
197. Jane E. Mangan, *Trading Roles: Gender, Ethnicity, and the Urban Economy in Colonial Potosí* (Durham: Duke University Press, 2005), 43–44.
198. Universidad de Oviedo, Fondo Antiguo, Relación del Viaje de fray Diego de Ocaña por el Nuevo Mundo, 180r.
199. Relación del Viaje de fray Diego de Ocaña, 181r.
200. Relación del Viaje de fray Diego de Ocaña, 181r.
201. James Lockhart, *Nahuas and Spaniards: Postconquest Central Mexican History and Philology* (Stanford: Stanford University Press, 1991),18, 144–145.
202. Lockhart, *Spanish Peru*, 142.
203. Lockhart, *Spanish Peru*, 218; ADC, Corregimiento: Causas Ordinarias, Legajo 1–18.

204. AHP, Escrituras Notariales, V.8, 1204–1206v; Nora Jaffary and Jane Mangan, *Women in Colonial Latin America, 1526 to 1806: Texts and Contexts* (Indianapolis: Hackett, 2018), 33–36.
205. Karen M. Powers, "Resilient Lords and Indian Vagabonds," *Ethnohistory* 38, no. 3 (1991): 225–249, 229.
206. Bronner, "Elite Formation," 21; Helen Nader, "Noble Income in Sixteenth-Century Castile," *Economic History Review* n.s., 30, no. 3 (1977): 411–428, 413.
207. Mörner, "Economic Factors," 350.
208. Mörner, "Economic Factors," 332.
209. Bronner, "Elite Formation," 21.
210. Bronner, "Elite Formation," 24.
211. AGI, Lima 28A, "Por las cartas," February 27, 1558.
212. José F. De La Peña, "Los mercaderes y el cabildo de Guatemala, 1592–1623," in *La formación de América Latina: La época colonial*, ed. Manuel Miño Grijalva (Mexico: El Colegio de Mexico, 1992), 129–165, here 162.
213. Eduardo R. Saguier, "The Contradictory Nature of the Spanish American Colonial State and the Origin of Self-Government in the Rio De La Plata Region: The Case of Buenos Aires in the Early Seventeenth Century," *Revista de Historia de América* no. 97 (1984): 23–44, here 30.
214. Luis Eduardo Wiesner, "Ciudad y poder en la provincia de Tunja" (PhD diss., Universidad de Pablo de Olavide de Sevilla, 2012), 297–298.
215. Louisa Schell Hoberman, "Merchants in Seventeenth-Century Mexico City: A Preliminary Portrait," *Hispanic American Historical Review* 57, no. 3 (1977): 479–503, 481; Manuel Alvarado Morales, "El cabildo y regimiento de la Ciudad de México en el siglo xvii," *Historia Mexicana* 28, no. 4 (1979): 489–514, 497.
216. Hoberman, "Merchants in Seventeenth-Century," 482; Bronner, "Elite Formation," 22.
217. Hoberman, "Merchants in Seventeenth-Century," 482.
218. John Lynch, "The Institutional Framework of Colonial Spanish America," *Journal of Latin American Studies* 24, no. S1 (1992): 69–81, here 73–77; J. H. Parry, *The Sale of Public Office in the Spanish Indies under the Hapsburgs* (Berkeley: University of California Press, 1953); Francisco Tomás y Valiente, *La venta de oficios en Indias* (Madrid: INAP, 1982).
219. François Chevalier, *Land and Society in Colonial Mexico: The Great Hacienda*, trans. Alvin Eustis (Berkeley: University of California Press, 1963), 2, 251.
220. Chevalier, *Land and Society*, 256–260.
221. Chevalier, *Land and Society*.
222. Chevalier, *Land and Society*, 251–254.
223. Chevalier, *Land and Society*, 234.
224. AGN-Madrid, Inquisición L.1050, 50r.
225. AGI, Mexico 98. For *mulato* and Black men and women, AGI, Panama 42, N.1; Miguel A. Valerio, "The Spanish Petition System, Hospital/ity, and the Formation of a Mulato Community in Sixteenth-Century Mexico," *The Americas* 78, no. 3 (2021): 415–437. Among many others, see Norah L. A. Gharala, *Taxing Blackness: Free Afromexican Tribute in Bourbon New Spain* (Tuscaloosa: University of Alabama Press, 2019); Ben Vinson III, *Before Mestizaje: The Frontiers of Race and Caste in Colonial Mexico* (Cambridge: Cambridge University Press, 2019); Martínez, *Genealogical Fictions*.
226. For a nonexhaustive list of works on this *nación*, see Luis Glave Testino, especially *Memoria y memoriales: La creación del programa político de la nación indiana (siglos xvi–xviii)* (Cusco: Centro de Estudios Regionales Andinos Bartolomé de Las Casas, 2023); Alcira Dueñas, "The Lima Indian Letrados: Remaking the República de Indios in the Bourbon Andes," *The Americas* 72, no. 1 (2015): 55–75; and de la Puente Luna, *Andean Cosmopolitans*.

227. Nancy E. van Deusen, *Global Indios: The Indigenous Struggle for Justice in Sixteenth-Century Spain* (Durham: Duke University Press, 2015); David Dery, "'Papereality' and Learning in Bureaucratic Organizations," *Administration & Society* 29, no. 6 (1998): 677–689.
228. AGI, México 217, N.26, 30v; Diego Muñoz Camargo, *Historia de Tlaxcala,* ed. Luis Reyes García (Tlaxcala: Centro de Investigaciones y Estudios Superiores, 1998), 14–15.
229. AGI, Indiferente 1399, "Diego Muñoz," May 6, 1585.
230. AGI, Mexico 1091, L.11, 101r-v, 106r-v, 127r-v, 132r, 139r-v, 147v–148v, 204r–205r.
231. Muñoz Camargo, *Historia de Tlaxcala,* 321.
232. Muñoz Camargo, *Historia de Tlaxcala,* 300, 307.
233. Muñoz Camargo, *Historia de Tlaxcala,* 58–59.
234. Muñoz Camargo, *Historia de Tlaxcala,* 51, 59.
235. Muñoz Camargo, *Historia de Tlaxcala,* 38.
236. Muñoz Camargo, *Historia de Tlaxcala,* 38–39.
237. Muñoz Camargo, *Historia de Tlaxcala,* 45–51.
238. AGI, Mexico 1091, L.11, 196v–197r.
239. Muñoz Camargo, *Historia de Tlaxcala,* 297, 304–305, 308, 311.
240. Muñoz Camargo, *Historia de Tlaxcala,* 296–297, 302.
241. Muñoz Camargo, *Historia de Tlaxcala,* 301, 305, 306, 311, 315, 316, 318, 322, 330.
242. Muñoz Camargo, *Historia de Tlaxcala,* 326.
243. For more information on Luis de Arciniega, see *Arquitectura del renacimiento en Nueva España* (Mexico: Iberoamericana, 2009), 20–23; Efraín Castro Morales, "Luis de Arciniega, maestro mayor de la catedral de Puebla," *Anales del Instituto de Investigaciones Estéticas* VII, no. 27 (1958): 17–32.
244. Muñoz Camargo, *Historia de Tlaxcala,* 305, 311, 324.
245. AGI, Indiferente 2063, N.119; Indiferente 1952, L.3, 28v; Muñoz Camargo, *Historia de Tlaxcala,* 298, 314, 323.
246. AGI, Indiferente 2063, N.119; Muñoz Camargo, *Historia de Tlaxcala,* 302, 308, 311, 314, 325.
247. AGN-Mexico, Indios 2, 108r, Exp.453/454.
248. AGI, Mexico 1092, L.12, 176r-v.
249. AGI, Mexico 1092, L.13, 12r–13r.
250. AGI, Mexico 1091, L.11, 221r–228v.
251. Muñoz Camargo, *Historia de Tlaxcala,* 18.
252. Muñoz Camargo, *Historia de Tlaxcala,* see "Testament of Leonor Vázquez," 381–385.
253. Muñoz Camargo, *Historia de Tlaxcala,* 366.
254. Peter Villella, *Indigenous Elites and Creole Identity in Colonial Mexico, 1500–1800* (New York: Cambridge University Press, 2016), 220–221.
255. José Carlos de la Puente, "Felipe Guaman Poma y el problema de la apropiación de tierras en el Perú colonial," *Boletín del Instituto Francés de Estudios Andinos* 37, no. 1 (2008): 123–149.
256. For evidence of this unusual reading of Guaman Poma's *Nueva corónica,* see Jorge Cañizares-Esguerra and Adrian Masters, "From Poor Indian Lázaro to Don Felipe Guaman Poma de Ayala: Rethinking a Commoner-Prince's Manifesto against the Andean Archive," *The Americas* 82, no. 3 (2025).
257. Poma, *Nueva corónica,* 5–7.
258. Juan Osio, "Nuevas miradas a los textos escondidos en el manuscrito temprano de fray Martín de Murúa," in *Vida y Obra de Fray Martín de Murúa,* ed. Thomas Cummins and Juan Osio (Lima: Lettera Gráfica, 2019), 261–276, here 270–271.
259. Poma, *Nueva corónica,* 6–7, 368.
260. For a transcription of the AGI documents on this case, see Víctor Manuel Maurtúa, *Juicio de límites entre el Perú y Bolivia: Organización audiencial sudamericana. Vol. 8: Chunchos* (Madrid: Imprenta de Henrich y Comp., 1906), 171–248.

261. Memorial, AGI, Indiferente del Perú 631, 1–20v.
262. Información de las misiones dominicas en el cerro de la Sal hecha for fray Antonio de Olmedo, in *Revista del Archivo Nacional* 20 (1956): 66–84; Información de las misiones dominicas en el cerro de la Sal hecha for fray Diego González de Valdosera (1661), in *Revista del Archivo Nacional* 21 (1957): 82–98.
263. The paperwork on Pedro and the politics of Tucuman is large and can be found in AGI, Charcas 58, 121, 122. For an account of Pedro's many changing identities, see Pedro Lozano, *Historia de la Conquista del Praguay, Rio de la Plata y el Tucumán* (1784–85) *V. 5: Tucumán* (Buenos Aires: Imprenta Popular, 1875). Ana María Lorandi, *De quimeras, rebeliones y utopías. La gesta del inca Pedro Bohorques* (Lima: PUCP, 1997), also studies Pedro's entries in the Amazon in search for the Inca of Paititi.
264. Nicanor Domínguez Faura, "Betanzos y los Quipucamayos en la época de Vaca de Castro (Cuzco, 1543)," *Revista Andina* 46 (2008): 155–192; Catherine Julien, "Polo de Ondegardo y el 'Discurso sobre la descendencia y gouierno de los ingas.'" *Histórica* 33, no. 2 (2009): 7–28; Nicanor Domínguez Faura, "El licenciado Polo: ¿ fuente del 'Discurso sobre la descendencia y govierno de los ingas' (ms. 1602/1603–1608)?," *Histórica* 34, no. 1 (2010): 131–144.
265. De la Puente, *Andean Cosmopolitans*, 155–192.
266. José Carlos De la Puente Luna, "What's in a Name? An Indian Trickster Travels the Spanish Colonial World," (PhD diss., Texas Christian University, 2006). For a sweeping survey of the paperwork produced by the *Nación Indiana* in the seventeenth and eighteenth centuries, see Glave, *Memoria y memoriales.*
267. ANE, Indígenas, Caja 8, Exp.19, 81. For a study of this case, see Carlos Espinosa Fernández de Córdova, *El Inca barroco. Política y estética en la Real Audiencia de Quito, 1630–1680* (Quito: Flacso Ecuador, 2015). Fernández Córdova has transcribed the 81 folios in ANE, and we draw from his transcription. Our emphasis, unlike his, is on falsification.
268. AGI, Lima 197, no. 3.
269. ANE, Indígenas, Caja 8, Exp.19, 52r–53v.
270. ANE, Indígenas, Caja 8, Exp.19, 2r, 6r, 31r, 41r, 43r.
271. ANE, Indígenas, Caja 8, Exp.19, 13r–14r.
272. Voluntary and under torture interrogations of Roque Ruiz revealing networks of couriers and letters: ANE, Indígenas, Caja 8, Exp.19, 54r–59r; 62r–v; 65r–66r.
273. AGI, Mexico 2346. The file has been studied by Rocio Quispe-Agnoli, *Nobles de papel: Identidades oscilantes y genealogías borrosas en los descendientes de la realeza Inca* (Madrid: Iberoamericana-Vervuet, 2016) from a literary perspective overlooking the issues of credibility and forgery. See also Laura Escobari de Querejazu, *Caciques, yanaconas y extravagantes: la sociedad colonial en Charcas, s. XVI–XVIII* (La Paz: Editor: Institut français d'études andines, 2005), 77–92.
274. AGI, Mexico 2346, 14r–14v (reproduced in Quispe Agnoli, *Nobles de papel*, 212–213).
275. AGI, Mexico 2346, 15v (Quispe Agnoli, *Nobles de papel*, 214).
276. AGI, Mexico 2346, 132v–137r (Quispe Agnoli, *Nobles de papel*, 231–234).
277. Escobari de Querejazu, *Caciques*, 89. For the Crown prosecutor's own doubts, see AGI, Mexico 2346, n. 25, 372.
278. AGI, Mexico 2346, 109v–113r (Quispe Agnoli, *Nobles de papel*, 228–231).
279. Viceroy duke of Santa Fe would even increase the annual pension a year later to thousand pesos; see AGN-Mexico, Tributos 30, Exp.2, 140–145.
280. Escobari de Querejazu, *Caciques*, 89.
281. José María Portillo, "Dionisio Inca Yupanqui: A 'Lord' in Spain's Cortes de Cádiz," in *Unexpected Voices in Imperial Parliaments*, ed. Josep M. Fradera, José María Portillo, and Teresa Segura-García (London: Bloomsbury Academic, 2021), 53–73.

282. John Howland Rowe, "Probanza de los incas nietos de conquistadores," *Histórica* 9, no. 2 (1985): 193–245.
283. De la Puente, *Andean Cosmopolitans*, 155–192.
284. David. Cahill, "First among Incas: The Marquesado de Oropesa Litigation (1741–1780) en route to the Great Rebellion," *Jahrbuch für Geschichte Lateinamerikas* 41, no. 1 (2004): 137–166; John Howland Rowe, "Genealogía y rebelión en el siglo XVIII," *Histórica* 6, no. 1 (1982): 65–85.
285. Iván Escamilla, "Lorenzo Boturini y el entorno social de su empresa historiográfica," in *El caballero Lorenzo Boturini: Entre dos mundos y dos historias* (Mexico: Museo de la Basílica de Guadalupe, 2010), 168–202.
286. For an inventory of Boturini's massive collection, see John B. Glass, "29. The Boturini Collection," in *Handbook of Middle American Indians*, vols. 14 and 15, *Guide to Ethnohistorical Sources, Parts Three and Four*, ed. Robert Wauchope, Howard F. Cline, Charles Gibson, and H. B. Nicholson (Austin: University of Texas Press, 1975), 473–486. On Boturini's Viconian theories, Indigenous evolutionary history of writing, and the miracle of Our Lady of Guadalupe, see Jorge Cañizares-Esguerra, *How to Write the History of the New World* (Stanford: Stanford University Press, 2001), 135–155.
287. Rolena Adorno, "La Nueva corónica y buen gobierno de Guaman Poma: Del manuscrito autógrafo del siglo XVII a su reproducción digital del siglo XXI," *Recial* 13, no. 22 (2022): 34–47.
288. Mariano Téllez-Girón y Beaufort de Osuna, *Pintura del gobernador, alcaldes y regidores de México* (Madrid: Imprenta de Manuel Hernández, 1878).

CONCLUSION

1. Octavio Paz, *Sor Juana Inés de la Cruz, o las trampas de la fe*, 6th ed. (Mexico: Planeta Mexicana, 1993), 23.
2. Paz, *Sor Juana*, 23.
3. Paz, *Sor Juana*, 53.
4. Mónica L. Espinosa Arando, *La civilización montés: La vision india y el trasegar de Manuel Quintín Lame en Colombia* (Bogotá: Universidad de los Andes, 2009), 143; Joanne Rappaport, *The Politics of Memory: Native Historical Interpretation in the Colombian Andes* (Cambridge: Cambridge University Press, 1990), 124.
5. Espinosa Arando, *Civilización montés*, 144.
6. Rappaport, *Politics*, 104.
7. Rappaport, *Politics*, 116; Fernando Romero Loaiza, *Manuel Quintín Lame Chantre: El indígena ilustrado, el pensador indigenista* (Pereira: Universidad de Pereira, 2005).
8. Espinosa Arando, *Civilización montés*, 25.
9. Paulo Ilich Bacca, "Tras las huellas de Manuel Quintín Lame," in *La Quintiada (1912–1925): La rebelión indígena liderada por Manuel Ouintín Lame en el Cauca. Recopilación de fuentes primarias*, ed. Julieta Lemaitra (Bogotá: Universidad de los Andes, 2013), 299–332, here 303 and 303n3.
10. Espinosa Arando, *Civilización montés*, 159.
11. Lemaitra, *Quintiada*, 25–26.
12. Lemaitra, *Quintiada*, 38.
13. Lemaitra, *Quintiada*, 135.
14. Lemaitra, *Quintiada*, 146; see also Gonzalo Castillo-Cárdenas, *Liberation Theology from Below* (Maryknoll: Orbis, 1987), 125.
15. Castillo-Cárdenas, *Liberation*, 60; Rappaport, *Politics*, 60–81, 114–126.
16. Lemaitra, *Quintiada*, 70.
17. Lemaitra, *Quintiada*, 73.
18. Manuel Quintin Lame, *La lucha del indio que bajó de la montaña* (Bogotá: Comité de Defensa del Indio, 1973), 27.

19. Espinosa Arando, *Civilización montés,* 159.
20. Espinosa Arando, *Civilización montés,* 159.
21. Espinosa Arando, *Civilización montés,* 29.
22. Marcela Piamonte Cruz, *Escuelas y resguardos indígenas* (Cauca: Universidad del Cauca, 2020), 101n100; Lemaitra, *Quintiada,* 126, 137.
23. Espinosa Arando, *Civilización montés,* 178–186.
24. Rappaport, *Politics,* 125.
25. Luz Ángela Núñez Espinel, "Quintín Lame: Mil batallas contra el olvido," *Anuario Colombiano de Historia Social y de la Cultura* 35 (2008): 91–124.
26. "32 Congreso Asocajas. El desafío de la participación, más allá de la inclusión por Jesús Piñacué," posted October 4, 2022, YouTube, https://www.youtube.com/watch?v=hJlvD4cMwVA.
27. Gloria Patricia Lopera Mesa, "We Have the Land Titles: Indigenous Litigants and Privatization of Resguardos in Colombia, 1870s–1940s" (Phd. diss., University of Florida, 2021), 2n3.
28. Juan Houghton, "La problemática de tierras de los pueblos indígenas," in *La tierra contra la muerte: Conflictos territoriales de los pueblos indígenas en Colombia,* ed. Juan Houghton (Bogotá: CECOIN, 2008), 83–144, here 85.
29. Lopera, "Land Titles," 1. José María Campo Serrano was an important lawyer and interim president of Colombia (1886–1887) who ratified the 1886 Constitution of the Republic of Colombia.
30. Choque Canqui with Quisbert, *Lucha desigual,* 149. For an overview of these movements and scholarly work on them, see Rossana Barragán, "Los títulos de la corona de España de los indígenas," *Boletín Americanista* LXII 2, no. 65 (2012): 15–33.
31. Roberto Choque Canqui and Cristina Quisbert Quispe, *Historia de una lucha desigual. Los contenidos ideológicos y políticos de las rebeliones indígenas de la pre y post revolución nacional* (La Paz: Unidad de Investigaciones Históricas Unih-Pakaxa, 2012), 54–55.
32. Choque Canqui with Quisbert, *Lucha desigual,* 55, "que se haga mérito a las antiguas leyes de la Corona de España."
33. Marka T'ula, *El indio Santos Marka Tula, Cacique Principal de los ayllus de Qallapa y apoderado general de las comunidades originarias de la República* (La Paz: Taller de Historia Oral Andina, 1984) 37–49; Laura Gotkowitz, *A Revolution for Our Rights: Indigenous Struggles for Land and Justice in Bolivia, 1880–1952* (Durham: Duke University Press, 2007), 49.
34. Gotkowitz, *A Revolution,* 51.
35. Marka T'ula, "El Indio," 31.
36. Marka T'ula, "El Indio," 31.
37. Marka T'ula, "El Indio," 32.
38. Marka T'ula, "El Indio," 34.
39. Marka T'ula, "El Indio," 52–53.
40. Marka T'ula, "El Indio," 53–54; Gotkowitz, *A Revolution,* 50.
41. Tristan Platt, "Un archivo campesino como 'acontecimiento de terreno,'" *Americanía: Revista de Estudios Latinoamericanos* 2 (2015): 158–185, here 183.
42. In Bolivia, for instance, indigenous leaders' and commoners' efforts prompted President Villarroel to pass a series of decrees that met their demands. Implementation issues caused further unrest, however; see see Choque Canqui with Quisbert, *Lucha desigual,* 116–129.
43. John Womack Jr., *Zapata and the Mexican Revolution* (New York: Vintage Books, 1970), 372.
44. Womack Jr., *Zapata,* 373.
45. Regina Olmedo Gaxiola, *Catálogo de documentos históricos del Archivo General Agrario* (Mexico: CIESAS, 1998), 1:19–34.
46. Marcos Sánchez Tranquilino, "Foreword," in *The Chicano Codices: Encountering the Art of the Americas* (San Francisco: Mexican Museum, 1992), 3–19, here 3.

47. Dylan A. T. Miner, *Creating Aztlán: Chicano Art, Indigenous Sovereignty, and Lowriding across Turtle Island* (Tucson: University of Arizona Press, 2014), 26.
48. Roberto Cintli Rodríguez, "Introduction," in *Cantos al sexto sol,* ed. Cecilio Xilo García-Camarillo, Roberto Rodríguez, and Patrisia Gonzales (San Antonio: Wings, 2002), xxxvi–xlix, here xxxix.
49. Marka T'ula, "El Indio," 60.

ACKNOWLEDGMENTS

This book has been over ten years in the making. Adrian presents it as an offering to his loved ones, and also as an offering to writing—a strange force keeping them together and also apart. Saint Jerome, in a letter to his friend Heliodorus, once lamented, "We write letters and send replies, our messages cross the seas, and as the ship cleaves a furrow through the waves the moments that we have to live grow less."* Jerome knew that writing both gives and takes, unites and distances. Sometimes writing has imitated real conversations Adrian wishes he was having. At other times, writing has been the boat itself. The centuries-old manuscripts Adrian began studying years ago have long since rewritten his life—upending his ideas, routines, friendships, and location. They took him away from Costa Rica to New York to Texas, Mexico, Peru, Spain, and most recently to Germany.

Adrian thanks his mentors and friends Renate Dürr, Philip Hahn, and Damien Tricoire, who skippered voyages across the Atlantic, the Neckar, the Rhein, and the Mosel. He found havens at the University of Texas at Austin's History Department and Institute for Historical Studies; the Eberhard Karls Universität Tübingen; the Special Research Cluster (Sonderforschungsbereich) 923- Threatened Orders, Universität Trier; the Forschungszentrum Europa, Team Forschungsservice; and

* Saint Jerome, *Select Letters of St. Jerome*, ed. T. E. Page, E. Capps, and W. H. D. Rouse, letter LXVII (London: William Heinemann, 1933), 309.

the Bundesministerium für Forschung, Technologie und Raumfahrt. He thanks his wife and travel companion, Altina Hoti, for her company and her mantra that no minute of life should go to waste. Adrian thanks Jorge for his radical generosity and friendship, and above all, for coming with him on this long journey of writing. It has been a thrilling crossing into the unknown.

Born to *ladino* parents who switched nations and languages constantly, Jorge learned to master new cultural scripts to survive from an early age. He grew up in Colombia, Mexico, and Ecuador but has spent most of his life in too many towns and cities in the United States to count. For him, the joy and sorrow of being *ladino* has always lain in mastering the language of others until they become his to contest and rewrite. It was this background that allowed him to establish ties of kinship and affection with the individuals this book explores. Jorge dedicates this book to his youngest child, Nico, a *ladino* despite himself.

For friendship and guidance, Jorge thanks Jim Sidbury, Mark Thurner, Carlos Jáuregui, Juan Pimentel, Ana Mariella Bacigalupo, Mireya Salgado, Alberto Martínez, José Carlos de la Puente, Ramón Mujica Pinilla, Bruce Kruger, Alex Chaparro, María Monterroso, Francisco Ortega, Lina del Castillo, and his son Sebastian. But most of all, he thanks Adrian for a decade of the most stimulating conversations on both the past and the self.

For helping us rethink this manuscript in the early stages, we thank Cristina Soriano, Santiago Muñoz, Mario Graña Taborelli, Caroline Cunill, Luis Fernando Restrepo, Chloe Ireton, Carlos Espinosa Fernández, Mireya Salgado, and José Sovarzo. We also owe thanks to the participants in workshops at the University of Texas-Austin, Universidad Central del Ecuador (Rafael Polo), FLACSO, University of San Francisco (Carlos Gálvez and Margarita Suárez), and the Colegio de México, who generously engaged with earlier versions.

We are thankful to the countless librarians and archivists around the world who helped us access documents as well as the hundreds of scholars on whose work we built. We offer special thanks to Emily Silk, editor extraordinaire, and all those at Harvard University Press whose dedicated labor made this book possible.

INDEX

Page numbers in *italics* refer to illustrations.